Mathematics
of Accounting

ARTHUR B. CURTIS, *B.C.S., C.P.A.*

JOHN H. COOPER, *B. Accts., C.P.A.*

Revised by **WILLIAM JAMES McCALLION,** *M.A.*

*Associate Professor of Mathematics
and Director of Extension, McMaster
University, Hamilton, Ontario*

FOURTH EDITION

Englewood Cliffs, N. J. **PRENTICE-HALL, INC.**

PRENTICE-HALL ACCOUNTING SERIES

H. A. Finney, Editor

©, 1925, 1934, 1947, 1961, BY

PRENTICE-HALL, INC.

ENGLEWOOD CLIFFS, N. J.

Current Printing (last digit)

19 18 17

LIBRARY OF CONGRESS
CATALOG CARD NO.: 61-7601
PRINTED IN THE UNITED STATES OF AMERICA
56390-C

Preface

This revision was undertaken with three main objectives: to bring the major portion of the content up to date, to introduce a sound mathematical basis to business mathematics, and to make the book more useful to Canadian readers.

The first objective is achieved by securing more current statistics and by including new approaches, new examples, and new problems. The second objective is achieved by giving a more mathematical treatment of simple interest, compound interest, and annuities. These subjects are presented as an exploitation of simple formulae, each of which contains four unknowns, with a solution found for the fourth unknown when values are assigned to the other three. The third objective is attained by including special notes and explanations where the Canadian theory differs significantly from the theory in the United States.

It is hoped that this revision will be useful as a textbook for courses in the mathematics of finance without losing any of its value as a reference book for accountants. Emphasis has been placed on the reference-book aspect by including completely detailed examples of a wide variety.

The author is indebted to Professor John L. Zimka, Department of Accounting, Fairleigh Dickinson University, Rutherford, New Jersey, who read the manuscript and made many valuable suggestions, to Miss Lillian Margot and the Editorial Department of Prentice-Hall for their helpful encouragement and conscientious assistance, and to the secretarial staff of the Department of University Extension, McMaster University, for the careful typing of the manuscript and proofreading.

Tables III, IV, V, VI, and VII are from Glover's *Tables of Applied Mathematics*. The author acknowledges his debt to Professor James W. Glover and his publisher, Mr. George Wahr, for their permission to use them.

WILLIAM J. McCALLION

Contents

any two mixed numbers ending in $\frac{1}{2}$; To multiply a mixed number by a mixed number; Decimal fractions; Approximate numbers; Calculations with exact numbers; Calculations with approximate numbers; To change a decimal fraction to an equivalent common fraction; To change a common fraction to a decimal; Aliquot parts; The use of aliquot parts; Multiplication by aliquot parts; Division by aliquot parts.

Relation between percentage and common and decimal fractions; Applications; Definitions; Fundamental processes; Computations; Daily record of departmental sales; Per cent of returned sales by departments; Clerk's per cent of average sales; Per cent of income by source; Per cent of expense; Per cent of increase or decrease; Operating statistics; Budgeting; Profits based on sales; Commissions; Cash discount; Trade discount; Single discount equivalent to a series; Transportation charges on discount invoices; Anticipation.

Interest; Simple interest formula; Comparison of simple amount and simple present worth. EXACT AND ORDINARY SIMPLE INTEREST: Method using aliquot parts; The cancellation method; Dollars-times-days method, 6%; Interchanging principal and time; Exact or accurate interest. BANK DISCOUNT: Definition; Counting time; Finding the difference between dates by use of a table. PARTIAL PAYMENTS: Part payments on debts; Methods; United States Rule; Merchants' Rule. AVERAGING DATES OF INVOICES: Definition; Use; Term of credit; Average due date; Focal date; Methods; Rule for product method. EQUATION OF ACCOUNTS, OR COMPOUND AVERAGE: Definition; Rule for the product method; When to date forward or backward. INSTALLMENT PLANS AND PERSONAL LOANS: Equal monthly installments plan formula; Equal-monthly-installments-plus-an-odd-final-payment plan formula; Personal loans. ACCOUNT CURRENT: Definition; Methods. STORAGE: Definition; Running account.

Valuation of inventories; Cost or market, whichever is lower; Average cost method; "First-in, first-out" method of inventory; "Last-in, first-out" method of inventory; Merchandise turnover; Number of turnovers; Per cent of mark-down to net cost; Computation of inventory by the retail method; Determining the ratio of cost to retail.

Division of profits by first deducting interest on capital; Profits insufficient to cover interest on investment; Adjustments of capital contribution; Profit sharing in ratio of average investment; Liquidation of
partnership; Methods; Total Distribution; Periodic distribution.

Governmental functions; Purposes of taxes; Appropriations; Kinds of
taxes. PROPERTY TAX: Determination of tax rate; To find the
amount of tax.

PART TWO: *Commercial Algebra—Compound Interest—*
Applications

Explanation; Symbols and terms; Positive and negative numbers;
Addition of positive and negative numbers; The coefficient; Parentheses,
brackets, and braces; Subtraction; Multiplication; Division. EQUA-
TIONS: Simple equations; Fractions; Clearing of complex fractions;
Simultaneous equations with two or more unknowns.

Uses of logarithms; The working rules of logarithms; Proof of working
rules; Common logarithms; How to use a table of logarithms; To find a
number when the logarithm is given; To find a number whose mantissa is
not in the table; The use of logarithms in computation; Multiplication
by logarithms; Division by logarithms; Powers of numbers; Roots of
numbers; Combination of working rules; The slide rule; Use of slide rule;
Accuracy of calculations made by the slide rule; Theory of the slide rule;
How to learn to use the slide rule; Reading the slide rule; Construction of
model slide rule; Multiplication on the slide rule; Division on the slide
rule.

Charts and graphs; Circle chart; Comparison of circles; Bar chart; Line
or curve chart; Rules for coördinate charts; Logarithmic chart; Semilogarithmic or ratio charts. INDEX NUMBERS: Indicators of
business conditions; Index numbers; Price indexes; Quantity indexes;
Value indexes; Business activity indexes; Other indexes.

PART ONE

Commercial Arithmetic
Simple Interest
Applications

1

Fundamental Processes and Short Methods for the Accountant

Addition. Addition is the process of combining numbers of the same denomination. Quantities of such unlike measures as *dollars* and *yards* cannot be added; but quantities like *yards, feet,* and *inches* can be changed to like numbers and then added. *Like* numbers are numbers that express the same kind of units. The *sum* is the number resulting from adding two or more like numbers, and the *addends* are the different numbers to be added.

Addition is the most fundamental of all numerical operations. It is essential that the clerk, the businessman, and the accountant be able to add with precision and rapidity. The ability to recognize the sums of numbers instantly is acquired by constant practice and careful study.

Drill tables. Practice adding the columns of numbers in the following table until you can complete the operation in 25 seconds, without error. State sums only; that is, do not repeat the numbers to be added.

5	8	1	6	5	4	5	9	6	7	2	9	4	8	9
1	2	1	3	3	2	2	7	4	7	1	6	4	6	2

7	9	6	3	7	5	9	4	3	9	5	9	8	4	8
4	9	5	1	2	5	4	3	2	8	4	5	8	1	7

7	8	6	6	8	9	2	7	8	8	7	6	3	7	9
3	4	2	1	5	3	2	5	1	3	1	6	3	6	1

Practice stating the sums of the following columns of numbers until you can do all of them correctly in less than $2\frac{1}{2}$ minutes.

3	4	2	3	4	3	3	5	5	7	6	5	2	3	5	3	8
2	2	2	3	3	3	2	3	3	2	3	3	2	2	2	3	2
4	5	8	6	4	4	5	7	6	9	8	5	4	8	5	7	8

5	6	7	2	3	2	7	2	8	4	7	4	4	6	3	3	2
4	3	1	2	2	2	2	2	2	3	2	4	2	2	2	2	2
6	6	8	9	7	6	8	7	9	6	7	5	4	6	6	3	5

4	5	8	4	9	6	3	5	3	4	5	4	8	4	5	6	8
4	4	3	2	1	2	3	2	2	3	2	2	1	2	3	2	3
7	5	9	8	9	7	8	6	9	9	7	7	8	9	8	9	8

6	7	4	5	7	5	7	6	8	8	6	3	4	6	3	9	6
5	4	2	2	6	4	1	4	4	1	3	3	3	1	3	2	1
6	7	6	9	8	8	7	9	8	9	9	5	7	9	9	9	8

9	5	8	8	6	4	8	7	8	6	5	5	7	7	7	7	6
8	2	8	6	3	3	5	6	7	5	5	3	7	5	4	6	4
9	8	9	9	7	5	9	9	8	7	8	9	9	9	8	7	6

7	6	7	4	7	5	8	9	6	4	5	6	9	5	9	6	6
4	4	3	1	4	6	4	4	3	4	6	7	5	5	5	5	1
8	7	8	9	9	9	8	9	8	8	7	7	9	9	9	8	9

7	8	8	7	9	6	5	7	6	8	9	7	2	7	4	4	5
3	4	5	5	3	6	5	4	6	7	6	5	2	3	4	4	5
9	9	8	7	9	9	6	9	8	9	9	8	3	7	8	6	7

Streamline addition.   Omit unnecessary words: that is, do not name the number to be added; name only the sum.

```
 5
 7
 8
 4
 3
 2
 9
――
38
```

In the example at the left, a common way of adding would be (commencing at the top): 5 and 7 are 12, 12 and 8 are 20, 20 and 4 are 24, and so forth.   Instead of adding in this manner, proceed to the answer by saying (mentally), "12, 20, 24, 27, 29, 38."

Drill table.

3	4	2	6	7	5	1	8	3	5
2	5	9	8	9	3	4	7	2	8
7	3	7	7	2	6	8	6	7	1
4	6	6	9	5	8	6	9	6	3
5	9	3	3	8	7	2	4	9	9
6	8	4	2	6	2	5	7	4	6
1	5	8	4	3	9	7	5	3	7

Combinations whose sum is 10.   Combinations of two or more numbers whose sum is 10 are of frequent occurrence.   When these combinations are recognized, addition may be shortened by adding such combinations as 10.

4
7)
3)
2
5
9
5)
3)
2)
———
40

In this example, the addition may be performed as follows: (commencing at the top) 14, 16, 21, 30, 40.

Or, it may be added in this manner: 11, 21, 30, 40.

Do not try to form combinations. Unless they are instantly recognized, add the numbers in the regular manner.

Drill table.

7	3	5	3	2	6	4	1	9	2
2	5	6	8	8	9	2	5	8	7
1	6	2	2	5	5	4	9	7	4
5	4	7	7	4	4	7	8	3	5
6	9	1	6	3	1	5	3	6	1
4	8	4	3	7	7	3	7	3	7
9	2	8	1	5	8	2	6	1	5
8	7	2	8	2	2	6	4	2	5
2	4	5	7	3	9	8	2	5	9

Adding where the same number is repeated many times. In obtaining averages, in adding statistics, and in other work involving addition, often the same number is repeated many times. Use multiplication to save time in adding.

724
785
773
748
696
687
679
———
5092

In this example, 7 occurs four times and 6 occurs three times in the third column. The sum of the third column may be found as follows:

Carried	4
4 × 7	28
3 × 6	18
	——
	50

The work is actually performed mentally thus: 4 (28) 32, (18) 50. Where the columns are long, a side calculation may be necessary.

Drill table.

68	284	34.86	23.56	48.34	71.53
63	273	33.75	23.95	47.56	72.37
64	281	32.86	24.72	39.85	72.48
67	311	31.29	25.31	38.64	69.95
59	314	34.36	26.54	45.58	68.83
54	321	32.75	31.72	39.95	68.44
57	318	33.95	32.69	42.74	67.93
56	319	36.87	33.47	38.56	71.59

Group addition.   The most practical method of adding is to group or combine two or more figures mentally, and to name results only.

Mental Steps			
5			Instead of saying, "5 and
4	9		4 are 9, and 7 are 16, and 3
7			are 19, and 8 are 27, and 6
3	10	19	are 33, and 1 are 34, and 2 are
8			36," simply *think*, "9, 19,
6	14	33	33, 36."
1			
2	3	36	
36			

Drill table.

6	4	8	5	3	7	9	3	8	6	4	5	7	3	8	7	4	2	9
3	6	5	2	4	8	7	6	3	2	5	7	6	3	9	3	8	4	7
7	3	6	2	9	8	4	6	7	4	5	7	6	2	4	6	9	7	4
7	6	3	5	8	7	5	3	2	5	9	7	3	8	4	6	8	2	7
8	2	4	8	3	7	4	6	5	4	9	7	6	3	5	8	7	3	6
3	8	6	2	4	7	8	6	3	5	8	6	3	4	7	6	2	4	8
5	7	3	7	3	5	8	2	3	7	6	3	4	8	6	2	3	5	9
4	3	7	4	2	7	8	6	4	7	6	4	8	3	9	5	8	2	1
5	5	9	9	8	6	3	6	7	7	7	7	5	3	4	2	1	7	3

Addition of two columns at a time.   Two columns of figures may be added at the same time, as shown in the following illustration:

Mental Steps					*Explanation*		
56	*Tens*		*Units*		*Tens*		*Units*
28	*(1)* 76		*(2)* 84		*(1)* 56 and 20 = 76		*(2)* 76 and 8 = 84
43	*(3)* 124		*(4)* 127		*(3)* 84 and 40 = 124		*(4)* 124 and 3 = 127
21	*(5)* 147		*(6)* 148		*(5)* 127 and 20 = 147		*(6)* 147 and 1 = 148
148							

Drill table.

79	82	24	37	65	39	28	28
48	84	33	44	81	58	39	59
81	95	46	53	42	48	23	86
15	83	52	66	73	73	37	63

Recording addition by columns.   Accountants are subject to interruptions, but the time required to re-add a column of figures for the purpose of picking up the carrying figure may be saved if the total of each column is recorded separately.   The separate column totals are also convenient to use in checking the work; for instance, if in a final summary of additions there is an error of $100.00, the hundreds' columns of the subtotals may be verified quickly without the necessity of re-adding all the columns.

Example—Method 1	Example—Method 2	Example—Method 3
4572	4572	4572
3986	3986	3986
2173	2173	2173
5911	5911	5911
2765	2765	2765
4937	4937	4937
24	24	24
32	34	34
40	43	43
20	24	24
24344		24344

Explanation 1. Add each column separately, setting the sums one place to the left, as in the example. After the last column has been added, add the individual sums in regular order; that is, from right to left.

Explanation 2. In Method 2, a little time is saved by adding to each column the number carried from the column at the right.

Explanation 3. Method 3 differs from Method 2 in the writing of the columns' sums. It is somewhat easier to write the sums one below the other. This cannot be done in Method 1 because carrying figures are not used, and another step is required to complete the answer: that is, finding the grand total of the units, tens, hundreds, and so forth.

A modification of the third method is useful in adding columns of dollars and cents.

$ 644.22
821.94
314.26
712.84
976.54
592.28
$4,062.08

The total, $4,062.08, is obtained by adding each column separately as explained under Method 3. The computation will appear as follows, the purpose of the horizontal lines being to separate cents from dollars, and hundreds from thousands.

Sum of the first column...................................... 28
Sum of the second column, 28 plus 2, carrying number.......... 30
Sum of the third column, 19 plus 3, carrying number........... 22
Sum of the fourth column, 24 plus 2, carrying number.......... 26
Sum of the fifth column, 38 plus 2, carrying number........... 40
As there are no more columns, write the carrying number........ 4

The total, $4,062.08, is obtained by reading the numbers at the right, commencing at the bottom.

PROBLEMS

1.	2.	3.	4.	5.	6.	7.	8.
5273	5126	7952	1395	3688	$367.98	$786.42	$498.57
2191	8497	2975	2764	4932	421.74	518.49	822.56
8437	7934	8675	8351	7563	281.34	946.72	753.86
3426	9783	8437	6248	2898	633.46	881.92	629.75
7139	9126	2975	5347	6598	855.91	542.37	367.43
7895	8751	3826	4586	8877	769.25	787.66	521.54

PRACTICE PROBLEMS

Average weekly earnings from payroll reports.

1.	2.	3.	4.	5.	6.	7.	8.
33.20	35.72	30.85	33.20	28.28	37.61	22.53	23.25
25.13	29.88	21.99	35.72	28.24	29.97	35.62	35.25
37.41	39.24	35.31	42.28	22.61	31.36	16.22	32.18
31.65	33.47	28.89	31.56	21.46	21.34	31.91	37.17
31.40	35.29	27.89	29.82	23.91	33.34	14.16	35.99
22.93	23.22	19.11	37.33	22.41	31.78	27.14	36.66
32 16	33.49	19.15	28.97	17.99	34.73	31.62	35.96
26.37	28.34	18.96	54.61	25.21	26.74	33.84	37.37
36.52	33.64	30.73	39.06	33.26	22.88	30.89	18.17
32.05	34.60	30.70	28.29	28.72	28.09	39.04	29.64
32.58	26.49	18.95	26.87	19.49	28.20	15.76	15.82
23.60	28.81	33.45	27.01	18.64	20.80	20.87	29.87
23.44	37.92	31.60	39.52	37.12	37.53	38.72	27.84
36.37	41.54	30.41	41.86	31.04	28.94	37.16	36.83

Tabulation of advertising lineage.

9.	10.	11.	12.	13.	14.	15.	16.
26,228	29,207	22,107	14,849	10,049	57,104	13,022	10,755
13,818	17,588	15,977	11,966	14,745	71,075	15,223	16,850
27,122	28,267	39,082	36,021	8,562	119,035	17,058	15,573
17,077	15,095	9,644	7,888	5,575	28,857	18,048	10,259
32,094	36,072	23,449	19,634	12,376	39,190	26,174	19,635
32,936	32,835	18,930	15,033	2,175	16,085	28,169	24,572
21,499	18,116	46,520	43,778	7,531	15,484	14,949	15,057
20,655	24,094	25,140	19,271	8,650	28,192	24,478	19,445
22,338	10,365	8,015	13,412	15,530	14,711	22,175	24,493
13,412	60,475	38,795	93,323	23,680	22,865	23,680	37,335

Addition of dollars and cents, irregular items.

17.	18.	19.	20.	21.	22.
139.10	86.35	209.80	45.40	86.35	1,955.05
12.65	52.67	44.82	34.20	52.67	531.03
10.57	44.00	37.45	28.66	42.57	442.85
50.05	208.33	127.29	135.68	208.33	2,148.74
1,275.48	394.68	4,151.36	945.21	878.52	30,149.39
260.73	64.72	24.94	2.72	111.56	112.64
7.81	6.29	.72	118.61	6.46	509.74
78.13	27.33	71.97	.75	44.77	27.02
2.50	.62	12.09	32.49	.69	153.07
111.82	27.65	.35	8.58	3.07	1,512.34
29.53	7.33	160.31	33.55	70.63	1,002.90
54.53	16.29	45.15	8.45	5.37	282.51
15.36	4.59	128.60	24.85	35.15	66.66
147.62	111.52	41.51	138.34	9.98	146.43
5.27	59.68	46.43	92.54	214.34	641.51

Practical applications. In the following problems will be found examples of business records requiring addition for the completion of the record.

PROBLEM 1

In this problem, cash register tapes provided the source of the entries on Form 1. As the sales were registered, the classification was imprinted on the tape. At the end of the day, the classified items appearing on the tape were accumulated on Form 1, and the totals transferred to Form 2. At the end of the week, Form 2 was added; at the end of the month, the weekly totals were accumulated to monthly totals. Thus, sales for the month were analyzed by departments or classes.

Add the columns on Form 1 (Saturday's sales), transfer the totals to Form 2, and find the total sales for the week.

Form 1

Candy	Cigars	Soda	Drugs	Own Remedies	Patent Medicines	Toilet Articles
.35	.10	.10	.45	.75	1.25	.35
1.25	.25	.15	1.64	.45	.50	1.15
.80	.15	.20	.10	.15	1.50	.80
.45	.25	.45	.75	1.25	.89	2.65
.75	.50	.10	1.50	.90	.33	.75
.90	.25	.50	1.75	1.65	2.35	1.85

Form 2

Day	Candy	Cigars	Soda	Drugs	Own Remedies	Patent Medicines	Toilet Articles	Totals
Mon.	12.65	19.15	3.95	27.63	4.18	9.85	5.00	....
Tues.	8.50	16.10	6.80	33.98	2.47	12.20	3.65	....
Wed.	11.25	8.75	4.50	15.20	1.75	2.55	10.45	....
Thurs.	9.65	4.25	2.55	7.65	2.85	4.86	4.63	....
Fri.	10.35	5.55	3.75	12.84	3.68	5.49	3.85	....
Sat.	....	....	....	....	....	....	....	....
	....	....	....	....	....	....	....	....

Form 2 is self-proving—that is, the sum of the daily totals must equal the sum of the departmental or classification totals.

PROBLEM 2

The "peg board" is used for accumulating numbers having to do with many kinds of information. The numbers are entered on narrow forms which are attached to the "peg board." The forms are held in place and cross extension as well as "footings" are thus permitted.

In the following example, this arrangement is used to accumulate total departmental sales made by a salesman.

Salesman R. F.	Salesman R. F.	Salesman R. F.	Salesman R. F.	Salesman R . F.	Total Sales	Dept.
Date 4/2	Date 4/3	Date 4/4	Date 4/5	Date 4/6		
128.57	587.23	347.58	237.51	637.82	....	1
645.39	321.69	123.63	563.85	495.71	....	2
362.45	847.86	219.23	149.27	826.45	....	3
472.31	123.45	547.81	462.38	718.26	....	4
45.97	671.17	359.34	326.49	534.58	....	5
273.14	372.45	135.67	857.62	149.17	....	6
928.63	436.49	569.81	318.48	529.32	....	7
....	....	....	....	....	....	

(a) Find the total of each day's sales.
(b) Find the total sales for each department.
The answer in the lower right corner proves the work.

Subtraction. Subtraction is the process of finding the *difference* between two like numbers. The *minuend* is the number to be diminished, and the *subtrahend* is the number to be taken from the minuend.

Addition and subtraction are closely related. Subtraction by adding is the method used by the expert cashier and by money changers. The "making change" method of subtraction consists in adding to the amount of the purchase enough to make the sum equal to the amount tendered in payment.

Example. *Y* buys groceries to the value of $1.34 and gives the cashier two one-dollar bills in payment. How much change should he receive?

Solution. The cashier in making change may return to *Y* a penny, a nickel, a dime, and a half-dollar, saying: "$1.34, 35, 40, 50, $2.00," which means $1.34 + .01 = $1.35; $1.35 + .05 = $1.40; $1.40 + .10 = $1.50; and $1.50 + .50 = $2.00. Other coins than those mentioned may be returned by the cashier, but it is customary to make change in the largest coins possible.

Exercise. As the cashier, make change, using the largest denominations possible, assuming that each of the following purchases were made and two one-dollar bills were offered in payment.

1. $1.44	**5.** $1.64	**9.** $1.17	**13.** $1.43
2. 1.67	**6.** 1.32	**10.** 1.29	**14.** 1.38
3. 1.27	**7.** 1.82	**11.** 1.54	**15.** 1.49
4. 1.41	**8.** 1.11	**12.** 1.56	**16.** 1.05

Avoid errors. Many errors in subtraction are made in borrowing from the next higher order. When that order is reached, it is not uncommon to overlook the fact that borrowing has taken place. Errors of this kind can be avoided by changing subtraction to the process of addition; that is, by adding to the subtrahend the number required to make the subtrahend equal to the minuend.

Explanation. Instead of thinking, "7 from 16 is 9," think, "7 + 9 = 16." Write the 9. Add 1, the digit carried over, to the 8, making 9. 9 + 8 = 17. Write, 8, and add 1, the digit carried over, to 1, making 2. 2 + 0 = 2. Write 0. 3 + 5 = 8. Write 5. Answer: 5,089.

Example.
Minuend........ 8276
Subtrahend..... 3187
Difference...... 5089

PROBLEMS

1. 9574	**2.** 7436	**3.** 6175	**4.** 8147	**5.** 6328	**6.** 5317
5886	3569	2897	4368	2549	3428

Difference between a given minuend and several subtrahends. In instances similar to the following example, the final result can be found in one operation by the application of the foregoing method of subtraction.

Example. From a fund of $3,456, the following disbursements were made: $594, $375, and $286. What was the balance left in the fund?

Explanation. Write the problem as shown in the solution. Begin at the right, and add the units' column of subtrahends, (6 + 5 + 4), adding (and setting

down) enough (in this instance, 1) to make the units' figure of
the sum the same as the units' figure of the minuend. Add the
tens' column of the subtrahends, including the carrying figure,
$(1 + 8 + 7 + 9)$, adding (and setting down) enough (in this instance, 0) to make the tens' figure of the sum equal the tens'
figure of the minuend. Add the hundreds' column of the
subtrahends, including the carrying figure, $(2 + 2 + 3 + 5)$,
adding (and setting down) enough (in this instance, 2) to make
the hundreds' figure of the minuend. To the carrying figure, 1, add enough
(in this case, 2) to make the thousands' figure of the minuend; set down 2.

Solution.
$3,456
594
375
286
$2,201

PROBLEMS

1.	**2.**	**3.**	**4.**	**5.**
$1,562	$2,756 28	$5,987	$4,875	$2,975
437	52.70	235	365	762
122	7.55	789	1,529	194
254	528.75	1,526	284	275

Balancing an account.   In most cases, inspection will tell which side
of the account is the greater in amount.   Add the larger side, and put the
same footing on the smaller side, leaving space for the balance; then add
from the top downward, supplying the figures necessary to make the
column total equal to the footing previously placed there.

Example.

Debits		*Credits*
$ 1,956.18		$ 134.26
3,452.75		258.19
289.34		764.83
5,726.31		2,375.94
	Balance,	7,891.36
$11,424.58		$11,424.58

Explanation.   The balance, $7,891.36, was found as follows: Inspection showed
the debit side to be the larger in amount.   It was therefore added, and the
footing of the account, $11,424.58, was placed under both debit and credit
columns.   The first order of the credits—that is, the cents—adds to 22.
Insert 6 to make 28.   With 2, the digit carried over, the second order, the
dimes, adds to 22.   Insert 3 to make 25.   The third order, the dollars, with
the digit carried over, adds to 23.   Insert 1 to make 24.   The fourth order,
the tens of dollars, with the digit carried over, adds to 23.   Insert 9 to make
32.   The fifth order, the hundreds of dollars, with the digit carried over, adds
to 16.   Insert 8 to make 24.   The sixth order, the thousands of dollars, with
the digit carried over, adds to 4.   Insert 7 to make 11.

PROBLEMS

1.	*Debits*	*Credits*	**2.**	*Debits*	*Credits*	**3.**	*Debits*	*Credits*
	$856.73	$298.56		$725.14	$1,356.17		$3,586.28	$ 591.18
	345.96	264.39		239.51	691.35		192.75	2,751.26
	298.85	6.15		64.28	256.38		384.72	185.35
	142.31	....		....	75.19		265.54	....

Complement method.   The complement of a number is the difference between that number and the unit of a next higher order.   Thus,

the complement of 6 is 4; the complement of 8 is 2; and the complement of 68 is 32.

If, in subtracting a number less than 10 from a given number, its complement is added, the result will be 10 too large. If two complements are added, the result will be 20 too large; and if three complements are added, the result will be 30 too large.

To find the sum of a column containing numbers to be subtracted, add the complements of the subtractive items, and from the sum of each order deduct as many tens as there are subtractive items in the order.

Example. A practical application of the complement method of subtraction is that of finding the net increase in a statistical record such as the following:

Dept.	Sales This Mo.	Sales Last Mo.	Increase Decrease*
1	$ 427.95	$ 346.29	$ 81.66
2	515.86	457.75	58.11
3	395.57	385.86	9.71
4	402.75	416.87	14.12*
	$1,742.13	$1,606.77	$135.36

Solution. The difference between the sales this month and the sales last month for each department is shown as an increase or a decrease. The difference between the total sales this month and the total sales last month is $135.36. To prove that the departmental increases and decrease are correct, add the third column, beginning at the top and adding downward, using the complement each time on the last number. Thus, 8 and 8 are 16; write 6, and drop the 10, as one complement was added and the answer is 10 too large. 14 and 9 are 23; write 3 and carry 10, dropping one 10. 19 and 6 are 25; write 5 and carry 1, again dropping one 10. 14 and 9 are 23; write 13, dropping one 10 as before.

Example. Find the net increase of the following items:

Increase Decrease*
15.60
4.51*
17.20
61.96
29.00
8.62*
124.20
59.40
89.83*
199.30
113.79*
132.46
34.99
122.65
580.01

Solution. In this problem there are four items showing decreases; therefore, each time a complement is added, the final result will be 10 too large, and in this case, the final result will be 40 too large, so 40 is deducted each time. Begin at the top and add downward: 9 (comp.), 15, 23 (comp. was 8), 30, 31, 37, 46, 51, subtract 40, write 1 and carry 1.

Now the next column. 7 (6 and 1), 12, 14, 23, 27, 29, 33, 35, 38, 41, 45, 54, 60, subtract 40, write 0 and carry 2. Next column, 7, 13, 20, 21, 30, 32, 36, 45, 46, 55, 62, 64, 68, 70, subtract 40, write 0 and carry 3.

Adding the tens: 4 (1 and 3 carried), 5, 11, 13, 15, 20, 22, 31, 40, 43, 46, 48, but subtract 20 as only two complements were used, write 8 and carry 2. The complement 10 may be added each time there is no item, making the answer 68, then subtract 40, leaving 28 as before. Remember, subtract as many 10's as there are complements added.

Finally the hundreds' column. There are but five items in this column; therefore, with the 2 carried, proceed as follows: 3, 4, 13, 15, subtract 10 (only one complement was added) and write 5. Answer: 580.01.

PROBLEMS

The items to be subtracted are marked (*) in Problems 1 and 2.

1.	**2.**	**3.**	**4.**
$58.10	$122 65	$48.75 Gain	$20.25 Gain
19 66	175.50	31.25 Gain	4.50 Loss
45.55	89.88*	3.20 Loss	41.50 Gain
77.28	17.20	65.50 Gain	28.45 Gain
9 01*	1.48	15.25 Loss	38.47 Gain
16.11	8.62*	16.38 Gain	12.34 Loss
14.12*	36.95	26.65 Gain	49.82 Gain

Subtracting on an adding machine. If increase or decrease columns are being verified on an adding machine that does not have a direct subtraction device, add the complements of the numbers to be subtracted.

To subtract $219.48, set 780.52 on the keyboard and strike all nines to the left of the number; and to subtract $102.79, set 897.21 and strike all nines to the left of the number. Striking of the nines eliminates from the totalizers the number 1 that would otherwise be included in the answer.

Practical problems. In the following problems, both addition and subtraction have to be performed in order to complete the records.

PROBLEM 1

This problem illustrates a section of a twelve-month moving-average schedule used in cost accounting and other cumulative work. Assuming that twelve months covers a cycle of business changes due to seasonal variations, and so forth, the moving twelve months' total provides a fairly reliable amount for comparative purposes.

The earliest month's results are subtracted from the twelve months' total and the current month's results are added, making a current twelve-month accumulation. The record is self-proving.

	Dept. 1	*Dept. 2*	*Dept. 3*	*Dept. 4*	*Total*
Total, 12/31/63..	$125,275.93	$56,472.29	$4,207.23	$7,200.49	....
Deduct Jan., 1963	9,495.79	4,907.63	368.80	502.50	....
Add Jan., 1964...	8,805.67	4,480.25	358.79	588.79	....
12 mos. totals....	....	....	....	....	....
Deduct Feb., 1963	8,933.07	4,093.19	293.67	496.68	....
Add Feb., 1964...	9,033.48	4,123.97	235.80	517.90	....
12 mos. totals....	....	....	....	....	....
Deduct Mar., 1963	10,854.92	4,837.07	331.04	480.09	....
Add Mar., 1964...	8,588.37	4,001.18	334.17	521.72	....
12 mos. totals....	....	....	....	....	....

PROBLEM 2

From the following sales record, find the increase or decrease in sales by department.

Comparative Sales Record

Dept. No.	February, 2nd Year	February, 1st Year	Increase or Decrease†
1......	$ 7,134.95	$ 6,834.79	....
2......	6,225.19	5,764.87	....
3......	7,934.97	8,375.16	....
4......	6,354.76	5,986.35	....
5......	3,695.15	3,756.89	....
6......	9,767.98	9,475.18	....
7......	8,567.39	8,467.57	....
8......	5,607.18	4,865.84	....
9......	11,365.39	10,785.65	....
10......	14,572.86	13,764.16	....
Total..	....	....	....

PROBLEM 3

A daily business record may be prepared from cash register totals and other information. With the aid of the amounts given, complete the record for the day. Some of the sections contain items that are needed to complete other sections.

Cash Receipts
Rec'd. on Acc't.. $234.56
Other Receipts.. 59.32
Cash Sales...... 497.85

Total Receipts... ....

Sales
Cash Sales..... $.............
Credit Sales.... 152.35

Total Sales.... ....

Cash Paid Out
For Stock....... $ 85.42
For Expenses... 19.56
Personal........ 27.50
Deposit........ 652.80
Total......... ....

Cash on Hand
Opening Balance. $250.75
Receipts........ ....
Total.......... ....
Paid Out........ ....
Closing balance.. ....

Bank Account
Bal. for'd...... $2,872.63
Today's Dept.. ....
Total.......... ....
Today's Cks... 175.32
Balance....... ....

Accounts Receivable
Bal. for'd....... $481.52
Credit Sales.... ....
Total.......... ....
Rec'd. on Acc't.. ....
Balance........ ....

Accounts Payable
Bal. for'd...... $315.20
Invoices Today.. 262.35
Total.......... ....
Paid Today..... 136.57
Balance........ ....

Cash Sales Summary
Total for'd..... $2,542.75
Today's Cash
Sales.... ....
Total to for-
ward........ ....

Credit Sales Summary
Total for'd...... $638.47
Today's Credit
Sales........ ....
Total to forward ....

PROBLEM 4

In the following table of Gross Profits by Departments, add the Goods on Hand, March 1, 1st Year, to the Purchases for the Year, and from this sum subtract the Goods on Hand, March 1, 2nd Year. This gives the Cost of Goods Sold. The operation should be performed without transferring any of the figures. Use the complements of the numbers in the column Goods on Hand, March 1, 2nd Year.

The difference between the Cost of Goods Sold and the Sales will give the Profit or Loss.

To verify the work, add all the columns, and deal with the totals in the same way as with the figures for the departments. The difference between the totals of the Cost of Goods Sold column and the Sales column should equal the difference between the totals of the Profit and the Loss columns, showing the Net Profit of the ten departments for the year.

Gross Profits by Departments

Dept.	Goods on Hand March 1, 1st Year	Purchases for the Year	Goods on Hand March 1, 2nd Year	Cost of Goods Sold	Sales	Profit	Loss
1	$3,475.86	$ 9,846.37	$2,347.11	....	$12,678.92	....	....
2	1,357.10	6,725.40	1,475.86	....	6,188.90	....	....
3	3,276.84	10,326.85	3,827.84	....	8,297.63	....	....
4	5,475.90	11,176.98	5,874.13	....	13,586.47	....	....
5	4,276.83	9,798.34	4,207.16	....	10,508.92	....	....
6	3,785.47	8,376.41	3,648.10	....	8,756.13	....	....
7	2,986.17	9,386.57	3,014.74	....	8,964.85	....	....
8	3,275.83	8,724.18	2,817.56	....	9,575.34	....	....
9	2,976.95	9,543.34	2,734.15	....	10,789.18	....	....
10	3,532.25	10,217.60	3,375.89	....	12,756.84	....	....
Footings							

Multiplication. Multiplication is a short process of addition; that is, a number is to be taken as an addend a given number of times.

How many bushels of grain are in three bins each containing 146 bu.?

Addition	Multiplication
146	146
146	3
146	438
438	

Multiplication involves three numbers, the multiplicand (the number to be repeated, 146); the multiplier (the number showing the number of repetitions, 3); and the product (the number showing the result, 438).

The multiplicand and the product are always like numbers. 146 bushels multiplied by 3 equals 438 bushels.

PROBLEMS

1. What is the cost of 640 acres of land at $42.50 an acre?

2. How many minutes are there in an ordinary year?

3. A barrel of flour contains 196 pounds. What is the weight of flour produced in one day by a mill that produces 375 barrels?

4. Sound travels about 1,120 feet in a second. How far will it travel in 15 seconds?

5. How many peaches are in 12 crates, if there are 84 peaches in each crate?

Accuracy and speed in multiplication depend largely upon a thorough mastery of the multiplication tables. Tables previously learned should be reviewed. Continue with frequent drills on combinations up to 25×25. The following table of multiples from 12×12 to 25×25 is given for reference and drill. Tables of multiples prepared in this manner facilitate the work of pay roll extension, inventory extension, billing, and so forth.

TABLE OF MULTIPLES

	12	13	14	15	16	17	18	19	20	21	22	23	24	25
12	144	156	168	180	192	204	216	228	240	252	264	276	288	300
13	156	169	182	195	208	221	234	247	260	273	286	299	312	325
14	168	182	196	210	224	238	252	266	280	294	308	322	336	350
15	180	195	210	225	240	255	270	285	300	315	330	345	360	375
16	192	208	224	240	256	272	288	304	320	336	352	368	384	400
17	204	221	238	255	272	289	306	323	340	357	374	391	408	425
18	216	234	252	270	288	306	324	342	360	378	396	414	432	450
19	228	247	266	285	304	323	342	361	380	399	418	437	456	475
20	240	260	280	300	320	340	360	380	400	420	440	460	480	500
21	252	273	294	315	336	357	378	399	420	441	462	483	504	525
22	264	286	308	330	352	374	396	418	440	462	484	506	528	550
23	276	299	322	345	368	391	414	437	460	483	506	529	552	575
24	288	312	336	360	384	408	432	456	480	504	528	552	576	600
25	300	325	350	375	400	425	450	475	500	525	550	575	600	625

Contractions in multiplication. Contractions in multiplication may often be made by observing the peculiarities of the multiplier and the multiplicand and calling into use factors, multiples, complements, supplements, reciprocals, aliquots, and the like.

To multiply by factors of the multiplier. The ordinary method and the shorter method of multiplying by factors are shown in the following example. Observe that in the ordinary method there are two multiplications and an addition, while in the shorter method there are only two multiplications.

Example. Multiply 567 by 27.

Solution.

Ordinary Method	*Shorter Method*
567	567 $27 = 9 \times 3$
27	9
3969	5103
1134	3
15309	15309

PROBLEMS

Multiply:

1. 4,584 by 64.   3. 1,459 by 35.   5. 8,756 by 42.
2. 8,359 by 54.   4. 2,684 by 27.   6. 6,123 by 45.

To multiply when a part of the multiplier is a factor or multiple of another part.

Example.   Multiply 34,768 by 488.

Solution.

$$34768$$
$$\underline{488}$$
$$\overline{278144} \text{ product by 8}$$
$$\underline{16688640} \text{ product of 60 times product by 8}$$
$$\overline{16966784}$$

PROBLEMS

Multiply:

1. 45,692 by 549.	**3.** 21,347 by 497.	**5.** 84,123 by 248.
2. 49,871 by 648.	**4.** 33,546 by 355.	**6.** 13,456 by 153.

To multiply a number of two figures by 11.   Observation of the ordinary method shows that, in the answer, the sum of the two digits is written between the two digits.

Ordinary Method	*Shorter Method*
54	54
11	11
54	594
54	
594	

When the sum of the two digits is 10 or more, 1 must be carried to the digit at the left; for example, $64 \times 11 = 704$, and $93 \times 11 = 1,023$.

To multiply any number by 11.   Observation of the ordinary method shows that, in the answer, the units' digit of the multiplicand is the units' digit of the product; that the tens' digit of the product is the sum of the units' digit and the tens' digit of the multiplicand; that the hundreds' digit of the product is the sum of the tens' digit and the hundreds' digit of the multiplicand; and so on.   When the sum of two digits is 10 or more, 1 must be carried.

Ordinary Method	*Shorter Method*
8937	8937
11	11
8937	98307
8937	
98307	

Multiplying by 25.   Annex two ciphers to the multiplicand, and divide by 4.

Example. Multiply 7,562 by 25.

Solution.

$$\frac{4)756200}{189050}$$

PROBLEMS

Multiply each of the following by 25:

1. 3,874.   **2.** 3,948.   **3.** 7,981.   **4.** 5,426.

Multiplying by 15. Annex a cipher to the multiplicand, and increase the result by one-half of the multiplicand.

Example. Multiply 8,435 by 15.

Solution.

$$\begin{array}{r} 84350 \\ 42175 \\ \hline 126525 \end{array}$$

PROBLEMS

Multiply each of the following by 15:

1. 7,432.   **2.** 8,397.   **3.** 3,926.   **4.** 9,536.

Multiplying numbers ending with ciphers. Multiply the significant figures in each number, and to the product annex as many ciphers as there are final ciphers in both the multiplier and the multiplicand.

Example. Multiply 756,000 by 4,200.

Solution.

$$\begin{array}{r} 756 \\ 42 \\ \hline 31752 \end{array}$$

Annex five ciphers.   Answer: 3,175,200,000.

PROBLEMS

Multiply:

1. 325,000 by 2,300.   **3.** 24,100 by 4,200.
2. 370 by 480.   **4.** 8,300 by 2,100.

Multiplication by numbers near 100, as 98, 97, 96, and so forth, and by numbers near 1,000, as 997, 996, and so forth. This method is of value in finding the net proceeds of some amount less 2%, 3%, and so forth, and also in many other situations.

Example.   Multiply 3,247 by 97.

Solution.   Multiply the number by 100, and subtract 3 times the number.

$$324,700 = 3,247 \times 100$$
$$\underline{9,741} = 3,247 \times 3$$
$$314,959 = 3,247 \times 97$$

Multiplication by a number near 1,000 is accomplished in the same manner by multiplying by 1,000 instead of by 100.

PROBLEMS

Multiply:

1. 2,459 by 98.   **2.** 7,318 by 97.   **3.** 5,438 by 96.   **4.** 8,752 by 95.

Multiplication of two numbers each near 100, 1,000, and so forth.   Products of numbers in this class may be calculated mentally.

Example.   Multiply 96 by 98.

Explanation.   Step 1.   Multiply the complements of the two numbers, and if the product occupies units' place only, prefix a cipher. Result, 08.

Step 2. Subtract the complement of one number from the other number, and write the result at the left of the result in Step 1.   The complement of either number subtracted from the other number leaves the same remainder; as, 96 − 2 or 98 − 4 each equals 94. Answer: 9,408.

Solution.

	Complement
96	4
98	2
9408	

Example.   Multiply 92 by 88.

Solution.

	Complement
92	8
88	12
8096	

Explanation.   The product of the complements is 96, the last two figures of the answer.   88 − 8 or 92 − 12 = 80, the first two figures of the answer. Answer: 8,096.

Example.   Multiply 996 by 988.

Solution.

	Complement
996	4
988	12
984,048	

Explanation.   When numbers near 1,000 are multiplied, ciphers are prefixed to the product of the complements, so that the product occupies three places.

PROBLEMS

Multiply:

1. 97 by 96.   2. 88 by 98.   3. 995 by 992.   4. 997 by 994.

Multiplying by numbers a little larger than 100, as 101, 102, and so forth. Annex two ciphers to the multiplicand, and to this add the product of the multiplicand and the units' figure of the multiplier. Annex three ciphers for multipliers over 1,000.

Example. Multiply 3,475 by 104.

Solution.

$$
\begin{array}{l}
347500 \\
\underline{\ 13900} \quad (4 \times 3,475) \\
361400
\end{array}
$$

PROBLEMS

Multiply:

1. 2,875 by 102.   2. 3,496 by 105.   3. 2,972 by 1,004.   4. 4,568 by 1,006.

Multiplication of two numbers each a little more than 100. To the sum of the numbers (omitting one digit in the hundreds' column), annex two ciphers, and add the product of the supplements (excess over 100).

Example. Multiply 112 by 113.

Solution.

$$
\begin{array}{l}
112 \\
\underline{113} \\
12500 \quad \text{(sum of numbers, with one digit in the hundreds' column omitted)} \\
\underline{\ \ 156} \quad \text{(product of supplements, } 12 \times 13) \\
12656
\end{array}
$$

Explanation. In instances similar to the foregoing, a knowledge of the multiplication tables to 20 × 20 makes mental results possible, and is invaluable in inventory and other extensions.

PROBLEMS

Multiply:

1. 114 by 112.   2. 106 by 108.   3. 116 by 111.   4. 118 by 115.

Cross multiplication. When the multiplicand and the multiplier are each numbers of two figures, the work may easily be kept in mind and the partial products added without being written down.

Example.   Multiply 47 by 38.

Solution   *Graphic Solution*

47
38
———
1786

Explanation.   8 × 7 = 56.   Write 6, carry 5.   (8 × 4) + (3 × 7) + 5 = 58.
Write 8, carry 5.   (3 × 4) + 5 = 17.   Write 17.   Answer: 1,786.

PROBLEMS

Multiply:

1. 53 by 29.   **2.** 48 by 57.   **3.** 74 by 32.   **4.** 65 by 28.

To cross-multiply a number of three digits by a number of two digits.   A three-digit number may be multiplied by a two-digit number in a manner similar to that of multiplying a two-digit number by a two-digit number.

Example.   Multiply 346 by 28.

Solution.

346
28
———
9688

Explanation.   8 × 6 = 48.   Write 8,   carry 4.   4 (carried) + (8 × 4) + (6 × 2) = 48.   Write 8, carry 4.   4 (carried) + (8 × 3) + (4 × 2) = 36. Write 6, carry 3.   3 (carried) + (2 × 3) = 9.   Write 9.   Answer: 9,688.
A graphic presentation of the steps required appears as follows:

PROBLEMS

1. 324 × 28	**4.** 428 × 34	**7.** 289 × 85	**10.** 693 × 42
2. 543 × 42	**5.** 516 × 26	**8.** 356 × 48	**11.** 384 × 56
3. 658 × 56	**6.** 513 × 76	**9.** 785 × 34	**12.** 473 × 65

To cross-multiply a number of three digits by another number of three digits.   Comparison of the graphic presentation with that above shows that the first three steps are the same, the next three are new, and the final three are the same.

Example.   Multiply 428 by 356.

Solution   *Graphic Solution*

4 2 8
3 5 6
————
152,368

Explanation. $6 \times 8 = 48$. Write 8, carry 4.   4 (carried) $+ (6 \times 2) + (8 \times 5)$ $= 56$.   Write 6, carry 5.   5 (carried) $+ (6 \times 4) + (8 \times 3) + (2 \times 5) = 63$. Write 3, carry 6.   6 (carried) $+ (5 \times 4) + (2 \times 3) = 32$.   Write 2, carry 3. 3 (carried) $+ (3 \times 4) = 15$.   Write 15.   Answer: 152,368.

PROBLEMS

1. 124×251	6. 832×425	11. 436×579
2. 262×158	7. 639×256	12. 832×656
3. 328×245	8. 819×325	13. 295×638
4. 638×256	9. 677×283	14. 767×842
5. 784×364	10. 518×824	15. 698×476

Preparation of a table of multiples of a number. It is not uncommon to have to use the same number many times in making calculations, especially in cost accounting. A saving of time and increased accuracy in the work are achieved if a table of multiples of the number is constructed. Suppose that you have to perform a number of multiplications in which 326,834 is one of the factors. A table of multiples may be constructed with an adding machine by locking the repeat key. Sub-total after each pull of the handle. The sub-totals should check with the product column shown below. If the table is prepared by repeated additions, and not with an adding machine, the 10th product should be computed, as it will verify all, unless there are compensating errors in the work.

TABLE OF MULTIPLES

Multiplier	Product
1	326,834
2 (326,834 + 326,834)	653,668
3 (653,668 + 326,834)	980,502
4 (980,502 + 326,834)	1,307,336
5 (1,307,336 + 326,834)	1,634,170
6 (1,634,170 + 326,834)	1,961,004
7 (1,961,004 + 326,834)	2,287,838
8 (2,287,838 + 326,834)	2,614,672
9 (2,614,672 + 326,834)	2,941,506

Verification

10 (2,941,506 + 326,834)	3,268,340

Example. Multiply 326,834 by 5,249.

Solution.

$$
\begin{array}{rl}
2941506 & = 9 \text{ times } 326,834 \\
1307336 & = 4 \text{ times } 326,834 \\
653668 & = 2 \text{ times } 326,834 \\
\underline{1634170} & = 5 \text{ times } 326,834 \\
1715551666 & = \text{product}
\end{array}
$$

If the table is prepared without the use of an adding machine, proceed as follows.

1. Write 326,834 near the bottom of a slip of paper or a card.

2. Start the table by writing 326,834. Place the slip or card just above this number, thus:

$$\boxed{}$$
$$326,834$$

1.   326,834
2.   ....
3.   ....

3. Add the two numbers, placing the sum, 653,668, on line 2. This is two times the number.

4. Move the slip or card down one line and add again, placing the sum, 980,502, on line 3, forming three times the number.

5. Continue moving the slip or card down one line each time and adding.

6. When 9 times the number is obtained, check the accuracy of the work by repeating the process once more. The result should be ten times the number.

PROBLEMS

Set up a table of multiples of 245,386, and multiply 245,386 by the following numbers:

1. 2,465   **2.** 3,542   **3.** 2,498   **4.** 5,347   **5.** 6,173

Division. Division is the process of finding how many times one number is contained in another number. The *dividend* is the number to be divided, the *divisor* is the number by which we divide, and the *quotient* is the number showing how many times the dividend contains the divisor.

The *remainder* is a number less than the divisor, and results when the dividend does not contain the divisor exactly. It is an undivided portion of the dividend.

Short division is the method used when the products of the divisor and the digits of the quotient are omitted.

Example. Divide 3,476 by 2.

Solution.

$$2)\underline{3476}$$
$$1738$$

Long division is the method used when the work is written in full.

Example. Divide 5,839 by 24.

Solution.

$$24)5839(243$$
$$\underline{48}$$
$$103$$
$$\underline{96}$$
$$79$$
$$\underline{72}$$
$$7$$

To divide by 25, 50, or 125. The work of division can be lessened by making the operation one of multiplication.

Example.   Divide 1,400 by 25.

Solution. $14 \times 4 = 56$.

Explanation.   Divide 1,400 by 100 by dropping the zeros. But, 100 is 4 times the actual divisor; therefore, the quotient 14 is $\frac{1}{4}$ of the actual quotient, so 14×4 or 56 is the actual quotient.

In a similar manner, 1,400 divided by 50 is 28; and 14,000 divided by 125 is 112. (*Note:* Further reference to this method is given under the subject of division by aliquot parts of 100.)

Abbreviated division.   Instead of writing the product and then subtracting, the product of each digit of the divisor is subtracted mentally, using the "making change" method, and only the remainder is written.

$$
\begin{array}{r}
3285 \\
234)\overline{768756} \\
667 \\
1995 \\
1236 \\
66
\end{array}
$$

Use of tables in division.   If a number of divisions are to be made with the same divisor, it is advantageous to set up a table of multiples of the divisor.

Example.   Assume that 328 is to be used a number of times as a divisor, and that one of the dividends is 587,954.   A table of multiples could be set up thus:

TABLE OF MULTIPLES

Multiplier	Product
1	328
2	656
3	984
4	1,312
5	1,640
6	1,968
7	2,296
8	2,624
9	2,952

Explanation.   Inspection shows the first digit in the quotient to be 1.   The second partial dividend is 2,599.   The table of multiples shows the largest product contained therein to be 2,296, opposite 7.   The third partial dividend is 3,035, and the table of multiples shows the largest product contained therein to be 2,952, opposite 9.   The fourth partial dividend is 834, and the largest product contained therein is 656, opposite 2.   The remainder is 178.   The fraction $\frac{178}{328}$ may be reduced to $\frac{89}{164}$, or it may be changed to a decimal.

Solution.

$$
\begin{array}{r}
328)\overline{587954}(1792\tfrac{89}{164} \\
328 \\
\overline{2599} \\
2296 \\
\overline{3035} \\
2952 \\
\overline{834} \\
656 \\
\overline{178}
\end{array}
$$

$$\frac{178}{328} = \frac{89}{164}$$

Division in this manner is rapid, as no time is lost through selection of a quotient so large that when the product is found it exceeds the dividend, necessitating another trial.

PROBLEMS

Divide the following numbers by 144 after setting up a table of multiples of 144:

1. 374,825.   **2.** 628,256.   **3.** 496,287.

Reciprocals in division. The reciprocal of any number is found by dividing 1 by the number. The reciprocal of 5 is 1 ÷ 5, or .2, and the reciprocal of 25 is 1 ÷ 25, or .04.

The quotient in a division may be found by multiplying the dividend by the reciprocal of the divisor. Hence, in instances in which it is necessary to find what per cent each item is of the total of the items, the use of the reciprocal of the divisor will save time and provide a check on these computations.

To find what per cent each item is of the total of the items:

(*a*) Divide 1 by the total of the items to obtain the reciprocal of the total.

(*b*) Using the result obtained in (*a*) as a fixed multiplier, multiply each of the individual items, and the respective results obtained will be the per cents which the individual items are of the total sum.

Example. Find the per cent that each department's monthly expense is of the total monthly expense.

Department	Expense
A	$ 600.00
B	500.00
C	1,200.00
D	700.00
E	1,000.00
Total	$4,000.00

Solution. Divide 1 by 4,000 to obtain the reciprocal, .00025. Multiply the expense of each department by this reciprocal, and the product will be the per cent that the department's expense is of the total expense.

Department	Expense		Reciprocal		Per Cent
A	$ 600.00	×	.00025	=	15 %
B	500.00	×	.00025	=	$12\frac{1}{2}$%
C	1,200.00	×	.00025	=	30 %
D	700.00	×	.00025	=	$17\frac{1}{2}$%
E	1,000.00	×	.00025	=	25 %
Total	$4,000.00				100 %

The foregoing method of calculating the rate per cent has a great many applications in an accountant's work. Another illustration is given—

that of calculating the per cent that each item in a profit and loss statement is of net sales.

Quality Meat Market

PROFIT AND LOSS STATEMENT FOR THE YEAR

	Detail	Amount	Per Cent
Net sales.........................		$20,000.00	100.00
Cost of merchandise sold...........		15,712.00	78.56
Gross profit...................		$ 4,288.00	21.44
Expenses			
Salaries and wages................	$2,266.00		11.33
Advertising......................	22.00		.11
Wrappings.......................	172.00		.86
Refrigeration....................	210.00		1.05
Heat, light, and power............	54.00		.27
Telephone.......................	54.00		.27
Rent............................	338.00		1.69
Interest.........................	146.00		.73
Depreciation of store equipment....	152.00		.76
Repairs to store equipment.........	44.00		.22
Insurance.......................	10.00		.05
Taxes...........................	42.00		.21
Losses from bad debts.............	38.00		.19
Other expenses...................	284.00		1.42
Total expenses...............		3,832.00	19.16
Net profit....................		$ 456.00	2.28

Explanation. The foregoing is a simple statement, and the per cents can be determined mentally if each item is divided by the amount of net sales. For the purpose of illustration, however, find the reciprocal of $20,000.00, which is .00005 (1 ÷ 20,000); then multiply each item by this reciprocal, and the results will be as shown in the per cent column.

PROBLEMS

1. The floor space occupied by *Z* Manufacturing Company was as follows:

Service Department *X*...............................	600 sq. ft.
Service Department *Y*...............................	1,100 sq. ft.
Service Department *Z*...............................	550 sq. ft.
Producing Department *A*............................	2,000 sq. ft.
Producing Department *B*............................	1,568 sq. ft.
Producing Department *C*............................	2,234 sq. ft.
Sales Department...................................	600 sq. ft.
Administrative Offices...............................	550 sq. ft.
	9,202 sq. ft.

The Building and Maintenance Expense account shows a total of $2,982.50. What amount of this expense should be distributed to each of the departments?

2. In the following tabulation, find the per cent that each department's floor space is of the total floor space:

	Sq. Ft. Floor Space	Per Cent of Total
Dept. 1	2,456	....
Dept. 2	1,014	....
Dept. 3	875	....
Dept. 4	1,252	....
Dept. 5	748	....
	6,345	100.00

3. Calculate the per cent that each item is of net sales.

The Food Mart

PROFIT AND LOSS STATEMENT

Net Sales		$35,600	100.00%
Cost of Merchandise Sold		27,969	....
Gross Profit		$ 7,631	....

Expenses

Salaries and Wages	$4,080		....
Advertising	28		....
Wrappings	266		....
Refrigeration	308		....
Heat, Light, and Power	106		....
Telephone	81		....
Rent	416		....
Interest	203		....
Depreciation of Store Equipment	147		....
Repairs to Store Equipment	45		....
Insurance	21		....
Taxes	39		....
Losses from Bad Debts	119		....
Other Expenses	490		....
Total Expenses		6,349	....
Net Profit		$ 1,282	....

CHECKING COMPUTATIONS

Methods. Addition may be checked by adding the second time, adding from the bottom to the top if the first addition was from the top to the bottom. This is preferable to performing the work in the same way the second time, as a mistake once made is likely to be repeated.

Subtraction may be checked by adding the subtrahend and the remainder. The sum should equal the minuend.

Multiplication may be checked by interchanging the multiplier and the multiplicand and multiplying again.

Division may be checked by multiplying the divisor and the quotient, adding to this product any remainder. The answer should equal the dividend.

Rough check. Rough check is an approximate check and is often used to locate large errors. It is also used in determining approximate results.   It is especially useful in checking misplacement of the decimal point in multiplication and division of decimal fractions.

A rough check of addition may be made as follows:

Example	*Check*
54,892	55
36,071	36
53,784	54
21,342	21
76,854	77
242,943	243

If the required result is thousands, disregard the three columns at the right, except to increase the fourth-column sum by one if the digit in the third column is 5 or more.   The check shows the answer to be approximately 243,000.

Absolute check.   There is no such thing as an absolute check, because there are always possibilities of offsetting errors, but the use of several methods of checking computations makes the probability of error so slight that one may rely on the result as correct.

Check numbers obtained by casting out the nines.   A simple and easily remembered check is that of casting out the nines.   Add the digits of the number, divide the sum by nine, and use the remainder, which is called "the excess," as the check number.   In the number 4,875, the sum of the digits is 24, and 24 divided by 9 equals 2 with an excess of 6.

Verification of addition.

Explanation.   The sum of the digits of 8,342 is 17 ($8 + 3 + 4 + 2$).   Cast out 9 and set down 8.   If a number contains a 9, skip it in adding the digits; thus, in 8,967, $8 + 6 + 7$ equals 21.   Cast out the nines and set down the excess, 3.   Find the check number of each line in the same way.   Add the check numbers, and cast the nines out of their sum.   Find the check number of the sum of the column being verified.   The final check number in each case is 5.

Example

8342	8
8967	3
8378	8
9276	6
8431	7
43394—5	32—5

PROBLEMS

Add, and verify by casting out the nines:

1.	**2.**	**3.**	**4.**
2487	7452	4501	1231
3156	8129	2765	4567
2982	5758	4567	1085
4756	2253	8256	3426
8928	7685	2435	7531

Verification of subtraction.

Example.

$$
\begin{array}{cc}
7856 & 8 \\
2138 & 5 \\
\hline
5718 & \overline{3}
\end{array}
$$

Explanation. 7,856 checks 8, and 2,138 checks 5. 8 − 5 = 3, and 5,718 checks 3.

PROBLEMS

Subtract, and verify by casting out the nines:

1.	2.	3.	4.
7496	7428	4751	8237
2831	1956	3286	5129

Verification of multiplication.

Example.

$$
\begin{array}{cc}
482 & 5 \\
376 & 7 \\
\hline
181232\text{—}8 & \overline{35}\text{—}8
\end{array}
$$

Explanation. 482 checks 5, and 376 checks 7. 7 × 5 = 35. 35 checks 8, and the product, 181,232, also checks 8.

PROBLEMS

Multiply, and verify by casting out the nines:

1.	2.	3.	4.
456	412	832	765
287	654	254	414

Verification of division. Division may be verified by multiplication; that is, the product of the quotient and the divisor should equal the dividend.   Apply the same principle in verifying with check numbers.

Example.

```
13)76492(5884
   65
   ---
   114
   104
   ---
   109
   104
   ---
    52
    52
    ---
```

Explanation. 76,492 checks 1. 13 checks 4. 5,884 checks 7. 4 × 7 = 28, and 28 checks 1, which is also the check number of the dividend.

PROBLEMS

Divide, and verify by casting out the nines:

1. 11,550 by 42.   **2.** 60,882 by 73.   **3.** 11,049 by 127.   **4.** 9,854 by 26.

Verification of division where there is a remainder.   The check number of the remainder added to the product of the check number of the quotient and the check number of the divisor should equal the check number of the dividend.

Example.

```
32)75892(2371
   04
   ───
   118
    96
   ───
   229
   224
   ───
    52
    32
   ──
```

Explanation. Step 1: The remainder, 20, checks 2. The quotient, 2,371, checks 4 The divisor, 32, checks 5. $2 + (4 \times 5) = 22$, and 22 checks 4.

Step 2: The dividend, 75,892, checks 4.

Step 1 and Step 2 should produce the same check number.

PROBLEMS

Divide, and verify by casting out the nines:

1. 34,765 by 52.   **2.** 29,878 by 87.   **3.** 95,763 by 26.   **4.** 8,476 by 41

Check numbers obtained by casting out the elevens.   Because casting out nines does not reveal errors in computations if two digits have been transposed, some persons prefer to use eleven as a check number.

Begin with the left-hand digit of the first number, and subtract it from the digit to its immediate right.   If the digit to the right is smaller, add eleven before subtracting.   Using the remainder as a new digit, subtract it from the third digit from the left, first adding eleven if necessary.   Use this remainder as a new digit, and subtract it from the fourth digit from the left, first adding eleven if necessary.   Continue in this manner until all the digits in the number have been used.   The final remainder is the check number of the number.

Another method of checking results by means of the number eleven is to use alternate digits.   From the sum of the first, third, fifth, etc., digits (beginning at units' place) subtract the sum of the second, fourth, sixth, etc., digits.   If the subtraction cannot be performed, eleven is first added to the sum of the odd digits, and the sum of the even digits is subtracted, the remainder being the check number.

Verification of addition.

Explanation. Begin at the left with the number 4,324. 4 from 14 (3 + 11) = 10. 10 from 13 (2 + 11) = 3. 3 from 4 = 1, the check number of 4,324.

Example.

Take the second number, 8,689. 8 from 17 (6 + 11) = 9. 9 from 19 (8 + 11) = 10. 10 from 20 (9 + 11) = 10, the check number of 8,689.

Check all the numbers in the same manner. Add the check numbers. The sum of the check numbers checks 1, and the sum of the numbers checks 1.

4324	1
8689	10
6327	2
8964	10
3487	0
31791—1	23—1

PROBLEMS

Add, and verify by casting out the elevens:

1.	2.	3.	4.
3789	2456	9755	8307
5462	1279	8256	7165
9581	2075	3851	2693
3998	2754	8632	2198
5314	9287	6311	5183

Verification of subtraction.

Example.

7453	6
1289	2
6164	4

Explanation. 7,453 checks 6. 1,289 checks 2. 6 − 2 = 4 and 6,164 checks 4.

PROBLEMS

Subtract, and verify by casting out the elevens:

1.	2.	3.	4.
8795	3465	7985	3079
1560	2134	5698	1002

Verification of multiplication.

Example.

584	1
256	3
149504	3

Explanation. 584 checks 1. 256 checks 3. 3 × 1 = 3, and 149,504 checks 3.

PROBLEMS

Multiply, and verify by casting out the elevens:

1.	2.	3.	4.
346	4289	7437	287
275	324	2856	36

Verification of division.

Example 1	Example 2
24)89784(3741	31)75893(2448
72	62
177	138
108	121
98	149
96	124
24	253
24	248
	5

Explanation 1. 89,784 checks 2. 24 checks 2. 3,741 checks 1. 2 × 1 = 2, the check number of the dividend.

Explanation 2. 75,893 checks 4. 31 checks 9. 2,448 checks 6. The remainder checks 5. 5 + (9 × 6) = 59. 59 checks 4, the same check number as that of the dividend.

PROBLEMS

Divide, and verify by casting out the elevens:

1. 80,925 by 83. **2.** 124,392 by 142. **3.** 25,874 by 49. **4.** 28,769 by 135.

Check number thirteen. If thirteen is used as a check number, transpositions and shiftings of figures are readily detected. However, in checking by 13, it is necessary actually to divide by 13.

TABLE OF MULTIPLES

1	13	6	78
2	26	7	91
3	39	8	104
4	52	9	117
5	65	10	130

All the dividing is done mentally.

Example. Cast out 13 from 247,563.

Explanation. Begin with the two left-hand digits. 24 checks 11. 11, with the next digit, 7, is 117, and 117 checks 0. Use the next two digits. 56 checks 4. 4 with the next digit is 43, and 43 checks 4.

The verification of addition, subtraction, multiplication, and division is performed in the same manner as with 9 and 11. The difference is in the method of arriving at the check number, as has been outlined.

PROBLEMS

1. Add, and verify by check number 13:

$$24875$$
$$32986$$
$$79840$$
$$80475$$
$$13048$$
$$93476$$

2. Subtract, and verify by check number 13:

$$84756$$
$$21348$$

3. Multiply, and verify by check number 13:

$$4875$$
$$259$$

4. Divide, and verify by check number 13:

$$975,648$$
$$348$$

2

Factors, Multiples, and Common Fractions

Factors. The *factors* of a number are the integers whose product is the number. Thus, the factors of 6 are 2 and 3, and the factors of 18 are 3 and 6, or 2 and 9. A prime factor is a prime number, that is, a number not exactly divisible by any number except itself and 1.

Factoring is the process of separating a number into its factors.

Example. What are the prime factors of 315?

Solution.

$$
\begin{array}{r}
3)\overline{315} \\
3)\overline{105} \\
5)\overline{35} \\
\overline{7}
\end{array}
$$
The prime factors of 315 are, therefore, $3 \times 3 \times 5 \times 7$.

Example. What are the factors of 315?

Solution.

$$
\begin{array}{r}
9)\overline{315} \\
7)\overline{35} \\
\overline{5}
\end{array}
$$
The factors of 315 are, therefore, $9 \times 7 \times 5$.

Factoring is important for its assistance in the solution of problems in fractions, practical measurements, percentage, and all problems in which cancellation is used. One use of factors was given on page **17**, "to multiply by factors of the multiplier," and another on page **18**, "to multiply when a part of the multiplier is a factor or multiple of another part."

Tests of divisibility.   To be able to factor a number quickly, one must become thoroughly familiar with the tests of divisibility.

A number is divisible by:

1. Two, if it is an even number or if it ends in zero.
2. Three, if the sum of its digits is divisible by 3.   Thus, 41754 is divisible by 3 because the sum of the digits is 21, and 21 is divisible by 3.
3. Four, if the two right-hand figures are zeros, or if they express a number divisible by 4.   Thus, 13724 is divisible by 4 because 24 is divisible by 4.
4. Five, if the units' figure is either a zero or a 5.
5. Six, if it is an even number the sum of whose digits is divisible by 3. Thus, 846, 918, and 54252 are divisible by 6.
6. Eight, if the three right-hand digits are zeros, or if they express a number divisible by 8.   Thus, 2000 and 5624 are divisible by 8.
7. Nine, if the sum of its digits is divisible by 9.
8. Ten, if the right-hand figure is zero.

(There is no simple method of testing divisibility by 7.)

Greatest common divisor.   A common divisor of two or more numbers is a number that evenly divides each of them.   Thus, a common divisor of 16 and 24 is 4.

The greatest common divisor of two or more numbers is the greatest number that will evenly divide each of them.   It is the product of all their common factors.

Example.   Find the greatest common divisor of 36, 63, and 54.

Solution.

$$
\begin{array}{r}
3)\overline{36\ \ 63\ \ 54} \\
3)\overline{12\ \ 21\ \ 18} \\
\overline{\ \ 4\ \ \ \ 7\ \ \ \ 6}
\end{array}
$$

Since 4, 7, and 6 have no common factors, the G. C. D. is $3 \times 3 = 9$.

A practical application of the principles involved in finding the G. C. D. is in reducing common fractions to their lowest terms.

PROBLEMS

Find the G. C. D. of the following:

1. 64, 160, 320, 640   **3.** 32, 48, 128
2. 36, 54, 90   **4.** 81, 729, 2187

5. *X*, *Y*, and *Z* own land on a new street.   *X* has 600 feet frontage, *Y* has 720 feet, and *Z* has 900 feet.   If they wish to cut this land into lots of equal width, how wide will the lots be, and how many will each have?

6. If you have three coils of steel cable measuring, respectively, 2205, 2940, and 4704 feet, and wish to cut the whole quantity into pieces of the greatest equal length possible without waste or splices, what will be the length of each piece? How many lengths will be cut from each coil?

Least common multiple. A common multiple of two or more numbers is a number that is evenly divisible by each of them. Thus, 24 is a common multiple of 3 and 8.

The least common multiple of two or more numbers is the least number that is evenly divisible by each of them. Thus, 12 is the **L. C. M.** of 4 and 6.

Example. What is the L. C. M. of 12, 28, 30, 42, and 64?

Solution.

$$
\begin{array}{r}
2)\overline{12\ \ 28\ \ 30\ \ 42\ \ 64} \\
2)\overline{\ \ 6\ \ 14\ \ 15\ \ 21\ \ 32} \\
3)\overline{\ \ 3\ \ \ \ 7\ \ 15\ \ 21\ \ 16} \\
7)\overline{\ \ 1\ \ \ \ 7\ \ \ \ 5\ \ \ \ 7\ \ 16} \\
\ \ 1\ \ \ \ 1\ \ \ \ 5\ \ \ \ 1\ \ 16
\end{array}
$$

$$2 \times 2 \times 3 \times 7 \times 5 \times 16 = 6{,}720$$

Explanation. Notice that any number not divisible by the factor is brought down, and the process is repeated as long as at least two of the numbers have a common factor. Finally, the L. C. M. is the product of the factors and the numbers having no common factor.

PROBLEMS

Find the L. C. M. of the following:

1. 6, 18, 30, 42

2. 16, 24, 64, 96

3. 45, 63, 72, 99

4. 14, 35, 42, 28

Cancellation. Certain computations involving division can be shortened by removing or cancelling equal factors from both dividend and divisor.

Example. If 32 units of product sell for $57.60, what will 18 units of the same product sell for at the same rate?

Solution.

$$
\frac{\overset{9}{\cancel{18}} \times \overset{\overset{3.60}{\cancel{14.40}}}{\cancel{57.60}}}{\underset{\underset{4}{\cancel{16}}}{\cancel{32}}} = 32.40
$$

PROBLEMS

Using cancellation, divide:

1. $\dfrac{27 \times 48 \times 96 \times 38}{19 \times 16 \times 9 \times 2}$ \qquad **2.** $\dfrac{8 \times 12 \times 15 \times 6}{5 \times 4 \times 3 \times 18}$

3. If 15 tons of coal cost \$258.00, how much will 25 tons cost at the same rate?

4. A ship's provisions will last 36 men for 216 days. How long will they last 124 men?

COMMON FRACTIONS

Terms explained. A *unit* is a single quantity by which another quantity of the same kind is measured: 1 foot is the unit of 5 feet; 1 barrel is the unit of 10 barrels; 1 acre is the unit of 40 acres, and so forth.

These integral units are often divided into equal parts known as *fractional units*, as $\frac{1}{2}$ ft., $\frac{1}{4}$ bbl., $\frac{1}{3}$ A., and so forth.

A *fraction* is an expression for one or more of the equal parts of a unit, as $\frac{1}{2}$ ft., $\frac{3}{4}$ ft., $\frac{2}{3}$ bbl., $\frac{5}{6}$ A., and so forth.

The number above the line in the expression of a fraction is called the *numerator;* the number below the line is called the *denominator.*

The *denominator* indicates the number (and hence the size) of parts into which the unit is divided.

The *numerator* indicates the number of these parts taken.

A *proper fraction* expresses less than a unit, or its numerator is less than its denominator; as, $\frac{2}{3}$, $\frac{3}{4}$, $\frac{5}{6}$, and so forth.

An *improper fraction* is a fraction whose numerator is equal to or greater than its denominator; as, $\frac{3}{3}$, $\frac{5}{4}$, $\frac{9}{8}$, and so forth.

A *mixed number* is a number expressed by a whole number and a fraction; as, $2\frac{1}{4}$, $3\frac{1}{2}$, $16\frac{3}{4}$, and so forth.

Reduction of fractions. Reduction is the process of changing the numerator and the denominator of a fraction without changing the value of the fraction.

A fraction is reduced to *higher terms* when the numerator and the denominator are expressed in larger numbers.

A fraction is reduced to *lower terms* when the numerator and the denominator are expressed in smaller numbers, and it is reduced to its *lowest terms* when there is no common divisor of its numerator and denominator.

Principle. Multiplying or dividing both numerator and denominator of a fraction by the same number does not change the value of the fraction. Thus, $\frac{16}{24}$ may be reduced to the equivalent fraction $\frac{4}{6}$ by dividing both terms by 4. The fraction $\frac{16}{24}$ has been reduced to lower terms. Again, $\frac{16}{24}$ may be reduced to the equivalent fraction $\frac{2}{3}$ by dividing both terms by 8. Here the fraction $\frac{16}{24}$ has been reduced to lowest terms, since 2 and 3 do not have a common divisor.

Conversely, $\frac{2}{3}$ may be changed to an equivalent fraction whose denominator is 24 by multiplying both terms by 8 (obtained by dividing 24 by 3), or $\frac{16}{24}$. Thus, the fraction $\frac{2}{3}$ has been reduced to a higher given denominator.

Mixed numbers. It is sometimes desirable to change a mixed number to an improper fraction, or, conversely, to change an improper fraction to a mixed number.

To change a mixed number to an improper fraction. Multiply the whole number by the denominator of the fraction, add the numerator, and place the sum over the denominator; thus, $3\frac{1}{3}$ is $\frac{10}{3}$, $4\frac{2}{5}$ is $\frac{22}{5}$, and $6\frac{1}{3}$ is $\frac{19}{3}$.

To change an improper fraction to a whole or a mixed number, divide the numerator by the denominator; thus, $\frac{12}{3}$ is 4, $\frac{6}{5}$ is $1\frac{1}{5}$, $\frac{10}{9}$ is $1\frac{1}{9}$ or $1\frac{1}{3}$, and $\frac{19}{4}$ is $4\frac{3}{4}$.

PROBLEMS

1. Reduce to lowest terms: $\frac{8}{16}$, $\frac{6}{24}$, $\frac{4}{12}$, $\frac{16}{24}$, $\frac{18}{30}$, $\frac{72}{96}$, $\frac{42}{49}$, $\frac{36}{60}$, $\frac{13}{39}$, $\frac{25}{30}$.

2. Change to equivalent fractions having denominators as indicated:

$\frac{1}{2}$ to 8ths	$\frac{1}{5}$ to 15ths	$\frac{4}{5}$ to 25ths
$\frac{2}{3}$ to 6ths	$\frac{1}{6}$ to 24ths	$\frac{5}{16}$ to 48ths
$\frac{4}{5}$ to 20ths	$\frac{3}{8}$ to 24ths	$\frac{3}{8}$ to 32nds
$\frac{1}{4}$ to 8ths	$\frac{5}{9}$ to 36ths	$\frac{7}{12}$ to 36ths.

3. Reduce to equivalent fractions whose denominators are 24: $\frac{1}{12}$, $\frac{2}{3}$, $\frac{5}{6}$, $\frac{3}{4}$, $\frac{7}{8}$, $\frac{7}{6}$.

4. Change to improper fractions: $4\frac{1}{8}$, $3\frac{1}{5}$, $1\frac{1}{2}$, $7\frac{1}{4}$, $8\frac{2}{3}$, $6\frac{1}{4}$, $3\frac{2}{3}$, $5\frac{3}{4}$, $5\frac{5}{9}$, $9\frac{4}{5}$.

5. Change to whole or mixed numbers: $\frac{48}{8}$, $\frac{12}{7}$, $\frac{32}{6}$, $\frac{20}{8}$, $\frac{72}{12}$, $\frac{16}{3}$, $\frac{8}{5}$, $\frac{64}{7}$, $\frac{96}{11}$, $\frac{17}{3}$.

6. Is the number of fractional units increased or decreased when we reduce $\frac{9}{12}$ to $\frac{3}{4}$? Is the size of the fractional unit increased or decreased when we reduce $\frac{9}{12}$ to $\frac{3}{4}$?

Addition and subtraction of fractions. Similar fractions are fractions that have a common denominator. Only similar fractions can be added or subtracted.

To add fractions, reduce the fractions to similar fractions having a common denominator and add the numerators.

To subtract fractions, reduce the fractions to similar fractions having a common denominator and subtract the numerators.

Example. Add: $\frac{1}{2}$, $\frac{2}{3}$, and $\frac{1}{4}$.

Solution.

$$\frac{17}{12} = 1\frac{5}{12}$$

Explanation. Inspection shows that 12 is the least common denominator. $\frac{1}{2}$ is $\frac{6}{12}$, $\frac{2}{3}$ is $\frac{8}{12}$, and $\frac{1}{4}$ is $\frac{3}{12}$. Adding the numerators of the similar fractions gives 17, and $\frac{17}{12}$ is $1\frac{5}{12}$.

Example. Subtract: $\frac{3}{4} - \frac{5}{16}$.

Solution.

$$\frac{3}{4} = \frac{12}{16}$$
$$\frac{12}{16} - \frac{5}{16} = \frac{7}{16}$$

Multiplication of fractions. (*a*) To multiply a fraction by a whole number, multiply the numerator or divide the denominator of the fraction by the whole number.

Example. Multiply $6 \times \frac{5}{12}$.

Solution.

$$6 \times \frac{5}{12} = \frac{30}{12} = 2\frac{1}{2}$$
$$\text{or}$$
$$12 \div 6 = 2, \text{ and } \frac{5}{2} = 2\frac{1}{2}$$

(*b*) To multiply a whole number by a fraction, multiply the whole number by the numerator of the fraction and write the product over the denominator. Cancel when possible.

Example. Find $\frac{2}{5}$ of 35.

Solution.

$$\frac{2}{5} \times 35 = \frac{70}{5} = 14$$
$$\text{or}$$
$$\frac{2 \times \overset{7}{\cancel{35}}}{\cancel{5} \times 1} = 14$$

(*c*) To multiply a fraction by a fraction, multiply the numerators to obtain the numerator of the answer, and multiply the denominators to obtain the denominator of the answer. Cancel when possible.

Example. Find $\frac{2}{3}$ of $\frac{15}{16}$.

Solution.

$$\frac{2}{3} \times \frac{15}{16} = \frac{30}{48} = \frac{5}{8}$$
$$\text{or}$$
$$\frac{\cancel{2} \times \overset{5}{\cancel{15}}}{\cancel{3} \times \underset{8}{\cancel{16}}} = \frac{5}{8}$$

(*d*) To multiply a mixed number by a mixed number, reduce each mixed number to an improper fraction and proceed as in (*c*).

Example. Find the product of: $3\frac{1}{2} \times 4\frac{1}{8}$.

Solution.

$$\frac{7}{2} \times \frac{33}{8} = \frac{231}{16} = 14\frac{7}{16}$$

Example. Find the product of: $6\frac{2}{5} \times 5\frac{1}{8}$.

Solution.

$$\frac{\overset{4}{\cancel{32}} \times 41}{5 \times \cancel{8}} = \frac{164}{5} = 32\frac{4}{5}$$

PROBLEMS

Find:

1. $9 \times \frac{5}{18}$ 3. $\frac{2}{5}$ of 35   5. $\frac{2}{3}$ of $\frac{15}{16}$ 7. $3\frac{1}{4} \times 4\frac{1}{2}$
2. $24 \times \frac{3}{4}$ 4. $\frac{5}{12}$ of 16   6. $\frac{4}{5}$ of $\frac{25}{28}$ 8. $12\frac{3}{4} \times 8\frac{1}{4}$

Division of fractions. (*a*) To divide a fraction by a whole number, divide the numerator or multiply the denominator by the whole number.

Example. Divide $\frac{25}{28}$ by 5.

Solution.

$$25 \div 5 = 5 \quad \text{Answer: } \frac{5}{28}$$
$$\text{or}$$
$$\frac{\overset{5}{\cancel{25}} \times 1}{28 \times \cancel{5}} = \frac{5}{28}$$

(*b*) To divide any quantity—a whole number, a mixed number, or a fraction, by a fraction, invert the divisor and multiply.

Example. Divide 8 by $\frac{2}{3}$.

Solution.

$$\frac{\overset{4}{\cancel{8}} \times 3}{1 \times \cancel{2}} = 12$$

Example. Divide $16\frac{1}{4}$ by $\frac{5}{6}$.

Solution.

$$\frac{\overset{13}{\cancel{65}} \times \overset{3}{\cancel{6}}}{\underset{2}{\cancel{4}} \times \cancel{5}} = \frac{39}{2} = 19\frac{1}{2}$$

Example. Divide $\frac{3}{4}$ by $\frac{1}{2}$.

Solution.

$$\frac{3 \times \cancel{2}}{\underset{2}{\cancel{4}} \times 1} = \frac{3}{2} = 1\frac{1}{2}$$

PROBLEMS

Divide:

a. $\frac{18}{35}$ by 3   c. 8 by $\frac{2}{3}$ e. $16\frac{3}{4}$ by $\frac{1}{8}$ g. $3\frac{1}{2}$ by $1\frac{1}{2}$
b. $\frac{36}{43}$ by 9   d. 9 by $\frac{3}{5}$ f. $18\frac{4}{5}$ by $\frac{5}{9}$ h. $9\frac{3}{4}$ by $3\frac{1}{4}$

1. How many pieces of wire each $8\frac{3}{4}$ inches long can be cut from 40 feet of wire?

2. If $\frac{2}{3}$ of a ton of coal costs \$12.75, what is the cost of one ton?

3. How many sash weights each weighing $2\frac{1}{2}$ pounds can be cast from 120 pounds of pig iron, if $\frac{1}{8}$ of the quantity of pig iron is wasted in the casting operation?

4. A room is $18\frac{5}{8}$ feet long and $14\frac{1}{2}$ feet wide. The width of the room is what part of the length of the room?

5. A carpenter has a board that is 20 feet long, but it is $\frac{1}{4}$ longer than he needs. How long a board does he need?

6. What is the cost of $7\frac{1}{2}$ tons of coal at $\$14\frac{1}{4}$ a ton?

7. A house and lot are valued at \$13,200. If the lot is worth $\frac{3}{8}$ as much as the house, what is the value of each?

8. If a man can earn $\$10\frac{3}{4}$ a day, how long will it take him to earn $\$247\frac{1}{4}$?

9. A table is 20 feet long. How many people can be seated on the two sides if you allow $1\frac{2}{3}$ feet for each person?

10. Henry's time book shows that his working time for one week was as follows: Monday, $7\frac{1}{2}$ hours; Tuesday, $8\frac{1}{4}$ hours; Wednesday, 8 hours; Thursday, $9\frac{1}{4}$ hours; Friday, $8\frac{1}{2}$ hours; Saturday, $6\frac{2}{3}$ hours.

He is paid straight time for 8 hours or less and time and a half for hours in excess of 8 each day other than Saturday, when he receives double-time pay for hours worked. How much did he earn at $\$1\frac{5}{8}$ an hour?

11. The shipping clerk reported that he dispatched 320 packages averaging $28\frac{3}{4}$ pounds each. What was the total weight of packages dispatched?

12. A cubic foot of water weighs $62\frac{1}{2}$ pounds, and there are approximately $7\frac{1}{2}$ gallons to the cubic foot. Estimate the weight of water that a 10-gallon keg will contain.

To find the product of any two mixed numbers ending in $\frac{1}{2}$.

(a) *When the sum of the whole numbers is an even number.* To the product of the whole numbers, add one-half of their sum, and annex $\frac{1}{4}$.

Example. Multiply $24\frac{1}{2}$ by $8\frac{1}{2}$.

Solution.

$$
\begin{array}{r}
24\frac{1}{2} \\
8\frac{1}{2} \\
\hline
192 \\
16 \\
\hline
208\frac{1}{4}
\end{array}
\quad
\begin{array}{l}
(8 \times 24) \\
(\frac{1}{2} \text{ of the sum of 24 and 8}) \\
(\frac{1}{4} \text{ annexed})
\end{array}
$$

PROBLEMS

Multiply:

1. $8\frac{1}{2}$ by $4\frac{1}{2}$.   **3.** $28\frac{1}{2}$ by $12\frac{1}{2}$.   **5.** $18\frac{1}{2}$ by $18\frac{1}{2}$.

2. $12\frac{1}{2}$ by $8\frac{1}{2}$.   **4.** $16\frac{1}{2}$ by $14\frac{1}{2}$.   **6.** $10\frac{1}{2}$ by $34\frac{1}{2}$.

(b) *When the sum of the whole numbers is an odd number.* To the product of the whole numbers, add one-half of their sum, less 1, and annex $\frac{3}{4}$.

Example. Multiply $15\frac{1}{2}$ by $6\frac{1}{2}$.

Solution.

$$
\begin{array}{ll}
15\frac{1}{2} & \\
\underline{6\frac{1}{2}} & \\
90 & (6 \times 15) \\
\underline{10} & (\frac{1}{2} \text{ of } 15 + 6 - 1) \\
100\frac{3}{4} & (\frac{3}{4} \text{ annexed})
\end{array}
$$

PROBLEMS

Multiply:

1. $18\frac{1}{2}$ by $5\frac{1}{2}$.   **3.** $38\frac{1}{2}$ by $5\frac{1}{2}$.   **5.** $23\frac{1}{2}$ by $4\frac{1}{2}$.
2. $14\frac{1}{2}$ by $7\frac{1}{2}$.   **4.** $13\frac{1}{2}$ by $8\frac{1}{2}$.   **6.** $19\frac{1}{2}$ by $6\frac{1}{2}$.

To multiply a mixed number by a mixed number.

Example. Multiply $524\frac{1}{2}$ by $27\frac{1}{3}$.

Solution.

$$
\begin{array}{ll}
524\frac{1}{2} & \\
\underline{27\frac{1}{3}} & \\
14148 \quad 6 & = \text{common denominator of fractions} \\
174\frac{2}{3} \quad 4 \;\Big\} & \\
13\frac{1}{2} \quad 3 \;\Big\} & = \text{numerators of changed fractions} \\
\underline{\frac{1}{6} \quad 1\;\Big)} & \\
14336\frac{1}{3} \quad \frac{8}{6} & = 1\frac{1}{3}
\end{array}
$$

Explanation. Multiply 524 by 27, obtaining the first part of the answer, 14,148. Next, take $\frac{1}{3}$ of 524, obtaining $174\frac{2}{3}$. Then take $\frac{1}{2}$ of 27, obtaining $13\frac{1}{2}$. Finally, take $\frac{1}{3}$ of $\frac{1}{2}$, obtaining $\frac{1}{6}$. Add the four partial products, and the complete product is $14,336\frac{1}{3}$.

PROBLEMS

Multiply:

1. $247\frac{2}{3}$ by $39\frac{1}{4}$.   **3.** $59\frac{1}{7}$ by $15\frac{1}{3}$.   **5.** $181\frac{3}{4}$ by $6\frac{2}{3}$.
2. $849\frac{1}{6}$ by $28\frac{1}{2}$.   **4.** $176\frac{5}{8}$ by $34\frac{2}{7}$.   **6.** $56\frac{1}{2}$ by $12\frac{2}{3}$.

Decimal fractions. A decimal fraction is a fraction whose denominator is some power of ten, indicated by a decimal point placed just to the right of the units' place. Thus, .1 is $\frac{1}{10}$, .05 is $\frac{5}{100}$, and .25 is $\frac{25}{100}$ or $\frac{1}{4}$.

Approximate numbers. Since many of the numbers we work with are approximate numbers, it is important that the student learn to recognize approximate numbers and to appreciate the limitations of results obtained by using approximate numbers.

All measurements are approximate numbers. If a surveyor measures a distance and finds it to be 124.7 feet, it would not be correct to say that the distance is exactly 124.7 feet. We would say that the distance, correct to four significant figures, is 124.7 feet. By more accurate methods the distance might be found to be 124.73 feet, which would be correct to five significant figures.

A measurement of 20.006 has five significant figures. There are two significant figures in .00043, the three zeros being merely "space-fillers" put in to locate the decimal point.

In 53,000 the number of significant figures is uncertain. When we say that the population of a city is 53,000, we do not usually mean that the population is exactly 53,000, but rather that the population is closer to 53,000 than it is to 52,000 or 54,000. In this case, only the 5 and the 4 are significant. On the other hand, the population may actually be 53,000 in which case the number has five significant figures. It follows that the number might also have three or four significant figures.

The number .05600 has four significant figures. The initial zero is a "space-filler," but the last two zeros show that the number is correct to the nearest one-hundred-thousandth.

The following table gives further examples.

Approximate Number	Number of Significant Digits
325	3
127,000	3 to 6
2.73	3
630	2 or 3
.0005	1
350.0	4
.00370	3
50,000	1 to 5
50,001	5

To round off an approximate number to a number of less accuracy, the following rule is used:

When the digit immediately to the right of the last retained digit is 5 or more, the last retained digit should be increased by one; when the digit immediately to the right of the last retained digit is less than 5, the last retained digit is left unchanged.

For example,

4.01738 rounded off to three decimal places would be 4.017.
3.78 rounded off to one decimal place would become 3.8.
3.065 rounded off to two places would become 3.07.

Measurements are not the only approximate numbers. Almost all numbers which appear in mathematical tables are approximate. A table of square roots shows that

$$\sqrt{7} \text{ is } 2.64575$$

and a table of logarithms shows that

$$\log 35.4 \text{ is } 1.54900.$$

These are approximations, both to six significant figures.

PROBLEMS

1. For each of the following approximate numbers, state the number of significant figures and round off to one less significant figure.

(a) 14.76	(f) .00079
(b) .0393	(g) 20.0
(c) 1740.5	(h) 4.3008
(d) .010007	(i) 12.04
(e) 2.400	(j) 1.999

2. Round off each of the following numbers to two places of decimal.

(a) 24.768 (b) .033 (c) 6.5439 (d) .006 (e) .255

Calculations with exact numbers. If it is found by counting that there are twelve people in a room, then 12 is an exact number. If a man writes a check for $500.00, then $500.00 is an exact number. If a calculation is performed with exact numbers, the answer will be exactly correct.

Addition and subtraction. To add or to subtract decimals, write the numbers so that the decimal points fall vertically in a line and proceed as in whole numbers.

Example. Add: .01, 4.72, 78.25, and .005.

Solution.

```
   .01
  4.72
 78.25
   .005
 82.985
```

Example. Subtract: 47.02 − .92.

Solution.

```
 47.02
   .92
 46.10
```

PROBLEMS

1. Add: 25.679, .0356, 2.78, and .017.

2. Add: 136.2, 28.348, .004 and 1.356.

3. Subtract: 13.48 from 27.049.

4. Subtract: .003 from .47

Multiplication. To multiply decimal fractions, multiply as in whole numbers and point off as many decimal places in the product as there are places in both multiplicand and multiplier.

Example. Multiply 3.06 × .8.

Solution.

$$
\begin{array}{r}
3.06 \\
.8 \\
\hline
2.448
\end{array}
$$

Explanation. Since there are three decimal places in both the multiplicand and the multiplier, point off three decimal places in the product.

Example. Multiply: 23.8564 by 6.72.

Solution.

$$
\begin{array}{r}
23.8564 \\
6.72 \\
\hline
477128 \\
1669948 \\
1431384 \\
\hline
160315008
\end{array}
$$

Explanation. As there are six decimal places in the multiplicand and the multiplier, point off six decimal places in the product. The answer is 160.315008. Rough check: 24 × 7 = 168.

Division. Proceed as with whole numbers, annexing zeros to the dividend if necessary. The number of decimal places in the quotient must equal the number in the dividend minus the number in the divisor.

Example. Divide: 54.864 by .24.

Solution.

$$
\begin{array}{r}
.24)54.864(228.6 \\
6\,8 \\
2\,06 \\
144 \\
0
\end{array}
$$

Explanation. Divide by writing the remainders only. The quotient is 2286. As there are three decimal places in the dividend and two decimal places in the divisor, point off one decimal place in the quotient. The answer is therefore, 228.6.

Example.   Divide: 256.7894 by 5.23.

Solution.

$$
\begin{array}{r}
49.099 \\
5.23{\overline{)256.78940}} \\
47\ 58 \\
5194 \\
4870 \\
163
\end{array}
$$

Explanation. Predetermine the placing of the decimal. As there are two decimals in the divisor, place the decimal point over the third decimal place in the dividend. Place the first figure of the quotient over the last figure of the partial dividend. One zero has been annexed to the dividend in order to obtain a quotient to three decimals. Rough check: 49 × 5 = 245.

PROBLEMS

Multiply:

1. 34.278 × 1.45
2. 395.264 × .035
3. 74.26 by .00423
4. .056 by .083
5. 18.42 × .045

Divide:

6. 5.8769 by 1.34
7. .0084 by 1.5
8. 45.87 by .0056
9. 8.45 by 25.3
10. 956 by 4.87

Calculations with approximate numbers.   In calculations with approximate numbers, the results are, of course, approximate numbers. To avoid giving a false appearance of accuracy, such results should be rounded off according to the following rules:

Addition and subtraction.   The sum or difference obtained in adding or subtracting approximate numbers cannot be accurate to more decimal places than the least accurate of the numbers.   Hence, before adding two or more approximate numbers, the numbers should be rounded off to the number of decimal places in the least accurate of the numbers.

Multiplication and division.   The product or quotient obtained in multiplication or division with approximate numbers should not contain more significant figures than the least accurate of the numbers.

Example.   Find the sum of 3.875, 24.6, 13.45, and 45.30.

Solution.   Here all numbers should be rounded off to one decimal place, since the least accurate number (24.6) has one decimal place.

$$
\begin{array}{r}
3.9 \\
24.6 \\
13.5 \\
45.3 \\
\hline
87.3
\end{array}
$$

Example.   Subtract 34.706 − 17.30522.

Solution. Here 17.30522 should be rounded off to three decimal places.

$$
\begin{array}{r}
34.706 \\
17.305 \\
\hline
17.401
\end{array}
$$

Example. A firm which employs eight men has a monthly payroll of $2226.50. What is the average pay for the employees of this company?

Solution. $2226.50 \div 8 = \$278.3125.$

Since these numbers are exact, it is correct to say that the average pay is exactly $278.3125.

Example. Find the area of a hall which measures 83.5 ft. by 9.3 ft.

Solution. Multiplying length by width we get:

$$
\begin{array}{r}
83.5 \\
9.3 \\
\hline
25\ 05 \\
751\ 5 \\
\hline
776.55
\end{array}
$$

Since the factors are approximate numbers, this product must be rounded off to two significant figures, giving 780 sq. ft., where the zero is not significant.

Example. If there are 16 people in a room of 1041 cu ft., how much space per person is there?

Solution. $1041 \div 16 = 65.0625$

Since the number 1041 is approximate, the answer must be rounded off to 65.06 cu. ft.

NOTE: In calculations involving both approximate and exact numbers, the exact number may be regarded as having an infinite number of significant figures. In the above problem, 16 should be thought of as 16.0000000000 . . .

PROBLEMS

1. In the following, all numbers are approximate. Perform the operations indicated, retaining the proper number of significant figures.

(a) 20.4×1.13

(b) $13.94 + 2.8 + 7.092 + .65$

(c) $571.2 \div 2.8$

(d) $.05614 \div 7$

(e) $176.30 + 2.47 + .98765$

(f) 24300×70, where none of the zeros is significant.

(g) $.9 \times .05$

(h) $2.976 - .8437$

(i) $58.363 - 24.2$

(j) 110.0×50001

(k) $\dfrac{35.8 \times 9.86}{136}$

(l) $\dfrac{9.008 \times 3.3}{4.6}$

2. In each of the following, assume the left-hand number to be exact and all others to be approximate. Perform the operations indicated, retaining the proper number of significant figures.

(a) 92.41 × 40.1
(b) 2 + .03 + .037
(c) 3012 ÷ 1.2
(d) 2.7 − 1.04
(e) 13 × 486.9

In the following problems, be careful to give answers to the proper number of significant digits.

3. A silver collection taken at a Sunday concert amounted to $252.75. It was estimated that 700 people attended. What was the average contribution?

4. A racing car is clocked at 5.6 seconds for a distance of 1535 feet. Find its average speed in feet per second.

5. What is the area of a table top which measures 2.3 ft. by 5.7 ft.?

Contracted multiplication. For students performing multiplications and divisions of decimal numbers as read from logarithm tables, interest tables, annuity tables, and so forth, which are correct to a designated number of decimal places only, another time-saving method of multiplication is presented.

Let us multiply 4.7892 × 3.1765 using the regular method:

$$
\begin{array}{r}
4.7892 \\
3.1765 \\
\hline
239460 \\
287352 \\
335244 \\
47892 \\
14\ 3676 \\
\hline
15.21289380 \\
\end{array}
$$

Recall that, if two numbers are correct to four decimal places each, the product cannot be assumed to be correct beyond four decimal places. The product above is written to eight decimal places, whereas only four decimal places can be considered correct. We have, therefore, performed unnecessary work on the last four decimal places.

The above multiplication could be written in the following manner:

4.7892	= multiplicand
3.1765	= multiplier
.0023|9460	= 4.7892 × .0005
.0287|352	= 4.7892 × .006
.3352|44	= 4.7892 × .07
.4789|2	− 4.7892 × .1
14.3676|	= 4.7892 × 3
15.2128|9380	

Obviously, everything to the right of the vertical line is unnecessary. This multiplication could be performed in the reverse order, as below.

4.7892	= multiplicand
5.6713	= multiplier reversed
14.3676	= 4.7892 × 3
.4789$\vert$2	= 4.7892 × .1
.3352$\vert$44	= 4.7892 × .07
.0287$\vert$352	= 4.7892 × .006
.0023$\vert$9460	= 4.7892 × .0005
15.2128$\vert$9380	

If we discard everything to the right of the vertical line, the solution is unaffected.

$$
\begin{array}{r}
4.7892 \\
5.6713 \\
\hline
14\ 3676 \\
4789 \\
3352 \\
287 \\
24 \\
\hline
15.2129
\end{array}
$$

It should be noted that the decimal point in the answer lies directly below the decimal point in the multiplicand.

The steps involved in this solution can now be outlined:

(*a*) Prepare the multiplier. This is done by moving the decimal point either to the left or to the right so that the multiplier has one non-zero digit to the left of the decimal place.

(*b*) Adjust the multiplicand. This is done by moving the decimal point either to the right or to the left so that the problem remains identical with the original.

$$30.657 \times 20.342 = 306.57 \times 2.0342$$
$$365.2422 \times 364.31 = 36524.22 \times 3.6431$$
$$.003657 \times 19.57 = .03657 \times 1.957$$
$$567.93 \times .00213 = .56793 \times 2.13$$

It should be noted that if the decimal place is moved x places to the right in the multiplier, then it is moved x places to the left in the multiplicand; if it is moved x places to the left in the multiplier, then it is moved x places to the right in the multiplicand.

(*c*) Write the multiplier down in reverse order under the multiplicand, with the right-hand digit under the xth decimal place in the multiplicand if x decimal places are desired in the answer.

(*d*) Multiply through normally by the first digit on the right.

(*e*) Cancel the digit you have multiplied by and the digit directly above it.

(*f*) Multiply through by the next digit 1, saying, $1 \times 2 = 2$, which gives 0 to carry since $2 < 5$ but we write nothing. Then, $1 \times 9 = 9$, which is written directly under the first digit on the right of the first line in the solution.

(*g*) Cancel the digit you have multiplied by and the digit directly above it.

(*h*) Multiply through by the next digit 7, saying, $7 \times 9 = 63$ so we carry 6; $7 \times 8 = 56$ and 6 to carry give 62. Write the 2 down directly under the first digit on the right of the first line in the solution and carry 6, and so forth, getting 3352.

(*i*) Carry through the multiplication by each digit in like manner.

(*j*) Total the result, getting 152129.

(*k*) Place the decimal point in the answer directly under the decimal place in the multiplicand (adjusting the multiplier permits this), getting 15.2129 as the answer.

Example. Multiply 0.47869347 by 72.5 and obtain the product correct to three decimal places.

Solution. $0.47869347 \times 72.5 = 4.7869347 \times 7.25$.

$$
\begin{array}{r}
4.7869347 \\
527 \\
\hline
33\ 508 \\
957 \\
239 \\
\hline
34.704
\end{array}
$$

PROBLEMS

1. Evaluate 5.987654×3.147, correct to four decimals.

2. Evaluate 3.596×14.57, correct to three decimals.

3. Evaluate 44.187542×6.2434 correct to four decimals.

4. Calculate to the nearest cent the value of each of the following:
(*a*) $2,376.205 \times 3.53710872$.
(*b*) $2,811.362 \times 2.69159903$.
(*c*) $1,000.00 \times 4.18635404 \times 12.56709979$.
(*d*) $30,265. \times 15.67362495$.

Contracted division. Many times an accountant has to do a rather complicated division, and so a time-saving method of division is presented.

Let us divide 3768.943 by 57.68429 using the regular method of long division. For the purpose of comparing this with contracted division, the decimal points are adjusted so that the divisor has one figure to the left of its decimal point.

```
                        65.337|
         5.768429  |376.894|3
                    346.105|74
                    ───────────
                     30.788|560
                     28.842|145
                    ───────────
                      1.946|4150
                      1.730|5287
                    ───────────
                       .215|88630
                       .173|05287
                    ───────────
                       .042|833430
                       .040|379003
                    ───────────
                       .002|454427
```

It should be noted immediately that the digits to the right of the vertical line do not contribute anything to the required answer.   The proposed contracted division permits the carrying out of a long division to the desired degree of accuracy without unnecessary labor.

The procedure is:

(*a*) Prepare the divisor.   This is done by moving the decimal point either to the left or to the right so that the divisor has one non-zero digit to the left of the decimal place.

(*b*) Adjust the dividend.   This is done by moving the decimal point either to the left or to the right so that the problem remains identical with the original.

$$30.657 \div 20.342 = 3.0657 \div 2.0342$$
$$.003657 \div 19.57 = .0003657 \div 1.957$$
$$567.93 \div .00213 = 567930. \div 2.13$$

It should be noted that if the decimal place is moved x places to the right in the divisor, then it is moved x places to the right in the dividend; and if it is moved x places to the left in the divisor, then it is moved x places to the left in the dividend.

(*c*) Lay out the problem in the ordinary long-division fashion:

$$5768429 \overline{)376.8943}$$

The decimal point in the divisor may be omitted, since the decimal point in the answer will lie directly above the decimal point in the dividend.   (Adjusting the divisor permits this.)

(*d*) Since the answer is required correct to two decimal places, the problem should be worked to three decimal places and the answer rounded off to two decimal places.   Since we are working to three decimal places, we shall use only the first six digits of the dividend and shall cross off the 3.   We shall, therefore, use only the first five digits of the divisor, since any more digits would give us a number which would not be contained in the six-digit dividend.

$$5768\cancel{429} \overline{)376.894\cancel{3}}$$

(*e*) Divide 57684 into 376894. Since it goes six times, place a 6 over the 7 in the dividend and a 6 under the 4 in the divisor.

$$
\begin{array}{r}
6 \\
5768\cancel{4}\cancel{2}\cancel{9}\overline{)376.894\cancel{3}} \\
6
\end{array}
$$

(*f*) Multiply the divisor by 6 and include the carryover from 6 × 2 (the 2 in the divisor which was crossed off). Subtract:

$$
\begin{array}{r}
6 \\
5768\cancel{4}\cancel{2}\cancel{9}\overline{)376.894\cancel{3}} \\
6 \quad 346\ 105 \\
\overline{30\ 789}
\end{array}
$$

(*g*) Cross off the 4 in the divisor and divide 5768 into the new dividend 30789. Since it goes five times, place 5 next to the 6 in the quotient and under the 8 in the divisor. Multiply by 5, remembering to add the carryover from 5 × 4.

$$
\begin{array}{r}
65 \\
5768\cancel{4}\cancel{2}\cancel{9}\overline{)376.894\cancel{3}} \\
56 \quad 346\ 105 \\
\overline{30\ 789} \\
28\ 842 \\
\overline{1\ 947}
\end{array}
$$

(*h*) Continue this process until the quotient is evaluated to three decimal places. By this time, all the digits in the divisor will have been crossed out.

$$
\begin{array}{r}
65.337 \\
\cancel{5}\cancel{7}\cancel{6}\cancel{8}\cancel{4}\cancel{2}\cancel{9}\overline{)376.894\cancel{3}} \\
73356 \quad 346\ 105 \\
\overline{30\ 789} \\
28\ 842 \\
\overline{1\ 947} \\
1\ 730 \\
\overline{217} \\
173 \\
\overline{44} \\
40 \\
\overline{4}
\end{array}
$$

(*i*) Round the answer off to two decimal places. The answer is, therefore, 65.34.

Example 1. Divide 7.24464613 by 5.38287878 and obtain the answer correct to 8 decimal places.

Solution.

```
                              1.34586834
                5.38287878 7.24464613
                4 38685431 5 38287878
                           1 86176735
                           1 61486363
                             24690372
                             21531515
                              3158857
                              2691439
                               467418
                               430630
                                36788
                                32297
                                 4491
                                 4306
                                  185
                                  161
                                   24
                                   21
                                    3
```

Example 2. Evaluate $\dfrac{42.3}{673.58}$ correct to four decimal places.

Solution. Here we shall work to five places of decimals, since the answer is required to four places. It is necessary to add two zeros to the end of the dividend, since the dividend has only three digits in it.

```
                    .06280
          67358 .42300
          0826   40415
                  1885
                  1347
                   538
                   538
```

This rounds off to .0628.

Example 3. Divide .76839 by .234 correct to two decimal places.

Solution.

```
                    3.283
          2340 7.6839
               7 020
                 663
                 468
                 195
                 187
                   8
                   7
                   1
```

Here it was necessary to add a zero to the end of the divisor so that the divisor would have as many digits as the dividend.

PROBLEMS

Evaluate correctly to the nearest cent:

1. $2,394.291 ÷ 3.497572
2. $9,093.255 ÷ 2.57284313
3. $14,300.4671 ÷ 9.231049

To change a decimal fraction to an equivalent common fraction. Write the denominator of the decimal, omit the decimal point, and reduce to lowest terms. Thus, to reduce to common fractions in lowest terms or to mixed numbers:

$$.75 = \tfrac{75}{100} = \tfrac{3}{4} \qquad .025 = \tfrac{25}{1000} = \tfrac{1}{40}$$
$$6.25 = 6\tfrac{25}{100} = 6\tfrac{1}{4} \qquad 4.125 = 4\tfrac{125}{1000} = 4\tfrac{1}{8}$$

To change a common fraction to a decimal. A common fraction may be regarded as an indicated division. Thus: $\tfrac{2}{5}$ may be regarded as $2 ÷ 5$; therefore, $\tfrac{2}{5}$ expressed as a decimal is .4; similarly, $\tfrac{1}{7}$ is $.14\tfrac{2}{7}$, $\tfrac{3}{8}$ is .375, and $\tfrac{7}{16}$ is .4375.

Aliquot parts. An aliquot part of any number is a number that is contained in it an integral number of times. Thus, 5, 10, 20, and 50 are aliquot parts of 100; that is, $5 = \tfrac{1}{20}$ of 100, $10 = \tfrac{1}{10}$ of 100, and so forth.

The use of aliquot parts. As a means of saving time in multiplication and in division, it is useful to know the decimal equivalents of common fractions, or, conversely, to know the common-fraction equivalents of decimal fractions. Aliquot parts are of value in addition and subtraction if an adding machine or a calculating machine is used, because machines are not adapted for general work involving common fractions.

TABLE OF ALIQUOT PARTS OF 1

Common Fraction	Decimal Equivalent	Common Fraction	Decimal Equivalent
$\tfrac{1}{2}$	.50	$\tfrac{1}{9}$	$.11\tfrac{1}{9}$
$\tfrac{1}{3}$	$.33\tfrac{1}{3}$	$\tfrac{1}{10}$	.10
$\tfrac{2}{3}$	$.66\tfrac{2}{3}$	$\tfrac{1}{11}$	$.09\tfrac{1}{11}$
$\tfrac{1}{4}$	.25	$\tfrac{1}{12}$	$.08\tfrac{1}{3}$
$\tfrac{3}{4}$	.75	$\tfrac{5}{12}$	$.41\tfrac{2}{3}$
$\tfrac{1}{5}$	.20	$\tfrac{7}{12}$	$.58\tfrac{1}{3}$
$\tfrac{1}{6}$	$.16\tfrac{2}{3}$	$\tfrac{11}{12}$	$.91\tfrac{2}{3}$
$\tfrac{5}{6}$	$.83\tfrac{1}{3}$	$\tfrac{1}{15}$	$.06\tfrac{2}{3}$
$\tfrac{1}{7}$	$.14\tfrac{2}{7}$	$\tfrac{1}{16}$	$.06\tfrac{1}{4}$
$\tfrac{2}{7}$	$.28\tfrac{4}{7}$	$\tfrac{3}{16}$	$.18\tfrac{3}{4}$
$\tfrac{3}{7}$	$.42\tfrac{6}{7}$	$\tfrac{5}{16}$	$.31\tfrac{1}{4}$
$\tfrac{4}{7}$	$.57\tfrac{1}{7}$	$\tfrac{7}{16}$	$.43\tfrac{3}{4}$
$\tfrac{5}{7}$	$.71\tfrac{3}{7}$	$\tfrac{9}{16}$	$.56\tfrac{1}{4}$
$\tfrac{6}{7}$	$.85\tfrac{5}{7}$	$\tfrac{11}{16}$	$.68\tfrac{3}{4}$
$\tfrac{1}{8}$	$.12\tfrac{1}{2}$	$\tfrac{15}{16}$	$.93\tfrac{3}{4}$
$\tfrac{3}{8}$	$.37\tfrac{1}{2}$	$\tfrac{1}{25}$	.04
$\tfrac{5}{8}$	$.62\tfrac{1}{2}$	$\tfrac{1}{32}$	$.03\tfrac{1}{8}$
$\tfrac{7}{8}$	$.87\tfrac{1}{2}$	$\tfrac{9}{32}$	$.09\tfrac{3}{8}$

The fractions in the above table can be extended as decimals as far as the work demands.

PROBLEMS

Express the following as decimal fractions; non-terminating fractions should be carried to the sixth decimal place and the common fraction annexed:

$\frac{2}{3}$	$\frac{1}{9}$	$\frac{1}{32}$	$\frac{3}{14}$	$\frac{5}{16}$	$\frac{11}{12}$
$\frac{3}{4}$	$\frac{1}{3}$	$\frac{1}{8}$	$\frac{2}{7}$	$\frac{6}{7}$	$\frac{2}{9}$
$\frac{5}{6}$	$\frac{1}{15}$	$\frac{1}{7}$	$\frac{15}{16}$	$\frac{1}{14}$	$\frac{1}{10}$
$\frac{8}{9}$	$\frac{1}{16}$	$\frac{2}{5}$	$\frac{1}{24}$	$\frac{3}{7}$	$\frac{1}{20}$
$\frac{5}{7}$	$\frac{4}{7}$	$\frac{3}{16}$	$\frac{5}{8}$	$\frac{5}{6}$	$\frac{3}{32}$

Multiplication by aliquot parts.

Example.   Find $16\frac{2}{3}\%$ of \$475.34.

Solution.

$$6)\$475.34$$
$$\overline{\$79.22}$$

Explanation.   Since $.16\frac{2}{3}$ equals $\frac{1}{6}$, find $\frac{1}{6}$ of \$475.34.

Example.   Find the cost of 256 units at $37\frac{1}{2}¢$ each.

Solution.

$$256 \times \frac{3}{8} \times \$1 = \$96$$

Explanation. $37\frac{1}{2}¢$ is $\frac{3}{8}$ of \$1.   Therefore, $256 \times \frac{3}{8} \times \$1 = \$96$.

PROBLEMS

Extend the following items mentally:

1. 72 @ $.12\frac{1}{2}$	9. 18 @ $.33\frac{1}{3}$	17. 64 @ $.25$	25. 72 @ $.83\frac{1}{3}$
2. 45 @ $.11\frac{1}{9}$	10. 39 @ $.66\frac{2}{3}$	18. 27 @ $.22\frac{2}{9}$	26. 32 @ $.87\frac{1}{2}$
3. 24 @ $.08\frac{1}{3}$	11. 55 @ $.09\frac{1}{11}$	19. 32 @ $.18\frac{3}{4}$	27. 36 @ $.41\frac{2}{3}$
4. 36 @ $.50$	12. 16 @ $.75$	20. 96 @ $.03\frac{1}{8}$	28. 27 @ $.44\frac{4}{9}$
5. 15 @ $.06\frac{2}{3}$	13. 49 @ $.28\frac{4}{7}$	21. 48 @ $.56\frac{1}{4}$	29. 12 @ $.75$
6. 75 @ $.93\frac{1}{3}$	14. 32 @ $.43\frac{3}{4}$	22. 60 @ $.58\frac{1}{3}$	30. 14 @ $.07\frac{1}{7}$
7. 48 @ $.16\frac{2}{3}$	15. 28 @ $.57\frac{1}{7}$	23. 48 @ $.37\frac{1}{2}$	31. 18 @ $.16\frac{2}{3}$
8. 32 @ $.06\frac{1}{4}$	16. 24 @ $.62\frac{1}{2}$	24. 35 @ $.14\frac{2}{7}$	32. 16 @ $.87\frac{1}{2}$

Division by aliquot parts.   It is difficult to divide a number by a mixed number.   If the divisor is an aliquot part, the quotient may be found by multiplication, as follows:

Example.   Divide 4,875 by $16\frac{2}{3}$.

Solution.

$$48.75$$
$$\underline{6}$$
$$292.50$$

Explanation. Since $16\frac{2}{3}$ is $\frac{1}{6}$ of 100, divide 4,875 by $\frac{1}{6}$ of 100, or $\frac{100}{6}$. This is the same as multiplying by $\frac{6}{100}$. Therefore, divide by 100 by pointing off two decimal places from the right, and multiply the result by 6. The answer is 292.50, or $292\frac{1}{2}$.

Example. The production cost of 1,250 units is $3,170. Find the cost per unit.

Solution.

$$
\begin{array}{r}
.3170 \\
8 \\
\hline
2.5360
\end{array}
$$

Explanation. 1,250 is $\frac{1}{8}$ of 10,000. Divide $3,170 by 10,000 by pointing off 4 decimal places from the right; then multiply the result by 8. The cost per unit is found to be $2.536.

PROBLEMS

Divide:

1. 1,342 by $11\frac{1}{9}$.
2. 2,578 by $12\frac{1}{2}$.

3. 3,126 by $33\frac{1}{3}$.
4. 384 by 25.

5. 158 by $6\frac{1}{4}$.
6. 4,275 by $14\frac{2}{7}$.

PROBLEMS

1. A manufacturer pays dividends amounting to $\frac{3}{16}$ of his capital. If the dividends amount to $37,500, what is the capital?

2. A fuel dealer had 36 cords of wood and sold $\frac{2}{9}$ of it. How many cords did he sell?

3. If a merchant buys an article for $12\frac{1}{2}$ and sells it for $16, the profit is what fraction of the selling price? What fraction of the cost price?

4. A crate containing 10 dozen oranges cost $4.50. If they are sold at the rate of 65 cents a dozen, but $\frac{1}{2}$ dozen are spoiled, the profit is what fraction of the selling price?

5. A man has $37\frac{1}{2}$ and spends $12\frac{1}{2}$. What fraction of his money does he keep?

6. A factory normally employed 48 men. During a dull period 16 received temporary layoffs. What fraction of the force continued to work?

7. The last reading of a gas meter was 67,324 cu. ft.; the previous reading was 64,815 cu. ft. At $1.45 a thousand cubic feet, find the amount of the gas bill.

8. An investment of $18,000 produces an annual income of $720. At the same rate, what should an investment of $25,000 produce?

9. Tires costing $18.75 were installed when the speedometer registered 18,985 miles. The four tires were replaced when the speedometer registered 34,652 miles. $1.00 was allowed for each old tire. What was the average tire cost per mile, correct to the nearest tenth of a mill?

10. An excavation 8 feet in depth required the removal of 5,328 cu. ft. of earth and rock. The average depth of earth was 5 ft., and the cost of earth removal was $1\frac{1}{4}$ a cu. yd. The remainder was rock and cost $4\frac{7}{8}$ a cu. yd. for removal. What was the cost of making the excavation?

3

Percentage and Applications

Relation between percentage and common and decimal fractions. Percentage is a continuation of the subject of fractions. It is the process of computing by hundredths, but instead of the term *hundredths*, the Latin expression *per cent* is used. The sign (%) generally replaces the words *per cent*, thus, 5%, 10%, and so forth.

Any per cent may be expressed either as a common fraction or as a decimal, thus:

	Common Fraction	*Decimally*
1%	$\frac{1}{100}$	.01
5%	$\frac{5}{100}$	.05
$12\frac{1}{2}$%	$\frac{12\frac{1}{2}}{100}$ or $\frac{125}{1000}$	$.12\frac{1}{2}$ or $.125$
100%	$\frac{100}{100}$	1.
300%	$\frac{300}{100}$	3.
$\frac{1}{2}$%	$\frac{\frac{1}{2}}{100}$ or $\frac{5}{1000}$	$.00\frac{1}{2}$ or $.005$
.05%	$\frac{\frac{5}{100}}{100}$ or $\frac{5}{10,000}$	.0005

Care should be taken in writing per cents. Do not write both the sign and the decimal point; thus, 2% and .02 are the same, but 2% and .02% are widely different, since the first is equivalent to $\frac{1}{50}$ and the second to $\frac{1}{5000}$.

Applications. Percentage admits of applications in many fields. Business operations are guided by carefully prepared statistics, and the relationships of items in statistics are often more clearly reflected when they are expressed in terms of percentage. There are numerous problems involving percentage besides those having to do with financial considerations, such as finding the per cent of increase or decrease in volume; per cent of shrinkage of material; per cent of waste in manufacturing operations; per cent of yield of crops.

Definitions. The *base* is the number or quantity represented by 100%. The base may be, for example, total sales, total expenses, the face value of a note, the par value of a bond, pounds of material used, capacity, and so forth.

The *rate* is the number of hundredths, or the per cent. The rate may be, for example, 6% or 25%, which are written decimally as .06 and .25.

The *percentage* is the product of the base and the rate. The percentage may be, for example, the interest cost of a sum of money, the departmental portions of an expense item, the increase in pounds of material used, and the like.

Fundamental processes. In percentage and its application, three fundamental mathematical principles are involved, namely: (1) to find a given per cent of a number; (2) to find what per cent one number is of another; and (3) to find a number when a certain per cent of it is known.

Computations. Computations in percentage are based on these principles.

Principle 1. The percentage is the product of the base and the rate.

$$\text{Base} \times \text{Rate} = \text{Percentage.}$$

Example. 6% interest on $500 is $30. (500 × .06 = 30).

PROBLEMS

In the following, convert the per cent either to a common fraction or to a decimal fraction, whichever is the easier.

Find:

1. 25% of 5,280 ft.
2. 10% of 846 lbs.
3. $16\frac{2}{3}$% of 24 bu.
4. $37\frac{1}{2}$% of $60.
5. 80% of 120 pp.

6. $2\frac{2}{5}$% of 180 lbs.
7. $\frac{3}{8}$% of 240 gal.
8. $\frac{3}{4}$% of $5,000.
9. 20% of 95 yds.
10. $14\frac{2}{7}$% of 42 in.

11. If an expense item of $16.00 is reduced $6\frac{1}{4}$%, what will be the amount of this item after the reduction?

12. A commission of $12\frac{1}{2}$% was earned on a $240 sale. What was the commission?

13. A sample of grain showed $2\frac{2}{3}$% weed seed. How many bushels of weed seed are in 600 bushels of this grain?

14. An item sells for 40 cents. What will be the selling price after a reduction of 15%?

15. Anticipated requirements for copper will exceed the manufacturer's stock by 35%. If 185 pounds are on hand, how many pounds will have to be purchased?

Principle 2.   The rate may be found by dividing the percentage by the base.

$$\text{Percentage} \div \text{Base} = \text{Rate}.$$

Example. $30 \div $500 = .06 or 6%.

PROBLEMS

In the following find what per cent of:

1. 72 is 24		**6.** 12 is 20
2. 60 is 50		**7.** 64 is 8
3. 180 is 120		**8.** 90 is 10
4. 360 is 90		**9.** 150 is 25
5. 50 is 20		**10.** 125 is 25

11. Last year's taxes on a house were $520.   This year's taxes were $640. What per cent were this year's taxes of last year's taxes?

12. A pile of lumber contained 4,500 feet, and 3,300 feet were used.   What per cent remained?

13. Wages are increased from $1.50 an hour to $1.75 an hour.   Find the per cent of increase.

14. A new style of packaging reduced the shipping weight from 130 lbs. to 121 lbs.   What was the per cent of saving in shipping weight?

15. The inspector rejected 5 items out of 140 produced.   What was the per cent of rejects?

Principle 3.   The base may be found by dividing the percentage by the rate.

$$\text{Percentage} \div \text{Rate} = \text{Base}.$$

Example.   30 ÷ .06 = 500.

PROBLEMS

Find the number of which:

1. 25 is 20%		**6.** 86 is 43%
2. 125 is $16\frac{2}{3}$%		**7.** 374 is 17%
3. 240 is 75%		**8.** 375 is $\frac{5}{8}$%
4. 48 is $\frac{1}{4}$%		**9.** $4\frac{1}{2}$ is $\frac{3}{8}$%
5. 72 is $12\frac{1}{2}$%		**10.** 26 is 40%

11. The fire insurance premium on a house was $22.50.   The house was insured for 80% of its value at $\frac{3}{8}$%.   Find the value of the house.

12. Sales increased each year over the preceding year as follows: 15% the second year, 20% the third year, and 25% the fourth year.   If the fourth year's sales were $21,562.50, what were the first year's sales?

13. A bankrupt can pay his creditors 72 cents on the dollar. If his assets are \$13,475.28, what are his liabilities?

14. The gross income of a rental property is \$1,800 a year. Expenses are \$500. If the net income is a return of $6\frac{1}{2}\%$ on the investment, find the value of the property.

15. One workman completes a unit in $7\frac{1}{2}$ hours. Another workman completes a similar unit in $5\frac{3}{4}$ hours. The first workman took what per cent more time than the second workman to complete the unit?

MISCELLANEOUS PROBLEMS

1. A machine that cost \$50 was marked up 30%. What was the marked price?

2. After a clerk's salary was increased $6\frac{1}{4}\%$, he received \$850 a year. What was his former salary?

3. A 4-apartment building cost \$18,000. Repairs average $1\frac{1}{3}\%$ of the cost; taxes, $2\frac{1}{4}\%$; insurance on 90% valuable, $\frac{3}{8}\%$; other expenses amount to \$114.25. What should the annual rental income be in order to return the owner 8% on his investment? What should be the average monthly rental of each apartment?

4. A product shrinks 16% in processing. How many pounds of raw material will be required to process 252 pounds of finished product?

5. A creditor received \$637.73 from a bankrupt estate paying 68 cents on the dollar. What was the creditor's loss on the account?

6. In a certain school 1250 pupils are enrolled. If 725 are boys, what per cent of the pupils are girls?

7. A bushel of wheat weighs 60 pounds and contains 0.6% potash, 1.1% phosphoric acid, and 2.1% nitrogen. How many pounds of each constituent are removed from the farm with 200 bushels of wheat?

8. In a year a businessman's sales amount to \$57,325.19. If salaries amount to \$15,829.40, wages to \$6,324.29, machinery to \$10,000, and incidentals to \$3,272.17, what per cent of sales is required to meet the overhead expenses?

9. How many pounds of cream containing 30% butter fat can be produced from 625 pounds of milk containing 3.9% butter fat?

10. An apartment house of 11 suites was bought for \$200,000.00. Taxes, repairs, insurance, and heating cost \$8,023.00 per year. Six suites are rented at \$125.00 per month, 4 at \$110.00 per month, and 1 suite at \$220.00 per month. What per cent is realized on the investment per year?

Daily record of departmental sales. The following tabulation is designed to show the total daily sales by department and the total sales for the week, both by department and for the business as a whole. After Saturday's sales have been entered, the total departmental sales for the week may be found and also the per cent that each department's sales is of total sales. The per cent that each day's sales is of total sales for the week is also obtainable.

Daily Record of Departmental Sales

Dept.	Mon.	Tues.	Wed.	Thurs.	Fri.	Sat.	Total	Per Cent
A	$475.86	$275.83	$329.86	$424.83	$387.92	$412.15	....	....
B	324.18	174.82	274.19	285.27	304.14	319.28	....	....
C	456.19	259.80	179.86	258.24	286.39	305.74	....	....
D	421.40	268.75	142.56	280.22	178.90	260.57	....	....
E	175.60	125.34	156.85	210.05	162.50	187.50	....	....
Total	....	....	....	....	....	....	....	100.00%
Per Cent	....	....	....	....	....	..............100.00%		

PROBLEM

Prepare a form similar to the above, enter the sales in the proper columns, and find: (a) the total sales for each day in all departments (add downward); (b) the total sales for each department for the week (add across); (c) in two ways, the total sales in all departments for the entire week; (d) the per cent of grand total sales made each day (total for each day divided by the grand total); (e) the per cent of grand total sales made in each department (total of each department divided by the grand total).

Per cent of returned sales by departments. In some lines of business it is important to keep a close check on the volume of returned sales. This may be done advantageously by means of per cents derived from tabulated results.

PROBLEM

Prepare a form similar to the following, enter the data, and find: (a) the net sales for each department and the net sales for all the departments; (b) the per cent of returned sales in each department and the total per cent of returned sales.

Sales and Returned Sales by Department

Dept.	Sales	Returned Sales	Net Sales	Per Cent of Sales Returned
A	$ 24,863.95	$ 756.82	....	....
B	110,356.80	1,328.95	....	....
C	53,768.21	975.32	....	....
D	16,135.40	628.74	....	....
E	9,356.24	256.48	....	....
Total	....	....	....	....

Clerk's per cent of average sales. As a measure of efficiency, the following tabulation may be made for a department, and each clerk's weekly or monthly sales compared with the average weekly or monthly sales.

Monthly Sales of Clerks—Dept. A

Clerk's Number	Monthly Sales	Per Cent of Average
1	$2,756.80	....
2	1,954.36	....
3	2,075.83	....
4	2,634.87	....
5	2,315.62	....
Total	....	100.00%
Average	....	

PROBLEM

Prepare a form similar to the above, enter the data, and find: (*a*) the total monthly sales; (*b*) the average monthly sales per clerk; and (*c*) what per cent each clerk's sales are of the average sales per clerk.

Per cent of income by source. In accounting for the income of a public service enterprise, it is desirable to show the per cent of income from each source when the company's activities are varied.

PROBLEMS

1. In the following tabulation of gross earnings of a public utility corporation, find what per cent the earnings from each source are of the total gross earnings.

Source	Gross Earnings	Per Cent
Electric light and power..................	$15,817,324.00	....
Electric and steam railroads.............	6,763,656.00	....
City railways and bus lines..............	4,248,824.00	....
Gas......................................	3,191,720.00	....
Heat.....................................	672,394.00	....
Bridges..................................	589,691.00	....
Ice......................................	254,670.00	....
Water....................................	88,303.00	....
Miscellaneous............................	21,816.00	....
	$31,648,398.00	100.00%

2. In the following tabulation of the revenue from transportation of an interurban railway, find what per cent each item of revenue is of the total revenue.

Revenue from Transportation

Source	Amount	Per Cent
Passengers...............................	$657,855.00	....
Baggage..................................	550.00	....
Parlor and chair cars....................	9,894.00	....
Special cars.............................	25.00	....
Mail.....................................	1,500.00	....
Express..................................	21,962.00	....
Milk.....................................	1,666.00	....
Freight..................................	264,214.00	....
Miscellaneous............................	269.00	....
	$957,935.00	100.00%

Per cent of expense. Items of operating expenses and their relation to total expenses are more easily compared if expressed in terms of percentage.

PROBLEMS

1. In the following report of an interurban railway company, find what per cent each group of expenses is of total operating expenses.

Operating Expenses

Item	Amount	Per Cent
Way and structures	$228,690.00	
Equipment	98,979.00	
Power	105,890.00	
Conducting transportation	249,427.00	
Traffic	52,823.00	
General and miscellaneous	141,560.00	
Transportation for investment (credit)	8,403.00	
	$868,966.00	100.00%

2. In the following statement of the operating expenses of a restaurant for a period of one month, find what per cent each item of expense is of total operating expenses.

Operating Expenses

Item	Amount	Per Cent
Superintendent's labor	$ 75.00	
General labor	1,776.00	
Extra labor	160.00	
Supplies	200.00	
Electricity	58.00	
Fuel	75.00	
Laundry	103.00	
Ice	22.00	
Repairs and renewals—equipment	110.00	
Meals to employees	340.00	
Music	75.00	
Miscellaneous	66.00	
Total	$3,060.00	100.00%

Per cent of increase or decrease. Percentage is often employed to find the relation between numbers; that is, to find how much larger or smaller one number is than another.

PROBLEMS

1. In the following departmental sales tabulation, find: (a) the increase or the decrease in monthly sales by departments; (b) each department's per cent of increase or decrease (divide increase or decrease in each department by that department's monthly sales for *This Month Last Year*).

Dept.	This Month This Year	This Month Last Year	Increase	Decrease	Per Cent Increase	Per Cent Decrease
A	$2,973.69	$2,795.84				
B	1,426.85	1,852.18				
C	3,752.89	3,565.62				
D	2,581.28	2,678.15				
E	2,076.82	1,825.38				
Total						

2. In the following condensed balance sheet of a municipal railway, find the increase or decrease for each item, and also the per cent of increase or decrease.

Assets	This Year	Last Year	Increase, Decrease†	Per Cent Inc., Dec.†
Capital Assets	$ 7,912,526	$7,610,139		
Current Assets	2,174,925	2,241,395		
Deferred Assets	132,124	132,125		
Total Assets	$10,219,575	$9,983,659		

Liabilities, Reserves, and Surplus				
Funded Debt	$ 3,992,000	$4,192,000		
Current Liabilities	269,720	343,126		
Reserves	1,568,469	1,615,743		
Surplus	4,389,386	3,832,790		
Total Liabilities, etc	$10,219,575	$9,983,659		

3. In the following tabulation of advertising expenditures and direct sales resulting therefrom, compute the totals, the increase, and the per cent of increase.

	This Year Advertising	Sales	Last Year Advertising	Sales
Jan	$2,238.00	$4,251.44	$ 1,769.64	$ 3,762.00
Feb	2,154.00	7,461.60	1,787.96	5,067.16
Mar	2,435.86	8,773.84	1,769.53	5,232.48
Apr	2,425.46	7,292.12	1,840.26	7,818.00
May	2,293.12	8,709.04	1,831.70	4,867.20
June	2,035.76	8,412.28	1,825.49	4,673.12
July	none	7,383.46	none	5,083.20
Aug	none	7,656.80	none	4,454.56
Sept	none	8,227.84	none	4,650.88
Oct	2,212.56	4,298.70	1,142.04	4,976.40
Nov	785.24	5,260.84	1,306.26	2,682.00
Dec	none	5,683.96	none	3,542.80
Total				
Year ago			$10,607.52	$37,650.77
Increase				
% Increase				

4. In the following statement, find the increase or decrease of revenues and expenses and the per cent of increase or decrease:

	This Year	Last Year	Increase, Decrease†	Per Cent
Railway operating revenue	$866,197	$970,060		
Other operating revenue	8,218	7,820		
Total operating revenue	$874,415	$977,880		
Railway operating expense:				
Way and structures	$ 91,380	$ 85,569		
Equipment	64,249	61,866		
Power	108,313	114,906		
Conducting transportation	196,259	211,144		
Traffic	9,496	10,157		
General and miscellaneous	128,849	128,887		
Depreciation	17,324	44,645		
Taxes (except income taxes)	26,185	29,840		
Total	$642,055	$687,014		
Operating income	$232,360	$290,866		
Non-operating income:				
Interest funded securities	2,579	5,105		
Interest unfunded securities	7,765	6,328		
Total	$ 10,344	$ 11,433		
Gross income	$242,704	$302,299		
Deductions from gross income:				
Interest	$160,318	$161,402		
Miscellaneous	3,216	3,257		
Total	$163,534	$164,659		
Net income	$ 79,170	$137,640		

Operating statistics. The operations of a public utility engaged in transportation afford an excellent opportunity for the presentation of statistics for managerial control. The following problem has been derived from the report of such an enterprise.

PROBLEM

From the following data, ascertain the required answers.

Section of Income Statement

Income	This Year	Last Year
Operating revenue:		
Railway operating revenue	$ 22,413,689	$ 21,678,906
Coach operating revenue	818,328	51,282
Total operating revenue	$ 23,232,017	$ 21,730,188
Non-operating income	184,273	141,767
Total revenue from all sources	$ 23,416,290	$ 21,871,955
Operating expenses:		
Railway operating expenses	$ 16,572,497	$ 15,383,494
Coach operating expenses	786,558	41,701
Total operating expenses	$ 17,359,055	$ 15,425,195
Net revenue from all sources	$ 6,057,235	$ 6,446,760

Statistics	This Year	Last Year
Railway revenue car-miles.........................	52,863,111	48,248,330
Coach revenue coach-miles........................	3,529,795	157,540
Railway revenue car-hours........................	5,692,190	5,267,176
Railway revenue passengers.......................	357,926,168	346,116,298
Railway transfer passengers.......................	123,310,526	111,445,912
Railway total passengers..........................	481,236,694	457,562,210
Coach revenue passengers.........................	10,564,723	978,782
Coach transfer passengers.........................	387,228	....
Coach total passengers............................	10,951,951	978,782
Total revenue and transfer passengers..............	492,188,645	458,540,992
Railway operating revenue per car-mile (cents)......	....	....
Coach operating revenue per coach-mile (cents)......	....	....
Railway operating expenses per car-mile (cents).....	....	....
Coach operating expenses per coach-mile (cents).....	....	....
Railway operating revenue per car-hour ($ and cents)	....	....
Railway operating expenses per car-hour ($ and cents)	....	....
Ratio of transfer passengers to revenue passengers— railway (per cent).............................	....	....
Ratio of transfer passengers to revenue passengers— coach (per cent)..............................	....	....
Railway revenue passengers per car-mile operated....	....	....
Railway transfer passengers per car-mile operated....	....	....
Total railway passengers per car-mile operated.......	....	....
Coach revenue passengers per coach-mile operated...	....	....
Coach transfer passengers per coach-mile operated...	....	....
Total coach passengers per coach-mile operated......	....	....
Ratio of railway operating expenses to railway operating revenue (per cent).....................	....	....
Ratio of coach operating expenses to coach operating revenue (per cent).............................	....	....

Budgeting. Percentage is also applied in budgeting, as shown by the following example from hotel accounting.

Example. Among the several items of the budget is China and Glassware, $3,500, to be distributed to four departments on the basis of the previous year's expense for this item in the four departments, as follows:

Department	Per Cent
Rooms..	11.29
Restaurant...	55.29
Coffee Shop...	14.86
Beverages...	18.56
Total...	100.00%

Solution.

Department	Per Cent	Budget
Rooms.....................................	11.29	$ 395.00
Restaurant................................	55.29	1,935.00
Coffee Shop..............................	14.86	520.00
Beverages................................	18.56	650.00
Total.....................................	100.00%	$3,500.00

PROBLEMS

1. The following year it was found that the actual disbursements for China and Glassware amounted to \$2,280.74, and other facts were as given in the tabulation below. Compute the per cent for the distribution of the budgeted amount for the next year, and the per cent that the expense of China and Glassware is of the income for each department.

Department	Gross Income	China and Glassware Expense	Per Cent of Expense	Per Cent of Income
Rooms	\$141,857.50	\$ 269.53	....	....
Restaurant	59,626.90	1,252.16	....	....
Coffee Shop	33,587.45	335.87	....	....
Beverages	9,061.65	423.18	....	....
	\$244,133.50	\$2,280.74	100.00%	....

2. The following budget is that of an estimated operating statement.

		Per Cent of Total Sales
Net sales:		
Class A	\$2,000,000	....
Class B	200,000	....
Class C	250,000	....
Class D	50,000	....
	\$2,500,000	100.00%

		Per Cent of Sales
Production costs:		
Class A	\$1,200,000	....
Class B	140,000	....
Class C	162,500	....
Class D	40,000	....
	\$1,542,500	....

		Per Cent
Gross margin	\$ 957,500	....
Selling:		
Sales administration	\$ 50,000	....
General sales department expense	12,500	....
Special promotion, etc	12,500	....
District operating expense	400,000	....
Advertising A	100,000	....
Advertising B	12,500	....
Advertising C	25,000	....
Selling cost	\$ 612,500	....
Net margin	\$ 345,000	....

Calculate: (*a*) the per cent of net sales in each class, as compared with total net sales; (*b*) the per cent of production cost in each class, based on sales of each class; (*c*) the per cent that selling cost is of total net sales; (*d*) the per cent that the net margin is of total net sales.

3. The following is the budget for the Water Department of a municipality. Find the per cent that each budget expenditure is of the total for the department.

	Amount	Per Cent
Pump station and filter plant salaries.........	$17,300.00	....
Office salaries and expenses...................	4,600.00	....
Chemicals, filter plant....................	1,000.00	....
Power—pump station and filter plant.........	15,000.00	....
Light, heat, and supplies...................	3,000.00	....
Water service.............................	3,000.00	....
Meters and installation....................	6,000.00	....
Water main extensions and fire hydrants......	3,000.00	....
Motor truck repairs	150.00	....
Interest on outstanding warrants............	4,246.00	....
Total..................................	$57,296.00	100.00%

4. Compute the increase or decrease and the per cent of increase or decrease in the following comparative budget.

Public Buildings and Utilities	This Year	Last Year	Inc.	Dec.	% Inc.	% Dec.
City hall engineers and janitors..	$ 5,060	$ 4,284	....	....	....	....
City hall fuel and supplies......	4,000	2,216	....	....	....	....
City hall maintenance and repairs	1,000	850	....	....	....	....
Detention hospital repairs.......	300	400	....	....	....	....
Detention hospital light and fuel.	900	700	....	....	....	....
Park light and fuel.............	1,200	1,050	....	....	....	....
Septic tank electric power.......	600	600	....	....	....	....
Septic tank repairs.............	100	100	....	....	....	....
Incinerator fuel and light.......	1,000	1,000	....	....	....	....
Electric lighting—streets, alleys.	14,500	14,000	....	....	....	....
Interest on warrants............	2,284	2,170	....	....	....	....
Contingent fund................	5,000	4,036	....	....	....	....
Detention hospital insurance....	....	433	....	....	....	....
Library insurance..............	....	281	....	....	....	....
Park insurance.................	....	104	....	....	....	....
	$35,944	$32,224	....	....	....	....

Profits based on sales. In the income statement, it is customary to base all percentage calculations on sales. With sales equalling 100%, cost of sales, overhead, and net profit are expressed as per cents of sales. Overhead expenses are those incurred in operating a business—such as salaries and wages, rent, heat, light and power, depreciation, taxes, insurance, advertising, telephone, postage, and so forth. In marking goods bought for resale, these expenses must be taken into consideration. A few items of overhead expense do not fluctuate, but many of them have a fairly constant ratio to gross sales. The merchant determines the ratio of overhead expenses to sales from his own experience and that of others engaged in similar businesses. This per cent of cost of doing business plus the per cent of profit decided upon deducted from 100% determines the per cent which the cost of goods plus freight and drayage bears to the selling price.

Sales = 100%		
Invoice Price plus Freight and Cartage 75%	Overhead 15%	Profit 10%
Cost of Sales 75%	Gross Profit on Sales 25%	

Example. If overhead charges amount to 15% of sales, and a profit of 10% on sales is desired, what is the selling price of an article with an invoice cost of $21.00 and freight and cartage of $1.50?

Solution.

$$15\% + 10\% = 25\%$$
$$100\% - 25\% = 75\%$$
$$\$21.00 + \$1.50 = \$22.50, \text{ the cost.}$$
$$\$22.50 \div 75\% = \$30.00, \text{ the selling price.}$$

Verification

$$25\% \text{ of } \$30.00 = \$7.50, \text{ the overhead and profit.}$$
$$\$30.00 - \$7.50 = \$22.50, \text{ the cost.}$$

PROBLEMS

1. An article that cost $15.00 was sold for $20.00. What is the profit per cent on the selling price?

2. With an overhead expense of 20%, what per cent of profit on sales is made by selling for $1.50 articles that have an invoice cost of $1.00?

3. What is the per cent of gross profit on sales in Problem 2?

4. How much must the article in Problem 2 be reduced to sell at cost? What per cent is this of the marked price?

5. A merchant sold an article for $12.00 and made a profit of $12\frac{1}{2}\%$ on the selling price. What was his profit in dollars?

6. Find the per cent of reduction of marked price to produce cost.

	Cost	Marked Price	Per Cent Reduction
a.	$ .20	$ .25	....
b.	2.50	2.75	....
c.	1.00	1.20	....
d.	.03	.05	....
e.	3.00	6.00	....
f.	.40	.50	....
g.	.09	.12	....
h.	15.00	25.00	....

7. Find the per cent of profit on the selling price.

	Cost	Selling Price	Per Cent Profit on Selling Price
a.	$ 1.00	$ 1.20	....
b.	10.00	15.00	....
c.	.60	.75	....
d.	3.50	7.00	....
e.	6.00	8.00	....
f.	150.00	175.00	....
g.	16.00	24.00	....
h.	75.00	125.00	....

8. The factory price of an automobile is $1,300. Freight charges from factory to dealer are $65.00. If the dealer's overhead is 20% and he expects a net profit of 15% on sales, what should be the selling price of the automobile?

9. A furniture dealer bought a shipment of 20 chairs at $30.00 each. He marked them to sell at a profit of 40% on cost. The entire shipment was sold in the fall clearance sale at 25% reduction from marked price. What was the profit or loss?

10. Complete the following:

	Cost	Selling Price	% on Cost	% on Selling Price
a.	$ 4.00	$ 6.00	....	....
b.	15.00	25.00	....	....
c.	.16	.20	....	....
d.	.04	.08	....	....
e.	.08	.10	....	....
f.	5.00	7.00	....	....
g.	500.00	750.00	....	....
h.	24.00	32.00	....	....

11. The invoice price of an article is $12.00. Freight is 75 cents. It costs 18% to do business and you desire a net profit of 10% on sales. What is the selling price of the article?

12. If the invoice cost is $28.00, freight $2.00, overhead 25%, net profit on sales 15%, what is the selling price?

13. A stock of merchandise valued at $8,750.00 was damaged by fire and water. The loss was estimated to be 25%. Find the value of the damaged merchandise.

14. A merchant's overhead, or cost of doing business, is $22\frac{3}{4}\%$. He desires to make a net profit of $7\frac{1}{4}\%$. What will be the selling price of an item that cost this merchant $4.90?

15. Merchandise is bought for $3.50 less 25% and sold at $3.50 net. What is the rate per cent of profit?

16. A tea and coffee merchant blends a 40¢ tea with a 70¢ tea in the ratio of 2 to 1. If the blend is sold at 65¢ a pound, what is the rate per cent of profit on cost?

17. A chair manufacturer finds the cost of material in a certain type chair to be $7.50. Manufacturing cost (labor and overhead) is $14.80. Selling and administrative expenses are 20% of sales. What is the manufacturer's price for this chair if he desires to net 10% on the selling price?

18. A clerk was ordered to mark a lot of suits so as to make a profit of 20% after allowing 5% discount for cash. By mistake he marked the suits $24.75 each, which resulted in a loss to the clothier of 8%. At what price should the suits have been marked?

Commissions. The commission business in this country is largely the result of our industrial and commercial development. Economic conditions demand that there shall be agents who shall represent either the buyer or the seller. The compensation paid the agent for his services is called a *commission*. The principles of percentage apply in commission.

The person who transacts business for another is the *agent*, and the one for whom the business is transacted is the *principal*. The fee, usually a per cent of the dollar volume of the transaction, is the *commission*.

PROBLEMS

1. An agent sells oil for $3,475.00 at $3\frac{1}{2}$% commission. What is the amount of the commission?

2. A merchant buys goods through an agent at a cost of $275.00. The agent charges $2\frac{1}{2}$% commission. What is the total cost of the goods to the merchant?

3. An agent sells a consignment of merchandise for $1,824, retaining his commission of 3%. How much does he remit to his principal?

4. If $302.75 was charged for selling $8,650.00 of merchandise, what was the rate of commission?

5. A realtor's fee for selling a house and lot was $375.00. If the rate was $2\frac{1}{2}$%, what was the amount received by the principal?

6. An agent's commissions for one week were $216.80. If his sales were $10,840.00, what rate did he charge?

7. The invoice price on a shipment of merchandise was $1,283.38, including agent's commission. If the agent's rate was 3%, what was the commission?

8. The proceeds of a sale received by the principal were $828.78. The commission deducted by the agent was $43.62. What was the rate?

9. The manufacturing cost of a certain type machine is $800.00. The manufacturer wishes to catalog this machine at a list price that will net a profit of 25% on sales after allowing a dealer's discount of 25% and agent's commission of $16\frac{2}{3}$%. Find the catalog list price.

10. A collector succeeded in collecting 80% of doubtful accounts, which amounted to $3,295.25. If his commission was 5% of the total he collected, how much did the principal realize?

11. If *A* remitted $5,297.00 including commission to his agent who purchased goods on a 2% commission, what investment in goods was made in *A*'s name?

12. An agent sold a consignment of wheat for \$5,280.00 and invested this sum less his commission in corn. His total commission on both transactions amounted to \$320.00. If his rate was the same in each case, what was this rate?

13. An agent sold wheat on a commission of $\frac{1}{2}\%$ and bought flour with the net proceeds on a commission of $\frac{1}{3}\%$. If his total commission was \$60.00, what was the cost of the flour?

Cash discount. Cash or time discount is a deduction for immediate payment, or for payment within a definite time. The deduction is a certain per cent of the invoice.

The expression "Terms: 2/10, 1/30, n/60" means that 2% of the invoice price may be deducted by the purchaser if payment is made within 10 days of the date of the invoice, that 1% may be deducted if the invoice is paid within 30 days from the date of the invoice, and that the invoice is due in 60 days without discount. In some cases notice is given to the effect that interest at a specified rate will be charged after the due date.

The acceptance of a cash discount is usually of advantage to the purchaser. The following table indicates the annual interest rates to which the usual cash discounts are equivalent:

$\frac{1}{2}\%$	10 days, net 30 days	= 9 per cent a year
1%	10 days, net 30 days	= 18 per cent a year
$1\frac{1}{2}\%$	10 days, net 30 days	= 27 per cent a year
2%	10 days, net 30 days	= 36 per cent a year
2%	10 days, net 60 days	= 14.4 per cent a year
2%	30 days, net 4 months	= 8 per cent a year

The rate per cent a year is calculated by taking the number of days between the discount date of payment and the end of the credit period, dividing the number of days in a year (360) by this number, and multiplying the quotient by the rate of discount under consideration.

$$\frac{360 \text{ Days}}{\substack{\text{Number of Days Between} \\ \text{Discount Date and} \\ \text{End of Credit Period}}} \times \text{Rate of Discount} = \text{Equivalent Annual Interest Rate}$$

PROBLEMS

1. Find the equivalent annual interest rate for the following terms:

2%	30 days, net 60 days
3%	10 days, net 30 days
3%	30 days, net 60 days
3%	10 days, net 4 months

2. To pay an invoice of \$1,500, with terms 2/10, n/30, the purchaser borrowed the money at 6% in order to take advantage of the 2% discount. What benefit did he secure by borrowing the money?

3. A merchant was able to obtain 5% discount on an invoice of $720 by borrowing the money at the bank for 90 days at 6% interest. How much was he able to save?

Trade discount. Mercantile or trade discounts are reductions from list prices, or from the amount of the invoice without regard to time of payment. By offering different rates of trade discounts to wholesalers and retailers, the manufacturer can send the same catalog to both classes of customers. Revised discount sheets are issued as prices fluctuate, but the same catalog may be used a year or more because the list prices are fixed.

Rules of percentage are applied in commercial discounts:

Invoice price = base
Per cent of discount = rate
Discount = percentage

Several discounts are sometimes given. These are known as *chain discounts* or *a series of discounts*.

The order in which the discounts are deducted will not affect the result; thus, a selling price stated as list price "less 10%, 20%, and 5%" is the same as a selling price stated as list price "less 5%, 20%, and 10%." This is shown in the following example, in which $100.00 is used as the base:

Example.

$100.00 × .10	$10.00	$100.00 × .05	$ 5.00
$100.00 − $10.00	$90.00	$100.00 − $5.00	$95.00
$ 90.00 × .20	$18.00	$ 95.00 × .20	$19.00
$ 90.00 − $18.00	$72.00	$ 95.00 − $19.00	$76.00
$ 72.00 × .05	$ 3.60	$ 76.00 × .10	$ 7.60
$ 72.00 − $3.60	$68.40	$ 76.00 − $7.60	$68.40
$100.00 − $68.40	$31.60	$100.00 − $68.40	$31.60

The total discount in each case is $31.60.

The dollar amount of discount determined from a series of rates is not the same as the amount of discount determined from a single rate equal to the sum of the series of rates. The sum of the series of rates is 35%; 35% of $100.00 is $35.00, whereas the correct discount is $31.60.

Single discount equivalent to a series. Since the rates of the discounts cannot be totalled to find the total discount as shown above, it is necessary to devise a means of evaluating the single discount which would produce the same price as a series of discounts.

A simple formula is derived.

Let L = list price

$d_1, d_2, \ldots, d_n$ = 1st, 2nd, $\ldots$, nth discount rates, respectively, expressed as decimal fractions.

$P_1, P_2, \ldots, P_n$ = 1st, 2nd, $\ldots$, nth reduced prices, respectively.

Then

$$P_1 = L - Ld_1$$
$$= L(1 - d_1)$$
$$P_2 = P_1 - P_1d_2$$
$$= L(1 - d_1) - L(1 - d_1)d_2$$
$$= L(1 - d_1)(1 - d_2)$$

. . . .

. . . .

. . . .

$$P_{n-1} = P_{n-2} - P_{n-2}d_{n-1}$$
$$= L(1 - d_1)(1 - d_2) \ldots (1 - d_{n-2}) - L(1 - d_1) \ldots (1 - d_{n-2})d_{n-1}$$
$$= L(1 - d_1)(1 - d_2) \ldots (1 - d_{n-1})$$
$$P_n = P_{n-1} - P_{n-1}d_n$$
$$= L(1 - d_1) \ldots (1 - d_{n-1}) - L(1 - d_1) \ldots (1 - d_{n-1})d_n$$
$$= L(1 - d_1)(1 - d_2) \ldots (1 - d_n)$$

Let d be the single discount rate equivalent to the series $d_1, d_2, \ldots, d_n$.

$$\therefore P_n = L - Ld$$
$$= L(1 - d)$$
$$\therefore L(1 - d) = L(1 - d_1)(1 - d_2) \ldots (1 - d_n)$$
$$\therefore 1 - d = (1 - d_1)(1 - d_2) \ldots (1 - d_n)$$
$$\therefore \mathbf{d = 1 - (1 - d_1)(1 - d_2) \ldots (1 - d_n)} \qquad (1)$$

Example 1. What single discount is equivalent to a series of discounts of 20%, 10%, and 10%?

Solution. Here $d_1 = .2$, $d_2 = .1$, and $d_3 = .1$. Substituting these values in the formula, $d = 1 - (1 - d_1)(1 - d_2)(1 - d_3) = 1 - (.8)(.9)(.9) = 1 - .648 = .352$ $\therefore$ single discount is 35.2%.

Example 2. What is the net price of an invoice of $600.00 less 30%, 20%, and 10%?

Solution. Here $d_1 = .3$, $d_2 = .2$, and $d_3 = .1$.

$$\therefore d = 1 - (1 - .3)(1 - .2)(1 - .1)$$
$$= 1 - (.7)(.8)(.9)$$
$$= 1 - .504 = .496.$$
$$\therefore \text{net price} = 600.00 - (600.00)(.496)$$
$$= 600.00 - 297.60 = \$302.40.$$

PROBLEMS

1. In each of the following, calculate by the short method the single discount that is equivalent to the series:

(*a*) 10% and 5%.   (*c*) 40% and 5%.   (*e*) 35% and 10%.
(*b*) 20% and 5%.   (*d*) 15% and 10%.   (*f*) 30% and 20%.

2. In each of the following, find the net price:

(*a*) $350.00, less 10%, 10%, and 5%.   (*c*) $480.00, less 20%, 10%, and 5%.
(*b*) $500.00, less $33\frac{1}{3}$%, 5%, and $2\frac{1}{2}$%.   (*d*) $1,200.00, less 5%, $2\frac{1}{2}$%, and 1%.
                      (*e*) $900.00, less 50%, 20%, and 5%.

3. The list price of an invoice is $750.00, with discounts of 10%, 5%, and $2\frac{1}{2}$%. The terms of the invoice are: 2/10, 1/30, and n/60. What amount will be necessary to pay the invoice: (*a*) within the 10-day period; (*b*) within the 30-day period?

4. *B* purchases merchandise listed at $3,500.00, less 20% and 25%. He sells this merchandise at the same list price, less 15%, 10%, and 5%. Does he gain or lose, and what amount?

5. A dealer offers merchandise at a list price of $5,000.00, less discounts of 25%, 10%, and 10%. Another dealer offers the same merchandise at a list price of $4,800.00, less discounts of 20%, 15%, and 5%. Which is the better offer, and by what amount?

6. Which is the better offer, and by what amount, on an invoice of $425.00; (*a*) 30%, 20%, and 10%; or (*b*) a single discount of 50%?

7. The list price of an item is $24.00. If bought at that price less $33\frac{1}{3}$% and 10%, and then sold at the same list price less 20% and 5%, what is the profit?

8. The net cost of an invoice of merchandise was $1,200.00. What was the list price, if the cost was 25% and 20% off list?

9. If the list price is $400.00, and the net price is $380.00, what is the single rate of discount?

10. What single discount is equivalent to 25%, 20%, and $12\frac{1}{2}$%?

Transportation charges on discount invoices. In some cases transportation charges are paid by the seller; in other cases, by the purchaser. If the purchaser is to pay the transportation charge, and as a matter of convenience the seller prepays it, the seller adds the charge to the invoice. The purchaser is not entitled to cash discount on the added charge.

If a shipment is made "freight allowed," the discount should be figured after the deduction for freight; otherwise, it would be equivalent to taking discount on the transportation charge.

PROBLEMS

1. An invoice of books amounts to $4.85, and parcel post charges are 79 cents, a total of $5.64. If terms are 2/10, what is the discount if paid within the 10-day period?

2. Complete the following invoice:

6 doz.	Items	@ $6.65	....
24 doz.	Articles	@ .45	....
6¼ doz.	Items	@ .47½	....
3 only	Items	@ 2.34	....
			....
	Less 15%		....
	Less freight allowance		....
	525 lbs. @ .45½ cwt.		....
	Net		....

If the terms of the above invoice are 1/10, n/30, what will be the discount if paid within 10 days?

3. An invoice for paper, freight allowed, amounted to $1,754.50. The freight bill paid by the purchaser was $238.54. If 2% discount was allowed for payment within 10 days, what was the amount of the check sent within the discount period?

Anticipation. In retail business, invoices for purchases often have *dating terms.* The terms may be 2/10, 90 days extra. If the merchandise is received within 10 days and checked by the receiving department, the purchaser will deduct 2% cash discount, and an anticipation discount on the balance computed at 6% (usually) for 90 days, which is equivalent to an additional discount of 1½%.

Another case is that of spring purchases of fall merchandise invoiced 2/10, November 1 dating. An invoice with these terms may be discounted 2% if paid before November 11, and if paid July 15 would be subject to anticipation discount for 119 days at the customary rate, say, 6%.

Example. An invoice billed April 2, for $3,250.75, terms 2/10, Nov. 1 dating, freight allowed, was paid April 28. Freight paid by the purchaser was $132.48. What was the amount of the check?

Solution.

Invoice..	$3,250.75
Less freight..	132.48
	$3,118.27
Less discount, 2%....................................	62.37
	$3,055.90
Less anticipation, 6% for 197 days....................	100.34
Amount of check......................................	$2,955.56

PROBLEMS

1. An invoice for $21.25 dated Dec. 28, terms 2/10, Feb. 26, was paid Jan. 7. What was the amount of the check?

2. What is the anticipation on an invoice for $475.50, dated June 10, terms 2/10, 90 days extra, if paid June 25?

3. Find the amount earned by paying an invoice for $1,275.25, dated July 12, terms 2/10, Oct. 1 dating, on July 28.

4

Simple Interest

Interest, as commonly defined, is a payment for the use of borrowed money or credit. This payment depends upon the rate per cent charged and upon the length of time for which interest is calculated. The sum loaned or the amount of credit used or the capital originally invested is the **principal.** The number of hundredths of the principal that is paid on the loan is the **rate of interest** and is usually expressed as a per cent. The length of time over which the principal is used is the **time,** and the principal plus the interest is the **amount.**

Simple interest formula. A simple formula for calculating simple interest should now be developed.

Let:
P = original principal.
n = time expressed as a fraction of a year.
i = interest rate expressed as a decimal fraction.
S = amount at the end of time n.
I = the total interest in dollars.

Then $$I = Pni \qquad (1)$$
Therefore, since $S = P + I$ by definition,
$$S = P + Pni$$
and therefore $$S = P(1 + ni) \qquad (2)$$

Analysis of the simple interest formula. An examination of the simple interest formula (2)

$$S = P(1 + ni)$$

reveals that it contains four variables, S, P, n, and i. If values are assigned to three of these variables, there remains a linear expression for the fourth variable which can, therefore, be easily evaluated. Since there are four ways of choosing three things at once from four things, there are four basic problems which can be solved by using the formula:

(*a*) Given P, n, i, solve to find S.
(*b*) Given S, n, i, solve to find P.
(*c*) Given P, S, n, solve to find i.
(*d*) Given P, S, i, solve to find n.

AMOUNT AT SIMPLE INTEREST

(*a*) Given *P*, *n*, *i*; to solve and find *S*.

Example 1. What is the amount of $100.00 for five years at 6%?

Solution. In this case $P = 100$, $i = .06$, and $n = 5$. Substituting these values in the formula,

$$S = P(1 + ni) = 100[1 + 5(.06)] = 100\ (1.30) = \$130.00.$$

Example 2. Find the simple interest for two months on $700.00 at 8%.

Solution. In this case $P = 700$, $i = .08$, and $n = \frac{1}{6}$. Substituting these values in the formula,

$$I = Pni = 700 \times \tfrac{1}{6} \times .08 = \$9.33.$$

PROBLEMS

1. A man borrows $500.00 for nine years at 4%. What amount of interest will he pay during this period? Write the formula and solution, as shown in the example above.

2. What is the amount of interest due on $300.00 at the end of ten years if the rate is 7%? Write the formula and solution, as shown in the example above.

3. What is the total amount of interest realized on two investments: $400.00 invested for five years at 6% and $750.00 invested for seven years at $4\frac{3}{4}$%?

4. What is the interest accumulation on a debt of $4,270.00 for eight years at 5% simple interest?

Write formulas and solutions for the following:

5. The amount of a $200.00 note due in six years; interest, 5%.

6. The amount due in six years on $530.00 at 6%.

7. The amount due on a note for $750.00 with 4% interest. No interest has been paid during a period of four years.

PRESENT VALUE AND SIMPLE DISCOUNT

(*b*) **Given *S*, *n*, *i*; to solve and find *P*.** This is the problem of finding what principal invested now will amount to a certain sum at a definite future time.

Example. What sum invested now at $4\frac{1}{2}\%$ will amount to $500.00 in three months?

Solution. In this case $S = 500$, $n = \frac{1}{4}$, $i = .045$. Substituting these values in the formula $P = \dfrac{S}{1 + ni}$, which is derived from formula (2) by a simple division,

$$P = \frac{S}{1 + ni} = \frac{500}{1 + \frac{1}{4}(.045)} = \frac{500}{1.01125} = \$494.44.$$

The result is commonly called the *present value* or present worth of $500.00 due in 3 months, money being worth $4\frac{1}{2}\%$ per annum.

In the theory of investment, money is never thought to be idle but continuously growing at some interest rate. A sum of money held at present is considered to have future worth (the amount at current interest) and a sum of money to be received in the future is considered to have present worth as shown in the example above. For practical purposes the terms present and future are relative only and may be considered as representative of any two given dates. Therefore, to evaluate a sum on a date later than that on which its value is known, multiply the known value by $(1 + ni)$; to evaluate a sum on a date earlier than that on which its value is known, divide the known value by $(1 + ni)$.

(i) *To move money forward through time multiply by $1 + ni$.*
(ii) *To move money backward through time divide by $1 + ni$.*

Present value of a debt which bears interest. If **any** debt bears interest then the **maturity value** of the debt differs from the **face value** of the debt.

If the present value of a debt bearing interest is calculated at the same interest rate, then the present value is the face value. If, however, the interest rate used in calculating the present value is different from the interest rate borne by the debt, there are two steps to the solution:

(i) Find the *maturity* value of the debt.
(ii) Evaluate the present value of the maturity value at the proper interest rate.

Example. A builder owes $1,000.00 to a wholesaler. His debt matures in three months and bears interest at 7% per annum. What is the present value at 6% per annum?

Solution. (i) To find the maturity value, $P = 1,000$, $n = \frac{1}{4}$, and $i = .07$. Substitute these values in the formula:

$$S = P\,(1 + ni) = 1,000\,[1 + \tfrac{1}{4}(.07)] = \$1,017.50.$$

(ii) Now, $S = 1,017.50$, $n = \frac{1}{4}$, and $i = .06$.
Substituting these values in the formula:

$$P = \frac{S}{1 + ni} = \frac{1,017.50}{1 + \frac{1}{4}(.06)} = \$1,002.46.$$

Comparison of simple amount and simple present worth. The following comparative chart is presented to illustrate the accumulation of simple interest on a sum and on the present worth of the same sum:

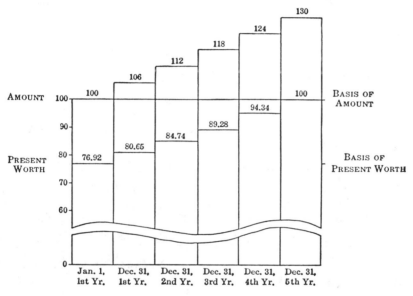

Fig. 4-1.

The amount starts at $100.00, and accumulates to $130.00 in 5 years. The present worth starts at $76.92, and accumulates to $100.00. The rate of interest is the same in each case, 6%.

PROBLEMS

1. What is the present value of a six-year note for $650.00 without interest, if money is worth 5%?

2. A note for $3,500.00, without interest, is due in five years. What is its present value, money being worth 6%?

3. Construct a comparative chart showing the difference in value of the amount and the present worth of $400.00 due in eight years, interest at 5%.

Simple discount or true discount. Simple discount or true discount is the difference between a sum and its earlier value or the difference between the sum due and its present worth. The purpose here is to distinguish simple discount from bank discount, which will be studied later.

In the example above, the simple discount on \$500.00 is \$500.00 − \$494.44 = \$5.56. It should be noted that \$5.56 is the simple interest on \$494.44 for three months at $4\frac{1}{2}\%$ per annum.

Simple discount formula. Since the present value of S due in time n at interest rate i is $\dfrac{S}{1 + ni}$, then

$$\text{Simple discount} = S - \frac{S}{1 + ni} = \frac{Sni}{1 + ni}. \qquad (3)$$

PROBLEMS

1. What is the true discount on a debt of \$750.00 due in three years, money being worth 4%? Write the formula and solution.

2. Find the difference between the present value and the face value of a non-interest-bearing note for \$500.00, due in four years, money being worth 6%.

3. Find the difference between the true discount and the simple interest on \$650.00 for eight years at 4%.

Equivalent discount and interest rates. The **equivalent discount rate** for a period of time is the discount rate which applied to S for that period of time would produce the same discount as the simple discount for the same period of time as calculated by formula (3).

The discount on S at interest rate i per period for time n is $\dfrac{Sni}{1 + ni}$ by formula (3). Let d be the *equivalent discount rate* for the same period. In this way, the discount is Snd.

Therefore, $$\frac{Sni}{1 + ni} = Snd$$

and therefore, $$d = \frac{i}{1 + ni}. \qquad (4)$$

Solve (4) for i and find

$$i = \frac{d}{1 - nd} \qquad (5)$$

Example 1. A dealer's business nets him 35% interest per annum on money invested in it. What cash discount can he afford to quote for payment of a bill one month before it is due?

Solution. In this case, $i = .35$, $n = \frac{1}{12}$. Substituting these values in the formula,

$$d = \frac{i}{1 + ni} = \frac{.35}{1 + \frac{1}{12}(.35)} = .3401.$$
$$\therefore d = 34.01\% \text{ interest per annum.}$$
$\therefore$ the discount rate for 1 month $= (34.01) \times \frac{1}{12} = 2.83\%$.

Alternative solution. Let the payment to settle the bill be $100.00.

∴ at 35% the interest on $100.00 for 1 month is $100 \times \frac{1}{12} \times .35 = \$2.92$.

∴ $100.00 settles a bill of $102.92.

∴ $2.92 is the discount on $102.92.

∴ the rate of discount $= \dfrac{2.92}{102.92} = 2.83\%$.

Example 2. A cash discount of 2% is given if a bill is paid a month before it is due. At what interest rate can a person afford to borrow money for one month to take advantage of the discount?

Solution. A discount of 2% is earned in one month. Therefore, the discount rate for 1 year is $.02 \times 12 = .24$.

Therefore, $d = 24$ and $n = \frac{1}{12}$. Substitute these values in the formula:

$$i = \frac{d}{1 - nd} = \frac{.24}{1 - \frac{1}{12}(.24)} = .245.$$

Therefore, $i = 24\frac{1}{2}\%$ per annum.

Alternative solution. Let the bill be $100.00. Then the discount if the bill is paid one month before it is due is $2.00.

∴ $98.00 is paid, and therefore $98.00 earns $2.00 in 1 month.

∴ the interest rate for 1 month is $\frac{2}{98}$.

∴ the interest rate for 1 year $= \frac{2}{98} \times 12 = .245$.

∴ $i = 24\frac{1}{2}\%$ per annum.

PROBLEMS

1. Money earns 25% per annum when invested in a certain business. What discount can be offered by this firm on an invoice of $600.00 for payment 40 days before it is due?

2. Find the interest rate per annum which is equivalent to a discount rate of 1% for payment of a bill 60 days before it is due.

3. The A. B. Hughes Co. estimates that money put into their business yields a net return of 18% per annum. Find the highest discount rate they can afford to allow for payment made one month before the net amount of an invoice is due.

RATE

(c) **Given P, S, n; to find i.** Since P and S are known in a rate problem, I can be calculated directly as $I = S - P$. In this way a rate problem can always be solved by means of the formula (1): $I = Pni$.

Example. At what interest rate per annum will $100.00 amount to $124.00 in 4 years?

Solution. Here $I = S - P = \$124.00 - \$100.00 = \$24.00$, $n = 4$, and $P = 100$.

Substituting these values in the formula,

$$i = \frac{I}{Pn} = \frac{24}{100 \times 4} = .06.$$

∴ the interest rate is 6% per annum.

TIME

(d) **Given P, S, i; to find n.** This solution is identical to the rate solution above, except that we use the formula $n = \dfrac{I}{Pi}$.

Example. How long will it take $325 to earn $2.60 if invested at 4% per annum?

Solution. In this case, $P = 325$, $I = 2.60$, and $i = .04$. Substituting these values in the formula,

$$n = \frac{2.60}{325 \times .04} = .2 = \frac{1}{5}.$$

Therefore, the time is $\frac{1}{5}$ of a year.

PROBLEMS

Write formulas and solutions for each of the following:

	Principal	Interest	Time	Rate
1.	$ 400.00	$ 48.00	3 years	....
2.	2,000.00	500.00	5 years	....
3.	800.00	336.00	6 years	....
4.	300.00	126.00	7 years	....
5.	150.00	40.50	6 years	....
6.	1,000.00	240.00	....	6%
7.	750.00	90.00	....	4%
8.	360.00	81.00	....	$4\frac{1}{2}$%

EXACT AND ORDINARY SIMPLE INTEREST

In practice, most business transactions involving simple interest are confined to periods of time which are shorter than one year. When evaluating n as a fraction of a year, there are two methods which are used:

(a) *Exact simple interest.* This is the method which uses a 365-day year and counts the exact number of days in each month.

(b) *Ordinary simple interest.* This is the method which uses a 360-day year. If we let I_e denote exact simple interest and I_o denote ordinary simple interest, it is easy to determine the relation between I_e and I_o for:

$$I_e = \frac{Pti}{365} \text{ and } I_o = \frac{Pti}{360},$$

where t = number of days.

Therefore,
$$\frac{I_e}{I_o} = \frac{Pti}{365} \times \frac{360}{Pti} = \frac{360}{365} = \frac{72}{73}.$$
$$\therefore I_e = \tfrac{72}{73} I_o \text{ or } I_o = \tfrac{73}{72} I_e. \tag{6}$$

NOTE: In Canada, exact interest and discount are used exclusively. In the United States of America, a 366-day year is used for time involving a leap year, whereas in Canada a 365-day year is used at all times.

In the United States of America, three days of grace are not allowed at any time, whereas in Canada three days of grace are always allowed on time drafts and "after sight" drafts as well as on promissory notes but not on demand or "at sight" drafts.

Computing the time for simple interest. If the duration of the loan is given between dates such as from January 29 to March 1, proceed as follows:

Time left in January........	2 days.
February.................	28 days (29 if leap year).
March..................	1 day.
	31 days (32 if leap year).

It should be noted that the first day, January 29, was not included but the last day, March 1, was included.

Methods of computing ordinary simple interest. There are a great many methods of computing simple interest, each of them possessing more or less merit. With the accountant, however, the chief consideration is not how many methods there are, but rather how accurately and how quickly he can solve a problem in interest.

The computation of the product of principal, rate, and time is the shortest method when the time is full years or fractional parts of a year, such as $\tfrac{1}{2}$, $\tfrac{1}{3}$, $\tfrac{1}{4}$, any number of 12ths, and so forth.

Sixty-day method. To find the interest at 6% for:

6 days, point off three additional places to the left of the decimal point in the principal.

60 days, point off two additional places to the left of the decimal point in the principal.

600 days, point off one additional place to the left of the decimal point in the principal.

For 6,000 days, the interest will be the same as the principal.

Justification:
$$\frac{\$ \times 6 \times .06}{360} = \$ \times .001$$

$$\frac{\$ \times 60 \times .06}{360} = \$ \times .01$$

$$\frac{\$ \times 600 \times .06}{360} = \$ \times .1$$

$$\frac{\$ \times 6,000 \times .06}{360} = \$ \times 1$$

Example. Find the interest on $256.75 for six days at 6%.

Solution. Pointing off three places to the left of the decimal point in the principal gives 25675, or 26¢.

Example. Find the interest on $345.65 for 36 days at 6%.

Solution. Point off three additional places to the left of the decimal point in the principal, and multiply by 6. The answer is $2.07.

This method may be used for any rate by adding to or subtracting from the interest computed at 6%, the fractional part thereof that the specified rate is greater or less than the 6% rate.

For 8%, increase the interest by $\frac{1}{3}$ of the amount computed at 6%
  7%, increase the interest by $\frac{1}{6}$ of the amount computed at 6%
  5%, decrease the interest by $\frac{1}{6}$ of the amount computed at 6%
  4%, decrease the interest by $\frac{1}{3}$ of the amount computed at 6%
  $4\frac{1}{2}$%, decrease the interest by $\frac{1}{4}$ of the amount computed at 6%

PROBLEMS

Find the interest at 6% on:

1. $180.00 for 60 days.
2. $150.00 for 54 days.
3. $262.50 for 24 days.
4. $32.75 for 36 days.
5. $65.50 for 12 days.

6. $26.50 for 18 days.
7. $752.25 for 6 days.
8. $15.80 for 54 days.
9. $75.40 for 30 days.
10. $12.85 for 24 days.

Method using aliquot parts.

Example. Find the interest on $275.84 for 124 days at 6%.

Solution.

$$
\begin{array}{r}
\$2|75.84 = \text{interest for 60 days} \\
2|75.84 = \text{interest for 60 days} \\
\underline{18.38 = \text{interest for 4 days}} \\
\$5|70.06 = \text{interest for 124 days}
\end{array}
$$

Explanation. Pointing off two decimals, as indicated by the vertical line, gives the interest for 60 days. Double this to find the interest for 120 days. Four days' interest is $\frac{1}{15}$ of 60 days' interest. The sum, $5.70, is the interest for 124 days.

Example. Find the interest on $754.90 for 137 days at 6%.

Solution.

$$
\begin{array}{r}
\$\ 7|54.90 = \text{interest for 60 days} \\
7|54.90 = \text{interest for 60 days} \\
1|50.98 = \text{interest for 12 days} \\
\underline{62.90 = \text{interest for 5 days}} \\
\$17|23.68 = \text{interest for 137 days}
\end{array}
$$

Explanation. Pointing off two decimal places gives the interest for 60 days. Double this to find the interest for 120 days. Twelve days is $\frac{1}{5}$ of 60 days; therefore, the interest for 12 days is $\frac{1}{5}$ of 60 days' interest, or \$1.5098. Five days is $\frac{1}{12}$ of 60 days, and the interest is $\frac{1}{12}$ of \$7.5490, or \$0.629. The sum, \$17.24, is the interest for 137 days.

After a little practice, any number of days can be resolved into 6- or 60-day periods and easy fractions thereof.

Example. Find the interest on \$247.64 for eight days at 6%.

Solution.

$$
\begin{array}{r}
\$|247\,.64 = \text{interest for 6 days} \\
|082\,.54 = \text{interest for 2 days} \\
\hline
\$|330\,.18 = \text{interest for 8 days}
\end{array}
$$

Explanation. To find the interest for six days, point off three decimals, as indicated by the vertical line. Two days' interest is $\frac{1}{3}$ of six days' interest. The answer is, therefore, 33¢.

For rates other than 6%, see adjustments under previous method.

PROBLEMS

Find the interest at 6% on:

1. \$286.75 for 9 days.
2. \$189.22 for 8 days.
3. \$256.35 for 27 days.
4. \$178.56 for 39 days.
5. \$38.29 for 40 days.

6. \$175.82 for 34 days.
7. \$38.95 for 19 days.
8. \$47.56 for 17 days.
9. \$29.10 for 2 days.
10. \$1,286.75 for 21 days.

The cancellation method. The cancellation method may be used to advantage in many interest calculations, especially in those having fractional rates and rates other than 6%.

Example. Find the interest on \$750.00 for 45 days at 5%.

Solution.

$$
\frac{\overset{125}{\cancel{750}} \times \overset{15}{\cancel{45}} \times \overset{.01}{\cancel{.05}}}{\underset{4}{\cancel{12}} \times \underset{6}{\cancel{30}}} = \frac{18.75}{4} = 4.687, \text{ or } \$4.69
$$

Explanation. Writing below the line 12 times 30, instead of 360 days, facilitates cancellation.

Example. Find the interest on \$345.75 for 90 days at $4\frac{1}{2}$%.

Solution.

$$\frac{345.75 \times \overset{3}{\cancel{90}} \times .09}{\underset{4}{\cancel{12}} \times \cancel{30} \times 2} = \frac{31.1175}{8} = \$3.889, \text{ or } \$3.89$$

PROBLEMS

Find the interest, by the cancellation method, on:

1. $840.00 for 12 days at 2%.
2. $320.00 for 15 days at 4%.
3. $160.80 for 16 days at 5%.
4. $275.75 for 74 days at 6%.
5. $112.50 for 85 days at 4%.
6. $284.00 for 34 days at 6%.
7. $368.00 for 56 days at 5%.

8. $775.14 for 79 days at 5%.
9. $250.00 for 91 days at 6%.
10. $500.00 for 102 days at 4%.
11. $360.80 for 38 days at $4\frac{1}{2}$%.
12. $312.32 for 45 days at $4\frac{3}{4}$%.
13. $1,000.00 for 40 days at $5\frac{1}{2}$%.
14. $1,600.00 for 75 days at $4\frac{1}{4}$%.

Dollars–times–days method, 6%. This method is rapid, and is particularly valuable when a calculating machine is used. It is a modification of the cancellation method, where 6% and 360 days are two of the factors. Thus:

$$\frac{\$ \times \text{Days} \times .\cancel{06}}{\cancel{360}}$$
$$6,000$$

Assume that there are no other items that can be cancelled. The number of dollars is multiplied by the number of days, and the product divided by 6,000. Any number may be divided by 6,000 by pointing off three decimals, and dividing the resultant number by 6.

Example. Find the interest on $256.50 for 28 days at 6%.

Solution. Multiply the number of dollars by the number of days, point off three decimal places in addition to the number of decimal places in the principal, then divide by 6.

$$\begin{array}{r} \$256.50 \\ 28 \\ \hline 6)7.182\ 00 \\ \hline 1.197 \end{array} \quad \text{or } \$1.20, \text{ the interest.}$$

For rates other than 6%, see adjustments under "Sixty-day method."

PROBLEMS

Find the interest on the following:

1. $275.12 for 73 days at 5%.
2. $132.86 for 28 days at 8%.
3. $280.60 for 70 days at 4%.

4. $138.42 for 28 days at $4\frac{1}{2}$%.
5. $276.95 for 17 days at 8%.
6. $640.64 for 56 days at 7%.

Interchanging principal and time. Under the 60-day method, the computations may often be shortened by interchanging the principal and the time.

Example. Find the interest on $6,000.00 for 31 days at 6%.

Solution. Interchanging the principal and the time, the problem becomes that of finding the interest on $31.00 for 6,000 days. Apply the 6%, 60-day method, and the interest is found to be $31.00, since the interest is equal to the principal when the rate is 6% and the time is 6,000 days.

PROBLEMS

Find the interest on the following:

1. $2,400.00 for 23 days at 6%.
2. $3,600.00 for 7 days at 6%.
3. $6,000.00 for 156 days at 6%.

4. $3,000.00 for 193 days at 6%.
5. $4,500.00 for 38 days at 6%.
6. $4,200.00 for 41 days at 6%.

Exact or accurate interest. Exact or accurate interest is that which is obtained when a year is taken as 365 days. For full years, all methods of computing interest give the same result—a certain per cent of the principal; hence the results differ only when fractional parts of a year are used.

Example. Find the exact interest on $1,200.00 for 93 days at 6%.

Solution. The cancellation method previously explained is the method used, as it is probably the most practical.

$$\frac{\overset{240}{\cancel{1200}} \times 93 \times .06}{\underset{73}{\cancel{365}}} = \frac{1,339.20}{73} = \$18.35$$

PROBLEMS

Find the exact interest on:

1. $750.00 for 45 days at 6%.
2. $1,200.00 for 68 days at 7%.
3. $1,600.00 for 73 days at $6\frac{1}{2}$%.
4. $273.00 at 4% from May 12, 1961 to October 4, 1961.
5. $1,600.00 at $2\frac{1}{2}$% from June 3, 1961 to December 17, 1961.
6. $1,103.00 at 6% from May 17, 1962 to September 9, 1962.
7. $12,235.00 at $4\frac{1}{2}$% from April 19, 1960 to August 20, 1960.
8. If the ordinary interest is $104.15, what is the exact interest?
9. What is the ordinary interest if the exact interest is $107.23?

Promissory notes. A promissory note is a written promise to pay on demand or at a stipulated time a sum of money to settle an obligation. It is signed by the debtor, who is called the *maker* of the note.

$2,000.00   Hamilton, Ont., May 17, 1962

Ninety days after date I promise to pay

to the order of   David J. Jones

Two thousand – – – – – – – – – – – – – – 100/xx Dollars

for value received with interest at 6% per annum.

                                        Kenneth Roy Brown

Fig. 4-2. A Promissory Note.

Drafts. A draft is a written order, signed by the creditor, called the *drawer*, requiring the debtor, called the *drawee*, to pay on demand or at a fixed or specified time in the future, a stipulated amount. The drawer sends it to the drawee for acceptance and the drawee writes "Accepted" across it, along with his signature, and returns it to the drawer. The draft does not bear interest. If the draft is an "after date" draft, the term begins with the date on the draft; if it is an "after sight" draft, the term begins with the date of acceptance.

Note to Canadian readers. Three days' grace is allowed on promissory notes, time drafts, and "after sight" drafts, but not on demand or "at sight" drafts.

$1,000.00   Hamilton, Ont. April 17, 1961

Ninety days after date pay to the order of   Myself

One thousand – – – – – – – – – – – – – 100/xx Dollars

Value received
        and charge the same to account of   Kenneth Roy Brown

To Samuel R. Green   Accepted

    Toronto, Ontario   Payable at Bank of Commerce
                                     Toronto, Ontario

Fig. 4-3. "After Date" Draft.

$5,000.00   Hamilton, Ont. Nov. 24, 1961

Ninety days after sight pay to the order of   Myself

                         xx

Five thousand – – – – – – – – – – – – – 100 Dollars

Value received
     and charge the same to account of   Douglas John Gray

To   Samuel R. Green   Accepted

       Toronto, Ontario   Payable at Bank of Commerce

                               Toronto, Ontario

Fig. 4-4. "After Sight" Draft.

Trade Acceptance. A trade acceptance is a draft arising from the sale of goods and is drawn by the seller of the goods on the purchaser. A trade acceptance bears no interest.

Buffalo, N.Y., Jan. 29, 1961 $2,317.45

ninety days after date pay to the order of OURSELVES

                                    45

Two thousand three hundred seventeen and 100 Dollars

     This obligation of the acceptor hereof is in payment of goods purchased from the drawer. The acceptor may make the acceptance payable at any bank or trust company in the United States.

To   N. L. White   Artistic Drapery Co.

     Columbus, Ohio   by *J. E. L. Graham, Manager*

Fig. 4-5. Trade Acceptance.

BANK DISCOUNT

Definition. Bank discount is a deduction made from the amount due at maturity on a note or draft, in consideration of its being converted into cash before maturity. If the note does not bear interest, its face value is the amount due at maturity. If the note does bear interest, the amount due at maturity is the face value plus interest on the face value for the period and at the rate specified in the note.

In bank discount, the time is the period from the date of discount to the date of maturity of the note. The date of maturity of a note is the day on which it is due. Notes due a given number of days after date mature after the exact number of days have elapsed. Notes due a given number of months after date mature on the same date so many months hence, except notes made on the 31st and falling due in a 30-day month, which mature on the 30th, and notes made on the 29th, 30th, or 31st of some month and falling due in February, which mature on the last day of February.

Example. A note due 30 days after January 31 will mature on March 2; but if the note is due in one month, it will mature on the last day of the succeeding month, or February 28. If the year should be a leap year, the maturity dates would be March 1 and February 29.

Counting time. In counting time, the usual method is to count the first succeeding day as one day. To illustrate, if a note is given on January 15 for 10 days, the 16th is counted as the first, the 17th as the second, the 18th as the third, and January 25 as the tenth day.

Finding the difference between dates by use of a table. By numbering the days of the year, a calendar may be made for determining the number of days between any two dates. A portion of such a table, and the use made of it, are illustrated now.

May 1	121	Nov. 1	305
2	122	2	306
3	123	3	307
4	124	4	308
5	125	5	309
6	126	6	310
7	127	7	311
8	128	8	312
9	129	9	313
10	130	10	314

The number of days between May 4 and November 9 is found as follows:

The table shows that November 9 is the 313th day of the year
The table shows that May 4 is the   124th day of the year
Therefore, the difference is   189   days, the time required

Another form of table is one that shows the number of days from any day of any month to the corresponding day of any other month not more than one year later.

	Jan.	Feb.	Mar.	Apr.	May	June	July	Aug.	Sept.	Oct.	Nov.	Dec.
January........	365	31	59	90	120	151	181	212	243	273	304	334
February.......	334	365	28	59	89	120	150	181	212	242	273	303
March.	306	337	365	31	61	92	122	153	184	214	245	275
April..........	275	306	334	365	30	61	91	122	153	183	214	244
May...........	245	276	304	335	365	31	61	92	123	153	184	214
June..........	214	245	273	304	334	365	30	61	92	122	153	183
July.......	184	215	243	274	304	335	365	31	62	92	123	153
August.........	153	184	212	243	273	304	334	365	31	61	92	122
September.	122	153	181	212	242	273	303	334	365	30	61	91
October.........	92	123	151	182	212	243	273	304	335	365	31	61
November......	61	92	120	151	181	212	242	273	304	334	365	30
December..... .	31	62	90	121	151	182	212	243	274	304	335	365

Example. A note due August 17 was discounted June 10. What was the term of discount?

Solution.

From the table, June 10 to August 10. . . . . 61 days

August 10 to August 17 . . . . 7 days

Total. . . . . 68 days

Exact bank discount is evaluated when a 365-day year is used and the exact number of days in each month is counted. This is the only method permitted in Canada, and the three days' grace must be included in the calculations.

Ordinary bank discount is evaluated when a 360-day year is used. This is the method which is always used in the United States.

Proceeds. The proceeds of a note is the difference between the amount due at maturity and the bank discount.

Bank discount and proceeds formulas.

Let S = maturity value.

n = time expressed as a fraction of a year.

d = discount rate expressed as a decimal fraction.

D_b = bank discount.

P_b = proceeds.

Then $$D_b = Snd \qquad (7)$$

but $$P_b = S - Snd \text{ by } def^n$$

$$\therefore P_b = S(1 - nd) \qquad (8)$$

Example 1. Find the bank discount and the proceeds if a non-interest-bearing note for \$420.00 is discounted 90 days before it is due at 6%.

Solution (United States). In this case $S = 420.00$, $n = \frac{90}{360}$, and $d = .06$. Substituting these values in formula (7),

$$D_b = Snd = (420.00)(\tfrac{90}{360})(.06) = \$6.30$$
$$\therefore P_b = \$420.00 - \$6.30 = \$413.70.$$

Solution (Canada). In this case $S = 420.00$, $n = \frac{93}{365}$, and $d = .06$. Substituting these values in formula (7),

$$D_b = Snd = (420.00)(\tfrac{93}{365})(.06) = \$6.42.$$
$$\therefore P_b = \$420.00 - \$6.42 = \$413.58.$$

Example 2. A note for $780.00 dated May 17, payable in six months with interest at 6%, is discounted at 6% on August 15. Find the bank discount and the proceeds.

Solution (United States).   Maturity value of note $= 780[1 + \frac{1}{2}(.06)] = \$803.40$

$$D_b = (803.40)(\tfrac{94}{360})(.06) = -12.59$$
$$\therefore P_b = \$803.40 - \$12.59 = \$790.81$$

Solution (Canada).   Maturity value of note $= 780[1 + \frac{1}{2}(.06)] = \$803.40$

$$D_b = (803.40)(\tfrac{97}{365})(.06) = \$12.81$$
$$P_b = \$803.40 - \$12.81 = \$790.59$$

PROBLEMS

Students in the United States should find the ordinary bank discount and students in Canada should find the exact bank discount, remembering to add the three days' grace. It would be good practice, however, to try some questions by both methods.

Find the bank discount and the proceeds on:

1. A note for $750.00, due May 17 without interest, and discounted Sept. 9 at 6%.

2. A note for $1,200.00, due December 4 without interest, and discounted Oct. 29 at 6%.

3. A note for $1,500.00 dated October 8 and due in 4 months with interest at 6%, discounted December 1 at 6%.

4. A note for $800.00, dated September 9 and due in 6 months with interest at 7%, discounted November 11 at 6%.

5. A note for $250.00, dated July 11 and due in 90 days with interest at $5\frac{1}{2}$%, discounted September 1 at 6%.

6. $443.03 was received as the proceeds of a 90-day note discounted at 6%. What was the face of the note?

7. For what sum must a 60-day note be drawn in order that the proceeds will be $600.00 when the note is discounted at 6%?

8. Find the date of maturity, the term of discount, the bank discount, and the proceeds of a 60-day note for $750.00, dated July 8 and discounted July 17 at 5%.

9. Find the date of maturity and the term of discount of a 90-day sight draft, dated May 14, accepted May 17, and discounted June 10.

10. Find the date of maturity, the term of discount, the bank discount, and the proceeds of a note for $650.00, dated November 30, due in three months, and discounted January 5 at 6%.

PARTIAL PAYMENTS

Part payments on debts.   A debtor may by agreement make equal or unequal payments on the principal at regular or irregular intervals. Any partial payment of a note or draft should be recorded on the back of the note or draft.

Methods.   There are two methods of applying payments of principal and interest to the reduction of an interest-bearing debt. The method adopted by the Supreme Court of the United States is termed the "United States Rule"; the other method, which has been widely adopted by businessmen, is termed the "Merchants' Rule."

United States Rule. The United States Rule is now a law in many of the states, having been made so either by statute or by court decision.

The court holds that when a part payment is made on an interest-bearing debt, the payment must first be used to discharge the accumulated interest, and what remains of the payment is then applied in cancellation of the principal. If the payment is smaller than the accumulated interest, no cancellation takes place, and the previous principal continues to draw interest until the accumulated payments exceed the accumulated interest.

Example. An interest-bearing note for $1,800.00 dated March 1, 1944, had the following indorsements:

September 27, 1959................................	$500.00
March 15, 1960....................................	25.00
June 1, 1960......................................	$700.00

How much was due September 1, 1960?

Solution.

	Yr.	Mo.	Da.	Yrs.	Mos.	Days
Date of note..................	1959	3	1			
First payment, $500.00........	1959	9	27		6	26
Second payment, $25.00.......	1960	3	15		5	18
Third payment, $700.00.......	1960	6	1		2	16
Settlement...................	1960	9	1		3	0
				1	6	0

Explanation. The time is found by successive subtractions of the first date from the second, the second from the third, and so on. The sum of the different times is equal to the time between the date of the note and the date of settlement.

Face of note, March 1, 1959......................................	$1,800.00
Interest on $1,800.00 at 6% from March 1 to Sept. 27, 6 months and 26 days..	61.80
Amount due Sept. 27, 1959.......................................	$1,861.80
Deduct payment...	500.00
Balance due Sept. 27, 1959......................................	$1,361.80

Interest on $1,361.80 at 6% from Sept. 27 to March 15, 5 months and 18 days, $38.13. As this interest is larger in amount than the payment made at March 15, the interest is not added and the payment is not deducted.

Interest on $1,361.80 at 6% from Sept. 27 to June 1, 1960, 8 months and 4 days..	55.38
Amount due June 1, 1960...	$1,417.18
Deduct sum of payments: March 15........................ $ 25.00	
June 1......................... 700.00	725.00
Balance due June 1, 1960...	$ 692.18
Interest on $692.18 at 6% from June 1 to Sept. 1, 3 months......	10.38
Balance due September 1, 1960...................................	$ 702.56

Merchants' Rule. Find the amount of the debt (principal and interest) to the date of final settlement, or, if the debt runs for more than one year, find the amount to the end of the first year. Deduct from this the sum of all the payments and interest on the same to the date of settlement or to the end of the year. The remainder will be the amount due at the date of settlement or at the beginning of the next year.

Example. For purposes of comparison, the same problem will be used here as was used to illustrate the United States Rule.

Solution.

Face of note, March 1, 1959		$1,800.00
Interest, 1 year at 6% to March 1, 1960		108.00
		$1,908.00
Deduct:		
First payment, Sept. 27, 1959	$500.00	
Interest at 6% to March 1, 1960, 5 months and 4 days	12.83	512.83
Balance due at beginning of second year		$1,395.17
Interest on $1,395.17 at 6%, March 1 to Sept. 1, 1960, 6 months		41.86
		$1,437.03
Deduct:		
Second payment, March 15, 1960	$ 25.00	
Interest at 6% from March 15 to Sept. 1, 1960, 5 months and 16 days	.69	
Third payment, June 1, 1960	700.00	
Interest at 6% from June 1 to Sept. 1, 1960, 3 months	10.50	736.19
Balance due		$ 700.84

The difference of $1.72 between the balance as computed by the Merchants' Rule and the balance as computed by the United States Rule is small, but a much greater difference will occur when the time is long and the amount large.

It is usual to compute the balance due on notes of one year or less by the Merchants' Rule.

Note to Canadian readers. In Canada both the Merchants' Rule and the United States Rule would be applicable using *exact simple interest* rather than ordinary simple interest as used in the examples.

PROBLEMS

(Readers in the United States should use ordinary simple interest for computations and readers in Canada should use exact simple interest for their computations.)

Solve each of the following problems by both the United States Rule and the Merchants' Rule and compare the results.

1. A note for $1,650.00 was dated May 20, 1959. The interest was 6% from date, and the following payments were indorsed:

Sept. 8, 1959	$ 45.00
Dec. 14, 1959	20.00
Feb. 26, 1960	50.00
July 5, 1960	90.00
Nov. 14, 1960	250.00

What amount was due December 17, 1960?

2. A note for $1,200.00 is dated June 20, 1961. The interest was 6% from date, and the following payments are indorsed:

Oct. 2, 1961	$120.40
February 8, 1962	29.50
May 23, 1962	56.40
December 11, 1902	388.75

What amount is due January 23, 1963?

3. A note for $1,000.00 was dated April 10, 1958. The interest is 7% from date, and the following payments are made:

November 10, 1959	$ 80.50
July 5, 1960	100.00
January 10, 1961	450.80
October 1, 1963	500.00

What amount is due January 1, 1964?

4. A note for $950.00 with interest at 6% was dated Feb. 3, 1960, and has the following indorsements:

March 1, 1960	$150.00
June 3, 1960	96.00
July 8, 1960	300.00
December 20, 1960	250.00

What amount is due January 17, 1961?

5. A note for $791.84 with interest at 6% was dated December 14, 1960, and bore the following indorsements:

January 3, 1961	$100.00
March 16, 1961	240.00
July 29, 1961	324.00
August 3, 1961	20.00

What amount is due November 14, 1961?

6. A note for $1,200.00 dated April 1, 1960, bore interest at 7% and had the following indorsements:

April 12, 1960	$161.08
July 19, 1960	224.14
July 28, 1960	17.90
January 29, 1961	100.25

What amount is due April 1, 1961?

AVERAGING DATES OF INVOICES

Definition. Averaging dates of invoices is the process of finding the date when several invoices due at different dates may be paid in one amount, without loss of interest to either debtor or creditor.   This date is called the *equated date of payment*.

Use.   The process of averaging the dates of invoices is most frequently used in bankruptcy settlements, where claims when filed with a trustee must show the average due date of the items if interest is to be obtained on overdue amounts.   In general, the equated date is important in the settlement of bills of long standing and in the fixing of the date of a note in settlement of invoices.

Term of credit.   A term of credit is the time elapsing between the date of a bill and the date on which it becomes due; as, "Bill purchased January 10, Term of Credit 10 days."   The due date would be January 20.

Average due date.   The average due date is the date on which settlement of the complete account should be made by payment of the amount of the invoices, without charge for interest on overdue items or allowance for discount on prepaid items.

Focal date.   The focal date is an assumed date of settlement with which the due dates of the several items may be compared, to determine the equated date of payment.

Any date may be used as the focal date, and the final result will be the same.   In the interest method, any rate per cent may be used, and the result will be the same.   However, 6% is usually used, as the computations are then less complicated.

In all calculations, use the nearest dollar.   For example, for $115.29, use $115.00; and for $161.84, use $162.00.

When several bills are sold, some of which have a term of credit, first find the due date of those with a term of credit, and then find the equated date of the several bills.

With respect to bills with terms of credit, the due date of such bills, rather than the invoice date, is used in computing the equated date.

Do not use fractions of a day in determining the average date.

Methods.   There are two methods in common use: the Product Method, and the Interest Method.

Rule for product method.   Use as the focal date the last day of the month preceding the first item.   Multiply each item by the number of days intervening between the assumed date and the due date of the item, and divide the sum of the several products by the sum of the account.   Count forward from the assumed date the number of days obtained in the quotient.   The result will be the average due date.

Example.   Find the date at which the following bills of merchandise may be paid in one amount without loss to either party: Due January 1, $150.00; February 14, $200.00; April 20, $155.00; June 15, $200.00.

Solution by Product Method

(*Focal date, Dec. 31*)

Due January 1............................. $150 × 1 = 150
Due February 14.......................... 200 × 45 = 9,000
Due April 20.............................. 155 × 110 = 17,050
Due June 15.............................. 200 × 166 = 33,200
                                                        705   59,400

59,400 ÷ 705 = 84 days.
84 days after December 31 is March 25.

Explanation. For convenience, assume December 31 as the date of settlement. On the first bill, which is due January 1, there would be interest for 1 day. On the second bill there would be interest from December 31 to February 14, or 45 days, which is equivalent to interest on $9,000.00 for 1 day. On the third bill there would be interest from December 31 to April 20, or 110 days, which is equivalent to interest on $17,050.00 for 1 day. On the fourth bill there would be interest from December 31 to June 15, or 166 days, which is equivalent to interest on $33,200.00 for 1 day.

If all the bills were paid December 31, the debtor would be entitled to interest on $59,400.00 for 1 day, or interest on $705.00, the amount of the account, for 84 days. It is evident that the bills could be paid at a time 84 days later than December 31, or March 25, without loss to either party.

Verification

The interest on $150.00 for 83 days is........................ $2.08
The interest on $200.00 for 39 days is........................ 1.30
   Total gain of interest to debtor........................... $3.38
The interest on $155.00 for 26 days is........................ $ .67
The interest on $200.00 for 82 days is........................ 2.72
   Total gain of interest to creditor......................... $3.39

The gain of interest to the debtor is on all bills paid after they are due.

The gain of interest to the creditor is on all bills paid before they are due. These two results should be equal, or within a few cents of the same amount. The reason for a little discrepancy is the fraction of a day which is disregarded in determining the due date of the account.

Interest Method

The solution by this method is as follows:

January 1.................. $150.00 for 1 day = $0.03, interest
February 14................ 200.00 for 45 days = 1.50, interest
April 20................... 155.00 for 110 days = 2.84, interest
June 15.................... 200.00 for 166 days = 5.53, interest
   Total interest.................................... $9.90

Interest on $705.00 for 1 day is $0.1175.

$9.90 ÷ $0.1175 = 84, or 84 days.

Explanation. Assume December 31, the last day of the month preceding the first item, to be the date of settlement. If the amount of the account, $705.00, is paid December 31, there will be a loss of interest to the debtor of $9.90. The interest on $705.00 for 1 day at 6% is $0.1175. It will take a principal of $705.00 as many days to produce $9.90 as the number of times that $0.1175 is contained in $9.90, or 84 days, the same result as was obtained by the product method.

Note to Canadian readers. It is to be remembered that ordinary simple interest is used in all calculations in this section, but in Canada exact simple interest would be used. Otherwise, the methods are identical.

PROBLEMS

1. Several invoices mature as follows:

April 12	$260.00	August 18	$120.00
May 25	500.00	September 2	300.00

At what date may the foregoing invoices be paid in one amount without loss to either party?

2. Calculate the average due date of the following invoices:

June 10	$400.00	August 15	$250.00
July 27	100.00	September 22	300.00

3. Calculate the average due date of the following invoices:

May 8	$275.00 on 60 days' credit
May 24	150.00 on 2 months' credit
June 10	300.00 on 90 days' credit
July 1	250.00 on 30 days' credit

EQUATION OF ACCOUNTS, OR COMPOUND AVERAGE

Definition. Equation of accounts, or compound average, is the process of finding the date when the balance of an account having both debits and credits can be paid without loss to either debtor or creditor. With respect to bills with terms of credit, the due date of the bill rather than the invoice date is used in computing the equated date. Credits other than for cash (such as noninterest-bearing notes) are extended to the due date thereof. Summarizing briefly, the date to be used for each debit and credit is the date when the item has a cash value of the amount shown in the entry.

Rule for the product method. After finding the date that each item has a cash value, use the last day of the month preceding the earliest date as the focal date for both sides of the account. Find the number of days between the focal date and the due date of each item; multiply each item by the number of days intervening between the focal date and the due date of the item. Find the sum of the products on both the debit and the credit sides of the account. Divide the difference between the sums of the debit and the credit products by the balance of the account. The quotient will be the number of days between the focal date and the average date of the account.

When to date forward or backward. The average date is forward from the focal date when the balance of the account and the excess of the products are on the same side (both debits or both credits); if they are on opposite sides, the average date is backward from the focal date.

Example. At what date may the balance of the following account be paid without loss of interest to either party?

Debits		Credits	
July 1. Mdse. 30 days........	$250.00	Aug. 15, Cash...............	$400.00
July 26, Mdse. 30 days........	425.00	Sept. 10, Cash...............	300.00
Aug. 15, Mdse. 60 days........	320.00	Sept. 20, Cash...............	150.00
Aug. 30, Mdse. 60 days........	500.00		

Solution by Product Method. Since the earliest date is July 31, the assumed focal date would be June 30. However, since July 31 is an end-of-month date, this date is used, as each multiplier is 31 less than it would be if June 30 were used.

July 31, $	250.00 × 0 =	$00,000	Aug. 15, $400.00 × 15 =	$ 6,000
Aug. 25,	425.00 × 25 =	10,625	Sept. 10, 300.00 × 41 =	12,300
Oct. 14,	320.00 × 75 =	24,000	Sept. 20, 150.00 × 51 =	7,650
Oct. 29,	500.00 × 90 =	45,000		
	$1,495.00	$79,625	$850.00	$25,950

Debit side................................	$1,495.00	$79,625.00	
Credit side...............................	850.00	25,950.00	
	$ 645.00	$53,675.00	

$$\$53,675.00 \div \$645.00 = 83.$$

The equated date is, therefore, 83 days after July 31, or October 22.

Explanation. First find the due date of each item. For convenience, assume July 31, the earliest due date, as the day of settlement for all the items on each side of the account. Proceed as in the process of averaging dates, which was described in the preceding chapter. With July 31 used as the focal date, there is a loss of interest on the total debits equivalent to the interest on $79,625.00 for 1 day, and a gain of interest on the total credits equivalent to the interest on $25,950.00 for 1 day; or a net loss of interest equivalent to the interest on $53,675.00 for 1 day, which is equal to the interest on $645.00 for 83 days. It is evident that the date when there would be no loss of interest to either party must be 83 days after July 31, or October 22.

Solution by Interest Method.

Debits

July 31, 0 days' interest on $ 250.00 = $ .00
Aug. 25, 25 days' interest on   425.00 =   1.77
Oct. 14, 75 days' interest on   320.00 =   4.00
Oct. 29, 90 days' interest on   500.00 =   7.50
                                 $1,495.00 $13.27

Credits

Aug. 15, 15 days' interest on $ 400.00 = $ 1.00
Sept. 10, 41 days' interest on   300.00 =   2.05
Sept. 20, 51 days' interest on   150.00 =   1.28
                                 $ 850.00 $ 4.33

Dr. $1,495.00   Interest, $13.27
Cr.   850.00   Interest,   4.33
6000)   645.00 $ 8.94
$ .1075, interest for one day.
$8.94 ÷ .1075 = 83.

The equated date of payment is, therefore, 83 days after July 31, or October 22.

Explanation. The explanation of the product method is applicable to the interest method. The variance is in finding interest on each item and dividing the interest balance by the interest for 1 day on the balance of the account.

Note to Canadian readers. Perform the same operations, using exact simple interest instead of ordinary simple interest.

PROBLEMS

Find the equated date in each of the following:

1.

Debits		Credits	
June 10, Mdse	$500.00	July 5, Cash	$300.00
Aug. 20, Mdse	100.00	Aug. 10, Cash	150.00
Oct. 30, Mdse	250.00	Sept. 25, Cash	200.00

2.

Debits		Credits	
May 3. Mdse. 60 days	$300.00	June 20, Cash	$150.00
June 15, Mdse. 60 days	250.00	July 1, Note, 30 days without	
July 20, Mdse. 30 days	175.00	int	200.00
Aug. 27, Mdse. 60 days	225.00	Aug. 10, Note, 60 days, int., 6%	300.00

3.

Debits		Credits	
Mar. 1, Mdse. 30 days	$225.00	Mar. 31, Cash	$150.00
Mar. 20, Mdse. 2 mos	300.00	Apr. 15, Cash	100.00
Apr. 5, Mdse. 60 days	150.00	May 10, Cash	200.00

INSTALLMENT PLANS AND PERSONAL LOANS

In recent years installment buying has increased rapidly, as has the practice of taking small personal loans from finance companies. Many purchases of household appliances, furniture, and automobiles are financed by the seller on an installment plan or are financed through an *acceptance corporation*. It has become important, therefore, to know how to calculate the equivalent rate of simple interest that is actually being charged, since it is quite different from the implied rate.

Equal monthly installments plan formula.

Let P = the balance owing immediately after the down payment has been made.

I = the interest or carrying charges.

m = the number of monthly installments.

i = the equivalent rate per annum of simple interest.

a = the amount of each monthly installment.

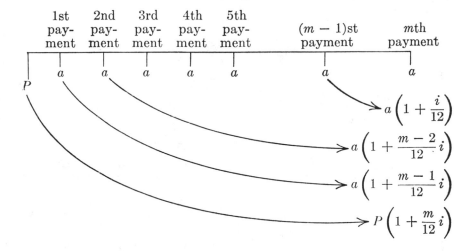

Obviously, from the chart, the amount of the principal P at rate i at the end of m months must be equal to the sum of the amounts of the installments at rate i at the right-hand end of the time scale.

$$\therefore P\left(1 + \frac{m}{12}i\right) = a + a\left(1 + \frac{i}{12}\right) + a\left(1 + \frac{2i}{12}\right) + \cdots$$

$$+ a\left(1 + \frac{m-2}{12}i\right) + a\left(1 + \frac{m-1}{12}i\right)$$

$$\therefore P + P\frac{m}{12}i = a + a + \frac{ai}{12} + a + 2\frac{ai}{12} + \cdots$$

$$+ a + \frac{(m-2)ai}{12} + a + \frac{(m-1)ai}{12}$$

$$\therefore P + P\frac{m}{12}i = ma + \frac{ai}{12}[1 + 2 + \cdots + (m-2) + (m-1)]$$

The terms in the square brackets form an arithmetic series whose sum is $\frac{m(m-1)}{2}$.

$$\therefore P + P\frac{m}{12}i = ma + \frac{m(m-1)ai}{24}$$

Since the sum of the installments is equal to the balance P plus the carrying charges I, we have

$$ma = P + I \text{ or } a = \frac{P+I}{m}.$$

$$\therefore P + P\frac{m}{12}i = m\left(\frac{P+I}{m}\right) + \frac{m(m-1)\left(\frac{P+I}{m}\right)i}{24}$$

$$\therefore P + P\frac{m}{12}i = P + I + \frac{(m-1)(P+I)i}{24}$$

$$\therefore P\frac{m}{12}i = I + \frac{mPi - Pi + (m-1)Ii}{24}$$

$$\therefore 2Pmi = 24I + Pmi - Pi + (m-1)Ii$$

$$\therefore P(m+1)i - (m-1)Ii = 24I$$

$$\therefore \{(m+1)P - (m-1)I\}i = 24I$$

$$\therefore i = \frac{24I}{(m+1)P - (m-1)I} \qquad (1)$$

Example 1. A washing machine which is listed as having a cash price of $120.00 may be purchased for $25.00 down and $20.00 per month for five months. What is the actual interest rate per annum?

Solution. In this case $P = 95$, $I = 5$, and $m = 5$. Substituting these values in the formula,

$$i = \frac{24I}{(m+1)P - (m-1)I} = \frac{24 \times 5}{6 \times 95 - 4 \times 5} = \frac{120}{550} = .2182$$

$\therefore$ The equivalent simple interest rate is 21.82% per annum.

Example 2. An article listed at $500.00 is sold for $50.00 down, plus a series of 12 monthly payments of $40.00 each, covering the $450.00 unpaid balance and the $30.00 installment charge. Find the equivalent simple interest rate per annum.

Solution. $P = \$450.00$, $m = 12$, and $I = \$30.00$.

$$i = \frac{24I}{(m+1)P - (m-1)I} = \frac{24 \times 30}{13 \times 450 - 11 \times 30} = .1304$$

$\therefore$ The equivalent simple interest rate is 12.18% per annum.

Example 3. A record player is worth $150.00 but is purchased on the following budget scheme. A down payment of $30.00 and an installment charge of $10.00, both paid at time of purchase, and ten monthly installments of $11.50 each. What is the equivalent simple interest rate?

Solution. $P = \$110.00$
$I = \$115.00 - \$110 = \$5.00$
$m = 10$

$$i = \frac{24I}{(m+1)P - (m-1)I} = \frac{24 \times 5}{11 \times 110 - 9 \times 5} = .103$$

∴ the equivalent simple interest rate is 10.3% per annum.

PROBLEMS

1. An article selling for $60.00 can be purchased on the installment plan with seven monthly installments of $9.00 each. Find the equivalent simple interest rate per annum.

2. A radio can be purchased for $100.00 cash or $0 down and ten monthly payments of $10.00 each. What is the equivalent simple interest rate per annum?

3. A fur coat is listed at $900.00 or $81.00 down and $50.00 per month for one and one-half years. Find the equivalent simple interest rate per annum.

4. A $4,000.00 mortgage is to be repaid over a period of four years through monthly payments of $100.00 each, such payments covering the mortgage and $800.00 carry charges. Find the equivalent simple interest rate per annum.

5. An article priced at $115.00 may be purchased for a cash payment of $20.00 and a $5.00 installment charge, both paid at the time of purchase, and eight monthly payments of $12.00 each. Find the equivalent simple interest rate per annum in this plan.

Equal-monthly-installments-plus-an-odd-final-payment plan formula. In the programming of an installment plan, it is frequently convenient to make all the installments equal except the last one. If, for example, $P + I = \$76.98$, then it could be convenient to have six payments of $12.00 each and an odd final payment of $4.98.

To develop a formula that is applicable for such a plan, the symbols in the previous section will be used with the same meanings, and the amount of the final payment will be denoted by f.

There are, therefore, $m - 1$ installments of a each and an mth or final payment of f.

Proceeding as in the previous section,

$$P + P\frac{m}{12}i = f + a\left(1 + \frac{i}{12}\right) + a\left(1 + \frac{2i}{12}\right) + \cdots$$
$$+ a\left(1 + \frac{m-1}{12}i\right)$$

$$\therefore P + P\frac{m}{12}i = f + (m-1)a + \frac{m(m-1)ai}{24}$$

Since the sum of the installments is equal to the balance P plus the carrying charges I, we have

$$f + (m - 1)a = P + I \text{ or } (m - 1)a = P + I - f$$

$$\therefore P + P\frac{m}{12}i = P + I + \frac{m(P + I - f)i}{24}$$

$$\therefore 2Pmi = 24I + Pmi + Imi - fmi$$

$$\therefore (P - I + f)mi = 24I$$

$$\therefore i = \frac{24I}{m(P - I + f)} \tag{2}$$

Example. Suppose a $600.00 article can be purchased for nine monthly payments of $70.00 and a tenth final payment of $10.00. Find the equivalent simple interest rate per annum.

Solution.

$$P = \$600$$
$$I = \$640 - \$600 = \$40$$
$$m = 10$$
$$f = \$10.00$$
$$\therefore i = \frac{24 \times 40}{10(600 - 40 + 10)} = .168$$

$\therefore$ The equivalent simple interest rate is 16.8% per annum.

PROBLEMS

1. A radio is priced at $70.00 cash or $7.00 down, $10.00 per month for six months, and a final payment of $8.00 at the end of the seventh month. Find the equivalent rate of simple interest.

2. A vacuum cleaner is for sale at $109.50 or $10.00 down, $15.00 per month for seven months and $3.50 at the end of the eighth month. Find the equivalent simple interest rate per annum.

3. A gas hot water heater is sold for $125.00 cash or $25.00 down, $10.00 per month for eleven months, and $8.00 at the end of the twelfth month. Find the equivalent simple interest rate per annum.

· 4. Mr. Smith purchased a washer-and-dryer combination for $592. After paying $100, he found that he could not pay the balance. This balance was financed by an acceptance corporation, with the following terms quoted: 23 monthly installments of $21.00 each plus a final payment of $9.00. Find the equivalent rate of simple interest.

Personal loans.

Formulas (1) and (2) developed in the previous sections apply equally well to personal loans which are repaid by monthly installments.

Example 1. Peter Smith borrows $600.00 from a finance company and contracts to repay with eight monthly installments of $78.00 each. What equivalent simple interest rate per annum is he paying?

Solution.

$$P = \$600$$
$$I = \$624 - \$600 = \$24$$
$$m = 8$$

Substituting these values in formula (1),

$$i = \frac{24I}{(m+1)P - (m-1)I} = \frac{24 \times 24}{9 \times 600 - 7} \times 24 = .11.$$

∴ the equivalent simple interest rate is 11% per annum.

Example 2. Miss Harris borrows $75.00 from a personal loan company and agrees to pay $8.00 per month for nine months and $6.75 in the tenth and final month. What simple interest rate per annum is she being charged?

Solution.
$$P = \$75.00$$
$$I = \$78.75 - \$75.00 = \$3.75$$
$$m = 10$$
$$f = \$6.75$$

Substituting these values in formula (2),

$$i = \frac{24I}{m(P - I + f)} = \frac{24 \times 3.75}{10(75 - 3.75 + 6.75)} = .116.$$

∴ Miss Harris is being charged 11.6% per annum.

PROBLEMS

1. The following table is taken from a newspaper advertisement of a small loan company. Calculate the equivalent simple interest rate per annum for each loan.

You Receive	Monthly Payment	Number of Payments
$ 147.16	$ 9.00	20
310.78	19.00	20
506.94	22.00	30
809.74	34.00	30
1,525.00	39.00	60

2. *A* borrowed $1,000.00 from *B* and promised to repay $100.00 per month for ten months and $50.00 in the eleventh month. What interest rate was *B* charging *A*?

ACCOUNT CURRENT

Definition. An *account current* is a transcript of the ledger account. It should show the dates on which sales were made, the term of credit for each item, cash payments, and, if settlements were made by note, the date and other details of each note.

Methods. Two methods are used in finding the amount due: the Interest Method, and the Product Method.

Example. Find the balance due January 1 on the following ledger account, which bears interest at 6%.

J. B. JOHNSON

Dr.		Cr.	
Sept. 1, Balance............	$1,200.00	Oct. 1, Cash..............	$1,000.00
Sept. 20, Mdse. 30 days......	400.00	Nov. 10, Cash..............	200.00
Oct. 30, Mdse. 30 days.	520.00	Dec. 3, Cash..............	400.00
Nov. 25, Mdse. 30 days......	350.00	Dec. 15, Note 10 days.......	300.00

Solution by Interest Method.

J. B. JOHNSON

Date Due	Dr. Amount	Days	Interest	Date	Cr. Amount	Days	Interest
Sept. 1	$1,200.00	122	$24.40	Oct. 1	$1,000.00	92	$15.33
Oct. 20	400.00	72	4.87	Nov. 10	200.00	52	1.73
Nov. 29	520.00	33	2.86	Dec. 3	400.00	29	1.93
Dec. 25	350.00	7	.41	Dec. 25	300.00	7	.35
	$2,470.00		$32.54		$1,900.00		$19.34
	1,900.00		19.34				
	$ 570.00	+	$13.20 = $583.20				

Explanation. The number of days opposite each entry is the actual number of days from the date of the item to January 1, the date which is taken as the focal date.

Solution by Product Method.

Date Due	Dr. Amount	Days		Product	Date	Cr. Amount	Days		Product
Sept. 1	$1,200	× 122	=	$146,400	Oct. 1	$1,000	× 92	=	$ 92,000
Oct. 20	400	× 73	=	29,200	Nov. 10	200	× 52	=	10,400
Nov. 29	520	× 33	=	17,161	Dec. 3	400	× 29	=	11,600
Dec. 25	350	× 7	=	2,450	Dec. 25	300	× 7	=	2,100
	$2,470			$195,210		$1,900			$116,100
	1,900			116,100					
	$ 570			$ 79,110					

The interest on $79,110 for 1 day = $ 13.20

$570.00 + $13.20 = $583.20

In some instances it is more convenient to find the equated due date, and then calculate the interest on the balance of the account from that date to the date of settlement.

PROBLEMS

1. Find the amount that will settle the following account Sept. 10, interest at 6%.

Dr.		Cr.	
Mar. 15, Mdse. 4 mos........	$450.00	July 5, Cash................	$400.00
Mar. 30, Mdse. 60 days.......	375.00	July 30, Cash................	375.00
Apr. 18, Mdse. 30 days.......	700.00	Aug. 15, Cash................	690.00
May 15, Mdse. 4 mos.........	620.00	Sept. 5, Cash................	615.00
May 30, Mdse. 4 mos.........	410.00		

2. Find the amount that will settle the following account on June 1, interest at 6%.

Dr.		Cr.	
Jan. 4, Mdse. 30 days......	$500.00	Feb. 20, Cash...............	$300.00
Jan. 30, Mdse. 30 days........	200.00	Feb. 28, Note, 60 days with	
Feb. 5, Mdse. 30 days........	600.00	interest at 6%......	300.00
Mar. 1, Mdse. 30 days........	400.00	Mar. 20, Cash...............	150.00

3. *A* borrowed $10,000.00 from a bank on January 2, for building a home, giving a note, secured by a mortgage, due in one year, with interest at 6%. From time to time the bank advanced him money to pay contractors' estimates. Before maturity the bank had actually advanced $9,000.00, as follows:

January 31.. $3,000.00
March 15.. 3,000.00
April 15.. 1,500.00
May 15.. 1,500.00

On June 1, the following year, the maker of the note desires to pay it. (*a*) How should interest be computed? (*b*) What amount is due June 1?

STORAGE

Definition. *Storage* is the charge made by a warehouse or depositary for the storing of goods until they are required for use or for transportation to some other point.

Running account. When goods are being received and delivered, the storage company keeps a running account, showing the dates at which goods are received and delivered, together with details of the number of packages, barrels, and so forth. Storage is charged for the average number of days for which one package, barrel, or box has remained in storage. The average number of days is divided by 30 to reduce the average number of days to months, or by 7 to reduce the average number of days to weeks, as the case may be; then the number of months or weeks is multiplied by the price per month or per week.

Example. The following is a memorandum of the quantity of salt stored with a storage company at 4¢ per barrel per term of 30 days' average storage.

Date	Receipts	Deliveries	Balance	Time in Storage	Equivalent for 1 Day
June 4	120 bbl.		120 bbl.	28 days	3,360 bbl.
July 2		20 bbl.	100 bbl.	18 days	1,800 bbl.
July 20	100 bbl.		200 bbl.	10 days	2,000 bbl.
July 30		50 bbl.	150 bbl.	11 days	1,650 bbl.
Aug. 10		100 bbl.	50 bbl.	15 days	750 bbl.
Aug. 25		50 bbl.	0 bbl.		
					9,560 bbl.

Explanation. 9,560 bbl. for 1 day are equivalent to 1 barrel for 9,560 days, and 9,560 divided by 30 (the number of days per term) equals $318\frac{2}{3}$ terms. In some cases a full month's storage is charged for any part of a month that goods remain in storage; in other cases, 15 days or less are called one-half of a month, and any period of over 15 days is counted as a whole month. $318\frac{2}{3}$ terms would be charged for as 319 terms, and $319 \times .04 = 12.76$. Therefore, $12.76 is the storage charge.

PROBLEMS

1. On the following memoranda, compute storage at 4¢ per barrel per term of 30 days' average storage:

Received		Delivered	
Feb. 10	300 bbl.	Feb. 20	150 bbl.
Feb. 19	150 bbl.	Mar. 5	200 bbl.
Mar. 12	500 bbl.	Mar. 15	400 bbl.
Mar. 30	300 bbl.	Apr. 14	300 bbl.

2. A grower stored 5,000 bushels of potatoes at $5\frac{1}{2}$¢ per cwt., the term being 30 days' average storage. The following is a memorandum of the transactions that occurred. Compute the amount of storage.

Received		Delivered	
Sept. 1	2,500 bushels	Nov. 4	500 bushels
Sept. 10	1,500 bushels	Dec. 10	600 bushels
Oct. 5	1,000 bushels	Jan. 15	750 bushels
		Feb. 1	1,500 bushels
		Mar. 18	750 bushels
		Apr. 2	900 bushels

5

Inventories

Valuation of inventories. The bases of inventory valuation most commonly used by business concerns are: (*a*) cost; and (*b*) cost or market, whichever is lower. However, the average cost method is used in some instances—the tobacco industry, for example—and market value as a basis is used in grain and cotton inventories and in inventories of dealers in securities.

Cost or market, whichever is lower. In valuing inventories at cost or market, whichever is lower, a comparison of inventory totals at the two values is not sufficient. It is necessary to consider each item or group of similar items purchased at the same price, and to make the extension at the cost or market price, whichever is lower.

Example. One hundred tons of sugar (200,000 lbs.) were purchased at 7¢ a pound, and later 50 tons (100,000 lbs.) were purchased at 6¢ a pound. The entire 150 tons were on hand at the close of the year, at which time the market value of sugar was 6½¢ a pound. Compute the inventory at: (*a*) cost; and (*b*) at cost or market, whichever is lower.

Solution.

(*a*)	200,000 lbs. @ .07	$14,000
	100,000 lbs. @ .06	6,000
	Inventory at cost	$20,000
(*b*)	200,000 lbs. @ .065	$13,000
	100,000 lbs. @ .06	6,000
	Inventory at cost or market, whichever is lower	$19,000

PROBLEMS

1. Given the following inventory of a retail shop for children's clothing, toys, and so forth (correct as to quantities and values), state the amount which should be shown on a balance sheet as merchandise inventory, adopting the method of valuing inventory at cost or market, whichever is lower.

	Value Per Unit		Total Value	
Item	Cost	Market	Cost	Market
150 knit towels..................	$ 0.38	$ 0.35	$ 57.00	$ 52.50
16 crepe de chine carriage sets....	10.00	12.50	160.00	200.00
125 lingerie and pongee hats.......	4.00	3.50	500.00	437.50
85 rubber bibs with sleeves.......	1.00	1.00	85.00	85.00
240 creepers.....................	3.05	2.98	732.00	715.20
200 spring coats.................	19.50	20.00	3,900.00	4,000.00
50 spring coats.................	27.50	29.50	1,375.00	1,475.00
8 play yards....................	18.00	17.25	144.00	138.00
8 desks used in office...........	110.00	120.00	880.00	960.00
140 shirts......................	4.50	5.00	630.00	700.00
200 boys' wash suits..............	6.20	5.98	1,240.00	1,196.00
125 bloomers....................	2.85	2.80	356.25	350.00
5 cribs........................	31.00	29.98	155.00	149.90
12 electric trains...............	19.00	19.00	228.00	228.00
Total.....................			$10,442.25	$10,687.10

2. You are called in by the X. Y. Z. Clothing Company to advise them on the calculation of their inventory. They have always followed the policy of cost or market, whichever is lower. You are informed that the inventory will be used for the tax return, as well as for the annual report to stockholders.

	Value per Unit		Total Value	
Item	Cost	Market	Cost	Market
13 suits, grade A....................	$120.00	$110.00	$1,560.00	$1,430.00
12 suits, grade B...................	80.00	75.00	960.00	900.00
17 suits, grade C...................	60.00	60.00	1,020.00	1,020.00
7 suits, grade D...................	40.00	44.00	280.00	308.00
24 overcoats, grade 1...............	150.00	160.00	3,600.00	3,840.00
5 overcoats, grade 2...............	80.00	90.00	400.00	450.00
10 overcoats, grade 3...............	60.00	50.00	600.00	500.00
6 topcoats, grade X...............	40.00	35.00	240.00	210.00
9 topcoats, grade Y...............	30.00	25.00	270.00	225.00
18 topcoats, grade Z...............	20.00	22.00	360.00	396.00
Total...........................			$9,290.00	$9,279.00

Which total figure would you advise the company to use for: (*a*) tax reports; (*b*) annual report to stockholders?

Average cost method. The general rule that the average cost method of valuing inventories will not be accepted for income tax purposes is subject to certain exceptions. In the tobacco industry, for example, tobacco is bought from the producer, usually in small quantities and at greatly varying prices. Different grades of tobacco are mixed and stored in hogsheads, and it is practically impossible to determine the exact cost of any particular hogshead. The inventory is therefore averaged monthly, according to grades, as follows:

First method. From the inventory of each grade at the beginning of the month is subtracted the amount of tobacco of that grade used, leaving so many pounds costing so many dollars; to this is added the tobacco of that grade purchased during the month, and a new average is determined. This is the inventory for the close of the month, and is consequently the opening inventory of the next month.

Example.

Stock Card

	RECEIVED				ISSUED			BALANCE		
Date	Quan-tity	Rate	Amount	Date	Quan-tity	Rate	Quan-tity	Rate	Amount
6–29	100,000	$1.00	$100,000				100,000	$1.00	$100,000
				9–1	80,000	$1.00	20,000	1.00	20,000
9–30	80,000	1.10	88,000				100,000	1.08	108,000
				12–5	30,000	1.08	70,000	1.08	75,600
12–10	125,000	.95	118,750				195,000	....	194,350
				12–18	20,000	1.08	175,000	....	172,750
Inv't 12–31	175,000	$0.987	$172,750						

Explanation. It will be noticed that the receipt of 125,000 at .95 on Dec. 10 was extended into the balance column in quantity and amount only, and that the issuance on Dec. 18 was made at the rate established on the first of the month. This is the method that is used when receipts are frequent, as it saves the time that would be required to compute a new rate after each receipt, and establishes a standard rate of issuance for the month.

Second method. When receipts are not frequent and are large in amount, a new average price is computed upon the entry of each receipt.

Example.

Stock Card

	RECEIVED				ISSUED			BALANCE		
Date	Quan-tity	Rate	Amount	Date	Quan-tity	Rate	Quan-tity	Rate	Amount
6–29	100,000	$1.00	$100,000				100,000	$1.00	$100,000
				9–1	80,000	$1.00	20,000	1.00	20,000
9–30	80,000	1.10	88,000				100,000	1.08	108,000
				12–5	30,000	1.08	70,000	1.08	75,600
12–10	125,000	.95	118,750				195,000	.99$\frac{1}{2}$	194,350
				12–18	20,000	.99$\frac{1}{2}$	175,000	.99$\frac{1}{2}$	174,450
Inv't 12–31	175,000	0.99\frac{1}{2}$	$174,450						

PROBLEMS

1. Rule two stock cards as in the preceding example, and enter the following data. Compute the balances: (*a*) by the first method; and (*b*) by the second method.

Received	*Issued*
July 5....... 80,000 units @ $0.90	Aug. 1........ 50,000 units
Aug. 15...... 20,000 units @ 1.00	Dec. 2........ 20,000 units
Sept. 1....... 30,000 units @ 1.10	Dec. 20....... 30,000 units
Dec. 8....... 20,000 units @ 1.20	

2. Complete the following stock ledger card, using the average-price method.

Stores Ledger

Actual Receipt Price		.15	.20			
Average Price		.15	.1708			

Name *Bushings 3" Mall*   Part No. *56-678*

Minimum *100*		Maximum *300*	Location *L3*
Drawing No.		Unit	

		REFERENCE		QUANTITY		ON HAND		
	Date	Number	Remarks	Received	Issued	Quantity	Value	
1	OCT 4	4523		100				1
2	OCT 10	34567			5			2
3	OCT 12	35654			10			3
4	OCT 13	38765			3			4
5	OCT 15	39458			12			5
6	OCT 16	4587		50				6
7	OCT 19	40156			10			7
8								8
9								9
10								10
11								11
12								12
13								13

"First-in, first-out" method of inventory. Where the same merchandise has been purchased at various prices during the year, and the goods on hand cannot be identified with specific invoices, the amount on hand at the end of the year may be inventoried at the latest purchase price. If, however, the quantity on hand is greater than the amount purchased at the last price, the balance may be inventoried at the next-to-the-last purchase price, and so on. This method is termed "first-in, first-out method" of inventory.

Example.

Inventory, December 31.............................	275,000 units
Invoices:	
November 10.......................	125,000 units @ $0.95 per C
September 5.......................	80,000 units @ 1.10 per C
June 10............................	70,000 units @ 1.00 per C

How should the foregoing inventory be valued?

Solution.

125,000 units @ $0.95 per C.......................... $1,187.50
 80,000 units @ 1.10 per C..........................   880.00
 70,000 units @ 1.00 per C..........................   700.00
275,000 units inventoried............................ $2,767.50

"Last-in, first-out" method of inventory. Under the "last-in, first-out" method, inventories are valued at the cost of goods earliest acquired, and in computing profits from sales the cost of goods last acquired is used. This method will show smaller profits when prices are rising and larger profits when prices are falling than the "first-in, first-out" method. Businesses which use raw materials or other goods includ able in inventory which are subject to sharp price fluctuations, businesses in which the value of inventory is large compared with other assets and sales, and businesses in which production consumes an extended period are most likely to benefit from the use of this method. (Consult the Internal Revenue Code relative to the requirements incident to adoption and use of this method.)

Example. *A* has an opening inventory of 10 units at 10 cents a unit, and during the year he makes purchases of 10 units as follows:

January... 1 @ .11 = .11
April... 2 @ .12 = .24
July.. 3 @ .13 = .39
October... 4 @ .14 = .56
                                                 10   1.30

His closing inventory shows 15 units. What is the value of the closing inventory?

Solution.

          10 @ .10   = 1.00
           1 @ .11 (Jan.) = .11
           2 @ .12 (Apr.) = .24
           2 @ .13 (July) = .26
Totals 15   1.61

PROBLEM

Value the closing inventory, using the "last-in, first-out" method.

    Opening inventory: 50 units at $1.00
    Production:
      First quarter: 50 units at $1.50
      Second quarter: 100 units at $1.75
      Third quarter: 50 units at $2.00
      Fourth quarter: 100 units at $2.25
    Closing inventory: 150 units

Merchandise turnover.   The number of times that the value of the inventory is contained in the cost of sales is the merchandise turnover.

The final inventory should not be used in computing turnover, unless it represents a normal inventory for the fiscal period or is the first inventory that has been taken.

If a perpetual inventory system is in use, the monthly inventories should be added to the inventory at the beginning of the period, and the sum divided by the number of months in the fiscal period plus one.   In a year there would thus be 13 inventories—the one at January 1, and the 12 inventories at the ends of the months.   When a perpetual inventory is not used, add the inventory at the beginning of the fiscal period to the one at the close of the period; then divide by 2.   The quotient will be the estimated average inventory for the period.   If semiannual inventories are taken, use three inventories and divide by 3.   If quarterly inventories are taken, use five inventories and divide by 5.

FORMULA

Cost of Sales ÷ Average Inventory at Cost = Rate of Turnover

Example.   A department store found the average inventory of Department A for the fiscal period to be $30,000.   The cost of sales for the same period was $120,000.

$120,000 ÷ $30,000 = 4, the rate of turnover.

An estimated inventory at the end of any period may be obtained by dividing the sales for the period by 100% plus the per cent of gross profit based on cost, and deducting the quotient from the total of purchases and first-of-period inventory.   A more complete discussion of the gross profit test is given in Chapter 7.

Example.   In the above example, assume that in Department A the total cost of merchandise was $150,000, that the sales were $144,000, and that the average profits were 20%.   Using the per cent of gross profits to determine the average inventory, the solution would be as follows:

$144,000 (sales) ÷ 120% = $120,000, the cost of sales.
$150,000 (total cost of goods) − $120,000
(cost of sales) = $30,000, the estimated inventory.
$120,000 (cost of sales) ÷ $30,000
(inventory) = 4, the rate of turnover.

Number of turnovers.   The number of turnovers varies in different lines of business.   Records show turnovers varying from 1 to more than 20, depending on the kind of business.   It is possible to make a larger profit by several turnovers with a small mark-up* than by 1 or 2 turnovers with a large mark-up.   Limited capital and frequent turnovers

---

* "Mark-up," as used in this text, refers to the addition made to the cost of merchandise to produce the selling price.

can produce a profit equal to that produced by a greater capital turned fewer times a year. If a merchant turns $1 eight times in the course of a year, he has used $\frac{1}{8}$ of the capital that would be required if the rate of turnover were 1.

Example 1. A merchant had a rate of mark-up of 50%, with a turnover of 1. He found that by using a rate of mark-up of 30%, he had a turnover of 2. If his former sales were $300,000 annually, how much were his gross profits increased, provided he continued to use the same investment in merchandise?

$$\$300,000 \div 150\% = \$200,000, \text{ cost of sales.}$$
$$\$300,000 - \$200,000 = \$100,000, \text{ gross profits.}$$

Under the new policy he turns the $200,000 twice, the equivalent of $400,000 annually.

$$\$400,000 \text{ at } 30\% = \$120,000, \text{ profits.}$$
$$\$120,000 - \$100,000 = \$20,000, \text{ increased profits due to lowering}$$
$$\text{the rate of mark-up and increasing}$$
$$\text{the rate of turnover.}$$

Example 2. What investment in merchandise would be required under the new policy to make the same amount of profits that was made under the old policy?

$100,000 \div 30\% = \$333,333.33$, cost of goods sold to make profits of $100,000.

Since there were two turnovers, the cost of goods sold was twice the amount of the average inventory. Therefore:

$$\$333,333.33 \div 2 = \$166,666.67, \text{ the average inventory.}$$

Hence, the merchant could make the same amount of gross profits with an investment $33,333.33 smaller than that required under his old policy.

PROBLEMS

1. A rate of mark-up of 30% results in two turnovers of an average inventory of $30,000. If the expenses of conducting the business are $8,000, what is the net profit?

2. A rate of mark-up of 20% results in three turnovers of an average inventory of $30,000. If expenses remain at $8,000, what is the net profit?

3. The cost of sales in Department B was $42,000. The average inventory was $12,000. What was the number of turnovers?

4. A merchant's sales amounted to $42,000. His average inventory was $10,000, and the average rate of mark-up was 40%. Find the number of turnovers.

5. Commodity X, with a rate of mark-up of 40%, had a turnover of 2. With a rate of mark-up of 30%, it had a turnover of 3. If prior sales were $56,000, find the sales and the increase in gross profit with the 30% rate of mark-up.

6. A rate of mark-up of 35% results in a turnover of 2 and in sales amounting to $540,000. A rate of mark-up of 20% results in a turnover of 4. How much

less capital under the latter plan is required to make as much profit as under the former plan?

7.* On January 1, a concern dealing in a single commodity had an inventory of merchandise which cost $20,000. The goods were marked to sell at 125% of cost, and all subsequent purchases during the six months ending June 30 were marked at the same rate. The selling price of the inventory at June 30 was $24,000. Purchases and sales by months were:

	Purchases (Cost)	Sales (Selling Price)
January	$ 8,000	$ 9,000
February	9,000	9,500
March	14,000	12,000
April	16,000	18,000
May	13,000	22,000
June	10,000	18,000

(a) Compute estimated inventories at cost price at the end of each of the six months.

(b) Compute the rate of turnover for the six months' period, using (1) the January 1 and June 30 inventories; (2) all the inventories.

(c) State which method gives the more accurate results.

Per cent of mark-down to net cost. If an item costs $1 and is marked $1.25, in order to sell the item for cost the price must be reduced 25¢. The marked price is the base when prices are reduced. 25¢ is $\frac{1}{5}$ of $1.25. $\frac{1}{5} = 20\%$.

An item costs $1 and is marked $1.50. 50¢ reduction is $\frac{1}{3}$ of $1.50, or $33\frac{1}{3}\%$.

PROBLEMS

Calculate the per cent of mark-down for each of the following items:

Item	Cost	Marked Price	Per Cent of Mark-down to Produce Cost
A	$ 2.00	$ 2.50	....
B	1.00	1.25	....
C	.35	.40	....
D	.80	1.00	....
E	15.00	25.00	....
F	3.50	4.00	....
G	.20	.30	....
H	5.00	7.00	....
I	.08	.10	....
J	2.00	4.00	....
K	40.00	75.00	....
L	12.00	18.00	....

Computation of inventory by the retail method. The need for frequent inventories has led many department stores to adopt the "retail method" of computing inventories. The accuracy of the inventory by this method depends upon the care exercised in recording the mark-ups

---

* American Institute Examination.

and the mark-downs of merchandise prices, and the classification of merchandise into departments and groups and sub-classes within the departments. In addition to the usual records showing sales (at selling price only), records are kept which show the opening inventory and purchases at cost and at retail (or selling) prices. An estimated inventory may be prepared from such records in the following manner.

INVENTORY COMPUTATION

	Cost	Retail
Inventory, beginning of period.................	$ 6,000	$ 8,000
Purchases during the period, including freight and cartage..................................	74,000	111,200
Totals..............................	$80,000	$119,200

(% Mark-on = $30,200 ÷ $110,200 or 32.8850 %.)

Sales......................................		104,200
Inventory at retail..........................		$ 15,000

Estimated inventory = $15,000 − ($15,000 × 32.8859%) = $10,067.

The foregoing illustration does not take into consideration changes in selling price after the original mark-up. Price changes must be dealt with, and the retail mercantile business has terms for these changes that are not generally understood; therefore, to prevent any misunderstanding, the diagram in Figure 5-1 is presented and the terms explained.

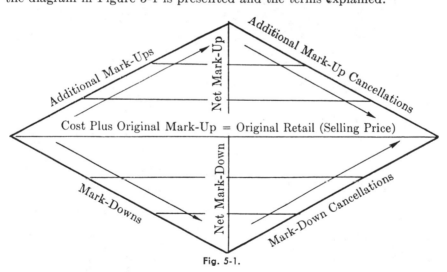

Fig. 5-1.

Original mark-up. The amount by which the original retail price of an article exceeds the cost is the original mark-up.

Additional mark-up. An amount that increases the original retail price is an additional mark-up.

Additional mark-up cancellation. A reduction in the additional mark-up is an additional mark-up cancellation, and the amount cannot exceed the amount of the additional mark-up.

Net mark-up. The sum of additional mark-ups minus the sum of additional mark-up cancellations is the net mark-up.

Mark-downs. Deductions from the original retail price to establish a new but lower retail price are mark-downs.

Mark-down cancellations. A reduction of the amount of a mark-down is a mark-down cancellation. Mark-down cancellations cannot exceed the total mark-downs. It is evident that the retail price of merchandise is increased when the mark-down is reduced, but such an increase is not to be considered as an additional mark-up.

Net mark-down. The difference between the sum of the mark-downs and the sum of the mark-down cancellations is the net mark-down.

Mark-on. The difference between cost and the original retail plus the net mark-up is the mark-on.

To illustrate the terms, let the following transactions be assumed.

Cost of Article $1.00	Original Mark-Up 50¢		
Original Retail (or Selling) Price $1.00 + .50 = $1.50			
$1.50	Addn'l Mark-Up 25¢		
1st Adjusted Retail Price $1.50 + .25 = $1.75			
2nd Adjusted Retail Price $1.75 − .10 = $1.65		*a* 10¢	*a.* Additional mark-up cancellation Net mark-up = 15¢ Mark-on = 65¢
3rd Adjusted Retail Price $1.65 − .15 = $1.50		*b* 15¢	*b.* Additional mark-up cancellation Net mark-up = 0 Mark-on = 50¢
4th Adjusted Retail Price $1.50 − .15 = $1.35		*c* 15¢	*c.* Mark-down
5th Adjusted Retail Price $1.35 − .35 = $1.00	*d* 35¢		*d.* Mark-down
$1.00	*e* 25¢		*e.* Mark-down cancellation Net mark-down = .15 + .35 − .25 = .25
6th Adjusted Retail Price $1.00 + .25 = $1.25			

Determining the ratio of cost to retail.   In determining the ratio of cost to retail, it is customary to include additional mark-ups and additional mark-up cancellations but to exclude mark-downs and mark-down cancellations.   To illustrate, let us assume the following facts:

```
Inventory at beginning of month:
    Cost...........................................  $30,000 00
    Retail.........................................   43,000.00
Purchases:
    Cost...........................................   46,000.00
    Retail.........................................   55,000.00
Returned purchases:
    Cost...........................................    1,000.00
    Retail.........................................    1,500.00
Additional mark-ups................................    5,500.00
Additional mark-up cancellations...................    2,000.00
Mark-downs.........................................    6,000.00
Mark-down cancellations............................    1,000.00
Sales at retail....................................   71,000.00
```

Compute the inventory by the retail method.

Solution.

	Cost	Retail
Inventory............................	$30,000.00	$ 43,000.00
Purchases............................	46,000.00	55,000.00
	$76,000.00	$ 98,000.00
Deduct: Returned purchases.............	1,000.00	1,500.00
	$75,000.00	$ 96,500.00
Additional mark-ups less cancellations thereof.........		3,500.00
		$100,000.00

$$\$100,000 - \$75,000 = \$25,000.$$
$$\$25,000 \div \$100,000 = 25\%.$$

Mark-downs less mark-down cancellations.............		5,000.00
		$ 95,000.00
Sales at retail...		71,000.00
End-of-month inventory at retail value...............		$ 24,000.00

$$\$24,000 \times 25\% = \$6,000.$$
$$\$24,000 - \$6,000 = \$18,000,$$ the cost value of the inventory.

PROBLEMS

1. From the records kept for Department B, the following information is obtained:

	Cost	Retail
Inventory at Beginning of Month..........	$15,000.00	$25,000.00
Purchases.............................	36,000.00	54,000.00
Returned Purchases......................	500.00	700.00
Additional Mark-Ups.....................		2,000.00
Additional Mark-Up Cancellations.........		1,000.00
Sales.................................		60,000.00

Calculate by the retail method of inventory the cost of the book inventory at the end of the month.

2.* In a certain department of a large dry-goods house, the purchases for one year were $30,000. They were in the first place marked up for selling purposes to $45,000. Later, additional mark-ups amounting to $2,000 were made, and mark-downs aggregating $5,000 were also recorded. At the end of the fiscal period there were found to be on hand goods of a marked selling value of $10,000. State how you would arrive at their inventory value for the purpose of closing the books, and calculate the amount. Explain fully.

---

* American Institute Examination.

6

Insurance

Insurance. There are at least 21 kinds of insurance applicable to the ordinary business being done in big cities and as many as 150 kinds of insurance covering all branches of human endeavor.

Policy. An insurance policy is a written contract. The consideration given for the protection promised consists of a premium to be paid in money and the fulfillment by the insured of acts of commission and omission according to the terms and conditions set forth in the policy.

Fire insurance. Fire insurance is guaranty of indemnity for loss or damage to property by fire. Insurance companies are liable for loss or damage resulting from the use of water or chemicals used in extinguishing the fire and from smoke. A fire loss is predicated on the sound value at the time the loss is sustained and not at the time the insurance is written.

Form of policy. With but a few exceptions, fire insurance companies use a State standard-form policy made mandatory by the State in which they operate. The New York State standard form of policy is the one that is generally used, as it embraces nearly all that is contained in other forms. The form attached to the policy is known as a *rider*. The rider form directly applies the insurance to fit the facts and conditions of the particular risk. It also amends the standard form, which is not a contract until completed by descriptions and amendments.

Rates. Probably no phase of insurance interests the businessman more than his insurance rate. Independent rating bureaus operate in different parts of the country. Their business is to inspect and to measure the hazards in terms of rates. Rate schedules are compiled for this purpose. The charges are in the nature of penalties for hazards.

Example. A particular building has been inspected and surveyed by the rater. The degree of municipal and local protection has been measured. This establishes the basic rate. Assume the basic rate to be .40, which is a charge commensurate with the degree of protection and covers all general hazards that cannot be segregated and measured. The better the city protection, the lower will be the basic rate.

Basic rate	.40
Area: 15,800 sq. ft.	.04
(The standard unit area is 1,000 sq. ft., and an additional charge is made for larger areas.)	
Parapet wall deficiency	.04
Skylights not standard construction	.02
Metal stacks through roof	.06
Outside wood cornices, loading docks, and wooden conveyor	.06
Gallery decks used for storage	.03
Occupancy hazard (woodworking mill)	.92
Shavings allowed to accumulate	.05
No cans for collecting waste	.05
No drip pans under machines	.05
Floor oil-soaked	.05
Total	1.77
Credit for open finish (inside walls)	.08
Building rate unexposed	1.69
Exposure:	
From buildings No. 2 and No. 5 at 18 ft .34	
From building No. 6 at 15 ft .02	
From office at 23 ft .05	
From buildings No. 9 and No. 10 .07	
Exposure charge	.48
Total building rate	2.17

If this assured would have the parapet wall brought up to the standard requirements, his rate would be reduced .04. By having the shavings removed daily, and by installing waste cans and drip pans under the machines, the rate could be reduced another .15. As a matter of fact, the owner makes his own rate—the rater simply measures the hazards in terms of rates.

To find the premium. Insurance companies charge a certain number of cents or dollars for insuring each $100.00 worth of property. Thus, the insurance rate in the foregoing example is $2.17 for each hundred dollars of insurance carried. If the building is valued at $65,000.00 and is insured for full value, the amount of the premium would be computed as follows:

$2.17	the rate per $100.00 of insurance.
× 6 50	the number of hundred dollars of insurance purchased.
$1,410.50	the premium, or cost of the insurance for one year.

Agent's commission. Local agents of the fire insurance companies are located in almost every city and town. They act as the representatives of the companies, soliciting the business and collecting the premiums. For this service they receive a certain per cent of the premiums.

Example. A store building valued at $10,000.00 was insured for 80% of its value, the rate being $1.25 a hundred. What was the agent's commission if he received 15% of the premium?

Solution.

$$80\% \text{ of } \$10,000.00 = \$8,000.00, \text{ the insured value.}$$
$$80 \times \$1.25 = \$100.00, \text{ the premium.}$$
$$15\% \text{ of } \$100.00 = \$15.00, \text{ the agent's commission.}$$

Cancellation of policies. Both the insurance company and the insured have the right to cancel an insurance policy at any time. When the policy is canceled by the insurance company, the portion of the premium to be repaid to the insured is determined pro rata.

Example. On April 10, the owner of a building insured his property for one year. The premium was $36.00. On October 20, the policy was canceled by the insurance company. What rebate did the insured receive for the unexpired term?

Solution. The time from April 10 to October 20 is 193 days, expired term of the policy. (See page 93 for table of number of days between dates.)

$$\tfrac{193}{365} \text{ of } \$36.00 \text{ is } \$19.04, \text{ amount of premium earned.}$$
$$\$36.00 - \$19.04 = \$16.96, \text{ amount of premium returned.}$$

When the policy is cancelled by the insured, the amount of premium returned is determined by the "short rate." The short rate is an arbitrary per cent fixed by the insurance companies, and is shown by a table like the one at the top of page 126.

Example. On May 2, a one-year policy was written on a shop. The premium was $38.75. On September 26, the policy was canceled at the request of the insured. What rebate did the insured receive?

Solution. From May 2 to September 26 is 147 days. The table shows that 60% of the premium is to be retained when the policy has been in force 150 days, which is the number of days next higher than 147. Then 40% of the premium will be returned.

$$\$38.75 \times .40 = \$15.50, \text{ the return premium.}$$

Coinsurance. This is a form of insurance in which the person who insures his property agrees to carry insurance equal to a certain percentage of the valuation of the property. If he fails to carry that percentage with an insurance company, he (the insured) becomes a coinsurer on the loss,

SHORT RATE CANCELLATION TABLE

Period exceeding 20 days and not exceeding 25 days, to be the rate of 25 days, and so on up to one year.

Policy in Force	Per Cent of Annual Prem.	Policy in Force	Per Cent of Annual Prem.
1 day	2%	55 days	29%
2 days	4%	60 days or 2 months	30%
3 days	5%	65 days	33%
4 days	6%	70 days	36%
5 days	7%	75 days	37%
6 days	8%	80 days	38%
7 days	9%	85 days	39%
8 days	9%	90 days or 3 months	40%
9 days	10%	105 days	46%
10 days	10%	120 days or 4 months	50%
11 days	11%	135 days	56%
12 days	11%	150 days or 5 months	60%
13 days	12%	165 days	66%
14 days	13%	180 days or 6 months	70%
15 days	13%	195 days	73%
16 days	14%	210 days or 7 months	75%
17 days	15%	225 days	78%
18 days	16%	240 days or 8 months	80%
19 days	16%	255 days	83%
20 days	17%	270 days or 9 months	85%
25 days	19%	285 days	88%
30 days or 1 month	20%	300 days or 10 months	90%
35 days	23%	315 days	93%
40 days	25%	330 days or 11 months	95%
45 days	27%	345 days	98%
50 days	28%	360 days or 12 months	100%

in the ratio which his lack of insurance bears to the amount he should have carried.

Illustration of 80% coinsurance clause:

Case 1.	Value of building and contents	$75,000
	Assured should carry 80% of value or	60,000
	Insurance actually carried	45,000
	Loss by fire	10,000
	Paid by insurance company, 75% of loss, or	7,500
	Assured must bear 25% of loss, or	2,500

Insurance carried was only 75% of what assured should have carried to comply with the 80% clause.

Case 2.	Value of property	$10,000
	Insurance required	8,000
	Insurance carried	9,000
	Losses up to $9,000	Paid in full
Case 3.	Value of property	$10,000
	Insurance required	8,000
	Insurance carried	8,000
	Losses exceeding $8,000	

Face of policy, $8,000, is paid.

Case 4. Value of property.............................. $10,000
Insurance required............................ 8,000
Insurance carried............................. 5,000
Losses exceeding $8,000.........................
Face of policy, $5,000, is paid.
Losses under $8,000.............................
Paid in the proportion that $5,000 bears to $8,000, or $\frac{5}{8}$ of the loss.

PROBLEMS

1. What premium must be paid on a policy for $3,760 at $1.50 a hundred?

2. A house worth $12,000 is insured for $\frac{3}{4}$ of its value for three years at $2.35 a hundred. How much is the premium?

3. An agent wrote a policy of $4,500 on a store building at a rate of 85 cents. If the agent's commission was 15%, what was the amount of his commission?

4. Find the amount paid by the insurance company under the 80% coinsurance clause in the following:

	(a)	(b)	(c)	(d)
Value of property	$50,000	$75,000	$100,000	$200,000
Insurance carried	40,000	60,000	80,000	80,000
Loss by fire	10,000	45,000	40,000	40,000
Paid by insurance company				

5. You are presented the following tornado insurance plan and are asked to select one of the four policies and to decide upon whether to insure for one or three years. In your opinion, what policy should be taken and for how long a term? The sound value of the property to be insured is $1,242,000.

Coinsurance	Amount of Insurance	One-Year Rate	Premium	Three-Year Rate	Premium
(1) None	$ 200,000	.20		.50	
(2) 50%	621,000	.102		.255	
(3) 80%	993,600	.0749		.1872	
(4) 90%	1,117,800	.0678		.1695	

Compute the premiums at the one-year rate and at the three-year rate. Find the average yearly premium on each policy at the three-year rate, and make comparisons in order to determine which policy to accept.

6. A one-year policy on a dwelling was dated June 5. The premium was $42.50. On October 1, the policy was canceled at the request of the insured. Find the amount of return premium.

Use and occupancy insurance. This kind of insurance is protection against loss due to interruption of business by fire or tornado. It is insurance against a loss that is suffered on account of destruction of the property.

The insurance recovery or indemnity is the profit that would have been made if business had not been interrupted and, in addition, the total of expenses that must continue during suspension of business. A business that is not profitable may be so insured in order to recover the continuing expenses.

Generally speaking, use and occupancy insurance insures gross profits plus the salaries of key employees kept on the payroll account. The policy excepts payroll (other than that of the key employees), heat, light, power, and expenses of maintaining properties not destroyed (such as taxes, depreciation, and maintenance thereof). These items can be picked up by analyzing the running expense accounts. In no event does the policy pay expenses required to be insured unless it is proved that they continue after the fire.

Coinsurance clauses are also applicable in use and occupancy insurance.

A simple procedure to arrive at use and occupancy value for the past twelve months is as follows:

```
Total Sales............................................  ................
Deduct:
  Cost of Merchandise
      (Opening Inventory + Purchases − Closing In-
      ventory).........................................  ............
  Ordinary Labor Payroll...............................  ............
  Light, Heat, and Power...............................  ............
      Total deductions...  ............................  ................
Actual 100% use and occupancy value for the period.......  ................
```

The foregoing procedure is predicated on the assumption that all expenses other than ordinary payroll and light, heat, and power will continue at the same cost as if the business were operating.

A more exact method is one considered in the light of a problem in arithmetic or algebra, as follows:

Let x = Use and Occupancy Insurable Interest Each Day
   a = Expenses That Do Not Continue During Suspension of Business
   b = Selling Price of Merchandise
   c = Cost of Merchandise
   d = Number of Working Days in the Month

Then:

$$\frac{b - c - a}{d} = x$$

Example.   The expenses of a business for a given month were determined as follows:

Item	Total	Part of Expense That Must Continue During Suspension	Part of Expense That Will Not Continue During Suspension
Payroll............................	$45,000		
Salaries and Wages of Key Employees Who Must Be Retained............		$20,000	
Salaries and Wages of Employees Not Retained........................			$25,000
Power.............................	750	—	750
Heat and Light....	525	225	300
Leasehold..........................	1,200	1,200	—
Advertising........................	1,725	725	1,000
Taxes.............................	950	950	—
Insurance.........................	1,375	500	875
Interest...........................	525	525	—
Other Expenses...................	1,950	875	1,075
	$54,000	$25,000	$29,000

Find the estimated amount of insurance to be carried for each day of the month if sales are estimated to be $181,500 and cost of merchandise sold $109,500. Average number of working days each month is 25.

Solution.

$$\frac{b - c - a}{d} = x \qquad \frac{181,500 - 109,500 - 29,000}{25} = 1,720$$

Therefore, on the basis of estimates, $1,720 is the amount of insurance to be carried for each day in the month.

The same result may be obtained in the following manner, using the estimates given:

Sales for the Month.....................................	$181,500
Less: Cost of Sales.....................................	109,500
Gross Profit..	72,000
Total Expenses..	54,000
Net Profit...	18,000
Add: Expenses That Must Continue During Suspension....	25,000
Use and Occupancy Value for the Month.................	$ 43,000

43,000 ÷ 25 = 1,720

PROBLEMS

1. The gross profit of a business was $200,000 after charging raw materials and payroll into manufacturing cost, but excluding light, heat, and power. Continuing payroll of key men was fixed at $20,000. If the policy contained the 80% clause, what was the required amount of insurance?

2. An audit of the expense accounts of the company insured in Problem 1 showed that items that would not have to be continued after the fire totaled $60,000. What amount would be collectible for a twelve-month period, other facts being as stated in Problem 1?

3. Assume that it takes 15 months to rebuild the plant. How much insurance would be collectible?

4. If a manufacturer on a Sept. 30 fiscal-year basis had a fire on April 1 and it is shown by previous experience that the following six months are the most profitable—in fact, that $66\frac{2}{3}\%$ of the net earnings are made in that period—would the adjustment take this into consideration, or would it be made on an average for the year?

5. If the conditions in Problem 4 were reversed, what earnings would the adjustment reflect?

6. Compute the use and occupancy value from the following data: Beginning inventory, $170,482.66; ending inventory, $171,721.77; manufacturing—including raw materials, labor, light, heat, and power, maintenance, depreciation, administration, insurance, taxes, interest, advertising, and all other expenses, $3,409,-658.42. Fixed charges that are included in the foregoing and that are expected to continue are: administrative salaries, $35,200; interest, $4,800; taxes, $9,961.22; dues and pledges, $6,150; credit information, $235; insurance, $7,918.49; salaries of office, supervisors, and foremen that will have to be retained, $237,075; miscellaneous expenses, $42,395.62. Sales were $3,551,708.81.

Group life insurance. Although this type of insurance is a part of the subject of life insurance, it is presented in this chapter because it is a common form of business insurance. The principles of life insurance are presented in another chapter.

Group life insurance affords employees of a business ordinary life insurance at low cost so long as they are employed by the particular employer, as the employer pays a part of the premium. The operation of this type of insurance is best explained by an example of an actual plan.

GROUP LIFE PLAN

1. *Eligibility.* The following plan of group life insurance is offered to all present employees of the company who will have completed six months or more of continuous service on November 11, 19—, and to all new employees after they have been with the company for six months.

2. *Amounts of insurance.* The amount of insurance available to each employee under age 65, nearest birthday, will be based on annual earnings as follows:

Class	Annual Earnings	Life Insurance
1. Less than $1,200		$1,000
2. $1,200, but less than $2,200		1,500
3. $2,200, but less than $2,800		2,000
4. $2,800, but less than $3,200		2,500
5. $3,200, but less than $3,800		3,000
6. $3,800, but less than $4,200		3,500
7. $4,200, but less than $4,800		4,000
8. $4,800, but less than $5,200		4,500
9. $5,200 and over		5,000

3. *Cost of insurance.* The monthly cost of the insurance will be based on the employee's insurance age on each anniversary date of the plan, as shown in the following schedule:

Attained Age on Policy Anniversary Each Year	Employee's Monthly Contribution per $1,000 of Insurance
Age 44 and under......................................	$0.70
Ages 45 to 54, inclusive...............................	1.00
Ages 55 to 59, inclusive...............................	1.50
Age 60 and over.......................................	1.80

PROBLEMS

1. Employee Y is 42 years of age and his earning classification is Class 5. What is the monthly deduction for his insurance?

2. If Y were 14 years older, what would be the monthly deduction?

3. B is 46 years of age and earns $3,000 a year. How much insurance is available to him, and what will be his monthly contribution?

4. Company X insures each of its employees for $1,000. Under age 50 the cost to the employee is 60 cents a month; at age 50 or over, the cost is $1.00 a month. There are 54 employees, classified as follows:

Age	Number
18...	1
22...	6
25...	10
29...	4
30...	7
45...	12
47...	8
52...	2
56...	3
58...	1

What is the amount of the monthly payroll deduction?

5. The manual shows the cost of group insurance on a monthly basis to be as follows:

Age	Premium
18...	$ .51
22...	.53
25...	.54
29...	.55
30...	.55
45...	.80
47...	.90
52...	1.26
56...	1.71
58...	2.00

With the number in each age group being that given in Problem 4, what is the amount of insurance premium that is borne by Company X?

Health insurance. Some plans are contributory and others non-contributory. In either case, the benefits are much the same; but in contributory plans the employee pays a part of the cost in the form of a monthly premium deducted from wages, while in the non-contributory plans the cost is borne by the employer. Few businesses have their own insurance departments, most of the plans being handled by insurance companies under a group plan.

Incapacities include sickness and non-occupational accidents (occupational accidents being covered by Workmen's Compensation Insurance), but the employer usually reserves the right to withhold benefits if the incapacity is the result of the employee's misconduct or negligence.

The following examples are illustrative of the many ways in which the factor of service is employed to favor the veteran worker.

Example 1.

Length of Service	*Amount and Duration of Disability Benefits*
Under 2 years......................	Such practice as the company may establish
2 but less than 5 years...............	Full pay 4 weeks, half-pay 9 weeks
5 but less than 10 years..............	Full pay 13 weeks, half-pay 13 weeks
10 years and over....................	Full pay 13 weeks, half-pay 39 weeks

Example 2.

Length of Service	*Amount and Duration of Disability Benefits*
1 but less than 10 years.............	50% of wages
10 but less than 30 years............	75% of wages
30 years and over...................	100% of wages
	Maximum: 26 weeks in 3 years

Example 3.

Length of Service	*Amount and Duration of Disability Benefits*
6 months but less than 1 year......	35% of wages; maximum: $35.00 per week, for 6 weeks
1 but less than 2 years.............	50% of wages; maximum: $50.00 per week, for 13 weeks
2 but less than 3 years.............	60% of wages; maximum: $60.00 per week, for 13 weeks
3 but less than 4 years.............	70% of wages; maximum: $70.00 per week, for 26 weeks
4 years and over..................	75% of wages; maximum: $75.00 per week for 26 weeks.

PROBLEMS

1. *A* was insured under the plan in Example 1. He was employed for 3 years and became incapacitated for a period of 6 weeks. His average weekly wage was $74.80. What amount of disability benefit was he entitled to receive?

2. *B* was insured under the plan in Example 2. He had been with the same employer for 12 years. Two years ago he drew compensation for 8 weeks, and last year for 12 weeks. This year he was again incapacitated for a period of 8 weeks. If his average weekly wage was $95.00, what amount of disability benefit was he entitled to this year?

3. *C* was employed by an employer using the plan in Example 3, and had worked for this employer for a period of 6 years. He became incapacitated when receiving a weekly salary of $110.00, and was unemployed for 10 weeks. What was the amount of compensation paid?

Workmen's compensation insurance. This type of insurance is financial protection against loss of time for the wage-earning group resulting from accident or occupational sickness while on duty. The cost is levied on the employer in the form of a premium on the payroll classified according to the hazard of occupation. A few states have their own Workmen's Compensation Insurance Departments, but in most states the insurance is carried by the insurance companies specializing in this type of insurance, generally referred to as *casualty insurance companies.*

PROBLEMS

Find the cost of workmen's compensation insurance on payrolls divided into four classifications with respective rates as follows:

1. $239,530.39 @ .611 per C
   75,535.62 @ .519 per C
   241,327.85 @ .081 per C
   99,791.48 @ .586 per C

2. $272,584.07 @ .611 per C
   91,856.68 @ .519 per C
   292,258.87 @ .081 per C
   148,735.42 @ .586 per C

3. $254,248.83 @ .581 per C
   79,950.31 @ .548 per C
   272,368.08 @ .085 per C
   105,553.36 @ .564 per C

4. A deposit of $100.00 was made on a public liability policy. The payroll audit was as follows:

   $381,839.77 @ .052 per C
   294,212.15 @ .026 per C
   138,631.05 @ .026 per C

What amount of additional premium was due on completion of the payroll audit?

7

Gross Profit Computations

Gross profit. The gross profit represents the margin between the sales and the cost of goods sold, and when expressed as a per cent of sales indicates to one who is familiar with trade practice whether a sufficient margin of profit is being made. Use of the per cent of gross profit to check the correctness of the value set upon the inventory is called the *gross profit test of inventory.*

Rate per cent of gross profit. The gross profit test is based on the supposition that, in normal times and under normal conditions, any business will produce approximately the same per cent of gross profit on sales in any one period of time as in any other corresponding period of time.

Procedure. Statements of the gross profit and sales for each of several prior periods should be obtained. The gross profit for any one period divided by the sales for the same period gives the rate of gross profit for that period, *based on sales.* Disregard any per cent that is abnormal. Add the remaining per cents, and divide by the number added. The quotient is the average per cent of gross profit in prior periods.

Uses. The per cent of gross profit may be used in two ways: first, to prove inventories, and second, to compute the estimated inventory when it is impossible or impracticable to take a physical inventory.

Example. Assume that the average gross profit for the past five years has been 40% of sales, and that an audit of the books shows that the inventory, taken prior to the beginning of the audit, and valued at $100,000, seems smaller than it should be, while the previous inventory and purchases amounted to $400,000. The sales for the period are $400,000. Show by comparative statement the possibility of error.

Solution. In the following set-up, both the average and the current per cents and results are shown. As the profit in prior years has been 40% of sales, the cost of goods sold has been 60% of sales. 60% of $400,000 (sales) = $240,000, cost of sales.

		CURRENT YEAR		CURRENT YEAR IN TERMS OF AN AVERAGE YEAR	
		Actual Amounts	*Current Per Cent*	*Test Amounts*	*Average Per Cent*
Sales.........................		$400,000	100	$400,000	100
Cost of Sales					
First-of-year inventory and purchases.......	$400,000				
Less: Current inv't.....	100,000	300,000	75	240,000	60
Gross profit..................		$100,000	25%	$160,000	40%

If the sales are correct, the cost of sales is $60,000 too high, unless the rate has really changed. This discrepancy may be caused by any of the following: the volume of sales may be incorrectly stated; the current inventory may be erroneous, and the cost of sales affected thereby; or there may be an abnormal increase in the cost of merchandise purchased, when compared with the 5-year average. The accountant should determine the reason for the discrepancy.

Cost of goods sold. The average rate per cent of gross profit, applied to the sales for the current period, will give the estimated gross profit for the current period. Deduction of the estimated gross profit from the sales gives the estimated cost of goods sold. This procedure may be reduced to a formula as follows:

AVERAGE FOR PRIOR PERIODS

1. *Sales − Cost of sales = Gross profit.*
2. *Gross profit ÷ Sales = Per cent of gross profit (based on sales).*

APPLICATION TO CURRENT PERIOD

3. *Sales × Per cent of gross profit (prior periods) = Estimated gross profit.*
4. *Sales − Estimated gross profit (current period) = Estimated cost of sales.*

Example.

	Sales	*Cost of Sales*	*Gross Profit*
First period......................	$400,000	$300,000	$100,000
Second period....................	450,000	340,000	110,000
Third period.....................	350,000	260,000	90,000
Fourth period....................	100,000	....	....

What was the cost of sales during the fourth period?

Solution.

AVERAGE FOR PRIOR PERIODS

First period, $100,000 ÷ $400,000 = 25.00%
Second period, 110,000 ÷   450,000 = 24.44%
Third period,   90,000 ÷   350,000 = 25.71%
                                      75.15%

75% ÷ 3 = 25%, the average rate of gross profit.

, APPLICATION TO CURRENT PERIOD

$100,000 × 25% = $25,000, estimated gross profit.
$100,000 − $25,000 = $75,000, estimated cost of sales.

Rate per cent of cost of sales.   If the rate of profit has been based on cost price instead of on selling price, the cost of sales may be tested by the following computations:

AVERAGE FOR PRIOR PERIODS

1. *Sales − Cost of sales = Gross profit.*
2. *Gross profit ÷ Cost of sales = Per cent of gross profit (based on cost of sales).*

APPLICATION TO CURRENT PERIOD

3. *Sales ÷ (100% + Per cent of gross profit) = Cost of sales.*

Example.

	Sales	Cost of Sales
First period...............................	$400,000	$300,000
Second period..............................	450,000	340,000
Third period...............................	350,000	260,000
Fourth period.............................	100,000	....

What was the cost of sales for the last period?

Solution.

AVERAGE FOR PRIOR PERIODS

First period, $100,000 ÷ $300,000 = 33.33%
Second period, 110,000 ÷   340,000 = 32.35%
Third period,   90,000 ÷   260,000 = 34.61%
                                      100.29%

100% ÷ 3 = $33\frac{1}{3}$%, average per cent of gross profit.

APPLICATION TO CURRENT PERIOD

$100,000 ÷ $1.33\frac{1}{3}$ $(1 + .33\frac{1}{3})$ = $75,000, cost of sales.
$100,000 − $75,000 = $25,000, gross profit.

It follows that if the cost of sales can be found, any element (inventory at beginning of period, purchases, closing inventory, and so forth) which goes to make up the cost of sales can be found, provided the other elements of the costs are given.

Fire losses. Insurance companies are generally willing to settle inventory losses resulting from fire on the basis of values determined by the gross profit method.

Example. The insurance company agrees that the following facts are to be the basis of its reimbursement to the insured for his fire losses:

> Average gross profit for 4 years, 40% of sales.
> Sales for this period to date of fire, $50,000.
> Cost of goods available for sale, $300,000.

Solution.

$50,000 (sales) $\times$ 40% (rate of gross profit) = $20,000, gross profit.
$50,000 (sales) $-$ $20,000 (gross profit) = $30,000, cost of goods sold.
$300,000 (goods available for sale) $-$ $30,000
(cost of goods sold) = $270,000, estimated inventory at date of fire.

Use of gross profit test in verification of taxpayer's inventory. Assessors make use of the gross profit test to determine the approximate inventory and to check the item of inventory in the schedule filed by the taxpayer, since assessment dates seldom coincide with closing dates. The following forms have been given to the taxpayer to fill out, the date of assessment being May 1.

For Merchants

1. Book value of last inventory of stock of merchandise............ ....
2. Add purchases since last inventory to May 1.................... ....
3. Add in-freight and cartage paid since last inventory to May 1.... ....
4.   Total of above three items............................. ....

Deduct from above total net result of following two items:

5. Amount of net sales from date of last inventory to May 1. ....
6. Less: Gross profit on sales estimated at ....%........... ....
    (Previous year % may be used where actual % is unknown.)
7. Net inventory of merchandise on May 1 (Item 4 less Item 6)..... ....

For Manufacturers

1. Book value of raw materials, finished goods, and work-in-process at last inventory. Date ....
2. Add purchases of raw materials and finished goods since last inventory to May 1... ....
3. Add amount paid for in-freight and cartage from last inventory to May 1... ....
4. Add amount paid for labor and manufacturing expenses from last inventory to May 1... ....
5.   Total of above four items................................ ....

Deduct from above total the net result of the following two items:

6. Amount of net sales from date of last inventory to May 1. ....
7. Less: Gross profit on sales estimated at ....%........... ....
    (Previous year % may be used where actual % is not known.) ....
8. Net value of raw materials, goods-in-process, and finished goods on May 1 (Item 5 $-$ Item 7).. ....

PROBLEMS

1. From the figures in the following tabulation, calculate the per cent of gross profit for each year, and by means of the average per cent of gross profit calculate the inventory at the end of the first half of the fifth year.

	Sales	Purchases	Opening Inventory	Closing Inventory	Per Cent of Gross Profit
First year	$120,000	$ 90,000		$10,000	....
Second year	150,000	100,000	10,000	12,000	....
Third year	165,000	110,000	12,000	10,000	....
Fourth year	180,000	122,000	10,000	11,000	....
Fifth year (6 mo.)	95,000	62,000	11,000	....	....

2. From the following facts, find the inventory as of December 31:

Inventory, January 15 following, $16,578.50.
Sales, December 31 to January 15, $2,890.00.
$765 of the above sales shipped and invoiced before December 31.
Purchases, December 31 to January 15, at cost, $1,256.50.
Average gross profit, 25% of cost.

3. The average gross profit of the X. Company for the past three years has been 45% of the sales. During the fourth year the sales amounted to $159,500. Goods were purchased to the amount of $105,000. Returned purchases totaled $5,000 for the period. Freight paid on purchases was $6,000. The inventory at the beginning of the period was $40,000. Current market prices are 10% above the purchase prices for the year. Find the cost of replacing the goods at the end of the year.

4. On April 30, the board of managers of the Ames Mercantile Company removed the superintendent on the general suspicion that his books misrepresented the true financial condition of the business. Prepare a statement showing the nature and the probable extent of the misrepresentations; also an approximate statement of income and profit and loss for the four months ending April 30. The following is a trial balance taken from the books, April 30:

Capital Stock		$ 75,000
Furniture and Fixtures	$ 10,000	
Inventory, January 1	128,600	
Cash	15,450	
Accounts Payable		39,000
Accounts Receivable	24,600	
Loans Payable		10,000
Sales		51,000
Purchases	40,700	
Salaries, Salesmen	2,200	
Advertising	1,650	
Salaries, Office	1,100	
Rent	400	
Interest	200	
Insurance, January 1 to December 31	999	
Stationery and Printing	105	
Reserve for Depreciation of Furniture & Fixtures		2,710
Surplus, January 1		48,294
	$226,004	$226,004

An analysis of the Purchases, Sales, and Inventory accounts revealed the following:

	Purchases	Sales	Opening Inv't	Closing Inv't
First year	$122,000	$153,750	$101,000	$100,000
Second year	123,000	153,170	100,000	102,000
Third year	121,000	154,722	102,000	128,600

5.* The books of a concern recently burned out contained evidence of purchases, including inventory, to the amount of $200,000, and sales of $40,800, since the last closing. Upon investigation, however, the auditor ascertained that a sale of merchandise had been made just prior to the fire, and not recorded in the books, at an advance of two-fifths over cost less a 10% cash discount; the profit on the transaction was $31,928. The past history of the business indicated an average gross profit of 50% on cost of goods sold.

(*a*) What amount should be claimed as fire loss?

(*b*) What rate of gross profit do the transactions finally yield?

6.† The store and stock of the Diamond Jewelry Company was destroyed by fire on November 1. The safe was opened, and the books were recovered intact. The trial balance taken off was as follows:

Cash in Bank	$ 1,000	
Accounts Receivable	10,000	
Accounts Payable		$ 30,000
Merchandise Purchases	90,000	
Furniture and Fixtures	7,500	
Sales		110,000
General Expense	18,000	
Insurance	1,500	
Salaries	5,500	
Real Estate—Store Lot	50,000	
Store Building	35,000	
Capital Stock		50,000
Surplus		28,500
	$218,500	$218,500

The average gross profit as shown by the books and accepted by the insurance companies was 40% of sales. The insurance adjuster agreed to pay 75% of the book value of furniture and fixtures, 90% of the book value of the store building, and the entire loss on merchandise stock.

Draft journal entries to include the account against the insurance companies.

Installment sales of personal property. The large increase in sales of personal property on the installment plan, and the option that the government allows a taxpayer coming within the definition of an installment dealer to return his gross income from sales on the installment basis are indications of the growing importance of this subject.

The installment plan of selling was devised for the purpose of stimulating sales, whereas the installment basis of reporting income was devised for the purpose of deferring from year to year the income to be

---

* American Institute Examination.
† C. P. A., Oklahoma.

realized from installment sales, with a view to the possible effect that this deferment might have upon the amount of federal income tax to be paid. It is, of course, essential that the latest Federal Income Tax Law be observed.

Computation of gross profit. The gross profit to be reported may be ascertained by taking that proportion of the total cash collections received in the taxable year from installment sales (such collections being allocated to the year against whose sales they apply) which the annual gross profit to be realized on the total installment sales made during each year bears to the gross contract price of all such sales made during that particular year.

Example. The books of the Model Credit Company, selling merchandise on the installment plan, show the following:

	First Year	Second Year	Third Year	Fourth Year
Sales....................	$ 80,000	$110,000	$130,000	$90,000
Cost of Sales				
Inventory (old)...........	$ 45,000	$ 40,000	$ 50,000	$48,000
Purchases...............	55,000	75,000	90,000	50,000
	$100,000	$115,000	$140,000	$98,000
Less: Inventory (new).....	40,000	50,000	48,000	40,000
Cost of sales...........	$ 60,000	$ 65,000	$ 92,000	$58,000
Gross profit.............	$ 20,000	$ 45,000	$ 38,000	$32,000

Collections were made in the fourth year on each year's contracts as follows:

First Year	Second Year	Third Year	Fourth Year
$1,600	$4,800	$25,000	$70,000

What was the gross profit to be reported for the fourth year?

Solution.

Per Cent of Gross Profit

First year, $20,000 (gross profit) ÷ $ 80,000 (sales) = 25.00%
Second year,   45,000   "   "   ÷   110,000   "   = 40.91%
Third year,   38,000   "   "   ÷   130,000   "   = 29.23%
Fourth year,   32,000   "   "   ÷   90,000   "   = 35.55%

Profit on Collections in Fourth Year

Collected on first-year contracts, $ 1,600 × 25.00% = $ 400.00
    "   " second-year   "   4,800 × 40.91% =   1,963.68
    "   " third-year   "   25,000 × 29.23% =   7,307.50
    "   " fourth-year   "   70,000 × 35.55% =   24,855.00
Gross profit realized in the fourth year............ $34,526.18

Reserve for unearned gross profit. The gross income to be realized on installment sales is credited to "Reserve for Unearned Gross Profit," and at this time this account is debited with the gross profit on collections. The balance of the account represents gross profit on installment sales contracts remaining unpaid at the date of closing.

Example. The books of the X.Y.Z. Company, selling merchandise on the installment plan, show the following:

	First Year	*Second Year*	*Third Year*	*Fourth Year*
Sales...................	$89,257.99	$111,825.86	$137,012.32	$97,912.26
Gross profits..............	29,962.89	48,068.37	38,128.63	39,168.71
Collections during the fourth year on each year's accts..	1,635.35	4,832.00	25,182.14	69,927.92

What amount should be credited to Reserve for Unearned Gross Profit to represent deferred income for the fourth year? What amount should be debited to Reserve for Unearned Gross Profit to represent income realized from the first, second, third, and fourth years' collections received in the fourth year?

Solution.

(a)   Per Cent of Gross Profit

First year................. $29,962.89 ÷ $ 89,257.99 = 33.57%
Second year............... 48,068.37 ÷ 111,825.86 = 42.98%
Third year............... 38,128.63 ÷ 137,012.32 = 27.83%
Fourth year............... 39,168.71 ÷ 97,912.26 = 40.00%

Profit on Collections

First-year accounts......... $ 1,635.35 × 33.57% = $ 548.99
Second-year accounts....... 4,832.00 × 42.98% =   2,076.79
Third-year accounts....... 25,182.14 × 27.83% =   7,008.19
Fourth-year accounts....... 69,927.92 × 40.00% =   27,971.17
Gross profit realized in 4th yr..................... $37,605.14

Journal entries

Installment Sales Contracts.............. $ 97,912.26		
Cost of Sales.......................	$ 58,743.55	
Reserve for Unearned Gross Profit......	39,168.71	
Cash................................ $101,577.41		
Installment Sales Contracts............	$101,577.41	
Reserve for Unearned Gross Profit........ $ 37,605.14		
Realized Gross Profit on Installment Sales	$ 37,605.14	

Bad debts. The bad debts written off during the year should be allocated by years, and a charge should be made to Reserve for Unearned Gross Profit for the percentage of gross profit in each year's write-off, and to Profit and Loss (Bad Debts) for the remainder, the entire credit being made to Installment Sales Contracts.

Example. During the fourth year, bad accounts were written off as follows:

First-Yr. Accts.	*Second-Yr. Accts.*	*Third-Yr. Accts.*	*Fourth-Yr. Accts.*
$67.65	$141.05	$65.62	$126.25

What amount should be charged to these accounts: Profit and Loss (Bad Debts), and Reserve for Unearned Gross Profit?

Solution.

	Unrealized Profit	Remainder
$ 67.65 × 33.57%............................	$ 22.71	$ 44.94
141.05 × 42.98%............................	60.62	80.43
65.62 × 27.83%............................	18.26	47.36
126.25 × 40.00%............................	50.50	75.75
	$152.09	$248.48
Reserve for Unearned Gross Profit............	$152.09	
Profit and Loss (Bad Debts).................	248.48	
Installment Sales Contracts...............		$400.57

PROBLEMS

1. The X.Y.Z. Company's books for the 5th year showed:

Sales... $128,642.60
Gross profit.................................... 42,975.12

Collections were made in the fifth year on each year's contracts as follows:

1st Yr.	2nd Yr.	3rd Yr.	4th Yr.	5th Yr.
$230.60	$1,590.31	$9,326.80	$21,256.30	$82,327.58

Calculate: (*a*) the per cent of gross profit for the fifth year; (*b*) the amount to be credited to Reserve for Unearned Gross Profit; (*c*) the amount to be debited to Reserve for Unearned Gross Profit. Use the rates given in the solution on page 141 for the first four years.

2. The analysis of bad debts written off during the 5th year was:

1st-Yr. Acct.	2nd-Yr. Acct.	3rd-Yr. Acct.	4th-Yr. Acct.	5th-Yr. Acct.
$8.35	$209.75	$910.40	$150.80	$470.62

What amounts should be charged to Reserve for Unearned Gross Profit and to Profit and Loss, respectively?

3. Results for the 6th year:

Sales... $140,695.39
Gross profit.................................... 54,541.07

Collections were made in the sixth year on each year's contracts as follows:

1st Yr.	2nd Yr.	3rd Yr.	4th Yr.	5th Yr.	6th Yr.
$62.70	$492.54	$2,798.30	$4,689.30	$2,657.80	$90,275.89

(*a*) Calculate the per cent of gross profit for the 6th year.
(*b*) Calculate for the 6th year the gross profit on collections made.

4. Accounts receivable were written off as follows:

1st Yr.	2nd Yr.	3rd Yr.	4th Yr.	5th Yr.	6th Yr.
$52.83	$31.50	$51.10	$150.00	$163.82	$108.28

Compute the charges to be made to Profit and Loss (Bad Debts) and to Reserve for Unearned Gross Profit.

5.* The "A & B" Company is engaged in the business of retailing musical merchandise. The majority of the sales consist of installment sales of pianos and hi-fi sets, on which the initial payment is less than 25% of the sales price and the balance is payable in monthly installments over a period of three to five years. The company was incorporated and began business on January 1. The following schedules are submitted on the various classes of merchandise:

Sales

	Piano Install-ment Sales	Hi-fi Install-ment Sales	Other Mdse Sales
First year..............	$148,650.00	$92,475.00	$38,337.60
Second year...........	163,520.00	88,535.00	39,543.50
Third year.............	180,400.00	94,256.00	40,731.15

Purchases

First year..............	106,322.37	67,432.18	27,108.88
Second year...........	120,987.41	55,116.92	27,224.35
Third year.............	140,125.25	60,013.22	27,469.33

Inventories

First year..............	20,103.14	10,248.31	8,323.64
Second year...........	32,105.86	15,012.83	15,299.41
Third year.............	39,294.44	18,144.77	13,521.31

Attention is called to the fact that "Other Merchandise Sales" are sales for cash, or credit sales other than installment sales.

No adjustments to Deferred Income account are made until the end of the year. Additions to this income are made at the end of the year on the basis of the balance due on the current year's installment sales, and deductions are made on the basis of cash received during the current year on installment sales of previous years. On December 31 of the third year, the unpaid balances on third-year piano installment sales amount to $110,425.50, and on third-year hi-fi installment sales to $60,475.00—exclusive of accrued interest. The following amounts were received during the third year on installment sales of previous years:

On first-year piano installment sales....................	$30,285.00
On second-year piano intallment sales....................	42,413.00
On first-year hi-fi installment sales.....................	25,386.00
On second-year hi-fi installment sales....................	26,285.00

The above amounts are exclusive of interest, which is credited direct to interest revenue.

Fractional percentages may be disregarded in the computation of ratios—over $\frac{1}{2}$ of 1% should be added, and less than $\frac{1}{2}$ of 1% should be dropped.

On first-year hi-fi installment sales, uncollectible balances amounting to $399.00 were charged on the books of the company to expense and credited to installment sales contracts.

Federal income taxes paid in the third year were charged to surplus.

---

* C. P. A., Michigan.

Depreciation is calculated at the following rates:

Buildings.................. 2%   Furniture and Fixtures..... 10%
                    Auto Trucks.................. 25%

The following is a copy of the trial balance as of December 31, end of third year, before closing and before apportionment of deferred income on installment sales:

Cash	$ 15,327.48	
Notes Receivable	2,000.00	
Accounts Receivable	20,842.11	
Installment Sales Contracts	265,418.50	
Inventories	62,418.10	
Government Bonds	5,000.00	
Real Estate	10,000.00	
Buildings	40,000.00	
Furniture and Fixtures	4,500.00	
Auto Trucks	3,000.00	
Notes Payable		$ 50,000.00
Accounts Payable		13,458.25
Deferred Income on Installment Sales		83,245.70
Reserve for Depreciation, Buildings		1,600.00
Reserve for Depreciation, Fur. & Fix		900.00
Reserve for Depreciation, Trucks		1,500.00
Capital Stock		150,000.00
Surplus		75,556.21
Sales		315,387.15
Piano Rentals		1,785.00
Interest on Installment Sales		2,035.23
Interest on Government Bonds		237.50
Cash Discounts on Purchases		2,452.07
Purchases	227,607.80	
Salaries, Officers	14,000.00	
Salaries, Store	8,101.46	
Light and Heat	717.68	
Advertising	4,015.71	
Truck Expense	508.53	
Sundry Store Expense	2,239.17	
Salaries, Office	2,020.00	
Traveling Expense	648.50	
Postage	472.30	
Telephone and Telegraph	441.40	
Insurance	1,309.06	
Real Estate and Personal Property Taxes	2,029.69	
Bad Debts, Accounts Receivable	709.66	
Bad Debts (first-year hi-fi installment sales)	399.00	
Repairs, Sundry	365.68	
Donations	200.00	
Cash Discounts on Sales	444.48	
State Franchise Tax	187.80	
Capital Stock Tax	233.00	
Interest Paid	3,000.00	
	$698,157.11	$698,157.11

You are asked to give: (*a*) the net taxable income (for federal tax purposes) for the third year; (*b*) a balance sheet of the "A & B" Company as of January 1, beginning of fourth year.

Deferring income; its effect on tax. The statement was made in the second paragraph of this subject that the installment basis of accounting defers income with a view to the possible effect that deferment may have on the amount of federal income tax to be paid. Since the income is deferred, the tax is deferred (not saved).

The amount of profit realized and to be realized from the sales of a particular year, if not taxed in that particular year, will be taxed eventually, and the saving of tax results from a possible reduction in the rate of tax or from the spreading of taxable income over several years. If it is anticipated that the rate of tax will be increased, it may not be wise to defer the income.

Second, a change from the accrual to the installment basis results in double taxation, for Section 44 (c) of the Internal Revenue Code provides as follows: "If a taxpayer entitled to the benefits of subsection (a) elects for any taxable year to report his net income on the installment basis, then in computing his income for the year of change or any subsequent year, amounts actually received during any such year on account of sales or other dispositions of property made in any prior year shall not be excluded."

The amount of gross income which may be deferred on installment sales is governed by:

(1) The terms of sale;

(2) Annual increase, if any, in sales;

(3) Per cent of year's sales collected in the current year; and

(4) Fluctuation of gross profits.

Example. Assume the terms of sale to be 10% down, and 10% a month; the annual increase in sales to be $10,000; the per cent of year's sales collected, and the sales throughout the year, to be uniform, and the per cent of gross profit to be fixed.

Year	Sales	Gross Profit on Sales
First.	$50,000	30%
Second.	60,000	30%
Third.	70,000	30%
Fourth.	80,000	30%
Fifth.	90,000	30%

Since it has been assumed that the sales are uniform throughout the year and that collections are met promptly, the second year's business may be analyzed as follows:

	Down Payments				*Installment Payments*			
Jan............	10% of $	5,000 = $		500				
Feb............	10% of	5,000 =		500	10% of $	5,000 = $		500
Mar............	10% of	5,000 =		500	10% of	10,000 =		1,000
Apr............	10% of	5,000 =		500	10% of	15,000 =		1,500
May............	10% of	5,000 =		500	10% of	20,000 =		2,000
June...........	10% of	5,000 =		500	10% of	25,000 =		2,500
July...........	10% of	5,000 =		500	10% of	30,000 =		3,000
Aug............	10% of	5,000 =		500	10% of	35,000 =		3,500
Sept...........	10% of	5,000 =		500	10% of	40,000 =		4,000
Oct............	10% of	5,000 =		500	10% of	45,000 =		4,500
Nov............	10% of	5,000 =		500	10% of	45,000 =		4,500
Dec............	10% of	5,000 =		500	10% of	45,000 =		4,500

Year's sales.................... $60,000

Down payments......................... $ 6,000

Install. payments..................... 31,500 $31,500

Total payments........................ $37,500

    Ratio of payments to sales: $37,500 ÷ $60,000 = 62.5%.

A comparison of the income to be reported on the accrual basis and on the installment basis may be made as follows:

Accrual Basis

	Second Year	Third Year	Fourth Year	Fifth Year
Sales..........................	$60,000	$70,000	$80,000	$90,000
Gross profit (%)................	30%	30%	30%	30%
Gross profit ($)................	18,000	21,000	24,000	27,000

Installment Basis

Collections:

	Second Year	Third Year	Fourth Year	Fifth Year
1st-year accounts..............	$18,750			
2nd-year accounts..............	37,500	$22,500		
3rd-year accounts.............		43,750	$26,250	
4th-year accounts.............			50,000	$30,000
5th-year accounts.............				56,250

Gross income to be reported:

	Second Year	Third Year	Fourth Year	Fifth Year
30% of 1st-year coll............	$ 5,625			
30% of 2nd-year coll...........	11,250	$ 6,750		
30% of 3rd-year coll...........		13,125	$ 7,875	
30% of 4th-year coll...........			15,000	$ 9,000
30% of 5th-year coll...........				16,875
Total income reported............	$16,875	$19,875	$22,875	$25,875
Income deferred.................	$ 1,125	$ 1,125	$ 1,125	$ 1,125

It may be observed from the foregoing analysis that with an annual increase of $10,000 in sales, and with a constant gross profit ratio of 30% the amount of income deferred from year to year is $1,125.

With an annual increase of $20,000 in sales, and other conditions the same, the amount of income deferred would be $2,250 (2 × $1,125).

PROBLEMS

1. Assume the terms of sale to be 10% down and 5% a month, the annual increase in sales $10,000, the per cent of year's sales collected and the sales throughout the year uniform, and the per cent of gross profit fixed.

Year	Sales	Gross Profit on Sales
First....................................	$50,000	30%
Second...................................	60,000	30%
Third....................................	70,000	30%
Fourth...................................	80,000	30%
Fifth....................................	90,000	30%

Show the amount of income deferred when the installment basis is used.

2. If the terms of payment were 5% down and 5% a month, and other conditions were the same as in Problem 1, what would be the amount of income deferred each year?

8

Analysis of Statements

Financial and operating ratios.   An analysis of the financial and the operating ratios of a business means a study of the relationships that are expressed in the statistics presented.   Well-known and commonly used ratios are those of expenses and earnings to sales, and of earnings on capital employed.   Other ratios, relationships, and turnovers that are indicators of the condition of a business should also be considered.

A summary of financial and operating ratios, relationships, and turnovers would include the following:

  (1) Ratio of costs and expenses to net sales.
  (2) Ratio of gross profit to net sales.
  ·(3) Ratio of operating profit to net sales.
  (4) Ratio of net profit to net sales.
  (5) Ratio of operating profit to total capital employed.
  (6) Ratio of net profit to net worth.
  (7) Earnings on common stockholders' investments.
  (8) Working capital ratio.
  (9) Sources of capital.
(10) Manner in which capital is invested.
(11) Turnover of total capital employed.
(12) Turnover of inventories.
(13) Turnover of accounts receivable.
(14) Turnover of fixed property investment.

There are many other ratios which are important measures of efficiency, but of which only brief mention can be made in this chapter. Depending on the type of business being analyzed, these other ratios might include the labor turnover, the unit of output per operative, the average wage per man, the average wage per hour, and other statistics.

Costs, expenses, and profits. Costs, expenses, and profits should be expressed as per cents of money values and, where possible, should be expressed in terms of dollars per production unit, such as the ton, pound, yard, or gallon. The per cents, compared with those of previous years, show whether sales prices have been adjusted proportionately to costs of production and distribution. The unit prices supplement the per cents and afford a direct comparison.

Ratio of gross profit to net sales. The ratio of gross profit to net sales is an indication of the spread between the cost of production and the selling price. The gross profit must be as large as possible, for out of it must come the expenses of selling, administration, finance, and other charges, before a net return is realized on capital.

Ratio of operating profit to net sales. The ratio of operating profit to net sales expresses the basic relationship between profits and sales. Operating profits represent the gain before the deduction of federal taxes, interest on borrowed money, and extraordinary losses but do not include miscellaneous income not attributable to ordinary operations.

Ratio of net profit to net sales. The ratio of net profit to net sales indicates the margin of profit on the selling price. The rapidity of stock turnover, and the capital invested in accounts receivable, in inventory, and in plant should be considered with this ratio.

Ratio of operating profit to total capital employed. The ratio of operating profit to total capital employed forms a ready basis for a comparison of the operating results of a business or of several plants under a single control. Capital employed includes plant, inventories, accounts receivable, cash balances, and so forth, regardless of the source of such capital, and is readily determined by referring to the asset side of the balance sheet.

Ratio of net profit to net worth. The ratio of net profit to net worth expresses the measure of earnings available to the stockholders or proprietors, and is the final indicator of the success or failure of any business.

Earnings on common stockholders' investments. The earnings on common stockholders' investments are based on the stockholders' share of the net profit, in relation to their interest in the net worth of the business. There are two ways in which these earnings may be stated: (*a*) as a per cent of the amount of such investments, and (*b*) in dollars earned per share outstanding.

Example. The following profit and loss statement, together with certain other facts, is presented to illustrate items 1–7 in the summary on page 148. The numbers in parentheses refer to the numbered ratios in the summary.

Blank Mercantile Company

PROFIT AND LOSS STATEMENT
FOR THE TWELVE MONTHS' PERIOD ENDED DECEMBER 31, 19—.

Sales:				
Gross Sales.............		$693,004.10		
Less: Sales Rebates and				
Allowances....... $	870.64			
Prepaid Freight.....	200.25			
		1,070.89		
Net Sales...............			$691,933.21	100.00%
Cost of Sales:				
Inventory, beginning of				
year................		$107,278.46		
Purchases.............	$624,225.28			
Freight...............	16,271.98			
	$640,497.26			
Less: Purchase Rebates and				
Allowances.......	630.81			
		639,866.45		
		$747,144.91		
Inventory, end of year....		124,814.04		
Cost of Sales............			622,330.87	89.94 *(1)*
Gross Profit..............			$ 69,602.34	10.06% *(2)*
Delivery Expenses:				
Salaries of Drivers........ $	3,414.34			
Dep'n on Equipment.....	2,839.57			
Auto Repairs...........	1,562.53			
Gasoline and Oil........	1,479.27			
Drivers' Expenses.......	119.40			
Drayage...............	66.84			
Total................ $		9,481.95		1.37 *(1)*
Selling Expenses:				
Salesmen's Salaries....... $	11,812.50			
Salesmen's Expenses......	1,942.06			
Advertising.............	844.32			
Telephone and Telegraph..	642.57			
Total................ $		15,241.45		2.20 *(1)*
General Expenses:				
Salaries................ $	8,722.33			
Expenses...............	613.36			
Executive Salaries........	3,600.00			
Taxes (other than federal).	1,906.23			
Insurance..............	1,723.46			
Depreciation............	1,259.54			
Light, Heat, and Water...	829.49			
Printing and Stationery...	444.50			
Postage................	408.52			
Collections.............	219.76			
Repairs................	115.91			
Storage................	22.69			
Miscellaneous...........	380.50			
Total................		20,246.29		2.93 *(1)*
Total Expense........			44,969.69	6.50% *(1)*
Net Operating Profit........			$ 24,632.65	3.56% *(3)*

Additions to Income:

Discount on Purchases....	$ 9,565.86		
Interest Earned.........	563.32		
Bad Debts Recovered.....	102.53		
Total...............		10,231.71	1.48
		$ 34,864.36	5.04%

Deductions from Income:

Discount on Sales........	$ 4,771.92		
Interest Paid for Money Borrowed...........	4,373.16		
Interest Paid on Building Contract...........	3,010.00		
Bad Debts Reserve.......	1,283.91		
Donations..............	162.00		
Total...............		13,600.99	1.97
Net Profit..............		$ 21,263.37	3.07% (4)

Supplemental

Total Capital Used (see Balance Sheet, below)..........	$276,317.34		
Ratio of Profit to Capital............................		7.69%	(5)
Net Worth (beginning of year).......................	124,252.36		
Ratio of Profit to Net Worth........................		17.11	(6)
Common Stock Outstanding........................	113,400.00		
Number of Shares ($50.00 par value).................	2,268		
Per cent earned....................................		18.75	(7)
Dollars earned per share............................		9.38	

Working capital ratio. This ratio is probably the best-known measure applied to financial statements, because more than any other it has been stressed by bankers and businessmen. It is computed by dividing the amount of the current assets by the amount of the current liabilities. If the quotient is 2, the current assets are said to be in a "2 to 1" ratio; that is, in a ratio of $2 of current assets to each $1 of current liabilities.

What the working capital ratio should be depends upon differences in types of business, location, and other factors the effect of which is to vary somewhat the proportions involved. While some lines of trade may be expected to maintain a 2-to-1 ratio, others may necessitate a proportion as high as 10 to 1.

The rapidity with which receivables and inventory are turned is a factor bearing on the adequacy of the working capital ratio. With respect to accounts receivable, there is a range of turnover from 3 days in some of the retail chain stores to 80 or 90 days in coal and heavy manufacturing industries. The turnover of inventories is most rapid in such industries as slaughtering and meat packing, retail chain stores, chemical products, and iron and steel, while the turnover of inventories is found to be slow in such industries as tobacco products, machinery manufacturing, leather products, and rubber goods.

Example. The following balance sheet is presented to illustrate the working capital ratio. It will also be referred to in later paragraphs, where the computation of other ratios is discussed.

Blank Mercantile Company

BALANCE SHEET
DECEMBER 31, 19—.

Assets

Current:

Cash in Banks	$ 13,598.85		
Cash on Hand	4,113.24	$ 17,712.09	
Accounts Receivable—Customers	$ 64,832.57		
Accounts Receivable—Others	647.92		
Notes Receivable—Customers	5,329.91		
Notes Receivable—Others	227.31		
Securities	1,274.34		
Accrued Interest	32.98		
Railroad Claims	93.76		
	$ 72,438.79		
Less: Reserve for Bad Debts	1,890.06	70,548.73	
Merchandise Inventory		124,814.04	
Total			$213,074.86

Fixed:

Land		$ 3,450.00	
Warehouse Building	$ 50,373.48		
Warehouse Equipment	545.77		
Delivery Equipment	14,090.39		
Furniture and Fixtures	2,488.85		
	$ 67,498.49		
Less: Accumulated Depreciation	9,152.48	58,346.01	
Total			$ 61,796.01

Deferred Charges:

Prepaid Insurance		$ 1,298.13	
Prepaid Interest		148.34	
Total			1,446.47
			$276,317.34

Liabilities

Current:

Payroll	$ 1,131.77	
Accounts Payable	16,177.08	
Notes Payable—Banks	50,000.00	
Notes Payable—Others	17,600.00	
Notes Payable—Stockholders	11,700.00	
Accrued Taxes	1,575.17	
Accrued Interest—Notes	1,393.92	
Accrued Interest—Contracts	3,010.00	
Total		$102,587.94

Fixed:

Warehouse Contract for Deed		43,000.00

Net Worth:

Capital Stock—Common	$113,400.00	
Surplus	17,329.40	130,729.40
		$276,317.34

In the foregoing balance sheet, the current assets are stated at $213,074.86, and the current liabilities are stated at $102,587.94.

$$213,074.86 \div 102,587.94 = 2.077.$$

The ratio of working capital is, therefore, 2.077.

Sources of capital., The sources of capital may be stated in a general way under four headings, as follows:

(1) Short-term borrowings and credits.
(2) Long-term borrowings and credits.
(3) Stockholders' investments.
(4) Surplus (earnings left in the business).

Summarizing the liability section of the foregoing blance sheet and dividing each section total by the total of all sections, the ratio of capital supplied by each source is as shown in the right-hand column of the following tabulation:

	Amount	Per Cent
Current Liabilities	$102,507.91	37.13
Fixed Liabilities	43,000.00	15.56
Capital Stock—Common	113,400.00	41.04
Surplus	17,329.40	6.27
	$276,317.34	100.00

Manner in which capital is invested. The manner in which the capital is employed in the business is shown by a summary of the asset sections.

	Amount	Per Cent
Current Assets	$213,074.86	77.12
Fixed Assets	61,796.01	22.36
Deferred Charges	1,446.47	.52
	$276,317.34	100.00

Turnover of total capital employed. This item expresses the relation of the net sales to the total capital employed. The average capital employed throughout the year should be used, but, in the absence of monthly statements, the capital at the beginning of the year and the capital at the end of the year should be added and divided by 2 to give an estimate of the average capital employed. In arriving at this average, investments not employed in operations should be eliminated from the total assets, for, as a rule, they represent a surplus not required in the conduct of the business. Income from such investments should be eliminated from the statement of earnings before the ratio is computed.

Total assets at beginning of year	$246,351.89
Total assets at end of year	276,317.34
	2)$522,669.23
Average capital employed (securities not eliminated, as the amount was negligible)	$261,334.61

The turnover of total capital employed is therefore:

$691,933.21 (net sales) ÷ $261,334.61 (average capital) = 2.64.

Turnover of inventories. The subject of inventory turnover was presented in Chapter 5.

The rate of turnover is computed as follows:

$622,330.87 (cost of sales) ÷ $112,131.69 (average inventory) = 5.55.

Turnover of accounts receivable. The normal credit period, whether it be 30, 60, or 90 days, is compared with the average number of days' sales uncollected obtained from the following formula, as a means of judging the efficiency of the collection department:

$$\frac{Accounts\ receivable\ at\ end\ of\ fiscal\ period}{Sales\ for\ fiscal\ period} \times Days\ in\ fiscal\ period$$
$$= Average\ number\ of\ days'\ sales\ uncollected.$$

The Accounts Receivable account showed $64,832.57 of outstanding accounts at the close of the fiscal period. The sales for the fiscal period of 12 months amounted to $691,933.21, and the average term of credit granted at time of sale was 30 days. The average number of days' sales represented in standing accounts is computed as follows:

$$\frac{64,832.57}{691,933.21} \times 365 = 34.$$

If the average number of days' sales uncollected is greater than the average term of credit, the presence of overdue accounts is indicated. This is true of the example just given.

Turnover of fixed property investment. This turnover expresses the relationship between the volume of business done and the capital invested in plant and equipment. Large investments in property and equipment increase the expense burden through charges for depreciation, insurance, taxes, and so forth, and may make a favorable or an unfavorable operating statement, depending on the volume of business handled.

The number of dollars of sales for each dollar of fixed property investment is calculated as follows:

$691,933.21 (net sales) ÷ $58,346.01 (net fixed property investment) = 11.86.

PROBLEMS

1. From the balance sheets and supplemental information, determine the ratios named following the balance sheets.

Assets	This Year	Last Year
Current Assets	$215,003.48	$213,074.86
Fixed Assets—Net	57,535.04	61,796.01
Deferred Charges	1,193.59	1,446.47
Total	$273,732.11	$276,317.34
Liabilities		
Current Liabilities	$ 86,229.30	$102,587.94
Fixed Liabilities	38,000.00	43,000.00
Total Liabilities	$124,229.30	$145,587.94

Net Worth

Capital Stock...........................	$124,300.00	$114,300.00
Surplus................................	25,202.81	16,429.40
Total Net Worth...................	$149,502.81	$130,729.40
Total............................	$273,732.11	$276,317.34
Annual Sales.........................	$688,167.98	$691,933.21
Annual Expense.......................	47,340.74	44,969.69

Ratios

Current Ratio.......................	....	....
Worth to Debt.......................	....	....
Worth to Fixed Assets................	....	....
Sales to Fixed Assets................	....	....
Sales to Current Debt................	....	....
Sales to Worth......................	....	....
Expense to Sales (%)................	....	....

2. The United Manufacturing Company's card in the credit file of the Second National Bank contained the data for the year ended January 31, 1960, and from their balance sheet and profit and loss statement you have entered the comparative figures for the year ended January 31, 1961. Compute the comparative ratios for 1961. (See Fig. 8-1.)

COMPARATIVE RATIOS

	1/31 1960	1/31 1961	19	19	19
FIXED ASSETS TO TANGIBLE NET WORTH	24.8				
CURRENT DEBT TO TANGIBLE NET WORTH	48.0				
NET WORKING CAPITAL REP BY FUNDED DEBTS					
NET SALES TO INVENTORY	4.3				
NET WORKING CAPITAL REP BY INVENTORY	107.7				
INVENTORY COVERED BY CURRENT DEBT	61.3				
AVERAGE COLLECTION PERIOD	42.5				
TURNOVER OF TANGIBLE NET WORTH	3.4				
TURNOVER OF NET WORKING CAPITAL	4.7				
NET PROFITS ON NET SALES	.52				
NET PROFITS ON TANGIBLE NET WORTH	1.8				
NET PROFITS ON NET WORKING CAPITAL	2.4				
CURRENT ASSETS TO CURRENT DEBT	2.5				
TOTAL DEBT INCLUDING N.W. TANGIBLE NET WORTH	148.0				
	$	$	$	$	$
SALES	388,553	394,774			
EXPENSES					
NET PROFIT	2,048	1,664			
WORKING CAPITAL	83,022	71,523			
TANGIBLE NET WORTH	113,983	114,649			
FIXED ASSETS	28,244	49,244			
FUNDED DEBT		8,280			

COMPARATIVE FINANCIAL STATEMENTS

ASSETS	1/31 1960	1/31 1961	19	19	19
CASH	3,206	1,862			
ACCOUNTS RECEIVABLE	45,199	42,267			
NOTES. TRADE ACCEPT RECV.					
INVENTORIES	89,342	83,218			
TOTAL CURRENT	168,709	127,349			
DUE FROM AFFILIATE OR SUBS'Y					
LAND. BUILDINGS					
MACHINERY-FIXTURES	28,244	49,248			
NOTES. ACC'TS (OFFICERS, PARTNERS)	2,716	2,156			
Organization Expense		999			
TOTAL ASSETS	168,709	179,754			
LIABILITIES					
ACCOUNTS PAYABLE-TRADE	34,037	32,671			
ACCEPT., NOTES PAYABLE					
BANKS PAYABLE	10,000	15,040			
PAYABLE AFFILIATE OR SUBS'Y					
ACCRUALS	2,557	2,793			
Due Officers	8,130	5,321			
TOTAL CURRENT	54,725	55,825			
MORTGAGES					
CHATTEL MORTGAGES					
Deferred Bank Loan		8,280			
TOTAL LIABILITIES	54,725	64,105			
CAPITAL STOCK	103,100	103,100			
SURPLUS	10,883	12,548			
TOTAL LIABILITIES & NET WORTH	168,709	179,754			

Fig. 8-1.

3. From the data given in the following balance sheet and profit and loss statement, together with the supplemental data, compute the 14 financial and operating ratios relationships, and turnovers outlined in the preceding sections of this chapter.

Blank Mercantile Company

BALANCE SHEET
DECEMBER 31, 19—

Assets

Current:
Cash in Banks...................... $ 13,771.58
Cash on Hand...................... 3,616.34 $ 17,387.92

Accounts Receivable—Customers....... $ 59,424.48
Accounts Receivable—Others........... 704.30
Notes Receivable—Customers.......... 3,746.76
Notes Receivable—Others............. 272.19
Securities........................... 994.64
Accrued Interest..................... 52.30
Railroad Claims...................... 50.95
                                    $ 65,245.62
    Less: Reserve for Bad Debts......... 3,852.57   61,393.05
    Merchandise Inventory........................... 136,222.51
        Total... $215,003.48
Fixed:
Land.. $ 3,450.00
Warehouse Building................... $ 50,180.55
Warehouse Equipment................. 545.77
Delivery Equipment................... 14,090.39
Furniture and Fixtures............... 2,503.85
                                    $ 67,320.56
    Less: Accumulated Depreciation...... 13,235.52   54,085.04   57,535.04

Deferred Charges:
Prepaid Insurance... 1,193.59
    Total... $273,732.11

Liabilities

Current:
Payroll.............................. $ 1,116.17
Accounts Payable..................... 13,325.73
Notes Payable—Banks................. 24,000.00
Notes Payable—Others............... 14,500.00
Notes Payable—Stockholders........... 26,700.00
Accrued Taxes........................ 1,641.97
Accrued Interest—Notes............... 2,285.33
Accrued Interest—Contracts........... 2,660.00
    Total.. $ 86,229.20
Fixed:
Warehouse Contract for Deed..................... 38,000.00
Net Worth:
Capital Stock—Common............... $123,400.00
Surplus............................ 26,102.91   149,502.91
    Total... $273.732.11

Blank Mercantile Company

PROFIT AND LOSS STATEMENT
FOR THE YEAR ENDED DECEMBER 31, 19—

Sales:
Gross Sales		$689,361.43	
Less: Sales Rebates and Allowances	$ 1,059.89		
Prepaid Freight	133.56		
		1,193.45	
Net Sales		$688,167.98	100.00%

Cost of Sales:
Inventory, beginning of year		$124,814.04	
Purchases	$611,332.45		
Freight	15,184.68		
	626,517.13		
Less: Pur. Rebates and Allowances	1,392.74		
		625,124.39	
		$749,938.43	
Inventory, end of year		136,222.51	
Cost of Sales		613,715.92	............%
Gross Profit		$ 74,452.06	............%

Delivery Expenses:
Salaries of Drivers	$ 3,874.27		
Dep'n on Equipment	2,818.08		
Auto Repairs	1,430.61		
Gasoline and Oil	1,231.29		
Drivers' Expenses	125.35		
Drayage	52.91		
Total		$ 9,532.51	............%

Selling Expenses:
Salesmen's Salaries	$ 12,300.00		
Salesmen's Expenses	2,015.78		
Advertising	1,357.83		
Telephone and Telegraph	536.21		
Total		16,209.82	............%

General Expenses:
Salaries	$ 8,797.50		
Expenses	265.43		
Executive Salaries	4,175.00		
Taxes (other than federal)	2,069.17		
Insurance	1,937.82		
Depreciation	1,264.96		
Light, Heat, and Water	826.33		
Printing and Stationery	516.70		
Postage	486.85		
Collections	238.65		
Repairs	106.47		
Storage	18.29		
Miscellaneous	895.24		
Total		$ 21,598.41	............%
Total Expense		47,340.74	............%
Net Operating Profit		$ 27,111.32	............%

Additions to Income:
    Discount on Purchases.................... $ 9,759.20
    Interest Earned..........................   1,348.60
    Bad Debts Recovered....................   10.65
        Total.......................................   11,118.45 ....%
                                                              $ 38,229.77 ....%
Deductions from Income:
    Discount on Sales........................ $ 4,523.98
    Interest Paid for Money Borrowed.........   4,443.87
    Interest Paid on Building Contract........   2,660.00
    Bad Debts Reserve.......................   3,446.80
    Donations...............................   269.20
        Total.......................................   15,343.85 ....%
Net Profit... $ 22,885.92 ....%

Supplemental

Total Capital Employed (see Balance Sheet).............. $........................
Ratio of Profit to Capital...............................   ....%
Net Worth (beginning of year)...........................   130,729.40
Ratio of Profit to Net Worth............................   ....%
Common Stock Outstanding (see Balance Sheet)...........   ....
Number of Shares ($50.00 per value)....................   ....
Per Cent Earned...   ....%
Dollars Earned Per Share................................   ....

9

Goodwill

Definition. Goodwill is an intangible asset, and may be defined in general terms as the value of any benefits or advantages which may accrue to a business from its being soundly established, bearing a good reputation, having a favorable location, and so forth. It results in the earning of a higher rate of net income than that of less fortunate concerns in the same line of business.

Basis of valuation. When two or more businesses are consolidated or merged, the payment made for each business depends upon:

(1) The value of the net assets of each business.

(2) The earning power of each business.

A committee should be formed, consisting of members from each of the businesses being consolidated or merged (proprietorship, firm, or corporation); this committee should have the assistance of an appraiser and an accountant in the preparation of a report dealing with the net assets and the earning power.

The report should contain a balance sheet of each business, stating the values at which it is proposed to take over the assets, and stating the liabilities to be assumed.

The value of the fixed assets and of the inventory should be determined by the appraiser. The accountant, after making an audit, should submit the other balance sheet items.

Earning power determined from profit and loss statements. The following points should receive consideration when earning power is being determined from profit and loss statements:

(1) *Number of years included.* The value of goodwill depends to some extent on whether profits have been uniform year after year, or

have steadily increased or decreased, or have fluctuated from year to year. Therefore, in order to show the trend of profits, it is necessary to have profit and loss statements for several years. A statement of average profits is insufficient, as it does not show the trend.

(2) *Adjustments to correct profits.* Adjustments may be necessary to correct errors, such as:

(a) Wrong classification of capital and revenue expenditures.
(b) Omission of provision for depreciation, bad debts, and so forth.
(c) Inadequate provision for repairs.
(d) Anticipation of profits on consignments and sales for future delivery.

(3) *Uniformity of methods.*

(a) If the methods of computing the manufacturing costs are not uniform, the cost statements should be revised and put on a uniform basis.
(b) The depreciation charges should be analyzed as to method and rate. If different methods and rates have been used, adjustments should be made so that the charges will have been calculated on a uniform basis.
(c) There may be a wide difference in the management salaries paid by the consolidating companies for the same services. The salaries should be adjusted. In a single proprietorship or partnership, salaries may not have been paid or credited; in that case they should be included at an arbitrary figure.
(d) If, in a partnership, interest on capital has been charged as an expense, the entries should be reversed and the item of interest on capital thus eliminated.

(4) *Eliminations.* Eliminations may have to be made for extraordinary and non-operating profits or losses.

Methods of valuing goodwill. Goodwill may be valued on the basis of:

(1) An appraisal of goodwill.
(2) A number of years' purchase price of the net profits.
(3) A number of years' purchase price of excess profits over interest on net assets.

Capitalization of profits in excess of interest on net assets is usually calculated as follows:

Net assets	$100,000.00
Profits	10,000.00
Interest on net assets @ 6%	6,000.00
Excess of profits over interest	4,000.00
Excess capitalized at 20% (4,000 ÷ .20)	20,000.00

Case illustrations.   The following four cases of goodwill valuation, taken from reports of consolidations, show how goodwill has been valued in practice.

Case 1.   The goodwill of the consolidating units was fixed at the sum of the profits for the two preceding years, plus an additional 10%.

Case 2.   The goodwill was based on the total profits for the five years preceding, less five years' interest on the net worth.

Case 3.   The goodwill was the average annual earnings for the four years preceding consolidation, less the following deductions:

(a) Profits on favorable contracts about to expire.
(b) $100,000 for the estimated value of services rendered by the retiring president.
(c) 6% interest on actual capital invested.

The remainder was capitalized on a 10% basis.

Case 4.   From the net profits of each company the following items were deducted:

(a) 7% on capital actually employed.
(b) $1\frac{1}{2}$% on sales.
(c) 2% depreciation on brick buildings.
(d) 4% depreciation on frame buildings.
(e) 8% depreciation on machinery.

The remainder was capitalized at 20%, or 5 times the amount of such earnings in excess of 7% on capital and other deductions agreed upon.

Valuation by appraisal.   There is no particular problem in the calculation of the value of goodwill by appraisal.   It may be appraised by a disinterested party; or, more often, it is the amount on which the vendor and the vendee agree.   They usually appraise the net assets, and agree that the purchase price shall be a certain amount in excess of the value of the net assets.   This excess is the payment for goodwill.

Valuation by number of years' purchase price of net profits. The goodwill may be estimated at so many years' purchase price of the net or gross profits of any one year, or at so many years' purchase price of the average profits of a number of years.

Example.   The consideration of the sale of a business, as agreed to between the parties, is four years' purchase price of the average profits for the preceding three years, plus the net value of the assets.

Net value of assets		$100,000
Profits of preceding three years:		
1st year	$20,000	
2nd year	15,000	
3rd year	28,000	

What is the selling price of the business?

Solution.

Net value of assets...............................		$100,000
Profits of preceding three years:		
1st year.....................................	$20,000	
2nd year....................................	15,000	
3rd year....................................	28,000	
	$63,000	
$63,000 ÷ 3 = $21,000, average profits for three years.		
$21,000 × 4 (goodwill).........................		84,000
Selling price.................................		$184,000

Valuation on basis of excess of profits over interest on net assets. The value of goodwill is calculated under this method by, first, deducting from the average profits a fair return of interest on the capital invested, and, second, by multiplying the remainder of the profits, or the excess, by an agreed number of years' purchase price.

Example. *A* agrees to buy a certain business, and to pay for it in cash. He agrees to give dollar for dollar of the value of the net assets, plus a six years' purchase price of the excess of the profits over the interest on capital at 6%. Net assets are valued at $100,000, and average profits are $18,000. What is the purchase price of the business, including goodwill?

Solution.

Net assets......................................		$100,000
Profits, average...............................	$18,000	
$100,000 × .06..............................	6,000	
Excess profits.................................	$12,000	
$12,000 × 6 (goodwill).....		72,000
Purchase price................................		$172,000

It would be more favorable to the seller to determine the value by using a higher rate of interest and capitalizing the excess profits at this rate; thus:

Net assets......................................		$100,000
Profits, average...............................	$18,000	
$100,000 × .08..............................	8,000	
Excess profits.................................	$10,000	
$10,000 ÷ .08 (goodwill)......................		125,000
Purchase price...		$225,000

$225,000 − $172,000 = $53,000, advantage to the seller.

In the foregoing example, the goodwill represents the capitalization of that portion of the profits which is not attributable to the net tangible assets. The rate to be used depends largely on the kind of business under consideration. In some lines of business the per cent may be as low as 6% or 8%; in others it may be 10%; and in still others, 15% or even 20%.

Basis of stock allotment. Since most phases of the calculation of the value of goodwill are found in consolidations, an example of consolidation is given. The matter of stock allotment is included, because when an agreement has been reached as to the valuation of the assets and as to the earning power of each of the businesses, the next question to decide is the method of making payment.

The following three typical methods will be presented:

(1) Payment entirely in common stock.

(2) Payment in preferred stock for the net assets; payment in common stock for the goodwill.

(3) Payment in bonds for the fixed assets, or for an agreed percentage thereof; payment in preferred stock for the balance of the net assets; payment in common stock for the goodwill.

In the allotment of securities, the fundamental rule is to distribute them in such a manner that, if the income of the consolidation is the same as the combined income of the several businesses, each of the old businesses, or the former owners or stockholders thereof, will receive the same net income as before the consolidation.

To illustrate how this principle would operate under each of the three methods outlined, assume that three companies are to be consolidated on the basis of the following statements:

	A	B	C	Total
Net assets..................	$40,000	$60,000	$120,000	$220,000
Average earnings...........	4,000	12,000	20,000	36,000
Rate of income on net assets.	10%	20%	$16\frac{2}{3}\%$	

Common stock only. When only common stock is to be issued, it must be issued in the ratio of the net earnings if the income of the consolidation is to be distributed in the ratio in which the companies contributed earnings. To determine the amount of stock which is to be issued, capitalize the earnings by dividing the income of each company by a rate of income agreed upon. Thus, if it is agreed that the rate be 10%, the distribution of common stock is made as follows:

	A	B	C	Total
Stock to be issued:				
A: $4,000 ÷ .10........	$40,000			
B: $12,000 ÷ .10......		$120,000		
C: $20,000 ÷ .10......			$200,000	
Total.................				$360,000
Less net assets transferred	40,000	60,000	120,000	220,000
Goodwill..............	0	$ 60,000	$ 80,000	$140,000

Ten per cent was chosen as the basic rate, because it was the lowest rate earned by any one of the three companies.

If the profits of the consolidation amount to $36,000, it will be possible to pay a 10% dividend, which would be distributed as follows:

```
A: 10% of $40,000......................................  $  4,000
B: 10% of $120,000.....................................    12,000
C: 10% of $200,000.....  ..............................    20,000
                                                          $36,000
```

This is an equitable division, so far as profits are concerned. However, it is objectionable because it gives each old company an interest in the assets which is proportionate to the profits earned before the consolidation, instead of an interest proportionate to the assets contributed. This might work a hardship in case of liquidation.

	Net Assets	Goodwill	Total	Fraction
A	$ 40,000	0	$ 40,000	$\frac{40}{360}$
B	60,000	$ 60,000	120,000	$\frac{120}{360}$
C	120,000	80,000	200,000	$\frac{200}{360}$
	$220,000	$140,000	$360,000	

Assume that after a number of years it is decided to liquidate the consolidated company, and that in the meantime, all of the profits have been paid out as dividends. The goodwill has no realizable value, so there is **$220,000** to be distributed as follows:

```
Former stockholders of A:  40/360 of $220,000............  $ 24,444.45
Former stockholders of B: 120/360 of  220,000............    73,333.33
Former stockholders of C: 200/360 of  220,000............   122,222.22
                                                           $220,000.00
```

The former stockholders of A would lose, and the former stockholders of B and C would profit.

Former Stockholders of Company	Assets Contributed	Liquidating Dividend	Gain	Loss
A	$ 40,000	$ 24,444.45		$15,555.55
B	60,000	73,333.33	$13,333.33	
C	120,000	122,222.22	2,222.22	
	$220,000	$220,000.00	$15,555.55	$15,555.55

Preferred stock for net assets. In order to avoid giving an advantage to one or more companies at the expense of the others, it is advisable to issue preferred stock for the net assets, and common stock for the goodwill. The goodwill should be allotted to the several companies in the ratio of the excess of the profits contributed over the dividends on the preferred stock.

Assume that in the above illustration 6% stock, preferred as to assets, is to be issued for the net assets, and that common stock is to be issued for the goodwill.

	A	B	C	Total
Earnings.....................	$4,000	$12,000	$20,000	$36,000
Less dividends on preferred stock:				
A: 6% of $ 40,000........	2,400			
B: 6% of 60,000........		3,600		
C: 6% of 120,000........			7,200	
Excess earnings..............	$1,600	$ 8,400	$12,800	

Common stock should be issued in the ratio of the excess earnings. If five years' purchase of the excess profits were agreed upon, the distribution of stock would be:

	A	B	C	Total
Preferred stock...........	$40,000	$60,000	$120,000	$220,000
Common stock...........	8,000	42,000	64,000	114,000

Assuming profits of $36,000 as before, the distribution of dividends would be:

Profits...	$36,000
Preferred dividends: 6% of $220,000......................	13,200
Balance available for common stock dividends..............	$22,800

Then, $22,800 ÷ $114,000 = 20%, the rate per cent which could be paid on the common stock.

	A	B	C
Preferred dividends:			
6% of $ 40,000.....................	$2,400		
6% of 60,000.....................		$ 3,600	
6% of 120,000.....................			$ 7,200
Common dividends:			
20% of $ 8,000.....................	1,600		
20% of 42,000.....................		8,400	
20% of 64,000.....................			12,800
Total dividends.....................	$4,000	$12,000	$20,000

These dividends are in each case equal to the profits contributed to the consolidation by the several companies.

It is important to note that goodwill should be based on the profits contributed minus the profits to be returned as preferred dividends, and not on the total profits.

Bonds, preferred stock, and common stock. If bonds are issued for a percentage of the net assets, preferred stock for the remaining net assets, and common stock for the goodwill, the goodwill should be based on the profits turned in minus the bond interest and the preferred dividends.

Assume that 5% bonds are to be issued for 80% of the net assets, 6% preferred stock for the remaining net assets, and common stock for the goodwill, which is to be computed by capitalizing at 20% the earnings of each company in excess of bond interest and preferred dividends to be paid to former stockholders.   The issues of the three classes of securities would be computed as follows:

	A	B	C	Total
Bonds:				
A: 80% of $ 40,000.......	· $32,000			
B: 80% of 60,000.......		$48,000		
C: 80% of 120,000.......			$96,000	
Total bonds.............				$176,000
Preferred Stock:				
A: 20% of $ 40,000.......		8,000		
B: 20% of 60,000.......			12,000	
C: 20% of 120,000.......			24,000	
Total preferred stock......				44,000

Common Stock:

A: Earnings.............		$ 4,000			
Bond interest..........	$1,600				
Pfd. dividend........ ..	480	2,080			
Excess...............		$ 1,920			
$1,920 ÷ .20..........			$ 9,600		
B: Earnings.............		$12,000			
Bond interest..........	$2,400				
Pfd. dividend..........	720	3,120			
Excess...............		$ 8,880			
$8,880 ÷ .20..........				$44,400	
C: Earnings.............		$20,000			
Bond interest..........	$4,800				
Pfd. dividend..........	1,440	6,240			
Excess..............		$13,760			
$13,760 ÷ .20.........					$68,800
Total common stock.......					$122,800

With profits of $36,000 before allowance for bond interest and preferred dividends, the former stockholders would receive interest and dividends as follows:

	A	B	C	Total
Bond interest:				
5% of $32,000......................	$1,600			
5% of 48,000......................		$ 2,400		
5% of 96,000......................			$ 4,800	
Total..............................				$ 8,800
Preferred dividends:				
6% of $ 8,000....	480			
6% of 12,000....................		720		
6% of 24,000....................			1,440	
Total.............................				2,640
Common dividends:				
20% of $ 9,600......................	1,920			
20% of 44,400......................		8,880		
20% of 68,800......................			13,760	
Total.............................				24,560
Total distribution......................	$4,000	$12,000	$20,000	$36,000

Conclusion. The illustrations given are merely indicative of the principles to be borne in mind in the distribution of stock and other securities; they cannot be accepted as procedures to be invariably followed, for several reasons.

First, in the illustrations, the profits of the consolidation are assumed to be the same as the combined profits of the separate companies before they were consolidated. However, consolidations are usually made with the object of increasing profits; hence the question is raised as to how the additional profits should be divided. Should the preferred stock be participating or non-participating?

Second, the question of control involves the matter of the voting rights of the several classes of stock.

These and other considerations would tend to cause modifications in the methods described, but the illustrations serve to indicate the basic principles which must be followed in security allotment in order that the stockholders of the several consolidating companies may preserve their interests in the assets and earnings of the consolidation.

PROBLEMS

1. *A*, *B*, and *C* are about to consolidate. The following data are presented:

	A	*B*	*C*	*Total*
Net Assets............	$250,000	$150,000	$600,000	$1,000,000
Average Profits........	50,000	15,000	150,000	215,000
Interest Rate..........				10%
Profit Rate.	20%	10%	25%	

Prepare tabulations showing the stock distribution:
(a) Preferred stock for the net assets, and common stock for the goodwill.
(b) Show the possible disadvantage of issuing only common stock.

2. Using the data in Problem 1, show the security allotment if 5% bonds are issued ·for 80% of the net assets, 6% preferred stock for the remainder, and common stock for the goodwill, which is to be based on excess earnings capitalized at 15%.

3. *A*, *B*, and *C* call upon you to draw up plans for their consolidation. They submit the following information:

Assets	*A*	*B*	*C*
Plants........................	$350,000	$200,000	$180,000
Materials......................	100,000	20,000	20,000
Accounts Receivable...............	80,000	60,000	40,000
Cash..........................	20,000	10,000	10,000
Liabilities			
Accounts Payable................	70,000	30,000	20,000
Capital........................	350,000	200,000	100,000
Surplus.......................	130,000	60,000	130,000
Average income.................	30,000	35,000	40,000

Upon your recommendation, the consolidation will issue: (a) 6% bonds for the fixed assets; (b) 7% preferred stock for the remaining net assets; (c) common stock for the goodwill, which is to be based on excess profits capitalized at 10%.

Assuming that the consolidation will have net profits amounting to $105,000, prepare statements showing the allotment of securities and the distribution of profits.

4.* The net worth and profits of three companies are as follows:

	X
Capital	$100,000
Profits	50,000
	Y
Capital	200,000
Profits	50,000
	Z
Capital	250,000
Profits	50,000

(*a*) Give your theory of how a consolidation should be made.

(*b*) Show the respective interests of X, of Y, and of Z in the consolidated company, using a factor of 6% to represent the normal value of money.

5.† A has agreed to sell to B the goodwill of the X. Y. Company on the basis of three years' profits of the business, which are to be determined by you, on sound principles of accounting and as accurately as possible, from the following statement handed you by A. You are required to compute the value of the goodwill, but are not expected to take into account any considerations except those presented by the statement.

Credits	1st Year	2nd Year	3rd Year
Sales (selling prices substantially uniform throughout period)	$638,400	$602,500	$ 564,000
Estimated value of construction work performed and charged to property	110,000	77,600	154,000
Appreciation of real estate upon revaluation by experts		80,000	
Profit on sale of Bethlehem Steel Co. stock			85,000
Inventory at end of period:			
Production material at cost	72,000	103,100	106,600
Finished goods at selling prices	76,500	114,000	150,000
	$896,900	$977,200	$1,059,600
Debits			
Production materials purchased	$233,000	$252,400	$ 220,300
Production labor	50,850	61,400	60,900
Production expense (including depreciation)	66,750	69,300	70,300
Selling expenses	52,500	55,650	62,800
Interest	96,000	94,000	98,500
Cost of construction work	74,600	49,000	86,000
Inventory at beginning of period:			
Production material at cost	51,400	72,000	103,100
Finished goods at selling prices	54,900	76,500	114,000
	$680,000	$730,250	$ 815,900
Balance, being profit claimed by A	$216,900	$246,950	$ 243,700

---

* C. P. A., Michigan.

† American Institute Examination.

6.* In the preceding problem, does the basis used for arriving at the value of the goodwill—three years' profits—appear to you to be reasonable in view of the facts disclosed to you? If not, what advice would you offer upon the question if *A* or *B* were your client?

7.* *A* and *B* are partners in business and have the following statement:

Store	$15,000	Accounts Payable	$10,000
Accounts Receivable	12,000	Bills Payable	5,000
Cash	9,000	A's Capital	30,000
Furniture and Fixtures	2,800	B's Capital	35,000
Merchandise	37,000		
Miscellaneous Equipment	4,200		
	$80,000		$80,000

C is admitted as a special partner, under the following arrangement: *C* is to contribute $30,000, and is to be entitled to one-third of the profits for 1 year. Before the contribution is made, the following changes are to be made in the books: store to be marked down 5%; allowance for doubtful accounts to be created, amounting to 2%; merchandise to be revalued at $35,000; furniture and fixtures to be revalued at $2,500. At the end of the year, the goodwill is to be fixed at 3 times the net profits for the year in excess of $20,000, this goodwill to be set up on the books and the corresponding credit to be to *A* and *B* equally. *A*, *B*, and *C* are each to draw $3,000 in cash, and the remaining profits are to be carried to their capital accounts.

During the year, the following transactions took place:

Merchandise bought on credit	$240,000
Cash purchases	25,000
Cash sales	125,000
Sales on credit	175,000
Accounts payable paid (face, $245,000; discount, 2%)	240,100
Accounts receivable collected (face, $170,000; all net except $50,000, on which 2% was allowed)	169,000
Buying expenses, paid cash	1,500
Selling expenses, paid cash	21,000
Delivery expenses, paid cash	9,000
Management expenses, paid cash	4,500
Miscellaneous expenses, paid cash	3,000
Interest on notes payable, paid cash	250

The partners each withdrew $3,000 cash, as agreed.

When the books were closed for the purpose of determining the profits and goodwill, the following were agreed upon:

Value of merchandise on hand	$60,000
Depreciation on store	285
Additional allowance for doubtful debts	165
Furniture and fixtures written down	200

The goodwill having been estimated and duly entered, *C* then contributes enough cash to make his capital account equal one-third of the total capital.

Prepare statements showing how the accounts are to be adjusted, and prepare the balance sheet after the final adjustment.

* American Institute Examination.

10

Business Finance

Stock rights. Corporations, in undertaking to secure additional capital, not infrequently offer additional stock to their stockholders at a price below the prevailing market quotation of the outstanding shares.

This privilege of subscribing has value as long as the market price of the old stock remains higher than the offering price of the new stock; and if the stockholders prefer not to exercise the rights, they may sell them in the market for whatever they will bring.

Example. A corporation has a capital stock of $100,000, divided into 1,000 common shares of $100 par value. The entire amount is outstanding, and the market quotation is $150. Finding that $50,000 additional capital is needed, the directors decide to offer to the stockholders 500 shares of new common stock at $125. They accordingly announce on August 1 that stockholders of record as of September 1 will have the privilege of subscribing for the new issue in the proportion of one share of the new stock for every two shares of the old stock held on the latter date. The subscriptions are payable on or before October 1 following, and transferable warrants for the rights are to be issued as soon as practicable after September 1. What is the value of a right?

Explanation. According to the conditions of this offer, every holder of two of the old shares at the close of business on September 1 will be entitled to subscribe to one of the new shares. He will therefore come into possession of two "rights," as that term is used on the New York Stock Exchange, or one right for every old share held. (On some stock exchanges the term right indicates the privilege of subscribing to one share of the new issue.)

Trading in the rights will begin following the declaration of the directors on August 1, and will continue until October 1. Until the warrants are in the hands of the stockholders—during the period from August 1 to September 1—the trading will be on a "when issued" basis; that is, delivery and payment for the rights will be made when the warrants are available. During this time the stock will sell "rights-on"; that is, the market value of the shares will include the value of the rights.

With the delivery of the warrants on September 1, the stock will sell "ex-rights," its price no longer including the value of the rights. With the issuance of the warrants, and until October 1, trading in the rights will be for immediate delivery and payment; that is, delivery and payment the day after the sale is made.

Should a holder of two shares exercise his privilege of subscription, he would own:

2 shares @ $150			$300
1 share @ 125			125
3 shares @ 141.67			$425

It will be noticed that the difference between the market price of the old stock and the average price of the three shares is $8.33, the value of a right; also that the difference between the market price of the old stock and the offering price of the new stock is $25.00, or three times the value of a right.

Therefore, the following formula may be used:

Formula

$$\frac{\text{Market price} - \text{Offering price}}{\text{Number of rights to purchase 1 share} + 1} = \text{Value of a right.}$$

Substitution

$$\frac{150 - 125}{2 + 1} = \frac{25}{3}, \text{ or } \$8.33.$$

During the second period—that is, while the stock is quoted ex-rights—the value of the rights may be ascertained as follows:

Formula

$$\frac{\text{Market price} - \text{Offering price}}{\text{Number of rights to purchase 1 share}} = \text{Value of a right.}$$

It will be found that the market price of the rights during the second period will tend to coincide with this value. Any appreciable difference opens an opportunity for a profit.

The foregoing discussion and example apply only to values on the market. The profit or loss resulting from the sale of rights, and the profit or loss from the sale of stock acquired by the exercise of rights, are governed by Section 29.22(a)-8, Regulations 111.

Sale of stock and rights, federal income tax. Ordinarily, a stockholder derives no taxable income from the receipt of rights to subscribe for stock, nor from the exercise of such rights, but if he sells the rights instead of exercising them, he may derive taxable income, or sustain a loss.

The following rule is stated in Sec. 29.22(a)-8, Regulations 111.

"(1) If the shareholder does not exercise, but sells, his rights to subscribe, the cost or other basis, properly adjusted, of the stock in respect of which the rights are acquired shall be apportioned between the rights and the stock in proportion to the respective values thereof at the time the rights are issued, and the basis for determining gain or loss from the sale of a right on one hand or a share of stock on the other will be the quotient of the cost or other basis, properly adjusted, assigned to the rights or the stock, divided, as the case may be, by the number of rights acquired or by the number of shares held."

Example. *A* purchased 100 shares of stock at $125.00 a share, and in the following year the corporation increased its capital by 20% *A*, therefore, received 100 rights, entitling him to subscribe to 20 additional shares of stock; the subscription price was $100.00 a share. Assume that at the time that the rights were issued the stock had a fair market value of $120.00 a share, and that the rights had a fair market value of $3.00 each. If, instead of subscribing for the additional shares, *A* sold the rights at $4.00 each, his taxable gain would be computed as follows:

100 shares @ $125.00.... $12,500.00, cost of stock in respect of which rights were issued.

100 shares @ $120.00.... $12,000.00, market value of old stock.

100 rights @ $3.00....... $300.00, market value of rights.

$\dfrac{12,000}{12,300}$ of 12,500......... $12,195.12, cost of old stock apportioned to such stock after issuance of rights.

$\dfrac{300}{12,300}$ of 12,500......... $304.88, cost of old stock apportioned to rights.

100 rights @ $4.00....... $400.00, sales price of rights.

$400.00 − $304.88....... $95.12, profit on sale of rights.

For the purpose of determining the gain or loss from the subsequent sale of the stock in respect of which the rights were issued, the adjusted cost of each share is $121.95—that is, $12,195.12 ÷ 100.

Rule 2 of Sec. 29.22(a)-8, Regulations 111, states:

"(2) If the shareholder exercises his rights to subscribe, the basis for determining gain or loss from a subsequent sale of a share of the stock in respect of which the rights were acquired shall be determined as in paragraph (1). The basis for determining gain or loss from a subsequent sale of a share of the stock obtained through exercising the rights shall be determined by dividing the part of the cost or other basis, properly adjusted, of the old shares assigned to the rights, plus the subscription price of the new shares, by the number of new shares acquired."

Example. *A* purchased 100 shares of stock at $125.00 a share, and in the following year the corporation increased its capital by 20%. *A*, therefore, received 100 rights entitling him to subscribe to 20 additional shares of stock; the subscription price was $100.00 a share. Assume that at the time that the rights were issued the stock had a fair market value of $120.00 a share, and that the rights had a fair market value of $3.00 each. *A* exercised his rights to subscribe, and later sold for $140.00 a share 10 of the 20 shares thus acquired. The profit is computed as follows:

Cost of old stock apportioned to rights in accordance
with the computation in the example under Rule 1 . . . $ 304.88
Subscription price of 20 shares at $100.00 a share. 2,000.00
Basis for determining gain or loss from sale of shares
acquired by exercise of rights. $2,304.88

$2,304.88 ÷ 20 = $115.24, basis for determining gain or loss from sale of
each share of stock acquired by exercise of rights.

Proceeds of sale:
10 shares @ $140.00. . . . . $1,400.00
Cost of stock sold:
10 shares @ $115.24. . . . .   1,152.40
Profit. . . . . $ 247.60

The basis for determining the gain or loss from the subsequent sale of the
remaining 10 shares of stock acquired on subscription is $115.24 a share; and
the basis for determining the gain or loss on the stock in respect of which the
rights were issued is $121.95 a share—that is, $12,195.12 ÷ 100, as in the
example under Rule 1.

PROBLEMS

1. A company has a capital stock of $1,000,000, divided into 10,000 common
shares of $100 par value. The entire amount is outstanding, and the market
quotation is $150 a share. Finding that $500,000 of additional capital is needed,
the directors decide to offer to the stockholders 5,000 shares of new common
stock at par. What is the approximate market value of a right if each stockholder may subscribe for one share of new stock for every two shares of the old
stock held?

2. A corporation offered, at $100 a share, one share of its new stock for each
six shares held. The stock was selling at $185 a share when the offer was
announced. What was the approximate market value of a right?

3. *W* owned 100 shares of Purity Baking Common that cost him $13,400.
Later, he received rights to subscribe to additional stock, but since he did not
care to increase his investment, he sold the rights at $3\frac{5}{8}$ less commission, receiving
therefore $357.30. At the date when the stock was quoted ex-rights, the average
market values were:

Stock. . . . . $124\frac{1}{2}$
Rights. . . . . $3\frac{5}{8}$

(*a*) What was *W*'s loss on the sale of the rights?
(*b*) What was the carrying value of the stock?

4. Smith owned 100 shares of common stock in the W. Corporation, which
offered rights to subscribe to new common stock at $100 a share, the basis of
the offering being one share for each five shares held. The average market
values on the date when the stock sold ex-rights were:

Stock. 150.50
Rights. 11.8125

Smith later sold his rights at $14.50.

(*a*) If Smith paid $120 a share for the original 100 shares, what is his profit on the sale of the rights?

(*b*) What is the carrying value of the 100 shares?

Working capital. One of the most difficult problems for anyone entering a new business is to know how much money will be required to finance the enterprise until the receipts will equal or exceed the disbursements. While this is strictly a question of finance, the accountant is often called upon to deal with it.

Example. A manufacturer gives you the following data, and requests that you estimate the amount of working capital required to finance the making and selling of an article:

```
Selling price, each................................. $100
Cost to make, each.................................   60
Selling expenses, each.............................   20
Overhead, each.....................................   10
Net profit, each...................................   10
Sales, first month.................................   50 articles
  "    second month................................  100   "
  "    third month..................................  150   "
  "    fourth month.................................  200   "
  "    each month thereafter........................  200   "
```

All the sales are installment sales, the payments being $10 per month. Assume arbitrarily that the complete cost of $90 on each article is incurred at the time that the sale is made.

What will be the largest amount of capital required, and in which month will it be required?

Solution.

Months	Total Costs Each Month	Total Receipts Each Month	Deficiency Each Month	Working Capital Required
First......................	$ 4,500	$ 500	$ 4,000	$ 4,000
Second....................	9,000	1,500	7,500	11,500
Third.....................	13,500	3,000	10,500	22,000
Fourth....................	18,000	5,000	13,000	35,000
Fifth.....................	18,000	7,000	11,000	46,000
Sixth.....................	18,000	9,000	9,000	55,000
Seventh......	18,000	11,000	7,000	62,000
Eighth....................	18,000	13,000	5,000	67,000
Ninth.....................	18,000	15,000	3,000	70,000
Tenth....	18,000	17,000	1,000	71,000
Eleventh....	18,000	18,500	500†	70,500
Twelfth..................	18,000	19,500	1,500†	69,000

† Receipts from collections are more than the costs for the month.

The above table shows in the last column the amount of working capital required to finance the business by months. The greatest amount required is found to be $71,000 in the tenth month. Thereafter, the collections are greater than the costs.

PROBLEMS

1. A company is about to be formed for the purpose of manufacturing a specialty. After careful investigation, the following estimates have been made:

Selling price, each.. $75
Cost to make, each... 35
Selling and administration expense............................... 14
Net profit... 26

Sales:
First month..................................... 30 machines
Second "   70   "
Third   "   180   "
Fourth "   200   "
Each month thereafter........................... 225   "

The terms of payment are $15 down, and $5 per month. What is the greatest amount of working capital that will be required, and in which month will this amount be needed?

2. The X Company plans to sell on the installment basis, direct from factory to consumer. Their product is a specialty retailing at $100, payable $10 with order and balance in nine equal installments.

Cost to manufacture:
Material... 40%
Labor.. 35%
Burden... 25%
Selling expense.................................... 15% of sales
Administration expense............................. 4% of sales
Other expense...................................... 1% of sales

Labor cost is expected to increase $14\frac{2}{7}\%$, which will decrease the profit 35%.

Estimated sales:
First month..................................... 50 machines
Second "   100   "
Third   "   150   "
Fourth "   200   "
Each month thereafter........................... 200   "

Assuming that all the expenses of a sale are paid during the month in which the sale is made, prepare a schedule showing the essential facts, and the amount of working capital needed monthly.

3.* On the basis of the following facts, determine, by months, the cash requirements of an installment dealer for the first year's operations:

1. Cost of article.................................... $50.00
2. Sales price....................................... 90.00
3. Selling expense................................... 15.00
4. Overhead... 15.00
5. Profit... 10.00
6. Sales for the first month were 100 articles
7. Sales for the second month were 200 articles
8. Sales for subsequent months were 300 articles per month
9. Merchandise paid for on the month following the sale
10. Expenses paid during the month of sale
11. Payments are received at the rate of $10 down and $10 per month; assume that no irregularities are experienced

4.† The A. B. Company acquired the right to sell musical instruments in a

---

* C. P. A., Wisconsin.
† C. P. A., Pennsylvania.

given territory.   They request you:

(a) To state how much capital will be required to carry on the business during the first year.

(b) To demonstrate by computation how your estimates would work out during the first six months.

Assume that the sales for the first year will total $180,000 from the sale of instruments, and $24,000 from service work (respectively, $15,000 and $2,000 monthly).   The overhead and direct selling costs are estimated at $30,000 for the year.   This amount includes all expenses except the cost of instruments sold and parts used in service, the latter being estimated at $12,000.

The instruments are purchased on 60 days' credit, at a discount of 30% from the price at which they are sold to the customer.   Twenty per cent of the instruments are sold for cash, and 80% on lease contracts.   When they are sold on lease contracts, 25% is required as a down payment, and the balance in 12 months.   All payments are made to the A. B. Company.   The leases are discounted at the bank, the charges by the bank being added to the price charged the customer.   The service charges are billed and payable in 30 days.

Cumulative voting.   Cumulative voting is a method whereby each shareholder is entitled to cast a number of votes equal to the product of the number of shares which he holds and the number of directors to be elected.   The shareholder may cast all his votes for any one or more of the directors to be elected, or may distribute his votes in any way that he desires.   Thus, the minority stockholders, by combining their votes, may elect a representative on the board of directors.

Example.   A corporation has an outstanding capital stock of $100,000, composed of 1,000 shares of common stock with a par value of $100 each.   The stockholders are to elect seven directors at the annual meeting.   Calculate the least number of shares required to elect three of the directors, provided that the cumulative method of voting is used.

Formula	*Substitution*
$$\frac{a \times c}{b + 1} + 1 = x.$$	$$\frac{1,000 \times 3}{7 + 1} + 1 = 376.$$

Explanation.

$a =$ Number of shares outstanding.

$b =$ Number of directors to be elected.

$c =$ Number of directors minority desires to elect.

$x =$ Required number of shares.

$1,000 \times 7 = 7,000$, total votes of 1,000 shares.

$376 \times 7 = 2,632$, total votes of 376 shares.

$2,632 \div 3 = 877$, the number of votes each of the three directors would receive if the holders of the 376 shares of stock cast all their votes for three directors.

$7,000 - 2,632 = 4,368$, balance of votes.

$4,368 \div 5 = 873$, the largest number of votes the remaining stockholders could cast for five directors.

By the same method of calculation, it will be found that the owners of 375 shares would have 875 votes for each of three directors, while the remaining stockholders would have 875 votes for each of five directors. This would give a tie vote, and neither side could elect the desired number.

PROBLEMS

1. In a corporation which uses the cumulative method of voting, how many of the seven directors can you safely seek to elect, if you own 1,501 out of the 4,000 voting shares?

2. Seven directors are to be elected by the X. Company, which has a voting capital of 5,000 shares. How many shares are necessary to elect four directors under the cumulative plan?

Book value of shares of stock. A corporation is owned by the stockholders, whose evidences of ownership are shares of stock. The book value of a share of stock is equal to the quotient of the net worth divided by the number of shares of stock outstanding.

Formula

$$\frac{\text{Assets} - \text{Liabilities}}{\text{Number of shares}} = \text{Book value per share}$$

Example. A corporation has assets of $340,000 and liabilities of $120,000. It has a capital stock of $200,000. If the shares have a par value of $100 each, what is their book value?

Solution.

$340,000 − $120,000 . . . . $220,000.00
$220,000 ÷ 2,000 shares 110.00

PROBLEMS

1. Find the book value of a share of stock in each of the following companies:

	Assets	Liabilities	Capital	Par Value of Shares
(a)	$350,829.75	$134,082.47	$100,000	$100
(b)	$575,850.00	$190,260.75	25,000 shares	No Par
(c)	$1,322,080.35	$110,809.20	$1,000,000	$50

2. A company has assets of $385,915.28 and liabilities of $158,910.75. If there are 5,000 shares outstanding, each with a par value of $50, what is the book value of each share?

Profits distribution. The distribution of profits in the partnership type of business organization is discussed under the subject of partnership (Chapter 11). The distribution of the profits of corporations is illustrated in the following examples.

Example 1. At the end of a certain year, a corporation had outstanding 2,250 shares of common stock, par value $100. A 2% dividend was declared.

Net earnings were $53,320.84. What was the amount of the dividend, and what amount of the year's profits, after the declaration of the dividend remained in surplus?

Solution.

2,250 shares @ $100	$225,000, capital stock
2% of $225,000	$4,500, dividend
$53,320.84 − $4,500	$48,820.84, credit to surplus

Example 2. A company had the following number of outstanding shares, each with a par value of $50: common, 858,860 shares; 6% cumulative preferred, 291,047 shares; 5% non-cumulative and non-participating preferred, 28,849 shares.

The company declared a 6% dividend on the common stock. What amount of profits was distributed to each class of stock? What amount of profits was necessary to cover the dividends?

Solution.

	Capital	*Dividends*
858,860 shares common @ $50	$42,943,000.00	
6% of $42,943,000		$2,576,580.00
291,047 shares 6% cumulative preferred @ $50	14,552,350.00	
6% of $14,552,350		873,141.00
28,849 shares 5% non-cumulative preferred @ $50	1,442,450.00	
5% of $1,442,450		72,122.50
Profits necessary to cover dividends		$3,521,843.50

PROBLEMS

1. Calculate the amount of dividends on the following stocks; each class has a par value of $100:

182,260 shares common @ 6%;
57,633 shares 7% cumulative preferred.

2. A company earned $2,850,460.03. It paid from this 8% dividends on $12,379,850 preferred stock outstanding. If the preferred stock was non-participating, what per cent was earned for the common stock, of which there was $10,600,000 outstanding? Par value in each case was $50 a share.

3. The outstanding stock of a corporation consists of:

Preferred *A* stock, without par value, series 1, cumulative dividends $7 per share	10,000 shares
Participating preference stock, without par value, cumulative dividends $8 per share	16,301 shares
Preferred *B* stock, without par value, non-cumulative dividends $3.50 per share	6,659 shares
Common stock without par value	198,145 shares

The participating preference stock entitles the holder to receive, among other things, participating dividends equal share for share to any dividends paid from time to time on the common stock.

If, in the course of a year, 50¢ is paid on each share of common stock, what will be the total amount of dividends paid?

11

Partnership

Definition. A partnership association is defined by Chancellor Kent as follows: "A contract of two or more competent persons to place their money, effects, labor, and skill, or some or all of them, in lawful commerce and business, and to divide the profits and bear the losses in certain proportions."

Mathematical calculations. The most important mathematical calculations in partnership accounting are concerned with:

(1) Division of profits.
(2) Division of assets upon liquidation.
(3) Calculation of goodwill.

Goodwill. The calculation of goodwill also has to be considered in connection with the other types of business organizations—namely, the individual proprietorship and the corporation—when changes in ownership, reorganizations, consolidations, and so forth, are made; see Chapter 9.

Profit-sharing agreements. Profits may be shared in many ways. A few of the most common methods of profit distribution are:

(1) Arbitrary ratios.
(2) In the ratio of capital invested at organization of business.
(3) In the ratio of capital accounts at the beginning or at the end of each period.
(4) In the ratio of average investments.
(5) Part of the profits may be distributed as salaries or as interest on capital invested, and the remainder in some other ratio.

(6) If the investment is less than the amount agreed upon, interest is charged on the shortage; and if the investment is more than the amount agreed upon, interest is credited on the excess; the resulting profit or loss is then distributed in a ratio agreed upon.

Lack of agreement. If the partners have failed to include in their articles of co-partnership an agreement as to the method by which profits are to be distributed, the law provides that the profits shall be divided equally, regardless of the ratio of the partners' respective investments.

Losses. If losses are incurred and no provision has been made for their distribution, the profit-sharing ratio governs.

Arbitrary ratio.

Example. *A* and *B* are partners. *A* has \$3,000.00 invested, while *B* has \$2,500.00 invested. *A* is to receive $\frac{2}{3}$ of the profits, and *B* is to receive $\frac{1}{3}$. The profits for the year are \$2,400.00. What is each partner's share?

Solution.

Net profits	\$2,400.00
A's share, $\frac{2}{3}$ of \$2,400.00	1,600.00
B's share, $\frac{1}{3}$ of \$2,400.00	800.00

PROBLEMS

A and *B* were partners. Gain or loss was to be divided $\frac{3}{5}$ and $\frac{2}{5}$, respectively. *A* invested \$3,500.00, and *B* invested \$2,400.00. During the year, *A* withdrew \$500.00, and *B* withdrew \$700.00. At the end of the year the books showed the following assets and liabilities:

Cash on Hand and in Bank	\$8,000.00
Inventory of Merchandise	7,500.00
Notes Receivable	790.00
Accounts Receivable	840.00
Notes Payable	4,700.00
Accounts Payable	7,240.00

(*a*) What has been the gain or loss? (*b*) What is each partner's net capital at the end of the year?

Ratio of investment.

Example.

January 1, *A*'s investment	\$10,000.00
January 1, *B*'s investment	6,000.00
January 1, *C*'s investment	4,000.00
Total	\$20,000.00
December 31, Profits	\$ 4,000.00

Profits are to be shared in the ratio of investments at the beginning of the year.

Solution.

	Investment	Ratio	Profits	Shares
A	$10,000	$\frac{10}{20}$	$4,000	$2,000
B	6,000	$\frac{6}{20}$	4,000	1,200
C	4,000	$\frac{4}{20}$	4,000	800
	$20,000	$\frac{20}{20}$		$4,000

Explanation. Add the beginning-of-year investments of the partners, and take for the numerator of the fraction representing each partner's share his investment at the beginning of the year, and for the denominator the total capital. Using these fractions, calculate the fractional parts of the net profit or loss, and these will be the partners' shares.

PROBLEMS

In each of the following, show the division of net profit or net loss, which is to be calculated in the ratio of investments:

	INVESTMENTS				
	A	B	C	NET PROFIT	NET LOSS
1.	$4,000	$4,000	$2,000	$2,500	
2.	5,000	3,000	1,500		$1,200
3.	6,000	7,500	2,500	2,000	
4.	2,000	3,500	1,500	1,400	
5.	3,500	2,500	1,000	750	

Division of profits by first deducting interest on capital.

Example.

January 1, A's investment		$10,000
January 1, B's investment		6,000
January 1, C's investment		4,000
December 31, Net profits		4,000

By agreement, each partner is to receive 5% interest on his investment (this interest to be deducted from total profits), and the balance of the profits is to be distributed equally.

Solution.

A's investment, $10,000, × .05	$ 500, interest
B's investment, 6,000, × .05	300, interest
C's investment, 4,000, × .05	200, interest
Total	$1,000

Net profits, $4,000 − $1,000 = $3,000, to be divided equally. $3,000 ÷ 3 = $1,000, each partner's share after interest is deducted.

	Interest	Profit	Total Credit
A	$500	$1,000	$1,500
B	300	1,000	1,300
C	200	1,000	1,200
Total			$4,000

PROBLEMS

Show the division of profits in each of the following:

	INVESTMENTS			NET PROFITS	RATE OF INT. ON INVESTMENT	BALANCE TO BE DIVIDED
	A	B	C			
1.	$ 8,000	$ 4,250	$ 3,700	$4,000	5%	Equally
2.	9,750	3,500	10,000	6,000	6%	Equally
3.	4,725	5,300	5,250	5,300	6%	Equally
4.	12,000	6,000	4,000	4,500	4%	$\frac{4}{7}, \frac{2}{7}, \frac{1}{7}$
5.	20,000	10,000	5,000	5,000	6%	$\frac{1}{2}, \frac{1}{3}, \frac{1}{6}$

Profits insufficient to cover interest on investment. If it is agreed that each partner is to be credited with interest on his investment, the interest must be credited to each partner, even though the total profits are not large enough to cover the credit. Any over-distribution incurred by the distribution of the interest should be divided among the partners in accordance with the agreement as to the division of profits. The same rule applies where there is a loss before interest is credited.

Example.

January	1, A's investment	$10,000
January	1, B's investment	6,000
January	1, C's investment	4,000
December 31, Business profits		700

By agreement, each partner is to receive 5% interest on his investment, and the profits are to be shared equally.

Solution.

A's investment, $10,000, × .05	$ 500, interest
B's investment, 6,000, × .05	300, interest
C's investment, 4,000, × .05	200, interest
Total interest to be credited	$1,000
Profits earned	700
Net loss	$ 300

Since the loss is to be shared equally, each partner's loss is $100.

	Credit Interest	Debit Loss	Net Credit
A	$500	$100	$400
B	300	100	200
C	200	100	100
Total			$700

PROBLEMS

Find the net credit or debit to each partner in each of the following:

	INVESTMENTS			PROFIT OR LOSS	INTEREST	BALANCE TO
	A	B	C	BEFORE INTEREST	RATE	BE DIVIDED
1.	$ 8,000	$ 8,000	$ 4,000	Profit, $ 800	6%	Equally
2.	5,000	7,000	2,000	Profit, 140	6%	$\frac{5}{14}, \frac{7}{14}, \frac{2}{14}$
3.	3,800	4,200	5,000	Loss, 200	6%	Equally
4.	10,000	7,500	5,000	Profit, 2,150	6%	$\frac{5}{9}, \frac{3}{9}, \frac{1}{9}$
5.	15,000	15,000	10,000	Profit, 2,000	6%	Equally

Adjustments of capital contribution. If the partners do not invest the agreed amounts, adjustments may be made, provided the contract so states. Partners may be charged with interest on the amount of the shortage of their investment from the agreed amount, and may be credited with interest on the excess of their investment over the agreed amount. These adjustments should be made before the profits for the period are prorated. If interest adjustments result in an over-distribution of profits, the amount over-distributed is divided in the ratio of the division of profits, unless otherwise agreed.

Example.

	Agreed to Invest	Invested
January 1, A.	$10,000	$12,000
January 1, B.	6,000	5,000
January 1, C.	4,000	2,000
December 31, Profits for the year, $3,100.		

By agreement, A is to be allowed 5% interest on his excess investment, and B and C are to be charged 5% interest on their shortages. After these adjustments have been made, profits are to be divided equally.

Solution.

A's excess, $2,000, × .05.	$100, interest	
B's shortage, $1,000, × .05.	50, interest	
C's shortage, $2,000, × .05.	100, interest	
Charge to B's account.	50	
Charge to C's account.	$100	$150
Credit to A's account.		100
Net amount of interest.		$ 50

The net amount of interest, $50, is added to net profits. Profits before distribution:

Net profits.	$3,100
Add net interest.	50
Total.	$3,150

$3,150 ÷ 3 = $1,050, each partner's share after interest adjustment.

A's $\frac{1}{3}$ profits...................	$1,050	
Add interest...................	100	$1,150, total credit of A
B's $\frac{1}{3}$ profits....................	$1,050	
Less interest...................	50	1,000, net credit of B
C's $\frac{1}{3}$ profits....................	$1,050	
Less interest...................	100	950, net credit of C
Total profits........................		$3,100

PROBLEMS

1. Prepare a statement of profit distribution from the following facts:

	A	B	C	D
Agreed investment..............	$6,000	$6,000	$8,000	$4,000
Investment.....................	7,000	6,000	6,000	2,500
Profit ratio after adjustment of 6% interest on excess or deficiency of investment..................	25%	25%	$33\frac{1}{3}$%	$16\frac{2}{3}$%

Net profits before adjustments for interest, $6,500.

2. Prepare a statement or profit distribution from the following facts:

	X	Y	Z
Agreed investment......................	$5,000	$4,500	$4,500
Investment.............................	4,000	4,000	6,000

Profits to be shared equally after adjustments for 6% interest. Profits before adjustments for interest, $600.

3. The capital of a certain organization was to be $40,000.00, of which A and B were to contribute one-half each, A to receive 55% of the profits and B to receive 45%. A, being short of funds, invested only $15,000.00, and, the firm being short of capital, B put in the balance until A could make up his shortage, with the provision that he be allowed 6% interest on the excess of his investment over the agreed amount. The profits for the year were $12,000.00. Show the distribution of profits.

Profit sharing in ratio of average investment.

First method. Multiply the original investment by the number of days or months during which the amount was in the business without change. The product may be termed Day-Dollars or Month-Dollars. The ratio of any product to the total of the products is the average capital ratio for that partner.

When the capital is changed, either by additional investment or by withdrawal, the changed capital is multiplied by the number of days or months to find its value in day-dollars or month-dollars, and for each change a new calculation is made. The ratio of the total of the day-dollars or month-dollars for each partner to the sum of the day-dollars or month-dollars for all the partners gives the ratio of each partner's investment to the total investment.

Example.

A

Debit		Credit	
Feb. 1..................	$1,000	Jan. 1..................	$10,000
June 1..................	1,500	May 1..................	4,000
Nov. 1.................	500	July 1.................	1,000

B

July 1..................	$1,000	Jan. 1..................	$ 6,000
Dec. 1..................	1,000	Aug. 1.................	4,000
		Oct. 1.................	2,000

Net profits of the business for the year were $4,530.

Solution.

A

INVESTED	MONTHS IN BUSINESS		MONTH-DOLLARS
Jan. 1, $10,000	× 1 month....................		$10,000
Feb. 1, 9,000	× 3 months...................		27,000
May 1, 13,000	× 1 month....................		13,000
June 1, 11,500	× 1 month....................		11,500
July 1, 12,500	× 4 months...................		50,000
Nov. 1, 12,000	× 2 months...................		24,000
A's month-dollars investment...........................			$135,500

B

Jan. 1, $ 6,000 × 6 months....................		$36,000
July 1, 5,000 × 1 month....................		5,000
Aug. 1, 9,000 × 2 months....................		18,000
Oct. 1, 11,000 × 2 months....................		22,000
Dec. 1, 10,000 × 1 month....................		10,000
B's month-dollars investment...........................		$ 91,000
Total month-dollars investment........................		$226,500
A's share of profits, $\frac{135,500}{226,500}$ of $4,530.............		$ 2,710
B's share of profits, $\frac{91,000}{226,500}$ of $4,530.............		1,820
		$ 4,530

If the average investment is desired, it can be found by dividing the month-dollars by 12, as:

A's month-dollars, $135,500 ÷ 12......................	$11,291.67
B's month-dollars, $91,000 ÷ 12......................	7,583.33
Total average monthly investment....................	$18,875.00

The ratios of the average monthly investments are the same as the ratios of the month-dollars investments.

Second method. Multiply each investment by the number of months from the date made until the end of the period; find the sum of the products obtained. Likewise, multiply each withdrawal by the number of months from the date withdrawn until the end of the period; find the sum of the products obtained.   Deduct the sum of the withdrawal products from the sum of the investment products; the result for each partner should be the same as the month-dollars obtained by the first method.

The example under the first method is used in the following solution.

Solution.

A

INVESTMENTS		TIME TO END OF	MONTH-
Date	*Amount*	YEAR	DOLLARS
Jan. 1	$10,000 ×	12 months =	$120,000
May 1	4,000 ×	8 months =	32,000
July 1	1,000 ×	6 months =	6,000
			$158,000

WITHDRAWALS			
Feb. 1	$ 1,000 ×	11 months =	$ 11,000
June 1	1,500 ×	7 months =	10,500
Nov. 1	500 ×	2 months =	1,000
			22,500

A's month-dollars...................... $135,500

B

INVESTMENTS			
Jan. 1	$ 6,000 ×	12 months =	$ 72,000
Aug. 1	4,000 ×	5 months =	20,000
Oct. 1	2,000 ×	3 months =	6,000
			$ 98,000

WITHDRAWALS			
July 1	$ 1,000 ×	6 months =	$ 6,000
Dec. 1	1,000 ×	1 month =	1,000
			7,000

B's month-dollars...................... $ 91,000

The distribution of the profits is the same as in the preceding example.

PROBLEMS

1. *A, B,* and *C* began business January 1.   Their accounts for the year appear as follows:

A

Jan. 1..................	$ 7,500
July 1.................	2,500

B

May 1.................. $4,000	Jan. 1................. $10,000

C

Oct. 1................ .... $7,000	Jan. 1................. $10,000
	Aug. 1................. 3,000

Their profits for the year were $3,310.   Determine the share of each partner, if profits were divided on the basis of average investment.

2. Ames and Brown engaged in the hardware business, and at the end of the first year their books showed a profit of $2,357.01. They had agreed to share profits and losses equally, after allowing 6% interest on average investment. Their investments and withdrawals for the year were:

Ames

July 1................	$ 500	Jan. 1................	$3,000
		Sept. 15..............	1,500

Brown

Sept. 15...............	$1,000	Jan. 1...............	$2,500
		July 1...............	250

Determine the net capital of each partner at the end of the year.

3. C. H. John and C. B. Arthur formed a partnership. John invested $15,000, but four months later withdrew $3,000. Arthur invested $10,000, and eight months later withdrew $2,000. Interest at 6% was to be credited on average investment; the remainder of the profits was to be distributed in proportion to original investments. The first year's profits, before interest adjustment, were $2,500. What was the net capital of each partner at the beginning of the second year?

Liquidation of partnership. Because of the nature of the association, a partnership must necessarily be terminated on or before the death of any one of the partners. It is not necessary to discuss here the various causes of dissolution, but only the problems met with at the time of settlement. The purpose of the formation of a partnership is the making of profits, and the division of losses is governed by the same general rule as the division of profits. Profits should be credited and losses should be charged before any division of assets is made. If this rule were not followed, an unfair distribution of capital would result.

When dissolution is accompanied by liquidation, each of the partners has an equal obligation to share in the work. But since it does not usually require the time of all the partners, any one of the partners, or an outsider, may liquidate the business.

In liquidation, profits or losses must first be divided in the profit or loss ratio, and the remaining capital should then be shared by the partners in the capital ratio.

In insolvency, partners must share losses in the profit and loss ratio, and not in the capital ratio. This may at times result in a deficit in capital for some one or more of the partners. Each partner with a deficit should contribute to the firm the amount of his deficit. But if he is totally unable to pay into the firm any portion of his deficit, the remaining partners must bear this loss in the profit and loss ratio.

The governing profit and loss ratio, when a partner is unable to pay, should be stated in fractions, of which the numerators are the profit-and-loss-sharing per cents of the partners with credit balances, and the denominators are the sum thereof. It is evident that it is incorrect to compute

Partnership

the loss division by multiplying the loss by the profit and loss per cents, since the full amount of the loss would not be distributed.

Methods. Liquidation may be accomplished in two ways:

(1) All the assets may be converted, all the liabilities paid, the profits or losses distributed, and all the capital divided at one time.

(2) A periodic distribution of the capital may be made before all the assets are converted.

Total Distribution. The first method of liquidation does not involve any very difficult calculations.

Example. From the following figures, show the amount of capital distributed to each partner at dissolution:

	A	B	C
Capital balances before conversion of assets.	$10,000	$6,000	$4,000
Profit ratio..............................	40%	40%	20%
Assets converted into cash..............	$30,000		
Liabilities to be paid....................	14,000		

Solution.

$$\begin{array}{ccccc} Assets & & Liabilities & & Net\ Assets \\ \$30,000 & - & \$14,000 & = & \$16,000 \end{array}$$

Total Investment, $20,000, less Net Assets, $16,000 = Loss, $4,000

	A (40%)	B (40%)	C (20%)	Total (100%)
Capital balances before conversion of assets...	$10,000	$6,000	$4,000	$20,000
Distribution of loss........................	1,600	1,600	800	4,000
Balances..................................	$ 8,400	$4,400	$3,200	$16,000
Cash distributed..........................	8,400	4,400	3,200	16,000

Periodic distribution. Periodic distribution may result from either of two causes:

(1) The desire of the partners to reduce the capital of the firm, or to completely dissolve the firm, even though it is still solvent.

(2) Forced liquidation.

As the assets are converted into cash, and the debts are paid, the balance of cash should be distributed periodically to the partners. This should be done in such a way as to reduce the accounts to the profit and loss ratio existing among the partners. The distribution is made on the assumption that all book assets may be a total loss until converted into cash.

The following example illustrates the adjustment of capital ratios to profit and loss ratios.

Example. From the following data, show the periodic distribution of the cash collected:

	A	B	C
Capital balances before conversion of assets.....................	$10,000	$6,000	$4,000
Profit ratio.....................	40%	40%	20%

First period:	
Net loss......................	$ 1,000
Cash collected...............	9,000
Assets unrealized.	10,000

Second period:	
Net loss......................	1,000
Cash collected..........	5,000
Assets unrealized.............	4,000

Third period:	
Cash collected...............	2,000
All other assets uncollectible ...	

Solution.

	A	B	C	Total
1. Capital balances before conversion of assets	$10,000	$6,000	$4,000	$20,000
2. Distribution of loss....................	400	400	200	1,000
3. Balance after distribution of loss........	$ 9,600	$5,600	$3,800	$19,000
For the purpose of making a test, it will be assumed that the unrealized assets will never be realized.				
4. Test loss in profit and loss ratio.........	(4,000)	(4,000)	(2,000)	(10,000)
5. After the test loss has been deducted, the remaining amounts will show the proper distribution of the cash balance (3 − 4).	5,600	1,600	1,800	9,000
6. Balance at the end of the first period (3 − 5)	$ 4,000	$4,000	$2,000	$10,000
7. Net loss for second period..............	400	400	200	1,000
8. Balance after distribution of loss........	$ 3,600	$3,600	$1,800	$ 9,000
The balances of the accounts are now in the profit and loss ratio.				
9. Distribution of cash....................	2,000	2,000	1,000	5,000
10. Balance at end of second period.........	$ 1,600	$1,600	$ 800	$ 4,000
11. Net loss for third period................	800	800	400	2,000
12. Balance after distribution of loss........	$ 800	$ 800	$ 400	$ 2,000
13. Cash distribution......................	800	800	400	2,000

The following example illustrates the adjustment of capital to the profit and loss ratio where a deficiency of one partner is involved.

Example. Show how each period's cash should be distributed in the following:

	A	B	C
Capital balances before conversion of assets.....................	$10,000	$8,000	$2,000
Profits to be shared equally.			

First period:	
Net loss......................	$1,500
Cash to be distributed.........	8,000

Second period:	
Net loss......................	1,500
Cash to be distributed.........	3,000

Third period:	
Remaining assets sold for.......	4,000

Solution.

	A	B	C	Total
Capital balances before conversion of assets..	$10,000	$8,000	$2,000	$20,000
First period's loss distributed...............	500	500	500	1,500
Balance after distribution of loss...........	$ 9,500	$7,500	$1,500	$18,500
Test loss of amount of the remaining assets...	(3,500)	(3,500)	(3,500)	(10,500)

It will be observed from the test loss that *C's* possible loss is $2,000 greater than his capital. If the test loss should become an actual loss, *C* will owe the firm $2,000, and if *C* should be unable to pay in this $2,000, *A* and *B* would be required to bear this additional loss.   To provide against this contingency, a further test loss charge of $2,000 is made against *A*

| and *B*................................. | (1,000) | (1,000) | 2,000 | |

When the sum of the two test losses, $4,500 ($3,500 + $1,000), is deducted from *A's* investment of $9,500, it can be seen that *A* should receive $5,000; it can also be seen that the sum of *B's* test losses deducted from his investment gives the amount of cash which is payable to him.

Cash distribution.........................	$ 5,000	$3,000		$ 8,000
Balance of capital undistributed............	$ 4,500	$4,500	$1,500	$10,500
Second period's loss distributed............	500	500	500	1,500
Balance after distribution of loss...........	$ 4,000	$4,000	$1,000	$ 9,000
Test loss of unrealized assets..............	(2,000)	(2,000)	(2,000)	(6,000)

What applied above applies again here.   *C's* account shows a possible loss, and the amount must be distributed as a test loss to be taken up by the other partners.

Test loss for *C's* account..................	(500)	(500)	1,000	
Cash distribution.........................	1,500	1,500		3,000
Balance undistributed.....................	$ 2,500	$2,500	$1,000	$ 6,000
Third period's net loss....................	667	667	666	2,000
Cash on hand.............................	$ 1,833	$1,833	$ 334	$ 4,000
Cash distributed..........................	1,833	1,833	334	4,000

The following example illustrates a return of investments and loans of partners which is complicated by the accounting principle that "loans must be paid before capital is returned to partners."

Example.

Partners	Capital Accounts	Loan Accounts	Profit Ratio
A....................	$33,000	$10,500	40%
B....................	28,500	10,000	30%
C....................	18,000	21,000	20%
D....................	10,500	18,500	10%
	$90,000	$60,000	100%

The partners have decided upon a dissolution, and after paying all their liabilities, they have:

Cash..	$ 30,000
Other assets..	110,000
Net loss..	10,000

How should the cash be distributed among the partners, assuming that no member of the firm has private property with which to repay a capital account that has been reduced by losses to a debit balance?

Solution.

	A	B	C	D	Total
Profit and loss ratio	40%	30%	20%	10%	100%
Capital balances before conversion of assets	$33,000	$28,500	$18,000	$10,500	$90,000
Loss distributed	4,000	3,000	2,000	1,000	10,000
Balance of capital	$29,000	$25,500	$16,000	$ 9,500	$80,000
Test loss of assets	(44,000)	(33,000)	(22,000)	(11,000)	(110,000)
Possible deficiency of capital	$15,000	$ 7,500	$ 6,000	$ 1,500	$30,000

By applying the possible loss of unrealized assets against capital accounts, it is found that the possible loss is greater than the capital invested.

In practice, as long as the firm has assets and owes each partner money on a loan account, a partner will generally not pay cash into the firm, since the firm would have to pay it back immediately. The problem states that none of the members of the firm has money other than that invested in the firm. As the shortages are debts due the firm, and as the partners have loan accounts, these loan accounts will undoubtedly be used as a set-off. Therefore, the shortages will be deducted as follows:

	A	B	C	D	Total
Loans by partners	$10,500	$10,000	$21,000	$18,500	$60,000
Less possible shortages	15,000	7,500	6,000	1,500	30,000
Each partner's standing in the business after distribution of the test loss	($4,500)	$ 2,500	$15,000	$17,000	$30,000

As *A*'s loan is not enough to take up the possible shortage, and as the problem states that *A* has no other property, it is necessary to distribute *A*'s test shortage to the other partners.

	A	B	C	D	Total
Ratio of distribution		$\frac{30}{60}$	$\frac{20}{60}$	$\frac{10}{60}$	
Balances after distribution of test loss	($4,500)	$2,500	$15,000	$17,000	$30,000
A's test shortage distributed	4,500	(2,250)	(1,500)	(750)	
Balances	0	$ 250	$13,500	$16,250	$30,000
Cash distribution	0	250	13,500	16,250	30,000

The accounts of the partnership now stand:

Net assets		$110,000
A's capital		$ 29,000
B's capital		25,500
C's capital		16,000
D's capital		9,500
A's loan		10,500
B's loan	$10,000	
Less payment	250	9,750
C's loan	$21,000	
Less payment	13,500	7,500
D's loan	$18,500	
Less payment	16,250	2,250
	$110,000	$110,000

PROBLEMS

1. *A*, *B*, and *C* decided to dissolve partnership.   On the basis of the following facts, show the proper distribution for each period:

	A	B	C
Capital.........................	$8,000	$4,000	$6,000
Ratios.........................	$44\frac{4}{9}\%$	$22\frac{2}{9}\%$	$33\frac{1}{3}\%$
First period:			
Net loss......................			$4,000
Assets uncollected..............			9,000
Cash.........................			5,000
Final period:			
Assets converted..............			7,000
Losses.......................			2,000

2. Show the periodic cash distribution based on the following facts:

	Capital	Loans	Ratio	
X............................	$22,000	$2,000	50%	
Y............................	8,000	3,000	$33\frac{1}{3}\%$	
Z............................	4,000	1,000	$16\frac{2}{3}\%$	
First period:				
Cash........................				$ 4,000
Assets uncollected.............				36,000
Second period:				
Cash........................				10,000
Assets uncollected.............				24,000
Loss........................				2,000
Third period:				
Cash........................				21,000
Loss........................				3,000

C. P. A. PROBLEMS

1.* The capital of a partnership is contributed as follows:

A..	$90,000
B..	45,000
C..	15,000

The partnership agreement provides for profit sharing in the following ratios:

A..	50%
B..	30%
C..	20%

The partners' salaries are as follows:

A..	$5,000
B..	3,000
C..	2,000

* C. P. A., Maryland.

At the end of the first year's business, C dies. The books are closed, and the net assets of the business are shown to be $152,500. A and B liquidate the affairs of the partnership, and distribute the surplus as follows:

First distribution...................................... $42,410.20
Second distribution.................................... 74,622.30
Final distribution..................................... 31,967.50

Prepare a statement of the partners' accounts, showing how the distribution of assets should be made and how the losses should be apportioned.

2.* A, B, C, and D enter into partnership with a capital of $100,000. A invests $40,000; B, $30,000; C, $20,000; and D, $10,000. They are to share profits or losses in the following proportions: A, 35%; B, 28%; C, 22%; and D, 15%. They are also to receive stipulated salaries chargeable to the business.

At the end of six months, there is a loss of $8,000, and meantime the partners have drawn against prospective profits as follows: A, $400; B, $600; C, $600; and D, $400.

They dissolve partnership, and agree to distribute the proceeds of firm assets monthly as realized. C and D enter other businesses, and A and B remain to wind up the firm's affairs, it being stipulated that from all moneys collected and paid over to C and D, a commission of 5% be deducted and divided equally between A and B for their services in liquidating the partnership.

The realization and liquidation lasts four months, and the transactions are as follows:

	Assets Realized	Liabilities Liquidated	Expenses and Losses on Realization, Exclusive of Commissions
First month..................	$ 30,190	$ 7,900	$ 400
Second month...............	50,300	6,100	750
Third month................	20,010	3,800	340
Fourth month..............	9,500	2,200	110
	$110,000	$20,000	$1,600

Prepare partners' accounts, showing the amount payable monthly to each partner.

3.† A, B, C, and D formed a personal-service partnership, the clientele of the firm being personal clients of the respective partners.

All fees received and all expenses were pooled by the firm, and the partnership agreement stated that the net earnings for the year were to be shared as follows:

A... $33\frac{1}{3}$%
B... 40%
C... $16\frac{2}{3}$%
D... 10%

On August 31, as a result of a dispute, a supplementary agreement covering the remainder of the year was made between the partners. This agreement provided that the distribution of net earnings was to be made on the basis of the above percentages, except that in the distribution of the net earnings for

---

* C. P. A., New York.
† American Institute Examination.

the last four months of the year, so far as C and D were concerned, a net earning was to be assumed on the basis of payment by the clients of A and B of gross fees of $175,000 and $250,000, respectively, instead of the amounts actually received from those clients.

The deficiency in A's gross fees was to be charged to him, and the excess in B's gross fees credited to him.

No adjustment for expenses was to be applicable to either the deficiency or the excess.

The net income from January 1 to August 31 was $75,000.

From September 1 to December 31, the following gross fees were received:

From clients of A	$110,000
From clients of B	290,000
From clients of C	15,000
From clients of D	25,000

The operating expenses for the last four months were $55,000.

Determine the total net income of each partner for the year, taking into account the supplementary agreement.

4.* On January 1, 19—, Adams, Burk, and Cline became partners in the operation of a dry goods business in Scranton, Pa.

At December 31 of the same year, the trial balance of the partnership, before any adjustments were made, was as follows:

Adams, capital		$ 50,000
Burk, capital		30,000
Cline, capital		20,000
Inventory of merchandise, January 1	$125,000	
Accounts receivable, customers	75,000	
Accounts receivable, employees	3,000	
Cash	6,000	
Notes payable		60,000
Accounts payable		15,000
Sales		500,000
Purchases, including freight	323,000	
Salaries and store expenses	125,000	
Bad debts written off	2,500	
Interest paid on notes payable	6,000	
Salary to Mr. Adams	2,500	
Salary to Mr. Burk	4,000	
Salary to Mr. Cline	3,000	
	$675,000	$675,000

Prepare a balance sheet as of December 31, a profit and loss statement for the year ended the same date, and a statement of the partners' accounts after the following adjustments have been made:

Interest to be credited on partners' capital at 6% per annum.

Mr. Adams owns the store, which the partnership occupies under an agreement providing for an annual rent of $10,000 payable in monthly installments in advance. No rent has been paid during the year. The year's rent should therefore be credited to Adams, together with $325 interest on unpaid monthly installments.

---

* C. P. A., Pennsylvania.

Of the interest paid on notes payable, $2,000 applies to the period subsequent to December 31; accrued taxes, $1,000; accrued wages, $1,500. A reserve of $1,500 is required to cover possible losses from doubtful accounts.

Ten per cent of the profits, if any, after the foregoing adjustments have been made, is to be credited to "Bonuses to department managers and salesmen."

The remaining profits or losses are to be apportioned to the partners as follows:

Mr. Adams... 40%
Mr. Burk.. 33⅓%
Mr. Cline... 26⅔%

5.* A partnership composed of two members divides its profits equally, after all items of income and expense for each calendar year have been determined. One of the items of income is interest on partners' withdrawals, which is calculated and charged to each partner at the end of the year. By agreement, the interest calculation is made on the partners' average monthly balances as shown by the books. Partner A's account for the calendar year 19—, before interest is charged to him, is found to be as follows:

	Debits	*Credits*
January 1, 19—, Balance.................	$ 1,080.21	$............
January account........................	6,000.00	550.00
February account.......................	2,500.00	550.00
March account..........................	3,052.74	550.00
April account..........................	13,009.81	9,550.00
May account............................	5.45	550.00
June account...........................	1,154.20	550.00
July account...........................	1,500.00	550.00
August account.........................	1,500.00	550.00
September account......................	500.00	550.00
October account........................	1,000.00	4,050.00
November account.......................	1,014.10	550.00
December account.......................	1,000.00	550.00

Show a statement of the interest which partner A should be charged at December 31, 19—; simple interest, 6% per annum.

6.† A and B are in partnership. A receives two-thirds and B one-third of the profits. On November 30, 1961, the Profit and Loss account (after interest on capital has been charged at 5%) shows a profit of $6,000. On December 1, 1960, the start of the year under audit, A had a capital of $10,000.00 in the business, and during the year he has drawn out $4,500.00. B on the same date had a capital of $8,000.00 and during the year has drawn out $1,000.00.

Make up the two capital accounts as they should appear on November 30, 1961.

7.† A, B, and C formed a partnership. A agreed to furnish $5,000, B and C each $3,500. A was to manage the business, and was to receive one-half of the profits; B and C were each to receive one-quarter. A supplied merchandise valued at $4,250, but no additional cash. B turned over to A, as manager, $4,500 cash, and C turned over $2,750. The business was conducted by A for some time, but exact books were not kept. While manager, A purchased additional merchandise amounting in all to $37,500 and made sales amounting to $50,000. The cash received and paid out for the partnership was not kept separate from *A*'s personal cash. *B* took over the management to straighten out the affairs. He found accounts receivable amounting to $10,000. Of these he collected $2,250. The remaining merchandise he sold for $250. These receipts he deposited to the firm's credit in the bank. The balance of accounts receivable proved worthless. The outstanding accounts payable amounted to $1,000, of which $750 had been incurred in purchasing merchandise, while $250 represented expenses. *B* paid these accounts.

A presented receipted claims, showing that during his management he had paid other expenses of $1,200. By mutual agreement, *B* was held to be entitled to $50 on account of interest on excess capital contributed, and *A* and *C* were each charged $37.50 for shortage of contributed capital.

(*a*) Prepare the Trading and Profit and Loss accounts and the accounts of each of the partners, including the final adjustments to be made at the close of the partnership.

(*b*) Show how the above final adjustments would be modified if *A* proved to have no assets or obligations other than those of the partnership.

8*. *A* and *B*, who are partners in a trading firm, decide to admit *C* as from January 1, 1962.

They make an agreement with *C*, as follows:

C is unable to contribute any tangible assets as his capital investment, but agrees to allow his share of the profits to be credited to his capital account until he shall have one-fifth interest. *C* is to share profits and losses to the extent of one-fifth.

C is to receive a salary of $30,000 per annum, payable monthly, in addition to his share of the profits.

The balance sheet of *A* and *B* at December 31, 1961, is as follows:

Assets		Liabilities		
Cash	$ 1,500	Accounts Payable		$ 8,000
Accounts Receivable	10,000	Capital Accounts:		
Merchandise	7,500	*A*	$10,000	
Furniture and Fixtures	1,500	*B*	5,000	
Goodwill	2,500			15,000
	$23,000			$23,000

During the six months ended June 30, 1962, the business has sustained unusual losses, and it is decided to dissolve the partnership.

The balance sheet at that date is as follows:

Assets		Liabilities		
Cash	$ 500	Accounts Payable		$12,500
Accounts Receivable	12,500	Capital Accounts:		
Merchandise	5,000	*A*	$10,000	
Furniture and Fixtures	1,500	*B*	5,000	
Goodwill	2,500			15,000
Deficit: Being loss on trading for				
6 mos	5,500			
	$27,500			$27,500

---

* American Institute Examination.

Accounts receivable were sold for $9,000, the buyer assuming all responsibility for collection and loss, if any.

Merchandise realized $6,500, and furniture and fixtures $500.

You are asked to make an examination of the accounts from January 1, and to prepare statements showing the realization of assets, the adjustment of the partnership accounts, and the distribution of funds.

In your examination, you find that C has not drawn his salary for four months, and that B has advanced to the partnership $2,500 as a temporary loan. You find that these liabilities are included in the sum of $12,500 shown as accounts payable.

C is ascertained to have no assets.

9.* A, B, and C were in partnership, A's capital being $90,000, B's $50,000, and C's $50,000. By agreement, the profits were to be shared in the following ratio: A, 60%; B, 15%; C, 25%. During the year, C withdrew $10,000. Net losses on the business during the year were $15,000, and it was decided to liquidate. It is uncertain how much the assets will ultimately yield, although none of them is known to be bad. The partners therefore mutually agree that as the assets are liquidated, distribution of cash on hand shall be made monthly in such a manner as to avoid, so far as feasible, the possibility of one partner's being paid cash which he might later have to repay to another. Collections are made as follows: May, $15,000, June, $13,000; July, $52,000. After this no more can be collected. Show the partners' accounts, indicating how the cash is distributed in each installment; the essential feature in the distribution is the observance of the agreement given above.

10.† Brown, Green, and Black engage in a soliciting business under an agreement that Brown is to receive a salary of $200 per month, Green a salary of $150 per month, and Black a salary of $100 per month; that the earnings are to be determined at any time at the request of any partner; and that the profits of the business are to be divided on the basis of the amount of business secured by each.

The partnership is in business nine (9) months, and the business record for that period is as follows:

Brown's business	$4,500.00
Green's business	2,800.00
Black's business	3,000.00

Net profits of the business amount to $5,026.50.

The partners then decide to rescind the agreement as to salaries, and to divide the profits on the basis of business secured individually, treating all salaries drawn as advances.

Drawings:

Brown	$1,600.00
Green	1,200.00
Black	900.00

You find that the following errors have occurred during the nine months:

---

* American Institute Examination.
† C. P. A., Indiana.

Office furniture charged to expense........................ $ 65.00
Accts. rec. (Green's business) worthless.................... 210.00
Cash advanced by Black—credited to his account as business
   secured... 400.00
Items not paid nor entered in the books:
   Brown's salary.............................. $200.00
   Green's salary.............................. 150.00
   Advertising................................. 27.50
   Clerk hire.................................. 130.00
   Telephone................................... 6.00
   Rent.. 50.00
   Stationery and supplies—exp................. 15.00

Show the journal entries necessary to readjust the accounts. Make up a statement of the Profit and Loss account, showing all corrections and the distribution of the profits.

11.* Brown and Green entered into a joint venture.

On May 1, 19—, they purchased 5,000 tons of coal in Philadelphia at $18 per ton, f.o.b., for which they gave notes on May 10 for one-half at 3 months and for the other half at 6 months. The coal was shipped to Mexico City on May 15, the freight, and so forth, amounting to $8,000.

A joint banking account was opened on May 10, each party contributing $10,000.

The freight was paid by check on May 20, and on May 25 a check was drawn for $1,000 for charges at Mexico City.

The coal was sold at $25 per ton, and the proceeds used to purchase a cargo of timber, which was shipped to Philadelphia. Freight and other charges thereon, amounting to $3,750, were paid by check June 30.

During July, four-fifths of the timber was sold for $110,000. This amount was received and paid into the joint account August 2.

In order to close the transaction, Brown agreed to take over the remaining one-fifth at cost price, including freight and charges, and he paid a check for this into the joint account August 10.

The first note fell due and was paid August 13, and on the same day the other note was paid under discount at the rate of 6% per annum.

Prepare accounts showing the results of the foregoing transactions; disregard interest on capital contributions.

---

* American Institute Examination.

12

Public Finance and Taxation

Governmental functions. Governmental functions are divided among three major classes of governmental units—the federal government, the fifty state governments, and thousands of local government bodies, including counties, towns, townships, cities, villages, and such special units as drainage, levee, irrigation, and park districts.

Purposes of taxes. Federal government taxes are used to pay the army and navy, the salaries of governmental personnel, pensions, and other goverment expenses such as education, highways, economic development, social welfare, and so forth. Expenses of the federal government in 1959 amounted to more than 80 billion dollars; most of this was for national defense, which cost 42 billions. The budget included over a billion dollars for aid to agriculture and a necessary item for interest on the public debt.

State government taxes are used to pay the salaries of state government personnel, the support of schools, universities and asylums and for sundry other state expenses. The largest single item in state expenditures for the states during any given year is usually for operation and maintenance, of which a sizeable proportion is for operation and maintenance of schools.

County taxes are used to pay the salaries of county employees, the cost of roads, charities, and miscellaneous other county expenses.

City taxes are used to pay the salaries of city employees, police and fire protection, support of schools, and other city expenses.

Town taxes are used to pay the salaries of town employees, support of schools, and other town expenses.

Taxes levied by special units are for the purpose of paying for and maintaining the special units.

Appropriations.   Funds deemed to be necessary for the conduct of government are set up by the respective governing bodies as appropriations.   The size of the appropriations may result from modifications in the quantity and/or quality of governmental activities and from changes in commodity prices and wage and salary levels.   To meet these appropriations, taxes are levied upon persons and property.

Kinds of taxes.   Commodity taxes may be limited in their scope, applying to particular commodities, such as taxes on tobacco, liquors, and so forth; or they may be general, applying to the manufacture and sale of all or most commodities, such as sales taxes, manufacturers' excise taxes, and so forth.

Highway taxes are best known as the motor vehicle tax or license, and the motor vehicle fuel tax known as the gasoline tax.

The general property tax and the special property taxes are the major sources of revenue for state and local governments.   The tax rate imposed on the assessed value of a piece of property is a total of a series of separate tax rates imposed by local and state governments.   Real property is listed and valued by the assessor, while personal property is usually listed by the taxpayer, who sets his own value on the articles he lists, although the assessor may change the values if investigation proves them to be incorrect.

Taxes on business consist of state bank taxes and state taxes on insurance companies, railroads, and public service enterprises such as telephone and light and power companies.   There are also state taxes on business in general in the form of license fees and franchise taxes.

Income taxes are levied on the income of both persons and business. The first income tax was a federal tax, but now most of the states have income tax laws.   The excess profits tax (repealed in 1946) is a tax on the excess profits of a corporation and is a federal tax.

Death taxes on transfer of property of a deceased person to his beneficiaries or heirs are levied by the federal government and by most of the state governments.   One form is the federal estate tax; another is the state inheritance tax.   To prevent distribution of large holdings of property in order to escape estate and inheritance taxes, the gift tax was enacted by the federal government.   Several of the states also have gift taxes.

Income, inheritance, estate, and gift taxes are complex and constitute complete studies in themselves; also, rates and regulations are frequently undergoing changes.   Therefore, these subjects will not be presented in this text.

PROPERTY TAX

Determination of tax rate.   The amount of money needed divided by the assessed valuation of the property determines the rate to be levied. For example:

State tax:
    Budget............................ $ 3,750,000
    Assessed value of property in state....... 1,250,000,000
            3,750,000 ÷ 1,250,000,000 =   .30%, State rate
County tax:
    Budget............................ $ 90,000
    Assessed value of property in county......   4,500,000
            90,000 ÷ 4,500,000   =   2.00%, County rate
City tax:
    Budget............................   75,000
    Assessed value of property in city........ 2,500,000
            75,000 ÷ 2,500,000   =   3.00%, City rate
                                                 5.30%, Total rate

To find the amount of tax. Multiply the assessed valuation by the rate. Tax rates may be expressed: as so many mills on the dollar; as a certain rate per cent; or as dollars on the thousand.

Example. Property is assessed at $8,500; the tax rate is $40.60 a thousand. Find the tax.

Solution.

                $ 40.60, rate on each thousand.
                  8.5 , number of thousands assessed.
                $345.10, the tax.

PROBLEMS

1. What is the total tax rate on the following?

    State:
        Budget.................................... $ 5,500,000
        Assessed valuation........................ 2,500,000,000
    County:
        Budget....................................   72,000
        Assessed valuation........................   6,000,000
    City:
        Budget....................................   125,000
        Assessed valuation........................   3,750,000
    School District:
        Budget....................................   35,000
        Assessed valuation........................   1,750,000

2. In a certain town the tax rate on $1,000 was as follows:

    State... $ 1.20
    County..   30.00
    Town:
        Library....................................... $1.24
        Revenue.......................................   .91
        Road and Bridge............................... 2.74
        Road Drag.....................................   .91
                                                         5.80
    School District...................................   1.00
        Total rate.................................... ....

If the assessed value of X Company's property in this town was $93,960, what was the amount of property tax?

3. If property is assessed at $6,880 and the tax rate is $100.30 a thousand, what is the tax?

4. If the tax rate is $100.30 a thousand, what is the rate per cent? What is this rate in mills on the dollar?

5. A tax rate of $99.20 a thousand is made up of the following rates:

State:
Debt	$ 7.33
Road, Bridge, and Soldiers' Relief	1.10
School	1.23
Teachers' Retirement	.04

County:
Revenue	27.09

City:
Revenue	61.41
School District	1.00
Total	

Property valued at $75,000 is assessed at $\frac{3}{5}$ of its value. What per cent of the total tax applies to each division?

6. In a certain city taxes are due January 1, but may be paid in two installments, the first on or before May 31 and the second on or before Oct. 31.

If the first half is not paid on or before May 31, the following penalties will attach: During June, 3%; July, 4%; August, 5%; September, 6%; October, 7%. During November and December, the penalty is 8% computed on any amount unpaid.

The second one-half cannot be paid until the first one-half has been paid.

If the tax rate is $96.50 a thousand, find the total tax paid on the following:
(a) Property with assessed value of $35,000, both installments paid on August 10.
(b) Property with assessed value of $7,500, the first installment paid July 15 and the second installment paid December 15.

7.* A city with an assessed valuation of $1,000,000 and estimated receipts for current expenses from miscellaneous sources of $50,000 and of $2,000 from sinking fund investments has submitted to you the following budget of expenditures for the year:

Mayor and other Commissioners	$20,000
Water Department	15,000
Bond Interest	5,000
Fire Department	20,000
Police Department	21,000
Health Department	15,000
Retirement of Bonds	10,000
Street Department	18,000
General Government	25,000

What tax levy must be made to provide the necessary revenue?

---

* C. P. A., North Carolina.

8. * The assessed valuation of the taxable property of the State of W., as determined by the Tax Commission for a certain year, was $4,068,268,534.

What would a citizen whose property was assessed at $507,374 have to pay for each of the following purposes, and what would be the amount of his total tax bill?

Purposes—Total Amount to Be Raised

Interest on Certificates of Indebtedness............. $	199,339.42
Free High Schools.................................	175,000.00
State Graded Schools..............................	200,000.00
Highway Improvements...........................	1,700,000.00
General Purposes.................................	100.00

In addition to the above, the following mill taxes are assessed:

University......................	$\frac{3}{0}$ mill
Normal Schools..	$\frac{1}{6}$ mill
Common Schools.......................................	$\frac{7}{10}$ mill

---

* Adapted from C. P. A. Examination.

PART TWO

Commercial Algebra
Compound Interest
Applications

13

Fundamentals of Algebra

Explanation. The work of an accountant is complicated in many particulars and requires technical calculations. It is extremely difficult to make some of these calculations by arithmetic. On the other hand, if the fundamentals of algebra are understood, the calculations may be made with comparative ease. Only the more common and more useful principles of algebra will be discussed in this chapter.

Symbols and terms. In algebra, the letters of the alphabet are usually employed as symbols to represent numbers.

The following signs have the same meaning in algebra as in arithmetic:

$+$ is read "plus"
$-$ is read "minus"
$\times$ is read "times" or "multiplied by"
$\div$ is read "divided by"
$=$ is read "equals"

An *exponent* is a number or symbol written at the right of another number or symbol and a little above it, to show how many times the latter is to be used as a factor and to indicate its power. For example, "25^3" = $25 \times 25 \times 25 = 15,625$. When no exponent is indicated, 1 is understood to be the exponent.

An *equation* is an expression of equality between two numbers.

An *axiom* is a statement which is admitted to be true without any proof. Algebraic operations make use of the following axioms:

(1) The equality of the two sides of an equation is not destroyed by the addition of the same number to both sides.

(2) The equality of the two sides of an equation is not destroyed by the subtraction of the same number from both sides.

(3) The equality of the two sides of an equation is not destroyed by the multiplication of both sides by the same number.

(4) The equality of the two sides of an equation is not destroyed by the division of both sides by the same number.

Positive and negative numbers. A positive or negative state of any concrete magnitude may be expressed without reference to the unit; thus, numbers that are greater than zero are positive, and numbers that are less than zero are negative.

A number which has a " $+$," or positive, sign prefixed to it is called a positive number; for example, $+5$. If a " $-$ " sign precedes the unit, it is called a negative number and is written thus: -5.

Addition of positive and negative numbers. When two or more positive and negative numbers are combined into a single number, the result is called the *sum* of the numbers.

Example.

The sum of $+6$ and -4 is $+2$.
"   "   " $+4a$ and $-2a$ is $+2a$.
"   "   " $+2$ and -6 is -4.
"   "   " $+3a$ and $-7a$ is $-4a$.
"   "   " -4 and -3 is -7.
"   "   " $-3a$ and $-4a$ is $-7a$.

From the foregoing, the following rules may be derived:

(1) To add two numbers or terms of different signs, subtract the smaller number or term from the larger, and prefix the sign of the larger.

(2) To add two negative numbers, add their absolute values and prefix the negative sign.

Example. Add $+4a$, $-3a$, $+6a$. The problem may be restated thus: $(+4a) + (-3a) + (+6a)$.

Solution.

$$
\begin{array}{r}
+\ 4a \\
+\ 6a \\
\hline
+10a \\
-\ 3a \\
\hline
+\ 7a
\end{array}
$$

The addition of positive quantities is made in the same way as in ordinary addition.

The addition of a positive and a negative number is equivalent to deducting the smaller number from the larger and retaining the sign of the larger.

PROBLEMS

Find the sum of each of the following:

1. $+4, -3, +7, -2, +6, +4, -8, -6.$
2. $-4, -8, +6, +5, -4, -3, -2, -7.$
3. $+1, -4, -6, +2, +7, +6, +4, +5.$

The coefficient. The number or letter put before a mathematical quantity, known or unknown, to show how often it is to be taken, is called the *coefficient*. In adding terms which are multiples of the same letter, add the coefficients of these terms and prefix the proper sign. Thus, $+6a, +7b, -5a, +6b$ becomes:

$$\begin{array}{ll} +6a & +\ 7b \\ -5a & +\ 6b \\ \hline \text{Added: } +\ a & +13b \end{array}$$

It is convenient to arrange the terms in columns, so that like terms stand in the same column.

PROBLEMS

Find the sum of each of the following:

1. $+4a, +3b, -4a, -2b.$
2. $+6a, +4b, -6c, +3a, -4b, +4c.$
3. $+4x, -4y, +4z, -3x, +3y, +2z.$
4. $-5x, +3y, +4z, +4x, -4y, -4z.$
5. $-x, +4x, +3x, -12x, -4x, +x.$
6. $+4x, +3x, -6x, +2x, -12x, +2x.$
7. $+4a, +3b, +3c, -4c, +4b, -a.$
8. $-a, -b, +c, +b, -c, +a, -c.$
9. $+c, +x, -z, +y, -2c, +6x, -3z.$
10. $+x^2, +2x^2, -xy, -x^2, -3x, +y.$

Hereafter, when a term is not preceded by a positive or a negative sign, it is to be understood as a positive term.

Parentheses, brackets, and braces. Parentheses, brackets, and braces are used to indicate that the part inclosed is to be employed as a single term or as a single unit.

Since the same rules apply to all signs of aggregation, in the explanation given hereafter only parentheses will be mentioned.

RULES. (*a*) When a term in parentheses is preceded by a "$+$," or positive, sign, the parentheses may be removed without any change in the signs of the inclosed terms.

(*b*) If a term in parentheses is preceded by a "$-$," or negative, sign, when the parentheses are removed it is necessary to change each of the positive and the negative signs of the terms inclosed.

Examples.

$$a + b + (c - d) = a + b + c - d$$
$$a + b - (c - d) = a + b - c + d$$
$$(a - b) + (c - d) - (e - f) = a - b + c - d - e + f$$
$$(4a + 3b - c) - (d + 4e - f) = 4a + 3b - c - d - 4e + f$$

Wherever possible, like terms should be combined, as:

$$(3a - 3b + 4c) - (2a - 3c) = a - 3b + 7c$$

If several algebraic expressions are inclosed one within the other by inclosure signs, such as parentheses or brackets, eliminate the innermost pair of inclosure signs first.

Example 1.
$$a + [b - (c - d)] = a + [b - c + d]$$
$$= a + b - c + d.$$

Example 2.

$$a + b - [- (b + c) + (c - d)] = a + b - [-b - c + c - d]$$
$$= a + b + b + c - c + d$$
$$= a + 2b + d.$$

PROBLEMS

Simplify the following by removing all signs of aggregation:

1. $x + y + (x + y) - (2x + 2y)$.
2. $3a + (b - 4c) - (4a - b - c)$.
3. $42 + (37 + 6) - (40 + 20)$.
4. $30 - [20 + (3 + 4) - (4 + 2)]$.
5. $(3x - 4y) - (6x + 2y) + (4x - 3y)$.
6. $-3a + [4b - (6c + 7a) - 5b + 6c]$.
7. $-3b^2 + 4a^2 - (2b^2 - 4a^2) + 4a$.
8. $a + b + c + d - (2a + 2b - 2c + 2c)$.
9. $-x - y - (z - x) - y - z(x + y + z)$.
10. $(8a - 4b) + (3c + d) - (3a + b + c)$.

Subtraction. *Subtraction* is the process of determining one of two numbers when their sum and one of the numbers are given.

The *minuend* is the sum of the two numbers.

The *subtrahend* is the number to be deducted.

The *remainder* is the required number.

To subtract, change the sign of the subtrahend and add the subtrahend and the minuend.

Example 1. Subtract $8x$ from $4x$.

Solution.
$$8x \text{ from } 4x = (+4x) - (+8x)$$
Removing parentheses:
$$= 4x - 8x$$
$$= -4x$$

Example 2. Deduct $-8x$ from $-4x$.

Solution.

$$-8x \text{ from } -4x = (-4x) - (-8x)$$

Removing parentheses:
$$= -4x + 8x$$
$$= +4x$$

Example 3. Deduct $-8x$ from $4x$.

Solution.

$$-8x \text{ from } 4x = (+4x) - (-8x)$$

Removing parentheses:
$$= 4x + 8x$$
$$= +12x$$

To subtract algebraic expressions having two or more terms, change the sign of each term of the subtrahend and proceed as in addition.

Example. Subtract $3a - 5c - 3d$ from $7c - 16a - 2d$.

Solution. The changing of the signs of the subtrahend is usually done mentally; thus,

$$\begin{array}{r} -16a + 7c - 2d \\ 3a - 5c - 3d \\ \hline -19a + 12c + d \end{array}$$

PROBLEMS

Subtract:

1. $17x$ from $28x$.
2. $13x$ from $3x$.
3. $16a$ from $-18a$.
4. $-6a$ from $18a$.
5. $a + 2a$ from $8a - 3a$.
6. $4a - 3b$ from $3a + 4b$.
7. $16a - 14b + 3c$ from $-13a + 2b - 4c$.
8. $-16a + 4b + 2c$ from $18a - 14b + 3c$.
9. $3cs - 5bz$ from $-6cs + 7bz$.
10. $3p + 4q$ from $4p - 4q$.

Multiplication. When two or more numbers are multiplied, the result is called the *product* of the numbers.

When two numbers with like signs, either positive or negative, are multiplied, the product is positive.

Examples.

$$(+a) \times (+b) = +ab$$
$$(-a) \times (-b) = +ab$$
$$(-4) \times (-4) = +16$$

When two numbers with unlike signs are multiplied, the product is negative.

Examples.

$$(+a) \times (-b) = -ab$$
$$(+4) \times (-3) = -12$$

The exponent to be used in the product is equal to the sum of the exponents appearing in the multiplier and the multiplicand.

Examples.

$$(a)^1 \times (a)^1 = a^2$$
$$(a^4) \times (-a^3) = -a^7$$
$$(-3a^2) \times (-2a^3) = +6a^5$$

PROBLEMS

Multiply the following:

1. a^2 by a^2.
2. a^3 by a^6.
3. $-a^3$ by a^4.
4. ab by ab.
5. a^2 by b^2.
6. $a + b + c$ by 5.

7. $3a + 100$ by 6.
8. $3(a + b)$.
9. $1,000 + s - b$ by 6.
10. $(100 - c) - b$ by 4.
11. $[20,000 - (2,000 + x)]$ by $12\frac{1}{2}$.
12. $[40,000 - (T - B - 2,000)]$ by 12.

Division.   *Division* is the process of finding one of two numbers when the other number and the product of the two numbers are given. When the dividend and the divisor have like signs, either positive or negative, the quotient is a positive number.

Examples.

$$ab \div a = b$$
$$-ab \div -b = a$$
$$-14 \div -7 = 2$$

When the dividend and the divisor have unlike signs, the quotient is a negative number.

Examples.

$$-ab \div a = -b$$
$$ab \div -b = -a$$
$$-10 \div 5 = -2$$
$$10 \div 5 = 2$$

The exponent to be used in the quotient is equal to the difference between the exponent in the dividend and the exponent in the divisor.

Examples.

$$a^7 \div a^2 = a^5$$
$$-ab^2 \div b = -ab$$
$$8a^6b^4 \div -2ab^3 = -4a^5b$$
$$20^5 \div 20^2 = 20^3$$

PROBLEMS

Divide the following:

1. 63 by 9.
2. -40 by 8.

3. -125 by -5.
4. $48a$ by $12a$.

5. a^2b by a.
6. $9a^2$ by $3a$.
7. $5a^2 - 60b$ by 5.
8. $50a^{10} - 25a^{15}$ by 5.

9. $20,000 - (2,000 - 5x)$ by 5.
10. $1,600 - (200 + 4x)$ by 4.
11. $60a^{28} - 30a^{24} + 15a^{20}$ by $15a^5$.
12. $72a^8 - 18a^{10} - 54a^6$ by $9a^2$.

EQUATIONS

Simple equations. An *equation* is an expression of equality between two magnitudes or operations. The members of the equation are separated by the sign of equality, " $=$," which means "is equal to." Either member of an equation may contain numerals, letters, or both. A *simple equation* is an equation of the first degree and contains but one unknown.

Example.

Simple equation: $\qquad\qquad x = 50$
Or: $\qquad\qquad\qquad 10x = 500$

If the same number is added to or subtracted from both sides of an equation, the equality is not destroyed.

Examples.

Simple equation: $\qquad\qquad\qquad x = 50$
Adding 10 to each side: $\qquad x + 10 = 60$
Simple equation: $\qquad\qquad\qquad 10x = 500$
Subtracting 10 from each side: $10x - 10 = 490$

If both sides of an equation are multiplied by or divided by the same number, the equality is not destroyed.

Example 1.

$$3x = 15$$
Multiplied by: $\qquad\qquad\qquad\quad 5$
$$\overline{15x - 75}$$
Simplifying, or dividing by 15: $\quad x = 5$

Example 2.

$$4)\overline{20x = 40}$$
Divided by 4: $\qquad\qquad\quad 5x = 10$
Simplifying, or dividing by 5: $\quad x = 2$

Any term of either member of an equation may be transposed from one side to the other by changing the sign of the term, and the equality of the two sides of the equation is not destroyed. This operation is equivalent to either adding the same quantity to or subtracting the same quantity from both sides of the equation.

Example 1.

Simple equation: $\qquad\qquad\quad 10x - 10 = 490$
Transposing the " -10 " to
the right side of the equation, and changing the
sign: $\qquad\qquad\qquad\qquad\qquad 10x = 490 + 10$
Or: $\qquad\qquad\qquad\qquad\qquad\qquad 10x = 500$

Example 2.

Simple equation: $\qquad\qquad\qquad x + 5 = 15$
Transposing: $\qquad\qquad\qquad\qquad x = 15 - 5$
Or: $\qquad\qquad\qquad\qquad\qquad\qquad x = 10$

Example 3.

Solve the equation, $10x - 14 = 6x + 2$.

Solution.

The equation: $\qquad\qquad\qquad 10x - 14 = 6x + 2$
Transposing " $6x$ " to the
left side, and changing
the sign to " $-$ ": $\qquad\quad 10x - 6x - 14 = +2$
Transposing " -14 " to
the right side, and
changing the sign: $\qquad\quad 10x - 6x = 14 + 2$
Uniting similar terms: $\qquad\qquad\quad 4x = 16$
Dividing by 4: $\qquad\qquad\qquad\quad x = 4$

Verification

	Left side		*Right side*
	$10x = \quad 40$		$6x = 24$
	$-14 = -14$		$2 = \quad 2$
Adding:	$\overline{26}$	Adding:	$\overline{26}$

Therefore, the two sides of the equation are equal, and $x = 4$.

PROBLEMS

In the following equations, solve for the unknown quantities, and check your results:

1. $40x - 20 = 10x + 10$.
2. $10x + 5 = 25$.
3. $8a + 8 = 2a + 32$.
4. $16 + 5a = 8a + 1$.
5. $49b - 4 = 37b + 8$.

6. $2x + 6(4x - 1) = 98$.
7. $39 + 4(a + 6) = 8a - 1$.
8. $2,000 - (5x + 500) = 2,500$.
9. $8b - 5(4b + 3) = 1 - 4(2b - 7)$.
10. $18y - (10y - 8) = 20y - (6y + 4)$.

Example. How can 90 be divided into two parts in such a way that one part will be four times the other?

Solution.

Let:	x = the smaller part
Then:	$4x$ = the larger part
Adding:	$5x = 90$
Dividing each member of the equation by 5:	$x = 18$, the smaller part
	$4x = 72$, the larger part

Example. How many dimes and cents are there in $2.40, if there are 60 coins in all?

Solution.

Let:	x = the number of dimes
Then:	$60 - x$ = the number of cents
Therefore:	$10x$ = the value of the dimes
But:	$60 - x$ = the value of the cents
Simplifying:	$10x + 60 - x = 240$
Transposing:	$9x = 180$
	$x = 20$, or there are 20 dimes
	$60 - x = 40$, or there are 40 cents

Verification

$$\begin{aligned} 20 \text{ dimes} &= \$2.00 \\ 40 \text{ cents} &= \quad .40 \\ \hline 60 \text{ coins} &= \$2.40 \end{aligned}$$

Example. The P. Q. Company wrote off depreciation on its building, which cost $50,000, at the rate of 2% of the original cost per annum. This amount was included in the General Administration Expense account and constituted $\frac{1}{10}$ of that account.

The purchases cost two and one-half times the old inventory. The value of the old inventory was twice the amount of the selling expense. The Selling and General Administration Expense accounts each equalled 10% of the sales. The new inventory was valued at an amount equal to the selling expense.

The interest and discount costs were $\frac{1}{5}$ of the selling expense. Set up a profit and loss statement showing the net profit from operations.

Solution.

$$\$50,000 \times 2\% = \$1,000, \text{ Depreciation}$$
$$\$1,000, \text{ Depreciation} = \tfrac{1}{10} \text{ of General Adm. Expense}$$

Multiplying by 10:
$$\$1,000 \times 10 = \$10,000 = \text{General Adm. Expense}$$
$$\$10,000 = \text{Selling Expense}$$
$$\text{Selling Expense} = \tfrac{1}{10} \text{ of Sales}$$

Multiplying by 10:
$$\$10,000 \times 10 = \$100,000, \text{ or Sales}$$
$$2 \times \$10,000 = \$20,000, \text{ or Old Inventory}$$
$$2\tfrac{1}{2} \times \$20,000 = \$50,000, \text{ Purchases}$$
$$\tfrac{1}{5} \text{ of } \$10,000 = \$2,000, \text{ Interest and Discount}$$

The P. Q. Company
PROFIT AND LOSS STATEMENT
DECEMBER 31, 19—.

Sales...		$100,000
Cost of Sales:		
Old Inventory.............................	$20,000	
Purchases................................	50,000	
Total.................................	$70,000	
Less New Inventory........................	10,000	60,000
Gross Profit.................................		$ 40,000
Selling Expense..............................	$10,000	
General Administrative Expense................	10,000	20,000
Operating Profit.............................		$ 20,000
Interest and Discount........................		2,000
Net Profit...................................		$ 18,000

PROBLEMS

1. How can 640 be divided into two parts in such a way that one part will be seven times the other?

2. How many quarters and cents are there in $4.00, if there are 40 coins in all?

3. A sum of money, $10.00, is made up of dimes and quarters, the total number of coins being 88.   How many dimes and quarters are there?

4. In a certain dairy, the ice cream contains 14% cream.   If the mixture is to be made from coffee cream of 20% butter fat and milk which tests 4%, what portion of each will have to be used in a mixture of 100 lbs.?

5. How many pounds of coffee worth 65¢ per pound must a grocer mix with other coffee worth 92¢ per pound to make a mixture worth 74¢ per pound? The total quantity desired is 50 lbs.

6. Barnes has $6,000 invested in 5% bonds.   How much must he invest in 8% stock to make his average net income 6%?

7. An estate of $33,120 was to be divided among the mother, three sons, and three daughters.   The mother was to receive four times as much as each son, and each son three times as much as each daughter.   How much was each to receive?

8. In the making of candy, a mixture of 75% sugar at 10¢ per pound and 25% corn syrup at 4¢ per pound is used.   If the price of sugar advances to 14¢ per pound, what must be the ratio of sugar and corn syrup to be used, if the cost of production is to remain the same?

9. A vinegar manufacturer makes various grades of vinegar, ranging from 50% to 100% pure cider vinegar.   How much 100% pure cider vinegar must be mixed with 63% pure to make 100 gallons of 75% pure?

10. How much milk with a butter fat test of 3.5% must be mixed with milk testing 4.65% to fill 75 quart bottles which are to test 3.95%?

Fractions. In many accounting problems it is necessary to use simple fractions in algebraic form, such as "$\frac{1}{10}$ of x" or "$\frac{4}{5}$ times a," which when simplified are written $\dfrac{x}{10}$ or $\dfrac{4a}{5}$.

Example. Divide 129 into two parts, in such a way that $\frac{2}{9}$ of one part will equal $\frac{3}{8}$ of the other.

Solution.

Let: x = one part

Then: $129 - x$ = the other part

The problem states that:
$$\frac{2x}{9} = \frac{3}{8}(129 - x)$$

The common denominator of the fractions, as seen by inspection, is 72, and by the process of changing the fractions to a common denominator, the result is:
$$\frac{16x}{72} = \frac{27}{72}(129 - x)$$

Multiplying each side of the equation by 72, to clear the equation of the fractions, the result is:
$$16x = 27(129 - x)$$

Eliminating the parentheses: $16x = 3{,}483 - 27x$

Transposing: $43x = 3{,}483$

Dividing by 43: $x = 81$

$$129 - x = 48$$

Verification

$\frac{2}{9}$ of 81 = 18

$\frac{3}{8}$ of 48 = 18

Example. The superintendent of a certain plant was hired under a contract which provided that he was to receive 10% of the net profits of the business as a salary, after his salary had been deducted as an expense. The profits for the year were \$13,200. Compute the superintendent's salary.

Solution.

Let: s = the amount of salary

The problem is stated: $s = \frac{1}{10}(\$13{,}200 - s)$

Clearing of fractions by multiplication: $10s = \$13{,}200 - s$

Transposing: $11s = \$13{,}200$

Dividing by 11: $s = \$1{,}200$

Verification

Net Profits... $13,200
Less Salary.. 1,200
$12,000
Dividing by 10... 1,200

Clearing of complex fractions. To clear an equation of a complex fraction, multiply the opposite term of the equation by the denominator of the complex fraction, and solve the resulting equation by the usual methods.

Example. Find the value of $(1.06)^{10}$ in the following equation:

$$\frac{1 - \frac{1}{(1.06)^{10}}}{.06} = \$7.3600871$$

Solution.

STEPS

$$\frac{1 - \frac{1}{(1.06)^{10}}}{.06} = \$7.3600871$$

Multiplying right-hand
term by .06: $\quad 1 - \dfrac{1}{(1.06)^{10}} = 7.3600871 \times .06 \quad$ (1)

Clearing: $\quad 1 - \dfrac{1}{(1.06)^{10}} = .4416052 \quad$ (2)

Transposing and changing
signs: $\quad \dfrac{1}{(1.06)^{10}} = 1 - .4416052 \quad$ (3)

Clearing: $\quad \dfrac{1}{(1.06)^{10}} = .5583947 \quad$ (4)

Changing and dividing: $\quad (1.06)^{10} = 1 \div .5583947 \quad$ (5)
Clearing: $\quad (1.06)^{10} = 1.790847 \quad$ (6)

PROBLEMS

1. One-half of a certain number exceeds one-sixth of the same number by 8. What is the number?

2. Find the value of $(1.05)^{10}$ in the following complex fraction:

$$\frac{1 - \frac{1}{(1.05)^{10}}}{.05} = 7.72173.$$

3. Find the value of $(1.03)^{15}$ in the following complex fraction:

$$\frac{(1.03)^{15} - 1}{.03} = 18.598913.$$

4. Find the value of $(1.04)^{20}$ in the following:

$$\frac{1}{\dfrac{1 - \dfrac{1}{(1.04)^{20}}}{.04}} = .0735818$$

5. Find the value of $(1.005)^{48}$ in the following:

$$\frac{1 - \dfrac{1}{(1.005)^{48}}}{.005} = 42.5803178.$$

Simultaneous equations with two or more unknowns. When each of two equations contains two or more unknown quantities, and every equation containing those unknowns may be satisfied by the same set of values for the unknown quantities, the equations are said to be simultaneous.

The value of the unknown quantities in two or more simultaneous equations may sometimes be found by combining the equations into a single equation containing only one unknown quantity.

This combining may be done in several different ways, and is known as *elimination*.

The method of elimination by addition and subtraction is probably the most simple, and will therefore be the one used here.

It is often necessary to multiply one, or sometimes both, of the equations by a number that will make the terms that contain one of the unknowns in each equation of equal absolute value. Substitute known values where possible.

Add or subtract the resulting equations, and the sum or remainder will be an equation containing one unknown less than the previous equations.

The chief difficulty in the practical application of these rules is the expression of the unknowns in the form of equations. It seems advisable to make a written statement of each condition, equation, or unknown, and also a similar statement of each of the knowns.

After each statement, a symbol or letter should be used to represent each unknown or known. In algebra, the letters "x," "y," and "z" are commonly used, but it seems to be more practical to use the initial letter of the name of the thing whose value is to be found.

Example 1. Carol has five times as much money as Mary. Together they have $60. How much money has each?
 Statement of equations:

$$M = \text{the number of dollars belonging to Mary}$$
$$C = 5M, \text{ or five times as much as belongs to Mary}$$
$$M + C = \$60$$

Solution.

Substitution of $5M$ for C: $M + 5M = 60$
Combining: $6M = 60$
Dividing by 6: $M = 10$
                                  $C = 5M$, or \$50

Example 2.   It cost \$98.50 to manufacture and sell a certain article.   The cost of the labor was equal to the cost of the material used.   The cost of the overhead was \$9.50 more than the expenses.   The overhead and expenses totaled \$2.50 more than the material.   Find the cost of each item.
    Statement of equations:

		STEPS
	$M = $ Cost of Material	*(1)*
	$L = $ Cost of Labor	*(2)*
	$O = $ Cost of Overhead	*(3)*
	$E = $ Cost of Expenses	*(4)*
$M + L + O + E = $ \$98.50		*(5)*

Solution.

$$M = L \qquad\qquad\qquad\qquad\qquad\qquad\qquad\qquad (6)$$
$$O = E + \$9.50 \qquad\qquad\qquad\qquad\qquad\qquad (7)$$
$$M = O + E - \$2.50 \qquad\qquad\qquad\qquad\quad (8)$$
$$M = E + \$9.50 + E - \$2.50 \qquad\qquad (9)$$
$$M = 2E + \$7.00 \qquad\qquad\qquad\qquad\qquad (10)$$
$$M = 2E + \$7.00 \text{ in terms of } E \qquad (11)$$
$$L = 2E + \$7.00 \;\text{“}\quad\text{“}\quad\text{“ “}\qquad (12)$$
$$O = E + \$9.50 \;\text{“}\quad\text{“}\quad\text{“ “}\qquad (13)$$
$$E = E \qquad\quad\text{“}\qquad\text{“}\quad\text{“ “}\qquad (14)$$

Adding *(11)*, *(12)*, *(13)*, and *(14)*: $M + L + O + E = 6E + \$23.50$ *(15)*
Substituting: \$98.50 $= 6E + \$23.50$ *(16)*
Transposing: $6E = \$98.50 - \$23.50$ *(17)*
Dividing by 6: $E = \$12.50$ *(18)*

    Substituting in *(11)*, *(12)*, and *(13)*, the value of each of the remaining items may be found.

Example 3.   In the following simultaneous equations, solve for the values of a and b:

	STEPS
$10a - 6b = 38$	*(1)*
$14a + 8b = 4$	*(2)*

Solution.

Multiplying *(1)* by 7: $70a - 42b = 266$ *(3)*
Multiplying *(2)* by 5: $70a + 40b = 20$ *(4)*
Subtracting *(4)* from *(3)*: $-82b = 246$ *(5)*
Dividing by 82: $-b = 3$ *(6)*
Or: $b = -3$ *(7)*
Substituting the value of b in *(1)*: $10a + 18 = 38$ *(8)*
Transposing 18 in step *(8)*: $10a = 20$ *(9)*
Dividing by 10: $a = 2$ *(10)*

Example 4.   The following are the condensed balance sheets of three companies who wish to know their true worth as of December 31:

	Company A	Company B	Company C
Assets, exclusive of intercompany investments..........................	$200,000.00	$500,000.00	$300,000.00
Investment in Company B (50%).......	350,000.00		
" " Company C (20%).......	250,000.00		
" " Company C (20%).......		100,000.00	
" " Company A (10%).......			100,000.00
	$800,000.00	$600,000.00	$400,000.00
Capital Stock........................	$500,000.00	$400,000.00	$300,000.00
Surplus.............................	300,000.00	200,000.00	100,000.00

As each company owns stock in each of the others, there are three unknown quantities. The true worth may be found as follows:

Solution.

Summary of Ownership

	Net Assets	Company A	Company B	Company C
Company A owns........	$200,000.00		50%	20%
Company B owns........	500,000.00			20%
Company C owns........	300,000.00	10%		

Let: A = Net Worth of Company A
Let: B = Net Worth of Company B
Let: C = Net Worth of Company C

Statement of equations:

$$A = 200,000 + \tfrac{1}{2}B + \tfrac{1}{5}C$$
$$B = 500,000 + \tfrac{1}{5}C$$
$$C = 300,000 + \tfrac{1}{10}A$$

Solution.

			STEPS
	$A - \tfrac{1}{2}B - \tfrac{1}{5}C =$	200,000.00	(1)
	$B - \tfrac{1}{5}C =$	500,000.00	(2)
	$-\tfrac{1}{10}A \quad\quad + C =$	300,000.00	(3)
Adding:	$\tfrac{9}{10}A + \tfrac{1}{2}B + \tfrac{3}{5}C =$	1,000,000.00	(4)
Multiplying (4) by 10:	$9A + 5B + 6C =$	10,000,000.00	(5)
Multiplying (2) by 5:	$+ 5B - C =$	2,500,000.00	(6)
Subtracting (6) from (5):	$9A \quad + 7C =$	7,500,000.00	(7)
Multiplying (3) by 7:	$-\tfrac{7}{10}A + 7C =$	2,100,000.00	(8)
Subtracting:	$9\tfrac{7}{10}A =$	5,400,000.00	(9)
Multiplying (9) by 10:	$97A =$	54,000,000.00	(10)
Dividing by 97:	$A =$	556,701.03	(11)
Using (3) and substituting the value of $-\tfrac{1}{10}A$:	$-55,670.10 + C =$	300,000.00	(12)
Transposing:	$C =$	355,670.10	(13)
Using (2) and substituting the value of $-\tfrac{1}{5}C$:	$B - 71,134.02 =$	500,000.00	(14)
Transposing:	$B =$	571,134.02	(15)

Verification

	A	B	C	Total
Assets, exclusive of inter-company investments...	$200,000.00	$500,000.00	$300,000.00	
A owns: $\frac{1}{2}$ of B..........	285,567.01			
$\frac{1}{5}$ of C..........	71,134.02			
Total worth of A..........	$556,701.03			$ 556,701.03
B owns: $\frac{1}{5}$ of C..........		71,134.02		
Total worth of B........		$571,134.02		571,134.02
C owns: $\frac{1}{10}$ of A..........			55,670.10	
Total worth of C........			$355,670.10	355,670.10
Total value of the three companies..............				$1,483,505.15

PROBLEMS

1. For a certain piece of advertising, the total cost of printing, envelopes, and postage is $14.50. The envelopes cost $1.50 more than the postage. The cost of printing is $0.50 more than the combined costs of postage and envelopes. Find the separate costs.

2. At the end of the year, the books of the Blank Company showed a net profit of $12,247.50. The treasurer was to receive $12\frac{1}{2}\%$ of the net profits as a bonus. The treasurer defaulted, and it was found that his account was short $4,847.55. Show: (*a*) the true profit; and (*b*) the treasurer's account balance.

3. A man has $7,000 invested at 5%. How much must he invest at $6\frac{1}{2}\%$ to make his total income equal to 6% on his total investment?

4. In a gallon of a certain kind of paint there are equal parts of pigment and oil. How much oil must be added to a gallon of this paint to make a paint of $\frac{2}{5}$ pigment and $\frac{3}{5}$ oil?

5. A merchant made 25% on his capital the first year, excluding his salary. He withdrew $1,800 for his personal expenses, and had $9,153.13 left. Find the amount of his investment.

6. A certain candy contains 40% corn syrup and 60% sugar. The syrup costs 2¢ per pound and the sugar 5¢ per pound. If sugar advances to 6¢ and the cost of the syrup is unchanged, in what proportions must the ingredients of the mixture be used in order to keep the cost the same?

7. A and B were partners, and agreed to share profits in proportion to the capital invested. The profits were $20,000. A owned a $\frac{2}{5}$ interest plus $4,000, and his share of the profits was $9,000. What was the value of the business and the capital of each partner?

8. The audited statements of a company show the following: The cash is $2,400 more than the expenses. The accounts receivable equal twice the amount of cash less $8,000. The cash and the accounts receivable together exceed the expenses by $10,000. Find the amount of cash, accounts receivable, and expenses.

9. The following is the balance sheet of the B. Company:

Assets			*Liabilities*	
Cash.........................	$	200	Accounts Payable............	$ 5,000
Accounts Receivable..........		2,500	Capital Stock...............	10,000
Plant and Equipment.........		18,000	Surplus or Net Profits........	13,200
Officers' Accounts:				
President Smith............		3,000		
Treasurer Brown............		4,500		
		$28,200		$28,200

By agreement, the president was to receive, in lieu of salary, 15% of the net profits, and the treasurer was to receive 10% of the net profits. Both the deductions were to be included in expenses.

The treasurer, who was not bonded, has disappeared, and you are now requested to state the amount of Smith's and of Brown's accounts and also the true amount to be credited to surplus.

10. You are requested to find the value, for consolidated purposes, of the following balance sheets, all as of the same date:

	A	B	C
Assets, other than stock............	$400,000	$200,000	$200,000
Stock in B Company..............	60,000		20,000
Stock in C Company..............	60,000	20,000	
Deficit...........................		40,000	
	$520,000	$260,000	$220,000
Liabilities.......................	$200,000	$160,000	$ 40,000
Capital Stock..................	300,000	100,000	100,000
Surplus.	20,000		80,000
	$520,000	$260,000	$220,000

The investments in stock were at par and cost, there being neither surplus nor deficit at the date of purchase.

11. Three companies agree to consolidate, and each agrees to accept its pro rata share in the capital stock of the new corporation, D. Corporation D is formed with 500,000 shares of no par value stock.

A

Total Assets..............	$ 750,000	Total Liabilities..........	$ 125,000
		Capital Stock.............	500,000
		Surplus...................	125,000
	$ 750,000		$ 750,000

B

Total Assets..............	$1,000,000	Total Liabilities..........	$ 375,000
		Capital Stock.............	375,000
		Surplus...................	250,000
	$1,000,000		$1,000,000

C

Total Assets..............	$1,750,000	Total Liabilities..........	$ 550,000
		Capital Stock.............	1,000,000
		Surplus...................	200,000
	$1,750,000		$1,750,000

Stock Ownership

	A	B	C
A owned..		15%	15%
Current at....................................		$50,000	$150,000
B owned..	15%		10%
Current at....................................	$75,000		$ 37,500
C owned..	5%	5%	
Current at....................................	$25,000	$30,000	

What percentage of the capital stock of Corporation D will each incorporator receive, and what will be the book value of each company's interest in Corporation D?

PROBLEMS

1. A corporation wishes to create an insurance fund equal to 25% of the net profits after deduction of the insurance fund and of the manager's bonus of 10% of the profits, the bonus and the insurance fund both to be considered as expenses. The profits are $47,250. Find the amount of the bonus, the insurance fund, and the balance to be carried to surplus.

2. The assets and liabilities of two companies are as follows:

	Smith Company	Jones Company
Assets, exclusive of intercompany investments...	$360,000	$320,000
Due from Jones Company.....................	20,000	
Due from Smith Company....................		80,000
Deficit.......................................	100,000	160,000
	$480,000	$560,000
Liabilities, exclusive of intercompany investments	$400,000	$540,000
Due to Jones Company.......................	80,000	
Due to Smith Company.......................		20,000
	$480,000	$560,000

Both companies having failed, you are required to state how many cents on the dollar each firm can pay.

3. Three companies, M, N, and O, agree to consolidate. Their balance sheets show assets as follows:

$$M: \text{Other assets, } \$ \ 425,000 + 10\%N + 15\%O$$
$$N: \text{Other assets, } \ \ \ 462,500 + 15\%M + 15\%O$$
$$O: \text{Other assets, } \ 1,145,000 + 12\tfrac{1}{2}\%M + 5\%N$$

What are the assets of each company?

14

Logarithms

Uses of logarithms. The use of logarithms greatly simplifies the multiplying and dividing of numbers, the raising of numbers to powers, and the finding of the roots of numbers. The possibility of such simplification is illustrated by the following:

$$5^2 \times 5^4 = 5^{2+4} = 5^6 \text{ and } 5^8 \div 5^3 = 5^{8-3} = 5^5$$

Two powers of 5 are multiplied by adding their powers or exponents and are divided by subtracting their powers or exponents. If all positive numbers were expressed as powers of 5, therefore, multiplication could be replaced by an addition, and division could be replaced by a subtraction. This is the basis of the use of exponents or, as they are called, *logarithms*, in computation.

DEFINITION: *The logarithm of a number to a given base is the exponent indicating the power to which the base must be raised to equal the given number.*

Since $3^4 = 81$, 4 is the logarithm of 81 to the base 3. If $b^l = n$, then l is the logarithm of n to the base b. Instead of $b^l = n$, an alternative notation is $\log_b n = l$, which is read: *the logarithm of* n *to the base* b *is* l. Thus, the following alternative forms are indicated:

$$10^3 = 1,000 \qquad \log_{10} 1,000 = 3$$
$$2^3 = 8 \qquad \log_2 8 = 3$$
$$10^4 = 10,000 \qquad \log_{10} 10,000 = 4$$
$$10^5 = 100,000 \qquad \log_{10} 100,000 = 5$$

225

The working rules of logarithms.   Since a logarithm is simply an exponent, the rules of operation with logarithms are furnished by the laws of exponents in algebra.   In the following table, the four working rules of logarithms are summarized and the law of exponents from which each is derived is indicated.

Let $X = a^x$, $Y = a^y$.

	OPERATIONS	LAWS OF EXPONENTS	RULES OF LOGARITHMS
i	Multiplication	$XY = a^x \cdot a^y = a^{x+y}$	$\log_a (XY) = \log_a X + \log_a Y$
ii	Division	$X/Y = a^x/a^y = a^{x-y}$	$\log_a (X/Y) = \log_a X - \log_a Y$
iii	Raising to a power	$X^n = (a^x)^n = a^{nx}$	$\log_a (X^n) = n \log_a X$
iv	Taking a root	$\sqrt[n]{X} = X^{\frac{1}{n}} = (a^x)^{\frac{1}{n}} = a^{\frac{1}{n}x}$	$\log_a (\sqrt[n]{X}) = \frac{1}{n} \log_a X$

Proof of working rules.

Let $X = a^x$, then $\log_a X = x$

" $Y = a^y$, " $\log_a Y = y$

i) $$XY = a^x \cdot a^y = a^{x+y}$$

Therefore, $\log_a XY = x + y = \log_a X + \log_a Y$.

ii) $$X/Y = a^x/a^y = a^{x-y}$$

Therefore, $\log_a X/Y = x - y = \log_a X - \log_a Y$.

iii) $$X^n = (a^x)^n = a^{nx}$$

Therefore, $\log_a (X^n) = nx = n \log_a X$.

iv) $$\sqrt[n]{X} = X^{\frac{1}{n}} = (a^x)^{\frac{1}{n}} = a^{\frac{1}{n}x}$$

Therefore, $\log_a (\sqrt[n]{X}) = \frac{1}{n} x = \frac{1}{n} \log_a X$.

These working rules are so important that the student should be able to express them in words as well as in symbols.

i) The logarithm of a product is the sum of the logarithms of the factors.

ii) The logarithm of a quotient is the logarithm of the upstairs minus the logarithm of the downstairs.

iii) The logarithm of a number raised to the nth power is n times the logarithm of the number.

iv) The logarithm of the nth root of a number is $\frac{1}{n}$ times the logarithm of the number.

These working rules permit us to express the logarithm of a quantity which involves products, quotients, powers, and roots of numbers in terms of the logarithms of the separate numbers.

$$\log_a \frac{XY}{Z} = \log_a X + \log_a Y - \log_a Z$$
$$\log_{10} (1.06)^{15} = 15 \log_{10} (1.06)$$
$$\log_{10} [(1.05)^{-5}(1.07)^8] = 8 \log_{10}(1.07) - 5 \log_{10} (1.05)$$

PROBLEMS

1. Write the following statements in logarithmic notation:

$$2^4 = 16, \ 4^2 = 16, \ 3^5 = 243, \ 10^2 = 100, \ \sqrt{100} = 10,$$
$$\sqrt[3]{27} = 3, \ a^0 = 1, \ a^1 = a.$$

2. Write the following statements in exponent notation:

$$\log_2 8 = 3, \ \log_5 125 = 3, \ \log_{10} 1,000 = 3$$
$$\log_{16} 10 = 1, \ \log_a 1 = 0, \ \log_{10} \sqrt{10,000} = 2$$
$$\log_{10} \sqrt[3]{1,000,000} = 2.$$

3. Evaluate:

$$\log_{10} 100, \ \log_{10} \sqrt{100}, \ \log_{10} 100^2, \ \log_3 81, \ \log_5 625, \ \log_9 9,$$
$$\log_4 64.$$

4. Express as simply as possible in terms of sums and differences of logarithms:

$$\log_{10} (1.05)^{20}, \ \log_{10} \frac{(1.05)^{15}}{.05}, \ \log_{10} (1.06)^{-15},$$

$$\log_{10} \frac{(1.06)^{-15}}{.06}, \ \log_{10} [(1.045)^{10}(1.06)^8], \ \log_{10} [(1.06)^8(1.05)^{-8}]$$

Common logarithms. Any positive number different from 1 could be used as the base of a system of logarithms. There is great advantage in using 10, however, as base. This produces the system known as the *common* or *Briggs'* system of logarithms.

Whenever, in writing the logarithm of a number, the base is omitted, base 10 will be understood. Thus, "log 25" means "$\log_{10} 25$."

To see the advantage of base 10, write the successive-positive integral powers of 10 and their logarithms in the following fashion:

$10^0 = 1$	$\log 1 = 0$
$10^1 = 10$	$\log 10 = 1$
$10^2 = 100$	$\log 100 = 2$
$10^3 = 1,000$	$\log 1,000 = 3$
$10^4 = 10,000$	$\log 10,000 = 4$
$10^5 = 100,000$	$\log 100,000 = 5$

The logarithms given here are integers; but if a number lies between two successive numbers in the list, the logarithm of that number is not an integer.   Thus, 73 lies between 10 and 100, and therefore log 73 lies between 1 and 2.   It is 1.863323.   Similarly, 7300 lies between 1,000 and 10,000, and therefore log 7300 lies between 3 and 4.   It is 3.863323.

The logarithm of any number, therefore, in general consists of two parts.   The whole-number part, or integral part, is called the *characteristic*.   The decimal fraction part is called the *mantissa*.

If the number is 1 or more but less than 10, the characteristic of its logarithm is 0.

If the number is 10 or more but less than 100, the characteristic of its logarithm is 1.

If the number is 100 or more but less than 1,000, the characteristic of its logarithm is 2.

If the number is 100,000 or more but less than 1,000,000, the characteristic of its logarithm is 5.

This produces the following rule:

If N *is greater than 1, then the characteristic of log* N *is one less than the number of digits preceding the decimal point in* N.

PROBLEMS

Write the characteristics of the logarithms of the following numbers:

1. 32	**6.** 32.3
2. 320	**7.** 32.00067
3. 1,000,006	**8.** 9.3456
4. 5673	**9.** 872.00002
5. 92734	**10.** 10,000.25

Now write the negative integral powers of 10 and their logarithms in the following fashion:

$$10^0 = 1 \qquad\qquad \log 1 = 0$$
$$10^{-1} = .1 \qquad\qquad \log .1 = -1$$
$$10^{-2} = .01 \qquad\qquad \log .01 = -2$$
$$10^{-3} = .001 \qquad\qquad \log .001 = -3$$
$$10^{-4} = .0001 \qquad\qquad \log .0001 = -4$$
$$10^{-5} = .00001 \qquad\qquad \log .00001 = -5$$

It can be seen that, if a number N lies between 1 and .1, then log N lies between 0 and -1.   We can look at log N in two ways, then:

log $N = 0 -$ a decimal fraction, or log $N = -1 +$ a decimal fraction.

For example, log $.73 = 0- .136677$ or log $.73 = -1 + .863323$.

We shall arbitrarily establish the rule:

> *The mantissa of the logarithm of a number will always be positive.*

Therefore, we shall always use the second way of looking at log .73. In order to make the rule explicit, we shall write: log .73 = $\bar{1}$.863323, which stands for log .73 = $-1 + 8.63323$ and is read "bar 1.863323."

Similarly, .073 lies between .1 and .01, and therefore log .073 lies between -1 and -2. It is $\bar{2}$.863323 in our notation. Similarly, numbers between .01 and .001 have logarithms of the form $\bar{3}$................. Thus, log .0073 = $\bar{3}$.863323.

If the number is .1 or more but less than 1, the characteristic of its logarithm is $\bar{1}$.

If the number is .01 or more but less than .1, the characteristic of its logarithm is $\bar{2}$.

If the number is .001 or more but less than .01, the characteristic of its logarithm is $\bar{3}$.

If the number is .000001 or more but less than .00001, the characteristic of its logarithm is $\bar{6}$.

This produces the following rule:

> *If N is positive and less than 1, the characteristic of log N is negative and its numerical value is one more than the number of zeros between the decimal point and the first non-zero digit of N.*

PROBLEMS

Write the characteristics of the logarithms of the following numbers:

1. .45
2. .0045
3. .03009
4. .000027

5. 200.003
6. .600003
7. 3.1412
8. .000000327

It has been determined that the characteristic of the logarithm of any positive number can be written at sight. It is sufficient, then, to tabulate the mantissa:

If   log 125 = 2.096910,
then   log 125000 = log (125)(1,000) = log 125 + log 1,000
                        = 2.096910 + 3 = 5.096910.

Hence, log 125 and log 125000 differ only in their characteristics. This reasoning is quite general and leads to the conclusion:

> *If two numbers have the same sequence of digits and differ only in the positions of their decimal points, the logarithms of the two numbers have the same mantissa.*

Examples of Numbers and Their Complete Logarithms

(Characteristic and Mantissa)

log	1235.	= 3.09167
"	123.5	= 2.09167
"	12.35	= 1.09167
"	1.235	= 0.09167
"	.1235	= $\bar{1}$.09167
"	.01235	.= $\bar{2}$.09167
"	.001235	= $\bar{3}$.09167

The table given in Appendix III of this book is called a *six-place* table. This means that the mantissas as given are accurate to the sixth place. However, it does not necessarily follow that by the use of a six-place table calculations can be performed accurately to the sixth place. Tables of logarithms accurate to six, eight, or even ten places are sometimes used, but the six-place table is sufficient for ordinary purposes. If the accountant has many computations involving large numbers, he should procure a more extended table.

How to use a table of logarithms.

For numbers of one significant figure. Table 12 shows only the mantissa of each logarithm. If it is desired to find the mantissa of a number such as 2, 20, 200, 2,000, or of any number whose only significant figure is 2, it is necessary to turn to the table and in the column at the left, headed "*N*," run down the line until the number 200 is reached. To the right of this number, in the column headed "0," the mantissa .301030 is found. This is the mantissa for the logs of 2, 20, 200, or .2, .02, .002, and so forth. The mantissa for, any other number of one significant figure may be found in a similar manner. In order to obtain the complete logarithm of a number it is necessary to supply the characteristic. The characteristic of the log of 2 is 0. Hence, the complete logarithm of 2 is 0.301030.

For numbers of two significant figures. If it is desired to find the logarithm of a number containing two significant figures—as, 17, 170, or 1.7—it is necessary to look in the column at the left of the table, headed "*N*," and run down the column until 170 is reached. In the column to the right of 170, headed "0," the mantissa .230449 is found. Keep in mind that this is the mantissa for the logs of 17, 170, 1,700, and so forth.

For numbers of three significant figures. Assume that the logarithm of 118 is desired. In the left-hand column of the table, headed "*N*," find the number 118. To the right of this number, in the column headed "0," the mantissa .071882 is given. This, of course, is the mantissa for the logs of 118, 1.18, 11,800, and so forth. In the foregoing illustrations, the mantissa only was found. By the rules previously given, the characteristic of the log of 118 is ascertained to be 2. Therefore, the logarithm of the number 118 is 2.071882.

For numbers of four significant figures. To illustrate: It is required to find the logarithm of 1,648. Find the number 164 at the left of the table, in the column headed "*N.*" On the horizontal line to the right of 164, in the column headed "8," the mantissa found is .216957. The characteristic for the log of 1,648 is 3. The complete logarithm of 1,648 is 3.216957.

Interpolation for numbers of five or more significant figures. The logarithm of a number of five or more significant figures may be found by the process of interpolation. This method is based upon the assumption that the differences of the mantissas are proportional to the differences of the numbers given. This proportion is not strictly exact, for the differences really grow smaller as the mantissas themselves grow larger. However, the results obtained deviate only slightly from the true results, and are sufficiently accurate for most purposes.

Example. Find the logarithm of 131,525.

Solution.

$$100 \begin{cases} 25 \begin{cases} \log 131500 = 5.118926 \\ \log 131525 = \end{cases} d \\ \log 131600 = 5.119256 \end{cases} .000330$$

$$\therefore \frac{d}{.000330} = \frac{25}{100}$$

$$\therefore d = \tfrac{1}{4}(.000330) = .0000825$$

Thus, log 131525 = 5.118926 + .000082 = 5.119008.

PROBLEMS

Find the logarithms of the following (express your answers in the form: "log 118 = 2.071882"):

1. 4	6. 5	11. 1.127	16. .82378
2. 20	7. 82	12. 1,275	17. .03264
3. 30	8. 775	13. 1,482	18. .000382
4. .06	9. 827	14. 739.82	19. 1.00375
5. 25	10. 8.37	15. 68,439	20. 2.48765

To find a number when the logarithm is given. If the above process of finding the logarithm from a number is reversed, the number can easily be found from the logarithm. This process is called finding the antilogarithm. It is necessary first to find the digits of the number, and this must be done from the mantissa. If the mantissa can be found in the table, take the digits corresponding to the mantissa, and point off these digits decimally as indicated by the characteristic.

Example. Find the number whose logarithm is 0.281033.

Solution. In the table, the mantissa, .281033, is found in the vertical column headed "0," opposite the number 191. This indicates that the sequence of digits, ignoring possible initial or final zeros, is 191. Using the characteristic for the correct placing of the decimal, the number is found to be 1.91.

To find a number whose mantissa is not in the table. If the mantissa is not given in the table, it is necessary to reverse the process of interpolation.

Example. Find the number whose logarithm is 5.119008.

Solution.

$$100 \begin{cases} d \begin{cases} \log 131500 = 5.118926 \\ \log \quad X \quad = 5.119008 \end{cases} .000082 \\ \log 131600 = 5.119256 \end{cases} .000330$$

$$\therefore \frac{d}{100} = \frac{.000082}{.000330}$$

$$\therefore d = \frac{82}{330}(100) = 24.9$$

$$\therefore X = 131500 + 24.9 = 131524.9$$

PROBLEMS

Find the numbers whose logarithms are:

1. 1.658011	**8.** 3.624076	**15.** $\bar{3}$.432488
2. 2.711807	**9.** 5.638988	**16.** 7.363048
3. 0.681241	**10.** $\bar{2}$.675432	**17.** 4.637540
4. $\bar{1}$.672098	**11.** 1.800236	**18.** 2.682085
5. 2.707570	**12.** $\bar{2}$.172019	**19.** $\bar{1}$.463794
6. $\bar{1}$.698970	**13.** $\bar{1}$.003891	**20.** 3.390791
7. 2.681784	**14.** $\bar{1}$.176091	**21.** 1.844334

The use of logarithms in computation. The four working rules provide the means of using logarithms for computing products, quotients, powers, roots, and combinations of these operations. Thus, if we wish to find a product, we take the logarithms of the factors and add these logarithms together. We then find from the tables what number has this sum for logarithm. Similar statements can be formulated for the other operations.

Multiplication by logarithms.

Example 1. Multiply 635 by 22.

Solution.
$$
\begin{aligned}
\text{Let } N &= (635)(22) \\
\log 635 &= 2.802774 \\
\log \ 22 &= 1.342423 \\
\therefore \log N &= 4.145197
\end{aligned}
$$

In the table, the mantissa .145196 is found to correspond to the digits 1397. The characteristic 4 indicates that the product N has five digits preceding its decimal point.

$$\therefore N = 13,970$$

Example 2. Compute $N = 497.2 \times 0.4256$.

Solution.

$$\log 497.2 = 2.696531$$
$$\log 0.4256 = \overline{1}.629002$$
$$\log N = \overline{2.325533}$$

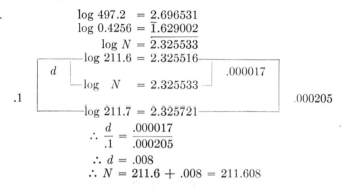

$$\therefore \frac{d}{.1} = \frac{.000017}{.000205}$$
$$\therefore d = .008$$
$$\therefore N = 211.6 + .008 = 211.608$$

PROBLEMS

Multiply:

1. 25 by 25
2. 42 by 37
3. 240 by 381
4. 762 by 431
5. 42.5 by 49.2
6. 34.7 by 1.42
7. 1,430 by .249

8. 1.43 by .032
9. 1,480 by .138
10. 92.7 by 8.75
11. 3.39 by 8.92
12. 9.293 by 48.67
13. 143.9 by 1.478
14. 1.278 by 3.84

15. 145.3 by 6.296
16. .003 by .002
17. 100.05 by 100.25
18. 47.2 by 200
19. .999 by 647.2
20. 3.8 by 4.9

Division by logarithms.

Example 1. Divide 875 by 37.

Solution.

$$\text{Let } N = \tfrac{875}{37}$$
$$\log 875 = 2.942008$$
$$\log 37 = 1.568202$$
$$\log N = \overline{1.373806}$$

$$\begin{array}{c}
\rule{0pt}{0pt}\\
\log 23.64 = 1.373647 \\
d \quad \log N = 1.373806 \quad .000159 \\
.01 \qquad\qquad\qquad\qquad .000184 \\
\log 23.65 = 1.373831
\end{array}$$

$$\therefore \frac{d}{.01} = \frac{.000159}{.000184}$$
$$\therefore d = .008$$
$$\therefore N = 23.64 + .008 = 23.648$$

Example 2. Evaluate $N = \dfrac{269}{239000}$.

Solution.
$$\log 269 \quad = 2.429752$$
$$\log 239000 = 5.378398$$
$$\log N = \overline{3}.051354$$

$$\log .001125 = \overline{3}.051153$$
$$d$$
$$\log \quad N \quad = \overline{3}.051354 \quad\quad .000201$$
$$.000001$$
$$\log .001126 = \overline{3}.051538 \quad\quad .000385$$

$$\therefore \frac{d}{.000001} = \frac{.000201}{.000385}$$
$$\therefore d = .0000005$$
$$\therefore N = .001125 + .0000005 = .0011255$$

Example 3. Evaluate $N = \dfrac{14200}{.000191}$.

Solution.
$$\log 14200. \quad = 4.152288$$
$$\log .000191 = \overline{4}.281033$$
$$\therefore \log N \quad = \overline{7}.871255$$
$$N = 74,345,000 \text{ (correct to five significant places)}$$

PROBLEMS

Divide:

1. 128 by 64
2. 2,160 by 150
3. 344 by 8
4. 93 by .31
5. 649.4 by 24.3
6. 8.42 by 2.48
7. .3472 by 124

8. 2.486 by 3.45
9. .6843 by 89
10. 9.278 by 12.43
11. 6 by 2
12. 89 by 47
13. 2.1 by 48
14. 3.875 by 238.7

15. 1.425 by 892.7
16. 147.25 by 9,276
17. .03 by 6,000
18. .0125 by 3,427
19. 1.005 by 927.8
20. 2.4255 by 384.275
21. 6,497.8 by 2.874

Powers of numbers.

Example 1. Evaluate $N = 26^4$.

Solution.
$$\log 26 = 1.414973$$
$$4 \log 26 = 5.659892$$
$$\therefore \log N = 5.659892$$
$$\therefore N = 456,975$$

Example 2. Find $N = (.025)^5$.

Solution.
$$\log .025 = \overline{2}.397940$$
$$5 \log .025 = \overline{9}.989700$$
$$\therefore \log N = \overline{9}.989700$$
$$\therefore N = .00000000976562$$

PROBLEMS

Find the value of:

1. 5th power of 25
2. 4th power of 35
3. 5th power of 2
4. 7th power of 1.25

5. 4th power of 2.47
6. 3rd power of 575
7. 9th power of 4
8. 12th power of 7

9. 12^3
10. 14^2
11. $9,200^6$
12. 18^3

13. 147^2	**16.** 146^5	**19.** 30^3
14. $.015^2$	**17.** $.07^2$	**20.** 27^4
15. 8.92^3	**18.** $.97^5$	**21.** 9^5

Roots of numbers.

Example 1.   Evaluate $N = \sqrt[3]{875}$.

Solution.
$$\log 875 = 2.942008$$
$$\tfrac{1}{3} \log 875 = 3\overline{|2.942008} = 0.980669$$
$$\therefore \log N \ = 0.980669$$
$$\therefore N \ = 9.5646$$

Example 2.   Evaluate $N = \sqrt[4]{.125}$.

Solution.
$$\log .125 = \overline{1}.096910$$
$$\tfrac{1}{4} \log .125 = 4\overline{|\overline{1}.096910} = 4\overline{|\overline{4} + 3.096910} = 1.774228$$
$$\therefore \log N \ = \overline{1}.774228$$
$$\therefore N \ = .59460$$

PROBLEMS

Find the value of the following to five significant places:

1. Square root of 64.	**8.** 10th root of 10.	**15.** $\sqrt[3]{42^2}$.
2. Square root of 97.	**9.** $\sqrt[3]{125}$.	**16.** $\sqrt[3]{19^2}$.
3. Square root of .64.	**10.** $\sqrt[10]{1}$.	**17.** $\sqrt{9 \times 97}$.
4. Cube root of 81.	**11.** $\sqrt[3]{3.89}$.	**18.** $\sqrt[3]{\frac{47}{929}}$.
5. Cube root of .081.	**12.** $\sqrt[5]{89.27}$.	**19.** $506 \times \sqrt[4]{40}$.
6. 6th root of 49.	**13.** $\sqrt{.9643}$.	**20.** $3.87^2 \times \sqrt[3]{\frac{1}{2}}$.
7. 7th root of 750.	**14.** $\sqrt[10]{2980}$.	**21.** $\sqrt[5]{225} \times \sqrt[10]{781}$.

Combination of working rules.

Example.   Evaluate $N = \dfrac{231.24 \times (1.05)^4}{(1.06)^5 \times \sqrt{(1.05)}}$.

Solution. $\log N = \log 231.24 + 4 \log 1.05 - 5 \log 1.06 - \tfrac{1}{2} \log 1.05$

In carrying out the operations indicated in this line, it is advisable to make a skeleton of the whole solution before looking up any logarithms.   The skeleton and the completed solution are both outlined below.

$\log 231.24 \ =$ $\log 1.05 \ =$ $4 \log 1.05 \ =$ _____ $=$ $\log 1.06 \ =$ $5 \log 1.06 \ =$ $\log 1.05 \ =$ $\tfrac{1}{2} \log 1.05 \ =$ _____ $=$ _____ $\log N \ =$ $N \ =$	$\log 231.24 \qquad = 2.364007$ $\log 1.05 = 0.021189$ $4 \log 1.05 \qquad = 0.084756$ $\qquad\qquad\qquad\qquad = 2.448763$ $\log 1.06 = 0.025306$ $5 \log 1.06 \qquad = 0.126530$ $\log 1.05 = 0.021189$ $\tfrac{1}{2} \log 1.05 \qquad = .010595$ $\qquad\qquad\qquad\qquad = .137125$ $\log N = 2.311638$ $N = 204.9$

PROBLEMS

1. Compute the value of $\dfrac{2.715 \times \sqrt{0.7125}}{0.04720 \times 1.432}$.

2. Evaluate $(1.05)(1.07)^4 \, (1.06)^{-6}$.

3. Find $\sqrt{\dfrac{23.2}{(1.07)^2}}$.

4. Find $27.50(1.045)^{20}$.

5. Compute the value of $\sqrt{(0.07654)^3}$.

The slide rule. This is an old device, yet it is used to only a limited extent by accountants in general. It has been described as "logarithms on a stick." In its simple form, this mechanical device consists of a grooved base rule into which a slide rule is fitted. A third part is the runner. The graduations on the upper part of the base and slide are called "upper scale," while those on the lower part of the base and slide are called "lower scale." These graduations are for different purposes, and because of the different requirements they are graduated differently.

Use of slide rule. The slide rule is used either to check figures or for original calculations. It may be used to check or compute any operation involving multiplication, division, raising to powers, or extracting of roots. It has a great many applications in business, although it is generally considered as a device used only by engineers.

The slide rule should appeal to the accountant as a device which may be carried in the pocket or the brief case; its weight is negligible.

Accuracy of calculations made by the slide rule. It is possible, after having attained proficiency in the handling of the slide rule, to obtain results in which the margin of error will not be more than one-quarter of 1%. This is satisfactory for most business problems. As in logarithms, when the slide rule is used, the digits are taken from the left to the right of a number, regardless of the value of the number. The slide rule is as nearly accurate in the calculation of decimal numbers as it is in the calculation of whole numbers of large denominations. It will give correct answers of two places, and if careful computations have been made, a three-place solution of a good degree of accuracy may be expected. If extreme care is used in the computation of a problem, an answer of four places may be had with a fair degree of accuracy. Of course, a long and carefully graded slide rule will give better results than either a short or a carelessly graded rule.

Theory of the slide rule. The theory of the slide rule is indicated very roughly in the following simple example and illustration.

Example. Find the sum of 4 and 6.

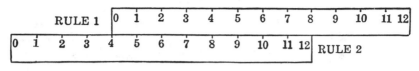

RULE 1 | 0 1 2 3 4 5 6 7 8 9 10 11 12

0 1 2 3 4 5 6 7 8 9 10 11 12 | RULE 2

Fig. 14-1.

Solution. Above are two ordinary rulers, set opposite each other. To find the sum of 4 and 6, perform the following steps:

(1) Set the "0" on Rule 1 over the "4" on Rule 2.
(2) Observe the figure "6" on Rule 1.
(3) On Rule 2, immediately below the "6" on Rule 1, will be found "10"— the sum of 4 and 6.

The process of subtraction may be shown as follows.

Example. Find the difference between 9 and 4.

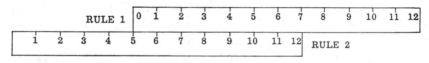

RULE 1 | 0 1 2 3 4 5 6 7 8 9 10 11 12

1 2 3 4 5 6 7 8 9 10 11 12 | RULE 2

Fig. 14-2.

Solution.

(1) Locate the subtrahend "9" on Rule 2.
(2) On Rule 1, locate the minuend "4," and place it immediately over the subtrahend "9" on Rule 2.
(3) On Rule 2, the number immediately below the "0" on Rule 1 will be the remainder, which in this case is 5.

The foregoing examples show that addition and subtraction of small numbers can be performed on two ordinary rulers. The principle of the slide rule is similar.

On the common slide rule, the graduations are made according to logarithms. Hence, if any two numbers on the slide rule are added, the result obtained is the sum of two logarithms.

The addition of the logarithms of numbers results in multiplication of the numbers; and the subtraction of the logarithms of numbers results in division of the numbers.

How to learn to use the slide rule. Practice is without doubt the only efficient method of learning how to use the slide rule. If possible, a slide rule should be obtained for use in this chapter. If, however, a slide rule is not available, a cardboard model may be made for practice. Care must be used to have the markings as accurate as possible, in order to obtain fair results. A model such as the following can be used very conveniently for the practice material.

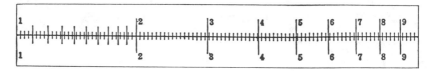

Fig. 14-3.

Reading the slide rule. In reading the numbers, go over the rule from left to right, as follows: 1, 2, 3 . . . 10; then, beginning at 1 again and calling it 10, read 10, 20, 30 . . . 100; then, again beginning at 1 and calling it 100, read 100, 200, 300 . . . 1,000. It is possible to do this because the mantissa for 10 is the same as that for 100, 1,000, and so on.

It will be noticed in Figure 4 that the spaces decrease from left to right. These decreases should correspond exactly to the differences between the logarithms from 1 to 10. Assume that you divide your model rule into 1,000 equal parts. Then, since log 2 = .301, the 2 would be placed at the 301st graduation. Log 3 = .477; therefore, 3 would be placed at the 477th graduation. Log 4 = .602; therefore, 4 would be placed at the 602nd graduation. Similarly, 5 would be placed at the 698th; 6 at the 778th; 7 at the 845th; 8 at the 903rd; and 9 at the 954th.

Marks can be put in to show the mantissas for the logarithms of 1.5, 2.5, 3.5, and so on, but they will not be half the distance between the previous graduations because log 1.5 is 0.176, and this is not half the difference between log 1 and log 2.

It will be noticed that the distance from 1 to 2 is divided into 10 divisions. These are read from left to right, like telephone numbers, thus: one-one, one-two, one-three, and so forth, to one-nine; then 2. These are understood as 1.1, 1.2, 1.3, and so forth. Consulting the table of logarithms for the logs of 110, 120, 130, and so forth, we find that the marks will be placed at the following graduations: 41, 79, 113, 146, 176, 204, 230, 255, and 278.

Construction of model slide rule. Obtain a piece of cardboard $12\frac{1}{2}$ inches long and 1 inch in width. Rule a line midway along the full length, and mark it off in graduations of one-eighth inch. This will make a measure with 100 graduations instead of 1,000, but for the purpose of this work, it will be satisfactory.

Since log 2 = .301, mark 2 at 30.1
log 3 = .477, mark 3 at 47.7
log 4 = .602, mark 4 at 60.2
log 5 = .698, mark 5 at 69.8

log 6 = .778, mark 6 at 77.8
log 7 = .845, mark 7 at 84.5
log 8 = .903, mark 8 at 90.3
log 9 = .954, mark 9 at 95.4

Between 1 and 2 are 1.1, 1.2, 1.3, . . . 1.9, as previously explained.

Since log 1.10 = .041, mark at 4.1
log 1.20 = .079, mark at 7.9
log 1.30 = .113, mark at 11.3
log 1.40 = .146, mark at 14.6
log 1.50 = .176, mark at 17.6
log 1.60 = .204, mark at 20.4
log 1.70 = .230, mark at 23.0
log 1.80 = .255, mark at 25.5
log 1.90 = .278, mark at 27.8

For closer graduations, you will find that you can make 10 indentations with a sharp pin in a one-eighth-inch space. By carefully counting the points placed, you can use the full logarithm and make a fairly accurate slide rule.

Having completed the graduations, cut the cardboard lengthwise on the medial line. This will give two pieces with measurements exactly the same. These two measures may now be used as Rule 1 and Rule 2 in the following simple problems.

Multiplication on the slide rule. Add the logarithms of the numbers to be multiplied.

Example. Multiply 2 by 3.

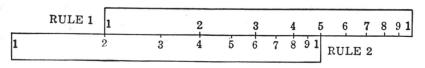

Fig. 14-4.

Solution.

(1) Locate "2" on Rule 2.
(2) Place "1" on Rule 1 over "2" on Rule 2.
(3) Locate "3" on Rule 1.
(4) Read the number on Rule 2 immediately below, which is "6."

PROBLEMS

Multiply:

1. 2 by 4. **2.** 3 by 4. **3.** 2 by 5. **4.** 3 by 2. **5.** 4 by 2. **6.** 3 by 3.

If the problem is of such a nature that the rules cannot be operated by placing the left-hand "1" on Rule 1 over the number on Rule 2, it is necessary to use the right-hand "1" on Rule 1.

Example. Multiply 4 by 5.

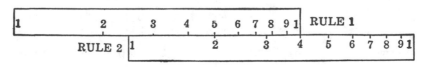

Fig. 14-5.

Solution.

(1) Locate "4" on Rule 2.
(2) Place "1" on Rule 1 over "4" on Rule 2, so that the "5" on Rule 1 is over Rule 2. In this case it is necessary to use the "1" on the right-hand side of Rule 1.
(3) Read the number immediately under "5" on Rule 1, which is "2." "2" may be either 2., .2, .02, 20, 200, or any other number in which the left-hand digit is "2." In this case the number can be determined by inspection to be 20.

PROBLEMS

Multiply:

1. 5 by 8. **2.** 4 by 5. **3.** 3 by 10. **4.** 20 by 20. **5.** 40 by 5. **6.** 2 by 30.

Division on the slide rule. Subtraction of logarithms results in the division of the numbers.

Example. Divide 9 by 6.

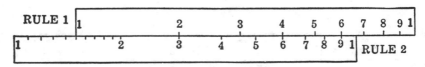

Fig. 14-6.

Solution.

(1) Locate "9" on Rule 2.
(2) Place "6" on Rule 1 over "9" on Rule 2.
(3) Read on Rule 2 immediately below "1" on Rule 1. As the "1" is over the 5th graduation on Rule 2, the digits will be 15, and by inspection the answer is determined to be 1.5.

PROBLEMS

Divide:

1. 6 by 2. **4.** 6 by 4. **7.** 35 by 7. **10.** 95 by 5.
2. 8 by 4. **5.** 9 by 4. **8.** 25 by 5. **11.** 18 by 12.
3. 5 by 2. **6.** 64 by 8. **9.** 12 by 4. **12.** 36 by 18.

Another type of problem is that of multiplying two or more numbers and dividing their product by another number.

Example. $8 \times 9 \div 4 = ?$

Solution.

(1) Set Rule 1 so that the "1" on the right is over "8" on Rule 2.
(2) Read the number immediately under "9" on Rule 1, which is "72."
(3) Set "4" on Rule 1 over "72" on Rule 2.
(4) Read the number on Rule 2 immediately under "1" on Rule 1, and the answer is found to be 18.

PROBLEMS

Solve the following by the use of the slide rule:

1. $16 \times 6 \div 32$
3. $35 \times 35 \div 5$
5. $37 \times 19 \div 13$
7. $8 \times 14 \div 12$
2. $20 \times 40 \div 8$.
4. $45 \times 12 \div 8$.
6. $44 \times 34 \div 27$.
8. $4 \times 7 \div 200$.

The following problems illustrate some of the practical applications of the slide rule.

PROBLEMS

1. *Payroll calculation.* Brown's time card for a particular day showed the following:

Job No.	Time H	Time M
12	3	30
21	2	10
32		50
45	1	30
	8	00

If Brown was paid $1.54 an hour, what was the labor cost chargeable to each job?

2. *Prorating expense.* The power cost of a small plant is to be distributed to the departments on the basis of horsepower hours, as follows:

Dept. A...	45 horsepower
Dept. B...	35 horsepower
Dept. C...	90 horsepower
Dept. D...	20 horsepower
Dept. E...	5 horsepower
Dept. F...	5 horsepower
Total...	200 horsepower

The total power cost was $450. What was the cost of power in each department?

3. The air fare from X to Y is $40. The traveler goes over three divisions of airway, respectively 380, 230, and 190 miles in length. Find the amount of the fare to be apportioned to each division.

4. An article that cost $25 is sold for $50 less 20%. Find the per cent of gain on the cost. Find the per cent of gain on the selling price.

5. Given:

Sales. $500
Cost of Goods Sold.   300
Selling Expenses.   75
General Expenses.   50
Profit. . . . .

What per cent of the sales is each item?

6. Work the following:

	Cost	% on Selling Price	Selling Price
(a)	$ 5.00	20	....
(b)	8.00	40	....
(c)	12.00	25	....
(d)	20.00	20	....
(e)	16.00	30	....

7. The list price of an article is $25, less 10% and 5%.   Find the net cost.

8. Find the interest on $600 at 5% for 3 years 6 months.

9. A field is 40 rods wide and 80 rods long.   How many acres does it contain?

10. Find the cost of 80 items at $1.50 a dozen.

15

Graphs and Index Numbers

Charts and graphs. Charts and graphs are becoming increasingly popular as a means of presenting the results of accounting and mathematical computations. Accountants, credit men, production managers, sales managers, advertising men, and general business executives are realizing more and more how greatly graphic charts may help them in their work. The reason is obvious. Long rows of figures must be thoroughly studied if the relations between quantities are to be grasped. This is a tedious task. On the other hand, pages of valuable data may be presented on a simple chart that will convey more real information than the most elaborately written report. It is necessary, however, to distinguish between important and unimportant data. Furthermore, a method of presentation must be chosen that will convey a correct impression, for it is quite possible to prepare misleading charts from correct data. Two important points must, therefore, be borne in mind:

(1) The selection of the data;
(2) The selection of the design.

Circle chart. This type of chart is used extensively for popular presentation, and is designed to exhibit the true proportions of the component parts of a group total. It is adapted to such purposes as exhibiting the distribution of disbursements, the sources of receipts, and the allocation of appropriations in government finance.

The circle with sectors, however, is not so desirable a form of presentation as the bar chart, described in later paragraphs, since the circle chart does not possess the same degree of flexibility. With a circle chart it is impossible, for instance, in a profit and loss analysis, to exhibit a loss.

243

Moreover, it does not always permit a convenient arrangement of captions, which must sometimes be written in at an angle.   Another disadvantage is that the figures are not easily compared.   For these reasons, it is probably best to limit the circle chart to the illustration of facts which are not intended to be compared from period to period.   However, the sector method is so widely used that it is perhaps better understood generally than any other.

The circle is segmented on the basis of 100°, not 360°, as geographic circles are segmented.   The reason is that the chart circle is designed to exhibit a percentage scale.

Example.   Distribution of the expense dollar.

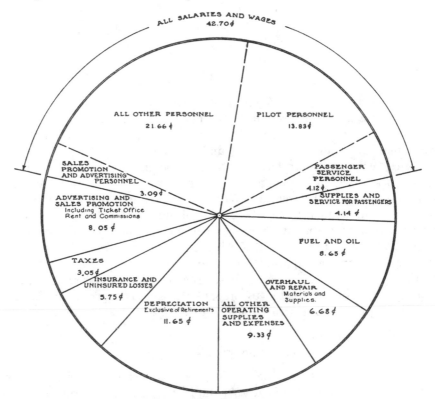

Fig. 15-1.   Circle Chart.

Comparison of circles.   Comparisons in magnitude are sometimes made by presenting circles of different sizes.   The objection to this method is the resulting confusion in the mind of the reader as to whether the area or the diameter is used as the basis of measurement.

It is impossible to estimate accurately the difference between the diameters of two circles by merely looking at them.   When comparative diameters are being estimated, the circles themselves have to be subordinated in the mind of the reader while the diameters are visualized. Charts were devised because of their ease of comprehension, and their purpose is defeated when conflicting mental processes are involved. For this reason, circles of different sizes should never be used for comparative purposes.

The same criticism applies to squares and cubes. A cube whose edge is twice that of another will possess eight times the cubic content and four times the outside area of the smaller one, and unless the basis of measurement is carefully explained, the comparison may easily be misleading.

PROBLEMS

1. Using the figures in the following condensed operating statement, prepare a circle chart showing the distribution of the "sales dollar."

Sales	$66,734.49
Plant Operating Expenses	21,464.91
Payroll	18,055.22
Taxes	1,055.07
Depreciation	14,252.63
Depletion	4,667.20
Net Profit	7,239.46

2. Prepare a circle chart to illustrate the following accounts receivable analysis.

Current to 60 days old	47.08%
90 days old	11.69%
120 days old	6.62%
4 to 6 months old	10.65%
6 months to 1 year old	8.54%
Over 1 year old	15.42%

3. Prepare a circle chart to illustrate the distribution of the sales dollar.

Raw materials	$.55
Wages and salaries	.25
Direct taxes	.07
Selling, advertising, and miscellaneous expense	.05
Reinvestment in the business	.03
Wear and tear on equipment	.02½
Dividends	.02½

Bar chart. The bar chart, like the circle chart, is designed to exhibit the true proportions of the component parts of a group total.

Bars used in charting may consist of single heavy lines or they may be widened into rectangles. Three ways of presenting data by means of bars are in common use:

(1) Comparisons are made by presenting a series of bars of different lengths, each bar representing a different magnitude (see Figure 15-2).

(2) A single bar is subdivided into component parts (see Figure 15-3).

(3) A combination of (1) and (2) may be employed (see Figure 15-4).

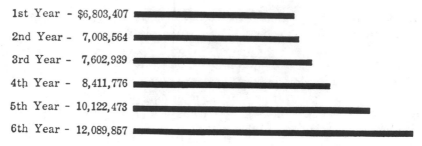

1st Year - $6,803,407

2nd Year - 7,008,564

3rd Year - 7,602,939

4th Year - 8,411,776

5th Year - 10,122,473

6th Year - 12,089,857

Fig. 15-2. Bar Chart Showing Sales for 6-year Period.

Where color is not used, bars or parts of a bar may be differentiated by crosshatching and also by the use of solid black and white. Crosshatching consists of the fine parallel lines drawn across the face of the bar at various angles and sometimes crossed into small rectangles.

In making comparisons by means of parallel bars, it is essential that the bars be of the same width in order that measurement of length be not confused with that of area.

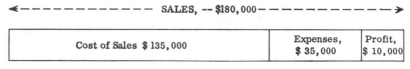

◄ ── ── ── ── ── ── SALES, ── $180,000 ── ── ── ── ── ── ── ►

Cost of Sales $ 135,000	Expenses, $ 35,000	Profit, $ 10,000

Fig. 15-3.

Bars may be placed in either horizontal or vertical position.

In the bar method of charting, figures may be placed at the side or in the bar and decimal points kept in line; it is thus easy to foot the figures representing the various components and to verify the total (Figure 15-3).

Because of its decimal divisions, a millimeter scale is most convenient in constructing these charts.

PROBLEMS

1. Chart the following data, using vertical bars.

Period	Amount
1	40,000
2	50,000
3	60,000
4	75,000
5	80,000
6	90,000
7	95,000
8	100,000
9	105,000
10	110,000

2. Chart the following data, using the single bar subdivided into component parts.

Sales........................	$1,000,000
Cost of Sales................	550,000
General Expenses............	200,000
Selling Expenses.............	150,000
Net Profit...................	100,000

3. Chart the following, using horizontal bars.

Period	Amount
1	2,931
2	9,052
3	13,541
4	16,403
5	20,919
6	28,063
7	36,365
8	41,393
9	49,404
10	56,615

4. Chart the following similarly to Figure 15-4.

GROWTH IN NUMBER OF EMPLOYEES

Year	No. Employees	No. Male	No. Female
1st	6,587	1,859	4,728
2nd	6,893	2,081	4,812
3rd	7,205	2,270	4,935
4th	7,581	2,317	5,264
5th	7,810	2,168	5,642
6th	8,104	2,278	5,826

Line or curve chart. The line or curve chart is probably adaptable to a greater variety of uses than any other type of graphic presentation. It is used particularly to exhibit trends and fluctuations in data, the abnormal conditions being shown by unusual "peaks" and "valleys."

On line charts, the scale is indicated by vertical and/or horizontal rulings. If the coördinate type of ruling is used, the lines in each direction are spaced an equal distance apart, horizontal lines marking the vertical scale and vertical lines marking the horizontal scale.

All rectilinear charts have two axes—the horizontal, called the *x*-axis, and the vertical, called the *y*-axis.

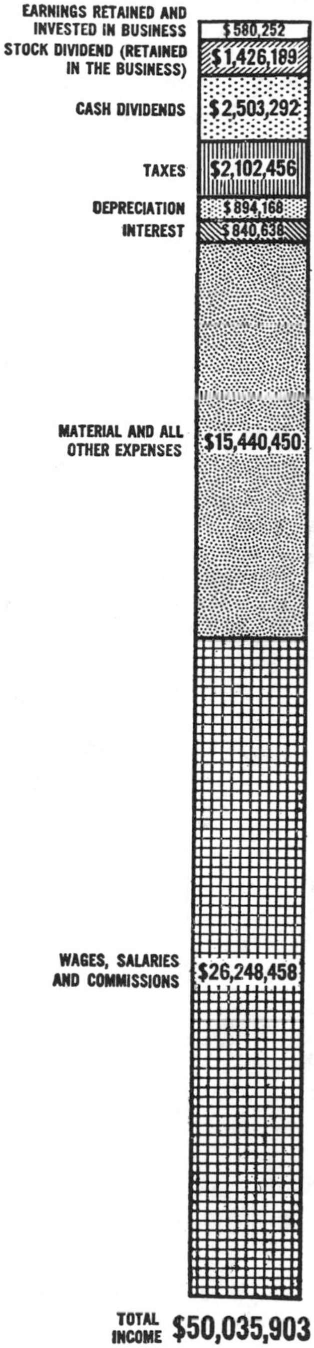

EARNINGS RETAINED AND INVESTED IN BUSINESS $580,252

STOCK DIVIDEND (RETAINED IN THE BUSINESS) $1,426,189

CASH DIVIDENDS $2,503,292

TAXES $2,102,456

DEPRECIATION $894,168
INTEREST $840,638

MATERIAL AND ALL OTHER EXPENSES $15,440,450

WAGES, SALARIES AND COMMISSIONS $26,248,458

TOTAL INCOME $50,035,903

Fig. 15-4.

Rules for coördinate charts. Custom has established certain rules governing the construction of coördinate charts which must be observed if they are to be plotted in accordance with good usage.

(1) The zero line should always appear, or attention should be specifically called to its omission.

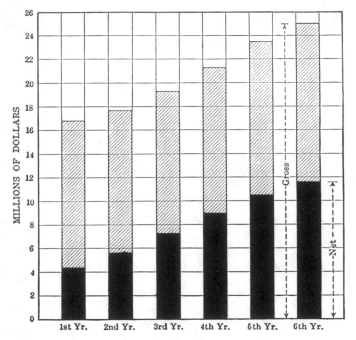

Fig. 15-5. Bar Chart Showing Annual Gross and Net Income.

(2) The time element should always be expressed by the horizontal scale and magnitude by the vertical scale.

(3) The curves should be sharply distinguished from the ruling.

(4) Figures and lettering should be so placed that they are read from the bottom or from the right-hand side.

(5) Exact data should be inserted at the top of the chart, the figures in each case appearing immediately above the corresponding point on the curve.

(6) The figures of the vertical scale should be placed on the left. In wide charts they may be repeated on the right.

(7) The horizontal scale should read from left to right, and the vertical scale from bottom to top.

It is considered good practice to make the zero line heavier than the other coördinate rulings. In percentage charts the 100% line is also accentuated by heavier ruling.

Example.   The earnings of a corporation over a period of years were as follows:

1st year..	$39,202,000
2nd year..	37,555,000
3rd year...	28,621,000
4th year...	30,438,000
5th year...	28,693,000
6th year...	27,319,000
7th year...	28,358,000
8th year....	35,941,000
9th year..	31,772,000
10th year......................................	34,249,000

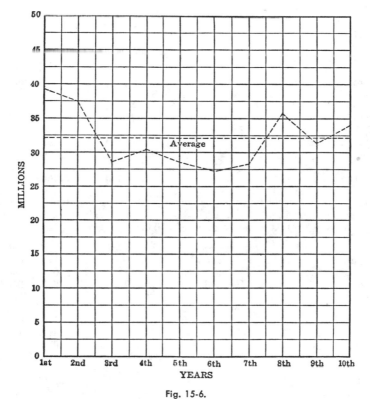

Fig. 15-6.

NOTE: Limited space does not permit insertion of exact figures (Rule 5).

PROBLEMS

1. Construct a line graph showing the total sales of the Acid Chemical Company from the following data.

Year	1951	1952	1953	1954	1955	1956	1957	1958	1959	1960
Total Sales in Millions of Dollars	82	90	99	100	140	162	173	154	180	205

2. Construct a line graph showing the production in millions of gallons of the Redi Paint Company from the data as given in the 1960 report of the directors.

Year	1951	1952	1953	1954	1955	1956	1957	1958	1959	1960
Production in Millions of Gallons	2.5	3.2	5.4	8.7	11.5	15.0	17.5	19.4	18.1	20.2

3. Using the following data, prepare a line chart showing the corporation's earnings and the dividends paid over a period of years.

Year	Net Income	Dividends Paid
1st	$28,154,431	$16,354,000
2nd	35,422,514	16,360,632
3rd	49,129,417	16,369,400
4th	28,684,916	16,404,509
5th	31,548,606	17,478,459
6th	32,070,274	18,209,281
7th	30,618,778	20,639,196
8th	32,600,150	20,662,854
9th	44,552,482	20,662,854
10th	35,419,903	20,943,094
11th	35,657,410	22,609,650

4. From the information given in the following table, prepare a line graph of the Bonded Debt Limit and the Net Bonded Indebtedness of the City of *X* for the 15-year period. (Scale, 1 in. = $2,000,000.)

Year	Assessed Valuation	Bonded Debt Limit	Net Bonded Indebtedness
1st	$442,932,255	$15,887,062	$10,698,500
2nd	460,548,763	18,272,142	9,321,050
3rd	486,424,005	20,804,104	10,577,500
4th	496,342,170	23,291,794	11,101,500
5th	505,713,510	23,919,607	11,921,000
6th	521,239,125	24,702,675	14,730,750
7th	539,457,120	25,491,759	16,566,000
8th	574,020,559	26,367,724	16,534,750
9th	588,556,266	27,289,865	18,254,800
10th	675,611,540	28,988,846	22,030,250
11th	681,198,160	30,588,436	23,965,500
12th	677,070,755	27,750,500	24,800,000
13th	725,603,037	29,033,300	27,403,300
14th	755,229,851	30,773,800	25,023,500
15th	810,509,504	33,974,550	25,744,500

Logarithmic chart. The common logarithms of the Briggs' table, being the expressions of numbers in terms of the power of 10, are particularly adapted to the presentation of percentage relationships. This fact has led to the construction of a chart in which percentage relationships are revealed by a comparison of different sets of data plotted in terms of numerical magnitude.

The logarithmic chart is a variation of the rectilinear type. The ruling differs from that of the customary coördinate chart in that the data lines representing the scale are not evenly spaced but conform to certain proportions expressed by the first ten numbers in a table of common logarithms.

Figure 15-7 illustrates the method of laying out such a scale. The first column of figures is purely for drafting purposes, and consists of the first ten figures of a logarithmic table, only the first two decimal digits being used in each case.

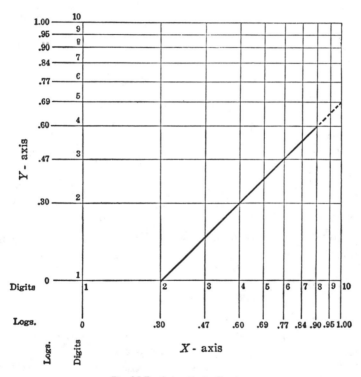

Fig. 15-7.   Logarithmic Chart.

The condensed table of logarithms of numbers, page 252, will be of assistance in preparing a logarithmic chart.

In the vertical scale, each horizontal line is spaced the distance from the base of the scale which represents the proportion that its scale number bears to 100; that is, the first line above the base line is 30 one-hundredths of the total height of the scale; the next line is 47 one-hundredths', and so on, the top line representing 100.   A ruler having a 100-millimeter scale may be conveniently used for making these horizontal lines.

The second vertical column represents the numerical magnitude scale and is numbered from 1 to 10, or some multiple thereof, the ruled lines being spaced according to the logarithms of these numbers. The result is that when data are plotted on such a chart in terms of numerical magnitude, the relationships shown between the various groups of data plotted will be correct percentage relationships. This does not hold true where data are plotted numerically on an ordinary coördinate chart; where the curves represent widely differing magnitudes, an attempted comparison of the fluctuations in the data will be misleading. In order that data plotted on a coördinate chart may present correct percentage relationships, the lines must represent a percentage, not a numerical, scale.

LOGARITHMS OF NUMBERS

Number	Logarithm	Number	Logarithm	Number	Logarithm	Number	Logarithm
1	0.00	10	1.00	100	2.00	1,000	3.00
2	0.30	20	1.30	200	2.30	2,000	3.30
3	0.47	30	1.47	300	2.47	3,000	3.47
4	0.60	40	1.60	400	2.60	4,000	3.60
5	0.69	50	1.69	500	2.69	5,000	3.69
6	0.77	60	1.77	600	2.77	6,000	3.77
7	0.84	70	1.84	700	2.84	7,000	3.84
8	0.90	80	1.90	800	2.90	8,000	3.90
9	0.95	90	1.95	900	2.95	9,000	3.95
						10,000	4.00

In comparing on a logarithmic scale data of widely differing magnitudes, it is necessary to use more than one grouping of logarithmic rulings. Each such grouping is called a *cycle*, because it represents 10, or some multiple thereof. For instance, if data represented by figures in the hundreds group and data running into the thousands were to be compared, it would be necessary to use two cycles; if the figures ran into the ten-thousands group, it would be necessary to use three cycles.

It will be noticed that the base line in a logarithmic chart is numbered 1, instead of 0. This is done because in the tables the log of 1 is .0. Therefore, in a logarithmic chart there is no zero line.

To illustrate the use of a full logarithmic chart, a simple example in multiplication may be cited. Applying the principle that in multiplication the logarithm of the product of two numbers is the sum of the logarithms of the numbers, the addition may be performed graphically on a logarithmic chart. By doubling the distance of any number represented by a digit, the square of the digit is obtained. Thus, the distance from 1 to 9 is twice the distance from 1 to 3, because 9 is the square of 3.

Since the scales of the two axes are the same, lines projected at right angles from identically numbered points on both axes will complete a square the diagonal of which is 45°, to the right of any point on the base of the *x*-axis; for instance, any horizontal line which intersects this diagonal will, if projected downward from the intersecting point to the base line of the *x*-axis and at right angles thereto, record on the *x*-axis digit scale the product of the two numbers representing the starting points of the diagonal and the horizontal lines.

Figure 15-7 illustrates a computation of this kind, and affords a mechanical demonstration of the logarithmic principle referred to. A diagonal line is projected upward at an angle of 45° from the digit 2 on the *x*-axis. The point at which it intersects the horizontal line numbered 4 on the *y*-scale is directly above digit 8 on the *x*-scale, and 2 times 4 is 8. Likewise, the sum of the distances 1 to 2 on the *x*-axis and 1 to 4 on the *y*-axis will, if laid off by a pair of dividers, arrive at point 8 on either scale.

Semilogarithmic or ratio charts. Semilogarithmic charts are extremely useful in plotting some time series data, such as gross sales or payroll for a number of years. These charts are used where it is the *rate of change* rather than the amount of change that is important.

Consider the following series of hypothetical data for annual sales of a firm:

	Sales
Year	*(in thousands of dollars)*
1954	$ 20
1955	40
1956	80
1957	160
1958	320
1959	640

These data can be plotted as an ordinary graph and the result will be a curve becoming steeper and steeper in the late 1950's.

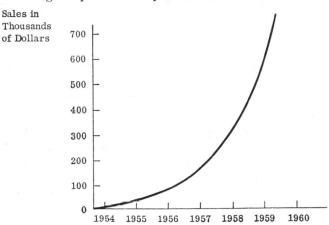

Fig. 15-8.

Inspection of the data will show, however, that, while the absolute amount of increase from one year to the next is quite different, in each case sales for one year were exactly double those of the preceding year. This will show up at once if, instead of plotting actual sales, the logarithms of the sales are plotted. In this case the result will be a straight line, and the constant slope of the line will show the constant *rate* of growth.

	Logarithm of Sales
Year	*(in thousands of dollars)*
1954...............	1.30103
1955...............	1.60206
1956...............	1.90309
1957...............	2.20412
1958...............	2.50515
1959...	2.80618

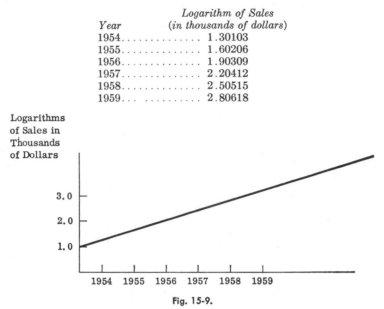

Fig. 15-9.

It will make no difference whether the logarithms of the original numbers are plotted or whether the logarithms of the numbers expressed in thousands of dollars are plotted. The position of the line will be different, but it will have the same slope. The slope is the only part which is relevant, and for this reason zero does not appear on a semilogarithmic chart.

Instead of plotting the logarithms of the numbers, exactly the same graph can be obtained by using "semilogarithmic graph paper," which has an ordinary horizontal scale but a special vertical scale constructed in such a way that, when the number is plotted, it is equivalent to plotting the logarithm of the number. Semilog paper comes with from one to seven cycles. The first cycle is from 1 to 10, the next cycle is from 10 to 100, the next from 100 to 1,000 and so forth, so that each cycle allows for an increase of 10 times the basic number. The vertical scale on any semilogarithmic paper can be multiplied by any convenient positive number if all values are multiplied by this number. Thus, a one-cycle semilogarithmic graph, which has a vertical scale reading from 1 to 10, can be multiplied by 30 and used for plotting data which vary between 30 to 300. In this case the number 60 would be plotted corresponding to 2 on the original scale, the number 273 would be plotted corresponding to 9.1 on the original scale.

To determine the number of cycles needed for graphing a particular series, find the minimum and maximum values of the series. Multiply the minimum value by 10 successively until the figure is as great as or greater than the maximum. If one multiplication by 10 is sufficient, one-cycle paper is adequate. If the minimum must be multiplied by 10 twice, two-cycle paper is needed. A series with values between 3.7 and 648.3 will require three-cycle paper, while a series with values between .0013 and .0097 can be put on one-cycle paper. It is always possible to use graph paper with more cycles than needed; the only disadvantage is that the resulting graph is smaller and hence more difficult to read. Two- or three-cycle paper will handle most series.

NOTE: *Since the logarithms of zero and of negative numbers are not defined, series which involve these numbers cannot be placed on semilogarithmic paper.*

When plotted on two-cycle semilogarithmic graph paper, the sales data of the above example would look like Figure 15-9, but the vertical scale would be in the original units. (See Figure 15-10.)

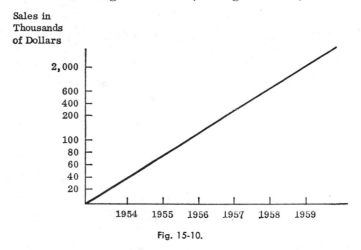

Fig. 15-10.

In this plotting, the 1.0 point of the logarithmic scale was taken as 20.0 thousand dollars. Each number printed on the first cycle of the vertical scale of the semilogarithmic paper was therefore multiplied by 20 and each number in the second cycle by 200. By this device the chart can be used for years subsequent to 1959 without adding a third cycle until sales pass $2,000,000 ($2,000 thousand) per annum.

As was explained above, when plotted on semilogarithmic paper, a series that is increasing or decreasing at a constant rate will appear as a straight line. The greater the rate of increase or decrease, the steeper the slope of the line will be. If the resulting curve is not a straight line, but one that slopes progressively upward at a steeper angle, the series is one that is increasing at an increasing rate. Conversely, if the slope is steep at the beginning and gradually decreases as the curve moves upward, the series is increasing at a decreasing rate. If the line is horizontal, the series is neither increasing nor decreasing. The chart (in Figure 15-11) shows the various possibilities.

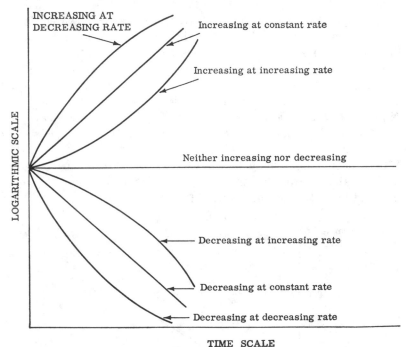

TIME SCALE

Fig. 15-11.

Another use of semilogarithmic paper is in comparing the rates of change in two different series on the same chart. For example, Figure 15-12 compares the change in the money supply with the rate of money turnover to indicate the changes in the forces affecting the inflationary potential of the early 1950's. This chart has the disadvantage that not only are there two different scales (one on the right and one on the left), but the scales are in different units. The differences in scales and units make comparisons of the movements of the two series difficult. If, however, the two series had been plotted on semilogarithmic graph paper, attention would have been focused on the rate of change in each series. When this is done, differences in units or scales do not matter, for it is percentage changes that are being compared. If the two series are parallel when plotted on semilogarithmic scale, they are changing at the same rate. If one series has a greater upward slope than the other, it is increasing at a greater rate. Thus, differences in the rate of change in the two series can be seen directly from the chart when semilogarithmic scale is used, and the possibility that the use of different scales may mislead the reader is eliminated.

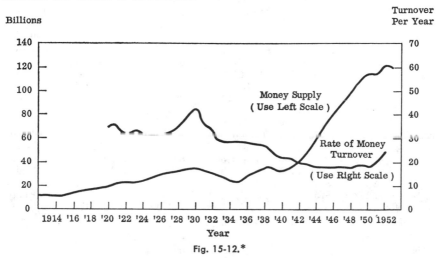

Fig. 15-12.*

PROBLEMS

1. Transfer the information from Figure 15-12 to a semilogarithmic chart.

2. Plot the following data by using (a) an arithmetic scale, and (b) semilogarithmic paper.

Year	Average Weekly Earnings
1949	$23.86
1950	25.20
1951	29.58
1952	36.65
1953	43.18
1954	46.12
1955	44.59
1956	43.97
1957	49.85
1958	54.23
1959	59.70

3. Prepare a ratio chart to illustrate the following condensed operating statements:

	1st Year	2nd Year	3rd Year	4th Year	5th Year	6th Year
Sales	$61,960.29	$74,401.38	$80,598.00	$72,887.60	$79,647.14	$65,315.48
Cost of Sales	27,745.59	32,967.89	48,935.10	41,660.83	48,945.54	33,414.53
Gross Profit	34,214.70	41,433.49	31,662.90	31,226.77	30,701.60	31,900.95
Expenses	31,152.64	33,308.86	28,640.73	30,580.32	30,342.26	29,736.02
Net Profit	3,062.06	8,124.63	3,022.17	646.45	359.34	2,164.93

* Federal Reserve Board.

4. Prepare a ratio chart to illustrate the following comparative income accounts of a public utility company:

Year	Gross Earnings	Maintenance and Renewals	Power-Opr., Conducting Transportation, and General	Taxes	Fixed Charges	Net Income
1st	$22,147,974	$3,661,198	$ 8,627,973	$1,591,523	$ 8,827,988	$ 560,708†
2nd	23,282,408	3,492,361	9,097,061	1,659,518	8,961,126	72,342
3rd	24,240,592	3,636,088	9,081,213	1,660,236	9,324,559	538,496
4th	23,961,398	3,594,209	8,825,665	1,808,951	9,531,232	201,341
5th	24,315,455	3,647,318	8,677,465	1,783,540	9,622,631	584,501
6th	27,279,517	4,091,928	9,382,587	1,812,541	9,614,908	2,377,553
7th	29,726,927	4,459,039	10,723,912	2,106,769	9,573,522	2,863,685
8th	31,704,427	4,755,664	13,355,575	2,428,819	9,629,553	1,534,816
9th	36,039,520	4,955,124	17,287,117	2,345,750	9,735,652	1,715,877
10th	39,400,341	5,965,409	20,628,504	2,601,253	9,823,110	382,065
11th	42,911,040	8,560,400	19,874,369	2,798,821	9,870,158	1,807,292
12th	43,235,972	8,560,400	20,407,117	2,586,001	9,853,177	1,829,277
13th	45,552,031	8,560,400	22,479,553	2,695,708	10,016,370	1,800,000
14th	46,215,488	8,560,400	22,678,896	2,760,903	10,404,924	1,810,365

† Loss.

5. Prepare a ratio chart to show the following expenses:

Salaries.. 5.0%
Rent.. .8
Credit Losses... .5
Heat.. .1
Light 1
Taxes... .3
Shipping and Receiving.................................. .5
Depreciation.. 2.5
Miscellaneous Expenses.................................. 1.0
Power... .5
Freight... .5
Delivery Expense.. .1
Insurance... .1

HINT.   Rearrange items from highest to lowest per cent.

INDEX NUMBERS

Indicators of business conditions.   Numerous indicators of business conditions are regularly published in the *Survey of Current Business*, in the *Federal Reserve Bulletin*, in the *Monthly Labor Review*, and in financial papers, trade journals, business magazines, and daily newspapers.

The most comprehensive indicator is the Gross National Product (GNP), which is estimated by the Department of Commerce and in Canada is published quarterly by the Dominion Bureau of Statistics.

The Gross National Product measures the market value of the goods and services produced during a year and is adjusted in two separate ways to reveal the significance of movements in the aggregate. One adjustment is designed to eliminate the effect of price changes. In 1950 the GNP for the United States in current inflated dollars was $282,630,000,000, whereas in constant 1939 dollars it was only $154,300,000,000. A second adjustment takes into account the seasonal pattern of production, and the GNP is deflated or inflated to allow for the fact that seasonally influenced production is either high or low in a particular period in relation to the average for a year.

Index numbers. An *index number* is a number that is used for measuring trends in prices or in other movements which can be quantitatively expressed by means of statistical data. If, for example, Peter Smith's income in 1950 was $3,000.00 and in 1959 was $4,500.00, his 1959 income is 150 per cent of what it was in 1950. This percentage figure of 150 is an index number. Some year—1950 in the above example—is selected as the *base year* (or base period) and is given the value of 100. The figures in all other years are then expressed as percentages of the base-year figure, so that the index number for a specific year indicates the percentage increase or decrease from the base year.

Price indexes. One common use of index numbers is to measure the change in price level that occurs over a period of time. The simplest example is that of a single commodity whose nature and quality have not changed during the period. For example, the price per quart of homogenized milk delivered to a household by Dairy *A* in Toronto could be expressed as an index (Jan. 31, 1958 = 100) as follows:

1958	*Price per Quart*	*Index*
January 31	20	100
February 28	21	105
March 31	22	110
April 30	23	115
May 31	21	105
June 30	19	95

Such *price relatives* enable one to read immediately that the price on April 30 was 15 per cent higher than the price on January 31. To ensure that this price comparison is valid, care must be taken that the same article is priced at all times and that no quality change, change in place priced, and so forth, has occurred. Moreover, if different prices did exist for different dairies (unlikely for a standard commodity delivered to the household), some averaging technique would have to be employed.

If an index is to be constructed for more than one commodity, an averaging problem also occurs. Suppose that the index is to reflect the change in the cost of milk and butter delivered to Peter Smith's household, and that on January 31 the price of butter (first grade) was 90 cents a pound and on February 28 it was 85 cents a pound. The price of homogenized milk, as specified above, was 20 cents and 21 cents, respectively. A naïve approach would be to say that, since one pound of butter plus one quart of milk cost $1.10 on January 31 and $1.01 on February 28, the price of these items to the consumer (Peter Smith) had *decreased* by 8.2 per cent, that is, that the February 28 index (Jan. 31 = 100) was 91.8. Suppose, however, that in one week Peter Smith's family consumed one pound of butter and 12 quarts of milk. The logical thing to do is to *weight* the prices by the quantities consumed in a week. Thus, at January 31 prices, a week's supply of milk and butter would cost 12 × 20¢ + 90¢ = $3.30; while at February 28 prices, the cost would be 12 × 21¢ + 85¢ = $3.37. The weighted price of these consumer goods to Peter Smith has thus increased by 2.11 per cent.

Expressed as a formula, this *weighted aggregative index* is:

$$\frac{\Sigma p_n q_0}{\Sigma p_0 q_0}$$

where p_0 = price of an item in the base period,

q_0 = quantity of an item consumed in the base period,

p_n = price of the item in period n, which is some period other than the base period,

Σ indicates that the values (price and quantity) for each item are summed.

The Department of Commerce index of retail prices and the Bureau of Labor Statistics indexes of wholesale prices and consumer prices, along with the Consumer Price Index published monthly by the Dominion Bureau of Statistics, are illustrations of this type.

The Consumer Price Index is of obvious interest to all consumers as an important indicator of inflationary pressures in the economy and is of importance in many wage negotiations. This index measures the percentage change through time in the cost of purchasing a constant "basket" of goods and services representing the consumption of a particular population group during the period of a year. So that the meaning of the index may be understood, the various parts of the definition must be spelled out.

(i) *Family Coverage.* From the results of a sample survey, a group of families was chosen whose changes in living costs resulting from price change could be represented by one index.

(ii) *Base Period.* A year of relatively stable price levels is used as the base period for a series of index numbers, including the Consumer Price Index.

(iii) *Basket of Goods and Services.* Two criteria for an item to be included in the "basket" of goods and services whose price change is measured by the index are: (a) the item must have a price, and (b) the price must be identified with a specific quantity of a good or service. No distinction is made between "luxuries" and "necessities." As long as an item is purchased by families defined in (i), and as long as the item meets the above price criteria, it is included in the index on the grounds that consumers do purchase it. Thus, inclusion in the index of an item that was formerly excluded does *not* reflect official recognition that it is now a necessity. It merely means that now enough urban families purchase the item to give it a weight in the index.

Since a large number of commodities are purchased by families meeting the requirements above, only a sample of all the commodities is used for the index. One item will be selected to represent a group of similar commodities. The weight given to this price is, however, the weight of the group—not of the one item selected from the group for pricing. Thus, one item of cotton clothing may represent several different types of cotton clothing whose prices all move in about the same way. Similarly, one cut of beef may be used to represent a group of similar cuts of beef. Use of a sample here has two advantages: (1) the obvious advantage of economy, since a large expenditure is involved in collecting data, and (2) the perhaps more important advantage of making the resulting index available much sooner than would otherwise be possible.

This also explains some of the changes in the commodities included in the index. Sometimes new commodities are bought in appreciable quantities by the group in question; and sometimes it is found that an item is no longer satisfactorily represented as part of a group of commodities. Thus, the addition of wieners to the items priced for the United States index a few years ago was not made because wieners were only then being purchased, but because the price change of wieners was no longer related to that of any other meat item priced in the index.

(iv) *Weights.* To construct an index of the price change in a basket of goods requires that the various items be weighted. (See the example of Peter Smith's expenditure on butter and milk earlier in this chapter.) A continuing program of small sample surveys attempts to keep the weights up to date. As time passes, however, the base-year pattern of family expenditures becomes less and less representative of consumer purchases, even when adjustments are made. Ultimately another detailed survey of families' expenditures will be taken and a new set of weights and a new base period determined for the Index. It should be remembered that these weights may be subject to all the various types of error that enter into estimates from a sample survey.

(v) *Formula.* Since the weights used are percentages of total family expenditure, the formula used is the *weighted average of price relatives:*

$$\frac{\sum \left[p_0 q_0 \left(\dfrac{p_n}{p_0} \right) \right]}{\Sigma p_0 q_0}$$

rather than the weighted aggregate index used earlier, which is appropriate when the weights are physical quantities. Simple cancellation of the p_0's in the numerator of the second formula shows that it gives results identical with those of the first formula.

(vi) *Prices.* The prices which enter into the index are the retail prices to the consumer, inclusive of all sales and excise taxes. These prices are collected from retail outlets in the cities covered by the index and relate to specified descriptions of each commodity and service. The procedure of pricing by specification is followed to facilitate distinction between price change and quality change. If a measurable quality change occurs without an actual price change, a comparable price change is computed.

(vii) *Seasonality.* Food consumption is subject to a seasonal pattern, and, therefore, the weight for items such as tomatoes in the Consumer Price Index is not fixed but changes during the year according to the seasonal pattern of consumer purchases of the item.

Quantity indexes. As the name implies, indexes which measure changes in quantities produced, sold, shipped, or consumed are referred to as *quantity indexes.* Automobile production, building construction, electric power output, and steel production are samples.

Value indexes. *Value* is the product of price and quantity; a low price and a large quantity could represent the same value as a high price and a small quantity. Therefore, a value index which remains stable for a period of time may reflect (1) stable prices and stable quantities or (2) increasing prices and decreasing quantities or (3) decreasing prices and increasing quantities. The Gross National Product is a value index.

Business activity indexes. These indexes are frequently constructed by combining independent indicators or indexes of prices, production, trade, employment, finance, and other series. Selection of series to be included in such indexes and assignment of weighting factors are largely matters of judgment. Although these indexes are easy to criticize, they nevertheless serve a useful purpose in reflecting the approximate trend of general business activity. The index of business activity published in *Business Week* magazine is an example of this type of index. Several university bureaus of business research publish indexes of business activity for states or regions.

Other indexes. Indexes or other indicators are available for almost all types of business activity. Specialized indexes have been developed for most major industries. For example, in the transportation industry indicators are published for: (1) railroad freight, (2) scheduled air carrier operations, (3) ton-miles of railway freight, (4) freight carloadings, (5) steam locomotives undergoing or awaiting repairs, and other phases of operations. Among indicators in the retail industry are: (1) retail sales, (2) department store sales, (3) department store stocks, (4) ratio of stocks to sales of department stores, and (5) men's clothing (ratio of

INDUSTRIAL PRODUCTION* (1947–1949 = 100)

Year or Month	Total (Adj.)	Major Industry Groupings			Major Market Groupings			
					Final Products			Mate-rials (Adj.)
		Manu-facturing (Adj.)	Mining (Adj.)	Utilities (Adj.)	Total (Adj.)	Con-sumer Goods (Adj.)	Equip-ment (Adj.)	
1947	99	99	101	91	99	98	100	100
1948	103	103	106	101	102	101	105	104
1949	98	97	94	108	99	101	94	96
1950	113	113	105	123	112	115	102	114
1951	123	123	115	140	121	114	142	124
1952	127	127	114	152	130	116	170	125
1953	138	139	117	166	138	124	182	137
1954	130	129	113	178	132	123	161	128
1955	146	145	125	199	144	136	172	147
1956	151	150	132	218	150	139	188	151
1957	152	150	132	233	152	141	189	151
1958	141	139	120	244	145	140	165	138
1959	159	158	126	268	162	156	188	157
1959 Aug.	157	157	120	269	166	158	194	148
Sept.	157	156	119	272	165	158	194	149
Oct.	155	154	120	272	165	157	194	146
Nov.	156	154	126	274	162	154	192	152
Dec.	165	164	130	279	166	159	194	165
1960 Jan.	168	168	129	280	170	164	195	167
Feb.	166	166	126	282	167	160	194	166
Mar.	166	165	125	288	167	160	196	164
Apr.	165	164	129	288	168	162	194	163
May	167	166	128	285	171	164	197	162
June	166	165	128	289	r 171	r 165	196	161
July	166	165	r 128	291	170	164	197	r 161
Aug.	165	163	128	291	169	163	196	159
Sept.	p 162	p 161	p 126	p 294	p 169	p 162	p 193	p 157

p Preliminary.   r Revised.   Adj. = adjusted for seasonal variation.
* Source: *Federal Reserve Bulletin*, October, 1960.

stocks to sales). Financial indicators include numerous measures of changes in (1) bond prices, (2) bond yields, (3) stock prices, (4) stock yields, (5) bank debits, (6) bank clearings, (7) loans, (8) reserves, (9) money supply, and (10) rate of money turnover. Similar listings could be made for commodity prices, employment and earnings, construction activity, and many phases of industrial and agricultural production.

Most of the indexes listed in the foregoing are expressed statistically; therefore, their trends can be measured mathematically.

The nature of the particular business primarily determines the indexes most useful to it. To answer the question, "How is business?" recourse may be had for purposes of comparison to some index of general business conditions, for example, to the Federal Reserve index of industrial production, a national summary charted for a period of years, illustrated on the preceding page.

PROBLEMS

1. Corn and barley are two principal feed grains used in fattening hogs for market. From the following figures calculate the weighted index for 1958, using 1945 as the base year.

	Pork and Lard (lbs.)	Corn (bu.)	Barley (bu.)
Total production in 1945........	12,763,000	2,868,795,000	266,994,000
Average price in 1945 (cents)....	13.80	107.0	102.0
Average price in 1958 (cents)....	18.50	93.1	85.5

2. Calculate the individual price indexes for pork, corn, and barley. Did the price of pork keep pace with the price of corn? How about the price of pork and the price of barley? If both feeds were available, which would be the more profitable to use, assuming that each has the same feed value for pork production?

3. Find the weighted index for the three following fresh fruits sold in large quantities for home canning.

	Apples (bu.)	Peaches (bu.)	Pears (bu.)
Total production in 1949....	139,379,000	64,222,000	29,279,000
Average price in 1949......	$ .64	$ .82	$ .70
Average price in 1952......	$1.38	$1.49	$1.57

16

Series of Numbers—The Progressions

Definition. *A* **sequence** *or series of numbers is a set of numbers arranged in a definite order and formed according to a definite law. The successive numbers are called the* **terms** *of the series.*

Examples.

Series	Laws
1, 2, 3, . . .	Add 1 to each preceding term.
2, 4, 8, 16, . . .	Multiply each preceding term by 2.
2, 4, 16, . . .	Square each preceding term.
4, 7, 10, 13, . . .	Add 3 to each preceding term.
−1, −3, −9, . . .	Multiply each preceding term by 3.
10, 6, 2, −2, −6, . . .	Add −4 to each preceding term.
12, 4, $\frac{4}{3}$, $\frac{4}{9}$, . . .	Multiply each preceding term by $\frac{1}{3}$.

PROBLEMS

1. Continue each of the following series three terms further so as to preserve the law of the series.

(a) $1 + 3 + 5 + 7 + \cdots$.
(b) $1 + 4 + 16 + 64 + \cdots$.
(c) $2 + 5 + 10 + 17 + \cdots$.
(d) $1 - \frac{1}{2} + \frac{1}{3} - \frac{1}{4} + \cdots$.
(e) $10 + 5 + 0 - 5 \cdots$.
(f) $18 + 9 + \frac{9}{2} + \frac{9}{4} + \cdots$.
(g) $-25 - 15 - 5 + 5 + \cdots$.

The arithmetic progression. *A series in which each term, after the first term, is obtained by adding the same quantity to the preceding term is called an* **arithmetic series** *or an* **arithmetic progression** *or an* **A.P.** *The quantity which is added each time is called the* **common difference.**

265

The series (*a*), (*e*), and (*g*) in the above set of problems are, therefore, arithmetic progressions. The common difference can obviously be obtained by subtracting any term from the term following it.

Symbols. The five elements of an arithmetical progression are represented by certain well-established symbols:

Number of terms . . . . *n*
First term . . . . *a*
Last term . . . . *l*
Common difference . . . . *d*
Sum of the terms . . . . *s*

Relation of elements. The five elements whose symbols are indicated above are so related that if any three of them are given, the remaining two may be found. According to the above symbols, any arithmetic series may be represented by

$$(1)\ a,\ a + d,\ a + 2d,\ a + 3d,\ \ldots,\ l$$

and its sum by

$$(2)\ s = a + (a + d) + (a + 2d) + \ldots,\ + l$$

Formulas for an arithmetical progression. From an observation of (1) above, it is immediately obvious that if we let t_n represent the *n*th term, then

$$t_n = a + (n - 1)d. \tag{A}$$

If the *n*th term is denoted by *l* when it is the last term,

$$l = a + (n - 1)d. \tag{B}$$

From (2), let S_n denote the sum of *n* terms of the series:

$$S_n = \quad a + (a + d) + (a + 2d) + \cdots + (l - 2d) + (l - d) + l,$$

and by reversing (2),

$$S_n = \quad l + (l - d) + (l - 2d) + \cdots + (a + 2d) + (a + d) + a$$

$$\therefore 2S_n = \underbrace{(a + l) + (a + l) + (a + l) + \cdots + (a + l) + (a + l) + (a + l)}_{n \text{ terms}}$$

$$\therefore 2S_n = n(a + l)$$

$$\therefore S_n = \frac{n}{2}(a + l). \tag{C}$$

From (B) above, $$S_n = \frac{n}{2}(a + a + \overline{n - 1}d)$$

$$\therefore S_n = \frac{n}{2}(2a + \overline{n - 1}d). \tag{D}$$

Example 1. Find the number of terms of the series $2 + 5 + 8 + \cdots + 35$.

Solution. Using formula (B), $l = a + (n - 1)d$, and substituting,

$$35 = 2 + (n - 1)3$$
$$n - 1 = 11$$
$$n = 12$$

Example 2. Find the number of terms of the series $7 + 3 - 1 - 5 \cdots -21$.

Solution. Using formula (B), $l = a + (n - 1)d$, and substituting,

$$-21 = 7 - (n - 1)4$$
$$n - 1 = 7$$
$$n = 8$$

Example 3. Find the 10th term (t_{10}) for the series $2 + 5 + 8 + \cdots$.

Solution. Using formula (A),

and substituting,
$$t_n = a + (n - 1)d,$$
$$t_{10} = 2 + 9 \times 3$$
$$t_{10} = 29$$

Example 4. Evaluate $S_n = 1 + 2 + 3 + \cdots + 100$.

Solution. In this example the last term $(l = 100)$ is given, and therefore we use formula (C), $S_n = \dfrac{n}{2}(a + l)$.

Substituting $n = 100$, $a = 1$, and $l = 100$,

$$S_{100} = \tfrac{100}{2}(1 + 100) = 50(101) = 5050.$$
$$1 + 2 + 3 + \cdots + 100 = 5050.$$

Example 5. Find the sum of 50 terms of the series $2 + 4 + 6 + \cdots$.

Solution. Since the last term is not given, use formula (D),

$$S_n = \frac{n}{2}[2a + (n - 1)d].$$

Substituting $n = 50$, $a = 2$, and $d = 2$,

$$S_{50} = \tfrac{50}{2}(4 + 49 \times 2) = 25(4 + 98) = 25 \times 102 = 2550.$$
$$2 + 4 + 6 + \cdots \text{ to 50 terms} = 2550.$$

PROBLEMS

1. Determine which of the following series are arithmetic progressions:
(i) $7 + 12 + 17 + \cdots$
(ii) $2 - 1 - 4 \cdots$
(iii) $4 - 6 + 8 + 10 + 12 \cdots$
(iv) $1 - \frac{1}{2} + \frac{1}{4} - \frac{1}{8} + \cdots$
(v) $1 - 2 - 5 - 8 \cdots$

2. Find the value of a and d for each series in (1) which is arithmetic.

3. Find the thirtieth term of $5 + 9 + 13 + \cdots$

4. Find a, d, and t_{20} for the series $0.8 - 0.4 - 1.6 - \cdots$

5. Given $a = 7$, $l = 65$, and $d = 2$; find n.

6. Which term of the series $3 + 7 + 11 + 15 + \cdots$ is 115?

7. How many multiples of 7 are there between 0 and 100?

8. Given $a = 2$, $n = 6$, $l = 12$; find d and s.

9. Find the sum of all the even numbers from 10 to 80 inclusive.

10. The first term of a progression is 6, the number of terms is 15, the common difference is 7; find the last term and the sum.

11. Given $n = 12$, $l = -17$, $s = -72$; find d and a.

12. The first term is 6, the last term is 181, and the common difference is 7; find the number of terms.

Given $l = 57$, $n = 23$, $a = -9$; find d and s.

13. Find the sum of $.1 + .4 + .7 + \cdots$ to 21 terms.

14. Find the sum of the odd numbers between 50 and 150.

15. Evaluate $5 + 12 + 19 + \cdots + 68$.

16. A building is to be leased for a term of 21 years. The first year's rental is to be $10,000.00, equal increases in rent are to be made each year, and the rental for the twenty-first year is to be $30,000.00. Find: (a) the difference in each year's rental; (b) the total rental that will be paid during the period of 21 years.

17. *A* deposited $25.00 in his savings account on January 1, and on the first of each month thereafter deposited $5.00 more than the previous month. How many dollars did he deposit December 1, and what was the amount of the accumulated deposits? Do not take interest into consideration in solving this problem.

18. A punch board has 50 numbers in each section (numbers 1 to 50). A person pays the amount of the number punched. If the board has four sections, what will be the amount of revenue derived from the board?

19. A man invests his savings in the shares of a building and loan association, depositing $240.00 the first year. At the beginning of the second year he is credited with $16.80 interest, and deposits $223.20. At the beginning of the third year he is credited with $33.60 interest, and deposits $206.40. What is his credit at the end of ten years, and how much cash has he paid in?

20. A bond issue of $40,000.00 bearing interest at 4% is to be retired in 10 equal annual installments. What amount of interest will be paid during the life of the issue?

21. An employee started work for a company at $1,200.00 for the first year, with a guaranteed yearly increase of $100.00. What was his salary 12 years later? How much has the company paid him in the course of the 12 years?

The geometric progression. *A series in which each term, after the first term, is obtained by multiplying the preceding term by a fixed quantity is called a* **geometric series** *or a* **geometric progression** *or a* **G.P.** *The quantity used to multiply is called the* **common ratio.**

Elements. In a geometrical progression, there are five elements so related that, any three being given, the others may be found. These five elements, together with their symbols, are:

Number of terms . . . . n
First term . . . . a
Last term l
Sum of the series . . . . s
Ratio . . . . r

According to the above symbols, any geometric series may be represented by:

$$(1)' \ a, \ ar, \ ar^2, \ ar^3, \ \cdots, \ l$$

and its sum by

$$(2)' \ a + ar + ar^2 + ar^3 + \cdots + l$$

Formulas for a geometric progression. From an observation of (1)′ above it is immediately obvious that, if we let t_n represent the nth term, then

$$t_n = ar^{n-1}. \tag{A$'$}$$

If the nth term is denoted by l, when it is the last term,

$$l = ar^{n-1}. \tag{B$'$}$$

From (2)′, let S_n denote the sum of n terms of the series:

$$\begin{aligned} S_n &= a + ar + ar^2 + \cdots + ar^{n-1} \\ \text{Hence,} \qquad rS_n &= ar + ar^2 + ar^3 + \cdots + ar^{n-1} + ar^n \\ \therefore (1-r)S_n &= a \qquad\qquad\qquad\qquad\qquad\qquad\quad - ar^n \end{aligned}$$

$$\therefore \ S_n = \frac{a(1 - r^n)}{1 - r}. \tag{C$'$}$$

If we multiply upstairs and downstairs by -1,

$$S_n = \frac{a(r^n - 1)}{r - 1}. \tag{D$'$}$$

NOTE: Use formula (C)′ when r is less than 1 and formula (D)′ when r is greater than 1.

Example 1. If the sixth term of a G.P. is 96 and the common ratio is 2, what is the first term?

Solution. Using formula (A)′, $t_n = ar^{n-1}$, by substituting $t_6 = 96$, $r = 2$, and $n = 6$,

$$96 = a \, 2^5$$

$$\therefore \ a = \frac{96}{2^5} = \frac{96}{32} = 3.$$

Example 2. Evaluate: $3 + 6 + 12 + 24 + 48 + 96$.

Solution. Using formula (D)′, since $r > 1$,

$$S_n = \frac{a(r^n - 1)}{r - 1},$$

and substituting $n = 6$, $a = 3$, and $r = 2$,

$$S_6 = \frac{3(2^6 - 1)}{2 - 1} = \frac{3 \times 63}{1} = 189.$$

Progression problems solved by the use of logarithms. The use of logarithms replaces laborious calculations in solving problems in progression.

Example. What is the average yearly rate of increase if $100.00 placed at interest for ten years produces $179.08?

Algebraic Formula   *Arithmetical Substitution*

$$R = \sqrt[n]{\frac{\text{Value at end}}{\text{Value at beginning}}} - 1. \qquad \text{Rate} = \sqrt[10]{\frac{179.08}{100.00}} - 1.$$

Solution.

$$179.08 \div 100.00 = 1.7908$$
$$\log 1.7908 = 0.253047$$
$$\log 0.253047 \div 10 = \log 0.025305$$

In the table of logarithms, it is found that $\log 0.025305$ stands for 1.06.

$$1.06 - 1.00 = .06, \text{ or } 6\%$$

PROBLEMS

1. Determine which of the following series are geometric:

(a) 1, 4, 16, 64, . . .
(b) 160, −80, 40, −20, 10, . . .
(c) 1, 7, 13, . . .
(d) $\frac{2}{3}$, $\frac{1}{2}$, $\frac{3}{8}$, $\frac{9}{32}$, . . .

2. Write the next three terms in each geometric series in Problem 1.

3. What is the ninth term of the series 729, −243, 81, . . .

4. Which term of the series 729, 243, 81, . . . is $\frac{1}{27}$?

5. If the number of bacteria in milk doubles every three hours, by how much does the number of bacteria increase in one day? In one week?

6. Find the following sums:

(a) $4 + 20 + 100 + 500 + \cdots$ to 7 terms.
(b) $1 + 4 + 16 + 64 + \cdots$ to 12 terms.
(c) $1 + \frac{1}{3} + \frac{1}{9} + \frac{1}{27} + \cdots$ to 10 terme.

7. What is the value of $5 - 10 + 20 - 40 + \cdots + 5120 - 10240$?

8. An exhaust pump removes one-half the air from a closed tank at each stroke. What fraction of the original amount of air if left in the tank after seven strokes?

9. A machine costing $27,500.00 is found to be worth only $2,750.00 at the end of 12 years. Find the fixed percentage of diminishing value.

10. A building cost $80,000.00. At the end of each year the owners deducted 10% from its carrying value as estimated at the beginning of the year. What is the estimated value at the end of ten years? NOTE: The value at the end of the tenth year is the value at the beginning of the 11th year; therefore: Value = $80,000 \times (.9)^{11-1}$.

11. An asset that cost $15,000.00 has been written down 3% of the decreasing balance each year for ten years. At the end of the tenth year, what is its value as shown by the books?

12. If the population of a city increases in five years from 150,000 to 175,000, find the average rate of yearly increase.

13. If a savings bank pays 5% compounded annually, what will be the amount of $200.00 at the end of six years?

14. There are seven terms in a geometric progression of which the first term is 2 and the last term is 1.458. Find r and s.

15. Find a and s in a geometric progression where $r = 2$, $n = 9$, and $l = 256$.

16. Find r and s in a geometric progression where $a = 17$, $l = 459$, and $n = 4$.

17. If the bacteria in milk double every two hours, how many times will the number be multiplied in 24 hours?

The infinite geometric series.

DEFINITION. *The series* $a_1 + a_2 + a_3 + \cdots$, *in which it is understood that each term has a term immediately following it, is called an* **infinite series.** Thus, in an infinite series there is no last term.

Sums of infinite geometric series. If we consider the sum of the series

$$1 + 2 + 4 + 8 + 16 + \cdots,$$

it is clear that the terms become larger as we write more terms, and therefore the sum of terms is becoming increasingly large, or, as we say, the sum becomes infinite.

Next consider the series:

$$S_n = 1 + \tfrac{1}{2} + \tfrac{1}{4} + \tfrac{1}{8} + \cdots + (\tfrac{1}{3})^{n-1}$$

A useful representation of the sum of this series for different values of n may be obtained by the following graphical method.

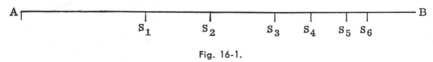

Fig. 16-1.

Let AB be a line 2 units in length. Starting from the point A on this line, mark off successive distances measured by the terms of the series. Thus, S_1 is one unit from A, so that AS_1 represents the sum of one term. The second point, S_2, is the mid-point of S_1B, so that S_1S_2 equals $\tfrac{1}{2}$ unit, and therefore AS_2 represents the sum of two terms. Similarly, AS_3 represents the sum of three terms, and so forth. The successive points S_1, S_2, S_3, . . . , approach B in such a way that, as n becomes infinite, S_n becomes arbitrarily close to B. This fact is expressed by saying that the point S_n approaches the point B as its limit as n becomes infinite, or that the sum S_n (represented by AS_n) approaches the limit 2 as n becomes infinite.

It should be emphasized that the sum of n terms of this series never reaches 2 for any value of n, regardless how large n becomes. Therefore, *2 is the limit toward which the sum of* n *terms tends as* n *becomes infinite* (*increases indefinitely*). The graphical representation makes this intuitively clear, since each of the points S_1, S_2, . . . is halfway between the preceding point and B, and therefore no point ever coincides with B.

This fact is expressed by saying that the *sum of the infinite series* $1 + \frac{1}{2} + \frac{1}{4} + \cdots$ is 2, and we write:

$$1 + \tfrac{1}{2} + \tfrac{1}{4} + \cdots = 2.$$

DEFINITION. *Whenever the sum of* n *terms of a series approaches a limit as* n *becomes infinite, the infinite series is said to* **converge** *or be* **convergent;** *otherwise, the series* **diverges** *or is* **divergent.**

It will now be shown that any infinite geometric series is convergent if the common ratio is numerically less than one.

If $r < 1$, then formula (C)′ is:

$$S_n = \frac{a(1 - r^n)}{1 - r},$$

which may be written:

$$S_n = \frac{a}{1 - r} - \frac{ar^n}{1 - r},$$

or

$$S_n = \frac{a}{1 - r} - \frac{a}{1 - r} r^n.$$

We have to examine the change in this function as n increases without limit. Since the first term does not include n, it is unchanged by any change in the value of n. In the second term, $\dfrac{a}{1 - r}$ is fixed with respect to n, and only r^n depends on n. Since r is less than 1, r^n approaches 0 as n increases indefinitely.

Therefore,

$$S_n = \frac{a}{1 - r} \qquad \text{for } n \text{ infinite.}$$

Example. Find the sum of the infinite geometric series $27 + 9 + 3 + 1 + \cdots$.

Solution. Here $a = 27$, $r = \frac{1}{3}$.

$$\therefore S = \frac{27}{1 - \frac{1}{3}} = \frac{27}{\frac{2}{3}} = 27 \times \frac{3}{2} = \frac{81}{2}.$$

17

Compound Interest

Compound interest. In transactions where simple interest computations are involved, the principal on which the simple interest is computed remains fixed or constant throughout the period involved. On a loan at simple interest, the interest becomes due at the termination of the loan or at the end of fixed or stated intervals throughout the term of the loan. If not paid when due, the interest becomes simply a non-interest-bearing debt and is never added to the principal.

In transactions where compound interest is involved, the principal is continually increasing by the addition of interest at stated intervals. The amount accumulated (principal + interest) at the end of some given time is the compound **amount.** The difference between the compound amount and the original principal is the **compound interest** for the period involved.

Compound interest is a logical approach to investments, for, if the periodic interest were paid to the lender, he would have this additional principal available for investment during the following period, and so on to the end of the last period.

Compound interest and simple interest compared. An illustration will serve to display the difference. Let us compute and compare the amount of debt at the end of three years if $1,000.00 is loaned at 7%.

Simple Interest		*Compound Interest*	
Original principal............	$1,000.00	Original principal............	$1,000.00
Interest for 1 year..........	70.00	Interest for 1st year.........	70.00
Interest for 3 years.........	210.00	Principal at end of 1st year..	1,070.00
		Interest for 2nd year........	74.90
		Principal at end of 2nd year..	1,144.90
Amount of debt at end of 3rd		Interest for 3rd year........	80.14
year....................	$1,210.00	Principal at end of 3rd year..	$1,225.04

273

The compound interest for the three years is $1,225.04 − $1,000.0 = $225.04. This is $15.04 more than the simple interest for the three years.

Actuarial science. *Actuarial science* is the mathematical science based upon compound interest and upon insurance probabilities (see Chapter 24). It deals with the investment of funds and also with the mortality tables used by insurance companies (see Table 1, page 433, in Appendix III). The actuary uses tables for the greater part of his work; yet he must also have a knowledge of the fundamentals of his science. The accountant's interest in actuarial science is that it enables him to give the best service to his clients by being able to compute investment values, prepare schedules of amortization, set up sinking fund accounts, and so forth.

Conversion period and the periodic rate. The accumulation of a principal at compound interest is dependent upon two factors: (a) the number of times the interest is added to the principal over the term of the loan, or the number of **conversion periods** or **compounding periods** or **interest periods**, and (b) the interest rate per conversion period, or the **periodic rate.**

Interest is converted into principal annually, semiannually, quarterly, monthly, or at any other regular periods. The number of times that interest is compounded or converted in one year is called the **frequency of conversion.**

Regardless of the frequency of conversion, the rate of interest is usually expressed as an annual rate, such as 6% per annum compounded quarterly. The periodic rate is found from the relation:

$$\text{Periodic rate} = \frac{\text{annual rate}}{\text{frequency}}.$$

Thus, the periodic rate at 6% per annum compounded quarterly is 6%/4, or 1.5%.

The term of the investment is usually expressed in years or in years and months. For calculating purposes, it is necessary to change the term into conversion or compounding periods.

Example.

Term	Rate	Frequency of Compounding	Number of Conversion Periods	Periodic Rate
1 year	7%	annually	1	7%
1 year	7%	semiannually	2	3.5%
1 year	6%	quarterly	4	1.5%
1 year, 6 months	6%	quarterly	6	1.5%
2 years	7%	semiannually	4	3.5%
3 years, 9 months	8%	quarterly	15	2%

Compound interest formula. On page 273 an arithmetical method was used to evaluate the compound amount. This method is tedious even when a small number of compounding periods is involved or when the periodic rate is a simple percentage to operate with. If the number of compounding periods increases, the arithmetical process becomes longer to perform. It behooves us, therefore, to find a simple formula which will perform some of this arithmetic for us. The formula to be derived is used by accountants and actuaries in actual practice.

Let

P = original principal

n − number of conversion periods or compounding periods

i = periodic rate expressed as a decimal fraction

S = compound amount at the end of n conversion periods.

Then,

Original principal	$= P$
Interest for 1st conversion period	$= Pi$
Principal at the end of 1st conversion period	$= P + Pi = P(1 + i)$
Interest for 2nd conversion period	$= P(1 + i)i$
Principal at the end of 2nd conversion period	$= P(1 + i) + P(1 + i)i$
	$= P(1 + i)(1 + i)$
	$= P(1 + i)^2$
Interest for 3rd conversion period	$= P(1 + i)^2 i$
Principal at the end of 3rd conversion period	$= P(1 + i)^2 + P(1 + i)^2 i$
	$= P(1 + i)^2 (1 + i) = P(1 + i)^3$

$$\cdot \quad \cdot \quad \cdot \quad \cdot \quad \cdot$$
$$\cdot \quad \cdot \quad \cdot \quad \cdot \quad \cdot$$
$$\cdot \quad \cdot \quad \cdot \quad \cdot \quad \cdot$$

Interest for $(n - 1)$st conversion period	$= P(1 + i)^{n-2} i$
Principal at the end of the $(n - 1)$st conversion period	$= P(1 + i)^{n-2} + P(1 + i)^{n-2} i$
	$= P(1 + i)^{n-2}(1 + i) = P(1 + i)^{n-1}$
Interest for nth conversion period	$= P(1 + i)^{n-1} i$
Principal at the end of the nth conversion period	$= P(1 + i)^{n-1} + P(1 + i)^{n-1} i$
	$= P(1 + i)^{n-1}(1 + i) = P(1 + i)^n$

Therefore, we have our basic or fundamental formula:

$$S = P(1 + i)^n. \qquad (1)$$

The quantity $1 + i$ in this formula is called the *ratio of increase*, because, as can be observed in the derivation of the formula, the principal at the end of any period is $(1 + i)$ times the principal at the end of the preceding period.

The quantity $(1 + i)^n$ in formula (1) is defined as the *accumulation factor*, because the compound amount of P at the end of n periods is found by multiplying P by $(1 + i)^n$. The accumulation factor is also called the *compound amount of 1*, because, as may be readily verified from (1), the compound amount of \$1 at periodic rate i at the end of n periods is $(1 + i)^n$.

Computation of compound amount of 1 by Table 3. To determine the compound amount of 1 by actual calculations would require considerable time. Much time can be saved by using a table such as Table 3 at the end of the book, where the compound amount of 1 can be read off for various numerical values of n and i. The letter n at the top of the first column on each page refers to the number of compounding periods. The per cent at the top of each of the other columns refers to the interest rate per period.

Example. What is the compound amount of 1 at 6% per period for 7 periods?

Solution. Find the column in Table 3 which is headed 6%. Read down in this column until you arrive at the entry in the row which contains 7 in the column headed n. $(1.06)^7 = 1.5036\ 3026$.

Table 3 gives the values of $(1 + i)^n$ to eight decimal places, although it is unnecessary to use all eight decimal places in each and every problem. The usual practice is to determine the answer to any question correct to the nearest cent; therefore, you read the entry in the table to as many decimal places as there are digits in the principal P when it is expressed in dollars and cents.

Example.

		Number of decimal places to use in
Principal P	*Number of digits in* P	*table entry*
\$3,000.00	6	6
\$ 552.25	5	5
\$ 61.03	4	4
\$ 9.99	3	3

Time beyond table limit. When the value of n is greater than the highest value of n which can be read directly from Table 3, the compound amount of 1 may still be evaluated by means of the table and the law of exponents, $a^x \cdot a^y = a^{x+y}$.

Example 1. What is the compound amount of 1 for 80 years at 7% per annum compounded annually?

Solution. $(1.07)^{80} = (1.07)^{40}(1.07)^{40}$
$= (14.97445784)(14.97445784)$
$= 224.23438760$

Example 2. What is the compound amount of 1 for 78 years at 4% per annum compounded semiannually?

Solution. $(1.02)^{156} = (1.02)^{50}(1.02)^{50}(1.02)^{50}(1.02)^{6}$
$= (2.69158803)^3(1.12616242) = (19.49960278)(1.12616242)$
$= 21.95971986$

The other approach to this problem is to evaluate the compound amount of 1 by using logarithm tables, as is outlined in the next article.

Computation of compound amount of 1 by the use of logarithms.

Example. What is the value of $(1.06)^7$?

Solution.
log 1.06	= 0.025306
multiply by exponent	7
log $(1.06)^7$	= 0.177142
antilog 0.177142	= 1.5036
$(1.06)^7$	= 1.5036

This method is especially valuable when the interest rate quoted is not to be found on Table 3.

PROBLEMS

Work the following problems by the two methods outlined.
Find the compound amount of:

1. $(1.04)^4$
2. $(1.06)^8$
3. $(1.005)^{30}$
4. $(1.025)^{17}$
5. $(1.04)^{50}$
6. $(1.03)^{75}$
7. $(1.0125)^{60}$
8. $(1.0725)^{78}$

Compound amount of 1 for fractional part of compounding period. In the problems thus far, the time contained an exact number of conversion intervals. How shall compound interest be computed when there is a fractional part of an interest period, for example, if the time is four years, two months, interest at 6% per annum convertible semiannually?

In actual practice, simple interest is customarily used for fractions of an interest period.

Compute the compound amount of 1 at the end of the last whole compounding period in the given length of time and add the simple interest on this amount at the periodic interest rate for the fractional part of the compounding period remaining.

Example.   What is the compound amount of 1 after six years and two months at 4% per annum compounded quarterly?

Solution.   Compound amount of 1 after 24 periods $= (1.01)^{24}$
$$= 1.26973465$$
Compound amount of 1 at end of six years two months
$$= 1.26973465 \; \{1 + \tfrac{2}{3}(.01)\}$$
$$= 1.278199544$$

Present value; Compound discount.   Starting with the compound interest formula:
$$S = P(1 + i)^n$$
and solving for P,

$$P = \frac{S}{(1 + i)^n} = S \frac{1}{(1 + i)^n} = S(1 + i)^{-n}$$
$$\therefore P = S(1 + i)^{-n}. \tag{2}$$

It is customary to denote the quantity $(1 + i)^{-n}$ in formula (2) by v^n and to define it as the **discount factor.**   The discount factor is also called the **present value of 1** for n periods at periodic rate i.   In other words, v^n is the amount that would accumulate to 1 if invested at periodic rate i for n periods.

Computation of present value of 1 by Table 4. v^n could be determined by evaluating $(1 + i)^n$ from Table 3 and performing the division $\frac{1}{(1 + i)^n}$.   Table 4, however, performs this division for us, and therefore $(1 + i)^{-n}$ can be read directly from this table.   The letter n at the top of the first column on each page refers to the number of compounding periods.   The per cent at the top of each of the other columns refers to the periodic interest rate.

Example.   What is the present value of 1 at 6% per period for seven periods?

Solution.   Find the column in Table 4 which is headed 6%.   Read down in this column until you arrive at the entry in the row which contains 7 in the column headed n.
$$(1.06)^{-7} = 0.6650 \; 5711.$$

Table 4 gives the values of $(1 + i)^{-n}$ to eight decimal places, although it is unnecessary to use all eight decimal places in each and every problem. The same practice is followed as for using the values of $(1 + i)^n$ from Table 3.

Time beyond table limit.   When the value of n is greater than the highest value of n which can be read directly from Table 4, the present value of 1 may still be evaluated by means of the table and the law of exponents, $a^{-x} \cdot a^{-y} = a^{-x-y} = a^{-(x+y)}$.

Example 1. What is the present value of 1 for 80 years at 7% per annum compounded annually?

Solution. $(1.07)^{-80} = (1.07)^{-40}(1.07)^{-40}$
$$= (.06678038)(.06678038)$$
$$= .00445962.$$

Example 2. What is the present value of 1 for 78 years at 4% per annum compounded semiannually?

Solution. $(1.02)^{-156} = (1.02)^{-50}(1.02)^{-50}(1.02)^{-50}(1.02)^{-6}$
$$= (.37152788)^3(.88797138) = (.05128309)(.88797138)$$
$$= .04553792$$

The logarithmic method may also be used to evaluate the present value of 1

Computation of present value of 1 by the use of logarithms.

Example. What is the value of $(1.06)^{-7}$?

Solution.

log 1		= 0.000000
log 1.06	= 0.025306	
7 log 1.06		= 0.177142
log $(1.06)^{-7}$		= $\overline{1}.822858$

antilog of $\overline{1}.822858 = .66505538$
$$(1.06)^{-7} = .66505538$$

This method is especially valuable when the interest rate quoted is not to be found on Table 4.

PROBLEMS

Work the following problems by the two methods outlined.
Find the present value of:

1. $(1.04)^{-4}$
2. $(1.06)^{-8}$
3. $(1.005)^{-30}$
4. $(1.025)^{-17}$

5. $(1.04)^{-50}$
6. $(1.03)^{-75}$
7. $(1.0125)^{-60}$
8. $(1.0725)^{-78}$

Nominal and effective rates. When the compounding period is other than a year, the stated annual rate of interest is termed the *nominal rate*. "6% per annum compounded quarterly" is a nominal rate of interest.

When the compounding period is one year, the annual rate of interest is termed the *effective rate*. "7% per annum compounded annually" is an effective rate of interest.

If two rates produce equal amounts of interest on the same principal in the same period of time, we say that the two rates are *equivalent rates* or *corresponding rates*.

Interest equation. Suppose that we have an interest rate quoted as i per annum compounded n times per year, and another interest rate

quoted as j per annum compounded m times per year which is equivalent
to the first rate stated.

Then, $$\left(1 + \frac{i}{n}\right)^n = \left(1 + \frac{j}{m}\right)^m. \tag{3}$$

Equation (3) is termed the *interest equation*. This interest equation
is valuable in determining the rate compounded a certain number of times
per year which is equivalent to a stated rate.

Example 1. What interest rate per annum compounded semiannually is
equivalent to 6% per annum compounded quarterly?

Solution (a). Let the interest rate be i per annum compounded semiannually.

Hence, $$\left(1 + \frac{i}{2}\right)^2 = (1.015)^4;$$

hence, $$1 + \frac{i}{2} = (1.015)^2$$
$$= 1.030225, \text{ from Table 3.}$$

Hence, $$\frac{i}{2} = .030225;$$
$$i = .060450.$$

Therefore, 6.045% per annum compounded semiannually is equivalent to
6% per annum compounded quarterly.

Solution (b).

$$1 + \frac{i}{2} = (1.015)^2$$
$$\log 1.015 = 0.006466$$
$$2 \log 1.015 = 0.012932$$
$$\text{antilog } 0.012932 = 1.0302$$
$$\frac{i}{2} = .0302$$
$$i = .0604$$

Example 2. What interest rate per annum compounded quarterly is equivalent
to 6% per annum compounded semiannually?

Solution (a). Let the interest rate be i per annum compounded quarterly.

Hence, $$\left(1 + \frac{i}{4}\right)^4 = (1.03)^2;$$

hence, $$1 + \frac{i}{4} = (1.03)^{\frac{1}{2}}$$
$$= 1.01488916 \text{ from Table 8;}$$

hence, $$\frac{i}{4} = .01488916$$
$$i = .05955664.$$

Therefore, 5.96% per annum compounded quarterly is equivalent to 6% per annum compounded semiannually.

Solution (b).

$$1 + \frac{i}{4} = (1.03)^{\frac{1}{2}}$$

$$\log 1.03 = 0.012837$$
$$\tfrac{1}{2} \log 1.03 = 0.0064185$$
$$\text{antilog } 0.0064185 = 1.0149$$
$$\frac{i}{4} = .0149$$
$$i = .0596.$$

The problem of finding the *effective rate* which is equivalent to some given *nominal rate* is simply a special application of the *interest equation* as is the problem of finding the *nominal rate* which is equivalent to some given *effective rate*.

Example. What is the effective rate equivalent to 7% per annum compounded semiannually?

Solution. Let the effective rate be *i*.

Hence, $1 + i = (1.035)^2 = 1.071225$ from Table 3;
hence, $i = .071225.$

Therefore, is the effective rate 7.12%.

PROBLEMS

1. Find the effective rate equivalent to:

    (a) 4% compounded quarterly.
    (b) 7% compounded semiannually.
    (c) 8% compounded quarterly.
    (d) 6% compounded monthly.

2. Complete the following table:

7% per annum compounded semiannually is equivalent to ....% per annum compounded quarterly.

5% per annum compounded quarterly is equivalent to ....% per annum compounded semiannually.

7% per annum compounded quarterly is equivalent to ....% per annum compounded annually.

6% per annum compounded monthly is equivalent to ....% per annum compounded annually.

8% per annum compounded annually is equivalent to ....% per annum compounded quarterly.

6% per annum compounded every four months is equivalent to ....% per annum compounded semiannually.

6% per annum compounded quarterly is equivalent to ....% per annum compounded every four months.

Compound amount of 1 and present value of 1 at changing rates. Up until now it has been assumed that the rate of interest has remained constant throughout the duration of the investment. Interest rates, however, may vary over the term of an investment. A savings bank which is paying 2% per annum compounded annually at the time of deposit may change the rate to $2\frac{3}{4}$% per annum compounded semiannually after three years and at a later date reduce it to $1\frac{1}{2}$% per annum compounded quarterly.

The final compound amount of 1 is the product of the required accumulation factors, each with its assigned values for i and n.

Example. Find the compound amount of 1 invested in a company which is paying 5% per annum compounded annually for the first five years, 6% per annum compounded semiannually for the next five years, and 4% per annum compounded quarterly for the remaining four years.

Solution. Compound amount of 1

$$\begin{aligned}
\text{at end of 14 years} &= (1.05)^5(1.03)^{10}(1.01)^{16} \\
&= (1.27628156)(1.34391638)(1.17257864) \\
&= 2.01122528.
\end{aligned}$$

The final present value of 1 is the product of the required discount factors, each with its assigned values for i and n.

Example. Find the present value of 1 invested in a company which is paying 5% per annum compounded semianually for the first four years, 4% per annum compounded annually for the next four years, and 6% per annum compounded quarterly for the remaining four years.

Solution.

Present	4 yrs.	8 yrs.	12 yrs.
$(1.015)^{-16}(1.04)^{-4}(1.025)^{-8}$	$(1.015)^{-16}(1.04)^{-4}$	$(1.015)^{-16}$	1

$$\begin{aligned}
\therefore \text{ present value of 1} &= (1.015)^{-16}(1.04)^{-4}(1.025)^{-8} \\
&= (.78803104)(.85480419)(.82074657) \\
&= 0.55286488.
\end{aligned}$$

Analysis of the compound interest formula. An examination of the compound interest formula (1),

$$S = P(1 + i)^n$$

reveals that it contains four variables: S, the compound amount at the end of n conversion periods; P, the original principal; n, the number of conversion periods or compounding periods; and i, the periodic rate expressed as a decimal fraction. Our algebra tells us that if we assign values to three of these variables, then the fourth can always be found. Since there are four ways of choosing three things from four things, we have four fundamental problems which can be solved by using this formula:

(a) Given P, n, i; solve to find S.
(b) Given S, n, i; solve to find P.
(c) Given P, S, n; solve to find i.
(d) Given P, S, i; solve to find n.

COMPOUND AMOUNT

(a) **Given P, n, i; to solve and find S.** This is the problem of finding the *compound amount* of any given principal which is invested at any given interest rate for any given period of time.

Example.1. Find the compound amount of $1,500.00 invested at $6\frac{1}{2}\%$ per annum compounded semiannually for five years.

Solution. In this case $P = 1500$, $i = 3\frac{3}{4}\% = .0375$, and $n = 10$. From Table 3, $(1.0375)^{10} = 1.44504394$. Substituting these values in the formula,

$$S = P(1 + i)^n$$
$$= 1500 \times 1.445044$$
$$= \$2,167.57.$$

Example 2. What is the **compound interest** earned by $100.00 if it is invested for four years at 6% per annum compounded annually?

Solution. Substituting in the formula,

$$S = P(1 + i)^n$$
$$= 100(1.06)^4$$
$$= 100 \times 1.26248$$
$$= \$126.25.$$

Therefore, the compound interest $I = S - P + \$126.25 - \$100.00 = \$26.25$.

PROBLEMS

1. Find the compound amounts of the following:

(a) $1,500.00 at 2% compounded quarterly for five years.
(b) $450.25 at 4% compounded semiannually for eight years.
(c) $1,250.00 at 3% compounded quarterly for ten years.

PRESENT VALUE

(b) **Given S, n, i; to solve and find P.** This is the problem of finding what principal invested now will amount to a certain sum at a definite future time.

Example. Find the amount of money that must be deposited now in a bank paying 2% per annum compounded semiannually so that the depositor will have $2,000.00 at the end of five years.

Solution. In this case, $S = 2,000$; $i = 1\% = .01$; and $n = 10$.

From Table IV, $(1.01)^{-10} = 0.90528695$. Substituting these values in the formula,

$$P = S(1 + i)^{-n}$$
$$= 2000 \times 0.90528695$$
$$= \$1,810.57.$$

PROBLEMS

Set up formulas, solutions, and verifications for the following:

1. What amount placed in the bank at 4%, interest compounded semi-annually, will accumulate to $2,000.00 in five years?

2. What principal will have to be placed at interest at $3\frac{1}{2}\%$, compounded semiannually, to accumulate to $3,000.00 in three years?

3. What amount of money will have to be placed on deposit to cancel a debt of $2,375.50 due in five years without interest, if the amount deposited is to be credited with interest at 4%, compounded quarterly?

Compound discount. The compound discount is the difference between 1 and the present worth of 1.

Procedure: (a) Calculate the compound discount by deducting from 1 the present worth of 1, $(1 - v^n) = D$.

(b) Multiply the compound discount on 1 by the number of dollars, $S(1 - v^n) = D$.

Example. What is the compound discount on $100.00 due in four years, if money can be invested at 6%, interest compounded annually?

Formula	*Arithmetical Substitution*
$S(1 - v^n) = D$	$100(1 - .792094) = \$20.79$

PROBLEMS

Construct formulas and write solutions for the following:

1. Find the compound discount on $500.00 due in four years, money being worth 5%.

2. Compute the compound discount on $600.00 due in five years, money being worth $4\frac{1}{2}\%$.

3. Required, the compound discount on $800.00 due in ten years, money being worth 4%.

RATE

(c) **Given S, n, P; to solve and find i.** This is the problem of finding at what interest rate a known amount of money has been invested in order to amount to a given sum at the end of a specified number of compounding periods. The *periodic rate* is always calculated and then adjusted to the proper expression by the interest equation.

There are two accepted methods for solving this problem: by logarithms and by interpolation on Table 3.

Example 1. If \$100.00 accumulates to \$265.00 after being invested for 20 years, what is the interest rate per annum compounded annually that the investment paid?

Solution by logarithms.

$$\text{From formula } S = P(1 + i)^n,$$
$$265 = 100 \ (1 + i)^{20}.$$

$$\therefore (1 + i)^{20} = \frac{265}{100} = 2.65.$$

$$\therefore \log (1 + i)^{20} = \log 2.65 = 0.423246$$
$$\therefore 20 \log (1 + i) = 0.423246$$
$$\therefore \log 1 + i = .0211623$$
$$\therefore 1 + i = 1.0499$$
$$\therefore i = .0499.$$

$\therefore$ Interest rate is 4.99% per annum compounded annually.

Solution by interpolation on Table 4.

$$\text{From formula } S = P(1 + i)^n,$$
$$265 = 100 \ (1 + i)^{20}.$$
$$\therefore (1 + i)^{20} = 2.65$$
$$\therefore \text{from Table 4,}$$

.005 $\quad d$ $\quad \begin{cases} (1.045)^{20} = 2.41171402 \\ (1 + i)^{20} = 2.65 \\ (1.05)^{20} = 2.65329771 \end{cases}$ .23828598 $\qquad$ .24158369

$$\therefore d = \frac{.23828598}{.24158369} (.005)$$

$$= .0049$$
$$\therefore i = .045 + .0049 = .0499$$
$$\therefore i = 4.99\% \text{ per annum compounded annually.}$$

Example 2. At what interest rate per annum compounded quarterly will money double itself in ten years?

Solution.

$$\text{From formula } S = P(1 + i)^n,$$
$$2 = (1 + i)^{40}$$
$$(1 + i)^{40} = 2$$

Either by logarithm or by interpolation on Table 3,

$$1 + i = 1.0175$$
$$i = .0175$$

$\therefore$ money doubles itself in ten years if invested at 7% (4 $\times$ 1$\frac{3}{4}$%) per annum compounded quarterly.

PROBLEMS

1. If \$100.00 amounts to \$130.70 in five years, what is the rate of interest?

2. If \$1,000.00 amounts to \$1,127.16 in two years, what is the rate of interest, compounded monthly? Set up the formula, the solution, and the verification.

3. Compute the annual rate of interest for each of the following:

	Principal	Amount	Time
(a)	\$ 100	\$ 133.82	5 years
(b)	200	310.59	10 years
(c)	80	212.26	20 years
(d)	1,000	2,830.75	25 years
(e)	40	68.10	18 years

4. At what nominal rate of interest per annum will \$200.00 amount to \$268.78 in five years, if interest is compounded semiannually?

5. At what rate of interest will any principal double itself in ten years?

TIME

(d) **Given S, P, i; to solve and find n.** This is the problem of finding the length of time required for a given sum of money to amount to a given sum at a stated rate of interest. The method will be presented by working an example.

Example. How long will it take \$1,000.00 to amount to \$1,600.00 if invested at 5% per annum compounded quarterly?

Solution.

$$\text{From formula } S = P(1 + i)^n,$$
$$1600 = 1000 \,(1.0125)^n$$
$$\therefore (1.0125)^n = 1.6$$

Now the question is: for what value of n is $(1.0125)^n = 1.6$?

$$\text{From Table 3, } (1.0125)^{37} = 1.58349312$$
$$(1.0125)^{38} = 1.60328678$$
$$\therefore 37 < n < 38$$

∴ the time correct to the nearest period (always less) is 37 quarters, or nine years and three months.

NOTE: At 5% per annum compounded quarterly, \$1,000.00 will amount to

$$\$1,000(1.0125)^{37} = 1000(1.58349312) = \$1,583.49$$

in nine years and three months. It would be possible to compute the length of time required for \$1,583.49 to amount to \$1,600.00 at the simple interest rate of 5%. This would give the time, correct to 1 day, for \$1,000.00 to amount to \$1,600.00 at 5% per annum compounded quarterly. In practice, however, the solution would be quoted as nine years and three months (correct to the nearest period slightly less than the required time).

PROBLEMS

Compute the time in each of the following:

	Principal	Amount	Rate	Compounded
(a)	$ 100	$ 240.66	5%	Annually
(b)	1,000	3,207.14	6%	Annually
(c)	200	533.17	4%	Quarterly
(d)	40	62.32	3%	Semiannually

Equation of value at compound interest. This is the problem of commuting one set of obligations into a second set of obligations. The two sets of obligations are said to be *equivalent* at a common date of comparison if the sum of the values of the obligations in one set at the common date is equal to the sum of the values of the obligations in the other set at the same common date. This common date, which is chosen arbitrarily, is called the *focal date*. By what has been shown previously, if the two sets are equivalent at *compound interest* at the chosen focal date, they are equivalent at any other date.

An equation expressing the equivalence of two sets at the chosen focal date is termed an *equation of value*.

Methods of handling the problems associated with equations of value will be illustrated by examples.

Example 1. A debt of $300.00 due in two years and a debt of $600.00 due in five years is to be paid by a single payment three years hence. If money is worth 5% per annum compounded annually, what should the single payment be?

Solution.

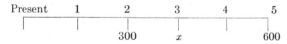

Select the end of the third year as the focal date. The equation of value becomes

$$x = 300(1.05) + 600(1.05)^{-2}$$
$$x = 315.00 + 600(.90702948)$$
$$= 315.00 + 544.22$$
$$= \$859.22$$

Therefore, single payment is $859.22.

Example 2. A man owes $1,000.00 due in three years interest-free and $2,000.00 due in ten years at 6% per annum compounded annually. He wishes to arrange payment of these two debts by making two equal payments, one four years hence and one eight years hence. What is the value of each of these payments if money is calculated to be 6% per annum compounded semiannually?

Solution.

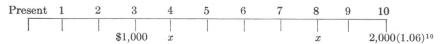

Select the end of the tenth year as focal date.   The equation of value becomes

$$x(1.03)^{12} + x(1.03)^4 = 1000(1.03)^{14} + 2000(1.06)^{10}$$
$$1.42576089x + 1.12550881x = 1000(1.51258972) + 2000(1.79084770)$$
$$\therefore 2.55126970x = 5094.29$$
$$\therefore x = \frac{5094.29}{2.55126970}$$
$$= \$1{,}996.76$$

Therefore, two payments of $2,035.98, one four years hence and one eight years hence, will discharge the debt.

Example 3.   A man owes a creditor a $5,000.00 non-interest-bearing note which is two years past due; a $5,000.00 five-year note bearing interest at 6% per annum compounded semiannually and due in two years; and a $10,000.00 ten-year note bearing interest at 7% per annum compounded annually and due in nine years.   He would prefer to discharge these responsibilities in eight equal annual payments, with the first one three years hence.   What is the annual payment if money is worth 5% per annum compounded annually?

Solution.

Select the end of the tenth year as focal date.   The equation of value is:

$$x(1.05)^7 + x(1.05)^6 + x(1.05)^5 + x(1.05)^4 + x(1.05)^3 + x(1.05)^2 + x(1.05) + x$$
$$= 5{,}000(1.05)^{12} + 5{,}000(1.03)^{10}(1.05)^8 + 10{,}000(1.07)^{10}(1.05)$$
$$\therefore x[(1.05)^7 + (1.05)^6 + (1.05)^5 + (1.05)^4 + (1.05)^3 + (1.05)^2 + (1.05) + 1]$$
$$= 5{,}000(1.79585633) + 5{,}000(1.34391638)(1.47745544)$$
$$+ 10{,}000(1.96715136)(1.05)$$
$$\therefore 9.54910887x = 8979.28 + 9927.88 + 20655.09$$
$$\therefore 9.54910887x = 39562.25$$
$$\therefore x = \frac{39562.25}{9.54910887} = \$4{,}143.04$$

PROBLEMS

1. What single payment six years hence will discharge debts of $900.00 and $700.00 due in five and ten years hence, respectively, if money is worth 6% per annum compounded quarterly?

2. A debt of $300.00 is two years overdue and another debt of $400.00 due in three years are to be paid now. If money is calculated to be worth 4% per annum compounded monthly, what is the value of this payment?

3. A house is sold for $6,000.00 cash and $2,000.00 a year for three years. What is the cash value of the house if money is worth $6\frac{1}{2}$% per annum compounded semiannually?

4. Solve Problem 1 if the $900.00 debt carries interest at 4% per annum compounded annually and the $700.00 debt carries interest at 5% per annum compounded semiannually.

REVIEW PROBLEMS FOR CHAPTER 17

1. Find the amount of $1,200.00 in five years at $4\frac{1}{2}$% per annum compounded annually.

2. What is the compound interest in Problem 1?

3. Find the present value of $926.00 due in four years if money is worth 5% per annum compounded annually.

4. On September 10, 1950 a boy was left $20,000.00 by his father, to be paid to him, with interest at 6% per annum compounded semiannually, when he reaches age 25. His birthday is November 11, 1938. How much does the boy inherit?

5. On the birthday of his first son, a father set aside $5,000.00 to provide a university education for him when the son should be 21 years old. The money was invested at 5% per annum compounded quarterly. How much is available when the boy turns 21?

6. Find the present value of $500.00 which is due in four years and bears interest at 4% per annum compounded semiannually, if money is calculated to be worth 6% per annum compounded annually.
(*To find the present value of a debt which bears interest, it is necessary to find the amount of the debt at maturity and determine the present value at the discount rate of this amount at maturity.*)

7. Find the value of $400.00 in ten years if it is invested at 6% per annum compounded annually for the first five years and at $6\frac{1}{2}$% per annum compounded semiannually for the last five years.

8. Find the effective rate equivalent to 7% per annum compounded quarterly.

9. Find the nominal rate, compounded monthly, which is equivalent to 6% per annum compounded annually.

10. A man deposits $3,000.00 now and $3,000.00 each year in a bank paying 3% per annum compounded annually. What is his bank balance after he makes his fourth deposit? Just prior to his making his sixth deposit?

11. What payment must be made now to discharge debts of $300.00 due in six months, $200.00 due in two years at 4% per annum compounded annually, and $600.00 due in three years and six months? Assume that money is worth $5\frac{1}{2}$% per annum compounded quarterly.

12. On October 1, 1960, I deposited $2,000.00 with a trust company which agreed to pay 4% per annum compounded semiannually on June 30 and December 31. If I withdraw this account on March 15, 1962, how much should I receive?

13. I have borrowed $2,000.00 at 8%, which I am to repay in four equal annual payments of principal and interest. What is the amount of each payment?

14. A mortgage of $6,000.00 bears interest at 6% per annum compounded semiannually and has four years to run. How much should an investor pay for this mortage if he is to earn $6\frac{1}{2}\%$ per annum compounded semiannually?

15. A deposit of $100.00 made 25 years ago has increased at such an interest rate compounded annually that the amount is now $250.00. What is the interest rate?

16. At what interest rate will a sum of money triple itself in 25 years?

17. How long will it take a sum of money to triple itself if invested at 9% per annum compounded quarterly?

18. $10.50 is the interest on a certain sum for the second year and $11.025 is the interest for the third year. Find the interest rate per annum compounded annually and the sum.

19. In settling the affairs of a grandfather, a person finds that the grandfather owes $1,000.00 due in one year, $2,000.00 due in two years at 3% per annum compounded quarterly, and $1,000.00 due in four years. These debts are to be paid by three equal annual payments commencing one year hence. What is the value of these payments if money is worth 6% per annum compounded annually?

18

Ordinary Annuities

Definition. An annuity is a series of equal payments made at equal intervals of time. Examples of annuities are: premiums of life insurance, interest payments on bonds or mortgages, rentals of property, pensions, sinking fund payments, regular preferred stock dividends, and so forth.

The word *annuity* suggests annual payments, but the broad meaning of the term is a series of equal payments made at equal stated intervals, whether these intervals are one year, six months, three months, or any other period of time.

Kinds of annuities. Annuities are of two kinds:

(1) *Ordinary annuity.* This is a series of payments where each periodical payment is made at the end of a period.

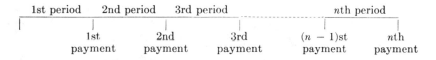

(2) *Annuity due.* This is a series of payments where each periodical payment is made at the beginning of the period.

1st period	2nd period	3rd period		nth period
1st payment	2nd payment	3rd payment	4th payment	nth payment

Ordinary annuities will be discussed in this chapter and annuities due in the next chapter.

ORDINARY ANNUITIES FORMULAS

It is obvious that it is desirable to evaluate, at any point along the time scale for an ordinary annuity, the series of payments constituting the annuity. When the series of payments is evaluated at the time of the final payment we say we have evaluated the *amount of the ordinary annuity* (point A, Figure 18-1) and when the series of payments is evaluated at the beginning of the first payment period we say we have evaluated *the present value of an ordinary annuity* (point $P.V.$, Figure 18-1).

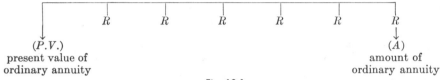

$(P.V.)$
present value of
ordinary annuity

(A)
amount of
ordinary annuity

Fig. 18-1.

Example. What is the amount and present value of three deposits of $1000.00 at the end of each of three years in a bank paying 3% per annum compounded annually?

Solution.

```
              1st year    2nd year    3rd year
               $1000       $1000       $1000
    (P.V.)                              (A)
```

To evaluate the amount is to find the sum of the values of the three payments at point (A) on the time scale.

Value of first payment at end of third year   = $1000(1.03)^2$ = 1060.90
Value of second payment at end of third year = $1000(1.03)$ = 1030.00
Value of third payment at end of third year   =   1000.00
               The amount of the ordinary annuity is $3090.90

To evaluate the present value is to find the present value of the amount $3090.90 at the beginning of the first year, which is

$$3090.90(1.03)^{-3} = (3090.90)(.91514166) - \$2828.61.$$

The present value may also be evaluated by finding the sums of the values of the three payments at point $(P.V.)$ on the time scale.

Value of first payment at beginning of first year   = $1000(1.03)^{-1}$ =   970.87
Value of second payment at beginning of first year = $1000(1.03)^{-2}$ =   942.60
Value of third payment at beginning of first year = $1000(1.03)^{-3}$ =   915.14
        ∴ the present value of the ordinary annuity is $2828.61

Amount of an ordinary annuity formula. In the previous example, an arithmetical method requiring only a knowledge of compound interest was used to evaluate the amount and present value of an ordinary annuity. If the number or complexity of periodic payments increases, the arithmetical process becomes long and cumbersome. Let us, therefore, find a simple formula which will accomplish much of this arithmetic for us.

For the purpose of developing this formula, it is necessary to consider *that the rental period of the annuity and the compounding period of the interest rate are equal in length.* The formula, therefore, will only be useful in solving problems in which the rental period and the interest period coincide in length. It should be noted, however, that the formula will be adjusted later to handle problems where the rental period and the interest period are of different lengths.

Let

R = periodic payment or rent.

n = number of periods or payments.

i = period rate of interest compounded per period expressed as a decimal fraction.

A = amount of the ordinary annuity at the end of n periods.

Then

The value of the first payment at the end of the nth period
$= R(1 + i)^{n-1}$.

The value of the second payment at the end of the nth period
$= R(1 + i)^{n-2}$.

$$\cdots \cdots \cdots$$

The value of the $(n - 1)$st payment at the end of the nth period
$= R(1 + i)$.

The value of the nth payment at the end of the nth period $= R$.

$\therefore$ the amount of the ordinary annuity is

$$A = R + R(1 + i) + R(1 + i)^2 + \cdots + R(1 + i)^{n-2} + R(1 + i)^{n-1}.$$

The right-hand side is a geometric series of n terms for which the first term is R and the common ratio is $1 + i$ which is larger than 1. Using the formula for the sum of a geometric series,

$$A = R \frac{(1 + i)^n - 1}{1 + i - 1} = R \frac{(1 + i)^n - 1}{i}.$$

$$\therefore A = R \left\{ \frac{(1 + i)^n - 1}{i} \right\}. \tag{1}$$

The quantity $\dfrac{(1 + i)^n - 1}{i}$ in Formula (1) is defined as the *compound amount of an ordinary annuity of 1 per period* and is denoted by $s_{\overline{n}|i}$ (read as *s* subscript *n* at rate *i*).

Then (1) becomes,

$$A = Rs_{\overline{n}|i} \qquad (2)$$

where
$$s_{\overline{n}|i} = \frac{(1 + i)^n - 1}{i}.$$

Computation of compound amount of an ordinary annuity of 1 per period by Table 5. To determine the compound amount of an ordinary annuity of 1 per period by actual calculations would require considerable time. Much can be saved by using a table such as Table 5 at the end of the book, where $s_{\overline{n}|i}$ can be read off for various numerical values of n and i. The letter n at the top of the first column on each page refers to the number of rental periods. The per cent at the top of each of the other columns refers to the interest rate per period.

Example. Evaluate $s_{\overline{7}|6\%}$.

Solution. Find the column in Table 5 which is headed 6%. Read down in this column until you arrive at the entry in the row which contains 7 in the column headed n.

$$s_{\overline{7}|6\%} = 8.39383765.$$

Table 5 gives the values of $s_{\overline{n}|i}$ to eight decimal places, although it is unnecessary to use all eight decimal places in each and every problem. Use the same practice here as was used for Table 3 (see page 276).

Time beyond table limit. When the value of n is greater than the highest value of n which can be read directly from Table 5, the value of $s_{\overline{n}|i}$ may still be evaluated by means of Tables 3 and 5 and the formula:

$$s_{\overline{n+m}|i} = s_{\overline{n}|i} + (1 + i)^n s_{\overline{m}|i} \qquad (3)$$

Proof of Formula (3):

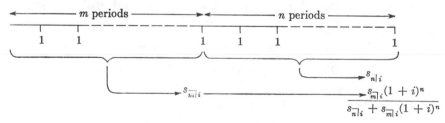

Example. Evaluate $s_{\overline{150}|4\%}$.

Solution.
$$\begin{aligned}
s_{\overline{150}|4\%} &= s_{\overline{100}|4\%} + s_{\overline{50}|4\%}(1.04)^{100} \\
&= 1237.62370461 + 152.66708366(50.50494818) \\
&= 1237.62370461 + 7710.44314903 \\
&= 8948.06685364.
\end{aligned}$$

Present value of an ordinary annuity formula. For the purpose of developing this formula it is necessary to restrict the lengths of the rental period and the compounding period in the same way that they were restricted for the amount formula—*the rental period of the annuity and the compounding period of the interest rate must be equal in length.*

Let R = periodic payment or rent.

n = number of periods or payments.

i = period rate of interest compounded per period expressed as a decimal fraction.

$P.V.$ = present value of an ordinary annuity of n periods.

Method 1.

The present value of an ordinary annuity for n payment periods is obviously the present value of the amount of an ordinary annuity for n payment periods. Therefore, using Formula (1),

$$P.V. = A(1 + i)^{-n}$$

$$P.V. = \frac{R(1 + i)^n - 1}{i}(1 + i)^{-n}$$

$$P.V. = R\left\{\frac{1 - (1 + i)^{-n}}{i}\right\} \tag{4}$$

Method 2.

The value of the first payment at the beginning of the first period $= R(1 + i)^{-1}$.

The value of the second payment at the beginning of the first period $= R(1 + i)^{-2}$.

$$\cdot \quad \cdot \quad \cdot \quad \cdot \quad \cdot$$
$$\cdot \quad \cdot \quad \cdot \quad \cdot \quad \cdot$$
$$\cdot \quad \cdot \quad \cdot \quad \cdot \quad \cdot$$

The value of the $(n - 1)$st payment at the beginning of the first period $= R(1 + i)^{-(n-1)}$.

The value of the nth payment at the beginning of the first period $= R(1 + i)^{-n}$.

$\therefore$ The present value of the ordinary annuity is,

$$P.V. = R(1 + i)^{-1} + R(1 + i)^{-2} + \cdots + R(1 + i)^{-(n-1)} + R(1 + i)^{-n}$$

The right-hand side is a geometirc series of n terms for which the first term is $R(1 + i)^{-1}$ and the common ratio is $(1 + i)^{-1}$, which is less than 1. Using the formula for the sum of a geometric series,

$$P.V. = R(1 + i)^{-1}\frac{1 - (1 + i)^{-n}}{1 - (1 + i)^{-1}} = R(1 + i)^{-1}\frac{1 - (1 + i)^{-n}}{i(1 + i)^{-1}}$$

$$P.V. = R\frac{1 - (1 + i)^{-n}}{i} \tag{4}$$

The quantity $\dfrac{1 - (1 + i)^{-n}}{i}$ in Formula (4) is defined to be *the present value of an ordinary annuity of 1 per period* and is denoted by $a_{\overline{n}|i}$ (read as a subscript n at rate i).

Then (4) becomes $P.V. = Ra_{\overline{n}|i},$ (5)

where, $a_{\overline{n}|i} = \dfrac{1 - (1+i)^{-n}}{i}.$

Computation of present value of an ordinary annuity of 1 per period by Table 6. In Table 6, $a_{\overline{n}|i}$ can be read off for various numerical values of n and i.

Example. Evaluate $a_{\overline{7}|\,6\%}$.

Solution. Find the column in Table 6 which is headed 6%. Read down in this column until you arrive at the entry in the row which contains 7 in the column headed n.

$$a_{\overline{7}|\,6\%} = 5.58238144.$$

Time beyond table limit. When the value of n is greater than the highest value of n which can be read directly from Table 6, the value of $a_{\overline{n}|i}$ may still be evaluated by means of the Tables 4 and 6 and the formula

$$a_{\overline{n+m}|i} = a_{\overline{n}|i} + (1+i)^{-n}a_{\overline{m}|i}$$ (6)

Proof of Formula (6):

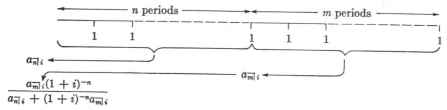

$$a_{\overline{m}|i}(1+i)^{-n}$$
$$a_{\overline{n}|i} + (1+i)^{-n}a_{\overline{m}|i}$$

Example. Evaluate $a_{\overline{150}|\,4\%}$.

Solution. $a_{\overline{150}|\,4\%} = a_{\overline{100}|\,4\%} + a_{\overline{50}|\,4\%}(1.04)^{-100}$
$\qquad\qquad = 24.50499900 + (21.48218462)(0.01980004)$
$\qquad\qquad = 24.50499900 + .42534809$
$\qquad\qquad = 24.93034709.$

Analysis of the ordinary annuities formulas. Each of the ordinary annuities formulas is similar to the compound interest formula in that each contains four variables, and therefore there are four fundamental problems which may be solved by each formula.

	1st	2nd		$(n-1)$st	nth	periods
	R	R	R	R	R	

$$P.V. = Ra_{\overline{n}|i} \qquad\qquad\qquad A = Rs_{\overline{n}|i}$$

where $a_{\overline{n}|}i = \dfrac{1-(1+i)^{-n}}{i}$ where $s_{n|i} = \dfrac{(1+i)^n - 1}{i}$

(a₁) Given R, n, i; solve to find $P.V.$ (a₂) Given R, n, i; solve to find A.
(b₁) Given $P.V., n, i$; solve to find R.   (b₂) Given A, n, i; solve to find R.
(c₁) Given $P.V., R, i$; solve to find n.   (c₂) Given A, R, i; solve to find n.
(d₁) Given $P.V., R, n$; solve to find i.   (d₂) Given A, R, n; solve to find i.

PRESENT VALUE AND COMPOUND AMOUNT
OF AN ORDINARY ANNUITY

(a₁) **Given R, n, i; to solve and find $P.V.$**   This is the problem of finding that single sum of money which, invested now at a given rate, will amount at the end of a given number of periods to the sum of the compound amounts of the payments, or of finding the sum of the present values of all the payments of the annuity.

Example. Find the present value of an ordinary annuity of $500 a year for 15 years if money is worth 6% per annum compounded annually.

Solution. In this case $R = 500$, $i = 6\% = .06$, and $n = 15$. From Table 6,

$$a_{\overline{15}|\,6\%} = 9.71224899.$$

Substituting these values in the formula,

$$P.V. = Ra_{\overline{15}|\,6\%} = 500 \times 9.71224899 = \$4856.14.$$

NOTE. If the given interest rate is not found on Table 6, then a logarithmic solution is possible. It should be noted that a subtraction is involved in evaluating $a_{\overline{n}|\,i}$, and therefore great care is necessary to avoid errors.

Example. Find the present value of an ordinary annuity of $10 per month for five years if money is worth 2% per annum compounded monthly.

Solution. The solution by formula becomes $P.V. = 10\,\dfrac{1 - (1.00166)^{-60}}{.00166}$.
Evaluate $(1.00166)^{-60}$ by using logarithms:

$$
\begin{aligned}
\log 1 &= 0.0000000 \\
\log 1.00166 &= 0.0007203 \\
60 \log 1.00166 &= 0.043218 \\
\therefore \log (1.00166)^{-60} &= \overline{1}.956782 \\
\therefore (1.00166)^{-60} &= .905275 \\
\therefore 1 - (1.00166)^{-60} &= .094725
\end{aligned}
$$

Thus,
$$P.V. = \frac{10 \times .094725}{.00166} = \frac{.947525}{.00166}$$
$$= \$570.51.$$

(a₂) **Given R, n, i; to solve and find A.**   This is the straightforward problem of finding the amount of an ordinary annuity.

Example 1.   Find the amount of an ordinary annuity of $500.00 a year for 15 years if money is worth 6% per annum compounded annually.

Solution.   In this case $R = 500$, $i = 6\% = .06$, and $n = 15$.   From Table 5,

$$s_{\overline{15}|\,6\%} = 23.27596988.$$

Substituting these values in the formula:

$$A = Rs_{\overline{15}|\,6\%} = 500 \times 23.27596988 = \$11,687.98.$$

Example 2.   Find the amount of an ordinary annuity of $10 per month for five years if money is worth 2% per annum compounded monthly.

Solution.   By formula, we have $A = 10\,\dfrac{(1.00166)^{60} - 1}{.00166}$.   Evaluate $(1.00166)^{60}$

by using logarithms:

$$
\begin{aligned}
\log 1.00166 \quad &= 0.0007203\\
60 \log 1.00166 \quad &= 0.043218\\
\therefore\ (1.00166)^{60} \quad &= \text{antilog } 0.043218 = 1.104633\\
\therefore\ (1.00166)^{60} - 1 &= .104633
\end{aligned}
$$

Thus,
$$A = \frac{10 \times .104633}{.00166} = \frac{1.04633}{.00166}$$
$$= \$630.32.$$

PROBLEMS

1. Find the amounts and the present values of the following ordinary annuities.   Verify your answers by compounding the present value in each case.

   (*a*) $200 per year for ten years at 3% per annum compounded annually.

   (*b*) $600 per annum for nine years at $6\frac{1}{2}$% per annum compounded annually.

   (*c*) $50 per month for twelve years at 5% per annum compounded monthly.

   (*d*) $250 every three months for twenty-five years at 6% per annum compounded quarterly.

   (*e*) $100 per year for ten years at $6\frac{1}{4}$% per annum compounded annually.

   (*f*) $235 per month for ten years at 2% per annum compounded monthly.

2. If for five years $250 is deposited at the end of every six months in a bank paying $3\frac{1}{2}$%, interest converted semiannually, what will be the amount credited to the account at the end of the term?   Set up a schedule showing: (*a*) number of periods; (*b*) amount deposited; (*c*) interest each period; (*d*) amount to be added to the account; (*e*) balance of the account each period.

3. *A* purchases a house, and agrees to pay $60 each month for one year.   If money is worth 6%, interest compounded monthly, what sum paid in one amount at the end of the year would be the equivalent of *A*'s total monthly payments?

4. By the terms of an annuity contract, $500 is to be paid at the end of each six months for four years.   Money is worth 6%, interest compounded semi-annually.   (*a*) Find the present value of the annuity.   (*b*) Submit solution and verification showing the applications each year of the payments as to interest, amortization of principal, and new principal against the present value of the annuity.

5. What is the value at the beginning of the first period of an annuity of $300 payable at the end of each year for ten years, money being worth 4%, interest compounded semiannually? Prepare columnar table.

6. A man purchases a house for $1,800 cash and sixteen notes of $400 each, without interest, one due at the end of each six months until all the notes are paid. If money is worth 4%, interest compounded semiannually, what is the cash value of the property?

7. What is the cash value of a contract which calls for the payment of $50 at the end of each month for five years, if money is worth 6%, interest convertible monthly?

AMORTIZATION AND SINKING FUNDS

(b₁) **Given P.V., n, i; solve to find R.** This is the problem of finding the periodic rent when the present value is known along with the number of periods and the interest rate.

Starting with the present value of an ordinary annuity formula,

$$P.V. = Ra_{\overline{n}|i}$$

and solving for R,

$$R = P.V. \cdot \frac{1}{a_{\overline{n}|i}} \tag{7}$$

The quantity $\dfrac{1}{a_{\overline{n}|i}}$ is called the *periodic rent of an annuity whose present value is 1.* Table 7 permits us to read off values for $\dfrac{1}{a_{\overline{n}|i}}$ for various values of n and i. If the value of i cannot be found on Table 7, a logarithmic solution is necessary.

Example. John's father deposited $10,000 in a fund paying 6% per annum compounded annually. How much may John withdraw at the end of each year for ten years if the fund is to be depleted after the tenth withdrawal is made?

Solution. In this case $P.V. = 10,000$, $n = 10$, $i = 6\% = .06$. From Table 7, $\dfrac{1}{a_{\overline{10}|6\%}} = 0.13586796$. Substituting these values in the formula:

$$R = P.V. \frac{1}{a_{\overline{10}|6\%}} = 10,000 \times 0.13586796 = \$1,358.68.$$

Repayment of a debt by the amortization method. The definition of the *amortization of an interest-bearing debt* in this book will consistently be the repayment of a debt, principal and interest, by a series of equal payments at equal intervals. The periodic payments form an ordinary annuity whose present value is equal to the principal of the debt.

The payment of a debt by the amortization method is based on the principle that the periodic payment shall be greater than the interest accrued· by the debt over the period. This excess of payment over the interest is applied to the reduction of the principal. Obviously the amount applied to the reduction of the principal increases each period since the interest is a reducing quantity each period.

The common amortization problem is to find the *amortization payment* when the principal of the debt, the number of payments, and the interest rate are known. This problem is a specific example of Problem $\mathbf{b}_1$.

Example. Mr. Smith buys a house for $10,000 and agrees to amortize the debt at 6% per annum compounded annually over the next ten years with the first payment made one year hence. What is the amortization payment?

Solution. In this case, $P.V. = 10,000$, $n = 10$, $i = 6\% = .06$. From Table 7, $\dfrac{1}{a_{\overline{10}|\,6\%}} = 0.13586796$. Substituting these values in the formula,

$$R = P.V. \cdot \frac{1}{a_{\overline{10}|\,6\%}} = 10{,}000 \times 0.13586796 = \$1358.68.$$

Therefore, the amortization payment is $1358.68 per year.

A second problem associated with the amortization method is that of finding the *book value of the debt* or the *outstanding principal* of the debt at any given time. This problem is important for account purposes.

The solution to this problem is to find the amortization payment first and then find the present value of the outstanding amortization payments.

Example. How much does Mr. Smith still owe on his house after making the fifth payment in the above example?

Solution. Mr. Smith's amortization payment from the above example is $1,358.68. The outstanding principal just after the fifth payment is made is the present value of an annuity of $1,358.68 at 6% per annum compounded annually for five years.

$$P.V. = 1{,}358.68 a_{\overline{5}|\,6\%}$$
$$= 1{,}358.68 \times 4.21236379$$
$$= \$5723.25$$

Thus, Mr. Smith owes $5,723.25 after his fifth payment is made.

An extremely important consideration for accounting purposes is that of preparing an *amortization schedule* which shows the distribution of each amortization payment into interest and principal.

Example. Construct an amortization schedule for Mr. Smith's debt in the previous example.

Solution.

AMORTIZATION SCHEDULE

Period	Outstanding principal at beginning of period	Interest due at end of period	Amortization payment	Principal payment	Outstanding principal at end of period
1	10000.00	600.00	1358.68	758.68	9241.32
2	9241.32	554.48	1358.68	804.20	8437.12
3	8437.12	506.23	1358.68	852.45	7584.67
4	7584.67	455.08	1358.68	903.60	6681.07
5	6681.07	400.86	1358.68	957.82	5723.25
6	5723.25	343.39	1358.68	1015.29	4707.96
7	4707.96	282.48	1358.68	1076.20	3631.76
8	3631.76	217.91	1358.68	1140.77	2490.99
9	2490.99	149.46	1358.68	1209.22	1281.77
10	1281.77	76.91	1358.68	1281.77	0000.00

(b₂) **Given A, n, i; solve to find R.** This is the problem of finding the periodic rent when the amount of the annuity is known along with the number of periods and the interest rate.

Starting with the amount formula for an ordinary annuity,

$$A = Rs_{\overline{n}|i}$$

and solving for R,

$$R = A \frac{1}{s_{\overline{n}|i}}. \tag{8}$$

The quantity $\frac{1}{s_{\overline{n}|i}}$ is called the *periodic rent of an annuity whose amount is 1.* It is necessary to relate $\frac{1}{s_{\overline{n}|i}}$ and $\frac{1}{a_{\overline{n}|i}}$ so that $\frac{1}{s_{\overline{n}|i}}$ can be evaluated by means of Table 7.

$$\frac{1}{s_{\overline{n}|i}} + i = \frac{i}{(1+i)^n - 1} + i = \frac{i(1+i)^n}{(+i)^n - 1} = \frac{i}{1 - (1+i)^m} = \frac{1}{a_{\overline{n}|i}}.$$

$$\therefore \frac{1}{s_{\overline{n}|i}} = \frac{1}{a_{\overline{n}|i}} - i. \tag{9}$$

Equation (9) is used to evaluate $\frac{1}{s_{\overline{n}|i}}$ after $\frac{1}{a_{\overline{n}|i}}$ has been found on Table 7.

Example.   What should be the amount of each equal annual payment into a fund which, in four years at 6% per annum compounded annually, is to amount to $1,000?

Solution.   In this case $A = 1000$, $n = 4$, $i = 6\% = .06$.   From Table 7,

$$\frac{1}{a_{\overline{4}|\,6\%}} = 0.28859149.$$

$$\therefore \frac{1}{s_{\overline{4}|\,6\%}} = \frac{1}{a_{\overline{4}|\,6\%}} - .06 = 0.22859149.$$

Substituting these values in the formula,

$$R = A\,\frac{1}{s_{\overline{n}|\,i}} = 1000 \times 0.22859149 = \$228.59.$$

Repayment of a debt by the sinking fund method.   There is a second method of discharging a debt to the amortization method outlined above.   In this method the entire principal is paid when the debt matures. The interest is paid at the end of each period and an amount of money is set aside periodically so that the debt can be discharged at maturity. This accumulation of money to discharge an obligation due at some future date is called a *sinking fund*.   Payments into a sinking fund may be of any amounts and made at any time.   In order to discuss the creation of a sinking fund as an example of an ordinary annuity, however, it is nec- essary to assume that payments into a sinking fund are equal in value and are deposited at equal intervals.   It is further necessary to assume that the amount of the sinking fund at maturity of the debt is exactly equal to the amount of the debt, and that the interest paid at the end of each period is not paid from the sinking fund but is paid as it falls due.

The common problem to solve for a sinking fund is that of finding the amount of the deposits in order that the sinking fund will discharge the liability at the time of maturity of the liability.   This is known as finding the *sinking fund payment* and is a specific example of problem b₂.

Example.   A company borrowed $2,500 for five years, and established a sinking fund to provide for the payment of the debt.   The contributions to the fund were to be made at the end of each year.   If money is worth 6% per annum compounded annually, what should be the amount of each annual contribution?

Solution.   In this case $A = 2,500$, $n = 5$, $i = 6\% = .06$.   From Table 7,

$$\frac{1}{a_{\overline{5}|\,6\%}} = 0.23739640.$$

Substituting these values in the formula,

$$R = A\,\frac{1}{s_{\overline{n}|\,i}} = 2500 \times 0.17739640 = \$443.49.$$

The periodic contribution to the sinking fund is not likely to be the only periodic responsibility. If the debt is carrying interest, this must also be paid periodically. The total amount which will make the periodic payment into the sinking fund, as well as pay the outstanding interest for the period, is called *the total periodic charge*.

Example. If the company borrowed the $2500 in the previous example at 4% per annum compounded annually what is the *total period charge for the debt*.

Solution. Periodic payment into sinking fund = $443.49 (from previous example)
Periodic interest because of the debt = $100.00
Total periodic charge = $543.49.

If the above debt had been amortized by five equal annual payments of principal and interest, the amortization payment would be,

$$2500 \frac{1}{a_{\overline{5}|4\%}} = 2500 \times 0.22462711 = \$561.57.$$

It should be noted that the amortization method has only one interest rate associated with it whereas the sinking fund method has two interest rates associated with it: (*a*) the interest rate which the borrower must pay and (*b*) the interest rate obtainable on sinking fund deposits. In the above example the sinking fund method is more to the advantage of the borrower than the amortization method, because the sinking fund is invested at an interest rate which is higher than the interest rate on the debt. The following is a handy rule to remember.

Sinking fund interest rate = interest rate of debt. *Sinking Fund Method = Amortization.*

Sinking fund interest rate > interest rate of debt. *Sinking Fund Method more advantageous to investor.*

Sinking fund interest rate < interest rate of debt. *Amortization Method more advantageous to investor.*

A second problem associated with the sinking fund method is that of evaluating the book value of the debt which is the difference between the principal of the debt and the amount in the sinking fund at that time.

It is important from an accounting standpoint to prepare a *sinking fund schedule* which outlines the accumulation of principal for the debt under consideration.

The following schedule is for the previous example.

SINKING FUND SCHEDULE

End of Period	Contribution to Sinking Fund	Interest Due at End of Period	Yearly Income	Total Fund
1	443.49	—	443.49	443.49
2	443.49	26.61	470.10	913.59
3	443.49	54.82	498.31	1411.90
4	443.49	84.71	528.20	1940.00
5	443.49	116.41	559.90	2500.00

PROBLEMS

1. If the present value of an annuity contract is $6,000, what amount must be paid at the end of each year for ten years to cancel the obligation, money being worth 4%, interest compounded annually?

2. An annuity contract is worth $12,000 at the present date. If the time to maturity is ten years, and money is worth 3%, interest compounded semi-annually, what periodic payment must be made at the end of every six months to cancel the contract in ten years?

3. The present value of a 12-year annuity contract is $8,000. If money is worth 4%, interest convertible quarterly, what amount must be paid at the end of each quarter to cancel the contract in 12 years?

4. A contracts for the purchase of a house, and agrees to pay for it in install-ments of equal amounts over a period of ten years. The cash value of the house is $10,000. If money is worth 5%, interest convertible quarterly, what should be the amount of each payment?

5. What annuity, payable quarterly for 20 years, would be required to repay a loan of $12,840, the nominal rate of interest being 4% per annum?

6. A debt of $3,500, with interest at 5%, compounded semiannually, will be discharged, principal and interest, by equal payments at the end of every six months for ten years. Determine the amount of each payment.

7. A house cost $15,000. The purchaser paid $3,000 cash, and agreed to pay the balance in equal quarterly payments, principal and interest, over a period of $8\frac{1}{2}$ years. If money is worth 6%, interest convertible quarterly, what is the amount of each payment?

8. A savings bank pays 2%, interest compounded quarterly. How much must be deposited at the end of each quarter in order to accumulate $400 at the end of two years? Prepare a schedule for verification.

9. A company owes $600, due in four years. How much must be set aside semiannually at 4%, interest compounded semiannually, to accumulate to the amount of the debt at maturity?

10. A company issued bonds for $30,000, due in ten years. Interest is at 5%, compounded quarterly. How much must the company set aside every three months in order to be able to meet the payments on the bonds when they become due?

11. A company has a debt of $20,000, due at the end of ten years. Money is worth 5%, interest compounded annually. How much must be set aside annually to accumulate to the amount of the debt?

12. At the age of 30, Y decides that he ought to deposit in the bank, every three months, an amount which will have accumulated to $25,000 by the time he is 55. The bank allows him 4%, interest compounded quarterly. What is the amount of Y's quarterly deposits?

13. A company establishes a sinking fund to provide for the payment of a debt of $8,000 maturing in 4 years. The contributions to the fund are to be made at the end of every six months. Interest at 4% is to be compounded semi-annually. What must be the amount of each semiannual contribution? Construct a sinking fund schedule.

14. A debt of $30,000 is due in four years. A sinking fund is to be established, and contributions are to be made at the end of every six months. What must be the amount of each semiannual contribution, if interest at 4% is compounded semiannually? Construct a sinking fund schedule.

15. A has an obligation of $8,000 maturing in three years. How much must be set aside each month at 6%, interest compounded monthly, in order to be able to pay the debt when due?

TERMS OF AN ORDINARY ANNUITY

(c_1) **Given $P.V., R, i$; to solve and find n.** This is the problem of finding the number of periods required to determine that an ordinary annuity of a fixed amount per period at a fixed periodic rate will have a present value of a fixed amount. This problem occurs frequently in real estate transactions. A buyer can offer a maximum amount per month to amortize the mortgage, and the mortgagor is anxious to know how long it will take to have the mortgage amortized.

Example. Find the term of an ordinary annuity whose present value is $600 and whose annual rent is $100 at 6% per annum compounded annually.

Solution. In this case $R = 100$, $i = 6\% = .06$, and $P.V. = 600$. From Formula (5),

$$a_{\overline{n}|i} = \frac{P.V.}{R}$$

$$\therefore a_{\overline{n}|6\%} = \frac{600}{100} = 6.$$

Now, from Table 6,

$$a_{\overline{7}|6\%} = 5.58238144$$
$$a_{\overline{8}|6\%} = 6.20979381$$
$$\therefore 7 < n < 8.$$

Therefore, there should be seven annual payments of $100 and an eighth partial payment, which we shall now find.

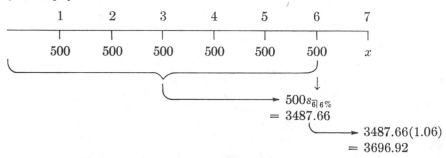

$$100a_{\overline{7}|\,6\%} \qquad = 558.24$$

$$x(1.06)^{-8}$$

$$\therefore\ 558.24 + x(1.06)^{-8} = 600$$
$$x(1.06)^{-8} = 41.76$$
$$x = 41.76(1.06)^8 = 41.76(1.59384807)$$
$$= 66.56.$$

Therefore, the eighth partial payment is \$66.56.

(c.) **Given A, R, i; to solve and find n.** When the rate of interest, the amount of the ordinary annuity and the size of each periodic payment are stated, it is possible to calculate the number of periodic payments to be made.

Example. In how many years will an annual investment of \$500 at 6% per annum, compounded annually, amount to \$3,800?

Solution. In this case $R = 500$, $i = 6\% = .06$, and $A = 3,800$. From Formula (2),

$$s_{\overline{n}|\,i} = \frac{A}{R}$$

$$\therefore\ s_{\overline{n}|\,6\%} = \frac{3800}{500} = 7.6.$$

Now, from Table 5,

$$s_{\overline{6}|\,6\%} = 6.97531854$$
$$s_{\overline{7}|\,6\%} = 8.39383765$$
$$\therefore\ 6 < n < 7.$$

Therefore, there should be six annual payments of \$500, and a seventh partial payment which is now found:

$$\therefore\ 3696.92 + x = 3800$$
$$x = 103.08.$$

Therefore, the seventh partial payment is $103.08.

NOTE: In this type of problem the final partial payment must be investigated carefully. There is always the possibility that when n is cornered on Table 5 such that $a < n < b$, and $Rs_{\overline{a}|i}$ is evaluated and this amount compounded for one period, this will exceed the quoted amount of the annuity. In this case an amount is added to the ath payment.

Example. In how many years will an annual investment of $400 at 4% per annum compounded annually amount to $2,700?

Solution. In this case $R = 400$, $i = 4\% = .04$, and $A = 2,700$. From Formula (2)

$$s_{\overline{n}|i} = A/R$$
$$\therefore s_{\overline{n}|4\%} = \frac{2,700}{400} = 6.75.$$

Now, from Table 5,

$$s_{\overline{6}|4\%} = 6.63297546$$
$$s_{\overline{7}|4\%} = 7.89829448$$
$$\therefore 6 < n < 7.$$

And now if we attempt to find the partial payment,

$$400s_{\overline{6}|4\%} = 400(6.63297546) = 2,653.19,$$

and $2,653.19(1.04) = 2,759.32$. This indicates that there can be no seventh partial payment.

The solution is therefore indicated as follows: there are five payments of $400 plus a sixth payment of:

$$\$400 + (\$2,700 - \$2,653.19) = \$400 + \$46.81 = \$446.81.$$

PROBLEMS

1. L. Miller purchased a house and lot for $7,800. He agreed to pay $2,800 cash and $50 at the end of each month until the debt should be paid. How many months will it take Miller to pay the debt, if each payment is to cancel the interest due, and the balance is to apply against the principal? The interest rate is 6% per annum compounded monthly.

2. B sells his residence for $10,500. He receives a down payment of $2,500. The balance is to be paid on the basis of $75 each month. Each monthly payment is to cancel the interest first, and the balance is to apply against the principal. The contract states that interest is at the rate of 6% per annum compounded monthly. How long will it take the buyer to pay off the debt?

3. Cole buys a farm for $18,000, and agrees to pay $6,000 down, the balance to draw interest at 6% per annum compounded quarterly. Any payments made are to apply on interest due to date, and if the payments exceed the interest due, the balance is to be applied to the reduction of the principal. Cole desires to know how long it will take him to pay for the farm if he makes equal quarterly payments of $400.

4. A man has saved $30,000, which is invested at $4\frac{1}{2}\%$ per annum compounded semiannually. He is planning to retire and wishes to know how long it will take to exhaust his funds if he spends $1,500 every six months.

5. If L. Miller deposits $250 a year in an investment syndicate which advertises a return of 5% per annum compounded annually, how long will it take to accumulate $20,000?

6. If Smith deposits $500 every year into a bank which pays $2\frac{3}{4}$% per annum compounded annually, how long will it be before he can purchase a new car for cash at $3,300?

RATE OF AN ORDINARY ANNUITY

(d_1) **Given *P.V.*, *R*, *n*; to solve and find *i*.** This is the problem of finding the interest rate on an ordinary annuity when the present value, periodic rent and number of periods are known. The periodic rate is always calculated and then adjusted to the correct expression on a per annum basis by the interest equation.

Example 1.   You are offered an annuity of $100 a year for 25 years for $1,500 cash.   What rate of interest is your investment earning?

Solution.   In this case, $R = 100$, $n = 25$, and $P.V. = 1500$.   By Formula (5),

$$a_{\overline{n}|i} = \frac{P.V.}{R}$$

$$\therefore a_{\overline{25}|i} = \frac{1500}{100} = 15.$$

By interpolation on Table 6,

$$.005 \quad d \left[\begin{array}{l} a_{\overline{25}|4\%} = 15.62207994 \\ a_{\overline{25}|i} \quad = 15 \\ a_{\overline{25}|4\frac{1}{2}\%} = 14.82820896 \end{array} \right. \quad \left. \begin{array}{c} \\ .62207994 \\ \\ \end{array} \right] \quad .79387098$$

$$\therefore d = \frac{.62207994}{.79387098}(.005) = .0039$$

$$\therefore i = .0439.$$

Therefore, the interest rate is 4.39% per annum compounded annually.

Example 2.   The purchaser of a house offers to pay $200 every three months for 15 years.   What is the interest rate earned on the mortgage if the cash value of the house is $7,500?

Solution.   In this case $R = 200$, $n = 60$, and $P.V. = 7500$.   By Formula (5),

$$a_{\overline{60}|i} = \tfrac{7500}{200} = 37.5$$

By interpolation on Table 6,

$$.0025 \quad d \left[\begin{array}{l} a_{\overline{60}|1\frac{1}{2}\%} = 39.38026889 \\ a_{\overline{60}|i} \quad = 37.5 \\ a_{\overline{60}|1\frac{3}{4}\%} = 36.96398552 \end{array} \right. \quad \left. \begin{array}{c} \\ 1.88026889 \\ \\ \end{array} \right] \quad 2.41628337$$

$$\therefore d = \frac{1.88026889}{2.41628337}(.0025) = .0019$$

$$\therefore i = .015 + .0019 = .0169$$

Therefore, the interest rate is 1.69 × 4 = 6.76% per annum, compounded quarterly.

(d₂) **Given *A*, *R*, *n*; to solve and find *i*.** This is the problem of finding the interest rate on an ordinary annuity when the amount, periodic rent, and number of periods are known. As in *d*, the *periodic rate* is always calculated and then adjusted to the correct expression on a per annum basis by the interest equation.

Example. At what rate per annum converted quarterly will an annuity of $100 every three months amount to $2250 in five years?

Solution. In this case $R = 100$, $n = 20$, and $A = 2,250$. From Formula (2),

$$s_{n|i} = \frac{A}{R}$$

$$\therefore s_{\overline{20}|i} = \frac{2250}{100} = 22.50$$

By interpolation on Table 5,

$$.00125 \quad d \begin{bmatrix} s_{\overline{20}|1\frac{1}{8}\%} = 22.28893519 \\ s_{\overline{20}|i} = 22.50 \\ s_{\overline{20}|1\frac{1}{4}\%} = 22.56297854 \end{bmatrix} \quad .21106481 \quad .27404335$$

$$d = \frac{.21106481}{.27404335}(.00125) = .00096$$

$$i = .01125 + .00096 = .01221$$

Therefore, the interest rate is 1.221 × 4 = 4.884% per annum compounded quarterly.

PROBLEMS

1. You are offered a 30-year annuity of $940 a year for $15,000 cash. What interest rate will you earn?

2. Find the interest rate when an annuity of $1,000 a year for 12 years amounts to $15,700.

3. If $5,400 purchases $500 every six months for eight years, what is the interest rate?

4. If $500 every six months amounts to $5,000 in four years, what is the interest rate?

REVIEW PROBLEMS FOR CHAPTER 18

1. Amos Brown sets aside $400 at the end of each year to provide a fund for his daughter's college expenses. If he invests the money at 3% per annum compounded annually, what will be the amount at the end of ten years?

2. Ben Told invests $200 at the end of each year. At the end of the fifth year, he has accumulated $1,040.81. Write the equation whose solution will give the rate of interest. Solve and check your answer as nearly as possible from the $s_{\overline{n}|i}$ table. Interest is convertible annually.

3. If in Problem 1 the interest realized had been $2\frac{1}{2}\%$, what would have been the amount?

4. An annuity of $1.00 a year amounted to $8.00 in seven years. What was the effective rate of interest?

5. If money can be invested at 3% effective, how many full years will be necessary to accumulate a fund of at least $2,000 from $100 set aside at the end of each year?

6. Find the amount of an annuity of $1,000 a year paid in four quarterly installments of $250 for six years if the interest rate is 4% per annum, compounded quarterly.

7. How long will it take to accumulate $1,500 by depositing $20 at the end of each month if the bank pays 6% per annum compounded monthly?

8. If you pay a paving tax of $52.17 at the end of each year for ten years and the rate of interest is 5%, what is the actual tax for the paving?

9. What is the present value of an annuity of $1,800 a year in monthly installments for ten years if money is worth 4% per annum compounded annually?

10. How long will it take to pay for a house and lot priced at $6,000 if you pay $1,000 down and $800 at the end of each year until full payment is made, assuming interest to be 6% effective?

11. If $750 invested at the end of each year for six years amounts to $4,912.62, what is the rate of interest?

12. An annuity of $100 a year for 8 years amounts to $900. Find the effective rate of interest, convertible annually.

13. Find the amount of an annuity of $500 for 10 years: (*a*) with effective rate 4%; (*b*) with a nominal rate of 4%, converted quarterly.

14. George Smith deposits $50 in a savings bank at the end of each six months. The bank pays 2% convertible semiannually. What will be the amount to Smith's credit at the end of five years?

15. Find the present value of an annuity of $500 a year for ten years if money is worth 4% effective.

16. A realtor offers a house for $4,000 cash and $1,000 a year for six years without interest. A buyer desires to pay cash. If money is worth 6% effective, what should be the cash price of the house?

17. Find the present value of an annuity of $2,000 a year for five years if money is worth 4% per annum compounded annually.

18. A realtor offers a house for $1,500 cash and $50 a month for ten years, without interest. If money is worth 6% per annum compounded monthly, what is the equivalent cash price?

19. What is the present value of an annuity of $840 a year in quarterly installments for six years if money is worth 4% nominal, convertible quarterly?

20. How many years will it take to accumulate $785 if $100 is invested at the end of each year at $4\frac{1}{2}\%$?

21. What half-yearly payment is equivalent to $3,000 per year if money is worth 7% per annum compounded semiannually?

22. Smith borrows $5,000 and wishes to repay the loan by making annual payments of $400. If money is worth 5% per annum compounded annually, how many full payments of $400 are made and what is the value of the partial payment?

23. Brown receives $20,000 worth of insurance and invests it at $6\frac{1}{2}\%$ per annum compounded annually. He spends $1,800 a year. How long will his capital last?

24. A man wishes to provide $8,000 at the end of 16 years for his son's education. He can invest his money at 4% per annum compounded annually. What are his annual payments?

25. A town borrows $200,000 at 3% per annum compounded annually, which is to be repaid in 15 years. A sinking fund is established which earns $4\frac{1}{2}\%$ per annum compounded annually. What are the annual payments into the sinking fund, and what is the annual commitment as a result of the debt?

26. A company wishes to borrow money by an issue of 4% bonds. They can pay $20,000 a year from revenue to finance the loan and to provide a sinking fund which earns 3% per annum compounded annually to redeem the bonds in ten years. If bonds are in denominations of $500, how many should they issue?

27. A man bought a farm for $10,000. He paid $3,000 cash and agreed to pay the balance with interest at 7% per annum compounded annually in ten equal annual installments, the first installment being due one year from date of purchase. Find the installment and construct the amortization schedule.

28. A mortgage for $15,000 with interest at 6% per annum compounded quarterly is to be repaid in 40 equal quarterly payments of principal and interest. Find the quarterly payment and construct a schedule for the first ten payments and calculate the amount of unpaid principal just after the twenty-fourth payment has been made.

29. An insurance policy provides the option at maturity of $10,000 cash or $350 at end of each six months for 20 years. If the interest rate is 5% per annum compounded semiannually, which is the better offer to accept?

30. A man buys a house for $16,000. He pays $4,000 cash and signs a mortgage in which he agrees to amortize the balance in monthly payments for 15 years at 6% per annum compounded monthly. Just after he makes his sixtieth payment, the mortgage is sold to an investor who is to realize 8% per annum compounded monthly on his investment. What was the purchase price of the mortgage?

19

Special Annuities

The special annuities discussed in this chapter are: *Annuity due* which is a series of payments in which eàch periodical payment is made at the beginning of the period; *deferred annuity* which is an ordinary annuity whose term begins a certain number of periods from the present and in which the payments are made at the *end of each period* after the term commences; *perpetuity*, which is an annuity whose term has become infinite or for which the payments continue forever.

ANNUITY DUE

Special formulas for the present value of an annuity due and the amount of an annuity due are developed in terms of Formulas (5) and (2) in Chapter 18 for ordinary annuities.

Amount of an annuity due formula. As was the case for the amount of an ordinary annuity formula, *the rental period of the annuity and the compounding period of the interest rate are equal in length.* A time scale should be constructed for each problem in order to avoid errors in counting periods.

There are two approaches leading to two formulas for the amount of an annuity due, and it can be shown that these two formulas produce the same result.

Let us start with a time scale where

R = periodic payment or rent.
n = number of periods or payments.
i = period rate of interest compounded per period and expressed as a decimal fraction.
A (due) = amount of the annuity due at the end of n periods.

(*a*) If we introduce an extra payment R at the end of the nth period and think of the annuity commencing one period prior to the commencing point indicated above, we would have

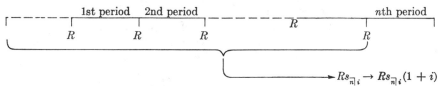

Fig. 19-1.

This obviously produces an ordinary annuity of $n + 1$ periods whose value at the end of the nth period is $Rs_{\overline{n+1}|i}$. This value is R too much because of the $(n + 1)$st R introduced at the end of the nth term. Thus,

$$A(\text{due}) = Rs_{\overline{n+1}|i} - R \text{ and}$$
$$A(\text{due}) = R(s_{\overline{n+1}|i} - 1). \tag{1}$$

(*b*) If we think of the annuity commencing one period prior to the commencing point, as indicated in Figure 19-1, without introducing an extra payment at the end of the nth period, we would have

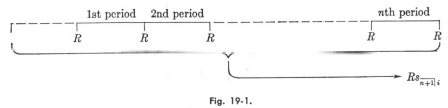

This obviously could be evaluated at the beginning of the nth period and would have the value $Rs_{\overline{n}|i}$. This amount could then be compounded through one period so as to produce an evaluation at the end of the nth term as required. Thus,

$$A(\text{due}) = Rs_{\overline{n}|i}(1 + i). \tag{2}$$

It can readily be shown that Formulas (1) and (2) are equivalent.

$$(s_{\overline{n+1}|i} - 1) = s_{\overline{n}|i}(1 + i)$$
$$s_{\overline{n+1}|i} - 1 = \frac{(1 + i)^{n+1} - 1}{i} = 1$$
$$= \frac{(1 + i)^{n+1} - 1 - i}{i} = \frac{(1 + i)^{n+1} - (1 + i)}{i}$$
$$= \left\{ \frac{(1 + i)^n - 1}{i} \right\} (1 - i) = s_{\overline{n}|i}(1 + i).$$

Present value of an annuity due formula. There are also two approaches to the present value problem leading to two formulas for the present value of an annuity due, and they can be shown to be equal.

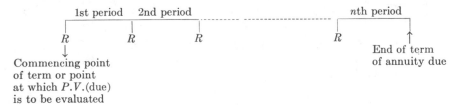

(*a*) If we think of the last $n - 1$ payments as forming an ordinary annuity of $n - 1$ payments, it can be evaluated at the beginning of the first period. If we add R to this quantity, we shall have the present value of an annuity due for n periods.

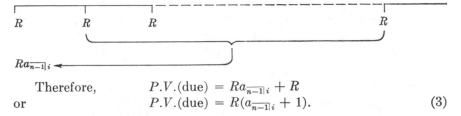

Therefore, $P.V.\text{(due)} = Ra_{\overline{n-1}|i} + R$

or $P.V.\text{(due)} = R(a_{\overline{n-1}|i} + 1).$ (3)

(*b*) If we think of the annuity commencing one period prior to the commencing point, as indicated in Figure 19-1, we could think of the n payments as an ordinary annuity of n payments, and it could be evaluated one period prior to the commencement of the term and compounded through one period so as to produce an evaluation at the beginning of the term of the annuity.

1st period   2nd period   nth period

$Ra_{\overline{n}|i}$

$Ra_{\overline{n}|i}(1 + i)$

Thus, $P.V.\text{(due)} = Ra_{\overline{n}|i}(1 + i).$ (4)

It can readily be shown that Formulas (3) and (4) are equivalent.

$$a_{\overline{n-1}|i} + 1 = \frac{1 - (1 + i)^{-n+1}}{i} + 1$$

$$= \frac{1 - (1 + i)^{-n+1} + i}{i} = (1 + i)\frac{1 - (1 + i)^{-n}}{i} = a_{\overline{n}|i}(1 + i).$$

Analysis of the annuity due formulas. Each of the four formulas for an annuity due contains four variables, and therefore the approach to the annuity due formulas is identical to the approach to ordinary annuities.

$$P.V.\text{(due)} = Ra_{\overline{n}|i}(1 + i) \quad (4)$$
$$P.V.\text{(due)} = R(a_{\overline{n-1}|i} + 1) \quad (3)$$

$$(2) \quad A\text{(due)} = Rs_{\overline{n}|i}(1 + i)$$
$$(1) \quad A\text{(due)} = R(s_{\overline{n+1}|i} - 1)$$

(a₁) Given R, n, i; solve to find $P.V.$(due).

(b₁) Given $P.V.$(due), n, i; solve to find R.

(c₁) Given $P.V.$(due), R, i; solve to find n.

(d₁) Given $P.V.$(due), R, n; solve to find i.

(a₂) Given R, n, i; solve to find A(due).

(b₂) Given A(due), n, i; solve to find R.

(c₂) Given A(due), R, i; solve to find n.

(d₂) Given A(due), R, n; solve to find i.

PRESENT VALUE AND COMPOUND AMOUNT OF AN ANNUITY DUE

(a₁) Given R, n, i; to solve and find $P.V.$(due).

Example. Under the terms of an annuity due, four annual payments of $100 each are to be made. If money is worth 6% per annum compounded annually, find the present value.

Solution. In this case, $R = 100$, $n = 4$, $i = 6\% = .06$.

(i) Using Formula (3), $P.V.\text{(due)} = R(a_{\overline{n-1}|i} + 1)$.
$$\therefore P.V.\text{(due)} = 100(a_{\overline{3}|6\%} + 1)$$
$$= 100(2.67301195 + 1)$$
$$= 100(3.67301195)$$
$$= \$367.30.$$

(ii) Using Formula (4), $P.V.\text{(due)} = Ra_{\overline{n}|i}(1 + i)$.
$$\therefore P.V.\text{(due)} = 100a_{\overline{4}|6\%}(1.06)$$
$$= 100(3.46510561)(1.06)$$
$$= \$367.30.$$

NOTES: It is apparent in the a₁ type of problem that Formula (3) is the better one to use.

If the given interest rate is not found on Table 6, then a logarithmic solution is possible.

(a_2) **Given R, n, i; to solve and find A(due).**

Example. Annuity payments of $100 are to be made at the beginning of each year for four years. If money is worth 6% per annum compounded annually, what is the amount of the annuity?

Solution. In this case $R = 100$, $n = 4$, $i = 6\% = .06$.

(i) Using Formula (1), $A(\text{due}) = R(s_{\overline{n+1}|i} - 1)$.
$$\therefore\ A(\text{due}) = 100(s_{\overline{5}|6\%} - 1)$$
$$= 100(5.63709296 - 1)$$
$$= 100(4.63709296)$$
$$= \$463.71.$$

(ii) Using Formula (2), $A(\text{due}) = Rs_{\overline{n}|i}(1 + i)$.
$$\therefore\ A(\text{due}) = 100s_{\overline{4}|6\%}(1.06)$$
$$= 100(4.37461600)(1.06)$$
$$= \$463.71.$$

NOTES: It is apparent in the a_2 type of problem that Formula (1) is the better one to use.

If the given interest rate is not found on Table 5, then a logarithmic solution is possible.

PROBLEMS

1. What is the present value of an annuity due in which $100 payments are to be made on the first day of each six months for ten years, if money is worth 5%, interest compounded semiannually? Prepare formula, solution, and verification.

2. The rents of an annuity due are $500 each, and are payable semiannually for ten years. If money is worth 6%, interest compounded semiannually, what is the value of the annuity at the date of the payment of the first rent? Prepare formula, solution, and verification.

3. A contract provides for the payment of $150 on the first of each quarter for a period of ten years. Interest is 4% compounded quarterly. What is the present value of the contract?

4. What is the present value of a contract which calls for the payment of $50 on the first of each month for a period of ten years, interest to be computed monthly at 6% per annum?

5. A is considering two propositions for the investment of $75,000 belonging to an estate. The first proposition offers him six 7% notes maturing as follows:

On July 1, 1963...	$ 5,000
On July 1, 1965...	5,000
On July 1, 1967...	5,000
On July 1, 1969...	5,000
On July 1, 1970...	5,000
On July 1, 1971...	50,000
Total......................................	$75,000

The second proposition offers him two 5% notes, maturing as follows:

On July 1, 1966	$25,000
On July 1, 1971	60,000
Total	$85,000

In each case, the loan is adequately secured, and the interest is payable semi-annually; each proposition is offered to *A* for $75,000 in cash in July, 1961.

A requests you to determine which proposition is the better one for him to accept. State your findings, and demonstrate the correctness of your answer.

6. An annuity contract calls for the payment of $1,000 at the beginning of each year for five years. Money is worth 6%, interest compounded annually. What is the amount of the annuity at the end of the fifth year?

7. For five years a man deposits in the bank $150 on the first of each quarter. The bank allows him 4% interest, compounded quarterly. What will be the amount of his savings in the bank at the end of the five-year period?

8. The X.Y.Z. Company deeds a house and lot to Smith. In return, Smith is to deposit with the company, over a period of ten years, $200 at the beginning of each six months. The rate of interest is to be 6%, compounded semiannually. What will be the amount of the accumulation at the end of the ten-year period?

RENT OF AN ANNUITY DUE

(b₁) **Given P.V.(due), n, i; to solve and find R.**

Starting with Formula (3), $P.V.\text{(due)} = R(a_{\overline{n-1}|i} + 1)$ and solving for R,

$$R = \frac{P.V.\text{ (due)}}{a_{\overline{n-1}|} + 1}. \tag{3'}$$

Starting with Formula (4), $P.V.\text{(due)} = Ra_{\overline{n}|i}(1 + i)$ and solving for R,

$$R = P.V.\text{ (due)} \frac{1}{a_{\overline{n}|i}} (1 + i)^{-1}. \tag{4'}$$

It becomes immediately apparent that Formula (4') is the better one to use, since $\frac{1}{a_{\overline{n}|i}}$ is found on Table 7 and $(1 + i)^{-1}$ is found on Table 4. Also, there are no divisions to perform, whereas Formula (3') involves one division.

Example. The present value of an annuity due of ten annual payments at 7% per annum compounded annually is $10,000. What is the periodic payment?

Solution. Here $P.V.\text{(due)} = 10,000$, $n = 10$, $i = 7\% = .07$. By formula (4'),

$$R = P.V.\text{(due)} \frac{1}{a_{\overline{n}|i}} (1 + i)^{-1}.$$

From Table 7, $\frac{1}{a_{\overline{10}|7\%}} = 0.14237750$.

From Table 4, $(1.07)^{-1} = 0.93457944$.

$$\therefore R = 10,000(0.14237750)(0.93457944)$$
$$= \$1,330.63.$$

(b$_2$) **Given A(due), n, i; to solve and find R.**
Starting with Formula (2), A(due) $= Rs_{\overline{n}|i}(1 + i)$ and solving for R,

$$R = A(\text{due}) \frac{1}{s_{\overline{n}|i}} (1 + i)^{-1}. \tag{2'}$$

The solution in this case is straightforward, since $(1 + i)^{-1}$ is found on Table 4 and $\frac{1}{s_{\overline{n}|i}}$ is found by using Formula (9), Chapter 18, and Table 7.

Example. If on his twenty-first birthday Mr. Brown deposits a sum of money in a bank which pays 3% per annum compounded annually and continues to deposit the same amount on each succeeding birthday up to and including his sixty-fourth birthday, what should be the amount of each deposit if he expects to have \$20,000 available on his sixty-fifth birthday?

Solution. In this case A(due) $= 20,000$, $n = 43$, $i = 3\% = .03$. From Table 7,

$$\frac{1}{a_{\overline{43}|3\%}} = 0.04169811.$$

$$\therefore \quad \frac{1}{s_{\overline{43}|3\%}} = \frac{1}{a_{\overline{43}|3\%}} - .03 = 0.01169811$$

and from Table 4, $(1.03)^{-1} = 0.97087379$.

Substituting in Formula (2'),

$$R = A(\text{due}) \frac{1}{s_{\overline{n}|i}} (1 + i)^{-1} = 20,000(0.01169811)(0.97087379).$$

Thus, $R = \$227.15$.

PROBLEMS

1. If the present value of an annuity contract is \$6,000, what amount must be paid at the beginning of each year for ten years to cancel the obligation, money being worth 4%, interest compounded annually?

2. An annuity contract is worth \$12,000 at the present date. If the time to maturity is ten years, and money is worth 3%, interest compounded semi-annually, what periodic payment must be made at the beginning of every six months to cancel the contract in ten years?

3. The present value of a 12-year annuity contract is \$8,000. If money is worth 4%, interest convertible quarterly, what amount must be paid at the beginning of each quarter to cancel the contract in 12 years?

4. A contracts for the purchase of a house and agrees to pay for it in installments of equal amounts over a period of 10 years. The cash value of the house is \$10,000. If money is worth 5%, interest convertible quarterly, what should be the amount of each payment at the beginning of each period?

5. What annuity due, payable quarterly for 20 years, would be required to repay a loan of \$12,840, the nominal rate of interest being 4% per annum?

6. A debt of $3,500, with interest at 5%, compounded semiannually, will be discharged, principal and interest, by equal payments at the beginning of each six months for ten years. Determine the amount of each payment.

7. A house cost $15,000. The purchaser paid $3,000 cash and agreed to pay the balance in equal quarterly payments at the beginning of each quarter, principal and interest, over a period of eight and a half years. If money is worth 6%, interest convertible quarterly, what is the amount of each payment?

8. A savings bank pays 2%, interest compounded quarterly. How much must be deposited at the beginning of each quarter in order to accumulate $400 at the end of two years? Prepare a schedule for verification.

9. A company owes $600, due in four years. How much must be set aside at the beginning of every six-month period at 4%, interest compounded semiannually, to accumulate to the amount of the debt at maturity?

10. A company issued bonds for $30,000, due in 10 years. Interest is at 5% compounded quarterly. How much must the company set aside at the beginning of every three-month period in order to be able to meet the payments on the bonds when they become due?

11. A company has a debt of $20,000, due at the end of ten years. Money is worth 5%, interest compounded annually. How much must be set aside at the beginning of each year to accumulate to the amount of the debt?

12. At the age of 30, Y decides that he ought to deposit in the bank at the beginning of every three months an amount which will have accumulated to $25,000 by the time he is 55. The bank allows him 4%, interest compounded quarterly. What is the amount of Y's quarterly deposits?

13. A company establishes a sinking fund to provide for the payment of a debt of $8,000 maturing in four years. The contributions to the fund are to be made at the beginning of every six months. Interest at 4% is to be compounded semiannually. What must be the amount of each semiannual contribution? Construct a sinking fund schedule.

14. A debt of $30,000 is due in four years. A sinking fund is to be established, and contributions are to be made at the beginning of every six months. What must be the amount of each semiannual contribution, if interest at 4% is compounded semiannually? Construct a sinking fund schedule.

15. A has an obligation of $8,000 maturing in three years. How much must he set aside at the beginning of each month at 6%, interest compounded monthly, in order to be able to pay the debt when due?

TERM OF AN ANNUITY DUE

(c₁) **Given *P.V.*(due), *R*, *i*; to solve and find *n*.** In this case it is wise to use Formula (4) to solve for

$$a_{\overline{n}|i} = \frac{P.V.(\text{due})}{R} (1 + i)^{-1}$$

because Formula (3) cannot as easily be solved for $a_{\overline{n-1}|i}$.

Example. Find the term of an annuity due whose present value is $600 and whose annual rent is $100 at 6% per annum compounded annually.

Solution.   In this case, $P.V.$(due) $= 600$, $R = 100$, $i = 6\% = .06$.
From Table 4, $(1.06)^{-1} = 0.94339623$
From Formula (4),

$$a_{\overline{n}|i} = \frac{P.V.(due)}{R}(1+i)^{-1}$$

$$\therefore \ a_{\overline{n}|6\%} = \tfrac{600}{100}(0.94339623) = 5.66037738.$$

Now from Table 6,

$$a_{\overline{7}|6\%} = 5.58238144$$
$$a_{\overline{8}|6\%} = 6.20979381$$
$$\therefore \ 7 < n < 8.$$

Therefore, there should be seven annual payments of $100 and an eighth partial payment, which is now found.

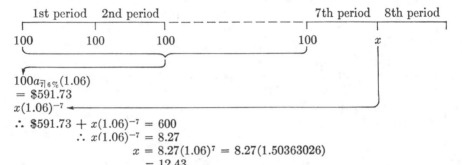

$$\therefore \ \$591.73 + x(1.06)^{-7} = 600$$
$$\therefore \ x(1.06)^{-7} = 8.27$$
$$x = 8.27(1.06)^7 = 8.27(1.50363026)$$
$$= 12.43.$$

Therefore, the eighth partial payment is $12.43.

(c₂) **Given A(due), R, i; to solve and find n.**   In this case it is wise
to use Formula (2) to solve for $s_{\overline{n}|i} = \dfrac{A(due)}{R}(1+i)^{-1}$ because Formula
(1) cannot as easily be solved for $s_{\overline{n+1}|i}$.

Example.   Mr. Jones invests $500 at the beginning of each year at 6% per annum
compounded annually. How many payments are required for the annuity
due to amount to $3800?

Solution.   In this case $R = 500$, $i = 6\% = .06$, and A(due) $= 3,800$.   From

Formula (2), $$s_{\overline{n}|i} = \frac{A(due)}{R}(1+i)^{-1}$$

$$\therefore \ s_{\overline{n}|6\%} = \tfrac{3800}{500}(1.06)^{-1}$$
$$= 7.6(0.94339623)$$
$$= 7.16981135.$$

Now from Table 5,

$$s_{\overline{6}|6\%} = 6.97531854$$
$$s_{\overline{7}|6\%} = 8.39383765$$
$$\therefore \ 6 < n < 7.$$

Therefore, there should be six annual payments of $500 and a seventh partial payment, which we shall now find.

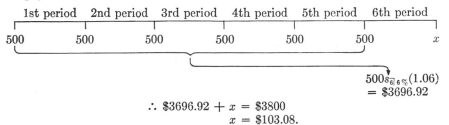

$$\therefore \$3696.92 + x = \$3800$$
$$x = \$103.08.$$

Therefore, the seventh partial payment is $103.08.

Note: Compare this example with the example on page 306, Chapter 18.

PROBLEMS

1. L. Miller purchased a house and lot for $7,800. He agreed to pay $2,800 cash and $50 at the beginning of each month until the debt should be paid. How many months will it take Miller to pay the debt, if each payment is to cancel the interest due and the balance is to apply against the principal? The interest rate is 6% per annum compounded monthly.

2. *B* sells his residence for $10,500. He receives a down payment of $2,500. The balance is to be paid on the basis of $75 at the beginning of each month. Each monthly payment is to cancel the interest first, and the balance is to apply against the principal. The contract states that interest is at the rate of 6% per annum compounded monthly. How long will it take the buyer to pay off the debt?

3. Cole buys a farm for $18,000, and agrees to pay $6,000 down, the balance to draw interest at 6% per annum compounded quarterly. Any payments made are to apply on interest due to date, and if the payments exceed the interest due, the balance is to be applied to the reduction of the principal. Cole desires to know how long it will take him to pay for the farm if he makes equal quarterly payments of $400 at the beginning of each quarter.

4. A man has saved $30,000, which is invested at $4\frac{1}{2}\%$ per annum compounded semiannually. He is planning to retire and wishes to know how long it will take to exhaust his funds if he withdraws $1,500 at the beginning of every six months.

5. If L. Miller deposits $250 at the beginning of each year in an investment syndicate, which advertises a return of 5% per annum compounded annually, how long will it take to accumulate $20,000?

6. If Smith deposits $500 at the beginning of every year into a bank which pays $2\frac{3}{4}\%$ per annum compounded annually, how long will it be before he can purchase a new car for cash at $3,300?

RATE OF AN ANNUITY DUE

(d₁) Given *P.V.*(due), *R*, *n*; to solve and find *i*.

Example. The purchaser of a house offers to pay $200 down and $200 every three months for 15 years. What is the interest rate earned on the mortgage if the cash value of the house is $7,500?

Solution.   In this case $R = 200$, $n = 60$, and $P.V.$(due) $= 7,500$.   By Formula (3),

$$a_{\overline{n-1}|i} = \frac{P.V.\text{(due)} - R}{R}$$

$$\therefore\; a_{\overline{59}|i} = 36.5.$$

By interpolation on Table 6,

$$.0025 \left\{ d \left[\begin{array}{l} a_{\overline{59}|1\frac{3}{4}\%} = 36.61085526 \\[6pt] a_{\overline{59}|i} \quad = 36.5 \\[6pt] a_{\overline{59}|2\%} = 34.45610441 \end{array} \right. \right. \quad .11085526 \quad \bigg] \quad 2.15475085$$

$$\therefore\; d = \frac{.11085526}{2.15475085}\,(.0025) = .00013$$

$$\therefore\; i = .0175 + .00013 = .01763.$$

Therefore, the interest rate is $1.763 \times 4 = 7.052\%$ per annum compounded quarterly.

NOTE: This result should be compared with the result in example 2 on page 308.

(d$_2$) Given A(due), R, n; to solve and find i.

Example.   At what rate per annum compounded quarterly will an annuity due of \$100 every three months amount to \$2,250 in five years?

Solution.   In this case, $R = 100$, $n = 20$ and A(due) $= 2,250$.   From Formula (1),

$$s_{\overline{n+1}|i} = \frac{A\text{(due)} + R}{R}$$

$$\therefore\; s_{\overline{21}|i} = \frac{2250 + 100}{100} = 23.50.$$

By interpolation on Table 5,

$$.00125 \left\{ d \left[\begin{array}{l} s_{\overline{21}|1\%} = 23.23919403 \\[6pt] s_{\overline{21}|i} \quad = 23.50 \\[6pt] s_{\overline{21}|1\frac{1}{8}\%} = 23.53968571 \end{array} \right. \right. \quad .26080597 \quad \bigg] \quad .30049168$$

$$\therefore\; d = \frac{.26080597}{.30049168}\,(.00125) = .00108$$

$$\therefore\; i = .01 + .00108 = .01108.$$

Therefore, the interest rate is $1.108 \times 4 = 4.432\%$ per annum compounded quarterly.

NOTE: This result should be compared with the result in the example on page 309.

PROBLEMS

1. You are offered a 30-year annuity of $940 at the beginning of each year for $15,000 cash. What interest rate will you earn?

2. Find the interest rate when an annuity of $1,000 at the beginning of each year for 12 years amounts to $15,700.

3. If $5,400 purchases $500 at the beginning of every six months for eight years, what is the interest rate?

4. If $500 at the beginning of every six months amounts to $5,000 in four years, what is the interest rate?

DEFERRED ANNUITIES

A *deferred annuity* is an annuity in which a number of periods are to expire before the periodic payments or rents are to begin.

The *amount of a deferred annuity* is the same as the amount of one which is not deferred, since no payments are made until after the time of deferment has expired. Therefore, the four problems which can be handled with the amount of a deferred annuity formula are identical to the four which can be handled by Formula (2), Chapter 18.

Present value of a deferred annuity formulas. Two formulas for the present value of an ordinary annuity for n periods deferred m periods are developed in terms of Formula (5), Chapter 18. It can be shown that the two formulas are actually equal.

Let R = periodic payment or rent.

n = number of periodic payments.

m = number of periods the annuity is deferred.

i = period rate of interest compounded per period and expressed as a decimal fraction.

$P.V.$(def) = present value of the deferred annuity deferred for m periods.

(*a*)   Interval of deferment.   Deferred annuity of n periods.

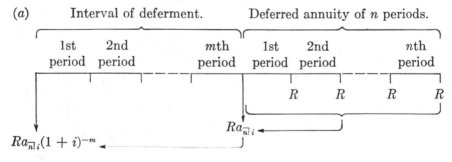

Therefore,

$$P.V.\text{(def)} = Ra_{\overline{n}|i}(1 + i)^{-m}. \tag{5}$$

(*b*)   Interval of deferment.   Deferred annuity of *n* periods.

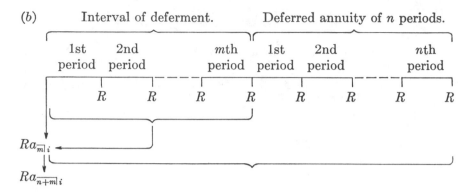

Therefore,

$$P.V.(\text{def}) = R(a_{\overline{n+m}|\,i} - a_{\overline{m}|\,i}). \tag{6}$$

It can readily be shown that Formulas (5) and (6) are equivalent.

$$a_{\overline{n+m}|\,i} - a_{\overline{m}|\,i} = \frac{1 - (1+i)^{-(n+m)}}{i} - \frac{1 - (1+i)^{-m}}{i}$$

$$= \frac{(1+i)^{-m} - (1+i)^{-n-m}}{i} = \frac{(1+i)^{-m}[1 - (1+i)^{-n}]}{i}$$

$$= \frac{1 - (1+i)^{-n}(1+i)^{-m}}{i} = a_{\overline{n}|\,i}(1+i)^{-m}.$$

Analysis of the present value of a deferred annuity formulas.
Each of the two formulas for the present value of a deferred annuity contains five variables; therefore, if the values for any four of the variables are given, it is possible to solve and find the value for the fifth variable. A time scale should be constructed for each problem in order to avoid errors in counting periods.

(a_1) **Given *R*, *n*, *m*, *i*; to solve and find *P.V.*(def).** This is the one of the five problems which occurs most frequently.

Example. Find the present value of an annuity contract which calls for five equal annual payments of $100 each, the first to be paid at the end of the seventh year, if money is worth 6% per annum compounded annually.

Solution 1.   1st   2nd   3rd   4th   5th   6th   1st   2nd   3rd   4th   5th

An analysis of the time scale shows that this is an ordinary annuity for five years deferred for six years.

In this case, $R = 100$, $n = 5$, $m = 6$, $i = 6\% = .06$. Substituting these values in Formula (5),

$$P.V.(\text{def}) = 100a_{\overline{5}|6\%}(1.06)^{-6}$$
$$= 100(4.21236379)(0.70496054)$$
$$= \$296.95.$$

Solution 2. Substituting these values in Formula (6),

$$P.V.(\text{def}) = 100(a_{\overline{11}|6\%} - a_{\overline{6}|6\%})$$
$$= 100(7.88687458 - 4.91732433)$$
$$= 100(2.96955025)$$
$$= \$296.95.$$

NOTE: It is obvious that Formula (6) is the better one to use, since it requires only one subtraction, rather than one multiplication, and also requires reading values from one table rather than from two tables.

(b₁) Given $P.V.(\text{def})$, n, m, i; to solve and find R.

Example. A father can invest \$5,000 now in a fund which pays 5% per annum compounded annually. His son is to receive 10 equal annual payments from this fund, with the first payment made at the end of the tenth year. How much will the son receive per year if the ten payments are to exhaust the fund?

Solution 1.

An analysis of the time scale shows that this is an ordinary annuity for ten years deferred nine years. In this case, $P.V.(\text{def}) = 5,000$, $n = 10$, $m = 9$, $i = 5\% = .05$.

From Formula (5), $R = P.V.(\text{def}) \dfrac{i}{a_{\overline{n}|i}} (1 + i)^m$.

Therefore,
$$R = 5000 \frac{1}{a_{\overline{10}|5\%}} (1.05)^9$$
$$= 5000(0.12950458)(1.55132822)$$
$$= \$1,004.52.$$

Solution 2. From Formula (6), $R = \dfrac{P.V.(\text{def})}{a_{\overline{n+m}|i} - a_{\overline{m}|i}}$.

Therefore,
$$R = \frac{5000}{a_{\overline{19}|5\%} - a_{\overline{9}|5\%}}$$
$$= \frac{5000}{12.08532086 - 7.10782168}$$
$$= \frac{5000}{4.97749918}$$
$$= \$1,004.52.$$

NOTE: It is obvious in this case that Formula (5) is the better one to use, since it requires no division, even though it requires reading from two tables rather than from one.

(c₁) **Given *P.V.*(def), *R*, *i*, *m*; to solve and find *n*.** The student is
referred to page 305, Chapter 18. Either formula works equally well,
and both are illustrated in the example.

Example. Find the term of an ordinary annuity, deferred five years, whose
present value is \$600 and whose annual rent is \$100 at 6% per annum compounded annually.

Solution 1.

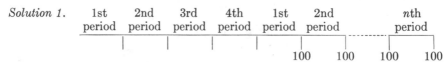

An analysis of the time scale shows that this is an ordinary annuity for *n*
periods deferred four periods.
Hence $P.V.(\text{def.}) = 600$, $R = 100$, $i = 6\% = .06$, $m = 4$.

From Formula (5), $a_{\overline{n}|i} = \dfrac{P.V.(\text{def.})(1 + i)^m}{R}$.

Therefore, $a_{\overline{n}|i} = \dfrac{600(1.06)^4}{100}$

$= 7.57486176.$

Now from Table 5,

$a_{\overline{10}|6\%} = 7.36008705$

$a_{\overline{11}|6\%} = 7.88687458$

$\therefore 10 < n < 11.$

Therefore, there should be ten annual payments of \$100 and an eleventh
partial payment, which is now found.

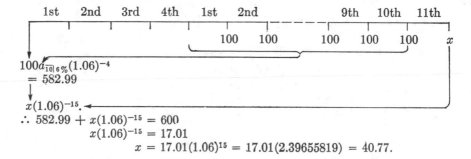

$\therefore 582.99 + x(1.06)^{-15} = 600$

$x(1.06)^{-15} = 17.01$

$x = 17.01(1.06)^{15} = 17.01(2.39655819) = 40.77.$

Therefore, the eleventh partial payment is \$40.77.

Solution 2. Substituting the given values for $P.V.(\text{def})$, R, i, and m into Formula
(6), we have

$$600 = 100(a_{\overline{n+4}|6\%} - a_{\overline{4}|6\%})$$

$$\therefore a_{\overline{n+4}|6\%} = 6 + a_{\overline{4}|6\%}$$

$$\therefore a_{\overline{n+4}|6\%} = 6 + 3.46510561$$

$$= 9.46510561.$$

Now from Table 6,

$$a_{\overline{14}|\,6\%} = 9.29498393$$
$$a_{\overline{15}|\,6\%} = 9.71224899$$
$$\therefore\ 14 < n + 4 < 15$$
$$\therefore\ 10 < n < 11$$

Therefore, there should be ten annual payments of $100 and an eleventh partial payment, which is now found.

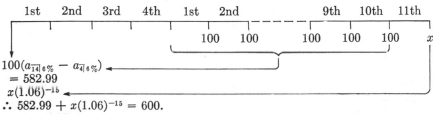

$$\therefore\ 582.99 + x(1.06)^{-15} = 600.$$
$$\therefore\ x = 40.77.$$

Therefore, the eleventh partial payment is $40.77.

(d₁) **Given P.V.(def), R, n, m; to solve and find i.** In this case, Formula (6) is the better one to use, and so it only is used in the example. The student might try to work the example using Formula (5), so that he may compare both solutions. This type of problem cannot be handled with the usual type of interpolation until the interest rate has been cornered between two values by a straight guessing process.

Example. The present value of an annuity contract which calls for five equal annual payments of $100 each, the first to be paid at the end of the seventh year, is $300. Find the interest rate.

Solution. 1st 2nd 3rd 4th 5th 6th 1st 2nd 3rd 4th 5th

An analysis of the time scale shows this to be an ordinary annuity for five years deferred for six years.

In this case, $P.V.(\text{def}) = 300, R = 100, n = 5, m = 6, i = ?$

Substituting these values in Formula (6),

$$300 = 100(a_{\overline{11}|\,i} - a_{\overline{6}|\,i})$$
$$\therefore a_{\overline{11}|\,i} - a_{\overline{6}|\,i} = 3.$$

Guess some interest rate, say, $i = .03$. Then $a_{\overline{11}|\,3\%} - a_{\overline{6}|\,3\%} = 3.83543267$. Since this value is higher than the required value for $a_{\overline{11}|\,i} - a_{\overline{6}|\,i}$, it indicates that the interest rate is higher than 3%. Try 4%, 4½%, 5%, 5½%, and so forth, until the value for $a_{\overline{11}|\,i} - a_{\overline{6}|\,i} < 3$. Then interpolate.

$$i = .04, \qquad a_{\overline{11}|\,4\%} - a_{\overline{6}|\,4\%} = 3.51833985.$$
$$i = .045, \qquad a_{\overline{11}|\,4\frac{1}{2}\%} - a_{\overline{6}|\,4\frac{1}{2}\%} = 3.37104444.$$
$$i = .05, \qquad a_{\overline{11}|\,5\%} - a_{\overline{6}|\,5\%} = 3.23072216.$$
$$i = .055, \qquad a_{\overline{11}|\,5\frac{1}{2}\%} - a_{\overline{6}|\,5\frac{1}{2}\%} = 3.09700592.$$
$$i = .06, \qquad a_{\overline{11}|\,6\%} - a_{\overline{6}|\,6\%} = 2.96955025.$$

Therefore, i lies between $5\frac{1}{2}\%$, and 6%. Now interpolate to find i.

$$
.005 \begin{cases} d \begin{cases} a_{\overline{11}|\,5\frac{1}{2}\%} - a_{\overline{6}|\,5\frac{1}{2}\%} = 3.09700592 \\ a_{\overline{11}|\,i} - a_{\overline{6}|\,i} = 3 \end{cases} \quad .09700592 \quad .2745567 \\ a_{\overline{11}|\,6\%} - a_{\overline{6}|\,6\%} = 2.96955025 \end{cases}
$$

$$\therefore d = \frac{.09700592}{.12745567}(.005) = .0038$$

$$\therefore i = .055 + .0038 = .0588.$$

$\therefore$ The interest rate is 5.88% per annum compounded annually.

NOTE: The smallest possible interval of interpolation should be used to give the best possible answer.

(e_1) **Given** *P.V.*(def), *R*, *n*, *i*; **to solve and find** *m*. This is a problem which is theoretically possible with our formulas (5) and (6); but, since it is a case which never occurs in practice, there is no example given. Mention of it here is simply for the sake of mathematical completeness.

This section on deferred annuities is closed with some examples of problems of a more general nature in which the deferred annuity formulas may be used advantageously.

Example 1. What is the present value of an annuity of $40 per month for ten years if the first payment is made at the end of five years and the interest rate is quoted as 6% per annum compounded monthly during the term of the annuity and annually during the deferred period?

Solution. Formula (5) is the better one to use. $R = 40$, $n = 120$, $m = 4$, and $i = .005$ during the term of the annuity and .06 during the deferred period.
From Formula (5),

$$
\begin{aligned}
P.V.(\text{def}) &= 40a_{\overline{120}|\,\frac{1}{2}\%}(1.06)^{-4} \\
&= 40(90.07345333)(0.79209366) \\
&= \$2{,}853.86.
\end{aligned}
$$

Example 2. What is the present value of an ordinary annuity of $100 per year for 30 years if the interest rate is quoted as 8% per annum compounded annually for the first ten years, 7% per annum compounded annually for the second ten years, and 6% per annum compounded annually for the last ten years?

Solution. A time scale is obviously helpful in making a complete analysis of the problem before beginning the work. Failure to make such a complete analysis is mainly responsible for most difficulties in the solutions of problems such as this one. Be sure to see each problem in all its parts before attempting to calculate the amounts.

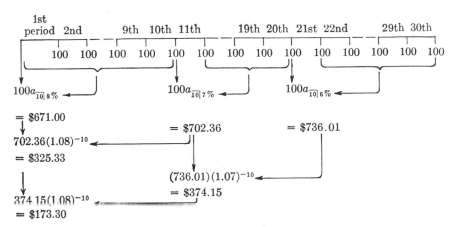

Therefore, the present value is $671.00 + $325.33 + $173.30 = $1,169.63.

Example 3. A lease has six years to run at $1,000.00 a year, with an extension for a further six years at $2,000.00 a year with the payments due at the end of each year. If money is worth 7% per annum compounded annually, what sum should be paid now in lieu of the 12 years' rent?

Solution. The solution depends upon seeing that two annuities are involved: an ordinary annuity of $1,000.00 per year for six years and an ordinary annuity of $2,000.00 per year for ten years deferred ten years.

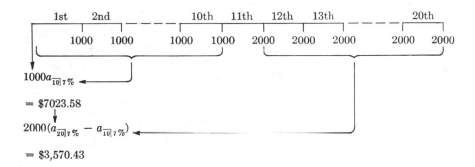

Therefore, the sum that should be paid now is $7,023.58 + $3,570.43 = $10,594.01.

PROBLEMS

Find the present value of each of the following deferred annuities. (NOTE: If interest is to be compounded semiannually, quarterly, or monthly, this same condition usually prevails during the period of deferment.)

	Payments	Payments Made	Rate	Number of Rents	Years Deferred
1.	$100	Annually	5%	5	5
2.	$500	Annually	4%	6	4
3.	$250	Semiannually	4%	10	5
4.	$200	Quarterly	6%	16	3
5.	$100	Quarterly	6%	12	5
6.	$ 50	Monthly	6%	48	3

Find the periodic payments of each of the following deferred annuities.

	Present Value	Payments Made	Rate	Number of Payments	Years Deferred
7.	$ 1,000	Annually	6%	6	6
8.	$10,000	Semiannually	$6\frac{1}{2}$%	10	4
9.	$ 6,000	Quarterly	5%	20	5
10.	$ 7,324.16	Monthly	6%	96	3

11. Mr. J. Jones purchases a house and lot for $19,800. He agreed to pay $6,600 cash and $100 at the end of each month, with the first payment payable six months from date of purchase. How many months will it take Jones to pay the debt, if each payment is to cancel the interest due and the balance is to apply against the principal? The interest rate is 6% per annum, compounded monthly.

12. B sells his residence for $16,500. He receives a down payment of $5,500. The balance is to be paid on the basis of $75 each month with the first payment payable three months from date of purchase. The interest rate is 6% per annum compounded monthly. How long will it take the buyer to pay off the debt?

13. Cole buys a farm for $50,000 with $20,000 down, the balance to draw interest at 8% per annum compounded quarterly. Any payments made are to apply on interest due to date; if the payments exceed the interest due, the balance is to be applied to the reduction of the principal. Cole desires to know how long it will take him to pay for the farm if he makes equal quarterly payments of $800, with the first payment payable one year from date of purchase.

14. A man has saved $30,000, which is invested at $4\frac{1}{2}$% per annum compounded semiannually. He is planning to retire in two years' time and wishes to know how long it will take to exhaust his funds if he spends $1,500 every six months.

15. Mr. Brown deposits $50 per month in a bank which pays 6% per annum, compounded monthly, for ten years. He starts to withdraw this fund ten years later at $150 per month. How long will his investment last before it is exhausted?

16. You are offered a 30-year annuity of $940 a year, with the first payment to be made five years from date of purchase for $15,000 cash. What interest rate will you earn?

17. If $5,400 purchases $500 every six months for eight years with the first payment payable two years from date of purchase, what is the interest rate?

18. What is the present value of an annuity contract in which the A.B. Company agrees to pay to Mr. Ladd a monthly installment of $40 for ten years, the first payment to be made ten years from date of purchase? Money is worth 6%, interest convertible monthly during the annuity period and annually during the deferred period.

19. A company is issuing $1,000,000 worth of 4%, 20-year bonds, which it wishes to pay at maturity by means of a sinking fund in which equal annual deposits are to be made. The board of directors wishes to assume that this fund will earn 5% interest for the first ten years and 4% for the last ten years. What is the annual deposit required?

20. A lease has five years to run at $1,200 a year, with an extension for an additional five years at $1,500 a year. The payments are due at the end of each year. If money is worth 5%, what should be the sum paid now in lieu of the ten years' rent?

21. On December 31, 1960, *A* is indebted to *B* in the following amounts:

(a) $1,500, due December 31, 1961, without interest.
(b) $3,500, due December 31, 1963, with interest at the rate of 6% payable annually.
(c) $5,000, due December 31, 1965, with interest at the rate of 6% from December 31, 1950, not payable until maturity of note but to be compounded annually.
(d) $6,000, due December 31, 1966, with interest at the rate of 5% payable annually.

On this date (December 31, 1960), *A* learns that on December 31, 1964, he will fall heir to $2,000,000, and he arranges with *B* to cancel the four notes in exchange for one note due in four years. It is then agreed that the new note shall include interest to maturity calculated at 5% compounded annually, and that *B* shall not lose by the exchange.
What will be the amount of the new note?

22. On January 1, 1960, *A* leased a building to *B* for the period ending December 31, 1974, at an annual rental of $7,000 payable annually in advance. Subject to this lease, *A* leased the same property to *C* on January 1, 1966, for a term of 50 years at an annual rental of $10,000, payable annually in advance, *C* to receive the rental of $7,000 payable by *B* during the remainder of *B*'s lease. For this lease *C* paid to *A* an additional $1,500 as a bonus.

Omitting all consideration of income tax questions, how should the various accounts appear on *C*'s books if he calculates interest on the investment at 6% per annum?

23. The Belgian pre-Armistice debt to the United States amounted to $171,-800,000. The settlement provided that no interest was to be charged on this part of the war debt and that graduated payments on account of principal were to be made totaling $9,400,000 by June 15, 1931, the balance to be payable at the rate of $2,900,000 per annum for 56 years.

Assuming an interest rate of 3% per annum, calculate the loss to the United States by the waiving of interest calculated at June 15, 1931.

24. A note, the face value of which is $1,000, bears interest at the rate of 8% per annum and is payable in monthly installments of $25, including interest. It is desired to discount this note at the bank so that the bank will have an effective rate of 12% per annum. What is the amount of the discount to be deducted by the bank?

PERPETUITIES

A *perpetuity* is defined as a series of periodic payments which are to run indefinitely. This form of annual payment is most often found as the effect of the establishment of an endowment fund, the rents of which are to be used for a special purpose. The amount of a perpetuity is not defined, because it increases beyond all bounds as time passes.

Present value of a perpetuity formula.   Suppose we consider a perpetuity of $R payable at the end of each k periods with the first payment due k periods hence.   Let the interest rate be i per period compounded periodically.   Define the *present value of the perpetuity* as that sum of money which, invested now at the rate i per period compounded periodically, will yield $R at the end of each k periods.   Denote the present value of the perpetuity as $P.V.$(per).   The interest payments $P.V.$(per) i per period constitute an annuity whose amount at the end of k periods must equal $R.

$$\therefore\ P.V.\text{(per)}\ i\ s_{\overline{k}|i} = R$$

$$\therefore\ P.V.\text{(per)} = \frac{R}{i}\frac{1}{s_{\overline{k}|i}} \tag{7}$$

It should be noted that if $k = 1$, then $s_{\overline{k}|i} = 1$ for all values of i, and,

therefore, $$P.V.\text{(per)} = \frac{R}{i}, \tag{8}$$

if we have a perpetuity of $R payable at the end of each period with the first payment one year hence with interest at rate i per period compounded periodically.

Example 1.   It is desired to establish a scholarship of $300 per year.   If the money can be invested at $4\frac{1}{2}\%$ per annum compounded annually, how much cash is required to establish the scholarship now so that the first award can be made one year hence?

Solution.   In this case $R = 300$ and $i = .045$.   Substituting these values in Formula (8),

$$P.V.\text{(per)} = \frac{300}{.045} = \$6666.66.$$

Example 2.   What is the present value of a perpetuity of $1,000 every five years if interest is 4% per annum compounded annually?

Solution.   In this case $R = 1,000$, $i = .04$, and $k = 5$.   Substituting these values in Formula (7),

$$P.V.\text{(per)} = \frac{1,000}{.04}\frac{1}{s_{\overline{5}|4\%}}$$

$$P.V.\text{(per)} = \$4,615.68.$$

PROBLEMS

1. If a farm produces a net annual income of $3,600, what is its present value if money is worth 5%?

2. What is the present value of a perpetuity of \$3,500 payable every five years, if money is worth 4% convertible semiannually?

3. Find the present value of a perpetuity of \$250 a year if money is worth 6%.

4. What is the present value of a perpetuity of \$600 a year if money is worth 4% convertible quarterly?

5. Find the annual rent of a perpetuity whose present value is \$15,000, if interest is 5% a year.

6. Find the present value of a perpetuity of \$10,000 payable every five years if money is worth $4\frac{1}{2}$% a year.

CAPITALIZED COST

The *capitalized cost* of an asset is the sum of the original cost plus the present value of all future replacements. This is the basis for determining whether one asset is more economical than another one or less economical. If the capitalized cost of asset A is more than the capitalized cost of asset B, then asset B is considered more economical than asset A, and vice versa. This is based on the assumption that asset A and asset B can be used for the same purpose and that the efficiency of both assets not be considered.

If $C.C.$ is the capitalized cost of an asset whose original cost is C, and which must be replaced every k periods at a cost of R, and if money is worth i per period compounded periodically, then,

$$C.C. = C + \frac{R}{i}\frac{1}{s_{\overline{k}|i}} \qquad (9)$$

Example. If money is worth 6% per annum compounded annually, what is the capitalized cost of an automobile which costs \$3,600.00 new and is replaced every three years for the trade-in plus \$1,200.00?

Solution. In this case $C = 3,600$, $R = 1,200$, $k = 3$, $i = 6\% = .06$. Substituting these values in Formula (9),

$$C.C. = 3,600 + \frac{1200}{.06}\frac{1}{s_{\overline{3}|6\%}}$$
$$= 3.600 + 20,000(0.31410981)$$
$$= 3,600 + 6282.20$$
$$= \$9,882.20.$$

PROBLEMS

1. A typewriter is purchased for \$500 and replaced each year for \$200. What is the capitalized cost of 12 typewriters at 4% per annum compounded annually?

2. \$25,000 worth of equipment must be replaced every five years at the same cost. Find the capitalized cost at 5% per annum, compounded annually.

3. A transport company operates 10 transports. Assuming money is worth $4\frac{1}{2}$% per annum, compounded annually, what is the capitalized cost of the transports if they cost $10,000 each and must be replaced every five years for trade-in plus $5,000?

4. A traffic light can be installed for $5,000 and it costs $500 per year to repair it. What must the traffic officer's salary be before it is economical to replace him with a traffic signal if money is worth 6% per annum compounded annually?

5. You can paint your house for $200 if you use brand x paint, and the job will last for two years. If brand y is used, the cost is $300 and the job will last for four years. Which brand is most economical?

6. A bridge can be erected for $9,000 with repairs of $3,000 every ten years. If money is worth $6\frac{1}{2}\%$ per annum compounded annually, how much can be spent on a permanent bridge which is equally economical?

REVIEW PROBLEMS FOR CHAPTER 19

1. Brown sets aside $500 at the beginning of each year to provide for his daughter's college education. If he invests the money at 3% effective, what will be the amount following the tenth payment?

2. Find the present value of a premium of $27.42, assuming that the insured will live to pay 20 premiums, money being worth 4% effective.

3. White bought a house, agreeing to pay $1,000 down and $500 each six months until he paid $8,000. If money is worth 5% effective, what should be the cash price of the house?

4. Find the present value of an annuity of $600 a year for ten years, if money is worth 4% effective and the annuity is deferred (*a*) five years, (*b*) eight years.

5. If you deposit $150 in a savings bank at the beginning of each quarter and the bank pays 3% nominal convertible quarterly, how much will you have to your credit at the end of five years?

6. Cole, at age 22, takes a 20-payment life insurance policy of $1,000 on which the premium is $27.42 payable at the beginning of each year. If he should die at the end of ten years just before the eleventh premium is due, by how much would his estate be increased by having taken the insurance, instead of having put the premiums into a savings bank paying 2% effective?

7. Find the present value of an annuity of $1,000 a year to be paid in quarterly installments for 12 years, deferred for five years, if money is worth 3% per annum compounded quarterly.

8. An insurance premium of $64.50 is payable semiannually in advance for 20 years. If interest is at 3% convertible semiannually, find the amount of the payments at the end of 20 years.

9. If it takes an orchard six years to reach profitable maturity, and for a period of 20 years it is expected to yield a net income of $3,500 a year, what is the cash value of the orchard if money is worth 4% effective?

10. Find the present value of an annuity due of $250 a year payable annually for six years, if money is worth 5% per annum compounded annually.

11. A farm is offered for sale for the cash value of 20 years' rental. The farm rents for $500 per year payable at the beginning of each year. What is the cash value of the farm if money is worth 6% per annum compounded annually?

12. An insurance company charges a premium of $27.50 per year for 20 years for a 20-payment life policy. If the company accumulates its funds at 5% per annum compounded annually, what is the amount of the premiums at the end of 20 years?

13. The rent of a store is $960 a year paid by monthly payments in advance. After paying no rent for three years, how much is due if money is worth 8% per annum compounded monthly?

14. A person who possessed a perpetuity of $2,000 per year left it to his son for 10 years, to his daughter for the next 15 years, and to a charitable organization forever after. What was the cash value of each bequest at the time of his decease, money being worth 5% per annum compounded annually?

15. A man wishes to present each of his three children, now aged 10, 13, and 16 years, with $2,000 at the age of 21. He plans on depositing equal sums, semi-annually, into a savings bank which pays 3% compounded semiannually on such deposits. The first deposit is to be made immediately, while the last one will be made on the youngest child's twentieth birthday. Assuming that the given ages are exact, find the amount of the semiannual deposit. Construct a schedule showing the status of the sinking fund for the last six years.

16. A debt of $10,000 bears interest at 6% per annum, compounded semi-annually. The principal, which is due in ten years, is to be discharged by making semiannual deposits into a sinking fund which accumulates at 4% per annum compounded semiannually, with the first payment made immediately. Find the semiannual expense on account of the debt. What rate of interest could the debtor afford to pay if he were to amortize the debt by semiannual payments each equal to his present semiannual expense caused by the debt?

17. A debt of $5,000 falls due in eight years. To extinguish the principal when due, the debtor deposits annually into a sinking fund which pays $4\frac{1}{2}\%$ per annum compounded annually. The first four payments are to be equal in amount, but each is to be $50 less than each of the last four. Find the amount of each of the eight deposits.

18. How much of an endowment would be required to provide a scholarship of $150, payable annually, if money can be invested at $3\frac{1}{2}\%$ per annum compounded annually?

19. A man at age 35 bought a life annuity of $2,000 annually, the first payment to be made on his sixtieth birthday. He was to pay for this annuity by making annual payments, the first payment immediately. Find the amount of the annual payment if money is worth 5% per annum compounded annually.

20. When the man in the previous problem has made ten payments, he wishes the annuity which he is buying changed so that the first payment will be made on his sixty-fifth birthday.

(*a*) Assuming that he continues to make the same annual payments for 15 years, what will be his annual income at age 65?

(*b*) Suppose that he wishes his annual income at 65 to be $2,000. What equal annual payments should he make from age 45 to 60? What equal annual payments should he make from age 45 to 65, if he decides to continue his payments for the extra five years?

20

Bond and Bond Interest Valuation

Definitions. A bond is a promise to pay a specified sum of money at a determinable future date. It differs from a note, in general, in that it is usually a long-term obligation. Bonds are generally issued by a city, state, nation, or corporation, and seldom by individuals. The sum written in the body of the instrument is known as the *face, par,* or *nominal par,* and is the amount on which interest is calculated. Bonds usually have a par of $100, $500, or $1,000.

Interest payments may be made annually, semiannually, or quarterly. These interest payments are known as *nominal interest,* or *cash interest.* The interest rate is known as the *coupon rate.*

The rate per cent earned on the actual money invested is termed the *effective* or *investment interest* or *yield rate.* The cash rate and the effective rate are not the same unless the bond is purchased at par. Quotations are sometimes made "on a basis," which means at an effective rate on the money invested. The price of a bond will usually be either above or below par; because the cash rate is either above or below the effective rate.

A bond is said to be "redeemed" when it is bought back by the company which issued it. If the market price of a bond is more than the par value, the bond is said to be above par; or if less, the bond is said to be below par. Bonds sold above par are said to be sold *at a premium,* and if sold below par, they are said to be sold *at a discount.*

Bonds are usually sold on the open market for whatever they will bring. Whether they bring more or less than par depends upon:

(1) The cash or coupon rate of interest.
(2) The redemption price.
(3) The current rate of interest.

(4) The length of time until maturity.

(5) The character of the security.

(6) The general economic situation.

Only the first four of the above can be mathematically considered.

The purchaser of a bond purchases the right to receive two future benefits:

(*a*) The face of the bond redeemable at the date of maturity.

(*b*) The interest payments at regular periods during the interval.

The concern issuing the bond has a responsibility to meet these two obligations.

Kinds of bonds. Bonds may be classified according to the security provided or according to the method of paying interest or according to the method of registering ownership of the bond.

Guaranteed bond—here the loan is secured by the guarantee of a third party.

Collateral trust bond—here the loan is secured by collateral deposited with a trustee.

Mortgage bond—here the loan is secured by hypothecated property with the deed of trust deposited with a trustee.

Debenture bond—here the loan is secured solely by the borrower's credit.

Coupon bond—a bond which has a detachable portion, called a coupon, for each interest payment and which can be cashed in a bank.

Registered bond—here the name of the owner is placed on the bond and a list of the bondholders is kept on the books of the corporation issuing the bond. A registered bond when sold must be transferred on the book of the corporation.

Fully Registered bond—here the bond is registered both as to principal and interest and the interest payments are paid by check to the registered holder.

Registered as to principal only bond—here the interest is paid as for coupon bonds.

Straight term bond—here the bond bears interest at a fixed rate until maturity when the face of the bond is redeemable.

Serial bond—here the capital is repaid at intervals during the term of the bond and interest is paid on the capital outstanding.

Annuity bond—here the principal and interest is paid in a definite number of equal installments.

Bonds sold at par. It is apparent that if a man desires to buy a certain bond which has a face value of $1,000, and this bond bears a cash rate of interest exactly the same as that which his money is worth on the market for other securities of the same general class, he will be willing to

pay $1,000 for the bond.   In such a case, the interest that he will receive
from this bond will be equivalent to the interest that he would receive
from any other investment of the same general class.   But if he considered the purchase of another bond of $1,000, which had a cash rate of
interest lower than that of other investments of the same general class,
it is apparent that he would not pay a full $1,000 for this bond.   And
again, if there were on the market securities of the same general class
paying a higher rate per thousand, he would be willing to pay more than
the par value for a bond of this class.

This may be illustrated graphically, as in Figure 20-1.

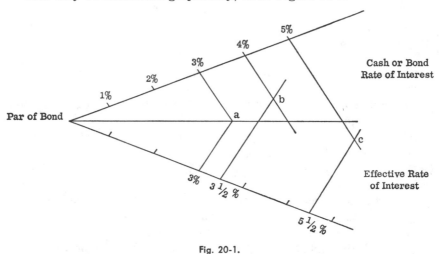

Fig. 20-1.

1. Cash or bond rate of interest has a tendency to lift the price of the
bond above par.

2. Effective rate of interest has a tendency to bring the price of the
bond below par.

a. This is an illustration of an equal pull of cash and effective interest.
If all other factors were equal, the result would be a price at par.

b. If the cash rate is larger than the effective rate, the price should be
above par.

c. If the effective rate is larger than the cash rate, the pull is below
par.

Bonds purchased at a discount or at a premium.   If a bond is
purchased at a discount, the effective rate is higher than the cash rate, for
two reasons: (*a*) the investment is less than par; and (*b*) the investor
makes additional income equal to the difference between the cost and the
par to be collected at maturity.   On the other hand, if a bond is purchased at a premium, the effective rate is lower than the cash rate, for
two reasons: (*a*) the investment is more than par; and (*b*) the investor

loses the difference between the price paid and the par to be collected at maturity.

Price and rate of yield. In business, the usual questions which arise with regard to bonds are: "What price should be paid for bonds if a certain investment rate of interest is desired by the investor?" and "What rate will a bond, purchased at a certain price produce?"

Purchase Price of a bond formula:

Let F = face value of the bond.

R = redemption value of the bond.

i = the yield rate of interest per dividend or coupon period.

c — the coupon rate of interest

C = the coupon value or periodic dividend payment.

P = purchase price.

n = the number of periods before redemption.

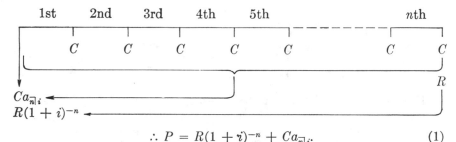

$$\therefore P = R(1+i)^{-n} + Ca_{\overline{n}|i}. \tag{1}$$

In deriving Formula (1), the following assumptions are inherent:

i) The bond is purchased on a dividend date.

ii) The purchaser holds the bond until maturity and therefore receives the full redemption value R.

iii) The purchaser receives the value of each coupon in full, with the first coupon redeemable at the close of the first period after the purchase date.

iv) The compounding period for the yield rate is equal to the compounding period for the coupon rate.

Example 1. Find the price of a 4% \$1,000 bond maturing in ten years to yield the buyer 5%.

Solution. In this case $F = 1,000$, $R = 1,000$, $c = 4\% = .04$, $C = 40$, $n = 10$, and $i = 5\% = .05$. Substituting these values in Formula (1),

$$P = 1,000(1.05)^{-10} + 40a_{\overline{10}|5\%}$$
$$= 1,000(0.61391325) + 40(7.72173493)$$
$$= 613.91 + 308.87$$
$$= \$922.78.$$

Example 2. A \$1,000 bond bearing interest at 5% per annum compounded semiannually is redeemable at 110 in ten years. Find the purchase price to yield the purchaser 4% per annum compounded semiannually.

Solution. In this case $F = 1,000$, $R = 1,100$, $c = 2\frac{1}{2}\% = .025$, $C = 25$, $n = 20$, and $i = 2\% = .02$. Substituting these values in Formula (1),

$$P = 1,100(1.02)^{-20} + 25a_{\overline{20}|2\%}$$
$$= 1,100(0.67297133) + 25(16.35143334)$$
$$= 740.27 + 408.79$$
$$= \$1,149.06.$$

PROBLEMS

In each of the following seven problems, find the purchase price of the given bond.

	Face Value	Redeemable	Coupon rate per annum	Yield rate per annum	Compounded
1.	\$ 1,000	At par in 20 yrs.	4%	4%	Annually
2.	\$ 1,500	At 110 in 25 yrs.	5%	4%	Semiannually
3.	\$ 2,000	At 105 in 10 yrs.	4%	5%	Quarterly
4.	\$10,000	At par in 20 yrs.	6%	7%	Semiannually
5.	\$10,000	At par in 20 yrs.	7%	6%	Semiannually
6.	\$ 500	At 102 in 30 yrs.	$2\frac{3}{4}\%$	$3\frac{1}{2}\%$	Annually
7.	\$ 200	At 108 in 10 yrs.	$2\frac{1}{2}\%$	4%	Quarterly

Premium and discount formulas. Formula (1) permits the calculation of the price of a bond whether it is redeemable at par or not. The premium $(P - F)$ or the discount $(F - P)$ can obviously be calculated directly. If, however, the bond is *redeemable at par*, simple formulas may be developed which permit the calculation of premium or discount more readily. In the case where the bond is redeemable at par, the bond will be sold at a premium if the yield rate is less than the coupon rate, and will be sold at a discount if the yield rate is greater than the coupon rate.

If $R = F$, then Formula (1) becomes:

$$P = F(1 + i)^{-n} + Ca_{\overline{n}|i}. \tag{2}$$

By definition, Premium = $P - F$.
Substituting the value of P from Formula (2),

$$\text{Premium} = F(1 + i)^{-n} + Ca_{\overline{n}|i} - F$$
$$= Ca_{\overline{n}|i} - F\{1 - (1 + i)^{-n}\}$$
$$= Ca_{\overline{n}|i} - Fi\left\{\frac{1 - (1 + i)^{-n}}{i}\right\}$$
$$\therefore \text{Premium} = (C - Fi)a_{\overline{n}|i}.$$
$$\text{Since } C = Fc,$$
$$\text{Premium} = F(c - i)a_{\overline{n}|i}. \tag{3}$$

By definition, Discount $= F - P$.
Therefore,

$$\text{Discount} = F(i - c)a_{\overline{n}|i}. \tag{4}$$

Example 1. A 6%, five-year $1,000 bond maturing April 1, 1963, with dividends payable April 1 and October 1, is purchased on April 1, 1958 to yield 5% per annum compounded semiannually. Find the premium.

Solution. In this case, $F = 1,000$, $n = 10$, $c = 3\% = .03$, $i = 2\frac{1}{2}\% = .025$. Substituting these values in Formula (3),

$$\begin{aligned}
\text{Premium} &= 1,000(.03 - .025)a_{\overline{10}|2\frac{1}{2}\%} \\
&= 1,000(.005)(8.75206393) \\
&= \$43.76.
\end{aligned}$$

Example 2. A 4%, ten-year $1,000 bond maturing January 1, 1965, with dividends payable January 1 and July 1, is purchased on January 1, 1957 to yield 6% per annum compounded semiannually. Find the discount.

Solution. In this case $F = 1,000$, $n = 16$, $c = 2\% = .02$, $i = 3\% = .03$. Substituting these values in Formula (4),

$$\begin{aligned}
\text{Discount} &= 1,000(.03 - .02)a_{\overline{16}|3\%} \\
&= 1,000(.01)(12.56110203) \\
&= \$125.61.
\end{aligned}$$

Accumulation of discount. When the coupon rate is less than the yield rate, the bond is bought at a discount and may be thought of as having a periodically increasing *book value* which approaches the redemption value at maturity. The periodic coupon value is less than the expected income at the yield rate for the period, and the deficit is applied each period to raise the book value of the bond. This process, known as *accumulation of discount*, raises the purchase price of the bond to the redemption value of the bond at maturity. A table showing the accumulation of discount may be constructed.

Example. Find the price of a $100, 5% bond with coupons payable January 1 and July 1 and redeemable at par on January 1, 1963 bought on January 1, 1959 to yield 6% per annum compounded semiannually. Construct a table showing the accumulation of discount.

Solution. In this case, $R = 100$, $n = 8$, $C = 2.50$, $i = .03$. Substituting in Formula 1,

$$\begin{aligned}
P &= 100(1.03)^{-8} + 2.50a_{\overline{8}|3\%} \\
&= 100(.78940923) + 2.50(7.01969219) \\
&= 78.94 + 17.55 \\
&= \$96.49.
\end{aligned}$$

Therefore, the discount to be accumulated is $100 - 96.49 = \$3.51$.

SCHEDULE FOR ACCUMULATION OF DISCOUNT

End of Period	Interest at Yield Rate	Coupon Interest	Accumulation of Discounts	Book Value
				$ 96.49
1	$2.89	$2.50	$.39	96.88
2	2.91	2.50	.41	97.29
3	2.92	2.50	.42	97.71
4	2.93	2.50	.43	98.14
5	2.94	2.50	.44	98.58
6	2.96	2.50	.46	99.04
7	2.97	2.50	.47	99.51
8	2.99	2.50	.49	100.00

Amortization of premium.   If the yield rate is less than the coupon rate, the bond will sell at a premium which means that it will be priced above par.   In this case the bond may be thought of as having a periodically decreasing *book value* which approaches the redemption value at maturity.   The periodic coupon value is greater than the expected income at the yield rate for the period and the excess is applied each period to decrease the book value of the bond.   This process, known as *amortization of premium* decreases the purchase price of the bond to the redemption value of the bond at maturity.   A table showing the amortization of premium may be constructed.

Example.   A $100, 6%, four-year bond with coupons in January 1 and July 1 is bought to yield the investor 5% per annum compounded semiannually.   Find the price of the bond and construct a table showing the amortization of premium.

Solution.   In this case, $R = 100$, $n = 8$, $C = 3.00$, and $i = .025$.   Substituting these values in Formula 1,

$$P = 100(1.025)^{-8} + 3.00a_{\overline{8}|\,2\frac{1}{2}\%}$$
$$= 100(0.82074657) + 3.00(7.17013717)$$
$$= 82.07 + 21.51$$
$$= \$103.58.$$

Therefore, the premium to be amortized is $3.58.

SCHEDULE FOR AMORTIZATION OF PREMIUM

End of Period	Interest at Yield Rate	Coupon Interest	Amortization	Book Value
				$103.58
1	$2.59	$3.00	$.41	103.17
2	2.58	3.00	.42	102.75
3	2.57	3.00	.43	102.32
4	2.56	3.00	.44	101.88
5	2.55	3.00	.45	101.43
6	2.54	3.00	.46	100.97
7	2.52	3.00	.48	100.49
8	2.51	3.00	.49	100.00

PROBLEMS

1. What should be the purchase price of a $1,000, five-year, 5% bond (interest payable semiannually) bought so that it will produce $6\frac{1}{4}\%$? Prove your work by means of the table.

2. If money is worth 6%, interest payable semiannually, what should be the purchase price of five $100 bonds, bearing a coupon rate of 5%, and having five years to run, coupon paid semiannually? Prove your answer by means of the table.

3. Construct in columnar form a table showing the book value, the coupon interest, the interest at yield rate, and the amortization of a five-year, 6% bond of $500, bought on a 7% basis (interest payable semiannually).

4. A $500 bond, maturing in six years and bearing interest at 6%, payable semiannually, is bought on an 8% basis. Construct a columnar table, as in Problem 3.

5. Show in columnar form the book value, the coupon interest, the interest at yield rate, and the accumulation of discount for a four-year bond the par value of which is $1,000. The bond bears 5% interest, payable semiannually; the effective rate is 6%, convertible semiannually.

Fill in the price in each of the following. The interest is payable semiannually.

	Face of Bond	Time to Run	Coupon Interest	Yield Interest	Price
6.	$ 100	5 years	6%	7%	$...............
7.	1,000	10 years	5%	6%	....
8.	5,000	15 years	$5\frac{1}{2}\%$	6%	....
9.	2,000	12 years	6%	$5\frac{1}{2}\%$	....
10.	3,000	6 years	$6\frac{1}{2}\%$	$4\frac{1}{2}\%$	....
11.	5,000	20 years	$5\frac{1}{2}\%$	5%	....

In Problems 12, 13, 14, and 15, set up a columnar table showing: (*a*) the number of periods; (*b*) the interest at yield rate; (*c*) the coupon value; (*d*) the amortization of premium or discount; and (*e*) the book value. The interest is payable semiannually.

	Face of Bond	Time to Run (Years)	Cash or Coupon Interest	Effective Interest	Price
12.	$ 100	4	5%	6%	$...............
13.	3,000	$3\frac{1}{2}$	6%	5%	....
14.	7,500	4	$6\frac{1}{2}\%$	$5\frac{1}{2}\%$	....
15.	5,000	5	4%	5%	....

16. A $10,000, 5% coupon bond is bought on a 4% basis. It is due one and a half years hence, and interest is payable semiannually. Find the cost of the bond.

17. What is the difference in the purchase prices of two $1,000, 20-year bonds, bought to yield 6%, if one of the bonds has a semiannual coupon of $25 while the other has a semiannual coupon of $35?

18. Davis died on April 1, 1933. His estate contained five $1,000 bonds of the X.Y.Z. Company bearing 6% interest, payable July 1 and January 1. The bonds were due on July 1, 1938 and are inventoried at $104\frac{1}{2}$. On July 1, 1933, the trustee purchased five more of the same bonds on a 5% basis. Compute the price paid by the trustee for the bonds.

19. Find the price for a $1,000 bond bearing interest at $5\frac{1}{2}$%, payable May 1 and November 1, maturing May 1, 1963, if bought on May 1, 1952 at a price to yield the purchaser 5%.

20. Suppose that the bond described in Problem 14 were bought to yield the purchaser 6%. Find the price.

Serial bonds. Many public and private corporations desire to pay off a portion of their bonds each year instead of setting up a sinking fund. Serial redemption bonds may be redeemed in equal or unequal periodic amounts.

If the bonds are not redeemed in equal periodic amounts, it is difficult to derive a formula or plan by which computations may be shortened or systematized. But if the redemptions are to be made in equal amounts and at regular periodic dates, formulas and solutions for finding the value of such an issue may be derived.

For the purpose of finding the present value of bonds to be redeemed in a series, it is well to analyze the issue into its component parts and to calculate the value of each component part separately. The following example will illustrate this point:

Example. What is the present value of a bond issue of $10,000 bearing 5% interest payable annually? These bonds are to be redeemed serially, $2,000 each year. Money is worth 6% per annum compounded annually.

Solution. This bond is equivalent to five separate bonds. For each bond, $R = 2,000$, $C = 100$, and $i = .06$. The bonds are redeemable 1, 2, 3, 4, and 5 periods hence, respectively. By Formula (1), we may calculate the price of each bond.

$$P_1 = 2,000(1.06)^{-1} + 100a_{\overline{1}|6\%} \qquad = 1981.13$$
$$P_2 = 2,000(1.06)^{-2} + 100a_{\overline{2}|6\%} \qquad = 1963.33$$
$$P_3 = 2,000(1.06)^{-3} + 100a_{\overline{3}|6\%} \qquad = 1946.54$$
$$P_4 = 2,000(1.06)^{-4} + 100a_{\overline{4}|6\%} \qquad = 1930.70$$
$$P_5 = 2,000(1.06)^{-5} + 100a_{\overline{5}|6\%} \qquad = 1915.76$$

$$P = P_1 + P_2 + P_3 + P_4 + P_5 = \$9737.46.$$

PROBLEMS

1. Compute the purchase price of $5,000 of serial bonds, issued January 1, 1960, with 5% interest payable annually, and dated to mature in five equal annual installments. Money is worth $5\frac{1}{2}$% per annum compounded annually.

2. Verify the solution of the above problem by setting up a columnar table showing: (*a*) date of maturity; (*b*) bonds outstanding; (*c*) coupon value each year; (*d*) interest at yield rate each year; (*e*) accumulation of discount; (*f*) book value.

3. Compute the purchase price of $50,000 of serial bonds, issued January 1, 1960, bearing 5% interest, coupons due annually. These bonds are to mature serially in equal annual payments, beginning January 1, 1961, and each year thereafter for ten years. Money is worth 4% per annum compounded annually.

4. Prepare a columnar table for Problem 3.

5. A $20,000 serial bond issue, with interest at $5\frac{1}{2}\%$, payable semiannually is redeemable in ten equal semiannual installments. Money is worth 5%, convertible semiannually. Set up a columnar table similar to that in Problem 2.

6. The Highway Department desires to know the value of a series of road bonds which it is about to issue. The bonds will have a par value of $200,000 and will bear 5% interest, payable semiannually. They are to be redeemed serially, in installments of $40,000. The first redemption payment is to be made one year from the date of issue, and the other payments are to be made annually thereafter. Money is worth 6%, interest compounded semiannually. Find the value of the bonds and draw up a table of analysis as a proof of your solution.

7. A corporation wishes to float an issue of serial bonds for $100,000. These bonds are to be redeemed in yearly installments of $20,000, the first redemption payment to be made at the beginning of the sixth year. The interest rate is 5%, payable semiannually, and the yield rate is $4\frac{1}{2}\%$, interest convertible semiannually. How much did the corporation realize from the issue?

8. An issue of serial bonds bearing 4% interest, payable semiannually, is to be redeemed serially in installments of $4,000. The first redemption payment is to be made at the end of the fifth year and the other payments are to be made annually thereafter. At what price must $20,000 of these serial bonds be purchased in order to net the purchaser 5% per annum compounded semiannually?

9. An issue of $50,000 of bonds bearing interest at 5% payable semiannually is sold to produce $5\frac{1}{2}\%$ per annum, convertible semiannually. The bonds are to be retired serially, as follows:

$10,000 at 104 in 6 years.
$10,000 at 103 in 7 years.
$10,000 at 102 in 8 years.
$10,000 at 101 in 9 years.
$10,000 at par in 10 years.

What amount is realized on the issue?

Annuity bonds. An *annuity bond* is one in which the capital is repaid in installments so that the sum of the capital repaid at each interest date, plus the periodic interest on the capital outstanding, is fixed. Finding the value of these payments in terms of their yielding a given interest rate, is a problem in annuities.

Example. A $1,000 annuity bond maturing in eight years, with interest at 5% per annum compounded semiannually, is purchased four years before maturity to yield the purchaser 6% per annum compounded semiannually. What price did the investor pay?

Solution. The first step is to determine the semiannual installment by using the formula

$$R = P.V. \cdot \frac{1}{a_{\overline{n}|\,i}}$$

$$\therefore R = 1,000 \frac{1}{a_{\overline{16}|\,2\frac{1}{2}\%}} = \$76.60.$$

The purchaser is buying an annuity of $76.60 every six months for four years to yield him 6% per annum compounded semiannually. Therefore, the price he pays is the present value of this annuity.

$$P.V. = Ra_{\overline{n}|\,i}$$
$$\therefore P.V. = 76.60a_{\overline{8}|\,3\%} = \$537.71.$$

Thus, he pays $537.71 to buy the remaining payments on the bond.

PROBLEMS

1. Bonds for $10,000, repayable principal and interest at 5% per annum payable annually in five equal annual installments, are sold to yield the buyer 6% per annum compounded annually. What is the price asked?

2. Find the price of a $20,000 annuity bond, 6% per annum compounded semiannually, repayable in 20 equal semiannual installments yielding 5% per annum, also compounded semiannually.

3. The principal of a $5,000 bond and interest at 6% per annum compounded annually are to be paid in ten equal annual payments. Find the price paid just after the fourth annual installment to yield the purchaser 5% per annum payable annually.

4. A $20,000, 10-year annuity bond, paying 5% per annum compounded semiannually, is redeemable in equal half-yearly installments of principal and interest. What is the purchase price of the bond five years before maturity to yield 6½% per annum compounded semiannually?

Bonds redeemable from a fund. Frequently, bonds are redeemed periodically from a fund; that is, as soon as money is put into the fund, or when money becomes available at the end of an interest period, it is at once used to redeem outstanding bonds. No difficulty would be encountered in making the computations necessary in this system of redemption except for the fact that bonds are usually issued in denominations of $100, $500, or $1,000, and the payments into the fund may exceed the expenditures from the fund for the redemption of bonds. A residue would then be left in the fund, and this residue should earn interest.

Example. The X.Y.Z. Company issues $100,000 of bonds, par value $100, and sets up a sinking fund for their periodic redemption. The bond interest and the sinking fund interest are each 6%. The bonds are to run for five years, with interest payable semiannually, and are to be kept alive in the treasury. Sinking fund payments are to be made semiannually. Interest is to be paid by the trustee on the balance remaining in the fund. Show: (a) the periodic payments into the sinking fund; (b) the interest accrued periodically on bonds redeemed; (c) the total amount that must be invested in the sinking fund each period; (d) the amount of bonds purchased periodically for the sinking fund; (e) the cash balance held in the treasury; and (f) the interest on the cash balance held in the treasury.

Solution. Let: i = the yield rate of interest per period.
And: n = the number of periods.

Therefore, from the formula, $R = P.V. \dfrac{1}{a_{\overline{n}|i}}$,

$$R = 100,000 \, \frac{1}{a_{\overline{10}|\, 3\%}} = \$11,723.05.$$

The remaining part of the solution can be derived from the following table:

Periodic Payment	Balance from Preceding Period	Total Amount Available	Bond Interest	Bonds Re-deemed	Cash Balance	Interest on Cash Balance	Bonds Out-standing $100,000
$11,723.05		$11,723.05	$3,000	$ 8,700	$23.05	$ .69	91,300
11,723.05	$23.74	11,746.79	2,739	9,000	7.79	.23	82,300
11,723.05	8.02	11,731.07	2,469	9,200	62.07	1.86	73,100
11,723.05	63.93	11,786.98	2,193	9,500	93.98	2.82	63,600
11,723.05	96.80	11,819.85	1,908	9,900	11.85	.36	53,700
11,723.05	12.21	11,735.26	1,611	10,100	24.26	.73	43,600
11,723.05	24.99	11,748.04	1,308	10,400	40.04	1.20	33,200
11,723.05	41.24	11,764.29	996	10,700	68.29	2.05	22,500
11,723.05	70.34	11,793.39	675	11,100	18.39	.55	11,400
11,723.06	18.94	11,742.00	342	11,400			

In the above example, the first payment into the fund is $11,723.05. The payment on the interest will be $3,000, leaving $8,723.05 to be used for the redemption of bonds. As the bonds issued are of $100 denomination, only $8,700 of this fund can be used for the redemption of bonds, leaving a balance of $23.05 cash in the hands of the trustee.

In order to verify the solution of a problem of this kind, it is necessary to charge the trustee with interest at the sinking fund rate on the balance remaining in his hands. The interest on $23.05, the cash balance in the trustee's hands, for six months at 3% is $.69. This interest added to the cash balance gives the balance from the preceding period.

PROBLEMS

1. A $200,000 bond issue, maturing in eight years, bears interest at 6%, payable semiannually. The par value of the bonds is $1,000. A sinking fund is set

up, and the trustee is to purchase bonds semiannually at par and keep them alive in the treasury. Money is worth 6%, interest convertible semiannually. Prepare a table, showing: (*a*) the semiannual periodic payments to the sinking fund; (*b*) the interest accrued on the bonds; (*c*) the par value of the bonds purchased semiannually; (*d*) the cash balance in the hands of the trustee; and (*e*) the interest on the cash balance.

2. An issue of $200,000 of 6%, ten-year bonds is floated by a corporation. The par value is $100, and the interest coupons are payable semiannually. The bonds are to be redeemed semiannually, and the sinking fund payments necessary for the redemption of the principal and the payment of the interest are placed in the hands of the trustee. The sinking fund rate is 6%. Prepare a table, as in Problem 1.

Values of bonds between interest dates. In the preceding articles, the price of a bond was found when the bond was purchased on a coupon payment date. Bonds, however, are usually bought between coupon dates. While there are several methods of computing the price of a bond bought between interest dates, the most common practice is to calculate the purchase price at yield rate on the preceding coupon date, and then accumulate this price through the time that has elapsed between the coupon date and the purchase date using simple interest at the yield rate.

Example 1. On March 1, 1960, what was the value of a $1,000, $4\frac{1}{2}$% bond, due January 1, 1965? Interest coupons are payable January 1 and July 1, and money is worth 6%, interest compounded semiannually.

Solution. Purchase price on January 1, 1960 is,

$$1000(1.03)^{-10} + 22.50a_{\overline{10}|3\%} = \$936.02.$$

From January 1, 1960, to March 1, 1960, is two months. The simple interest on $936.02 for two months is $936.02 \times \frac{1}{6} \times .06 = \$9.36$. Therefore, the purchase price on March 1, 1960 is $936.02 + \$9.36 or $945.38.

Example 2. On May 1, 1963, what should have been paid for a $1,000, 6% bond, due January 1, 1967, if interest coupons were payable January 1 and July 1 and money was worth 5%, interest compounded semiannually?

Solution. Purchase price on January 1, 1963, is

$$1,000(1.025)^{-8} + 30a_{\overline{8}|2\frac{1}{2}\%} = \$1035.85.$$

From January 1, 1963, to May 1, 1963 is four months. The simple interest on $1035.85 for four months at 5% is

$$1035.85 \times \tfrac{4}{12} \times .05 = \$17.26.$$

Therefore, the purchase price on May 1, 1963, is $1035.85 + $17.26 or $1053.11.

Flat price and "and interest" price of a bond. The actual price paid for a bond is the flat price. The quoted price of a bond in the daily paper is never the flat price except on a coupon date. On any other date, the quoted price is the price actually paid (flat price) less the portion of the coupon value which belongs to the seller of the bond for holding the bond beyond a coupon date. This price is called the *"and interest" price.*

The "and interest" price in Example 1 above is $945.38 $- \frac{1}{3}(22.50) =$ $937.88. The "and interest" price in Example 2 above is $1,053.11 $- \frac{2}{3}(30) = $1,033.11$.

PROBLEMS

1. A $100 bond bears 5% interest, payable semiannually, and is due in five years and four months. What price, plus accrued interest, should an investor pay for this bond if he wishes his investment to produce 4%?

2. A $1,000, 5% bond is due in six years and three months, and interest is payable semiannually. The effective interest rate is 6%. What is the value of the bond, with accrued interest?

3. A $1,000, $5\frac{1}{2}$% bond, with interest payable annually, is redeemable at par in 20 years and four months and is bought on a 6% basis. Find the flat price.

4. A $1,000, 5% bond, with interest payable semiannually, is redeemable at par in eight years and five months, and is bought on a $4\frac{1}{2}$% basis. Find the flat price.

5. Five $1,000, 6% bonds, with interest payable semiannually, are due in four years and four months and are purchased on a $4\frac{1}{2}$% basis. Find the value of the bonds.

6. Find the "and interest" price and the flat price of a $1,000 bond bearing interest at 5% per annum payable January 1 and July 1, redeemable January 1, 1968 and purchased April 1, 1960 to yield 6% per annum compounded semiannually.

7. Find the value of $2,000,000 worth of 6% bonds due October 1, 1965, with half-yearly coupons, April and October, purchased May 10, 1959 to yield 5% per annum compounded semiannually.

Approximate yield rate of interest on bonds. One question which is very important to the investor is, "What rate of interest will I receive on the bond?" The investor knows the amount of each interest coupon, but the coupon rate is based on the par value and not on the amount of money which has been invested.

Because the unknown effective interest rate must be used more than once in the algebraic formula for the calculation of the price of a bond, the absolute effective rate is difficult to find. There are, however, several methods which will give a close approximation to this exact yield rate. The most useful, and therefore, the most common method is the one now to be illustrated.

USE OF BOND TABLE AND INTERPOLATION METHOD

Example 1. If a $100, three year, 6% bond, bearing semiannual interest coupons, is bought at $105.38, what is the approximate yield rate of the investment?

SECTION OF BOND TABLE
CASH INTEREST PAYABLE SEMIANNUALLY

Effective Interest Rate	3%	$3\frac{1}{2}$%	4%	$4\frac{1}{2}$%	5%	6%	7%
3.75	$97.89	$99.30	$100.70	$102.11	$103.52	$106.33	$109.14
3.80	97.75	99.16	100.56	101.97	103.37	106.18	108.99
3.875	97.54	98.95	100.35	101.75	103.16	105.96	108.77
3.90	97.48	98.88	100.28	101.68	103.09	105.89	108.70
4.00	97.20	98.60	100.00	101.40	102.80	105.60	108.40
4.10	96.92	98.32	99.72	101.12	102.52	105.31	108.11
$4.12\frac{1}{2}$	96.86	98.25	99.65	101.05	102.45	105.24	108.04
4.20	96.65	98.05	99.44	100.84	102.23	105.02	107.82
4.25	96.51	97.91	99.30	100.70	102.09	104.88	107.67

Solution. In the 6% column of the section of the bond table given above will be found, opposite 4%, the price of $105.60; and opposite 4.1%, the price of $105.31. The rate is therefore somewhere between 4% and 4.1%. A more exact approximation may now be determined by interpolation.

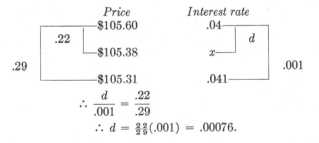

$$\therefore \frac{d}{.001} = \frac{.22}{.29}$$
$$\therefore d = \tfrac{22}{29}(.001) = .00076.$$

Therefore, the approximate yield rate is .04 + .00076, or 4.076% per annum compounded semiannually.

Example 2. What will be the rate of income on an investment in a 4%, semi-annual, three-year bond bought at $99.35?

Solution. By reference to the bond table above, the computation may be made as follows:

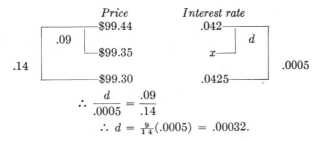

$$\therefore \ \frac{d}{.0005} = \frac{.09}{.14}$$

$$\therefore \ d = \tfrac{9}{14}(.0005) = .00032.$$

Therefore, the approximate yield rate is .042 + .00032, or 4.232% per annum compounded semiannually.

Computation when bond table is not available. The secret of the bond table and interpolation method is to corner the price paid between a higher and lower price found on the table and then approximate more closely by interpolation. If no bond table is available, it is still possible to corner the price paid between a lower price and a higher price, each of which is calculated by guessing yield rates and calculating the prices. Care must be exercised in the choice of the rates, which must be as close to the actual rate as it is possible to estimate.

Example. If a $100, 5%, five-year bond, with semiannual coupons, is bought at $97.31, what rate of interest will be realized on the investment?

Solution. The first step is to find the cost at an estimated yield rate. Guess the yield rate to be $5\frac{1}{2}\%$. Then the price is

$$100(1.0275)^{-10} + 2.50a_{\overline{10}|\,2.75\%} = \$97.84.$$

This price is too high; therefore, the rate guessed is too low. Guess the yield rate to be 5.75%. Then the price is

$$100(1.02875)^{-10} + 2.50a_{\overline{10}|\,2.875\%} = \$96.78.$$

Since we now have the price paid cornered between a higher and lower price, the yield rate can be approximated by interpolation.

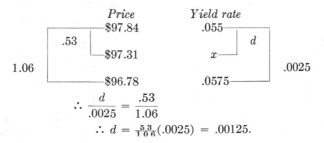

$$\therefore \ \frac{d}{.0025} = \frac{.53}{1.06}$$

$$\therefore \ d = \tfrac{53}{106}(.0025) = .00125.$$

Therefore, the approximate yield rate is .055 + .00125, or 5.625% per annum compounded semiannually.

PROBLEMS

In each of the following, find the approximate yield rate.

	Purchase Price	Nominal Rate	Par Value	Time in Years	Interest Payable
1.	$ 92.00	4%	$ 100.00	3	Semiannually
2.	1,015.00	4%	1,000.00	9	"
3.	9,750.00	4%	10,000.00	29	"
4.	545.00	5%	500.00	8	"
5.	925.00	5%	1,000.00	15	"
6.	983.75	5%	1,000.00	18	"
7.	9,732.50	$5\frac{1}{2}$%	10,000.00	5	"
8.	5,201.50	$5\frac{1}{2}$%	5,000.00	9	"
9.	96.85	6%	100.00	4	"
10.	73.55	6%	100.00	6	"

Amortization of discount, premium, or discount and expense on serial redemption bonds. The calculation of the amortization of bond discount, bond premium, or bond discount and expense, when bonds are to be redeemed serially, or in unequal amounts, is a problem which requires particular attention, since the distribution over the period of years must be equitable. The two methods which are most commonly used are:

(1) The bonds outstanding method.

(2) The scientific or effective-interest method.

Bonds outstanding method. It would be incorrect to write off the discount or premium, or the discount and expense, on serial redemption bonds or on a bond issue which has no regular redemption period, by the straight-line method. In some cases it is difficult to calculate the portion to be amortized by the scientific method. Because of the ease of the calculations and the fair degree of accuracy which it affords, the bonds outstanding method is the one most commonly used.

Procedure: (*a*) Find the sum of the bonds outstanding during each period of the life of the bond issue.

(*b*) Use the sum found in (*a*) as the denominator of a series of fractions, and use the sum of the bonds outstanding each period as successive numerators. The sum of all these fractions, of course, will in every problem be equal to 1.

(*c*) Multiply the total bond discount or the premium, or the total bond discount and expense, by the appropriate fraction, to obtain the portion of discount or premium to be amortized each period.

Example. An issue of ten bonds of $1,000 each, bearing 5% interest, payable semiannually, is to be redeemed as follows: $3,000 at the end of the sixth year; $3,000 at the end of the eighth year; and $2,000 at the end of each year thereafter. The bonds are sold at a discount of $400. Compute an equitable amortization of the discount over the life of the bonds.

Solution.

Periods of One-half Year Each	Bonds Outstanding	Fraction	Amortization Written Off	Discount on Bonds	Bonds Less Discount
	$10,000.00			$400.00	$9,600.00
1	10,000.00	10/160	$ 25.00	375.00	9,625.00
2	10,000.00	10/160	25.00	350.00	9,650.00
3	10,000.00	10/160	25.00	325.00	9,675.00
4	10,000.00	10/160	25.00	300.00	9,700.00
5	10,000.00	10/160	25.00	275.00	9,725.00
6	10,000.00	10/160	25.00	250.00	9,750.00
7	10,000.00	10/160	25.00	225.00	9,775.00
8	10,000.00	10/160	25.00	200.00	9,800.00
9	10,000.00	10/160	25.00	175.00	9,825.00
10	10,000.00	10/160	25.00	150.00	9,850.00
11	10,000.00	10/160	25.00	125.00	9,875.00
12	7,000.00	10/160	25.00	100.00	0,000.00
13	7,000.00	7/160	17.50	82.50	6,917.50
14	7,000.00	7/160	17.50	65.00	6,935.00
15	7,000.00	7/160	17.50	47.50	6,952.50
16	4,000.00	7/160	17.50	30.00	3,970.00
17	4,000.00	4/160	10.00	20.00	3,980.00
18	2,000.00	4/160	10.00	10.00	1,990.00
19	2,000.00	2/160	5.00	5.00	1,995.00
20	000.00	2/160	5.00	0.00	000.00
		160/160	400.00		

Scientific method. To find by the scientific method the amount of discount or premium to be amortized on an issue of serial redemption bonds, it is necessary to find the approximate effective rate of interest which these bonds will bear; and to find the approximate effective rate, it is necessary to use other approximations.

Procedure: (*a*) Determine the average life of the bonds, in periods.

(*b*) Determine, by the use of a bond table or by annuity calculations, the approximate effective interest rate for one bond having a life of the same number of periods as the average life found in (*a*).

(*c*) From a bond table or by annuity calculations, find the value of one bond at each of the annual redemption dates, at the approximate effective rate found in (*b*).

(*d*) By using the values found in (*c*), find the total value of the bonds redeemed at each redemption date.

(*e*) Add the values found in (*d*).

(*f*) Compare the sum found in (*e*) with the actual price received for the bonds.

(*g*) By the same process, determine another approximate rate.

(*h*) By interpolation, determine the error, using the approximate rates found above.

The computation of the periodic amortization is comparatively simple when the cost of the serial redemption bonds, the nominal or coupon rate, and the effective rate of interest are known. Valuation of each member of the series is equally simple. Refer to the table on page 355, which shows the amortization of discount for a series of serial redemption bonds. The periodic amortization is the difference between the effective income and the actual cash income. It may be observed that the difficulty of the whole calculation is the determination of the effective rate.

The example that was previously given under the bonds outstanding method would be solved by the scientific method as follows:

(*a*) *Solution.*

Bonds	Maturing In	Product
3	6 years	18
3	8 "	24
2	9 "	18
2	10 "	20
10		80

80 ÷ 10 = 8, or an average life of 8 years.
$9,600 ÷ 100 = $96, the average sales price per hundred.

(*b*) Refer to a bond table which shows the values at different effective rates of a 5% bond maturing in eight years, with interest payable semiannually. The price nearest to 96 is found to be 96.02. This amount is opposite the effective rate of $5\frac{5}{8}$%.

(*c*) The next step is to find the value at $5\frac{5}{8}$% of all the bonds in the series. To do this, refer to the bond table which shows a cash rate of 5% and an effective rate of $5\frac{5}{8}$%.

(*d*) The results will be:

Par Value of Bonds	Years to Run	Value at $5\frac{5}{8}$%	Total Value
$3,000.00	6	$96.85	$2,905.50
3,000.00	8	96.02	2,880.60
2,000.00	9	95.63	1,912.60
2,000.00	10	95.27	1,905.40

(*e*) Value of series............................ $9,604.10

(*f*) As the sales price of $9,600 for the bonds is below the price based on a $5\frac{5}{8}$% rate, the effective rate is a little larger than $5\frac{5}{8}$%. A test at $5\frac{3}{4}$% would result in the following:

(*g*)

Par Value of Bonds	Years to Run	Value at $5\frac{3}{4}$%	Total Value
$3,000.00	6	$96.24	$2,887.20
3,000.00	8	95.24	2,857.20
2,000.00	9	94.79	1,895.80
2,000.00	10	94.36	1,887.20

Value of series................ $9,527.40

(*h*) *Interpolation.*

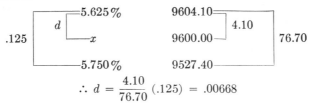

$$\therefore d = \frac{4.10}{76.70} (.125) = .00668$$

∴ rate is 5.625 + .00668 = 5.63168% per annum compounded semiannually, or 2.81584% per six months.

TABLE SHOWING AMORTIZATION OF DISCOUNT FOR SERIES OF SERIAL REDEMPTION BONDS

End of Period	Bonds Redeemed	Effective Rate, 2.815841%	Coupon Rate, 2.5%	Amortization of Discount	Bonds Less Discount
					$9,600.00
1		$270.32	$250.00	$20.32	9,620.32
2		270.89	250.00	20.89	9,641.21
3		271.48	250.00	21.48	9,662.69
4		272.09	250.00	22.09	9,684.78
5		272.71	250.00	22.71	9,707.49
6		273.35	250.00	23.35	9,730.84
7		274.01	250.00	24.01	9,754.85
8		274.68	250.00	24.68	9,779.53
9		275.38	250.00	25.38	9,804.91
10		276.09	250.00	26.09	9.831.00
11		276.83	250.00	26.83	9,857.83
12	$3,000.00	277.58	250.00	27.58	6,885.41
13		193.88	175.00	18.88	6,904.29
14		194.41	175.00	19.41	6,923.70
15		194.96	175.00	19.96	6,943.66
16	3,000.00	195.52	175.00	20.52	3,964.18
17		111.63	100.00	11.63	3,975.81
18	2,000.00	111.95	100.00	11.95	1,987.76
19		55.97	50.00	5.97	1,993.73
20	2,000.00	56.14	50.00	6.14	.13*

* Error caused by approximation and by the use of bond tables having only four places.

PROBLEMS

1. On January 1, 1960, a corporation floated a bond issue of $300,000 to be retired serially over a period of eight years as follows:

Dec. 31, 1960	$10,000	Dec. 31, 1964	$ 30,000
Dec. 31, 1961	15,000	Dec. 31, 1965	35,000
Dec. 31, 1962	20,000	Dec. 31, 1966	40,000
Dec. 31, 1963	25,000	Dec. 31, 1967	125,000

The discount and expense of issuing the bonds amounted to $33,000.

Draft a schedule, showing how much of such bond discount and interest you would claim as a deduction from gross income for federal income tax purposes for each of the years 1960 to 1967, inclusive.

2.* A city wishes to buy new fire equipment. The cost will be $500,000, and the equipment will have an estimated life of ten years, and no salvage value. It is necessary to issue bonds to pay for this purchase, although, at the present time, interest rates are high—6%, payable annually.

How would you suggest that these bonds be issued, and what will be the annual cost to the taxpayers?

It is expected that a sinking fund would not earn more than an average of 3%. The bonds will be issued in denominations of $100 and multiples thereof.

3.† A series of 5% bonds totalling $100,000, dated January 1, 1960, is redeemable at par by ten annual payments of $10,000 each, beginning December 31, 1970. What equal annual payments to a sinking fund are required to be provided on a 4% basis in order to pay off the bonds as they mature?

The first payment to the sinking-fund trustees is to be made on December 31, 1960, and the further payments are to be made annually thereafter.

What is the status of the sinking fund on December 31, 1969, 1970, and 1971?

4. On June 1, a corporation sold a $3,000,000 issue of 6%, first mortgage, 20-year bonds at a discount of $300,000. According to the terms of sale these bonds were to be retired at the rate of $150,000 each year, the purchases to be made in the open market. The first retirement in the amount of $75,000 was to be made on March 1 following the date of issue, and $75,000 was to be retired each six months thereafter.

Any premium paid or discount received on bonds purchased for retirement was to be added or deducted, whichever the case might be, to that year's portion of discount, and was to be amortized as shown by the schedule of amortization.

Prepare a schedule, showing the amortization of bond discount by the bonds outstanding method.

5. An issue of $175,000 of $6\frac{1}{2}$% bonds was sold for 95, the amount of the discount being $8,750. Other expenses pertaining to the issue of the bonds amounted to $596.67, making the total of bond discount and expense $9,346.67. These bonds are dated March 30, 1960, and the due dates are as follows:

$ 3,500 due April 15, 1960	$ 12,000 due April 15, 1965
5,000 due April 15, 1961	14,500 due April 15, 1966
7,000 due April 15, 1962	15,000 due April 15, 1967
8,000 due April 15, 1963	100,000 due April 15, 1968
10,000 due April 15, 1964	

Prepare a schedule, showing the annual charge for amortization of bond discount and expense as of the close of each year, December 31.

6.‡ On April 1, 1934, Southern Railway Equipment Gold $4\frac{1}{2}$'s, due serially on each successive coupon date in October and April between October 1, 1934, up to, and including, April 1, 1948, were sold to yield $4\frac{3}{4}$%. The Bank of Montrose purchased 2 bonds due April 1, 1937, 4 due October 1, 1938, 1 due October 1, 1942, 7 due April 1, 1943, and 1 due April 1, 1945.

(*a*) What was the total price paid? (*b*) Set up a schedule showing the investor's situation in regard to the book value of this investment at the beginning of each six-month period until the final maturity.

---

* American Institute Examination.
† American Institute Examination.
‡ Justin H. Moore, *Handbook of Financial Mathematics*. Englewood Cliffs, N. J.: Prentice-Hall, Inc., 1929.

7.* On November 1, 1933, an investor purchased 20 bonds, each with a par value of $1,000, and maturing as follows:

	Number of Bonds
May 1, 1934	1
Nov. 1, 1934	3
May 1, 1935	2
May 1, 1936	5
May 1, 1937	9

The price paid for the 20 bonds was $20,417.11. The coupon rate is 6%, payable May 1 and November 1.

(a) Determine the rate of yield. (b) Set up a schedule showing the investor's situation in regard to the book value of this investment at the beginning of each six-month period until the final maturity.

REVIEW PROBLEMS

1. A serial issue of $20,000 in denominations of $1,000 with interest at 4% has maturity of $1,000 at each interest date, March 1 and September 1. Find the price at the date of issue, March 1, to yield the purchaser $3\frac{1}{2}\%$.

2. If, in Problem 1, the first maturity were to occur two years following the date of issue, and then each six months thereafter, find the price at the date of issue, March 1, that would yield the purchaser $3\frac{1}{2}\%$.

3. A $1,000 bond with interest at $4\frac{1}{2}\%$, maturing April 1, 1954 and redeemable at 102 on any interest date after January 1, 1945, was sold on July 21, 1942 on a 5% basis. What price was paid for it?

4. A loan of $5,000 at 5% payable semiannually is repayable on each interest date in installments of $1,250. Find the purchase price to yield the investor 4%.

5. A loan of $5,000 with interest at 6% payable semiannually is to run five years and then be redeemed in annual installments of $1,000. What is the purchase price to yield 5% convertible semiannually?

---

* Justin H. Moore, *Handbook of Financial Mathematics*. Englewood Cliffs, N. J.: Prentice-Hall, Inc., 1929.

21

Asset Valuation Accounts

Asset valuation. At the moment when an asset is purchased for use, it is said to be worth *cost.* When this asset can no longer be used for the purpose for which it was purchased and can be sold for little or nothing, it is said to be worth *scrap value.*

Depreciation. *Depreciation* is the decline in value of a physical asset caused by wear, tear, action of the elements, obsolescence, supersession, or inadequacy. Depreciation results in an impairment of operating effectiveness. The difference between the original cost and the scrap value is the *total depreciation* or *wearing value* of the asset. The *book value* of an asset on a given date is the difference between the original cost and the amount of depreciation at that time.

Depletion. *Depletion* is the progressive extinction of a wasting asset by a reduction in the quantity. A gold mine is depleted year by year as the gold is mined.

Depreciation methods. There are many methods of calculating the *periodic depreciation charge.* Probably the following are the most serviceable:

1. Straight-line method.
2. Working-hours method or unit-product method.
3. Sum-of-digits method.
4. Sinking-fund method.
5. Annuity method.
6. Constant-percentage-of-book-value method.

The accountant should know how to calculate depreciation by each method, should be able to discuss the advantages and disadvantages of each method, and should be able to formulate tables of comparison showing the results of each method.

The following notation will be used in depreciation discussions.

C = the original cost.

S = the scrap value.

W = wearing value (total depreciation).

n = number of periods in the useful life of the asset.

D = periodic depreciation.

Straight-line method.   This is the simplest method and is the one that is most commonly used.   It is assumed that the periodic depreciation charge is to remain constant throughout the life of the asset.   The formula for the periodic depreciation charge is

$$D = \frac{W}{n} = \frac{C - S}{n}. \tag{1}$$

Example.   What will the annual depreciation charge be for an asset which costs $1,000.00 and which, after a useful life of ten years, has a scrap value of $100.00?   Calculate the book value at the end of each year.

Solution.   In this case, $C = 1,000$, $S = 100$, $n = 10$.   Substituting these values into Formula (1), $D = \dfrac{C - S}{n}$,

$$D = \frac{1000 - 100}{10} = \frac{900}{10} = 90.$$

∴ the annual depreciation is $90.00.

TABLE OF DEPRECIATION

At the End of Year	Annual Depreciation Charge	Accumulated Depreciation Fund	Book Value
0			$1,000.00
1	$90	$ 90	910.00
2	90	180	820.00
3	90	270	730.00
4	90	360	640.00
5	90	450	550.00
6	90	540	460.00
7	90	630	370.00
8	90	720	280.00
9	90	810	190.00
10	90	900	100.00

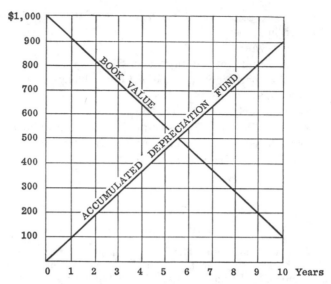

Fig. 21-1. Graphic Representation of Depreciation by the Straight-Line
Method.

PROBLEMS

1. Set up a table showing the annual depreciation, carrying value, and accumulated depreciation for an asset costing $3,500, and having a life of ten years and an estimated scrap value of $500.

2. Prepare tables showing by the straight-line method the depreciation on the following machines:

Assets	Cost	Estimated Scrap Value	Estimated Life in Years
Lathes........................	$5,000	$600	10
Milling machines...............	3,000	400	12
Power equipment...............	4,100	200	10
Furniture.....................	600	150	15

3. The following fixed assets belong to the Western Hardware Company:

Asset	Cost	Estimated Scrap Value	Estimated Life in Years
Buildings..................	$100,000	$35,000	20
Machinery.................	70,000	25,000	15
Tools.....................	20,000	5,000	10
Patterns..................	10,000	none	8

Compute the amount of annual depreciation by the straight-line method.

4. Complete the following schedule of fixed assets and depreciation, for the purpose of supporting an income tax return (allow six months' average on additions):

Asset	Previous Cost	Additions	Rate	Reserve	Current Depreciation
Land..................	$75,000.00	none	none	none	none
Brick buildings.........	92,519.61	$1,046.91	3%	$ 9,461.92	$..................
Wooden buildings.......	35,654.18	1,126.19	5%	12,319.14	....
Machinery and tools....	51,252.19	9,217.62	10%	11,463.21	....
Office furniture.........	3,469.52	417.51	10%	1,121.44	....
Automobile trucks......	3,219.52	1,750.19	25%	1,749.32	....
Spur track.............	712.92	none	5%	128.34	....
	$..................	$..................		$..................	$..................

Working-hours or unit-product method. This method is based on the number of hours which the asset is in use, or on the number of units produced.

Example. A certain one-purpose machine which costs $1,000, and has no scrap value, has been installed in a factory. A machine of this class produces 10,000 units of product during its life. Assuming that the annual production is as given below, set up a table showing the depreciation to be written off each year.

First year.........	1,000 units	Fifth year........	1,000 units
Second year.......	2,000 "	Sixth year........	1,200 "
Third year.......	1,800 "	Seventh year......	1,200 "
Fourth year.......	1,000 "	Eighth year.......	800 "

Solution.

TABLE OF DEPRECIATION

Year	Unit Fraction of Cost	Periodic Depreciation Charge	Accumulated Depreciation Reserve	Asset Value
				$1,000
1	1,000/10,000	$100	$ 100	900
2	2,000/10,000	200	300	700
3	1,800/10,000	180	480	520
4	1,000/10,000	100	580	420
5	1,000/10,000	100	680	320
6	1,200/10,000	120	800	200
7	1,200/10,000	120	920	80
8	800/10,000	80	1,000	0

PROBLEMS

1. Show in appropriate form the yearly depreciation, accumulated depreciation, and asset value of a machine which cost $7,400, and, which will have a scrap value of $200. Assume that machines of this class have a working-hour average life of 24,000 hours; also assume that the machine will be run as follows:

First year........ 2,000 hours	Sixth year........ 2,000 hours
Second year...... 2,000 "	Seventh year..... 3,000 "
Third year........ 1,800 "	Eighth year...... 3,000 "
Fourth year...... 2,600 "	Ninth year........ 3,000 "
Fifth year........ 2,800 "	Tenth year........ 1,800 "

2. An aircraft motor costing $7,700, and having an estimated scrap value of $1,000, is assumed to have a useful life of 2,000 hours. If this motor is operated 350 hours during a certain month, what should be the charge for depreciation in that month?

Sum-of-digits method. This method is very simple and has the advantage that it provides a diminishing charge for depreciation during the life of the asset. In finding the charge for depreciation, a certain fraction of the wearing value is calculated for each year.

If the life of the asset is n years, the depreciation charge for the first year is $\dfrac{n}{1 + 2 + 3 + \cdots + n}$ of the wearing value. The depreciation charge for the second year is $\dfrac{n - 1}{1 + 2 + 3 + \cdots + n}$ of the wearing value, and so on, until the depreciation charge for the nth year is

$$\frac{1}{1 + 2 + 3 + \cdots + n}$$

of the wearing value.

Example. An asset valued at $2,000.00 with a scrap value of $200.00 has an estimated life of eight years. What should the depreciation charges be?

Solution.

TABLE OF DEPRECIATION

Year	Fractional Part	Periodic Depreciation Charge	Accumulated Depreciation	Book Value
				$2,000.00
1	$\frac{8}{36}$	$400	$ 400	1,600.00
2	$\frac{7}{36}$	350	750	1,250.00
3	$\frac{6}{36}$	300	1050	950.00
4	$\frac{5}{36}$	250	1300	700.00
5	$\frac{4}{36}$	200	1500	500.00
6	$\frac{3}{36}$	150	1650	350.00
7	$\frac{2}{36}$	100	1750	250.00
8	$\frac{1}{36}$	50	1800	200.00

PROBLEMS

Construct the schedule for depreciation on the following assets, using the sum-of-the-digits method.

1. Motor vehicles costing $5,000.00 and having a scrap value of $200.00 after a life of eight years.

2. Printing machines costing $3,400.00 and having a scrap value of $100.00 after an estimated life of six years.

3. Boilers costing $2,500.00 and having a scrap value of $50.00 after a life of ten years.

4. A power lathe costing $1,200.00 and having a scrap value of $180.00 after a life of 12 years.

5. Compute the depreciation charges for the first five years of the life of a company whose assets are as follows. Also calculate the book value for each year.

Asset	Cost	Scrap value	Life of Asset (years)
Lathe	$1,300.00	$200.00	10
Hack Saw.................	350.00	38.00	12
Power Saw................	1,275.00	235.00	7
Boiler....................	2,700.00	180.00	6
Power equipment...........	800.00	50.00	5
Delivery equipment.........	2,100.00	560.00	5

Sinking-fund method. Under the sinking-fund method, the replacement of the asset when it is worn out is provided for by setting aside a fixed sum of money each year out of revenue. These payments when invested in a sinking fund at a certain rate will accumulate to a sum which, together with the scrap value, will replace the asset. The amount may be carried on the books of the company as an account on which interest is credited or it may be separately invested.

If the depreciation charge per year is D, with the scrap value $= S$, and the original cost $= C$, then, if the expected life is n years,

$$Ds_{\overline{n}|i} = C - S$$
$$D = (C - S)\,\frac{1}{s_{\overline{n}|i}}. \tag{2}$$

Example. A machine which cost $4,000.00 has a salvage value of $120.00 after an expected life of ten years. The depreciation charges under the sinking-fund method are invested at 5%. What is the annual depreciation charge?

Solution. In this case $C = \$4000.00$, $S = \$120.00$, $n = 10$, and $i = .05$. Substituting into the formula, $D = 3,880 \dfrac{1}{s_{\overline{10}|\,5\%}}$.

$$\therefore D = 3,880(.07950458)$$
$$= \$308.48.$$

$\therefore$ The annual depreciation charge is $308.48.

TABLE OF DEPRECIATION

Age in Years	Debit to Sinking Fund	Interest on Fund	Total Addition	Accumulation of Fund	Book Value of Asset
					\$4,000.000
1	\$308.478	0	\$308.478	\$ 308.478	3,691.522
2	308.478	\$ 15.424	323.902	632.380	3,367.620
3	308.478	31.619	340.097	972.477	3,027.523
4	308.478	48.624	357.102	1,329.579	2,670.421
5	308.478	66.479	374.957	1,704.536	2,295.461
6	308.478	85.226	393.704	2,098.238	1,901.757
7	308.478	104.911	413.389	2,511.627	1,488.368
8	308.478	125.581	434.059	2,945.686	1,054.309
9	308.478	147.284	455.762	3,401.448	598.547
10	308.478	170.072	478.550	3,879.998	119.997

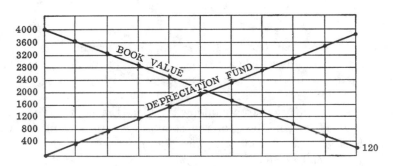

Fig. 21-2. Graphic Representation of Depreciation by the Sinking Fund Method.

PROBLEMS

1. Set up sinking fund depreciation tables for the following assets, using 5% as the sinking fund rate.

Asset	Cost	Scrap	Life
Office furniture........................	\$ 500	\$ 125	8 years
Factory furniture.....................	1,000	100	10 years
Machinery............................	15,000	3,000	8 years
Delivery equipment...................	4,000	500	5 years

2. A man buys a used car for $1,250. The life of the car is five years, and its scrap value $125. If money can be invested at 6%, find the annual replacement charge and the book value of the car at the end of each year.

3. A factory building costs $80,000 and has an estimated life of 50 years with a scrap value of $2,500. Determine the annual sinking fund payment on a 5% basis, and set up a schedule to show the amount in the fund for the first eight years.

4. A steam shovel cost $30,000 new and has a probable life of eight years and a scrap value of $2,000. If the fund can be invested at 5%, find the annual replacement charge and set up a schedule to show the condition of the fund and the book values.

5. A trucking company purchased six motor trucks worth $3,500 each, with a scrap value of $200 each and a probable life of six years. What amount should be set aside in a depreciation reserve fund each year if the fund earns 5% per annum? Set up a schedule to show accumulation of the fund.

Annuity method of depreciation. The theory applied in this method is that the depreciation charge should include, in addition to the amount credited to the reserve, interest on the carrying value of the asset.

The investment in property is regarded, first, as the amount of scrap value which draws interest, and second, as an investment in an annuity to be reduced by equal periodic amounts. The interest on the scrap value plus the equal periodic reduction of the investment is the charge to depreciation, offset by a credit to interest computed on the diminishing value of the property, and a credit to the reserve account for the balance. This charge to depreciation is the same each period during the life of the property. The theory of an investment in an annuity is that the annuity is to be reduced by equal periodic payments, and as the credits to interest will decrease, the credits to the reserve must correspondingly increase.

The formula for the annuity method of determining the annual depreciation charge is,

$$D = (C - S)\frac{1}{a_{\overline{n}| i}} + Si. \tag{3}$$

Example. Using the annuity method, what will the annual charge for depreciation be for an asset costing $2,000.00 and having a scrap value of $200.00 after a life of ten years if interest is calculated at 6%?

Solution. In this case, $C = \$2,000.00$, $S = \$200.00$, $n = 10$, and $i = .06$. Substituting into Formula (3),

$$\begin{aligned}
D &= 1800\,\frac{1}{a_{\overline{10}| 6\%}} + (200)(.06) \\
&= 1800(.13586796) + (200)(.06) \\
&= 244.562 + 12.00 \\
&= \$256.562.
\end{aligned}$$

DEPRECIATION TABLE

Age in Years	Book Value at End of Year	Interest on Book Value of Previous Year	Total Payment	Charge to Depreciation Fund
0	$2,000.00			
1	1,863.438	$120.000	$256.562	$ 136.562
2	1,718.682	111.806	256.562	144.756
3	1,565.240	103.120	256.562	153.442
4	1,402.592	93.914	256.562	162.648
5	1,230.185	84.155	256.562	172.407
6	1,047.433	73.810	256.562	182.752
7	853.717	62.846	256.562	193.716
8	648.378	51.223	256.562	205.339
9	430.718	38.902	256.562	217.660
10	199.999	25.843	256.562	230.719
				1,800.001

PROBLEMS

1. The Acme Manufacturing Company, believing that the annuity method of depreciation is the correct one, desires that you construct tables for the following machines (one table for each):

Assets	Cost	Scrap	Life	Interest Rate
Lathes.....................	$5,000	$ 500	10 years	5%
Milling machines..............	4,500	1,000	8 years	5%
Grinders....................	1,200	200	5 years	5%
Motors.....................	2,000	200	6 years	5%

2. Electric motors, costing $2,000 each, have a scrap value of $180 and an estimated life of eight years. Construct a table to show the interest charges and the accumulation of the depreciation fund by the annuity method. Interest at 6%.

3. A lathe costing $5,800 has a life of ten years and a scrap value of $400. Allowing interest at 5% on the book value, calculate the annual charge by the annuity method and prepare a schedule to show the state of the fund.

4. A building worth $56,000 has an estimated life of 30 years and a scrap value of $1,000. The owner wishes to allow interest at 5% on the book value of the property and to provide depreciation by the annuity method. Make out a schedule for the first six years.

5. A printing machine costs $4,000 and has an estimated life of eight years. Its scrap value is $800. Allowing interest on diminishing book values at 5%, construct the schedule.

Constant-percentage-of-book-value method. This method writes off at the end of each year a constant percentage of the book value at the beginning of that year. This percentage is determined in relation to the life of the asset and its scrap value.

Formula: Let r = constant percentage or percentage rate of depreciation, C = cost of asset, S = scrap value, and n = life in years.

Years	Book Value at Beginning of Year	Depreciation Fund Payment	Book Value at End of Year
1	C	Cr	$C - Cr = C(1 - r)$
2	$C(1 - r)$	$C(1 - r)r$	$C(1 - r) - C(1 - r)r = C(1 - r)^2$
. . .	. . .	. . .	. . .
n	$C(1 - r)^{n-1}$	$C(1 - r)^{n-1}r$	$C(1 - r)^{n-1} - C(1 - r)^{n-1}r = C(1 - r)^n$

Since the book value at the end of n years has to equal the scrap value,

$$C(1 - r)^n = S. \tag{4}$$

Obviously, the book value after k periods is,

$$C(1 - r)^k,$$

and the contribution to the depreciation fund during the $(k + 1)$st period is $C(1 - r)^k r$.

Example. A machine worth \$3,000.00 has a life expectancy of six years and a scrap value of \$50.00. Find the constant percentage by which depreciation should be charged and construct a depreciation table.

Solution. In this case $C = 3,000$, $S = 50$, and $n = 6$. Substituting these values in Formula (4),

$$3,000(1 - r)^6 = 50$$

$$(1 - r)^6 = \frac{50}{3,000}$$

$\therefore$ By logarithms, $6 \log (1 - r) = \log 50 - \log 3,000$
$\therefore \log (1 - r) = \frac{1}{6}(\log 50 - \log 3,000)$

$$
\begin{array}{rl}
\log 50 = & 1.698970 \\
\log 3,000 = & 3.477121 \\
\hline
6 \,\overline{\big)} & \overline{2}.221849 \\
\hline
& \overline{1}.703641
\end{array}
$$

$$
\begin{array}{rl}
\therefore \log (1 - r) = & \overline{1}.703641 \\
\therefore 1 - r = & .50540 \\
\therefore r = & .49460.
\end{array}
$$

DEPRECIATION TABLE

Age in Years	Depreciation Charge	Book Value at End of Year	Accrued Depreciation
0	0	$3,000.00	0
1	$1,483.20	1,516.80	$1,483.20
2	750.51	766.29	2,233.71
3	378.99	387.30	2,612.70
4	191.56	195.74	2,804.26
5	96.81	98.93	2,901.07
6	48.93	50.00	2,950.00

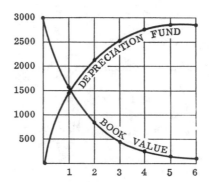

Fig. 21-3. Graphic Representation of Depreciation by the Constant Percentage of the Book Value Method.

PROBLEMS

1. A truck costing $5,000 has a scrap value of $200 at the end of ten years. Find the constant percentage reduction of the book value and construct a schedule for the depreciation fund.

2. Find the annual percentage under the reducing-balance method for a machine whose cost was $10,000 and which will be reduced to a scrap value of $1,000 after five years. Draw up a depreciation schedule showing the changes in book value.

3. An asset whose life is 20 years costs $40,000 new and has a scrap value of $4,000 when worn out. Find the annual rate of depreciation under the reducing-balance method.

4. In Problem 3, construct the schedule to show the accrued depreciation and the book value for the first ten years.

5. A machine when new cost $4,500 and has an estimated life of 12 years. Its salvage value will be $300. Find the constant annual rate of depreciation necessary to reduce the machine to scrap value in 12 years. Construct the schedule.

6. Construct a comparative columnar table showing the periodic depreciation charges computed by the straight-line, sum-of-digits, sinking-fund, annuity, and constant-percentage-of book-value methods for an asset costing $10,000, and having a probable life of ten years and a scrap value of $1,500. Use an interest rate of 4% per annum.

7. An asset costing $2,000 has a life of five years. It has no scrap value, but for the purposes of calculation, use $1. Money is worth 5%. Construct comparative columnar tables showing the carrying value and the annual depreciation charge computed by the straight-line, sum-of-digits, sinking-fund, annuity, and constant-percentage-of-book-value methods.

8. A businessman, having heard much about correct depreciation but understanding little of the methods of calculation used, calls on you to explain to him by means of comparison the five most important methods. As an illustration, use an asset costing $1,000, with a scrap value of $500 and a life of five years, and an interest rate of 6%.

Composite life. Often the depreciable assets of a business have wearing values (cost less scrap value) and terms of effective life that vary widely, yet it is desirable to ascertain the life of the plant as a whole, as when bonds secured by a mortgage on buildings and equipment are issued. The bonds should not be issued for a term of years exceeding the composite life of the plant; and, for a margin of safety, the term of the bonds should be considerably shorter than the composite life of the plant.

If interest *is not* a factor, the composite life is found by dividing the total wearing value by the total depreciation.

Unit	Life	Cost	Scrap	Wearing Value	Annual Charge
Bldg. (Brick)	50	$45,000	$5,000	$40,000	$ 800
Bldg. (Frame)	25	12,000	2,000	10,000	400
Heavy Machinery	25	30,000	5,000	25,000	1,000
Boiler	20	12,000	2,000	10,000	500
				$85,000	$2,700

85,000 ÷ 2,700 = 31.5, approximate years

If interest *is* a factor, as when depreciation is computed on the sinking fund basis, the annual charge for depreciation is the annual rent, the accumulation of which should equal the wearing value. Making use of the data from above and using 5% as the interest rate, we have:

Unit	Life	Wearing Value	Annual Charge
Bldg. (Brick)	50	$40,000	$ 191.07
Bldg. (Frame)	25	10,000	209.53
Heavy Machinery	25	25,000	523.81
Boiler	20	10,000	302.43
		$85,000	$1,226.84

Since the composite life of the plant is the time necessary for the total annual contribution to accumulate to the total wearing value at the given rate of interest, it is the time required for annual payments of $1,226.84 to amount at 5% to $85,000.00.

$$\therefore\ 1{,}226.84 s_{\overline{n}|5\%} = 85{,}000.00$$

$$\therefore\ s_{\overline{n}|5} = \frac{85000}{1226.84} = 69.3$$

$$1\ \begin{bmatrix} d\begin{bmatrix} s_{\overline{30}|5\%} = 66.4388 \\ \\ s_{\overline{n}|5\%} = 69.3 \end{bmatrix} 2.8612 \\ \\ s_{\overline{31}|5\%} = 70.7608 \end{bmatrix}\ 4.3220$$

$$\frac{d}{1} = \frac{2.8612}{4.3220} = .66$$

$\therefore$ the composite life is 30.66 years.

PROBLEMS

1. A company's plant consists of: (*a*) Buildings: cost, \$100,000; life, 40 years; scrap value, \$10,000. (*b*) Engine: cost, \$40,000; life, 25 years; scrap value, \$5,000. (*c*) Boiler: cost, \$12,000; life, 20 years; scrap value, \$2,000. (*d*) Electrical equipment: cost, \$7,500; life, 15 years; scrap value, \$1,500. Compute the charge for depreciation by the sinking fund method, on a 4% basis, and find the composite life of the plant.

2. Find the composite life of a plant consisting of the following:

Item	Cost	Scrap Value	Life
A	\$ 6,000	\$ 200	10 years
B	3,500	500	15 years
C	12,000	1,000	20 years
D	15,000	2,500	12 years

Interest at 5%.

Depletion. The provision for the extinction of wasting assets, such as mines, timber lands, or gravel pits, is called a provision for depletion.

We shall deal with two classes of problems; namely, the determination of the amount of depletion each year, and the capitalization of the wasting asset.

Calculation of depletion. The amount of depletion usually stands in the same proportion to the total cost of the wasting asset as the units of product removed stand to the total units of product that it was estimated the asset would produce when new; but if the property is leased and it is not possible to remove all the product before the lease expires, it is plain that depletion should be based on the quantity to be extracted during the period of the lease.

Valuation of wasting assets. Suppose that the value of a wasting asset is V, and the asset is estimated to yield a net annual income of R for n years more. Let i be the interest rate expected on the purchase price V, and the expected annual interest be Vi.

The net annual income, however, should build up a sinking fund which will contain an amount at the exhaustion of the asset which is equal to the original investment as well as paying the annual interest. If we assume that the sinking fund is invested at rate j, then the annual contribution to the sinking fund will be $V \dfrac{1}{s_{\overline{n}|j}}$.

$$\therefore R = Vi + V \frac{1}{s_{\overline{n}|j}} = V\left(i + \frac{1}{s_{\overline{n}|j}}\right)$$

$$\therefore V = \frac{R}{i + s_{\overline{n}|j}^{-1}}. \tag{5}$$

Example. A coal mine is expected to yield a net annual income of $25,000 for the next 25 years. Find the purchase price of the mine if the purchaser expects 7% on his investment and can invest in a sinking fund at 5%.

Solution. In this case $R = 25,000$, $i = .07$, $j = .05$, and $n = 25$. Substituting these values in Formula (5),

$$V = \frac{25,000}{.07 + s_{\overline{25}|5\%}^{-1}} = \frac{25,000}{.07 + 0.0209525} = \$274,868.75.$$

$\therefore$ the purchase price should be $274,868.75.

PROBLEMS

1. The estimated recoverable tonnage in a coal mine was placed at 2,214,363 tons. The value of "Coal Lands" was $96,443.62. Compute the depletion charge per ton of coal mined.

2. A tract of timber was valued at $25,965.86, and its footage was estimated at 17,228,000. The following year the timber cut was 5,184,336 feet. Compute the rate of depletion per thousand feet, and the depletion charge for the year.

3. A mining property was valued at $50,000, and the estimated recoverable tonnage placed at 1,000,000 tons.

During the next seven years, tonnage was removed as follows:

First year	50,000 tons
Second year	60,000 tons
Third year	70,000 tons
Fourth year	80,000 tons
Fifth year	80,000 tons
Sixth year	80,000 tons
Seventh year	80,000 tons

Prospecting and development toward the close of the seventh year cost $25,000, and resulted in an estimated recoverable tonnage of 2,000,000 tons. Appreciation due to discovery was placed on the books at $60,000.

The tonnage removed during the eighth and ninth years was 100,000 tons and 120,000 tons, respectively.

Calculate the annual charges for depletion.

[Suggestion: Set up two accounts, Mining Property (Cost), and Mining Property (Discovery Value), and credit these accounts with the proper depletion charges each year. This problem is illustrative of the complications that arise when there is more than one valuation on a particular property.]

4. What is the present value of a gold mine which will yield a net annual income of $8,000.00 for the next seven years if the purchaser wants 6% and he can invest in a sinking fund at 5%?

5. An oil well will produce $25,000.00 a year for the next 15 years. If the purchaser expects $7\frac{1}{2}$% on his investment and his sinking fund earns 6%, what is the price?

6. Find the capitalized value of a coal mine which will produce a net income of $20,000 a year for 30 years; the annual income rate is 6%, and a sinking fund is to be accumulated at 4%.

7. A tract of timber will yield an annual revenue of $20,000 for 20 years. If annual dividends are declared at 5%, and payments are made annually into a sinking fund which bears 4% interest, what is the value of the timber rights?

8. A gravel pit is estimated to contain 3,500,000 cubic yards of gravel. This pit is leased at a royalty of 10¢ per cubic yard of gravel extracted, and the average annual output is 150,000 cubic yards. If a 6% dividend is paid on the stock, and a fund equal to the capital stock is accumulated at 4%, what should be the capitalized value of the property?

REVIEW PROBLEMS

1. A railway purchased 12 pieces of equipment at a cost of $32,000 each. The probable life of the pieces is 30 years and their scrap value is estimated at $1,500 each. Calculate the annual charges for depreciation by

(a) The straight-line method,
(b) The constant-percentage method,

and calculate the sum of money in each fund at the end of ten years.

2. A shoe company installed in their factory two automatic machines at a cost of $12,500 each. Their estimated life is ten years, and scrap value $1,200 each. What will be their book value at the end of seven years if depreciation is figured

(a) By the straight-line method?
(b) By the constant-percentage method?

3. The Canadian Pacific Railway Co. purchased two machines at a cost of $95,000 each. It is estimated that their life will be 30 years and their scrap value $3,000 each. If depreciation is cared for by the sinking-fund method and the fund earns 5%, calculate the amount in the fund at the end of seven years.

4. An electric company installed a 30M-kilowatt generator at a cost of $350,000. It is estimated to have a life of 20 years and a scrap value of $18,000. If money is worth 5%, construct a schedule for ten years, using the interest-on-investment method.

5. The Alberta Anthracite Corporation installed an oil engine in their plant. The engine cost $64,000 and was estimated to have a life of 20 years and a scrap value of $4,000. Calculate the depreciation charges by the constant-percentage method and show the amounts for the first eight years.

6. The Hamilton Cotton Mills installed machinery worth $65,000 with an estimated life of 12 years and a scrap value of $5,000. Using the sum-of-the-digits method of depreciation, find the book value of the machinery after six years.

7. A company purchased a transformer costing $25,000 and having an estimated life of ten years and a scrap value of $2,000. Determine the charges for interest and depreciation for each year of the life of the machine, allowing interest at 5% on the remaining book value of the asset.

8. A building valued at $120,000 has an estimated life of 40 years and a scrap value of $5,000. Calculate the charges for depreciation by the sinking-fund method, assuming a six per cent interest rate.

9. A machine that cost $1,000 is estimated to have a life of ten years and a scrap value of $200. Compute the annual depreciation charge by:

   (*a*) The straight-line method.
   (*b*) The constant-percentage-of-book-value method.
   (*c*) The sinking-fund method, using 6% effective interest.
   (*d*) The annuity method, using 6% effective interest.

10. A mine with a net annual yield of $7,5,000 will be exhausted in 15 years at the present rate of output. What is the mine worth, on a 5% basis?

11. A certain make of bench drill costs $17.50 and lasts three years. How much can be paid for a better grade of drill that will last six years, money being worth 4%? (HINT: Capitalized costs must be equal. Solve for *x*.)

12. A roof made of one material will cost $300 and last for 20 years. If made of another type of material, it will last for the life of the building, which is estimated to be 75 years. How much can one afford to pay for the permanent type of roof if money is worth 5%?

13. Calculate the fixed percentage to be written off each year for an asset costing $2,400, estimated life six years and scrap value $400.

22

Permutations and Combinations

Fundamental principles.

I. *If an event can occur in* m *different ways, and after it has happened another event can occur in* n *different ways, then both events can occur in the stated order in* mn *different ways.* The principle can be extended to show that the number of different ways of three or more events occurring together is *mnp* . . . different ways.

Example. In how many ways can three positions as stenographers be filled if eight applicants applied?

Solution. Assuming that all applicants are qualified, there are eight ways of choosing the first stenographer. After she has been chosen, there are seven applicants left for the position of second stenographer. After the second stenographer is chosen, there are six applicants left for the position of third stenographer. Therefore, there are $8 \cdot 7 \cdot 6 = 336$ ways of filling the three positions.

II. *If one of two independent events can occur in* m *ways and the other can occur in* n *ways, then both can occur, disregarding their order, in* mn *ways.* The principle can be extended to show that the number of different ways that three or more independent events can occur together is *mnp* . . . .

Example. In how many ways can two positions, the one that of bookkeeper and the other that of stenographer, be filled when there are five applicants for the position of bookkeeper and three applicants for that of stenographer?

Solution. Assuming that all applicants are qualified, there are five ways of filling the position of bookkeeper, and for each of these there is a choice of three stenographers; hence, the two positions can be filled in $5 \cdot 3 = 15$ ways.

III. *If two events are mutually exclusive (cannot occur together), and the first can occur in* m *different ways and the second in* n *different ways, then either one or the other can occur in* m + n *different ways.* This principle can be extended to show that the number of different ways that three or more mutually exclusive events can occur is $m + n + p + \cdots$ different ways.

Example. A boy may purchase a suit or a sports coat. He enters a clothing store in which five different suits and six different sports coats fit him. How many ways has he of choosing one garment?

Solution. According to principle III, he has 5 + 6 = 11 choices.

Example. A boy is permitted to choose a suit or a combination sports coat and slacks ensemble. The store has five suits, six sports coats, and 11 pairs of slacks that fit him. How many ways has he of choosing an outfit?

Solution. According to principle II, he has $6 \cdot 11 = 66$ ways of choosing a sports coat and slacks ensemble.

Therefore, according to principle III, he has 5 + 66 = 71 ways of choosing an outfit.

Permutation. A *permutation* is each arrangement which can be made by using all or part of a number of things. The "number of permutations of n things taken r at a time," represented by the symbol $_nP_r$, is the number of arrangements of r things that can be formed from n things. Thus, using the three letters a, b, and c taken two at a time, the permutations are ab, ac, ba, bc, ca, and cb. Using all of them at the same time, the permutations are abc, acb, bac, bca, cab, and cba.

Since $_nP_r$ is used to denote the number of permutations of n things taken r at a time, its value is determined as follows:

For first place: any one of n things may be chosen;
For second place: any one of the remaining, or $n - 1$, things may be chosen;
For third place: any one of the remaining, or $n - 2$, things may be chosen;
For fourth place: any one of the remaining, or $n - 3$, things may be chosen;
and so forth;
For the last or
rth place: there remains a choice of

$$n - (r - 1) \text{ or } n - r + 1 \text{ things.}$$

Therefore, $_nP_r = n(n - 1)(n - 2)(n - 3) \cdots (n = r + 1).$ (1)

Take the three letters a, b, and c two at a time. For the first place, there is a choice of three letters; for the second place, there is a choice of

376   *Permutations and Combinations*

$3 - 1$ letters; therefore, $_3P_2 = 3(3 - 1) = 6$, the number of permutations of three letters taken two at a time, as shown in the first paragraph.

Using the three letters a, b, and c all at the same time, $r = n$. Therefore, the symbol may be expressed $_nP_n$ when all of the n things are taken at once, and

$$_nP_n = n(n - 1)(n - 2)(n - 3) \cdots \text{ (until } n \text{ factors are used).}$$

The symbol $n!$, called "factorial n," denotes the product of all integers from n to 1 inclusive, and the expression is abbreviated to $_nP_n = n!$. Solving the foregoing example, we have $_3P_3 = 3 \cdot 2 \cdot 1 = 6$, the number of permutations of the three letters taken three at a time, as shown in the first paragraph.

. . . placed on the line of writing indicates omission of the "in-between" factors.

Example 1. Determine the number of three-letter code words that can be made from the letters of the word *bunch*, not repeating a letter in any word.

Solution. The answer is the number of arrangements that can be made from five objects (the letters of the word *bunch*) taken three at a time.

Formula
$$_nP_r = n(n - 1) \cdots (n - r + 1)$$

Arithmetical Substitution
$$_5P_3 = 5(5 - 1)(5 - 2) = 5 \cdot 4 \cdot 3 = 60$$

Example 2. Determine the number of five-letter code words obtainable in the foregoing example.

Solution. The answer is the number of arrangements that can be made from five objects taken all at the same time, or $_nP_n = n!$; and, since $n!$ is the product of all the integers from n to 1, we have

$$n! = n(n - 1)(n - 2)(n - 3)(n - 4), \text{ or five factors in all.}$$

Arithmetical Substitution
$$_5P_5 = 5 \cdot 4 \cdot 3 \cdot 2 \cdot 1 = 120$$

Notice that the last factor $(n - r + 1)$ is one more than the difference between the number of things, n, and the number of places, r. Thus, if n is 7 and r is 5, the last factor is 3; also, the number of factors will be equal to r. So we may write the formula $_nP_r = n(n - 1)(n - 2) \cdots$ (until r factors are used).

Example 3. Five persons enter a doctor's waiting room in which there are seven vacant chairs. In how many ways can they take their places?

Solution.
Formula
$$_nP_r = n(n - 1)(n - 2) \cdots \text{ (until } r \text{ factors are used)}$$

Arithmetical Substitution

$$_7P_5 = 7(7-1)(7-2)(7-3)(7-4) \text{ (five factors)}$$
$$= 7 \cdot 6 \cdot 5 \cdot 4 \cdot 3 = 2,520$$

The formula (1) may be expressed as

$$_nP_r = \frac{n!}{(n-r)!}. \tag{2}$$

Using the data in Example 3, we have:

$$_7P_5 = \frac{7!}{(7-5)!}$$
$$= \frac{7 \cdot 6 \cdot 5 \cdot 4 \cdot 3 \cdot 2 \cdot 1}{2 \quad 1} = 2,520$$

Notice that the last two factors cancel the two below the line, and that the remaining factors are the same as in the preceding solution.

Using the three letters, a, b, and c two at a time, we have:

$$_nP_r = \frac{n!}{(n-r)!} = \frac{3!}{(3-2)!} = \frac{3 \cdot 2 \cdot 1}{1} = 6$$

The number of permutations of n things, taken all together when p of the things are alike and the rest different, is $\frac{n!}{p!}$. This can be seen if we let the number of arrangements be N and then replace the p similar things by p things which are all different from each other and from the rest. In this way each of the N arrangements gives rise to $p!$ arrangements by permuting the p things without disturbing the others. The number of arrangements has now become $N \times p!$, and since the n things are now all different,

$$N \times p! = n!$$

and

$$N = \frac{n!}{p!}$$

It follows, therefore, that the number of permutations of n things, taken all together, when p of the things are alike of one kind, q alike of another kind, r alike of another kind, and so on, is:

$$\frac{n!}{p!q!r! \cdots} \tag{3}$$

Example 1. How many permutations may be made of the letters of the word *Illinois?*

Solution. There are eight letters in the word *Illinois*, but three are i's and two are l's. Then we have:

$$\frac{8!}{3! \cdot 2!} = \frac{40,320}{12} = 3,360$$

Example 2. How many permutations may be made of the letters of the word *Indianola?*

Solution. There are nine letters in the word *Indianola*, but two are *a*'s, two are *i*'s, and two are *n*'s. Then we have:

$$\frac{9!}{2! \cdot 2! \cdot 2!} = \frac{362,880}{8} = 45,360$$

PROBLEMS

1. If three dice are thrown together, in how many ways can they fall?

2. There are eight vacant seats to be filled by five persons. In how many ways can they take their places?

3. How many five-place numbers can be made from the digits 1, 2, 3, 4, 5, 6, and 7?

4. What is the number of permutations of the letters (a) of the word *Indiana;* (b) of the word *Illiopolis?*

5. Using three letters at a time, how many permutations can be formed with the letters *abcd?*

6. (a) How many permutations of the letters *abcde* can be formed four at a time? (b) Five at a time? (c) Three at a time?

7. How many permutations may be made of six objects taken: (a) six at a time? (b) five at a time? (c) two at a time?

8. Given the numbers 2, 3, 4, 5, and 6. How many four-place numbers can be formed therefrom?

9. The Greek alphabet contains 24 letters. If no repetition of letters are allowed, how many three-letter fraternities can be named therefrom?

10. A signal man has five flags, no two of which are alike. (a) How many different signals can he make by placing them in a row using all five of them each time? (b) How many by using three at a time?

Combinations. A *combination* is a set or selection of r things out of a total of n things without reference to the order within the selection; therefore, *ab* and *ba* are the same combination. The "number of combinations that can be made from a total of n things taken r at a time" is denoted by the symbol nCr.

Clearly, any combination of n distinct things taken r at a time gives rise to $r!$ permutations, since each set of r things can be permuted among themselves in $r!$ ways.

$$\therefore\ r!{_n}C_r = {_n}P_r$$

$$\therefore\ {_n}C_r = \frac{{_n}P_r}{r!}$$

But
$$\qquad {_n}P_r = \frac{n!}{(n-r)!}, \text{ from (2).}$$

$$\therefore\ {_n}C_r = \frac{n!}{r!(n-r)!} \tag{4}$$

Example. Find the number of combinations which can be made with the four letters a, b, c, and d taken three at a time.

Solution.

$$_4C_3 = \frac{4!}{3!(4-3)!} = \frac{4 \cdot 3 \cdot 2 \cdot 1}{3 \cdot 2 \cdot 1} = 4$$

These combinations are: abc, abd, acd, and bcd. Notice in permutations that the three letters a, b, and c form six permutations, abc, acb, bac, bca, cab, and cba, but that there is only one combination abc, since all others are merely a rearrangement of the same letters. The addition of the fourth letter makes possible three more combinations.

Example. How many lines can be drawn connecting seven points no three of which are in the same straight line?

Solution. If we let the points be represented by the letters a, b, c, d, e, f, and g, and any line connecting two of them by the symbol ab, ac, and so on, we find that ab and ba is the same line, that ac and ca is another line, and so forth; therefore, the problem is that of finding the number of combinations of seven objects taken two at a time.

$$_7C_2 = \frac{7!}{2!(7-2)!} = \frac{7 \cdot 6}{2!} = 21$$

Note: The factors from *5* to *1* above the line cancel the same factors below the line, leaving the factors indicated in the solution.

If r is large and the difference between n and r is small, the following formula will save considerable work: $_nC_r = {}_nC_{n-r}$.

Example. Find the value of $_{25}C_{23}$.

Solution.

$$_{25}C_{23} = {}_{25}C_{25-23} = {}_{25}C_2 = \frac{25 \cdot 24}{1 \cdot 2} = 300$$

PROBLEMS

1. How many combinations can be made with the five letters a, b, c, d, and e taken three at a time?

2. If 12 members of an association are available for committee assignments, how many different committees of four each can be selected?

3. You have nine friends that you wish to invite to dinner parties of four guests each. How many dinner parties can you have without having the same company of four twice?

4. A committee consisting of two men and one woman is to be formed from a party of five men and four women. In how many ways can the committee be chosen?

23

Probability

Probability. One of the principal applications of permutations and combinations is found in the theory of probability. The probabilities for the occurrence of one or more events, in cases in which it is possible to count the number of equally likely ways in which the event can happen or fail, are known as *priori* probabilities.

Counting of some sort is the background of probability. For example, if a coin is tossed, the chances are even between heads and tails. If a die is thrown, the chances of throwing any one of the numbers 1 to 6 is 1 in 6, as there are six surfaces numbered from 1 to 6. The chance of drawing an ace from a well-shuffled pack of 52 cards is evidently 4 in 52.

If an event can occur in m ways and fail in n ways, and if each of these ways is equally likely, then the probability of its occurring is

$$p = \frac{m}{m + n},$$

and the probability of failure in an event is

$$q = \frac{n}{m + n}.$$

Example. Compute the probability of throwing a 3 in the first throw of a die.

Solution.

$$p = \frac{m}{m + n} = \frac{1}{1 + 5} = \frac{1}{6}$$

Example. Compute the probability of failing to throw a 3 in the first throw of a die.

Solution.

$$q = \frac{n}{m + n} = \frac{5}{1 + 5} = \frac{5}{6}$$

The mathematician computes the ratio of successes to the total number of ways in which the event can occur. For example, he would say that the chances of throwing a 4 in one toss of a die is "one chance in six." The average person usually calculates the ratio of the successes to the failures, and would say, "the odds are five to one against throwing a 4."

PROBLEMS

1. A bag contains 10 black balls and 15 white ones. What is the probability that a ball drawn at random will be black?

2. A box contains six times as many black balls as white ones, and one ball is drawn at random. What is the probability that the ball drawn will be black?

3. If you are to win a prize valued at $12.00 by throwing an ace in a single throw of a die, what is the value of your expectation?

Permutations and combinations in probability. The following examples will illustrate the statement made at the beginning of this chapter.

Example. What is the probability of obtaining a 6 if two dice are tossed?

Solution. Under permutations we learned that a succession of acts can be performed together in as many ways as the result of their continued product. Since each die has six faces, the two dice can fall in 6 × 6, or 36, ways. In these 36 ways, the sum 6 can appear in any one of the following five ways: 5 and 1, 1 and 5, 4 and 2, 2 and 4, 3 and 3. Therefore, the probability of throwing a 6 is $\frac{5}{36}$.

Example. If two cards are drawn from a complete deck of 52 cards, what is the probability that both are hearts?

Solution. First is the determination of the number of combinations of 52 objects taken two at a time.

$$_nC_r = \frac{n!}{r!(n-r)!} = \frac{52!}{2!(52-2)!} = 1,326$$

Second is the determination of the number of selections of two hearts.

$$_nC_r = \frac{13!}{2!(13-2)!} = 78$$

Therefore, the probability of selecting two hearts is $\frac{78}{1326}$ or $\frac{1}{17}$.

Example. Two prizes are offered in a lottery of 20 tickets. What is your probability of winning a prize if you hold five tickets?

Solution. First, determine the number of ways in which five tickets can be selected.

$$_nC_r = \frac{20!}{5!(20-5)!} = 15,504$$

If you hold the two prize tickets; the remaining tickets may be any three of the remaining 18, so the number of selections containing both prizes is

$$_nC_r = \frac{18!}{3!(18-3)!} = 816$$

Next, determine the number of selections containing the first prize and not the second.

$$_nC_r = \frac{18!}{4!(18-4)!} = 3,060$$

The number of selections containing the second prize and not the first is evidently the same, 3,060.

Therefore, the probability of winning a prize is

$$\frac{816 + (2 \times 3,060)}{15,504} = \frac{6,936}{15,504} = \frac{17}{38}$$

Example. In the foregoing example, what is the probability that you will not win a prize?

Solution. As two of the tickets are winners, 18 are not winners, and this is the number from which five tickets must be selected, then,

$$_nC_r = \frac{18!}{5!(18-5)!} = 8,568$$

As before,

$$_nC_r = \frac{20!}{5!(20-5)!} = 15,504$$

The probability that there will be no winner is

$$\frac{8,568}{15,504} = \frac{21}{38}$$

Checking the answer to the preceding problem, we have:

$$1 - \tfrac{21}{38} = \tfrac{17}{38}$$

PROBLEMS

1. A complete deck of cards numbers 52 and is made up of 13 cards in each of the four suits. If four cards are drawn, find the following probabilities:

(a) That all are hearts;
(b) That there is one card of each suit;
(c) That there are two diamonds and two clubs.

2. (a) In a single throw of two dice, what is the probability of throwing a ten? (b) What would be the probability in a single throw of three dice?

3. If you toss six coins, what is the probability that there are four heads and two tails?

4. The cash drawer contains five ten-dollar bills, six five-dollar bills, and seven one-dollar bills. How many different sums may be formed with three bills taken out at random?

Compound events. The joint occurrence of two or more simpler events in connection with one another is called a *compound event.* If two or more events occur without influencing one another, they are said to be independent; but if any of them does affect the occurrence of the others, they are said to be dependent. When the occurrence of any one of the events excludes the occurrence of any other on that occasion, the events are said to be mutually exclusive.

Independent events. The probability that n independent events will happen favorably on a given occasion (when all of them are in question) is the product of their separate probabilities. If the separate probabilities that an event can occur favorably are represented by $p_1, p_2, \ldots p_n$, and P equals the probability that all these events will happen together at a given trial, then,

$$P = p_1 \times p_2 \times \cdots \times p_n$$

Example. What is the probability that 2, 3, and 4 are thrown in succession with a die?

Solution. The probability of getting 2 is $\frac{1}{6}$, that of getting 3 is $\frac{1}{6}$, and that of getting 4 is $\frac{1}{6}$. As these are the probabilities of independent events, the joint probability will be $\frac{1}{6} \times \frac{1}{6} \times \frac{1}{6} = \frac{1}{216}$.

Example. What is the probability of getting 2, 3, and 4 in one throw with three dice?

Solution. Consider the three dice as being thrown separately. Then there are three chances in 6 of getting the first number, two chances in 6 of getting the second number, and one chance in six of getting the third number. Since these events are all independent of one another, the joint probability will be $P = \frac{3}{6} \times \frac{2}{6} \times \frac{1}{6} = \frac{1}{36}$.

Example. From a box containing five brown marbles and four green marbles, three marbles are drawn. What is the probability that all three will be brown?

Solution. Consider each drawing an independent event. Since there are at first nine marbles and five are brown, the probability on the first drawing will be $\frac{5}{9}$. If a brown marble has been drawn, then on the second drawing the probability will be $\frac{4}{8}$. Now, if two brown marbles have been drawn, on the third drawing the probability will be $\frac{3}{7}$. Since these three probabilities have been independent events, the joint probability is

$$P = \frac{5}{9} \times \frac{4}{8} \times \frac{3}{7} = \frac{5}{42}$$

Mutually exclusive events. Let the number of mutually exclusive events be represented by $p_1, p_2, \ldots p_n$. The probability that some one of these events will occur is equal to their sum; therefore,

$$P = p_1 + p_2 + \cdots p_n.$$

Example. Three horses are entered in a race. Snowball's chances of winning are $\frac{1}{6}$, Thunderbolt's chances are $\frac{1}{2}$, and Fleetwind's $\frac{1}{4}$. What is the probability that the race will be a tie?

Solution. The winning of the race by Snowball, Thunderbolt, or Fleetwind forms a set of mutually exclusive events, since only one can be the winner. The probability that one of them wins the race is

$$P = \tfrac{1}{6} + \tfrac{1}{2} + \tfrac{1}{4} = \tfrac{11}{12}$$

Since the race may be a tie, that probability is

$$q = 1 - \tfrac{11}{12} = \tfrac{1}{12}$$

Example. If my chance of completing a certain engagement is $\tfrac{1}{4}$, and your chance of completing it is $\tfrac{2}{3}$, what is the probability that the engagement will be completed if we both work independently of one another?

Solution. If we work together to complete the engagement,

$$p_1 = \tfrac{1}{4} \times \tfrac{2}{3} = \tfrac{2}{12}$$

If I complete the engagement and you fail to complete it,

$$p_2 = \tfrac{1}{4} \times (1 - \tfrac{2}{3}) = \tfrac{1}{12}$$

If you complete it and I fail,

$$p_3 = \tfrac{2}{3} \times (1 - \tfrac{1}{4}) = \tfrac{6}{12}$$

The sum of $p_1 + p_2 + p_3 = \tfrac{2}{12} + \tfrac{1}{12} + \tfrac{6}{12} = \tfrac{3}{4}$, the probability that the engagement will be completed by one or the other of us.

This result can be checked by assuming that both will fail:

$$(1 - \tfrac{1}{4})(1 - \tfrac{2}{3}) = \tfrac{1}{4}$$
$$\tfrac{4}{4} - \tfrac{1}{4} = \tfrac{3}{4}$$

Example. From a box containing five brown marbles and four green marbles, two marbles are drawn at random. What is the probability that both are of the same color?

Solution. The probability that the two are brown is determined as shown:

$$\frac{5!}{2!(5-2)!} = 10 \quad \text{and} \quad \frac{9!}{2!(9-2)!} = 36; \quad \frac{10}{36} = \frac{5}{18}$$

The probability that the two are green is determined in the same manner.

$$\frac{4!}{2!(4-2)!} = 6 \quad \text{and} \quad \frac{9!}{2!(9-2)!} = 36; \quad \frac{6}{36} = \frac{3}{18}$$

These two events are mutually exclusive; hence, the probability that both marbles are of the same color is

$$\tfrac{5}{18} + \tfrac{3}{18} = \tfrac{4}{9}$$

The probability that there will be one of each color is

$$\frac{5 \times 4}{\dfrac{9!}{2!(9-2)!}} = \frac{5 \times 4}{36} = \frac{5}{9}$$

PROBLEMS

1. *A* and *B* engage in a game of checkers. The probability that *A* will win a game is $\frac{2}{3}$ and that *B* will win a second game is $\frac{1}{5}$. What is the probability that both win?

2. From a bowl containing five red marbles and six white ones, four marbles are drawn at random. What is the probability that they are all white?

3. In Problem 2, what is the probability that the four marbles drawn at random are red?

4. In Problem 2, determine the probability that of the four marbles drawn, two are red and two are white.

5. If three cards are drawn from an ordinary pack of playing cards, what is the probability that all three will be spades?

6. In Problem 5, what is the probability that all three cards are black?

7. What is the probability that all three will be of the same suit?

8. If the cards are replaced after each drawing, what is the probability that the first three are hearts?

9. At an election, 500 of the registered voters in the precinct cast their ballots. Two hundred voted in favor of a certain amendment and 300 voted against it. If five voters are chosen at random, what is the probability that they all voted for the amendment?

Empirical probability. The practical application of probabilities leads to a consideration of probabilities which are derived from experience. These are called *empirical* probabilities. The connection between probability and statistics, a subject devoted to the analysis and interpretation of data, is found in empirical probability.

Example. The following table gives the average daily sales of 92 market gardeners in a certain public market.

Average Daily Sales	2.50–7.49	7.50–12.49	12.50–17.49	17.50–22.49	22.50–27.49	27.50–32.49	32.50–37.49	37.50–42.49	42.50–47.49	47.50–52.49
Number of Gardeners	2	8	27	21	16	3	11	2	1	1

What is the probability of a person engaging in market gardening in this market of having average daily sales of less than $17.50?

Solution. The table shows that of 92 gardeners, the number who make less than $17.50 average daily sales is $2 + 8 + 27 = 37$. The required probability is, therefore, $\frac{37}{92}$, expressed decimally as 0.402.

PROBLEMS

1. A study of market gardening showed that 100 gardeners had marketed in a particular market as follows:

Years	Number of Gardeners
1 to 5	31
6 to 10	22
11 to 15	10
16 to 20	19
21 to 25	6
26 to 30	3
31 to 35	5
36 to 40	3
41 to 45	1
	100

What is the probability of a gardener being in this market for 20 years or less?

2. A survey among farmers to determine their average income disclosed the following facts:

Income Range	Per Cent of Farmers
Negative income (Loss)	4.55
0 to $ 500	12.53
$ 500 to $ 1,000	21.89
$ 1,000 to $ 1,500	17.01
$ 1,500 to $ 2,000	14.69
$ 2,000 to $ 3,000	13.31
$ 3,000 to $ 4,000	7.66
$ 4,000 to $ 5,000	3.25
$ 5,000 to $ 7,500	3.17
$ 7,500 to $10,000	0.93
$10,000 and over	1.01
	100.00

Based on the above survey, what is C's probability of making $2,000 to $3,000 a year if he engages in farming?

3. A manufacturer of electric light bulbs made a test with 200 bulbs of uniform design. The results were tabulated as follows:

Life in Hours	400 to 500	500 to 600	600 to 700	700 to 800	800 to 900	900 to 1,000	1,000 to 1,100	1,100 to 1,200	1,200 to 1,300	1,300 to 1,400	1,400 to 1,500	1,500 to 1,600
Number of Bulbs	2	4	7	16	23	27	37	31	24	18	8	3

What is the probability that a bulb will burn out in less than 800 hours, based on the experience of the foregoing test?

4. If three new bulbs are placed in operation at the same time, what is the probability that all of them will last 1,200 hours?

HINT: Cube of a single probability.

5. Find the probability that a bulb will be "alive" between 900 and 1,300 hours.

24

Probability and Mortality

Life insurance. Life insurance is based upon probabilities determined by the actual study of large collections of mortality statistics. If an event has happened m times in n possible cases (where n is a large number), then, in the absence of further knowledge, it may be assumed for many practical purposes that $\dfrac{m}{n}$ is the best estimate of the probability of the event and that confidence in this estimate may increase as n increases. The fraction $\dfrac{m}{n}$ is called the *frequency ratio*.

According to the American Experience Table of Mortality (see page 433), of 69,804 men living at age 50, the number living ten years later will be 57,917. The probability that a man aged 50 will live ten years is taken to be

$$\frac{57{,}917}{69{,}804} = .8297$$

Mortality table. Application of the theory of probability is made in the study of problems involving the duration of human life, such as life insurance, life annuities, pensions, and so forth. Tables that show the number of deaths expected to occur during a given age are used in the solution of these problems. Census records and vital statistics gathered by governmental agencies are the basis of some mortality tables. Others are based upon the records of life insurance companies. Results based upon mortality tables are applicable only to large groups of individuals.

The table on page 388 is taken from the American Experience Table. (The entire table is given in Table 1, in the Appendix.)

Column (1) is the age column and contains the age of 100,000 people or their survivors.

Column (2) indicates the number of people living at the beginning of the year designated on the same line in column (1). The table starts with 100,000 people alive at age 10 and at age 11 shows that only 99,251 have survived. The number that have died in the interval, 749, is shown in column (3).

Column (4) is $\dfrac{749}{100,000}$ = .00749 at age 10, and so on for each age.

Column (5) is $\dfrac{99,251}{100,000}$ = .99251 at age 10, and so on for each age.

AMERICAN EXPERIENCE TABLE OF MORTALITY				
(1)	(2)	(3)	(4)	(5)
Age	Number Living	Number of Deaths	Yearly Probability of Dying	Yearly Probability of Living
x	l_x	d_x	q_x	p_x
10	100,000	749	0.007490	0.992510
11	99,251	746	0.007516	0.992484
12	98,505	743	0.007543	0.992457
13	97,762	740	0.007569	0.992431
14	97,022	737	0.007596	0.992404
15	96,285	735	0.007634	0.992366
16	95,550	732	0.007661	0.992339
17	94,818	729	0.007688	0.992312
18	94,089	727	0.007727	0.992273
19	93,362	725	0.007765	0.992235
20	92,637	723	0.007805	0.992195
30	85,441	720	0.008427	0.991573
50	69,804	962	0.013781	0.986219
70	38,569	2,391	0.061993	0.938007
90	847	385	0.454545	0.545455
95	3	3	1.000000	0.000000

Notation. For convenience, the letter l is used to designate entries in the "living" column. Subscripts appended to the l denote specific entries in this column; thus, l_{15} indicates the number living at age 15.

It is customary to refer to the age as x, that is, any age; therefore, l_x would apply to any entry in column (2).

The number dying is denoted by d, which with the subscript, as in d_{15}, indicates the number dying between the age indicated and the next. Since x stands for any year, d_x indicates any entry in column (3).

The probability of a person dying is expressed by q. With the subscript, as in q_{15}, it denotes the probability of a person of the age indicated dying before reaching the following age. Similarly, q_x stands for the probability of a person aged x dying before reaching age $x + 1$. This probability is shown in column (4).

The probability of living is denoted by the letter p, and p_{15} denotes the probability that a person aged 15 will live to become age 16. This probability is shown by the table, column (5), to be .992366. The symbol p_x denotes the probability that a person aged x will live to age $x + 1$.

For convenience, the symbols already explained and others based on them are shown in the following summation:

x = a person or a life aged x years
l_x = the number of persons living at age x
l_{x+1} = the number living at age $x + 1$
l_{x+n} = the number living at age $x + n$
d_x = the number of persons dying in the age interval x to $x + 1$
d_{x+1} = the number dying in the age interval $x + 1$ to $x + 2$
p_x = the probability that a person of age x will live one year
q_x = the probability that a person of age x will die within one year
$_np_x$ = the probability that a person of age x will live at least n years
$_n|q_x$ = the probability that a person of age x will not live n years
$_n|q_x$ = the probability that a person of age x will die within one year after reaching the age of $x + n$
p_{xy} = the probability that two persons, of ages x and y, respectively, will live at least a year
$_np_{xy}$ = the probability that two persons, of ages x and y, respectively, will live at least n years

Probability of living. On page 387 was shown the probability that a man aged 50 will live ten years is taken to be $\dfrac{57,917}{69,804} = .8297$.

The probability that a person aged 50 will survive 10 years is equal to the ratio between the number living at age 60 and the number living at age 50. Expressed as a formula,

$$_{10}p_{50} = \frac{l_{60}}{l_{50}}$$

The probability that a person aged x will live to age $x + 1$ is equal to the ratio of the number of people living at age $x + 1$ to the number living at age x, or

$$p_x = \frac{l_{x+1}}{l_x}$$

Example.   What is the probability that a person of age 30 will live at least a year?

Solution.

$$p_x = \frac{l_{x+1}}{l_x} = \frac{l_{31}}{l_{30}} = \frac{84721}{85441} = .991573$$

The probability that a person will live longer than one year or n years is expressed by the formula

$$_np_x = \frac{l_{x+n}}{l_x}$$

Example.   Determine the probability that a person of age 40 will live to be 60.

Solution.

$$_np_x = \frac{l_{x+n}}{l_x} = \frac{l_{60}}{l_{40}} = \frac{57917}{78106} = .7415$$

Probability of dying.   The probability that a person aged x will die within a year is expressed by

$$q_x = \frac{d_x}{l_x}$$

Example.   What is the probability that a person aged 40 will die within one year?

Solution.

$$q_{40} = \frac{d_{40}}{l_{40}} = \frac{765}{78106} = .009794$$

The probability that a person aged x will not live to age $x + n$ is ascertained by the following formula:

$$_{|n}q_x = \frac{l_x - l_{x+n}}{l_x}$$

Example.   What is the probability that a person aged 30 will not live to age 40?

Solution.

$$_{|10}q_{30} = \frac{l_{30} - l_{30+10}}{l_{30}}$$

$$= \frac{85441 - 78106}{85441}$$

$$= .085849$$

Since the sum of the probability of living and the probability of dying equals 1, or certainty, the foregoing example may be solved as follows:

$$|_nq_x = 1 - {_np_x}$$
$$|_{10}q_{30} = 1 - {_{10}p_{30}} = 1 - \frac{l_{40}}{l_{30}}$$
$$= 1 - \frac{78106}{85441}$$
$$= .085849$$

The probability that a person aged x will die within one year after reaching age $x + n$ is ascertained by the following formula:

$$_n|q_x = \frac{d_{x+n}}{l_x}$$

Example. What is the probability that a person aged 30 will die within one year after reaching age 40?

Solution.

$$_{10}|q_{30} = \frac{d_{40}}{l_{30}} = \frac{765}{85441} = .008959$$

Joint life probabilities. The probability that two persons (x) and (y) will survive at least a year is denoted by p_{xy}. As the probabilities of life, or of death, of two or more persons are assumed to be independent of each other, it follows that

$$p_{xy} = \frac{l_{x+1} \cdot l_{y+1}}{l_x \cdot l_y}$$

Example. A husband and wife are aged 37 and 32, respectively. What is the probability that both will be alive at the end of 20 years?

Solution. The probability that the husband will be alive at the end of 20 years is

$$\frac{62104}{80353}, \text{ or } 0.7729$$

The probability that the wife will be alive at the end of 20 years is

$$\frac{67841}{84000}, \text{ or } 0.8076$$

Since the probability of two separate and distinct events is the product of the probabilities of each event, the probability that both will be alive at the end of 20 years is

$$0.7729 \cdot 0.8076 = 0.6242$$

NOTE: Since (x) is used in life insurance to denote the age of a person, it is confusing to use it to represent *times*, or *multiplied by;* therefore, multiplication is indicated by the period placed above the line. The formula may also be written

$$p_{xy} = \frac{l_{x+1} \cdot l_{y+1}}{l_{xy}}$$

PROBLEMS

1. What is the probability that a child aged 12 will die between the ages 15 and 16?

2. A father and son are aged 35 years and 13 years, respectively. Find the probability that both will be living on the son's twenty-first birthday.

3. What is the probability that a man aged 35 will die within five years? What is the probability that he will die in the year after he reaches age 40?

4. A husband and wife are aged 42 and 40, respectively. The husband has purchased an annuity, the first payment to be on his 65th birthday. What is the probability that both will be living at that time?

5. What is the probability that neither will be living when the first payment of the annuity described in Problem 4 is due?

6. If the annuity described in Problem 4 is payable for 20 years, what is the probability that both husband and wife will be living when the twentieth payment is due?

7. A husband and wife are aged 26 and 24, respectively, at the date of their marriage. What is the probability that they will live to celebrate their golden wedding anniversary?

8. Y is aged 40 and Z is aged 35. Calculate the following:

(a) That Y will survive the first year but Z will not.
(b) That both will survive one year.
(c) That Z will survive the first year but Y will not.
(d) That both will survive 15 years.
(e) That both will die during the first year.

9. Find the probability that a person aged 50 will live to age 70.

10. Find the probability that a person aged 25 will not live to age 35. What is the probability that this person will die between the ages of 35 and 36?

25

Life Annuities

Factors involved. In Chapter 16 it is shown that the present value of a sum of money payable n years in the future depends upon the rate of interest which can be earned.

If the payment of this sum of money at a future time is contingent on some person being alive at such future time, the present value depends upon the rate of interest and also upon the probability that the person will be living. For example, if two equally good insurable risks aged 25 and 65, respectively, are to receive $1,000 each upon attaining ages 35 and 75, respectively, the present value of the promised payment to the person aged 25 would be relatively much greater than to the person aged 65.

Pure endowment. A pure endowment contract promises to pay to the holder thereof a definite sum of money if he is living at the end of a specified period, but nothing to his beneficiaries if he fails to survive this period.

The present value of an n-year pure endowment of 1 to a person now aged x is expressed by the symbol $_nE_x$, which is equivalent to the present value of 1 to be received at the end of n years, multiplied by the probability $_np_x$ that a person aged x will survive n years.

If $_nE_x$ denotes the present value of an n years' pure endowment to a person of age x, we have

$$_nE_x = \left[\frac{1}{(1+i)^n} \right] {_np_x} \qquad {_np_x} = \frac{l_{x+n}}{l_x}$$

OR

$$_nE_x = \frac{\left(\dfrac{1}{(1+i)^n} \right) l_{x+n}}{l_x}$$

Example. A person aged 20 is to receive \$5,000 upon attaining age 25. Find the present value of the probability, interest at $3\frac{1}{2}\%$.

Solution.

$$5{,}000\,{}_5E_{20} = 5{,}000 \left[\dfrac{\dfrac{1}{(1.03\frac{1}{2})^5}\, l_{25}}{l_{20}} \right]$$

The probability that the person will receive the money is

$${}_5p_{20} = \frac{l_{25}}{l_{20}} = \frac{89032}{92637} = .9610846$$

$\dfrac{1}{(1.03\frac{1}{2})^5} = .8419732$, the present value of 1 for 5 years at $3\frac{1}{2}\%$

The present value to the person aged 20 is, then,

$$\$5{,}000 \times .8419732 \times .9610846 = \$4{,}046.04$$

PROBLEMS

1. A girl aged 10 is to receive \$5,000 upon attaining age 18. Find the present value of the inheritance, interest at $3\frac{1}{2}\%$.

2. A person, aged 20, is to receive \$10,000 upon reaching age 30. Find the present value of his expectation on the basis of $3\frac{1}{2}\%$ interest and the American Experience Table of Mortality.

3. Find the present value of a pure endowment of \$2,000 to a person aged 30 payable if he reaches the age of 60, on a $3\frac{1}{2}\%$ basis.

Life annuity. A series of periodical payments during the continuance of one or more lives constitutes a life annuity. The simplest form of a life annuity to a person aged x is the payment of 1 at the end of each year so long as the person now aged x lives. Such an annuity consists of the sum of pure endowments of 1 each year. The symbol for a life annuity is a_x; therefore, $a_x = {}_1E_x + {}_2E_x + {}_3E_x \cdots + {}_nE_x \cdots$ to table limit.

Substituting these values gives:

$$a_x = \frac{v l_{x+1} + v^2 l_{x+2} + v^3 l_{x+3} \cdots + v^n l_{x+n}}{l_x} \cdots \text{ to table limit.}$$

Example. Find the value of a life annuity of \$1,000 a year to a person now aged 90, interest at $3\frac{1}{2}\%$.

$$a_{90} = \frac{[(1.035)^{-1}l_{91}] + [(1.035)^{-2}l_{92}] + [(1.035)^{-3}l_{93}] + [(1.035)^{-4}l_{94}] + [(1.035)^{-5}l_{95}]}{l_{90}}$$

Present values are found in Table 4 (Appendix III). Values of l_{90}, l_{91}, and so forth, are found in Table 1 (Appendix III).

Substituting all the indicated values and solving, we have

$$a_{90} = .8738$$
$$\$1,000 \times .8738 = \$873.80$$

PROBLEM

A life pension of \$500 a year, payable at the end of each year, is granted to a person now aged 91. What is the present value of this pension, interest at $3\frac{1}{2}\%$?

Commutation columns. In the examples and in the preceding problem, the computations are not particularly arduous, because the age of the annuitant made it necessary to make only a few computations. But in cases where the annuitant is younger—for example, age 20—it is evident that a great amount of work would be required in order to solve the problem. Much of this computation may be eliminated by the use of tables called "commutation columns" (see Table 2).

The first column of this table, the D_x column, has been constructed of the products of similar v's and l's and the product denoted by the letter D. The computation was therefore reduced to the addition of the values found in the D_x column. To save time in adding these values, another commutation column was formed, containing the sums of all the D's from any particular value of D_x to the table limit. This is the N_x column of Table 2.

Therefore, the work is materially reduced by using the tables and the formula:

$$a_x = \frac{N_{x+1}}{D_x}$$

The solution to the second example on page 394 now becomes:

$$a_x = \frac{N_{x+1}}{D_x} = \frac{N_{90+1}}{D_{90}} = \frac{33.47}{38.3047} = .8738$$
$$\$1,000 \times .8738 = \$873.80$$

Using the commutation tables, the present value of the pure endowment on page 393 may be found by the formula

$$_nE_x = \frac{D_{x+n}}{D_x}$$

Substituting the values for the first example on page 394, we have

$$_5E_{20} = \frac{37673.6}{46556.2} = .809207$$

and

$$\$5,000 \times .809207 = \$4,046.04$$

From the foregoing formula it may be found that 1 at age x will purchase an n-year pure endowment of

$$\frac{D_x}{D_{x+n}}$$

PROBLEMS

1. What is the present value of a life annuity of $3,000 to a person aged 30, interest at $3\frac{1}{2}\%$?

2. Find the value of a life annuity of $2,500 at $3\frac{1}{2}\%$ to a person aged 35.

Life annuities due. The principles of annuities apply in life insurance. The preceding illustration was that of a life annuity where the payment was made at the end of each year. When the payments are to be made at the beginning of each year, the life annuity is a *life annuity due*. Actuaries use the symbol a_x to represent the present value of an annuity; and, since an annuity due differs from an ordinary annuity by an additional payment made at the beginning of the period, the present value of an annuity due is $1 + a_x$, and the symbol becomes

$$a_x = 1 + a_x$$

using a different type "a" from that used in the ordinary life annuity. Since the different type "a" is somewhat difficult to make, the regular a may be used and distinguished by a bar over it, thus,

$$\bar{a}_n = 1 + a_x$$

Use of commutation table. Since $a_x = \dfrac{N_{x+1}}{D_x}$, the life annuity due formula may be written as

$$\bar{a}_x = 1 + \frac{N_{x+1}}{D_x}$$

and if for 1 we substitute $\dfrac{D_x}{D_x}$, we have

$$\bar{a}_x = \frac{D_x}{D_x} + \frac{N_{x+1}}{D_x}, \quad \text{or} \quad \bar{a}_x = \frac{D_x + N_{x+1}}{D_x}$$

which is equivalent to

$$\bar{a}_x = \frac{N_x}{D_x},$$

the formula for the present value of a life annuity due of 1 payable to a person aged x. The values may be obtained from the commutation table.

Example. Find $\bar{a}_{30}$.

$$\bar{a}_x = \frac{N_x}{D_x}$$

$$\bar{a}_{30} = \frac{N_{30}}{D_{30}}$$

$$\bar{a}_{30} = \frac{596804}{30440.8} \text{ from the table}$$

$\bar{a}_{30} = 19.6054$, also shown in the table in the $1 + a_x$ column.

PROBLEMS

(Use the commutation table.)

1. Find N_{20}.
2. Find D_{35}.
3. If $x = 75$, find D_x.
4. Find N_x if $x = 22$.
5. When $D_x = 25630.1$, what is the value of x?
6. When $N_x = 208510$, what is the value of x?
7. At what age does $N_x = 157{,}255$?
8. At what age does $D_x = 1987.87$?
9. What is the difference in value between $\bar{a}_{40}$ and a_{40}?
10. Find (1) $\bar{a}_{30}$; (2) a_{30}.

Deferred annuity. When the first payment under a life annuity is to be made after the lapse of a specified number of years (contingent upon the annuitant (x) being alive), instead of being made a year after the payment of the single premium, the annuity is *deferred*.

Since under an ordinary annuity the first payment is made at the end of one year, then if an annuity is *deferred* n *years*, the first payment is made at the end of $n + 1$ years; but an annuity providing for *the first payment at the end of* n *years* is deferred $n - 1$ years, for the annuity is entered upon at the end of $n - 1$ years, and the first payment is not made until one year later; and it is a deferred life annuity due.

The present value of a life annuity of \$1.00 deferred for n years is expressed by the symbol

$$_n|a_x$$

but in n years the annuitant's age will be $x + n$, and the value of the annuity will be a_{x+n}; and, since it is desired to find the value of this annuity *now*, we discount it by multiplying a_{x+n} by the regular present-value symbol, v^n.

However, three factors are to be considered as follows:

(*a*) The value of the life annuity, a_{x+n};
(*b*) The present value of 1 in *n* years, v^n;
(*c*) The probability that the person aged *x* will be living *n* years from now, $_np_x$.

Therefore, the formula becomes:

$$_n|a_x = (a_{x+n})(v^n)(_np_x)$$

and, making substitutions so that the solution may be obtained from the commutation table, we have

$$_n|a_x = \frac{N_{x+n+1}}{D_x}.$$

Example. What single premium will a person aged 30 have to pay to obtain a life annuity of $2,500, so that he will receive his first annuity payment at the end of his 46th year?

Solution.

$$_n|a_x = \frac{N_{x+n+1}}{D_x}$$

$$_{15}|a_{30} = \frac{N_{30+15+1}}{D_{30}}$$

$$_{15}|a_{30} = \frac{N_{46}}{D_{30}}$$

From the commutation tables, it is found:

$$_{15}|a_{30} = \frac{237972}{30440.8}$$

$$= 7.8175$$
$$\$2,500 \times 7.8175 = \$19,543.75$$

Deferred life annuity due. The first payment of an annuity due would be made one year before that of an ordinary deferred annuity; therefore, the deferred life annuity due is the equivalent of an ordinary life annuity deferred for $n - 1$ years, and the formula is

$$_n\bar{a}_x = {}_{n-1}|a_x \qquad \text{or} \qquad _n\bar{a}_x = \frac{N_{x+n}}{D_x}$$

Example. *Y* is aged 55, and he desires to purchase a life annuity of $2,500, the first payment to be made at age 65. What is the single premium payment?

Solution.

$$_n\bar{a}_x = \frac{N_{x+n}}{D_x}$$

and

$$_{10}\bar{a}_{55} = \frac{N_{55+10}}{D_{55}}$$

$$= \frac{48616.4}{9733.40}$$

$$= 4.9948$$

$$\$2,500 \times 4.9948 = \$12,487.00$$

PROBLEMS

1. A child 15 years of age is to receive $2,400 a year for life, the first payment to be made at age 21. Calculate the value of this annuity at $3\frac{1}{2}\%$.

2. What single premium payment will a person aged 35 have to pay to obtain a life annuity of $3,000 from which he will receive his first annuity payment at age 60?

Temporary life annuities. A temporary life annuity continues for n years, contingent on the annuitant living that long; hence, it is not an annuity certain. The symbol for a temporary life annuity is $a_{x\overline{n}|}$, and the formula is

$$a_{x\overline{n}|} = \frac{N_{x+1} - N_{x+n+1}}{D_x}$$

Example. Find the present value of a life annuity of $2,000 for 25 years, to a person aged 40.

Solution.

$$a_{x\overline{n}|} = \frac{N_{x+1} - N_{x+n+1}}{D_x}$$

$$a_{x\overline{n}|} = \frac{N_{41} - N_{66}}{D_{40}}$$

$$= \frac{324440 - 43343.1}{19727.4}$$

$$= 14.24906$$

$$\$2,000 \times 14.24906 = \$28,498.12$$

Temporary annuities due. The present worth of a temporary life annuity due, also termed an *immediate temporary annuity*, is equivalent to the difference between the present worth of a whole life annuity due and a deferred life annuity due, and may be expressed as

$$\bar{a}_{x\overline{n}|} = \bar{a}_x - {}_{n|}\bar{a}_x$$

Substituting values, the formula for use with commutation tables becomes

$$\bar{a}_{x\overline{n}|} = \frac{N_x - N_{x+n}}{D_x}$$

Example. *Y* buys a temporary life annuity of $1,200 for his widowed mother aged 50. Payments are to begin at once and to continue until age 75. What is the present value of this annuity due?

Solution.

$$\bar{a}_{x\overline{n}|} = \frac{N_x - N_{x+n}}{D_x}$$

$$\bar{a}_{50\,\overline{25}|} = \frac{N_{50} - N_{50+25}}{D_{50}}$$

$$= \frac{181663 - 11728.9}{12498.6}$$

$$= 13.59625$$

$$\$1,200 \times 13.59625 = \$16,315.50$$

PROBLEMS

1. Find the present value of a temporary life annuity of $1,500 for 5 years to a person aged 65.

2. Find the values of $a_{20\,\overline{10}|}$, $a_{15\,\overline{20}|}$, and $a_{35\,\overline{10}|}$.

3. Find the values of $_{10|}a_{20}$, $_{20|}a_{15}$, and $_{10|}a_{35}$.

Life annuities with payments *m* times a year. Annuity contracts often provide that payments shall be made more frequently than once a year, such as quarterly or monthly, the latter being more common. For an annuity payable *m* times a year, the symbol $a_x^{(m)}$ is used to denote its present value, and the formula used to determine the value when the payments are made at the end of the period is

$$a_x^{(m)} = a_x + \frac{m-1}{2m}$$

Example. Find the present value of a life annuity of $600 a year payable monthly, the first installment to be paid in one month, for a person 35 years of age.

Solution.

$$a_x^{(m)} = a_x + \frac{m-1}{2m}$$

Substituting values,

$$a_{35}^{(12)} = a_{35} + \tfrac{11}{24}$$

$$a_{35} = \frac{N_{36}}{D_{35}} = \frac{432326}{24,544.7}$$

$$= 17.6143$$

$$\tfrac{11}{24} = .4583$$

$$17.6143 + .4583 = 18.0726$$

$$\$600 \times 18.0726 = \$10,843.56$$

If the payments are made at the beginning of the period, they constitute an annuity due, and its present value will be:

$$\ddot{a}_x{}^{(m)} = \ddot{a}_x - \frac{m-1}{2m}$$

For a deferred life annuity of 1 a year, payable in m installments a year, the present value is

$$_n|a_{xn}{}^{(m)} = \frac{D_{x+n}}{D_x} \times a_{x+n}{}^{(m)}$$

For a temporary life annuity for n years, payable in m installments a year, the present value is

$$a_{\overline{xn|}}{}^{(m)} = a_{\overline{xn|}} + \frac{m-1}{2m}(1 - {}_nE_x)$$

Example. The value of a temporary life annuity of \$180 a year payable annually for 15 years to a person aged 45 is \$1,873.96.

What is the present value of an annuity of the same annual rent if paid in monthly installments of \$15 each, the first payment one month hence?

Solution.

$$\$180a_{45\,\overline{15|}} = \$1,873.96$$
$$a_{45\,\overline{15|}} = 10.4109$$
$$a_{45}{}^{(12)}{}_{\overline{15|}} = a_{45\,\overline{15|}} + \tfrac{11}{24}(1 - {}_{15}E_{45})$$
$$_{15}E_{45} = \frac{D_{60}}{D_{45}} = \frac{7351.65}{15773.6} = .46606$$

Therefore,

$$a_{45}{}^{(12)}{}_{\overline{15|}} = 10.4109 + \tfrac{11}{24}(.53394)$$
$$= 10.4109 + .2447 = 10.6556$$
$$\$180(10.6556) = \$1918.01$$

PROBLEMS

1. Find the present value of a pension of \$75 a month payable at the end of each three months to a pensioner aged 65.

2. A corporation executive aged 58 is to be retired at age 65. During retirement he will receive \$3,600 a year payable in monthly installments. Find the present value of this retirement allowance on a $3\tfrac{1}{2}\%$ basis.

3. A life annuity contract provided for a payment of \$750 a year for 15 years, the first payment to be made at age 60. At age 60 the annuitant desired monthly payments. Find the amount of the monthly payments.

4. A widow was to receive \$1,800 a year for life in annual payments, the first payment to be made one year after her husband's death. When the first payment was due, the widow was 65 and asked that the payments be made monthly. What amount should she receive monthly?

Forborne temporary annuity due. A forborne temporary annuity due is created when a person who is entitled to a life annuity due of 1 a year forbears to draw it and agrees that the unpaid installments are to accumulate as pure endowments until he is aged $x + n$.

On page 399 the present value of a temporary annuity due was found by the formula

$$\ddot{a}_{\overline{xn}|} = \frac{N_x - N_{x+n}}{D_x},$$

and on page 396 it is given that 1 at age x will purchase an n-year pure endowment of

$$\frac{D_x}{D_{x+n}}$$

Then the present value would buy a pure endowment equal to

$$\frac{D_x}{D_{x+n}} \times \frac{N_x - N_{x+n}}{D_x} \qquad \text{or} \qquad \frac{N_x - N_{x+n}}{D_{x+n}}$$

PROBLEMS

1. Find the amount at age 60 of a forborne temporary annuity due of 1 a year that is to be accumulated for a person now aged 40.

2. A man was to receive a life annuity of $1200 a year, the first payment to be made one year after his 60th birthday. At that time he was still employed at a good salary, and so decided to postpone the beginning of the annuity for five years. What yearly sum will he receive, the first payment to begin on his 66th birthday? (Use American Experience Table of Mortality and $3\frac{1}{2}\%$, and treat the postponed annuity as a forborne annuity.)

26

Net Premiums

Net single premium. The net single premium is equal to the present value of the benefit influenced by rates of mortality and interest.

The net single premium for a whole life policy (a policy payable at death only) is denoted by A_x. Solution of a problem of this type is simplified by use of the commutation columns M_x and D_x, thus:

$$A_x = \frac{M_x}{D_x}.$$

Example. Find the net single premium for $3,000 whole life insurance on a person aged 24.

Solution.

$$A_{24} = \frac{M_{24}}{D_{24}}$$

$$= \frac{11935.4}{39307.1} = .303644$$

$$\$3,000 \times .303644 = \$910.93$$

Annual premiums. Life insurance premiums are most frequently paid in equal annual payments, but they may be paid semiannually, quarterly, or monthly, and, in the case of industrial insurance, weekly. Rates other than annual are greater in proportion than annual rates, for they include interest and additional overhead or administrative costs.

On an ordinary life policy, payments continue throughout the life of the insured. On a limited payment life policy, the premium payments are limited to a certain number of years, such as 20 years on a 20-payment life policy.

The net annual premium is the annual payment made at the beginning of each policy year, the sum thereof being the equivalent of the net single premium. The annual premiums constitute an annuity due payable by the policy holder to the insurance company. P_x is the symbol used for the net annual premium and, using commutation columns,

$$P_x = \frac{M_x}{N_x}.$$

Example. Find the net annual premium for an ordinary life policy of $1,000 issued to a person aged 30.

Solution.

$$P_{30} = \frac{M_{30}}{N_{30}} = \frac{10259.0}{596804} = .017189.$$
$$\$1,000 \times .017189 = \$17.19.$$

If the premium-paying period is limited to a certain number of years, such as 10 years in a 10-payment life policy, then the payments are equivalent, interest and mortality considered, to the single net premium. $_nP_x$ is the symbol used for the net annual premium for an n-payment life policy to a person aged x, and, in terms of commutation columns:

$$_nP_x = \frac{M_x}{N_x - N_{x+n}}.$$

Example. Find the net annual premium for a 20-payment life policy for $2000 issued to a person aged 45.

Solution.

$$_{20}P_{45} = \frac{M_{45}}{N_{45} - N_{65}} = \frac{7192.81}{253745 - 48616} = \frac{7192.81}{205129} = .03506.$$
$$\$2000 \cdot .03506 = \$70.12.$$

Term insurance. Other than group life insurance, term insurance is the lowest-cost life insurance obtainable. The term may be one year, five years, or ten years, and so forth, and the face value of the policy is payable in the event of death within the stated term.

The net single premium for term insurance may be ascertained from commutation columns, using the formula

$$A'_{x\overline{n}|} = \frac{M_x - M_{x+n}}{D_x}.$$

Example. Find the net single premium for a 10-year term insurance of $5,000 at age 25.

Solution.

$$A'_{25\,\overline{10|}} = \frac{M_{25} - M_{35}}{D_{25}}$$

$$= \frac{11631.1 - 9094.96}{37673.6}$$

$$= \frac{2536.14}{37673.6} = .067318.$$

$$\$5,000 \times .067318 = \$336.59.$$

Annual premium for term insurance. The payments of premium constitute an annuity due for a definite term, and the net annual premium may be determined from commutation columns, using the formula

$$P'_{x\,\overline{n|}} = \frac{M_x - M_{x+n}}{N_x - N_{x+n}}.$$

Example. Find the net annual premium for a 10-year term insurance of $3,000 at age 20.

Solution.

$$P'_{20\,\overline{10|}} = \frac{M_{20} - M_{30}}{N_{20} - N_{30}}$$

$$= \frac{13267.3 - 10259.0}{984400 - 596804}$$

$$= \frac{3008.3}{387596} = .007761.$$

$$\$3,000 \times .007761 = \$23.38.$$

Net single premium for endowment insurance. An endowment policy provides for payment of the face value of the policy at the end of the stated period if the insured be living, or to the named beneficiary or beneficiaries should death occur before the end of the stated period.

Endowment insurance may be considered as term insurance of 1 for n years plus an n-year pure endowment of 1, and the net single premium may be found from commutation columns by the use of the following formula:

$$A_{x\,\overline{n|}} = \frac{M_x - M_{x+n} + D_{x+n}}{D_x}.$$

Example. Find the net single premium on a ten-year endowment policy for $5,000 at age 30.

Solution.

$$A_{30\,\overline{10|}} = \frac{M_{30} - M_{40} + D_{40}}{D_{30}}$$

$$= \frac{10259.0 - 8088.91 + 19727.4}{30440.8}$$

$$= \frac{21897.49}{30440.8} = .719346.$$

$$\$5,000 \times .719346 = \$3,596.73.$$

Annual premium for endowment insurance. The net annual premium for r years for an n-year endowment insurance of 1 may be found from commutation columns, using the formula

$$P_{x\overline{n}|} = \frac{M_x - M_{x+n} + D_{x+n}}{N_x - N_{x+n}}.$$

Example. Find the net annual premium on a 15-year endowment policy for $10,000 purchased at age 40.

Solution.

$$P_{40\,\overline{15}|} = \frac{M_{40} - M_{55} + D_{55}}{N_{40} - N_{55}}$$

$$= \frac{8088.91 - 5510.54 + 9733.40}{344167 - 124876}$$

$$= \frac{12311.77}{219291} = .056143$$

$$\$10,000 \times .056143 = \$561.43.$$

MISCELLANEOUS PROBLEMS

1. Find the net single premium for a whole life insurance of $1,000 at age 30.

2. What is the increase in the net single premium for a whole life insurance of $2,000 from age 25 to 26?

3. What is the present value of a life annuity of $1,000 a year at age 25?

4. Find the net annual premium for an ordinary life policy of $1,000 at age 20.

5. Find the net annual premium for a 20-payment life policy for $10,000 at age 30.

6. What is the net annual premium for a 10-payment life policy for $2,000 at age 60?

7. What is the net single premium for 10-year term insurance of $5,000 at age 20?

8. What is the net annual premium on a 10-year endowment policy for $5,000 at age 45?

9. Find the net annual premium for a 20-payment endowment at age 65 for $5,000 if the insured is 45 at date of issue.

10. Find the difference in annual premiums between a 20-payment life policy and a 20-year endowment policy, each for $5,000, issued at age 30.

27

Valuation of Life Insurance Policies

Mortality and the level premium. If the cost of insurance on a group of men were to be met each year by payment into a fund of just the amount necessary to meet the year's death loss, the amount would be low at first and finally prohibitive; hence the necessity of a level premium. In order to have a level premium, an excess over current death losses is collected during the early years to bear the burden of later years when losses exceed the premium income.

This excess premium is known as the "reserve." When calculated on the basis prescribed by law, it is called the "legal reserve," and "legal reserve" companies are referred to as "old line" companies.

Policy reserves. To show the meaning of insurance reserves, a simple illustration is given.

Assume that an ordinary life policy for $1,000 is purchased at age 20. The net annual premium, calculated from Table 9, would be,

$$P_{20} = \frac{M_{20}}{N_{20}} = \frac{13267.3}{984400} = .013487.$$

$$\$1,000 \times .013847 = \$13.85.$$

Term insurance for one year at the same age would be:

1st year:

$$A_{20} = \frac{C_{20}}{D_{20}} = \frac{351.07}{46556.2} = .00754.$$

$$\$1,000 \times .00754 = \$7.54.$$

5th year:

$$A_{25} = \frac{C_{25}}{D_{25}} = \frac{293.55}{37673.6} = .00779$$

$1,000 \times .00779 = \$7.79.$

and so on.

Comparing these premiums over a period of years, we have:

Age	Ordinary Life	One Year Term
20	$13.85	$ 7.54
25	13.85	7.79
30	13.85	8.14
35	13.85	8.64
40	13.85	9.46
45	13.85	10.79
50	13.85	13.32
55	13.85	17.94
60	13.85	25.79
65	13.85	38.77

The excess of the premium on ordinary life over one-year term insurance is the amount placed in the reserve to be accumulated for heavier losses which will occur. It will be noticed that between 50 and 55 and from that point on the ordinary life premiums will be insufficient; therefore, the reserves will be drawn upon to meet the difference.

Interest and the premium. Reserves are invested in securities and earn interest which increases the reserves. The amount of interest earned, therefore, is reflected in lower premiums. If a company assumes a rate of interest lower than the maximum permitted under insurance law, the premium is higher and a larger reserve is accumulated during the early policy years.

Loading. Using the mortality table and an assumed rate of interest to be earned on the reserve, the actuary arrives at the net level premium. To this must be added the expense of doing business, or overhead, which amount is called "loading." The net premium plus the loading is the premium rate to the purchaser of insurance.

Expenses are heaviest in the first policy year; therefore, the plan is modified to permit more of the premium to be used for expenses, and this is balanced by lowering the amount required for the reserve. Methods of modification* are not presented in this text.

Dividends and net cost. Mortality may differ from that shown by the table; interest may be earned in excess of the rate anticipated; the loading may exceed the actual costs. Such savings result in dividends

---

* An extended discussion of these methods will be found in Robert Riegel and Jerome S. Miller, *Insurance Principles and Practice*. Englewood Cliffs, N.J.: Prentice-Hall, Inc., 4th ed., 1959, p. 148.

to policy holders in mutual companies and to holders of participating policies issued by stock companies. The net cost of the insurance is the premium paid less these dividend refunds.

Terminal reserves. When a policy is issued, the mathematical expectation of the future premiums equals the benefit.

As the insured grows older, the value of the future premiums becomes less and the value of the benefit, conversely, becomes greater.

The value of the benefit is represented by A_{x+n}, and the net annual premium constitutes a life annuity with a value represented by $P_x(1 + a_{x+n})$; therefore, $_nV_x$, the terminal reserve, is found by the formula

$$_nV_x = A_{x+n} - P_x(1 + a_{x+n}).$$

The foregoing method of valuation is called the *prospective* method.

Example. Find the terminal reserve of the 20th policy year on an ordinary life policy of $1,000 issued at age 30.

Solution.

$$_{20}V_{30} = A_{50} - P_{30}(1 + a_{50})$$

$$A_{50} = \frac{M_{50}}{D_{50}} = \frac{6355.44}{12498.6} = .508492$$

$$a_{50} = \frac{N_{51}}{D_{50}} = \frac{169165}{12498.6} = 13.5347$$

$$1 + 13.5347 = \$14.5347$$

$$P_{30} = \frac{M_{30}}{N_{30}} = \frac{10259.0}{596804} = .017189.$$

Substituting values gives:

$$_{20}V_{30} = .50849 - (.017190 \times 14.5347)$$

$$= .25864$$

$$\$1,000 \times .25864 = \$258.64.$$

The surrender value is the sum which the insurance company pays the policy holder upon the surrender and cancellation of the policy. Whether the amount will be greater or less than an amount as calculated in the foregoing example is dependent on averages obtained from the company's records instead of the theoretical amount so calculated. Policies contain a table showing the company's contractual surrender value for each $1,000 of insurance.

PROBLEMS

1. Find the terminal reserve of the tenth year on an ordinary life policy of $3,000 taken at age 20.

2. Find the terminal reserve of the twentieth year on an ordinary life policy of $5,000 taken at age 30.

Retrospective method. Under this method the policy value is found by deducting the accumulated losses from the accumulated premiums. The formula is:

$$_nV_x = \frac{M_x}{N_x} \cdot \frac{N_x - N_{x+n}}{D_{x+n}} - \frac{M_x - M_{x+n}}{D_{x+n}}.$$

PROBLEMS

1. Check the answer to the example, using the retrospective formula.

2. Find the surrender value in Problems 1 and 2 on page 409 by the retrospective method.

Transformation. In computing the terminal reserve, the formula used was

$$_nV_x = A_{x+n} - P_x(1 + a_{x+n}),$$

and the net single premium at age x, denoted by A_x, was computed by the formula:

$$A_x = P_x(1 + a_x).$$

Then, substituting for A_x, we have:

$$_nV_x = P_{x+n}(1 + a_{x+n}) - P_x(1 + a_{x+n})$$
$$= (P_{x+n} - P_x)(1 + a_{x+n}),$$

which represents the policy value or reserve, for the policy value is equal to the present value of the difference between the net premiums for age $x + n$ and age x for the remainder of life.

To express the value of the reserve in terms of annuities, take the formula:

$$A_x = 1 - d(1 + a_x),$$

which denotes the present value of 1 payable at the end of the year in which a person dies (d being the value, at the beginning of the year, of the interest for each year on 1), and

$$P_x = \frac{1}{1 + a_x} - d,$$

which denotes the annual premium P_x, for an ordinary life policy expressed in terms of annuity values. Then substitute the values of A_x and P_x in the formula:

$$_nV_x = A_{x+n} - P_x(1 + a_{x+n}).$$

Following the algebraic processes of simplifying, the result is

$$_nV_x = 1 - \frac{1 + a_{x+n}}{1 + a_x}.$$

PROBLEMS

1. With the aid of the table of life annuities, calculate the terminal reserve of the twentieth policy year on an ordinary life policy for $1,000 issued at age 30.

2. Find the terminal reserve the tenth year on an ordinary life policy of $5,000 issued at age 25.

Reserve valuation for limited payment life insurance. In determining the reserve valuation for such policies as 10-payment life, 20-payment life, and so forth, the following principle is fundamental: the terminal reserve of the nth policy year equals the net single premium at the attained age of the insured minus the present value of the future net premiums. Using m to denote the number of annual payments, we have

$$n_{:m}V_x = A_{x+n} - {}_mP_x(1 + a_{x+n\ \overline{m-n-1}}),$$

but only when n is less than m. Where n is equal to or greater than m, the terminal reserve is simply equal to the net single premium.

For endowment insurance, the formula is

$$_nVE_{x\overline{r}|} = AE_{x+n:\overline{r-n|}} - PE_{x\overline{r}|}(1 + a_{x+n:\overline{r-n-1|}})$$

for an r-year endowment.

PROBLEMS

1. Find the terminal reserve of the fifteenth policy year for a $2,000 20-year pay-life policy issued at age 30.

2. Find the terminal reserve of the fifteenth policy year for a $3,000 20-year endowment issued at age 45.

Preliminary term valuation. Initial expenses of securing a policy, such as agents' commissions, medical and inspection fees, and other expenses, make it practically impossible to provide any reserve out of the first year's premium. Under the net level premium method, the loading is the same each year; therefore, expenses exceed income, and the deficit must be met from general funds. To avoid this, the preliminary term valuation is used, whereby the first year's premium becomes available for expenses and losses, the policy is renewed at the beginning of the second year, and policy values begin with that year. Therefore, the first year is simply term insurance.

Under this plan, assume an ordinary life policy of $1,000 at age 20, the premium being $16.50.

The net premium for the first year would be:

$$A^{1}_{20\,\overline{1}|} = \frac{C_{20}}{D_{20}} = \frac{351.07}{46556.2} = .00754.$$

$1,000 \times .00754 = \$7.54$.

$16.50 - \$7.54 = \$8.96$, the loading for the first year.

For the second and subsequent years, the net premium will be the level net premium based upon age 21:

$$P_{21} = \frac{M_{21}}{N_{21}} = \frac{12916.3}{937843} = .01377.$$

$1,000 \times .01377 = \$13.77$.

$16.50 - 13.77 = \$2.73$, the loading for each year after the first.

PROBLEMS

1. Find the loading for the first and second years on an ordinary life policy of \$2,000 at age 30, with an annual premium of \$42.60, using the preliminary term evaluation.

2. Using the preliminary term evaluation, find the loading for the first and second years on an ordinary life policy of \$1,000 at age 40, the premium being \$28.80.

APPENDIXES

Practical Business Measurements

Table of Weights, Measures, and Values

Mathematical Tables

I

Practical Business Measurements

Practical business measurements. The measurements discussed in this section are those of practical use, and include measurements of or pertaining to the following: angles; surfaces; triangles, rectangles, and other polygons; circles, including circumference, radius, diameter, and area; area of irregular figures; and solids, such as the sphere, cone, cylinder, cube, and prismatoid.

Rectilinear figures. An *angle* is the difference in the direction of two lines proceeding from a common point called the vertex.

A *right angle* is an angle formed by two lines perpendicular to each other, and is an angle of 90°.

An angle that is less than a right angle is an *acute angle,* and one that is greater is an *obtuse angle.* Acute and obtuse angles are also called *oblique angles.*

A surface has two dimensions—length and breadth.

A *plane,* or a plane surface, is a level surface. A straight edge will fit on it in any position.

A *plane figure* is a figure all of whose points lie in the same plane.

A *quadrilateral* is a plane figure bounded by four straight lines.

Quadrilaterals are of three classes or kinds: the *trapezium,* which has four unequal sides, no two of which are parallel; the *trapezoid,* which has two and only two sides parallel; and the *parallelogram,* which has two pairs of parallel sides.

The *altitude of a quadrilateral* having two parallel sides is the perpendicular distance between those sides.

The *diagonal of a quadrilateral* is the straight line connecting two of its opposite vertices.

Parallelograms are of three classes or kinds: the *rhomboid,* which has one pair of parallel sides greater in length than the other pair, and no right angles; *the rhombus,* all of whose four sides are equal; and the *rectangle,* whose angles are all right angles.

A *square* is a rectangle having four equal sides.   It is also a rhombus whose four angles are 90°.

A *triangle* is a plane figure bounded by three straight lines.   If the three sides are of equal length, the triangle is called *equilateral*.   If two sides are of equal length, it is called *isosceles*.   If the three sides are of different lengths, it is called *scalene*.   If one of the three angles is a right angle, the triangle is called a *right triangle*, and the side opposite the right angle is called the hypotenuse.

Plane figures may be regular or irregular.   A *regular plane figure* has all its sides and all its angles equal.   The smallest regular plane figure is an equilateral triangle; the next, a square; the next, a pentagon; and so on.   Each figure derives its name from the number of its angles or sides—hexagon, heptagon, octagon, nonagon, decagon, etc.

The *perimeter of a plane figure* is the sum of the lengths of its sides.

The *apothem of a polygon* is a perpendicular line drawn from the center of the figure to the middle of a side, the center being the point within the figure which is equally distant from the middle points of all the sides.

The *altitude of a plane figure* is the perpendicular distance from the highest point above the base to the base or to the base extended.

Circles.   A *circle* is a plane figure bounded by a curved line, called the circumference, every point of which is equally distant from a point within called the center.

The *diameter* of a circle is a straight line drawn through the center and terminated by the circumference.

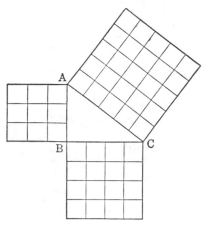

Fig. 1.

The *radius* of a circle is a straight line drawn from the center to the circumference, and is equal to one-half the diameter.

An *arc* of a circle is any portion of the circumference.

A *sector* of a circle is bounded by two radii and the intercepted arc.

A *chord* is the straight line joining the extremities of an arc.

A *segment* is bounded by an arc and its chord.

A *zone* is a portion of a circle bounded by two parallel chords.

A *tangent to a circle* is a straight line having only one point in common with the curve; it simply touches the circle.   A *secant* enters the figure from without.

An *ellipse* is a plane figure bounded by an oval curved line, and has a long and a short diameter or axis.

Measurement of triangles.   It is proved in geometry that the square erected on the hypotenuse of a right triangle is equal to the sum of the squares erected on the other two sides.   This may be illustrated as in Figure 1.

To find the length of the hypotenuse of a right triangle, the lengths of the other two sides being given, add the squares of the sides forming the right angle, extract the square root of the sum, and the result will be the length of the hypotenuse.

To find the length of either of the two sides other than the hypotenuse, from the square of the hypotenuse subtract the square of the given side, extract the square root of the remainder, and the result will be the length of the third side.

To find the area of a triangle, the base and the altitude being given, multiply the base by one-half the altitude.

To find the area of a triangle when the lengths of the three sides are given, from half the sum of the three sides, subtract the length of each side separately.   Find the continued product of the three remainders and the half sum.   The square root of the result will be the area.

Measurement of rectangles.   The area of a square or of a rectangle is the product of the length and the breadth.

Either dimension of a rectangle may be found by dividing the area by the given dimension.

Measurement of quadritalerals.   The area of a trapezium may be found by multiplying one-half the sum of the altitudes by the diagonal.

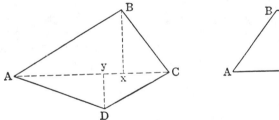

Fig. 2. Trapezium.

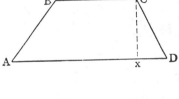

Fig. 3. Trapezoid.

The area of a trapezoid may be found by multiplying the sum of the parallel sides by one-half the altitude.

The area of a parallelogram may be found by multiplying the base by the altitude.

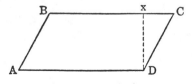

Fig. 4. Parallelogram.

The area of polygons having equal sides and equal angles may be found by multiplying the square by one of the equal sides by:

.433, if the figure is a triangle.
1.7205, if the figure is a pentagon.
2.5981, if the figure is a hexagon.
4.8284, if the figure is an octagon.

Measurement of circles. It is shown in geometry that the circumference of a circle bears a fixed ratio to its diameter. This constant ratio is represented by π (pronounced "pi"), and is 3.1416.

From this relation the following principles are derived:

The circumference = the diameter $\times$ 3.1416.
The diameter = the circumference $\div$ 3.1416.
The area = the circumference $\times$ half the radius.

The area of a circle is found by considering the surface to be composed of an infinite number of isosceles triangles, the bases of which, taken together, equal the perimeter of the circle. The common altitude of these triangles constantly approaches the radius of the circle, and will reach that length when the perimeter consists of very short straight lines; hence, perimeter (circumference) $\times \frac{1}{2}$ radius = area.

To find the circumference of a circle, multiply the diameter by 3.1416, or divide the area by one-fourth of the diameter.

To find the diameter of a circle, divide the circumference by 3.1416, or divide the area by .7854 and extract the square root of the result.

To find the area of a circle, multiply the circumference by one-half the radius; or, multiply the diameter by one-fourth of the circumference; or, multiply the square of the diameter by .7854; or, multiply the square of the radius by 3.1416.

To find the area of an ellipse, multiply the major axis by the minor axis, and that result by .7854.

To find the area of a sector of a circle, multiply one-half the length of the arc by the radius; or, take the same part of the area of the circle as the number of degrees in the arc is of 360°.

To find the area of a segment which is less than a semi-circle, from the area of a corresponding sector, subtract the area of the triangle formed by the chord and radii; to find the area of a segment which is greater than a semi-circle, add the area of the triangle formed by the chord and radii to the area of a corresponding sector.

To find the area of a zone, from the area of the circle subtract the areas of the segments not included in the zone.

PROBLEMS

1. Harry and George start from the same point, Harry going 4 miles due west, and George 3 miles due north; how far apart are they?

2. The base of a triangle is 12 inches, and the altitude is 8 inches. What is the area of the triangle?

3. The three sides of a triangular plot of land are 100 feet, 130 feet, and 150 feet. What is the area of the plot?

4. A rectangular piece of land is 40 rods long and 20 rods wide. What is the area in square rods?

5. Find the cost of fencing a field 40 rods wide and 55 rods long, if the fencing costs $2.25 a rod.

6. A field is in the form of a trapezium, having a diagonal of 90 rods, and altitudes of 25 rods and 40 rods. What is the area in square rods?

7. One of the parallel sides of a garden is 60 yards long, and the other is 80 yards long. The garden is 52 yards wide. How many square yards does it contain?

8. Find the area of a parallelogram whose base is 10 feet and whose altitude is 4 feet.

9. The side of a hexagonal building is 20 feet. What is the floor area?

10. A cylindrical tank is 12 feet in diameter. What must be the length of a piece of strap iron which is to be used to make a band around the tank, if 1 foot is allowed for overlapping?

11. The circumference of a circle is 44 feet. What is its diameter?

12. Find the area of the circle in Problem 11.

13. The diameters of an ellipse are 60 feet and 40 feet. What is the area?

14. How much belting will be required to make a belt to run over two pulleys, each 30 inches in diameter, if the distance between the centers of the pulleys is 18 feet?

15. If there is a steam pressure of 90 pounds to the square inch, what is the pressure on a 9-inch piston?

16. If pieces of sod are 12 inches by 14 inches, how many pieces will be required to sod a lawn 24 feet wide and 28 feet long?

17. Find the cost of painting the four side walls of a room 14 feet long, 10 feet 6 inches wide, and 8 feet high, at 18 cents a square yard, no allowance being made for openings.

18. A circular walk 5 feet wide is laid around a plot 20 feet in diameter. What is the cost of the walk at $2.50 a square foot?

19. Find the number of paving blocks required to pave a street one mile long and 35 feet wide, if the blocks are one foot long and five inches wide.

20. What part of an acre is a plot of land 78 feet long and 36 feet wide?

Solids. A *solid* is a magnitude which has length, breadth, and thickness. Solids include the prism, the cylinder, the pyramid, the cone, the polyhedron, and the sphere.

A *prism* is a solid whose upper and lower bases are equal and parallel polygons, and whose sides, or lateral faces, are parallelograms.

A *rectangular solid* is bounded by six rectangular surfaces.

A *cube* is a rectangular solid having six square faces.

A *triangular prism* is a prism whose bases are triangles.

A *cylinder* is a prism having an infinite number of faces or sides; the two bases are equal parallel circles.

A *pyramid* is a solid having for its base a polygon, and for its other faces three or more triangles which terminate in a common point called the vertex or apex.

A *cone* is a pyramid having an infinite number of faces; or, it is a solid whose base is a circle, and whose convex surface tapers uniformly to a point called the apex.

A *polyhedron* is a solid bounded by four or more faces.

A *sphere* is a solid bounded by a curved surface, every point of which is equally distant from a point within, called the center.

The *frustum of a pyramid* or of a cone is the solid which remains when a portion which includes the apex is cut off by a plane parallel to the base.

The *axis of a pyramid* or of a cone is a straight line that joins the apex to the center of the base.

The *altitude of a pyramid* or of a cone is the perpendicular height from its apex to its base.

The *slant height of a pyramid* is the distance from the apex to the midpoint of one side of its base.

The *slant height of a cone* is the distance from its apex to the circumference of its base.

The *diameter of a sphere* is a straight line drawn through its center and terminated at both ends by the surface.

The *radius of a sphere* is one-half of its diameter.

The *circumference of a sphere* is the greatest distance around the sphere.

A *hemisphere* is one-half of a sphere.

Measurement of solids. To find the contents of a prism or of a cylinder when the perimeter of the base and the altitude are given, multiply the area of the base by the altitude.

To find the convex surface of a prism or of a cylinder, multiply the perimeter of the base by the height.

To find the entire surface of a prism or of a cylinder, add the area of the bases to the area of the convex surface.

To find the convex surface of a cone, multiply the circumference of the base by one-half the slant height.

To find the entire surface of a cone, add the area of the base to the area of the convex surface.

The slant height of a pyramid or of a cone may be found by adding the square of the altitude to the square of the radius of the base, and extracting the square root of the sum.

To find the volume of a pyramid or of a cone, multiply the area of the base by one-third the altitude.

The volume of a pyramid is one-third as much as the volume of a prism that has the same base and altitude.

The volume of a cone is one-third as much as the volume of a cylinder that has the same base and altitude.

To find the convex surface of a frustum of a pyramid or of a cone, multiply one-half the sum of the perimeters of the two bases by the slant height.

To find the entire surface of a frustum of a pyramid or of a cone, add the area of the two bases to the area of the convex surface.

To find the volume of a frustum of a pyramid or of a cone, find the product of the areas of the two bases, and extract the square root thereof. This result is the area of a base which is a mean base between the other two. Add the three areas, and multiply by one-third the altitude.

To find the surface of a sphere, find the area of a great circle of the sphere, and multiply this area by 4.

To find the volume of a sphere, multiply the convex surface by one-third the radius.

The volume of a spherical shell (a hollow sphere) is equal to the volume of the outside sphere minus the volume of the inside sphere.

PROBLEMS

1. A cylindrical tank is 12 feet in diameter. If it is filled with water to a depth of 6 feet, what is the weight of the water? (1 cu. ft. of water weighs 62.5 pounds.)

2. How many square yards of sheet metal will be required for a smokestack 2 feet in diameter and 12 feet in height if 1 inch is allowed for overlapping?

3. Find the cost of painting the entire surface of a cylindrical tank 10 feet in diameter and 20 feet long, at 10¢ per square foot.

4. The boundary lines of the Fort Pembina Airport are marked by cone-shaped markers; each marker is 3 feet in diameter and has a slant height of 3 feet. If there are 120 of these markers, and 1 inch was allowed for overlapping, how many square feet of sheet metal were required for their construction?

5. If a freight car is 36 feet long and 8 feet 6 inches wide, inside measure, how many bushels of wheat will it contain when filled to a depth of 5 feet? (A cubic foot is approximately .8 of a bushel.)

6. How many tons of coal will fill a bin 20 feet, by 16 feet, by 8 feet, if there are 80 cubic feet to a ton?

7. The measurements of a railroad embankment are: length, 400 feet; height, 10 feet; width of base, 14 feet; and width of top, 8 feet. How many cubic yards of earth will be required?

8. The measurements of a funnel are as follows: larger diameter, 12 inches; smaller diameter, 1 inch; and slant height, 18 inches. How many square inches of sheet metal will be required?

9. One of the units of a grain elevator is a concrete cylinder 20 feet in diameter and 50 feet in height. The bottom is cone-shaped to facilitate the drawing off of the grain. The depth of this cone is 5 feet. If the wheat in this unit is leveled off at the 30-foot mark, how many bushels are in the unit, assuming that a cubic foot is approximately .8 of a bushel?

10. A bucket is 16 inches wide at the top, and 10 inches wide at the bottom. The depth is 12 inches. How many gallons of water will the bucket hold? (231 cu. in. = 1 gal.)

11. What number of square feet of sheet metal will be required to make 100 pails, each 10 inches deep, 8 inches in diameter at the bottom, and 11 inches in diameter at the top? The allowance for seams and for waste in cutting is 10%.

12. How many tiles 1 inch square will be required for the surface of a tiled dome in the form of a hemispherical surface, if the diameter of the dome is 24 feet?

13. The top of a vat is 9 feet square, and the base is 8 feet square. If the slant height is 10 feet, what is the capacity of the vat in cubic feet?

14. How many cubic feet are there in a spherical body whose diameter is 10 feet?

15. The base of a church steeple is in the form of an octagon measuring 6 feet on each side. The slant height of the steeple is 80 feet. What will be the cost of painting this steeple at 50¢ per square yard?

16. A tank is 8 feet long, 6 feet wide, and 3 feet deep. If a cubic foot of water weighs 62.5 pounds, what is the weight of water in this tank if it is two-thirds full?

17. If 38 cubic feet of coal weigh a ton, how many tons can be put into a bin 10 feet long and 8 feet wide, if the coal is leveled off at an average depth of 5 feet?

18. Find the number of square feet of sheet metal required to make 12 gross of pails, each 14 inches deep, 8 inches in diameter at the bottom, and 11 inches in diameter at the top, not allowing for seams or waste in cutting.

19. The diagram is that of a cross section of a concrete retaining wall 150 feet long. Find the number of cubic yards of material necessary to construct such a wall.

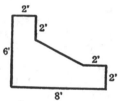

20. If 200 gallons of water flow through a pipe 2 inches in diameter in 4 hours, how much water will flow through a pipe 4 inches in diameter in the same time? HINT: The amounts of the liquids are to each other as the squares of the like dimensions.

21. A cylindrical hot water tank is 5 feet high and 11 inches in diameter. How many gallons will it contain?

22. A corn crib 32 feet by 10 feet by 8 feet is filled with ear corn. How many bushels will it contain if one bushel equals $1\frac{1}{2}$ cubic feet?

23. A barn loft is 36 feet by 24 feet by 8 feet. How many tons of hay will it hold if it is to be filled with: (a) clover hay weighing one ton for 600 cubic feet; (b) timothy hay weighing one ton for 500 cubic feet?

24. If a heaped bushel equals $1\frac{1}{4}$ cubic feet, how many bushels of potatoes may be stored in a bin that is 12 feet by 8 feet by 6 feet?

25. If a cubic foot of steel weighs 484 pounds, what is the weight of a hollow steel cylinder whose length is 10 feet and the radii of whose outer and inner circles are 3 feet and $2\frac{1}{2}$ feet, respectively?

II

Tables of Weights, Measures, and Values

Long Measure

U. S. and British Standard		*Metric System*	
12 inches............	1 foot	10 millimeters..........	1 centimeter
3 feet..............	1 yard	10 centimeters..........	1 decimeter
5½ yards, or 16½ feet..	1 rod	10 decimeters...........	1 meter
320 rods, or 5,280 feet..	1 mile	10 meters...............	1 dekameter
1,760 yards.............	1 mile	10 dekameters..........	1 hektometer
40 rods..............	1 furlong	10 hektometers.........	1 kilometer
8 furlongs..........	1 statute mile	10 kilometers...........	1 myriameter
3 miles..............	1 league		

Comparisons of Long Measures

1 inch..............	25.4001 millimeters	1 centimeter...........	.3937 inch
1 foot..............	.304801 meter	1 meter................	39.37 inches
1 yard..............	.914402 meter	1 meter................	3.28083 feet
1 rod..............	5.029 meters	1 meter................	1.093611 yards
1 mile.............	1.60935 kilometers	1 kilometer.............	.62137 mile

Square Measure

U. S. and British Standard

144 square inches...................	1 square foot
9 square feet...................	1 square yard
30¼ square yards...................	1 square rod
272¼ square feet...................	1 square rod
40 square rods...................	1 rood
4 roods...................	1 acre
160 square rods...................	1 acre
640 acres...................	1 square mile
43,560 square feet...................	1 acre
4,840 square yards...................	1 acre

Metric System

100 square millimeters......................	1 square centimeter
100 square centimeters......................	1 square decimeter
100 square decimeters.......................	1 square meter
100 square meters..........	1 square dekameter
100 square dekameters......................	1 square hektometer
100 square hektometers.....................	1 square kilometer
100 square kilometers.......................	1 square myriameter

Comparisons of Square Measures

1 sq. in	6.452 sq. cm.	1 sq. mm..............	.00155 sq. in.
1 sq. ft.................	.0929 sq. m.	1 sq. cm..............	.155 sq. in.
1 sq. yd.................	.8361 sq. m.	1 sq. m................	10.764 sq. ft.
1 sq. rd.................	25.293 sq. m.	1 sq. m................	1.196 sq. yds.
1 sq. mi.	2.59 sq. km.	1 sq. km..............	.3861 sq. mi.
		1 sq. km..............	247.11 acres
		1 sq. Dm., or 1 are......	1,076.41 sq. ft.
		100 ares = 1 hektare....	2.4711 acres

Solid or Cubic Measure (Volume)

U. S. and British Standard		*Metric System*	
1,728 cubic inches..	1 cubic foot	1,000 cubic millimeters......	1 cu. cm.
27 cubic feet. ...	1 cubic yard	1,000 cubic centimeters......	1 cu. dm.
128 cubic feet. ...	1 cord of wood	1,000 cubic decimeters......	1 cu. m.
$24\frac{3}{4}$ cubic feet ...	1 perch of stone	1,000 cubic meters..........	1 cu. Dm.
2,150.42 cubic inches..	1 standard bushel	1,000 cubic dekameters......	1 cu. Hm.
231 cubic inches ..	1 standard gallon	1,000 cubic hektometers.....	1 cu. Km.
40 cubic feet....	1 ton (shipping)	1,000 cubic kilometers.......	1 cu. Mm.

Comparisons of Solid or Cubic Measures (Volume)

1 cu. in......	16.3872 cu cm.	1 cu. cm.................	.061 cu. in.
1 cu. ft.......	.02832 cu. m.	1 cu. m..................	35.314 cu. ft.
1 cu. yd......	.7646 cu. m.	1 cu. m..................	1.3079 cu. yds.
		1 cu. dm. = 1 liter.........	61.023 cu. in.
		1 liter....................	1.05671 liquid quarts
		1 liter....................	.9081 dry quart
		1 hectoliter or decistere.....	3.5314 cu. ft. or 2.8375 U. S. Bushels
		1 stere, kiloliter, or cu. m...	1.3079 cu. yds. or 28.37 U. S. Bushels

Liquid Measure (Capacity)

U. S. and British Standard		*Metric System*	
4 gills.................	1 pint	10 milliliters.....	1 centiliter
2 pints................	1 quart	10 centiliters....	1 deciliter
4 quarts...............	1 gallon	10 deciliters.....	1 liter
$31\frac{1}{2}$ gallons...............	1 barrel	10 liters	1 dekaliter
2 barrels..............	1 hogshead	10 dekaliters....	1 hektoliter
1 U. S. Gallon..........	231 cubic inches	10 hektoliters....	1 kiloliter
1 British Imperial Gallon	277.274 cubic inches	10 kiloliters.....	1 myrialiter
7.4805 U. S. Gallons.........	1 cubic foot		
16 fluid ounces..........	1 pint		
1 fluid ounce..........	1.805 cubic inches		

U. S. and British Standard

1 fluid ounce...........	29.59 cubic centimeters
1.2 U. S. Quarts..........	1 Imperial Quart
1.2 U. S. Gallons.........	1 Imperial Gallon
1 gallon gasoline........	6 pounds (approx.)
1 gallon oil.............	$7\frac{1}{2}$ pounds (approx.)
1 gallon water..........	8.3 pounds (approx.)
1 liter gasoline..........	1.59 pounds (approx.)
1 liter gasoline..........	0.72 kilograms

Dry Measure

U. S. and British Standard		*Metric System*
2 pints.................	1 quart	
8 quarts...............	1 peck	
4 pecks................	1 bushel	[In the Metric System,
2,150.42 cubic inches..........	1 U. S. Standard Bushel	the same table is used
1.2445 cubic feet............	1 U. S. Standard Bushel	for both Liquid Meas-
2,218.192 cubic inches..........	1 British Imperial Bushel	ure and Dry Measure.]
1.2837 cubic feet............	1 British Imperial Bushel	

Comparisons of Liquid and Dry Measures

1 liquid quart..................	.94636 liter
1 liquid gallon.................	3.78543 liters
1 dry quart...................	1.1012 liters
1 peck.......................	8.80982 liters
1 bushel......................	.35239 hektoliters
1 milliliter....................	.03381 liquid ounce, or .2705 apothecaries' dram
1 liter = 1 cubic decimeter......	$\begin{cases} 61.023 \text{ cubic inches} \\ .03531 \text{ cubic foot} \\ .2642 \text{ U. S. Gallon} \\ 2.202 \text{ pounds of water at } 62° \text{ F.} \end{cases}$
28.317 liters...................	1 cu. ft.
4.543 liters...................	1 British Imperial Gal.
3.785 liters...................	1 U. S. Gal.

Avoirdupois Measure (Weight)

(Used for weighing all ordinary substances except precious metals, jewels, and drugs)

U. S. and British Standard		*Metric System*	
$27\frac{11}{32}$ grains...............	1 dram	10 milligrams........	1 centigram
16 drams...............	1 ounce	10 centigrams........	1 decigram
16 ounces.............	1 pound	10 decigrams........	1 gram
25 pounds.............	1 quarter	10 grams............	1 dekagram
4 quarters.............	1 hundredweight	10 dekagrams.......	1 hektogram
100 pounds.............	1 hundredweight	10 hektograms.......	1 kilogram
20 hundredweight.......	1 ton	10 kilograms.........	1 myriagram
2,000 pounds.............	1 short ton		
2,240 pounds.............	1 long ton		

Troy Measure (Weight)

(Used for weighing gold, silver, and jewels)

24 grains	1 pennyweight
20 pennyweights	1 ounce
12 ounces	1 pound

Apothecaries' Measure (Weight)

(Used for weighing drugs)

20 grains	1 scruple
3 scruples	1 dram
8 drams	1 ounce
12 ounces	1 pound

Comparison of Avoirdupois and Troy Measures

1 pound troy	5,760 grains	1 ounce troy	480 grains
1 pound avoirdupois	7,000 grains	1 ounce avoirdupois	$437\frac{1}{2}$ grains
	1 karat, or carat	3.2 troy grains	
	24 karats	pure gold	

Comparison of Avoirdupois and Troy Measures with Metric Weights

1 grain	.0648 gram	
1 ounce (avoir.)	28.3495 grams	1 gram .... $\begin{cases} 15.4324 \text{ grains} \\ .03527 \text{ ounce (avoir.)} \\ .03215 \text{ ounce (troy)} \end{cases}$
1 ounce (troy)	31.10348 grams	
1 pound (avoir.)	.45359 kilogram	
1 pound (troy)	.37324 kilogram	1 kilogram ..... $\begin{cases} 2.20462 \text{ pounds (avoir.)} \\ 2.67923 \text{ pounds (troy)} \end{cases}$
		1 tonne, or metric ton ... $\begin{cases} .9842 \text{ ton of 2,240 pounds,} \\ \text{or 19.68 hundredweight} \\ 1.1023 \text{ tons of 2,000 pounds} \end{cases}$
	1,000 kilograms	2,204.6 pounds
	1.016 metric tons, or 1,016 kilograms ..	1 ton of 2,240 pounds

Apothecaries' Fluid Measure (Capacity)

60 minims	1 fluid dram
8 fluid drams	1 fluid ounce
16 fluid ounces	1 pint
8 pints	1 gallon

Comparisons (Approximate Liquid Measure)

Apothecaries'	Common	Metric
1 minim	1 to 2 drops	0.06 cu. cm.
60 minims, or 1 fluid dram	1 teaspoonful	3.75 cu. cm.
2 fluid drams	1 dessertspoonful	7.50 cu. cm.
4 fluid drams	1 tablespoonful	15.00 cu. cm.
8 fluid drams	1 fluid ounce	28.39 cu. cm.
2 fluid ounces	1 wineglassful	59.20 cu. cm.
4 fluid ounces	1 teacupful	118.40 cu. cm.
16 fluid ounces	1 pint	473.11 cu. cm.

NOTE: Drops are not accurate measures, but for practical purposes it may be considered that one minim equals one drop of watery liquids and fixed oils, but two drops of volatile oils and alcoholic liquids, such as tinctures and fluid extracts.

MISCELLANEOUS TABLES
Surveyors' Long Measure

7.92 inches	1 link
25 links	1 rod
4 rods, or 100 links	1 chain
80 chains	1 mile

Surveyors' Square Measure

625 square links	1 square rod
16 square rods	1 square chain
10 square chains	1 acre
640 acres	1 square mile
36 square miles	1 township

Mariners' Measure

6 feet	1 fathom
120 fathoms	1 cable's length
7½ cable lengths	1 mile
5,280 feet	1 statute mile
6,080 feet	1 nautical mile, or British Admiralty knot
50.71$\frac{11}{15}$ feet	1 knot
120 knots, or 1.152$\frac{2}{3}$ statute miles	1 nautical or geographical mile
3 geographical miles	1 league
60 geographical miles, or 69.16 statute miles	1 degree of longitude on the equator, or 1 degree of meridian
360 degrees	1 circumference

NOTE: A knot is properly $\frac{1}{120}$ of a marine mile, but current usage makes it equivalent to a marine mile. Hence, when the speed of vessels at sea is being measured, a knot is equal to a nautical mile, or 6,086.08 feet, or 2,028.69 yards.

Circular or Angular Measure

60 seconds (60″)	1 minute (1′)
60 minutes (60′)	1 degree (1°)
30 degrees	1 sign
90 degrees	1 right angle or quadrant
360 degrees	1 circumference

NOTE: One degree at the equator is approximately 60 nautical miles.

Counting

12 units or things	1 dozen
12 dozen, or 144 units	1 gross
12 gross	1 great gross
20 units	1 score

Paper Measure

```
24 sheets.............................................. 1 quire
20 quires............................................. 1 ream
 2 reams.............................................. 1 bundle
 5 bundles............................................ 1 bale
```
NOSE: Although a ream contains 480 sheets, 500 sheets are usually sold as a ream.

Books

Books are printed on large sheets of paper, which are folded into leaves according to the size of the book.   The terms *folio, quarto, octavo*, and so forth, as applied to printed books, are based on sheets about 18 by 24 inches, or about half the size now generally used, and indicate the number of leaves into which each sheet is folded.

A sheet folded in	2 leaves is called	a folio	and makes	4 pages
" "	" " " 4 " " "	a quarto, or 4to	" "	8 "
" "	" " " 8 " " "	an octavo, or 8vo	" "	16 "
" "	" " " 12 " " "	a 12 mo	" "	24 "
" "	" " " 16 " " "	a 16 mo	" "	32 "
" "	" " " 24 " " "	a 24 mo	" "	48 "
" "	" " " 32 " " "	a 32 mo	" "	64 "

Sizes of Paper

Book Papers		*Bond, Ledger, and Writing Papers*	
25 × 38	38 × 50	14 × 17	20 × 28
30½ × 41	41 × 61	16 × 21	23 × 31
32 × 44	64 × 44	18 × 23	21 × 32
33 × 44	66 × 44	17 × 28	16 × 42
35 × 45	45 × 70	19 × 24	23 × 36
		17 × 22	22 × 34

MEASURES OF VALUE
United States Money

```
10 mills............................................... 1 cent
10 cents............................................... 1 dime
10 dimes............................................... 1 dollar
10 dollars............................................. 1 eagle
```

English Money

```
 4 farthings.......................................... 1 penny (d.)
12 pence.............................................. 1 shilling (s.)
20 shillings.......................................... 1 pound (£)
```
A pound sterling = $4.8665 (normal).

French Money

```
10 millimes (m.).................................... 1 centime (c.)
10 centimes......................................... 1 decime (d.)
10 decimes.......................................... 1 franc (fr.)
```
A franc = $0.193 (normal).

Comparison of Thermometer Scales

To convert from ° F to ° C, subtract 32 from ° F and divide by 1.8.
To convert from ° C to ° F, multiply ° C by 1.8 and add 32.

Temperature Equivalents

Degrees C	Degrees F	Remarks
−100	−148	
− 50	− 58	
− 40	− 40	
− 20	− 4	
− 17.77	0	
− 15	5	
− 10	14	
− 5	23	
0	32	. . . . Water freezes
5	41	
10	50	
15	59	
20	68	
25	77	
30	86	
35	95	
40	104	
45	113	
50	122	
55	131	
60	140	
65	149	
70	158	
75	167	
80	176	
85	185	
90	194	
95	203	
100	212	. . . . Water boils at sea level.
150	302	(With each 1,000 feet
190	374	altitude, boiling point of
200	392	water is reduced ap-
300	572	proximately 1° C.)

Approximate Weight of Substances

	Lbs. Per Cu. Ft.		Lbs. Per Cu. Ft.
Brick, pressed, best.	150	Lead.	709.6
Brick, common, hard.	125	Limestone, marble, ordinarily.	168
Brick, common, soft.	100	Limestone, marble, piled.	96
Coal, broken (anthra.), loose. .	52–56	Masonry, granite, dressed.	165
Coal, broken (bitu.), loose. . . .	47–52	Masonry, sandstone.	145
Cement, concrete, limestone. . .	148	Sand, pure quartz dry loose. . .	112–113
Cement, concrete, cinder.	112	lbs. per struck bu.	90–106
Cement, concrete, stone.	150	Sand, angular, large and small.	117
Cement, concrete, trap rock. . .	155	Sandstone, dry for building. . .	151
Granite.	170	Sandstone, quarried, piled. . . .	86
Hemlock, dry.	25	Shales, red or black.	162
Hickory, dry.	53	Shales, quarried, piled.	92
Ice.	57–60	Slate.	175
Iron, cast.	450	Soapstone or steatite.	170
Iron, wrought.	485	Steel, heaviest, lowest in carbon	490

WEIGHTS AND MEASURES
Solid Fuels

	Lbs. Per Cu. Yd.	Tons Per Cu. Yd.	Cu. Ft. Per Ton
Coal, anthracite egg	1514	.76	36
Coal, anthracite nut	1536	.77	36
Coal, anthracite stove	1521	.76	36
Coal, bituminous, Ill.	1275	.64	42
Coal, bit., Ind. block	1161	.58	43
Coal, bit., Iowa lump	1256	.63	42
Coal, bit., Pittsburgh	1255	.63	42
Coal, bit., Pocahontas egg and lump	1411	.71	38
Coal, cannel	1328	.66	49
Coke, loose	870–1026	.51	60–65
Charcoal, hardwood	513	.25	19
Charcoal, pine	486	.24	19
Peat, dry	1269	.63	42

Anthracite and Pocahontas, approximately 36 cu. ft. for 1 ton. Other bituminous coal, approximately 40½ cu. ft. for 1 ton. Coke, approximately 60–65 cu. ft. for 1 ton.

Bulk Materials

	Lbs. Per Cu. Yd.	Tons Per Cu. Yd.
Ashes	1080	.52
Asphalt	2700	1.35
Brick, soft clay	2718	1.35
Brick, hard clay	3397	1.69
Brick, pressed	3806	1.90
Bluestone	2970	1.48
Cement, Portland	2430	1.21
Cinders	1080	.54
Clay, dry	1701	.85
Clay, wet	2970	1.48
Earth, dry, loose	1890	.94
Earth, dry, shaken	2214	1.10
Earth and sand, dry, loose	2700	1.35
Earth and sand, dry, rammed	3240	1.62
Fire brick	3915	1.95
Fire clay	3510	1.75
Gravel, dry	2970	1.48
Granite	4536	2.26
Lime, quick, shaken	1485	.70
Limestone, loose	2592	1.29
Marble, loose	2592	1.29
Mud, river	2430	1.21
Pitch	1863	.93
Rip-rap, limestone	2160	1.08
Rip-rap, sandstone	2430	1.21
Rip-rap, slate	2835	1.41
Sand, dry, loose	2619	1.30
Sand, wet	3186	1.59
Slag, screenings	2700	1.35
Street sweepings	850	.42
Tar	1674	.83
Trap Stone	5049	2.52

III

Tables

TABLE I.—American Experience Table of Mortality

(Based on 100,000 living at age of 10)

Age x	Number living l_x	Number dying d_x	Yearly probability of dying q_x	Yearly probability of living p_x
10	100 000	749	0.007 490	0.992 510
11	99 251	746	0.007 516	0.992 484
12	98 505	743	0.007 543	0.992 457
13	97 762	740	0.007 569	0.992 431
14	97 022	737	0.007 596	0.992 404
15	96 285	735	0.007 634	0.992 366
16	95 550	732	0.007 661	0.992 339
17	94 818	729	0.007 688	0.992 312
18	94 009	727	0.007 727	0.992 273
19	93 362	725	0.007 765	0.992 235
20	92 637	723	0.007 805	0.992 195
21	91 914	722	0.007 855	0.992 145
22	91 192	721	0.007 906	0.992 094
23	90 471	720	0.007 958	0.992 042
24	89 751	719	0.008 011	0.991 989
25	89 032	718	0.008 065	0.991 935
26	88 314	718	0.008 130	0.991 870
27	87 596	718	0.008 197	0.991 803
28	86 878	718	0.008 264	0.991 736
29	86 160	719	0.008 345	0.991 655
30	85 441	720	0.008 427	0.991 573
31	84 721	721	0.008 510	0.991 490
32	84 000	723	0.008 607	0.991 393
33	83 277	726	0.008 718	0.991 282
34	82 551	729	0.008 831	0.991 169
35	81 822	732	0.008 946	0.991 054
36	81 090	737	0.009 089	0.990 911
37	80 353	742	0.009 234	0.990 766
38	79 611	749	0.009 408	0.990 592
39	78 862	756	0.009 586	0.990 414
40	78 106	765	0.009 794	0.990 206
41	77 341	774	0.010 008	0.989 992
42	76 567	785	0 010 252	0.989 748
43	75 782	797	0.010 517	0.989 483
44	74 985	812	0.010 829	0.989 171
45	74 173	828	0.011 163	0.988 837
46	73 345	848	0.011 562	0.988 438
47	72 497	870	0.012 000	0.988 000
48	71 627	896	0.012 509	0.987 491
49	70 731	927	0.013 106	0.986 894
50	69 804	962	0.013 781	0.986 219
51	68 842	1 011	0.014 541	0.985 459
52	67 841	1 044	0.015 389	0.984 611
53	66 797	1 091	0.016 333	0.983 667
54	65 706	1 143	0.017 396	0.982 604

TABLE I.—American Experience Table of Mortality

Age x	Number living l_x	Number dying d_x	Yearly probability of dying q_x	Yearly probability of living p_x
55	64 563	1 199	0.018 571	0.981 429
56	63 364	1 260	0.019 885	0.980 115
57	62 104	1 325	0.021 335	0.978 665
58	60 779	1 394	0.022 936	0.977 064
59	59 385	1 468	0.024 720	0.975 280
60	57 917	1 546	0.026 693	0.973 307
61	56 371	1 628	0.028 880	0.971 120
62	54 743	1 713	0.031 292	0.968 708
63	53 030	1 800	0.033 943	0.966 057
64	51 230	1 889	0.036 873	0.963 127
65	49 341	1 980	0.040 129	0.959 871
66	47 361	2 070	0.043 707	0.956 293
67	45 291	2 158	0.047 647	0.952 353
68	43 133	2 243	0.052 002	0.947 998
69	40 890	2 321	0.056 762	0.943 238
70	38 569	2 391	0.061 993	0.938 007
71	36 178	2 448	0.067 665	0.932 335
72	33 730	2 487	0.073 733	0.926 267
73	31 243	2 505	0.080 178	0.919 822
74	28 738	2 501	0.087 028	0.912 972
75	26 237	2 476	0.094 371	0.905 629
76	23 761	2 431	0.102 311	0.897 689
77	21 330	2 369	0.111 064	0.888 936
78	18 961	2 291	0.120 827	0.879 173
79	16 670	2 196	0.131 734	0.868 266
80	14 474	2 091	0.144 466	0.855 534
81	12 383	1 964	0.158 605	0.841 395
82	10 419	1 816	0.174 297	0.825 703
83	8 603	1 648	0.191 561	0.808 439
84	6 955	1 470	0.211 359	0.788 641
85	5 485	1 292	0.235 552	0.764 448
86	4 193	1 114	0.265 681	0.734 319
87	3 079	933	0.303 020	0.696 980
88	2 146	744	0.346 692	0.653 308
89	1 402	555	0.395 863	0.604 137
90	847	385	0.454 545	0.545 455
91	462	246	0.532 466	0.467 534
92	216	137	0.634 259	0.365 741
93	79	58	0.734 177	0.265 823
94	21	18	0.857 143	0.142 857
95	3	3	1.000 000	0.000 000

TABLE II.—Commutation Columns, $3\frac{1}{2}\%$

Age x	D_x	N_x	C_x	M_x	$1 + a_x$	A_x
10	70891.9	1575 535	513.02	17612.9	22.2245	0.24845
11	67981.5	1504 643	493.69	17099.9	22.1331	0.25154
12	65189.0	1436 662	475.08	16606.2	22.0384	0.25474
13	62509.4	1371 473	457.16	16131.1	21.9403	0.25806
14	59938.4	1308 963	439.91	15674.0	21.8385	0.26151
15	57471.6	1249 025	423.88	15234.1	21.7329	0.26508
16	55104.2	1191 553	407.87	14810.2	21.6236	0.26877
17	52832.9	1136 449	392.47	14402.3	21.5102	0.27261
18	50653.9	1083 616	378.15	14009.8	21.3926	0.27659
19	48562.8	1032 962	364.30	13631.7	21.2707	0.28071
20	46556.2	984 400	351.07	13267.3	21.1443	0.28497
21	44630.8	937 843	338.73	12916.3	21.0134	0.28940
22	42782.8	893 213	326.82	12577.5	20.8779	0.29399
23	41009.2	850 430	315.33	12250.7	20.7375	0.29873
24	39307.1	809 421	304.24	11935.4	20.5922	0.30365
25	37673.6	770 113	293.55	11631.1	20.4417	0.30873
26	36106.1	732 440	283.62	11337.6	20.2858	0.31401
27	34601.5	696 334	274.03	11054.0	20.1244	0.31947
28	33157.4	661 732	264.76	10779.9	19.9573	0.32512
29	31771.3	628 575	256.16	10515.2	19.7843	0.33097
30	30440.8	596 804	247.85	10259.0	19.6054	0.33702
31	29163.5	566 363	239.797	10011.2	19.4202	0.34328
32	27937.5	537 199	232.331	9771.38	19.2286	0.34976
33	26760.5	509 262	225.406	9539.04	19.0304	0.35646
34	25630.1	482 501	218.683	9313.64	18.8256	0.36339
35	24544.7	456 871	212.157	9094.96	18.6138	0.37055
36	23502.5	432 326	206.383	8882.80	18.3949	0.37795
37	22501.4	408 824	200.757	8676.42	18.1688	0.38560
38	21539.7	386 323	195.798	8475.66	17.9354	0.39349
39	20615.5	364 783	190.945	8279.86	17.6946	0.40163
40	19727.4	344 167	186.684	8088.92	17.4461	0.41003
41	18873.6	324 440	182.493	7902.23	17.1901	0.41869
42	18052.9	305 566	178.828	7719.74	16.9262	0.42762
43	17263.6	287 513	175.421	7540.91	16.6543	0.43681
44	16504.4	270 250	172.680	7365.49	16.3744	0.44628
45	15773.6	253 745	170.127	7192.81	16.0867	0.45600
46	15070.0	237 972	168.345	7022.68	15.7911	0.46600
47	14392.1	222 902	166.872	6854.34	15.4878	0.47626
48	13738.5	208 510	166.047	6687.47	15.1770	0.48677
49	13107.9	194 771	165.983	6521.42	14.8591	0.49752
50	12498.6	181 663	166.424	6355.44	14.5346	0.50849
51	11909.6	169 165	167.316	6189.01	14.2041	0 51967
52	11339.5	157 255	168.601	6021.70	13.8679	0 53104
53	10787.4	145 916	170.234	5853.10	13.5264	0 54258
54	10252.4	135 128	172.317	5682.86	13.1801	0.55430

TABLE II.—Commutation Columns, $3\frac{1}{2}\%$

Age	D_x	N_x	C_x	M_x	$1 + a_x$	A_x
55	9733.40	124876	174.646	5510.54	12.8296	0.56615
56	9229.60	115142	177.325	5335.90	12.4753	0.57813
57	8740.17	105912.8	180.167	5158.57	12.1179	0.59022
58	8264.44	97172.6	183.140	4978.40	11.7579	0.60239
59	7801.83	88908.2	186.340	4795.27	11.3958	0.61463
60	7351.65	81106.4	189.604	4608.93	11.0324	0.62692
61	6913.44	73754.7	192.909	4419.32	10.6683	0.63924
62	6486.75	66841.3	196.117	4226.41	10.3043	0.65155
63	6071.27	60354.5	199.109	4030.30	9.9410	0.66383
64	5666.85	54283.3	201.887	3831.19	9.5791	0.67607
65	5273.33	48616.4	204.457	3629.30	9.2193	0.68824
66	4890.55	43343.1	206.522	3424.84	8.8626	0.70030
67	4518.65	38452.5	208.022	3218.32	8.5097	0.71223
68	4157.82	33933.9	208.903	3010.30	8.1615	0.72401
69	3808.32	29776.1	208.858	2801.40	7.8187	0.73560
70	3470.67	25967.7	207.881	2592.54	7.4820	0.74698
71	3145.43	22497.1	205.639	2384.66	7.1523	0.75813
72	2833.42	19351.6	201.851	2179.02	6.8298	0.76904
73	2535.75	16518.2	196.436	1977.17	6.5141	0.77972
74	2253.57	13982.5	189.491	1780.73	6.2046	0.79018
75	1987.87	11728.9	181.253	1591.24	5.9002	0.80048
76	1739.39	9741.03	171.940	1409.99	5.6002	0.81062
77	1508.63	8001.63	161.889	1238.05	5.3039	0.82064
78	1295.73	6493.00	151.2646	1076.158	5.0111	0.83054
79	1100.647	5197.27	140.0891	924.894	4.7220	0.84032
80	923.338	4096.62	128.8801	784.805	4.4368	0.84997
81	763.234	3173.29	116.9588	655.924	4.1577	0.85940
82	620.465	2410.05	104.4881	538.966	3.8843	0.86865
83	494.995	1789.59	91.6152	434.478	3.6154	0.87774
84	386.641	1294.59	78.9565	342.862	3.3483	0.88677
85	294.610	907.95	67.0490	263.906	3.0819	0.89578
86	217.598	613.34	55.8566	196.857	2.8187	0.90468
87	154.383	395.74	45.1992	141.000	2.5634	0.91332
88	103.963	241.36	34.82425	95.8011	2.3216	0.92149
89	65.6231	137.398	25.09929	60.9768	2.0937	0.92920
90	38.3047	71.775	16.82244	35.8775	1.8738	0.93664
91	20.18692	33.4700	10.385393	19.05509	1.6580	0.94393
92	9.11888	13.2831	5.588150	8.66970	1.4567	0.95074
93	3.22236	4.16420	2.285784	3.08155	1.2923	0.95630
94	0.827611	0.94184	0.685393	0.79576	1.1380	0.96152
95	0.114232	0.114232	0.110369	0.110369	1.0000	0.96618

TABLE III.—Amount of 1 at Compound Interest

$$s = (1 + i)^n$$

n	$\frac{1}{4}\%$	$\frac{7}{24}\%$	$\frac{1}{3}\%$	$\frac{5}{12}\%$	n
1	1.0025 0000	1.0029 1667	1.0033 3333	1.0041 6667	1
2	1.0050 0625	1.0058 4184	1.0066 7778	1.0083 5069	2
3	1.0075 1877	1.0087 7555	1.0100 3337	1.0125 5216	3
4	1.0100 3756	1.0117 1781	1.0134 0015	1.0167 7112	4
5	1.0125 6266	1.0146 6865	1.0167 7815	1.0210 0767	5
6	1.0150 9406	1.0176 2810	1.0201 6741	1.0252 6187	6
7	1.0176 3180	1.0205 9618	1.0235 6797	1.0295 3379	7
8	1.0201 7588	1.0235 7292	1.0269 7986	1.0338 2352	8
9	1.0227 2632	1.0265 5834	1.0304 0313	1.0381 3111	9
10	1.0252 8313	1.0295 5247	1.0338 3780	1.0424 5666	10
11	1.0278 4634	1.0325 5533	1.0372 8393	1.0468 0023	11
12	1.0304 1596	1.0355 6695	1.0407 4154	1.0511 6190	12
13	1.0329 9200	1.0385 8736	1.0442 1068	1.0555 4174	13
14	1.0355 7448	1.0416 1657	1.0476 9138	1.0599 3983	14
15	1.0381 6341	1.0446 5462	1.0511 8369	1.0643 5625	15
16	1.0407 5882	1.0477 0153	1.0546 8763	1.0687 9106	16
17	1.0433 6072	1.0507 5732	1.0582 0326	1.0732 4436	17
18	1.0459 6912	1.0538 2203	1.0617 3060	1.0777 1621	18
19	1.0485 8404	1.0568 9568	1.0652 6971	1.0822 0670	19
20	1.0512 0550	1.0599 7829	1.0688 2060	1.0867 1589	20
21	1.0538 3352	1.0630 6990	1.0723 8334	1.0912 4387	21
22	1.0564 6810	1.0661 7052	1.0759 5795	1.0957 9072	22
23	1.0591 0927	1.0692 8018	1.0795 4448	1.1003 5652	23
24	1 0617 5704	1.0723 9891	1.0831 4296	1.1049 4134	24
25	1.0644 1144	1.0755 2674	1.0867 5344	1.1095 4526	25
26	1.0670 7247	1.0786 6370	1.0903 7595	1.1141 6836	26
27	1.0697 4015	1.0818 0980	1.0940 1053	1.1188 1073	27
28	1.0724 1450	1.0849 6508	1.0976 5724	1.1234 7244	28
29	1.0750 9553	1.0881 2956	1.1013 1609	1.1281 5358	29
30	1.0777 8327	1.0913 0327	1.1049 8715	1.1328 5422	30
31	1.0804 7773	1.0944 8624	1.1086 7044	1.1375 7444	31
32	1.0831 7892	1.0976 7849	1.1123 6601	1.1423 1434	32
33	1.0858 8687	1.1008 8005	1.1160 7389	1.1470 7398	33
34	1.0886 0159	1.1040 9095	1.1197 9414	1.1518 5346	34
35	1.0913 2309	1.1073 1122	1.1235 2679	1.1566 5284	35
36	1.0940 5140	1.1105 4088	1.1272 7187	1.1614 7223	36
37	1.0967 8653	1.1137 7995	1.1310 2945	1.1663 1170	37
38	1.0995 2850	1.1170 2848	1.1347 9955	1.1711 7133	38
39	1.1022 7732	1.1202 8648	1.1385 8221	1.1760 5121	39
40	1.1050 3301	1.1235 5398	1.1423 7748	1.1809 5142	40
41	1.1077 9559	1.1268 3101	1.1461 8541	1.1858 7206	41
42	1.1105 6508	1.1301 1760	1.1500 0603	1.1908 1319	42
43	1.1133 4149	1.1334 1378	1.1538 3938	1.1957 7491	43
44	1.1161 2485	1.1367 1957	1.1576 8551	1.2007 5731	44
45	1.1189 1516	1.1400 3500	1.1615 4446	1.2057 6046	45
46	1.1217 1245	1.1433 6010	1.1654 1628	1.2107 8446	46
47	1.1245 1673	1.1466 9490	1.1693 0100	1.2158 2940	47
48	1.1273 2802	1.1500 3943	1.1731 9867	1.2208 9536	48
49	1.1301 4634	1.1533 9371	1.1771 0933	1.2259 8242	49
50	1.1329 7171	1.1567 5778	1.1810 3303	1.2310 9068	50

TABLE III.—Amount of 1 at Compound Interest

$$s = (1 + i)^n$$

n	$\frac{1}{4}\%$	$\frac{7}{24}\%$	$\frac{1}{3}\%$	$\frac{5}{12}\%$	n
51	1.1358 0414	1.1601 3165	1.1849 6981	1.2362 2002	51
52	1.1386 4365	1.1635 1537	1.1889 1971	1.2413 7114	52
53	1.1414 9026	1.1669 0896	1.1928 8277	1.2465 4352	53
54	1.1443 4398	1.1703 1244	1.1968 5905	1.2517 3745	54
55	1.1472 0484	1.1737 2585	1.2008 4858	1.2569 5302	55
56	1.1500 7285	1.1771 4922	1.2048 5141	1.2621 9033	56
57	1.1529 4804	1.1805 8257	1.2088 6758	1.2674 4946	57
58	1.1558 3041	1.1840 2594	1.2128 9714	1.2727 3050	58
59	1.1587 1998	1.1874 7935	1.2169 4013	1.2780 3354	59
60	1.1616 1678	1.1909 4283	1.2209 9659	1.2833 5868	60
61	1.1645 2082	1.1944 1641	1.2250 6658	1.2887 0601	61
62	1.1674 3213	1.1979 0013	1.2291 5014	1.2940 7561	62
63	1.1703 5071	1.2013 9400	1.2332 4730	1.2994 6760	63
64	1.1732 7658	1.2048 9807	1.2373 5813	1.3048 8204	64
65	1.1762 0977	1.2084 1235	1.2414 8266	1.3103 1905	65
66	1.1791 5030	1.2119 3689	1.2456 2093	1.3157 7872	66
67	1.1820 9817	1.2154 7171	1.2497 7300	1.3212 6113	67
68	1.1850 5342	1.2190 1683	1.2539 3891	1.3267 6638	68
69	1.1880 1605	1.2225 7230	1.2581 1871	1.3322 9458	69
70	1.1909 8609	1.2261 3813	1.2623 1244	1.3378 4580	70
71	1.1939 6356	1.2297 1437	1.2665 2015	1.3434 2016	71
72	1.1969 4847	1.2333 0104	1.2707 4188	1.3490 1774	72
73	1.1999 4084	1.2368 9816	1.2749 7769	1.3546 3865	73
74	1.2029 4069	1.2405 0578	1.2792 2761	1.3602 8298	74
75	1.2059 4804	1.2441 2393	1.2834 9170	1.3659 5082	75
76	1.2089 6291	1.2477 5262	1.2877 7001	1.3716 4229	76
77	1.2119 8532	1.2513 9190	1.2920 6258	1.3773 5746	77
78	1.2150 1528	1.2550 4179	1.2963 6945	1.3830 9645	78
79	1.2180 5282	1.2587 0233	1.3006 9068	1.3888 5935	79
80	1.2210 9795	1.2623 7355	1.3050 2632	1.3946 4627	80
81	1.2241 5070	1.2660 5547	1.3093 7641	1.4004 5729	81
82	1.2272 1108	1.2697 4813	1.3137 4099	1.4062 9253	82
83	1.2302 7910	1.2734 5156	1.3181 2013	1.4121 5209	83
84	1.2333 5480	1.2771 6580	1.3225 1386	1.4180 3605	84
85	1.2364 3819	1.2808 9086	1.3269 2224	1.4239 4454	85
86	1.2395 2928	1.2846 2680	1.3313 4532	1.4298 7764	86
87	1.2426 2811	1.2883 7362	1.3357 8314	1.4358 3546	87
88	1.2457 3468	1.2921 3138	1.3402 3575	1.4418 1811	88
89	1.2488 4901	1.2959 0010	1.3447 0320	1.4478 2568	89
90	1.2519 7114	1.2996 7980	1.3491 8554	1.4538 5829	90
91	1.2551 0106	1.3034 7054	1.3536 8283	1.4599 1603	91
92	1.2582 3882	1.3072 7233	1.3581 9510	1.4659 9902	92
93	1.2613 8441	1.3110 8520	1.3627 2242	1.4721 0735	93
94	1.2645 3787	1.3149 0920	1.3672 6483	1.4782 4113	94
95	1.2676 9922	1.3187 4435	1.3718 2238	1.4844 0047	95
96	1.2708 6847	1.3225 9069	1.3763 9512	1.4905 8547	96
97	1.2740 4564	1.3264 4825	1.3809 8310	1.4967 9624	97
98	1.2772 3075	1.3303 1706	1.3855 8638	1.5030 3289	98
99	1.2804 2383	1.3341 9715	1.3902 0500	1.5092 9553	99
100	1.2836 2489	1.3380 8856	1.3948 3902	1.5155 8426	100

TABLE III.—Amount of 1 at Compound Interest

$$s = (1 + i)^n$$

n	$\frac{1}{4}\%$	$\frac{7}{24}\%$	$\frac{1}{3}\%$	$\frac{5}{12}\%$	n
101	1.2868 3395	1.3419 9131	1.3994 8848	1.5218 9919	101
102	1.2900 5104	1.3459 0546	1.4041 5344	1.5282 4044	102
103	1.2932 7616	1.3498 3101	1.4088 3395	1.5346 0811	103
104	1.2965 0935	1.3537 6802	1.4135 3007	1.5410 0231	104
105	1.2997 5063	1.3577 1651	1.4182 4183	1.5474 2315	105
106	1.3030 0000	1.3616 7652	1.4229 6931	1.5538 7075	106
107	1.3062 5750	1.3656 4807	1.4277 1254	1.5603 4521	107
108	1.3095 2315	1.3696 3121	1.4324 7158	1.5668 4665	108
109	1.3127 9696	1.3736 2597	1.4372 4649	1.5733 7518	109
110	1.3160 7895	1.3776 3238	1.4420 3731	1.5799 3091	110
111	1.3193 6915	1.3816 5047	1.4468 4410	1.5865 1395	111
112	1.3226 6757	1.3856 8029	1.4516 6691	1.5931 2443	112
113	1.3259 7424	1.3897 2186	1.4565 0580	1.5997 6245	113
114	1.3292 8917	1.3937 7521	1.4613 6082	1.6064 2812	114
115	1.3326 1240	1.3978 4039	1.4662 3202	1.6131 2157	115
116	1.3359 4393	1.4019 1742	1.4711 1946	1.6198 4291	116
117	1.3392 8379	1.4060 0635	1.4760 2320	1.6265 9226	117
118	1.3426 3200	1.4101 0720	1.4809 4327	1.6333 6973	118
119	1.3459 8858	1.4142 2001	1.4858 7979	1.6401 7543	119
120	1.3493 5355	1.4183 4482	1.4908 3268	1.6470 0950	120
121	1.3527 2693	1.4224 8166	1.4958 0212	1.6538 7204	121
122	1.3561 0875	1.4266 3057	1.5007 8813	1.6607 6317	122
123	1.3594 9902	1.4307 9157	1.5057 9076	1.6676 8302	123
124	1.3628 9777	1.4349 6471	1.5108 1006	1.6746 3170	124
125	1.3663 0501	1.4391 5003	1.5158 4609	1.6816 0933	125
126	1.3697 2077	1.4433 4755	1.5208 9892	1.6886 1603	126
127	1.3731 4508	1.4475 5731	1.5259 6858	1.6956 5193	127
128	1.3765 7794	1.4517 7935	1.5310 5514	1.7027 1715	128
129	1.3800 1938	1.4560 1371	1.5361 5866	1.7098 1181	129
130	1.3834 6943	1.4602 6042	1.5412 7919	1.7169 3602	130
131	1.3869 2811	1.4645 1951	1.5464 1678	1.7240 8992	131
132	1.3903 9543	1.4687 9103	1.5515 7151	1.7312 7363	132
133	1.3938 7142	1.4730 7500	1.5567 4341	1.7384 8727	133
134	1.3973 5609	1.4773 7147	1.5619 3256	1.7457 3097	134
135	1.4008 4948	1.4816 8047	1.5671 3900	1.7530 0485	135
136	1.4043 5161	1.4860 0204	1.5723 6279	1.7603 0903	136
137	1.4078 6249	1.4903 3621	1.5776 0400	1.7676 4365	137
138	1.4113 8214	1.4946 8302	1.5828 6268	1.7750 0884	138
139	1.4149 1060	1.4990 4252	1.5881 3889	1.7824 0471	139
140	1.4184 4787	1.5034 1472	1.5934 3269	1.7898 3139	140
141	1.4219 9399	1.5077 9968	1.5987 4413	1.7972 8902	141
142	1.4255 4898	1.5121 9743	1.6040 7328	1.8047 7773	142
143	1.4291 1285	1.5166 0801	1.6094 2019	1.8122 9763	143
144	1.4326 8563	1.5210 3145	1.6147 8492	1.8198 4887	144
145	1.4362 6735	1.5254 6779	1.6201 6754	1.8274 3158	145
146	1.4398 5802	1.5299 1707	1.6255 6810	1.8350 4588	146
147	1.4434 5766	1.5343 7933	1.6309 8666	1.8426 9190	147
148	1.4470 6631	1.5388 5460	1.6364 2328	1.8503 6978	148
149	1.4506 8397	1.5433 4293	1.6418 7802	1.8580 7966	149
150	1.4543 1068	1.5478 4434	1.6473 5095	1.8658 2166	150

TABLE III.—Amount of 1 at Compound Interest

$$s = (1 + i)^n$$

n	¼%	⁷⁄₂₄%	⅓%	⁵⁄₁₂%	n
151	1.4579 4646	1.5523 5889	1.6528 4212	1.8735 9591	151
152	1.4615 9132	1.5568 8660	1.6583 5160	1.8814 0256	152
153	1.4652 4530	1.5614 2752	1.6638 7943	1.8892 4174	153
154	1.4689 0842	1.5659 8169	1.6694 2570	1.8971 1358	154
155	1.4725 8069	1.5705 4913	1.6749 9045	1.9050 1822	155
156	1.4762 6214	1.5751 2990	1.6805 7375	1.9129 5580	156
157	1.4799 5279	1.5797 2403	1.6861 7566	1.9209 2645	157
158	1.4836 5268	1.5843 3156	1.6917 9625	1.9289 3031	158
159	1.4873 6181	1.5889 5253	1.6974 3557	1.9369 6752	159
160	1.4910 8021	1.5935 8697	1.7030 9369	1.9450 3821	160
161	1.4948 0791	1.5982 3493	1.7087 7067	1.9531 4254	161
162	1.4985 4493	1.6028 9645	1.7144 6657	1.9612 8063	162
163	1.5022 9129	1.6075 7157	1.7201 8146	1.9694 5264	163
164	1.5060 4702	1.6122 6032	1.7259 1540	1.9776 5869	164
165	1.5098 1214	1.6169 6274	1.7316 6845	1.9858 9893	165
166	1.5135 8667	1.6216 7888	1.7374 4068	1.9941 7351	166
167	1.5173 7064	1.6264 0878	1.7432 3215	2.0024 8257	167
168	1.5211 6406	1.6311 5247	1.7490 4292	2.0108 2625	168
169	1.5249 6697	1.6359 1000	1.7548 7306	2.0192 0469	169
170	1.5287 7939	1.6406 8140	1.7607 2264	2.0276 1804	170
171	1.5326 0134	1.6454 6672	1.7665 9172	2.0360 6645	171
172	1.5364 3284	1.6502 6600	1.7724 8035	2.0445 5006	172
173	1.5402 7393	1.6550 7928	1.7783 8862	2.0530 6902	173
174	1.5441 2461	1.6599 0659	1.7843 1658	2.0616 2347	174
175	1.5479 8492	1.6647 4799	1.7902 6431	2.0702 1357	175
176	1.5518 5488	1.6696 0350	1.7962 3185	2.0788 3946	176
177	1.5557 3452	1.6744 7318	1.8022 1929	2.0875 0129	177
178	1.5596 2386	1.6793 5706	1.8082 2669	2.0961 9921	178
179	1.5635 2292	1.6842 5518	1.8142 5411	2.1049 3338	179
180	1.5674 3172	1.6891 6760	1.8203 0163	2.1137 0393	180
181	1.5713 5030	1.6940 9433	1.8263 6930	2.1225 1103	181
182	1.5752 7868	1.6990 3544	1.8324 5720	2.1313 5483	182
183	1.5792 1688	1.7039 9096	1.8385 6539	2.1402 3547	183
184	1.5831 6492	1.7089 6094	1.8446 9394	2.1491 5312	184
185	1.5871 2283	1.7139 4541	1.8508 4292	2.1581 0793	185
186	1.5910 9064	1.7189 4441	1.8570 1240	2.1671 0004	186
187	1.5950 6836	1.7239 5800	1.8632 0244	2.1761 2963	187
188	1.5990 5604	1.7289 8621	1.8694 1311	2.1851 9683	188
189	1.6030 5368	1.7340 2909	1.8756 4449	2.1943 0182	189
190	1.6070 6131	1.7390 8667	1.8818 9664	2.2034 4474	190
191	1.6110 7896	1.7441 5901	1.8881 6963	2.2126 2576	191
192	1.6151 0666	1.7492 4614	1.8944 6352	2.2218 4504	192
193	1.6191 4443	1.7543 4811	1.9007 7840	2.2311 0272	193
194	1.6231 9229	1.7594 6496	1.9071 1433	2.2403 9899	194
195	1.6272 5027	1.7645 9673	1.9134 7138	2.2497 3398	195
196	1.6313 1839	1.7697 4347	1.9198 4962	2.2591 0787	196
197	1.6353 9669	1.7749 0522	1.9262 4912	2.2685 2082	197
198	1.6394 8518	1.7800 8203	1.9326 6995	2.2779 7299	198
199	1.6435 8390	1.7852 7393	1.9391 1218	2.2874 6455	199
200	1.6476 9285	1.7904 8098	1.9455 7589	2.2969 9565	200

TABLE III.—Amount of 1 at Compound Interest

$$s = (1 + i)^n$$

n	½%	⁷⁄₁₂%	⅝%	⅔%	n
1	1.0050 0000	1.0058 3333	1.0062 5000	1.0066 6667	1
2	1.0100 2500	1.0117 0069	1.0125 3906	1.0133 7778	2
3	1.0150 7513	1.0176 0228	1.0188 6743	1.0201 3363	3
4	1.0201 5050	1.0235 3830	1.0252 3535	1.0269 3452	4
5	1.0252 5125	1.0295 0894	1.0316 4307	1.0337 8075	5
6	1.0303 7751	1.0355 1440	1.0380 9084	1.0406 7262	6
7	1.0355 2940	1.0415 5490	1.0445 7891	1.0476 1044	7
8	1.0407 0704	1.0476 3064	1.0511 0753	1.0545 9451	8
9	1.0459 1058	1.0537 4182	1.0576 7695	1.0616 2514	9
10	1.0511 4013	1.0598 8865	1.0642 8743	1.0687 0264	10
11	1.0563 9583	1.0660 7133	1.0709 3923	1.0758 2732	11
12	1.0616 7781	1.0722 9008	1.0776 3260	1.0829 8951	12
13	1.0669 8620	1.0785 4511	1.0843 6780	1.0902 1950	13
14	1.0723 2113	1.0848 3662	1.0911 4510	1.0974 8763	14
15	1.0776 8274	1.0911 6483	1.0979 6476	1.1048 0422	15
16	1.0830 7115	1.0975 2996	1.1048 2704	1.1121 6958	16
17	1.0884 8651	1.1039 3222	1.1117 3221	1.1195 8404	17
18	1.0939 2894	1.1103 7182	1.1186 8053	1.1270 4794	18
19	1.0993 9858	1.1168 4899	1.1256 7229	1.1345 6159	19
20	1.1048 9558	1.1233 6395	1.1327 0774	1.1421 2533	20
21	1.1104 2006	1.1299 1690	1.1397 8716	1.1497 3950	21
22	1.1159 7216	1.1365 0808	1.1469 1083	1.1574 0443	22
23	1.1215 5202	1.1431 3771	1.1540 7902	1.1651 2046	23
24	1.1271 5978	1.1498 0602	1.1612 9202	1.1728 8793	24
25	1.1327 9558	1.1565 1322	1.1685 5009	1.1807 0718	25
26	1.1384 5955	1.1632 5955	1.1758 5353	1.1885 7857	26
27	1.1441 5185	1.1700 4523	1.1832 0262	1.1965 0242	27
28	1.1498 7261	1.1768 7049	1.1905 9763	1.2044 7911	28
29	1.1556 2197	1.1837 3557	1.1980 3887	1.2125 0897	29
30	1.1614 0008	1.1906 4069	1.2055 2661	1.2205 9236	30
31	1.1672 0708	1.1975 8610	1.2130 6115	1.2287 2964	31
32	1.1730 4312	1.2045 7202	1.2206 4278	1.2369 2117	32
33	1.1789 0833	1.2115 9869	1.2282 7180	1.2451 6731	33
34	1.1848 0288	1.2186 6634	1.2359 4850	1.2534 6843	34
35	1.1907 2689	1.2257 7523	1.2436 7318	1.2618 2489	35
36	1.1966 8052	1.2329 2559	1.2514 4614	1.2702 3705	36
37	1.2026 6393	1.2401 1765	1.2592 6767	1.2787 0530	37
38	1.2086 7725	1.2473 5167	1.2671 3810	1.2872 3000	38
39	1.2147 2063	1.2546 2789	1.2750 5771	1.2958 1153	39
40	1.2207 9424	1.2619 4655	1.2830 2682	1.3044 5028	40
41	1.2268 9821	1.2693 0791	1.2910 4574	1.3131 4661	41
42	1.2330 3270	1.2767 1220	1.2991 1477	1.3219 0092	42
43	1.2391 9786	1.2841 5969	1.3072 3424	1.3307 1360	43
44	1.2453 9385	1.2916 5062	1.3154 0446	1.3395 8502	44
45	1.2516 2082	1.2991 8525	1.3236 2573	1.3485 1559	45
46	1.2578 7892	1.3067 6383	1.3318 9839	1.3575 0569	46
47	1.2641 6832	1.3143 8662	1.3402 2276	1.3665 5573	47
48	1.2704 8916	1.3220 5388	1.3485 9915	1.3756 6610	48
49	1.2768 4161	1.3297 6586	1.3570 2790	1.3848 3721	49
50	1.2832 2581	1.3375 2283	1.3655 0932	1.3940 6946	50

TABLE III.—Amount of 1 at Compound Interest

$$s = (1 + i)^n$$

n	$\frac{1}{2}\%$	$\frac{7}{12}\%$	$\frac{5}{8}\%$	$\frac{2}{3}\%$	n
51	1.2896 4194	1.3453 2504	1.3740 4375	1.4033 6325	51
52	1.2960 9015	1.3531 7277	1.3826 3153	1.4127 1901	52
53	1.3025 7060	1.3610 6628	1.3912 7297	1.4221 3713	53
54	1.3090 8346	1.3690 0583	1.3999 6843	1.4316 1805	54
55	1.3156 2887	1.3769 9170	1.4087 1823	1.4411 6217	55
56	1.3222 0702	1.3850 2415	1.4175 2272	1.4507 6992	56
57	1.3288 1805	1.3931 0346	1.4263 8224	1.4604 4172	57
58	1.3354 6214	1.4012 2990	1.4352 9713	1.4701 7799	58
59	1.3421 3946	1.4094 0374	1.4442 6773	1.4799 7918	59
60	1.3488 5015	1.4176 2526	1.4532 9441	1.4898 4571	60
61	1.3555 9440	1.4258 9474	1.4623 7750	1.4997 7801	61
62	1.3623 7238	1.4342 1246	1.4715 1736	1.5097 7653	62
63	1.3691 8424	1.4425 7870	1.4807 1434	1.5198 4171	63
64	1.3760 3016	1.4509 9374	1.4899 6881	1.5299 7399	64
65	1.3829 1031	1.4594 5787	1.4992 8111	1.5401 7381	65
66	1.3898 2486	1.4679 7138	1.5086 5162	1.5504 4164	66
67	1.3967 7399	1.4765 3454	1.5180 8069	1.5607 7792	67
68	1.4037 5785	1.4851 4766	1.5275 6869	1.5711 8310	68
69	1.4107 7664	1.4938 1102	1.5371 1600	1.5816 5766	69
70	1.4178 3053	1.5025 2492	1.5467 2297	1.5922 0204	70
71	1.4249 1968	1.5112 8965	1.5563 8999	1.6028 1672	71
72	1.4320 4428	1.5201 0550	1.5661 1743	1.6135 0217	72
73	1.4392 0450	1.5289 7279	1.5759 0566	1.6242 5885	73
74	1.4464 0052	1.5378 9179	1.5857 5507	1.6350 8724	74
75	1.4536 3252	1.5468 6283	1.5956 6604	1.6459 8782	75
76	1.4609 0069	1.5558 8620	1.6056 3896	1.6569 6107	76
77	1.4682 0519	1.5649 6220	1.6156 7420	1.6680 0748	77
78	1.4755 4622	1.5740 9115	1.6257 7216	1.6791 2753	78
79	1.4829 2395	1.5832 7334	1.6359 3324	1.6903 2172	79
80	1.4903 3857	1.5925 0910	1.6461 5782	1.7015 9053	80
81	1.4977 9026	1.6017 9874	1.6564 4631	1.7129 3446	81
82	1.5052 7921	1.6111 4257	1.6667 9910	1.7243 5403	82
83	1.5128 0561	1.6205 4090	1.6772 1659	1.7358 4972	83
84	1.5203 6964	1.6299 9405	1.6876 9920	1.7474 2205	84
85	1.5279 7148	1.6395 0235	1.6982 4732	1.7590 7153	85
86	1.5356 1134	1.6490 6612	1.7088 6136	1.7707 9868	86
87	1.5432 8940	1.6586 8567	1.7195 4175	1.7826 0400	87
88	1.5510 0585	1.6683 6134	1.7302 8888	1.7944 8803	88
89	1.5587 6087	1.6780 9344	1.7411 0319	1.8064 5128	89
90	1.5665 5468	1.6878 8232	1.7519 8508	1.8184 9429	90
91	1.5743 8745	1.6977 2830	1.7629 3499	1.8306 1758	91
92	1.5822 5939	1.7076 3172	1.7739 5333	1.8428 2170	92
93	1.5901 7069	1.7175 9290	1.7850 4054	1.8551 0718	93
94	1.5981 2154	1.7276 1219	1.7961 9704	1.8674 7456	94
95	1.6061 1215	1.7376 8993	1.8074 2328	1.8799 2439	95
96	1.6141 4271	1.7478 2646	1.8187 1967	1.8924 5722	96
97	1.6222 1342	1.7580 2211	1.8300 8667	1.9050 7360	97
98	1.6303 2449	1.7682 7724	1.8415 2471	1.9177 7409	98
99	1.6384 7611	1.7785 9219	1.8530 3424	1.9305 5925	99
100	1.6466 6849	1.7889 6731	1.8646 1570	1.9434 2965	100

TABLE III.—Amount of 1 at Compound Interest

$$s = (1 + i)^n$$

n	½%	⁷⁄₁₂%	⅝%	⅔%	u
101	1.6549 0183	1.7994 0295	1.8762 6955	1.9563 8585	101
102	1.6631 7634	1.8098 9947	1.8879 9624	1.9694 2842	102
103	1.6714 9223	1.8204 5722	1.8997 9621	1.9825 5794	103
104	1.6798 4969	1.8310 7655	1.9116 6994	1.9957 7499	104
105	1.6882 4894	1.8417 5783	1.9236 1788	2.0090 8016	105
106	1.6966 9018	1.8525 0142	1.9356 4049	2.0224 7403	106
107	1.7051 7363	1.8633 0768	1.9477 3824	2.0359 5719	107
108	1.7136 9950	1.8741 7697	1.9599 1161	2.0495 3024	108
109	1.7222 6800	1.8851 0967	1.9721 6105	2.0631 9377	109
110	1.7308 7934	1.8961 0614	1.9844 8706	2.0769 4840	110
111	1.7395 3373	1.9071 6676	1.9968 9010	2.0907 9472	111
112	1.7482 3140	1.9182 9190	2.0093 7067	2.1047 3335	112
113	1.7569 7256	1.9294 8194	2.0219 2923	2.1187 6491	113
114	1.7657 5742	1.9407 3725	2.0345 6629	2.1328 9000	114
115	1.7745 8621	1.9520 5822	2.0472 8233	2.1471 0927	115
116	1.7834 5914	1.9634 4522	2.0600 7785	2.1614 2333	116
117	1.7923 7644	1.9748 9865	2.0729 5333	2.1758 3282	117
118	1.8013 3832	1.9864 1890	2.0859 0929	2.1903 3837	118
119	1.8103 4501	1.9980 0634	2.0989 4622	2.2049 4063	119
120	1.8193 9673	2.0096 6138	2.1120 6464	2.2196 4023	120
121	1.8284 9372	2.0213 8440	2.1252 6504	2.2344 3784	121
122	1.8376 3619	2.0331 7581	2.1385 4795	2.2493 3409	122
123	1.8468 2437	2.0450 3600	2.1519 1387	2.2643 2965	123
124	1.8560 5849	2.0569 6538	2.1653 6333	2.2794 2518	124
125	1.8653 3878	2.0689 6434	2.1788 9685	2.2946 2135	125
126	1.8746 6548	2.0810 3330	2.1925 1496	2.3099 1882	126
127	1.8840 3880	2.0931 7266	2.2062 1818	2.3253 1828	127
128	1.8934 5900	2.1053 8284	2.2200 0704	2.3408 2040	128
129	1.9029 2629	2.1176 6424	2.2338 8209	2.3564 2587	129
130	1.9124 4092	2.1300 1728	2.2478 4385	2.3721 3538	130
131	1.9220 0313	2.1424 4238	2.2618 9287	2.3879 4962	131
132	1.9316 1314	2.1549 3996	2.2760 2970	2.4038 6928	132
133	1.9412 7121	2.1675 1044	2.2902 5489	2.4198 9507	133
134	1.9509 7757	2.1801 5425	2.3045 6898	2.4360 2771	134
135	1.9607 3245	2.1928 7182	2.3189 7254	2.4522 6789	135
136	1.9705 3612	2.2056 6357	2.3334 6612	2.4686 1635	136
137	1.9803 8880	2.2185 2994	2.3480 5028	2.4850 7379	137
138	1.9902 9074	2.2314 7137	2.3627 2559	2.5016 4095	138
139	2.0002 4219	2.2444 8828	2.3774 9263	2.5183 1855	139
140	2.0102 4340	2.2575 8113	2.3923 5196	2.5351 0734	140
141	2.0202 9462	2.2707 5036	2.4073 0416	2.5520 0806	141
142	2.0303 9609	2.2839 9640	2.4223 4981	2.5690 2145	142
143	2.0405 4808	2.2973 1971	2.4374 8950	2.5861 4826	143
144	2.0507 5082	2.3107 2074	2.4527 2380	2.6033 8924	144
145	2.0610 0457	2.3241 9995	2.4680 5333	2.6207 4517	145
146	2.0713 0959	2.3377 5778	2.4834 7866	2.6382 1681	146
147	2.0816 6614	2.3513 9470	2.4990 0040	2.6558 0492	147
148	2.0920 7447	2.3651 1117	2.5146 1916	2.6735 1028	148
149	2.1025 3484	2.3789 0765	2.5303 3553	2.6913 3369	149
150	2.1130 4752	2.3927 8461	2.5461 5012	2.7092 7591	150

TABLE III.—Amount of 1 at Compound Interest

$$s = (1 + i)^n$$

n	½%	7/12%	5/8%	2/3%	n
151	2.1236 1276	2.4067 4252	2.5620 6356	2.7273 3775	151
152	2.1342 3082	2.4207 8186	2.5780 7646	2.7455 2000	152
153	2.1449 0197	2.4349 0308	2.5941 8944	2.7638 2347	153
154	2.1556 2648	2.4491 0668	2.6104 0312	2.7822 4896	154
155	2.1664 0462	2.4633 9314	2.6267 1814	2.8007 9729	155
156	2.1772 3664	2.4777 6293	2.6431 3513	2.8194 6927	156
157	2.1881 2282	2.4922 1655	2.6596 5472	2.8382 6573	157
158	2.1990 6344	2.5067 5448	2.6762 7756	2.8571 8750	158
159	2.2100 5875	2.5213 7722	2.6930 0430	2.8762 3542	159
160	2.2211 0905	2.5360 8525	2.7098 3558	2.8954 1032	160
161	2.2322 1459	2.5508 7908	2.7267 7205	2.9147 1306	161
162	2.2433 7566	2.5657 5921	2.7438 1437	2.9341 4448	162
163	2.2545 9254	2.5807 2614	2.7609 6321	2.9537 0544	163
164	2.2658 6551	2.5957 8037	2.7782 1923	2.9733 9681	164
165	2.2771 9483	2.6109 2242	2.7955 8310	2.9932 1945	165
166	2.2885 8081	2.6261 5280	2.8130 5550	3.0131 7425	166
167	2.3000 2371	2.6414 7203	2.8306 3710	3.0332 6208	167
168	2.3115 2383	2.6568 8062	2.8483 2858	3.0534 3883	168
169	2.3230 8145	2.6723 7909	2.8661 3063	3.0738 4038	169
170	2.3346 9686	2.6879 6796	2.8840 4395	3.0943 3265	170
171	2.3463 7034	2.7036 4778	2.9020 6922	3.1149 6154	171
172	2.3581 0219	2.7194 1906	2.9202 0715	3.1357 2795	172
173	2.3698 9270	2.7352 8233	2.9384 5845	3.1566 3280	173
174	2.3817 4217	2.7512 3815	2.9568 2381	3.1776 7702	174
175	2.3936 5088	2.7672 8704	2.9753 0396	3.1988 6153	175
176	2.4056 1913	2.7834 2954	2.9938 9961	3.2201 8728	176
177	2.4176 4723	2.7996 6622	3.0126 1149	3.2416 5519	177
178	2.4297 3546	2.8159 9760	3.0314 4031	3.2632 6623	178
179	2.4418 8414	2.8324 2426	3.0503 8681	3.2850 2134	179
180	2.4540 9356	2.8489 4673	3.0694 5173	3.3069 2148	180
181	2.4663 6403	2.8655 6559	3.0886 3580	3.3289 6762	181
182	2.4786 9585	2.8822 8139	3.1079 3977	3.3511 6074	182
183	2.4910 8933	2.8990 9469	3.1272 6440	3.3735 0181	183
184	2.5035 4478	2.9160 0608	3.1469 1043	3.3959 9182	184
185	2.5160 6250	2.9330 1612	3.1665 7862	3.4186 3177	185
186	2.5286 4281	2.9501 2538	3.1863 6973	3.4414 2265	186
187	2.5412 8603	2.6973 3444	3.2062 8454	3.4643 6546	187
188	2.5539 9246	2.9846 4389	3.2263 2382	3.4874 6123	188
189	2.5667 6242	3.0020 5431	3.2464 8834	3.5107 1097	189
190	2.5795 9623	3.0195 6630	3.2667 7890	3.5341 1571	190
191	2.5924 9421	3.0371 8043	3.2871 9627	3.5576 7649	191
192	2.6054 5668	3.0548 9732	3.3077 4124	3.5813 9433	192
193	2.6184 8397	3.0727 1755	3.3284 1462	3.6052 7029	193
194	2.6315 7639	3.0906 4174	3.3492 1722	3.6293 0543	194
195	2.6447 3427	3.1086 7048	3.3701 4982	3.6535 0080	195
196	2.6579 5794	3.1268 0440	3.3912 1326	3.6778 5747	196
197	2.6712 4773	3.1450 4409	3.4124 0834	3.7023 7652	197
198	2.6846 0397	3.1633 9018	3.4337 3589	3.7270 5903	198
199	2.6980 2699	3.1818 4329	3.4551 9674	3.7519 0609	199
200	2.7115 1712	3.2004 0404	3.4767 9172	3.7769 1880	200

TABLE III.—Amount of 1 at Compound Interest

$$s = (1 + i)^n$$

n	$\frac{3}{4}\%$	$\frac{7}{8}\%$	1%	$1\frac{1}{8}\%$	n
1	1.0075 0000	1.0087 5000	1.0100 0000	1.0112 5000	1
2	1.0150 5625	1 0175 7656	1.0201 0000	1.0226 2656	2
3	1.0226 6917	1.0264 8036	1.0303 0100	1.0341 3111	3
4	1.0303 3919	1.0354 6206	1.0406 0401	1.0457 6509	4
5	1.0380 6673	1.0445 2235	1.0510 1005	1.0575 2994	5
6	1.0458 5224	1.0536 6192	1.0615 2015	1.0694 2716	6
7	1.0536 9613	1.0628 8147	1.0721 3535	1.0814 5821	7
8	1.0615 9885	1.0721 8168	1.0828 5671	1.0936 2462	8
9	1.0695 6084	1.0815 6327	1.0936 8527	1.1059 2789	9
10	1.0775 8255	1.0910 2695	1.1046 2213	1.1183 6958	10
11	1.0856 6441	1.1005 7343	1.1156 6835	1.1309 5124	11
12	1.0938 0690	1.1102 0346	1.1268 2503	1.1436 7444	12
13	1.1020 1045	1.1199 1773	1.1380 9328	1.1565 4078	13
14	1.1102 7553	1.1297 1701	1.1494 7421	1.1695 5186	14
15	1.1186 0259	1.1396 0203	1.1609 6896	1.1827 0932	15
16	1.1269 9211	1.1495 7355	1.1725 7864	1.1960 1480	16
17	1.1354 4455	1.1596 3232	1.1843 0443	1.2094 6997	17
18	1.1439 6039	1.1697 7910	1.1961 4748	1.2230 7650	18
19	1.1525 4009	1.1800 1467	1.2081 0895	1.2368 3611	19
20	1.1611 8414	1.1903 3980	1.2201 9004	1.2507 5052	20
21	1.1698 9302	1.2007 5527	1.2323 9194	1.2648 2146	21
22	1.1786 6722	1.2112 6188	1.2447 1586	1.2790 5071	22
23	1.1875 0723	1.2218 6042	1.2571 6302	1.2934 4003	23
24	1.1964 1353	1.2325 5170	1.2697 3465	1.3079 9123	24
25	1.2053 8663	1.2433 3653	1.2824 3200	1.3227 0613	25
26	1.2144 2703	1.2542 1572	1.2952 5631	1.3375 8657	26
27	1.2235 3523	1.2651 9011	1.3082 0888	1.3526 3442	27
28	1.2327 1175	1.2762 6052	1.3212 9097	1.3678 5156	28
29	1.2419 5709	1.2874 2780	1.3345 0388	1.3832 3989	29
30	1 2512 7176	1.2986 9280	1.3478 4892	1.3988 0134	30
31	1.2606 5630	1.3100 5636	1.3613 2740	1.4145 3785	31
32	1.2701 1122	1.3215 1935	1.3749 4068	1.4304 5140	32
33	1.2796 3706	1.3330 8265	1.3886 9009	1.4465 4398	33
34	1.2892 3434	1.3447 4712	1.4025 7699	1.4628 1760	34
35	1.2989 0359	1.3565 1366	1.4166 0276	1.4792 7430	35
36	1.3086 4537	1.3683 8315	1.4307 6878	1.4959 1613	36
37	1.3184 6021	1.3803 5650	1.4450 7647	1.5127 4519	37
38	1.3283 4866	1.3924 3462	1.4595 2724	1.5297 6357	38
39	1.3383 1128	1.4046 1843	1.4741 2251	1.5469 7341	39
40	1.3483 4861	1.4169 0884	1.4888 6373	1.5643 7687	40
41	1.3584 6123	1.4293 0679	1.5037 5237	1.5819 7611	41
42	1.3686 4969	1.4418 1322	1.5187 8989	1.5997 7334	42
43	1.3789 1456	1.4544 2909	1.5339 7779	1.6177 7079	43
44	1.3892 5642	1.4671 5534	1.5493 1757	1.6359 7071	44
45	1.3996 7584	1.4799 9295	1.5648 1075	1.6543 7538	45
46	1.4101 7341	1.4929 4289	1.5804 5885	1.6729 8710	46
47	1.4207 4971	1.5060 0614	1.5962 6344	1.6918 0821	47
48	1.4314 0533	1.5191 8370	1.6122 2608	1.7108 4105	48
49	1.4421 4087	1.5324 7655	1.6283 4834	1.7300 8801	49
50	1.4529 5693	1.5458 8572	1.6446 3182	1.7495 5150	50

TABLE III.—Amount of 1 at Compound Interest

$$s = (1 + i)^n$$

n	¾%	⅞%	1%	1⅛%	n
51	1.4638 5411	1.5594 1222	1.6610 7814	1.7692 3395	51
52	1.4748 3301	1.5730 5708	1.6776 8892	1.7891 3784	52
53	1.4858 9426	1.5868 2133	1.6944 6581	1.8092 6564	53
54	1.4970 3847	1.6007 0602	1.7114 1047	1.8296 1988	54
55	1.5082 6626	1.6147 1219	1.7285 2457	1.8502 0310	55
56	1.5195 7825	1.6288 4093	1.7458 0982	1.8710 1788	56
57	1.5309 7509	1.6430 9328	1.7632 6792	1.8920 6684	57
58	1.5424 5740	1.6574 7035	1.7809 0060	1.9133 5259	58
59	1.5540 2583	1.6719 7322	1.7987 0960	1.9348 7780	59
60	1.5656 8103	1.6866 0298	1.8166 9670	1.9566 4518	60
61	1.5774 2363	1.7013 6076	1.8348 6367	1.9786 5744	61
62	1.5892 5431	1.7162 4766	1.8532 1230	2.0009 1733	62
63	1.6011 7372	1.7312 6483	1.8717 4443	2.0234 2765	63
64	1.6131 8252	1.7464 1340	1.8904 6187	2.0461 9121	64
65	1.6252 8139	1.7616 9452	1.9093 6649	2.0692 1087	65
66	1.6374 7100	1.7771 0934	1.9284 6015	2.0924 8949	66
67	1.6497 5203	1.7926 5905	1.9477 4475	2.1160 2999	67
68	1.6621 2517	1.8083 4482	1.9672 2220	2.1398 3533	68
69	1.6745 9111	1.8241 6783	1.9868 9442	2.1639 0848	69
70	1.6871 5055	1.8401 2930	2.0067 6337	2.1882 5245	70
71	1.6998 0418	1.8562 3043	2.0268 3100	2.2128 7029	71
72	1.7125 5271	1.8724 7245	2.0470 9931	2.2377 6508	72
73	1.7253 9685	1.8888 5658	2.0675 7031	2.2629 3994	73
74	1.7383 3733	1.9053 8408	2.0882 4601	2.2883 9801	74
75	1.7513 7486	1.9220 5619	2.1091 2847	2.3141 4249	75
76	1.7645 1017	1.9388 7418	2.1302 1975	2.3401 7659	76
77	1.7777 4400	1.9558 3933	2.1515 2195	2.3665 0358	77
78	1.7910 7708	1.9729 5292	2.1730 3717	2.3931 2675	78
79	1.8045 1015	1.9902 1626	2.1947 6754	2.4200 4942	79
80	1.8180 4398	2.0076 3066	2.2167 1522	2.4472 7498	80
81	1.8316 7931	2.0251 9742	2.2388 8237	2.4748 0682	81
82	1.8454 1691	2.0429 1790	2.2612 7119	2.5026 4840	82
83	1.8592 5753	2.0607 9343	2.2838 8390	2.5308 0319	83
84	1.8732 0196	2.0788 2537	2.3067 2274	2.5592 7473	84
85	1.8872 5098	2.0970 1510	2.3297 8997	2.5880 6657	85
86	1.9014 0536	2.1153 6398	2.3530 8787	2.6171 8232	86
87	1.9156 6590	2.1338 7341	2.3766 1875	2.6466 2562	87
88	1.9300 3339	2.1525 4481	2.4003 8494	2.6764 0016	88
89	1.9445 0865	2.1713 7957	2.4243 8879	2.7065 0966	89
90	1.9590 9246	2.1903 7914	2.4486 3267	2.7369 5789	90
91	1.9737 8565	2.2095 4496	2.4731 1900	2.7677 4867	91
92	1.9885 8905	2.2288 7848	2.4978 5019	2.7988 8584	92
93	2.0035 0346	2.2483 8117	2.5228 2869	2.8303 7331	93
94	2.0185 2974	2.2680 5450	2.5480 5698	2.8622 1501	94
95	2.0336 6871	2.2878 9998	2.5735 3755	2.8944 1492	95
96	2.0489 2123	2.3079 1910	2.5992 7293	2.9269 7709	96
97	2.0642 8814	2.3281 1340	2.6252 6565	2.9599 0559	97
98	2.0797 7030	2.3484 8439	2.6515 1831	2.9932 0452	98
99	2.0953 6858	2.3690 3363	2.6780 3349	3.0268 7807	99
100	2.1110 8384	2.3897 6267	2.7048 1383	3.0609 3045	100

TABLE III.—Amount of 1 at Compound Interest

$$s = (1 + i)^n$$

n	1¼%	1⅜%	1½%	1¾%	n
1	1.0125 0000	1.0137 5000	1.0150 0000	1.0175 0000	1
2	1.0251 5625	1.0276 8906	1.0302 2500	1.0353 0625	2
3	1.0379 7070	1.0418 1979	1.0456 7838	1.0534 2411	3
4	1.0509 4534	1.0561 4481	1.0613 6355	1.0718 5903	4
5	1.0640 8215	1.0706 6680	1.0772 8400	1.0906 1656	5
6	1.0773 8318	1.0853 8847	1.0934 4326	1.1097 0235	6
7	1.0908 5047	1.1003 1256	1.1098 4491	1.1291 2215	7
8	1.1044 8610	1.1154 4186	1.1264 9259	1.1488 8178	8
9	1.1182 9218	1.1307 7918	1.1433 8998	1.1689 8721	9
10	1.1322 7083	1.1463 2740	1.1605 4083	1.1894 4449	10
11	1.1464 2422	1.1620 8940	1.1779 4894	1.2102 5977	11
12	1.1607 5452	1.1780 6813	1.1956 1817	1.2314 3931	12
13	1.1752 6356	1.1942 6880	1.2135 9244	1.2529 0050	13
14	1.1899 5475	1.2106 8773	1.2317 5573	1.2749 1682	14
15	1.2048 2918	1.2273 3469	1.2502 3207	1.2972 2786	15
16	1.2198 8955	1.2442 1054	1.2689 8555	1.3199 2935	16
17	1.2351 3817	1.2613 1843	1.2880 2033	1.3430 2811	17
18	1.2505 7739	1.2786 6156	1.3073 4064	1.3665 3111	18
19	1.2662 0961	1.2962 4316	1.3269 5075	1.3904 4540	19
20	1.2820 3723	1.3140 6650	1.3468 5501	1.4147 7820	20
21	1.2980 6270	1.3321 3492	1.3670 5783	1.4395 3681	21
22	1.3142 8848	1.3504 5177	1.3875 6370	1.4647 2871	22
23	1.3307 1709	1.3690 2048	1.4083 7715	1.4903 6146	23
24	1.3473 5105	1.3878 4451	1.4295 0281	1.5164 4279	24
25	1.3641 9294	1.4069 2738	1.4509 4535	1.5429 8054	25
26	1.3812 4535	1.4262 7263	1.4727 0953	1.5699 8269	26
27	1.3985 1092	1.4458 8388	1.4948 0018	1.5974 5739	27
28	1.4159 9230	1.4657 6478	1.5172 2218	1.6254 1290	28
29	1.4336 9221	1.4859 1905	1.5399 8051	1.6538 5762	29
30	1.4516 1336	1.5063 5043	1.5630 8022	1.6828 0013	30
31	1.4697 5853	1.5270 6275	1.5865 2642	1.7122 4913	31
32	1.4881 3051	1.5480 5986	1.6103 2432	1.7422 1349	32
33	1.5067 3214	1.5693 4569	1.6344 7918	1.7727 0223	33
34	1.5255 6629	1.5909 2419	1.6589 9637	1.8037 2452	34
35	1.5446 3587	1.6127 9940	1.6838 8132	1.8352 8970	35
36	1.5639 4382	1.6349 7539	1.7091 3954	1.8674 0727	36
37	1.5834 9312	1.6574 5630	1.7347 7663	1.9000 8689	37
38	1.6032 8678	1.6802 4633	1.7607 9828	1.9333 3841	38
39	1.6233 2787	1.7033 4971	1.7872 1025	1.9671 7184	39
40	1.6436 1946	1.7267 7077	1.8140 1841	2.0015 9734	40
41	1.6641 6471	1.7505 1387	1.8412 2868	2.0366 2530	41
42	1.6849 6677	1.7745 8343	1.8688 4712	2.0722 6624	42
43	1.7060 2885	1.7989 8396	1.8968 7982	2.1085 3090	43
44	1.7273 5421	1.8237 1999	1.9253 3302	2.1454 3019	44
45	1.7489 4614	1.8487 9614	1.9542 1301	2.1829 7522	45
46	1.7708 0797	1.8742 1708	1.9835 2621	2.2211 7728	46
47	1.7929 4306	1.8999 8757	2.0132 7910	2.2600 4789	47
48	1.8153 5485	1.9261 1240	2.0434 7829	2.2995 9872	48
49	1.8380 4679	1.9525 9644	2.0741 3046	2.3398 4170	49
50	1.8610 2237	1.9794 4464	2.1052 4242	2.3807 8893	50

TABLE III.—Amount of 1 at Compound Interest

$$s = (1 + i)^n$$

n	1¼%	1⅜%	1½%	1¾%	n
51	1.8842 8515	2.0066 6201	2.1368 2106	2.4224 5274	51
52	1.9078 3872	2.0342 5361	2.1688 7337	2.4648 4566	52
53	1.9316 8670	2.0622 2460	2.2014 0647	2.5077 8046	53
54	1.9558 3279	2.0905 8019	2.2344 2757	2.5518 7012	54
55	1.9802 8070	2.1193 2566	2.2679 4398	2.5965 2785	55
56	2.0050 3420	2.1484 6639	2.3019 6314	2.6419 6708	56
57	2.0300 9713	2.1780 0780	2.3364 9259	2.6882 0151	57
58	2.0554 7335	2.2079 5541	2.3715 3998	2.7352 4503	58
59	2.0811 6676	2.2383 1480	2.4071 1308	2.7831 1182	59
60	2.1071 8135	2.2690 9163	2.4432 1978	2.8318 1628	60
61	2.1335 2111	2.3002 9164	2.4798 6807	2.8813 7306	61
62	2.1601 9013	2.3319 2065	2.5170 6609	2.9317 9709	62
63	2.1871 9250	2.3639 8456	2.5548 2208	2.9831 0354	63
64	2.2145 3241	2.3964 8934	2.5931 4442	3.0343 0785	64
65	2.2422 1407	2.4294 4107	2.6320 4158	3.0884 2574	65
66	2.2702 4174	2.4628 4589	2.6715 2221	3.1424 7319	66
67	2.2986 1976	2.4967 1002	2.7115 9504	3.1974 6647	67
68	2.3273 5251	2.5310 3978	2.7522 6896	3.2534 2213	68
69	2.3564 4442	2.5658 4158	2.7935 5300	3.3103 5702	69
70	2.3858 9997	2.6011 2190	2.8354 5629	3.3682 8827	70
71	2.4157 2372	2.6368 8732	2.8779 8814	3.4272 3331	71
72	2.4459 2027	2.6731 4453	2.9211 5796	3.4872 0990	72
73	2.4764 9427	2.7099 0026	2.9649 7533	3.5482 3607	73
74	2.5074 5045	2.7471 6139	3.0094 4996	3.6103 3020	74
75	2.5387 9358	2.7849 3486	3.0545 9171	3.6735 1098	75
76	2.5705 2850	2.8232 2771	3.1004 1059	3.7377 9742	76
77	2.6026 6011	2.8620 4710	3.1469 1674	3.8032 0888	77
78	2.6351 9336	2.9014 0024	3.1941 2050	3.8697 6503	78
79	2.6681 3327	2.9412 9450	3.2420 3230	3.9374 8592	79
80	2.7014 8494	2.9817 3730	3.2906 6279	4.0063 9192	80
81	2.7352 5350	3.0227 3618	3.3400 2273	4.0765 0378	81
82	2.7694 4417	3.0642 9881	3.3901 2307	4.1478 4260	82
83	2.8040 6222	3.1064 3291	3.4409 7492	4.2204 2984	83
84	2.8391 1300	3.1491 4637	3.4925 8954	4.2942 8737	84
85	2.8746 0191	3.1924 4713	3.5449 7838	4.3694 3740	85
86	2.9105 3444	3.2363 4328	3.5981 5306	4.4459 0255	86
87	2.9469 1612	3.2808 4300	3.6521 2535	4.5237 0584	87
88	2.9837 5257	3.3259 5459	3.7069 0723	4.6028 7070	88
89	3.0210 4948	3.3716 8646	3.7625 1084	4.6834 2093	89
90	3.0588 1260	3.4180 4715	3.8189 4851	4.7653 8080	90
91	3.0970 4775	3.4650 4530	3.8762 3273	4.8487 7496	91
92	3.1357 6085	3.5126 8967	3.9343 7622	4.9336 2853	92
93	3.1749 5786	3.5609 8916	3.9933 9187	5.0199 6703	93
94	3.2146 4483	3.6099 5276	4.0532 9275	5.1078 1645	94
95	3.2548 2789	3.6595 8961	4.1140 9214	5.1972 0324	95
96	3.2955 1324	3.7099 0897	4.1758 0352	5.2881 5429	96
97	3.3367 0716	3.7609 2021	4.2384 4057	5.3806 9699	97
98	3.3784 1600	3.8126 3287	4.3020 1718	5.4748 5919	98
99	3.4206 4620	3.8650 5657	4.3665 4744	5.5706 6923	99
100	3.4634 0427	3.9182 0110	4.4320 4565	5.6681 5594	100

TABLE III.—Amount of 1 at Compound Interest

$$s = (1 + i)^n$$

n	2%	2¼%	2½%	2¾%	n
1	1.0200 0000	1.0225 0000	1.0250 0000	1.0275 0000	1
2	1.0404 0000	1.0455 0625	1.0506 2500	1.0557 5625	2
3	1.0612 0800	1.0690 3014	1.0768 9063	1.0847 8955	3
4	1.0824 3216	1.0930 8332	1.1038 1289	1.1146 2126	4
5	1.1040 8080	1.1176 7769	1.1314 0821	1.1452 7334	5
6	1.1261 6242	1.1428 2544	1.1596 9342	1.1767 6836	6
7	1.1486 8567	1.1685 3901	1.1886 8575	1.2091 2949	7
8	1.1716 5938	1.1948 3114	1.2184 0290	1.2423 8055	8
9	1.1950 9257	1.2217 1484	1.2488 6297	1.2765 4602	9
10	1.2189 9442	1.2492 0343	1.2800 8454	1.3116 5103	10
11	1.2433 7431	1.2773 1050	1.3120 8666	1.3477 2144	11
12	1.2682 4179	1.3060 4999	1.3448 8882	1.3847 8378	12
13	1.2936 0663	1.3354 3611	1.3785 1104	1.4228 6533	13
14	1.3194 7876	1.3654 8343	1.4129 7382	1.4619 9413	14
15	1.3458 6834	1.3962 0680	1.4482 9817	1.5021 9896	15
16	1.3727 8571	1.4276 2146	1.4845 0562	1.5435 0944	16
17	1.4002 4142	1.4597 4294	1.5216 1826	1.5859 5595	17
18	1.4282 4625	1.4925 8716	1.5596 5872	1.6295 6973	18
19	1.4568 1117	1.5261 7037	1.5986 5019	1.6743 8290	19
20	1.4859 4740	1.5605 0920	1.6386 1644	1.7204 2843	20
21	1.5156 6634	1.5956 2066	1.6795 8185	1.7677 4021	21
22	1.5459 7967	1.6315 2212	1.7215 7140	1.8163 5307	22
23	1.5768 9926	1.6682 3137	1.7646 1068	1.8663 0270	23
24	1.6084 3725	1.7057 6658	1.8087 2595	1.9176 2610	24
25	1.6406 0599	1.7441 4632	1.8539 4410	1.9703 6082	25
26	1.6734 1811	1.7833 8962	1.9002 9270	2.0245 4575	26
27	1.7068 8648	1.8235 1588	1.9478 0002	2.0802 2075	27
28	1.7410 2421	1.8645 4499	1.9964 9502	2.1374 2682	28
29	1.7758 4469	1.9064 9725	2.0464 0739	2.1962 0606	29
30	1.8113 6158	1.9493 9344	2.0975 6758	2.2566 0173	30
31	1.8475 8882	1.9932 5479	2.1500 0677	2.3186 5828	31
32	1.8845 4059	2.0381 0303	2.2037 5694	2.3824 2138	32
33	1.9222 3140	2.0839 6034	2.2588 5086	2.4479 3797	33
34	1.9606 7603	2.1308 4945	2.3153 2213	2.5152 5626	34
35	1.9998 8955	2.1787 9356	2.3732 0519	2.5844 2581	35
36	2.0398 8734	2.2278 1642	2.4325 3532	2.6554 9752	36
37	2.0806 8509	2.2779 4229	2.4933 4870	2.7285 2370	37
38	2.1222 9879	2.3291 9599	2.5556 8242	2.8035 5810	38
39	2.1647 4477	2.3816 0290	2.6195 7448	2.8806 5595	39
40	2.2080 3966	2.4351 8897	2.6850 6384	2.9598 7399	40
41	2.2522 0046	2.4899 8072	2.7521 9043	3.0412 7052	41
42	2.2972 4447	2.5460 0528	2.8209 9520	3.1249 0546	42
43	2.3431 8936	2.6032 9040	2.8915 2008	3.2108 4036	43
44	2.3900 5314	2.6618 6444	2.9638 0808	3.2991 3847	44
45	2.4378 5421	2.7217 5639	3.0379 0328	3.3898 6478	45
46	2.4866 1129	2.7829 9590	3.1138 5086	3.4830 8606	46
47	2.5363 4351	2.8456 1331	3.1916 9713	3.5788 7093	47
48	2.5870 7039	2.9096 3961	3.2714 8956	3.6772 8988	48
49	2.6388 1179	2.9751 0650	3.3532 7680	3.7784 1535	49
50	2.6915 8803	3.0420 4640	3.4371 0872	3.8823 2177	50

TABLE III.—Amount of 1 at Compound Interest

$$s = (1 + i)^n$$

n	2%	2¼%	2½%	2¾%	n
51	2.7454 1979	3.1104 9244	3.5230 3644	3.9890 8562	51
52	2.8003 2819	3.1804 7852	3.6111 1235	4.0987 8547	52
53	2.8563 3475	3.2520 3929	3.7013 9016	4.2115 0208	53
54	2.9134 6144	3.3252 1017	3.7939 2491	4.3273 1838	54
55	2.9717 3067	3.4000 2740	3.8887 7303	4.4463 1964	55
56	3.0311 6529	3.4765 2802	3.9859 9236	4.5685 9343	56
57	3.0917 8859	3.5547 4990	4.0856 4217	4.6942 2975	57
58	3.1536 2436	3.6347 3177	4.1877 8322	4.8233 2107	58
59	3.2166 9685	3.7165 1324	4.2924 7780	4.9559 6239	59
60	3.2810 3079	3.8001 3479	4.3997 8975	5.0922 5136	60
61	3.3466 5140	3.8856 3782	4.5097 8449	5.2322 8827	61
62	3.4135 8443	3.9730 6467	4.6225 2910	5.3761 7620	62
63	3.4818 5612	4.0624 5862	4.7380 9233	5.5240 2105	63
64	3.5514 9324	4.1538 6394	4.8565 4464	5.6759 3162	64
65	3.6225 2311	4.2473 2588	4.9779 5826	5.8320 1974	65
66	3.6949 7357	4.3428 9071	5.1024 0721	5.9924 0029	66
67	3.7688 7304	4.4406 0576	5.2299 6739	6.1571 9130	67
68	3.8442 5050	4.5405 1939	5.3607 1658	6.3265 1406	68
69	3.9211 3551	4.6426 8107	5.4947 3449	6.5004 9319	69
70	3.9995 5822	4.7471 4140	5.6321 0286	6.6792 5676	70
71	4.0795 4939	4.8539 5208	5.7729 0543	6.8629 3632	71
72	4.1611 4038	4.9631 6600	5.9172 2806	7.0516 6706	72
73	4.2443 6318	5.0748 3723	6.0651 5876	7.2455 8791	73
74	4.3292 5045	5.1890 2107	6.2167 8773	7.4448 4158	74
75	4.4158 3546	5.3057 7405	6.3722 0743	7.6495 7472	75
76	4.5041 5216	5.4251 5396	6.5315 1261	7.8599 3802	76
77	4.5942 3521	5.5472 1993	6.6948 0043	8.0760 8632	77
78	4.6861 1991	5.6720 3237	6.8621 7044	8.2981 7869	78
79	4.7798 4231	5.7996 5310	7.0337 2470	8.5263 7861	79
80	4.8754 3916	5.9301 4530	7.2095 6782	8.7608 5402	80
81	4.9729 4794	6.0635 7357	7.3898 0701	9.0017 7751	81
82	5.0724 0690	6.2000 0397	7.5745 5219	9.2493 2639	82
83	5.1738 5504	6.3395 0406	7.7639 1599	9.5036 8286	83
84	5.2773 3214	6.4821 4290	7.9580 1389	9.7650 3414	84
85	5.3828 7878	6.6279 9112	8.1569 6424	10.0335 7258	85
86	5.4905 3636	6.7771 2092	8.3608 8834	10.3094 9583	86
87	5.6003 4708	6.9296 0614	8.5699 1055	10.5930 0696	87
88	5.7123 5402	7.0855 2228	8.7841 5832	10.8843 1465	88
89	5.8266 0110	7.2449 4653	9.0037 6228	11.1836 3331	89
90	5.9431 3313	7.4079 5782	9.2288 5633	11.4911 8322	90
91	6.0619 9579	7.5746 3688	9.4595 7774	11.8071 9076	91
92	6.1832 3570	7.7450 6621	9.6960 6718	12.1318 8851	92
93	6.3069 0042	7.9193 3020	9.9384 6886	12.4655 1544	93
94	6.4330 3843	8.0975 1512	10.1869 3058	12.8083 1711	94
95	6.5616 9920	8.2797 0921	10.4416 0385	13.1605 4584	95
96	6.6929 3318	8.4660 0267	10.7026 4395	13.5224 6085	96
97	6.8267 9184	8.6564 8773	10.9702 1004	13.8943 2852	97
98	6.9633 2768	8.8512 5871	11.2444 6530	14.2764 2255	98
99	7.1025 9423	9.0504 1203	11.5255 7693	14.6690 2417	99
100	7.2446 4612	9.2540 4630	11.8137 1635	15.0724 2234	100

TABLE III.—Amount of 1 at Compound Interest

$$s = (1 + i)^n$$

n	3%	3½%	4%	4½%	n
1	1.0300 0000	1.0350 0000	1.0400 0000	1.0450 0000	1
2	1.0609 0000	1.0712 2500	1.0816 0000	1.0920 2500	2
3	1.0927 2700	1.1087 1788	1.1248 6400	1.1411 6613	3
4	1.1255 0881	1.1475 2300	1.1698 5856	1.1925 1860	4
5	1.1592 7407	1.1876 8631	1.2166 5290	1.2461 8194	5
6	1.1940 5230	1.2292 5533	1.2653 1902	1.3022 6012	6
7	1.2298 7387	1.2722 7926	1.3159 3178	1.3608 6183	7
8	1.2667 7008	1.3168 0904	1.3685 6905	1.4221 0061	8
9	1.3047 7318	1.3628 9735	1.4233 1181	1.4860 9514	9
10	1.3439 1638	1.4105 9876	1.4802 4428	1.5529 6942	10
11	1.3842 3387	1.4599 6972	1.5394 5406	1.6228 5305	11
12	1.4257 6089	1.5110 6866	1.6010 3222	1.6958 8143	12
13	1.4685 3371	1.5639 5606	1.6650 7351	1.7721 9610	13
14	1.5125 8972	1.6186 9452	1.7316 7645	1.8519 4492	14
15	1.5579 6742	1.6753 4883	1.8009 4351	1.9352 8244	15
16	1.6047 0644	1.7339 8604	1.8729 8125	2.0223 7015	16
17	1.6528 4763	1.7946 7555	1.9479 0050	2.1133 7681	17
18	1.7024 3306	1.8574 8920	2.0258 1652	2.2084 7877	18
19	1.7535 0605	1.9225 0132	2.1068 4918	2.3078 6031	19
20	1.8061 1123	1.9897 8886	2.1911 2314	2.4117 1402	20
21	1.8602 9457	2.0594 3147	2.2787 6807	2.5202 4116	21
22	1.9161 0341	2.1315 1158	2.3699 1879	2.6336 5201	22
23	1.9735 8651	2.2061 1448	2.4647 1554	2.7521 6635	23
24	2.0327 9411	2.2833 2849	2.5633 0416	2.8760 1383	24
25	2.0937 7793	2.3632 4498	2.6658 3633	3.0054 3446	25
26	2.1565 9127	2.4459 5856	2.7724 6978	3.1406 7901	26
27	2.2212 8901	2.5315 6711	2.8833 6858	3.2820 0956	27
28	2.2879 2768	2.6201 7196	2.9987 0332	3.4296 9999	28
29	2.3565 6551	2.7118 7798	3.1186 5145	3.5840 3649	29
30	2.4272 6247	2.8067 9370	3.2433 9751	3.7453 1813	30
31	2.5000 8035	2.9050 3148	3.3731 3341	3.9138 5745	31
32	2.5750 8276	3.0067 0759	3.5080 5875	4.0899 8104	32
33	2.6523 3524	3.1119 4235	3.6483 8110	4.2740 3018	33
34	2.7319 0530	3.2208 6033	3.7943 1634	4.4663 6154	34
35	2.8138 6245	3.3335 9045	3.9460 8899	4.6673 4781	35
36	2.8982 7833	3.4502 6611	4.1039 3255	4.8773 7846	36
37	2.9852 2668	3.5710 2543	4.2680 8986	5.0968 6049	37
38	3.0747 8348	3.6960 1132	4.4388 1345	5.3262 1921	38
39	3.1670 2698	3.8253 7171	4.6163 6599	5.5658 9908	39
40	3.2620 3779	3.9592 5972	4.8010 2063	5.8163 6454	40
41	3.3598 9893	4.0978 3381	4.9930 6145	6.0781 0094	41
42	3.4606 9589	4.2412 5799	5.1927 8391	6.3516 1548	42
43	3.5645 1677	4.3897 0202	5.4004 9527	6.6374 3818	43
44	3.6714 5227	4.5433 4160	5.6165 1508	6.9361 2290	44
45	3.7815 9584	4.7023 5855	5.8411 7568	7.2482 4843	45
46	3.8950 4372	4.8669 4110	6.0748 2271	7.5744 1961	46
47	4.0118 9503	5.0372 8404	6.3178 1562	7.9152 6849	47
48	4.1322 5188	5.2135 8898	6.5705 2824	8.2714 5557	48
49	4.2562 1944	5.3960 6459	6.8333 4937	8.6436 7107	49
50	4.3839 0602	5.5849 2686	7.1066 8335	9.0326 3627	50

TABLE III.—Amount of 1 at Compound Interest

$$s = (1 + i)^n$$

n	3%	3½%	4%	4½%	n
51	4.5154 2320	5.7803 9930	7.3909 5068	9.4391 0490	51
52	4.6508 8590	5.9827 1327	7.6865 8871	9.8638 6463	52
53	4.7904 1247	6.1921 0824	7.9940 5226	10.3077 3853	53
54	4.9341 2485	6.4088 3202	8.3138 1435	10.7715 8677	54
55	5.0821 4859	6.6331 4114	8.6463 6692	11.2563 0817	55
56	5.2346 1305	6.8653 0108	8.9922 2160	11.7628 4204	56
57	5.3916 5144	7.1055 8662	9.3519 1046	12.2921 6993	57
58	5.5534 0098	7.3542 8215	9.7259 8688	12.8453 1758	58
59	5.7200 0301	7.6116 8203	10.1150 2635	13.4233 5687	59
60	5.8916 0310	7.8780 9090	10.5196 2741	14.0274 0793	60
61	6.0683 5120	8.1538 2408	10.9404 1250	14.6586 4129	61
62	6.2504 0173	8.4392 0793	11.3780 2900	15.3182 8014	62
63	6.4379 1379	8.7345 8020	11.8331 5016	16.0076 0275	63
64	6.6310 5120	9.0402 9051	12.3064 7617	16.7279 4487	64
65	6.8299 8273	9.3567 0068	12.7987 3522	17.4807 0239	65
66	7.0348 8222	9.6841 8520	13.3106 8463	18.2673 3400	66
67	7.2459 2868	10.0231 3168	13.8431 1201	19.0893 6403	67
68	7.4633 0654	10.3739 4129	14.3968 3649	19.9483 8541	68
69	7.6872 0574	10.7370 2924	14.9727 0995	20.8460 6276	69
70	7.9178 2191	11.1128 2526	15.5716 1835	21.7841 3558	70
71	8.1553 5657	11.5017 7414	16.1944 8308	22.7644 2168	71
72	8.4000 1727	11.9043 3624	16.8422 6241	23.7888 2066	72
73	8.6520 1778	12.3209 8801	17.5159 5290	24.8593 1759	73
74	8.9115 7832	12.7522 2259	18.2165 9102	25.9779 8688	74
75	9.1789 2567	13.1985 5038	18.9452 5466	27.1469 9629	75
76	9.4542 9344	13.6604 9964	19.7030 6485	28.3686 1112	76
77	9.7379 2224	14.1386 1713	20.4911 8744	29.6451 9862	77
78	10.0300 5991	14.6334 6873	21.3108 3494	30.9792 3256	78
79	10.3309 6171	15.1456 4013	22.1632 6834	32.3732 9802	79
80	10.6408 9056	15.6757 3754	23.0497 9907	33.8300 9643	80
81	10.9601 1727	16.2243 8135	23.9717 9103	35.3524 5077	81
82	11.2889 2079	16.7922 4195	24.9306 6267	36.9433 1106	82
83	11.6275 8842	17.3799 7041	25.9278 8918	38.6057 6006	83
84	11.9764 1607	17.9882 6938	26.9650 0475	40.3430 1926	84
85	12.3357 0855	18.6178 5881	28.0436 0494	42.1584 5513	85
86	12.7057 7981	19.2694 8387	29.1653 4914	44.0555 8561	86
87	13.0869 5320	19.9439 1580	30.3319 6310	46.0380 8696	87
88	13.4795 6180	20.6419 5285	31.5452 4163	48.1098 0087	88
89	13.8839 4865	21.3644 2120	32.8070 5129	50.2747 4191	89
90	14.3004 6711	22.1121 7595	34.1193 3334	52.5371 0530	90
91	14.7294 8112	22.8861 0210	35.4841 0668	54.9012 7503	91
92	15.1713 6556	23.6871 1568	36.9034 7094	57.3718 3241	92
93	15.6265 0652	24.5161 6473	38.3796 0978	59.9535 6487	93
94	16.0953 0172	25.3742 3049	39.9147 9417	62.6514 7529	94
95	16.5781 6077	26.2623 2856	41.5113 8594	65.4707 9168	95
96	17.0755 0559	27.1815 1006	43.1718 4138	68.4169 7730	96
97	17.5877 7076	28.1328 6291	44.8987 1503	71.4957 4128	97
98	18.1154 0388	29.1175 1311	46.6946 6363	74.7130 4964	98
99	18.6588 6600	30.1366 2607	48.5624 5018	78.0751 3687	99
100	19.2186 3198	31.1914 0798	50.5049 4818	81.5885 1803	100

TABLE III.—Amount of 1 at Compound Interest

$$s = (1 + i)^n$$

n	5%	5½%	6%	6½%	n
1	1.0500 0000	1.0550 0000	1.0600 0000	1.0650 0000	1
2	1.1025 0000	1.1130 2500	1.1236 0000	1.1342 2500	2
3	1.1576 2500	1.1742 4138	1.1910 1600	1.2079 4963	3
4	1.2155 0625	1.2388 2465	1.2624 7696	1.2864 6635	4
5	1.2762 8156	1.3069 6001	1.3382 2558	1.3700 8666	5
6	1.3400 9564	1.3788 4281	1.4185 1911	1.4591 4230	6
7	1.4071 0042	1.4546 7916	1.5036 3026	1.5539 8655	7
8	1.4774 5544	1.5346 8651	1.5938 4807	1.6549 9567	8
9	1.5513 2822	1.6190 9427	1.6894 7896	1.7625 7039	9
10	1.6288 9463	1.7081 4446	1.7908 4770	1.8771 3747	10
11	1.7103 3936	1.8020 9240	1.8982 9856	1.9991 5140	11
12	1.7958 5633	1.9012 0749	2.0121 9647	2.1290 9624	12
13	1.8856 4914	2.0057 7390	2.1329 2826	2.2674 8750	13
14	1.9799 3160	2.1160 9146	2.2609 0396	2.4148 7418	14
15	2.0789 2818	2.2324 7649	2.3965 5819	2.5718 4101	15
16	2.1828 7459	2.3552 6270	2.5403 5168	2.7390 1067	16
17	2.2920 1832	2.4848 0215	2.6927 7279	2.9170 4637	17
18	2.4066 1923	2.6214 6627	2.8543 3915	3.1066 5438	18
19	2.5269 5020	2.7656 4691	3.0255 9950	3.3085 8691	19
20	2.6532 9771	2.9177 5749	3.2071 3547	3.5236 4506	20
21	2.7859 6259	3.0782 3415	3.3995 6360	3.7526 8199	21
22	2.9252 6072	3.2475 3703	3.6035 3742	3.9966 0632	22
23	3.0715 2376	3.4261 5157	3.8197 4966	4.2563 8573	23
24	3.2250 9994	3.6145 8990	4.0489 3464	4.5330 5081	24
25	3.3863 5494	3.8133 9235	4.2918 7072	4.8276 9911	25
26	3.5556 7269	4.0231 2893	4.5493 8296	5.1414 9955	26
27	3.7334 5632	4.2444 0102	4.8223 4594	5.4756 9702	27
28	3.9201 2914	4.4778 4307	5.1116 8670	5.8316 1733	28
29	4.1161 3560	4.7241 2444	5.4183 8790	6.2106 7245	29
30	4.3219 4238	4.9839 5129	5.7434 9117	6.6143 6616	30
31	4.5380 3949	5.2580 6861	6.0881 0064	7.0442 9996	31
32	4.7649 4147	5.5472 6238	6.4533 8668	7.5021 7946	32
33	5.0031 8854	5.8523 6181	6.8405 8988	7.9898 2113	33
34	5.2533 4797	6.1742 4171	7.2510 2528	8.5091 5950	34
35	5.5160 1537	6.5138 2501	7.6860 8679	9.0622 5487	35
36	5.7918 1614	6.8720 8538	8.1472 5200	9.6513 0143	36
37	6.0814 0694	7.2500 5008	8.6360 8712	10.2786 3603	37
38	6.3854 7729	7.6488 0283	9.1542 5235	10.9467 4737	38
39	6.7047 5115	8.0694 8699	9.7035 0749	11.6582 8595	39
40	7.0399 8871	8.5133 0877	10.2857 1794	12.4160 7453	40
41	7.3919 8815	8.9815 4076	10.9028 6101	13.2231 1938	41
42	7.7615 8756	9.4755 2550	11.5570 3267	14.0826 2214	42
43	8.1496 6693	9.9966 7940	12.2504 5463	14.9979 9258	43
44	8.5571 5028	10.5464 9677	12.9854 8191	15.9728 6209	44
45	8.9850 0779	11.1265 5409	13.7646 1083	17.0110 9813	45
46	9.4342 5818	11.7385 1456	14.5904 8748	18.1168 1951	46
47	9.9059 7109	12.3841 3287	15.4659 1673	19.2944 1278	47
48	10.4012 6965	13.0652 6017	16.3938 7173	20.5485 4961	48
49	10.9213 3313	13.7838 4948	17.3775 0403	21.8842 0533	49
50	11.4673 9979	14.5419 6120	18.4201 5427	23.3066 7868	50

TABLE III.—Amount of 1 at Compound Interest

$$s = (1 + i)^n$$

n	5%	5½%	6%	6½%	n
51	12.0407 6978	15.3417 6907	19.5253 6353	24.8216 1279	51
52	12.6428 0826	16.1855 6637	20.6968 8534	26.4350 1762	52
53	13.2749 4868	17.0757 7252	21.9386 9846	28.1532 9377	53
54	13.9386 9611	18.0149 4001	23.2550 2037	29.9832 5786	54
55	14.6356 3092	19.0057 6171	24.6503 2159	31.9321 6963	55
56	15.3674 1246	20.0510 7860	26.1293 4089	34.0077 6065	56
57	16.1357 8309	21.1538 8793	27.6971 0134	36.2182 6509	57
58	16.9425 7224	22.3173 5176	29.3589 2742	38.5724 5233	58
59	17.7897 0085	23.5448 0611	31.1204 6307	41.0796 6173	59
60	18.6791 8589	24.8397 7045	32.9876 9085	43.7498 3974	60
61	19.6131 4519	26.2059 5782	34.9669 5230	46.5935 7932	61
62	20.5938 0245	27.6472 8550	37.0649 6944	49.6221 6198	62
63	21.6234 9257	29.1678 8620	39.2888 6761	52.8476 0251	63
64	22.7046 6720	30.7721 1994	41.6461 9967	56.2826 9667	64
65	23.8399 0056	32.4645 8654	44.1449 7165	59.9410 7195	65
66	25.0318 9559	34.2501 3880	46.7936 6994	63.8372 4163	66
67	26.2834 9037	36.1338 9643	49.6012 9014	67.9866 6234	67
68	27.5976 6488	38.1212 6074	52.5773 6755	72.4057 9539	68
69	28.9775 4813	40.2179 3008	55.7320 0960	77.1121 7209	69
70	30.4264 2554	42.4299 1623	59.0759 3018	82.1244 6327	70
71	31.9477 4681	44.7635 6163	62.6204 8599	87.4625 5339	71
72	33.5451 3415	47.2255 5751	66.3777 1515	93.1476 1936	72
73	35.2223 9086	49.8229 6318	70.3603 7806	99.2022 1461	73
74	36.9835 1040	52.5632 2615	74.5820 0074	105.6503 5856	74
75	38.8326 8592	55.4542 0359	79.0569 2079	112.5176 3187	75
76	40.7743 2022	58.5041 8479	83.8003 3603	119.8312 7794	76
77	42.8130 3623	61.7219 1495	88.8283 5620	127.6203 1101	77
78	44.9536 8804	65.1166 2027	94.1580 5757	135.9156 3122	78
79	47.2013 7244	68.6980 3439	99.8075 4102	144.7501 4725	79
80	49.5614 4107	72.4764 2628	105.7959 9348	154.1589 0683	80
81	52.0395 1312	76.4626 2973	112.1437 5309	164.1792 3577	81
82	54.6414 8873	80.6680 7436	118.8723 7828	174.8508 8609	82
83	57.3735 6322	85.1048 1845	126.0047 2097	186.2161 9369	83
84	60.2422 4138	89.7855 8347	133.5650 0423	198.3202 4628	84
85	63.2543 5344	94.7237 9056	141.5789 0449	211.2110 6229	85
86	66.4170 7112	99.9335 9904	150.0736 3875	224.9397 8134	86
87	69.7379 2467	105.4299 4698	159.0780 5708	239.5608 6712	87
88	73.2248 2091	111.2285 9407	168.6227 4050	255.1323 2349	88
89	76.8860 6195	117.3461 6674	178.7401 0493	271.7159 2451	89
90	80.7303 6505	123.8002 0591	189.4645 1123	289.3774 5961	90
91	84.7668 8330	130.6092 1724	200.8323 8190	308.1869 9448	91
92	89.0052 2747	137.7927 2419	212.8823 2482	328.2191 4912	92
93	93.4554 8884	145.3713 2402	225.6552 6431	349.5533 9382	93
94	98.1282 6328	153.3667 4684	239.1945 8017	372.2743 6441	94
95	103.0346 7645	161.8019 1791	253.5462 5498	396.4721 9810	95
96	108.1864 1027	170.7010 2340	268.7590 3028	422.2428 9098	96
97	113.5957 3078	180.0895 7969	284.8845 7209	449.6886 7889	97
98	119.2755 1732	189.9945 0657	301.9776 4642	478.9184 4302	98
99	125.2392 9319	200.4442 0443	320.0963 0520	510.0481 4181	99
100	131.5012 5785	211.4686 3567	339.3020 8351	543.2012 7103	100

TABLE III.—Amount of 1 at Compound Interest

$$s = (1 + i)^n$$

n	7%	7½%	8%	8½%	n
1	1.0700 0000	1.0750 0000	1.0800 0000	1.0850 0000	1
2	1.1449 0000	1.1556 2500	1.1664 0000	1.1772 2500	2
3	1.2250 4300	1.2422 9688	1.2597 1200	1.2772 8913	3
4	1.3107 9601	1.3354 6914	1.3604 8896	1.3858 5870	4
5	1.4025 5173	1.4356 2933	1.4693 2808	1.5036 5669	5
6	1.5007 3035	1.5433 0153	1.5868 7432	1.6314 6751	6
7	1.6057 8148	1.6590 4914	1.7138 2427	1.7701 4225	7
8	1.7181 8618	1.7834 7783	1.8509 3021	1.9206 0434	8
9	1.8384 5921	1.9172 3866	1.9990 0463	2.0838 5571	9
10	1.9671 5136	2.0610 3156	2.1589 2500	2.2609 8344	10
11	2.1048 5195	2.2156 0893	2.3316 3900	2.4531 6703	11
12	2.2521 9159	2.3817 7960	2.5181 7012	2.6616 8623	12
13	2.4098 4500	2.5604 1307	2.7196 2373	2.8879 2956	13
14	2.5785 3415	2.7524 4405	2.9371 9362	3.1334 0357	14
15	2.7590 3154	2.9588 7735	3.1721 6911	3.3997 4288	15
16	2.9521 6375	3.1807 9315	3.4259 4264	3.6887 2102	16
17	3.1588 1521	3.4193 5264	3.7000 1805	4.0022 6231	17
18	3.3799 3228	3.6758 0409	3.9960 1950	4.3424 5461	18
19	3.6165 2754	3.9514 8940	4.3157 0106	4.7115 6325	19
20	3.8696 8446	4.2478 5110	4.6609 5714	5.1120 4612	20
21	4.1405 6237	4.5664 3993	5.0338 3372	5.5465 7005	21
22	4.4304 0174	4.9089 2293	5.4365 4041	6.0180 2850	22
23	4.7405 2986	5.2770 9215	5.8714 6365	6.5295 6092	23
24	5.0723 6695	5.6728 7406	6.3411 8074	7.0845 7360	24
25	5.4274 3264	6.0983 3961	6.8484 7520	7.6867 6236	25
26	5.8073 5292	6.5557 1508	7.3963 5321	8.3401 3716	26
27	6.2138 6763	7.0473 9371	7.9880 6147	9.0490 4881	27
28	6.6488 3836	7.5759 4824	8.6271 0639	9.8182 1796	28
29	7.1142 5705	8.1441 4436	9.3172 7490	10.6527 6649	29
30	7.6122 5504	8.7549 5519	10.0626 5689	11.5582 5164	30
31	8.1451 1290	9.4115 7683	10.8676 6944	12.5407 0303	31
32	8.7152 7080	10.1174 4509	11.7370 8300	13.6066 6279	32
33	9.3253 3975	10.8762 5347	12.6760 4964	14.7632 2913	33
34	9.9781 1354	11.6919 7248	13.6901 3361	16.0181 0360	34
35	10.6765 8148	12.5688 7042	14.7853 4429	17.3796 4241	35
36	11.4239 4219	13.5115 3570	15.9681 7184	18.8569 1201	36
37	12.2236 1814	14.5249 0088	17.2456 2558	20.4597 4953	37
38	13.0792 7141	15.6142 6844	18.6252 7563	22.1988 2824	38
39	13.9948 2041	16.7853 3858	20.1152 9768	24.0857 2865	39
40	14.9744 5784	18.0442 3897	21.7245 2150	26.1330 1558	40
41	16.0226 6989	19.3975 5689	23.4624 8322	28.3543 2190	41
42	17.1442 5678	20.8523 7366	25.3394 8187	30.7644 3927	42
43	18.3443 5475	22.4163 0168	27.3666 4042	33.3794 1660	43
44	19.6284 5959	24.0975 2431	29.5559 7166	36.2166 6702	44
45	21.0024 5176	25.9048 3863	31.9204 4939	39.2950 8371	45
46	22.4726 2338	27.8477 0153	34.4740 8534	42.6351 6583	46
47	24.0457 0702	29.9362 7915	37.2320 1217	46.2591 5492	47
48	25.7289 0651	32.1815 0008	40.2105 7314	50.1911 8309	48
49	27.5299 2997	34.5951 1259	43.4274 1899	54.4574 3365	49
50	29.4570 2506	37.1897 4603	46.9016 1251	59.0863 1551	50

TABLE III.—Amount of 1 at Compound Interest

$$s = (1 + i)^n$$

n	7%	7½%	8%	8½%	n
51	31.5190 1682	39.9789 7698	50.6537 4151	64.1086 5233	51
52	33.7253 4799	42.9774 0026	54.7060 4084	69.5578 8778	52
53	36.0861 2235	46.2007 0528	59.0825 2410	75.4703 0824	53
54	38.6121 5092	49.6657 5817	63.8091 2603	81.8852 8444	54
55	41.3150 0148	53.3906 9004	68.9138 5611	88.8455 3362	55
56	44.2070 5159	57.3949 9179	74.4269 6460	96.3974 0398	56
57	47.3015 4520	61.6996 1617	80.3811 2177	104.5911 8332	57
58	50.6126 5336	66.3270 8739	86.8116 1151	113.4814 3390	58
59	54.1555 3910	71.3016 1894	93.7565 4043	123.1273 5578	59
60	57.9464 2683	76.6492 4036	101.2570 6367	133.5931 8102	60
61	62.0026 7671	82.3979 3339	109.3576 2876	144.9486 0141	61
62	66.3428 6408	88.5777 7839	118.1062 3906	157.2692 3253	62
63	70.9868 6457	95.2211 1177	127.5547 3819	170.6371 1729	63
64	75.9559 4509	102.3626 9515	137.7591 1724	185.1412 7226	64
65	81.2728 6124	110.0398 9729	148.7798 4662	200.8782 8041	65
66	86.9619 6153	118.2928 8959	160.6822 3435	217.9529 3424	66
67	93.0492 9884	127.1648 5631	173.5368 1310	236.4789 3365	67
68	99.5627 4976	136.7022 2053	187.4197 5815	256.5796 4301	68
69	106.5321 4224	146.9548 8707	202.4133 3880	278.3889 1267	69
70	113.9893 9220	157.9765 0360	218.6064 0590	302.0519 7024	70
71	121.9686 4965	169.8247 4137	236.0949 1837	327.7263 8771	71
72	130.5064 5513	182.5615 9697	254.9825 1184	355.5831 3067	72
73	139.6419 0699	196.2537 1675	275.3811 1279	385.8076 9678	73
74	149.4168 4047	210.9727 4550	297.4116 0181	418.6013 5100	74
75	159.8760 1931	226.7957 0141	321.2045 2996	454.1824 6584	75
76	171.0673 4066	243.8053 7902	346.9008 9236	492.7879 7543	76
77	183.0420 5451	262.0907 8245	374.6529 6374	534.6749 5335	77
78	195.8549 9832	281.7475 9113	404.6252 0084	580.1223 2438	78
79	209.5648 4820	302.8786 6046	436.9952 1691	629.4327 2195	79
80	224.2343 8758	325.5945 6000	471.9548 3426	682.9345 0332	80
81	239.9307 9471	350.0141 5200	509.7112 2101	740.9839 3610	81
82	256.7259 5034	376.2652 1340	550.4881 1869	803.9675 7067	82
83	274.6967 6686	404.4851 0440	594.5271 6818	872.3048 1418	83
84	293.9255 4054	434.8214 8723	642.0893 4164	946.4507 2338	84
85	314.5003 2838	467.4330 9878	693.4564 8897	1026.8990 3487	85
86	336.5153 5137	502.4905 8119	748.9330 0808	1114.1854 5283	86
87	360.0714 2596	540.1773 7477	808.8476 4873	1208.8912 1633	87
88	385.2764 2578	580.6906 7788	873.5554 6063	1311.6469 6971	88
89	412.2457 7558	624.2424 7872	943.4398 9748	1423.1369 6214	89
90	441.1029 7988	671.0606 6463	1018.9150 8928	1544.1036 0392	90
91	471.9801 8847	721.3902 1447	1100.4282 9642	1675.3524 1025	91
92	505.0188 0166	775.4944 8056	1188.4625 6013	1817.7573 6512	92
93	540.3701 1778	833.6565 6660	1283.5395 6494	1972.2667 4116	93
94	578.1960 2602	896.1808 0910	1386.2227 3014	2139.9094 1416	94
95	618.6697 4784	963.3943 6978	1497.1205 4855	2321.8017 1436	95
96	661.9766 3019	1035.6489 4751	1616.8901 9244	2519.1548 6008	96
97	708.3149 9430	1113.3226 1858	1746.2414 0783	2733.2830 2319	97
98	757.8970 4390	1196.8218 1497	1885.9407 2046	2965.6120 8016	98
99	810.9498 3698	1286.5834 5109	2036.8159 7809	3217.6891 0698	99
100	867.7163 2557	1383.0772 0993	2199.7612 5634	3491.1926 8107	100

TABLE IV.—Present Value of 1 at Compound Interest

$$v^n = (1 + i)^{-n}$$

n	$\frac{1}{4}\%$	$\frac{7}{24}\%$	$\frac{1}{3}\%$	$\frac{5}{12}\%$	n
1	0.9975 0623	0.9970 9182	0.9966 7774	0.9958 5062	1
2	0.9950 1869	0.9941 9209	0.9933 6652	0.9917 1846	2
3	0.9925 3734	0.9913 0079	0.9900 6630	0.9876 0345	3
4	0.9900 6219	0.9884 1791	0.9867 7704	0.9835 0551	4
5	0.9875 9321	0.9855 4341	0.9834 9871	0.9794 2457	5
6	0.9851 3038	0.9826 7726	0.9802 3127	0.9753 6057	6
7	0.9826 7370	0.9798 1946	0.9769 7469	0.9713 1343	7
8	0.9802 2314	0.9769 6996	0.9737 2893	0.9672 8308	8
9	0.9777 7869	0.9741 2875	0.9704 9395	0.9632 6946	9
10	0.9753 4034	0.9712 9580	0.9672 6972	0.9592 7249	10
11	0.9729 0807	0.9684 7110	0.9640 5620	0.9552 9211	11
12	0.9704 8107	0.9656 5460	0.9608 5335	0.9513 2824	12
13	0.9680 6171	0.9628 4630	0.9576 6115	0.9473 8082	13
14	0.9656 4759	0.9600 4617	0.9544 7955	0.9434 4978	14
15	0.9632 3949	0.9572 5418	0.9513 0852	0.9395 3505	15
16	0.9608 3740	0.9544 7030	0.9481 4803	0.9356 3656	16
17	0.9584 4130	0.9516 9453	0.9449 9803	0.9317 5425	17
18	0.9560 5117	0.9489 2682	0.9418 5851	0.9278 8805	18
19	0.9536 6700	0.9461 6717	0.9387 2941	0.9240 3789	19
20	0.9512 8878	0.9434 1554	0.9356 1071	0.9202 0371	20
21	0.9489 1649	0.9406 7191	0.9325 0236	0.9163 8544	21
22	0.9465 5011	0.9379 3627	0.9294 0435	0.9125 8301	22
23	0.9441 8964	0.9352 0857	0.9263 1663	0.9087 9636	23
24	0.9418 3505	0.9324 8881	0.9232 3916	0.9050 2542	24
25	0.9394 8634	0.9297 7696	0.9201 7192	0.9012 7012	25
26	0.9371 4348	0.9270 7300	0.9171 1487	0.8975 3041	26
27	0.9348 0646	0.9243 7690	0.9140 6798	0.8938 0622	27
28	0.9324 7527	0.9216 8864	0.9110 3121	0.8900 9748	28
29	0.9301 4990	0.9190 0820	0.9080 0453	0.8864 0413	29
30	0.9278 3032	0.9163 3556	0.9049 8790	0.8827 2610	30
31	0.9255 1653	0.9136 7068	0.9019 8130	0.8790 6334	31
32	0.9232 0851	0.9110 1356	0.8989 8468	0.8754 1577	32
33	0.9209 0624	0.9083 6416	0.8959 9802	0.8717 8334	33
34	0.9186 0972	0.9057 2247	0.8930 2128	0.8681 6599	34
35	0.9163 1892	0.9030 8847	0.8900 5444	0.8645 6364	35
36	0.9140 3384	0.9004 6212	0.8870 9745	0.8609 7624	36
37	0.9117 5445	0.8978 4341	0.8841 5028	0.8574 0372	37
38	0.9094 8075	0.8952 3231	0.8812 1290	0.8538 4603	38
39	0.9072 1272	0.8926 2881	0.8782 8528	0.8503 0310	39
40	0.9049 5034	0.8900 3288	0.8753 6739	0.8467 7487	40
41	0.9026 9361	0.8874 4450	0.8724 5920	0.8432 6128	41
42	0.9004 4250	0.8848 6365	0.8695 6066	0.8397 6227	42
43	0.8981 9701	0.8822 9030	0.8666 7175	0.8362 7778	43
44	0.8959 5712	0.8797 2444	0.8637 9245	0.8328 0775	44
45	0.8937 2281	0.8771 6604	0.8609 2270	0.8293 5211	45
46	0.8914 9407	0.8746 1508	0.8580 6249	0.8259 1082	46
47	0.8892 7090	0.8720 7153	0.8552 1179	0.8224 8380	47
48	0.8870 5326	0.8695 3539	0.8523 7055	0.8190 7100	48
49	0.8848 4116	0.8670 0662	0.8495 3876	0.8156 7237	49
50	0.8826 3457	0.8644 8520	0.8467 1637	0.8122 8784	50

TABLE IV.—Present Value of 1 at Compound Interest

$$v^n = (1 + i)^{-n}$$

n	¼%	⁷⁄₂₄%	⅓%	⁵⁄₁₂%	n
51	0.8804 3349	0.8619 7112	0.8439 0336	0.8089 1735	51
52	0.8782 3790	0.8594 6435	0.8410 9969	0.8055 6084	52
53	0.8760 4778	0.8569 6487	0.8383 0534	0.8022 1827	53
54	0.8738 6312	0.8544 7266	0.8355 2027	0.7988 8956	54
55	0.8716 8391	0.8519 8769	0.8327 4446	0.7955 7467	55
56	0.8695 1013	0.8495 0995	0.8299 7787	0.7922 7353	56
57	0.8673 4178	0.8470 3942	0.8272 2047	0.7889 8608	57
58	0.8651 7883	0.8445 7608	0.8244 7222	0.7857 1228	58
59	0.8630 2128	0.8421 1989	0.8217 3311	0.7824 5207	59
60	0.8608 6911	0.8396 7085	0.8190 0310	0.7792 0538	60
61	0.8587 2230	0.8372 2893	0.8162 8216	0.7759 7216	61
62	0.8565 8085	0.8347 9412	0.8135 7026	0.7727 5236	62
63	0.8544 4474	0.8323 6638	0.8108 6737	0.7695 4591	63
64	0.8523 1395	0.8299 4571	0.8081 7346	0.7663 5278	64
65	0.8501 8848	0.8275 3207	0.8054 8850	0.7631 7289	65
66	0.8480 6831	0.8251 2545	0.8028 1246	0.7600 0620	66
67	0.8459 5343	0.8227 2584	0.8001 4531	0.7568 5265	67
68	0.8438 4382	0.8203 3320	0.7974 8702	0.7537 1218	68
69	0.8417 3947	0.8179 4752	0.7948 3756	0.7505 8474	69
70	0.8396 4037	0.8155 6878	0.7921 9690	0.7474 7028	70
71	0.8375 4650	0.8131 9695	0.7895 6502	0.7443 6874	71
72	0.8354 5786	0.8108 3202	0.7869 4188	0.7412 8008	72
73	0.8333 7442	0.8084 7397	0.7843 2745	0.7382 0423	73
74	0.8312 9618	0.8061 2278	0.7817 2171	0.7351 4114	74
75	0.8292 2312	0.8037 7843	0.7791 2463	0.7320 9076	75
76	0.8271 5523	0.8014 4089	0.7765 3618	0.7290 5304	76
77	0.8250 9250	0.7991 1015	0.7739 5632	0.7260 2792	77
78	0.8230 3491	0.7967 8619	0.7713 8504	0.7230 1536	78
79	0.8209 8246	0.7944 6899	0.7688 2230	0.7200 1529	79
80	0.8189 3512	0.7921 5853	0.7662 6807	0.7170 2768	80
81	0.8168 9289	0.7898 5479	0.7637 2233	0.7140 5246	81
82	0.8148 5575	0.7875 5774	0.7611 8505	0.7110 8959	82
83	0.8128 2369	0.7852 6738	0.7586 5619	0.7081 3901	83
84	0.8107 9670	0.7829 8368	0.7561 3574	0.7052 0067	84
85	0.8087 7476	0.7807 0662	0.7536 2366	0.7022 7453	85
86	0.8067 5787	0.7784 3618	0.7511 1993	0.6993 6052	86
87	0.8047 4600	0.7761 7234	0.7486 2451	0.6964 5861	87
88	0.8027 3915	0.7739 1509	0.7461 3739	0.6935 6874	88
89	0.8007 3731	0.7716 6440	0.7436 5853	0.6906 9086	89
90	0.7987 4046	0.7694 2026	0.7411 8790	0.6878 2493	90
91	0.7967 4859	0.7671 8264	0.7387 2548	0.6849 7088	91
92	0.7947 6168	0.7649 5153	0.7362 7125	0.6821 2868	92
93	0.7927 7973	0.7627 2691	0.7338 2516	0.6792 9827	93
94	0.7908 0273	0.7605 0876	0.7313 8720	0.6764 7960	94
95	0.7888 3065	0.7582 9706	0.7289 5735	0.6736 7263	95
96	0.7868 6349	0.7560 9179	0.7265 3556	0.6708 7731	96
97	0.7849 0124	0.7538 9294	0.7241 2182	0.6680 9359	97
98	0.7829 4388	0.7517 0048	0.7217 1610	0.6653 2141	98
99	0.7809 9140	0.7495 1439	0.7193 1837	0.6625 6074	99
100	0.7790 4379	0.7473 3467	0.7169 2861	0.6598 1153	100

TABLE IV.—Present Value of 1 at Compound Interest

$$v^n = (1 + i)^{-n}$$

n	¼%	7⁄24%	⅓%	5⁄12%	n
101	0.7771 0104	0.7451 6128	0.7145 4681	0.6570 7372	101
102	0.7751 6313	0.7429 9421	0.7121 7290	0.6543 4727	102
104	0.7732 3006	0.7408 3345	0.7098 0688	0.6516 3214	103
104	0.7713 0180	0.7386 7897	0.7074 4872	0.6489 2827	104
105	0.7693 7836	0.7365 3075	0.7050 9839	0.6462 3562	105
106	0.7674 5971	0.7343 8879	0.7027 5587	0.6435 5415	106
107	0.7655 4584	0.7322 5305	0.7004 2114	0.6408 8380	107
108	0.7636 3675	0.7301 2352	0.6980 9416	0.6382 2453	108
109	0.7617 3242	0.7280 0019	0.6957 7491	0.6355 7630	109
110	0.7598 3284	0.7258 8303	0.6934 6336	0.6329 3905	110
111	0.7579 3799	0.7237 7203	0.6911 5950	0.6303 1275	111
112	0.7560 4787	0.7216 8718	0.6888 6229	0.6276 9734	112
113	0.7541 6247	0.7195 6842	0.6865 7470	0.6250 9279	113
114	0.7522 8176	0.7174 7578	0.6842 9372	0.6224 9904	114
115	0.7504 0575	0.7153 8923	0.6820 2032	0.6199 1606	115
116	0.7485 3441	0.7133 0875	0.6797 5448	0.6173 4379	116
117	0.7466 6774	0.7112 3431	0.6774 9616	0.6147 8220	117
118	0.7448 0573	0.7091 6591	0.6752 4534	0.6122 3123	118
119	0.7429 4836	0.7071 0353	0.6730 0200	0.6096 9086	119
120	0.7410 9562	0.7050 4714	0.6707 6611	0.6071 6102	120
121	0.7392 4750	0.7029 9673	0.6685 3765	0.6046 4168	121
122	0.7374 0399	0.7009 5229	0.6663 1660	0.6021 3279	122
123	0.7355 6508	0.6989 1379	0.6641 0292	0.5996 3431	123
124	0.7337 3075	0.6968 8122	0.6618 9660	0.5971 4620	124
125	0.7319 0100	0.6948 5456	0.6596 9761	0.5946 6842	125
126	0.7300 7581	0.6928 3379	0.6575 0592	0.5922 0091	126
127	0.7282 5517	0.6908 1890	0.6553 2152	0.5897 4365	127
128	0.7264 3907	0.6888 0988	0.6531 4437	0.5872 9658	128
129	0.7246 2750	0.6868 0669	0.6509 7445	0.5848 5966	129
130	0.7228 2045	0.6848 0933	0.6488 1175	0.5824 3286	130
131	0.7210 1791	0.6828 1778	0.6466 5623	0.5800 1613	131
132	0.7192 1986	0.6808 3202	0.6445 0787	0.5776 0942	132
133	0.7174 2629	0.6788 5203	0.6423 6665	0.5752 1270	133
134	0.7156 3720	0.6768 7780	0.6402 3254	0.5728 2593	134
135	0.7138 5257	0.6749 0932	0.6381 0552	0.5704 4906	135
136	0.7120 7239	0.6729 4656	0.6359 8557	0.5680 8205	136
137	0.7102 9664	0.6709 8950	0.6338 7266	0.5657 2486	137
138	0.7085 2533	0.6690 3814	0.6317 6677	0.5633 7745	138
139	0.7067 5843	0.6670 9246	0.6296 6788	0.5610 3979	139
140	0.7049 9595	0.6651 5243	0.6275 7596	0.5587 1182	140
141	0.7032 3785	0.6632 1804	0.6254 9099	0.5563 9351	141
142	0.7014 8414	0.6612 8928	0.6234 1295	0.5540 8483	142
143	0.6997 3480	0.6593 6613	0.6213 4181	0.5517 8572	143
144	0.6979 8983	0.6574 4857	0.6192 7755	0.5494 9615	144
145	0.6962 4921	0.6555 3659	0.6172 2015	0.5472 1609	145
146	0.6945 1292	0.6536 3017	0.6151 6958	0.5449 4548	146
147	0.6927 8097	0.6517 2929	0.6131 2583	0.5426 8429	147
148	0.6910 5334	0.6498 3394	0.6110 8887	0.5404 3249	148
149	0.6893 3001	0.6479 4410	0.6090 5867	0.5381 9003	149
150	0.6876 1098	0.6460 5976	0.6070 3522	0.5359 5688	150

TABLE IV.—Present Value of 1 at Compound Interest

$$v^n = (1 + i)^{-n}$$

n	¼%	⁷⁄₂₄%	⅜%	⁵⁄₁₂%	n
151	0.6858 9624	0.6441 8090	0.6050 1849	0.5337 3299	151
152	0.6841 8578	0.6423 0750	0.6030 0847	0.5315 1833	152
153	0.6824 7958	0.6404 3956	0.6010 0512	0.5293 1286	153
154	0.6807 7764	0.6385 7704	0.5990 0842	0.5271 1654	154
155	0.6790 7994	0.6367 1994	0.5970 1836	0.5249 2934	155
156	0.6773 8647	0.6348 6824	0.5950 3491	0.5227 5121	156
157	0.6756 9723	0.6330 2193	0.5930 5805	0.5205 8211	157
158	0.6740 1220	0.6311 8098	0.5910 8776	0.5184 2202	158
159	0.6723 3137	0.6293 4539	0.5891 2401	0.5162 7089	159
160	0.6706 5473	0.6275 1514	0.5871 6679	0.5141 2869	160
161	0.6689 8228	0.6256 9021	0.5852 1607	0.5119 9538	161
162	0.6673 1399	0.6238 7058	0.5832 7183	0.5098 7091	162
163	0.6656 4987	0.6220 5625	0.5813 3405	0.5077 5527	163
164	0.6639 8989	0.6202 4720	0.5794 0271	0.5056 4840	164
165	0.6623 3406	0.6184 4341	0.5774 7778	0.5035 5027	165
166	0.6606 8235	0.6166 4486	0.5755 5925	0.5014 6085	166
167	0.6590 3476	0.6148 5154	0.5736 4710	0.4993 8010	167
168	0.6573 9129	0.6130 6344	0.5717 4129	0.4973 0798	168
169	0.6557 5191	0.6112 8054	0.5698 4182	0.4952 4447	169
170	0.6541 1661	0.6095 0282	0.5679 4866	0.4931 8951	170
171	0.6524 8540	0.6077 3027	0.5660 6178	0.4911 4308	171
172	0.6508 5826	0.6059 6288	0.5641 8118	0.4891 0514	172
173	0.6492 3517	0.6042 0063	0.5623 0682	0.4870 7566	173
174	0.6476 1613	0.6024 4350	0.5604 3870	0.4850 5460	174
175	0.6460 0112	0.6006 9149	0.5585 7677	0.4830 4192	175
176	0.6443 9015	0.5989 4456	0.5567 2104	0.4810 3760	176
177	0.6427 8319	0.5972 0272	0.5548 7147	0.4790 4159	177
178	0.6411 8024	0.5954 6595	0.5530 2804	0.4770 5387	178
179	0.6395 8129	0.5937 3422	0.5511 9074	0.4750 7439	179
180	0.6379 8632	0.5920 0753	0.5493 5954	0.4731 0313	180
181	0.6363 9533	0.5902 8586	0.5475 3442	0.4711 4005	181
182	0.6348 0831	0.5885 6920	0.5457 1537	0.4691 8511	182
183	0.6332 2525	0.5868 5754	0.5439 0237	0.4672 3828	183
184	0.6316 4613	0.5851 5085	0.5420 9538	0.4652 9953	184
185	0.6300 7096	0.5834 4912	0.5402 9440	0.4633 6883	185
186	0.6284 9971	0.5817 5234	0.5384 9940	0.4614 4614	186
187	0.6269 3238	0.5800 6050	0.5367 1037	0.4595 3142	187
188	0.6253 6895	0.5783 7357	0.5349 2728	0.4576 2465	188
189	0.6238 0943	0.5766 9156	0.5331 5011	0.4557 2580	189
190	0.6222 5380	0.5750 1443	0.5313 7885	0.4538 3482	190
191	0.6207 0204	0.5733 4218	0.5296 1347	0.4519 5168	191
192	0.6191 5416	0.5716 7480	0.5278 5396	0.4500 7637	192
193	0.6176 1013	0.5700 1226	0.5261 0029	0.4482 0883	193
194	0.6160 6996	0.5683 5456	0.5243 5245	0.4463 4904	194
195	0.6145 3362	0.5667 0168	0.5226 1041	0.4444 9697	195
196	0.6130 0112	0.5650 5361	0.5208 7417	0.4426 5258	196
197	0.6114 7244	0.5634 1033	0.5191 4369	0.4408 1585	197
198	0.6099 4757	0.5617 7183	0.5174 1896	0.4389 8674	198
199	0.6084 2650	0.5601 3809	0.5156 9996	0.4371 6522	199
200	0.6069 0923	0.5585 0911	0.5139 8667	0.4353 5125	200

TABLE IV.—Present Value of 1 at Compound Interest

$$v^n = (1 + i)^{-n}$$

n	½%	⁷⁄₁₂%	⅝%	⅔%	n
1	0.9950 2488	0.9942 0050	0.9937 8882	0.9933 7748	1
2	0.9900 7450	0.9884 3463	0.9876 1622	0.9867 9882	2
3	0.9851 4876	0.9827 0220	0.9814 8196	0.9802 6373	3
4	0.9802 4752	0.9770 0302	0.9753 8580	0.9737 7192	4
5	0.9753 7067	0.9713 3688	0.9693 2750	0.9673 2310	5
6	0.9705 1808	0.9657 0361	0.9633 0683	0.9609 1699	6
7	0.9656 8963	0.9601 0301	0.9573 2356	0.9545 5330	7
8	0.9608 8520	0.9545 3489	0.9513 7745	0.9482 3175	8
9	0.9561 0468	0.9489 9907	0.9454 6827	0.9419 5207	9
10	0.9513 4794	0.9434 9534	0.9395 9580	0.9357 1398	10
11	0.9466 1489	0.9380 2354	0.9337 5980	0.9295 1720	11
12	0.9419 0534	0.9325 8347	0.9279 6005	0.9233 6145	12
13	0.9372 1924	0.9271 7493	0.9221 9008	0.9172 4649	13
14	0.9325 5646	0.9217 9780	0.9164 6840	0.9111 7200	14
15	0.9279 1688	0.9164 5183	0.9107 7604	0.9051 3775	15
16	0.9233 0037	0.9111 3686	0.9051 1905	0.8991 4346	16
17	0.9187 0684	0.9058 5272	0.8994 9719	0.8931 8886	17
18	0.9141 3616	0.9005 9923	0.8939 1025	0.8872 7371	18
19	0.9095 8822	0.8953 7620	0.8883 5802	0.8813 9772	19
20	0.9050 6290	0.8901 8346	0.8828 4027	0.8755 6065	20
21	0.9005 6010	0.8850 2084	0.8773 5679	0.8697 6224	21
22	0.8960 7971	0.8798 8816	0.8719 0736	0.8640 0222	22
23	0.8916 2160	0.8747 8525	0.8664 9179	0.8582 8035	23
24	0.8871 8567	0.8697 1193	0.8611 0985	0.8525 9638	24
25	0.8827 7181	0.8646 6803	0.8557 6135	0.8469 5004	25
26	0.8783 7991	0.8596 5339	0.8504 4606	0.8413 4110	26
27	0.8740 0986	0.8546 6782	0.8451 6378	0.8357 6931	27
28	0.8696 6155	0.8497 1118	0.8399 1432	0.8302 3441	28
29	0.8653 3488	0.8447 8327	0.8346 9746	0.8247 3617	29
30	0.8610 2973	0.8398 8395	0.8295 1300	0.8192 7434	30
31	0.8567 4600	0.8350 1304	0.8243 6075	0.8138 4868	31
32	0.8524 8358	0.8301 7038	0.8192 4050	0.8084 5896	32
33	0.8482 4237	0.8253 5581	0.8141 5205	0.8031 0492	33
34	0.8440 2226	0.8205 6915	0.8090 9520	0.7977 8635	34
35	0.8398 2314	0.8158 1026	0.8040 6976	0.7925 0299	35
36	0.8356 4492	0.8110 7897	0.7990 7554	0.7872 5463	36
37	0.8314 8748	0.8063 7511	0.7941 1234	0.7820 4102	37
38	0.8273 5073	0.8016 9854	0.7891 7997	0.7768 6194	38
39	0.8232 3455	0.7970 4908	0.7842 7823	0.7717 1716	39
40	0.8191 3886	0.7924 2660	0.7794 0693	0.7666 0645	40
41	0.8150 6354	0.7878 3092	0.7745 6590	0.7615 2959	41
42	0.8110 0850	0.7832 6189	0.7697 5493	0.7564 8635	42
43	0.8069 7363	0.7787 1936	0.7649 7384	0.7514 7650	43
44	0.8029 5884	0.7742 0317	0.7602 2245	0.7464 9984	44
45	0.7989 6402	0.7697 1318	0.7555 0057	0.7415 5613	45
46	0.7949 8907	0.7652 4923	0.7508 0802	0.7366 4516	46
47	0.7910 3390	0.7608 1116	0.7461 4462	0.7317 6672	47
48	0.7870 9841	0.7563 9884	0.7415 1018	0.7269 2058	48
49	0.7831 8250	0.7520 1210	0.7369 0453	0.7221 0654	49
50	0.7792 8607	0.7476 5080	0.7323 2748	0.7173 2437	50

TABLE IV.—Present Value of 1 at Compound Interest
$$v^n = (1+i)^{-n}$$

n	½%	⁷⁄₁₂%	⅝%	⅔%	n
51	0.7754 0902	0.7433 1480	0.7277 7886	0.7125 7388	51
52	0.7715 5127	0.7390 0394	0.7232 5849	0.7078 5485	52
53	0.7677 1270	0.7347 1809	0.7187 6620	0.7031 6707	53
54	0.7638 9324	0.7304 5709	0.7143 0182	0.6985 1033	54
55	0.7600 9277	0.7262 2080	0.7098 6516	0.6938 8444	55
56	0.7563 1122	0.7220 0908	0.7054 5606	0.6892 8918	56
57	0.7525 4847	0.7178 2179	0.7010 7434	0.6847 2435	57
58	0.7488 0445	0.7136 5878	0.6967 1985	0.6801 8975	58
59	0.7450 7906	0.7095 1991	0.6923 9239	0.6756 8518	59
60	0.7413 7220	0.7054 0505	0.6880 9182	0.6712 1044	60
61	0.7376 8378	0.7013 1405	0.6838 1796	0.6667 6534	61
62	0.7340 1371	0.6972 4678	0.6795 7064	0.6623 4968	62
63	0.7303 6190	0.6932 0310	0.6753 4970	0.6579 6326	63
64	0.7267 2826	0.6891 8286	0.6711 5499	0.6536 0588	64
65	0.7231 1269	0.6851 8594	0.6669 8632	0.6492 7737	65
66	0.7195 1512	0.6812 1221	0.6628 4355	0.6449 7752	66
67	0.7159 3544	0.6772 6151	0.6587 2651	0.6407 0614	67
68	0.7123 7357	0.6733 3373	0.6546 3504	0.6364 6306	68
69	0.7088 2943	0.6694 2873	0.6505 6898	0.6322 4807	69
70	0.7053 0291	0.6655 4638	0.6465 2818	0.6280 6100	70
71	0.7017 9394	0.6616 8654	0.6425 1248	0.6239 0165	71
72	0.6983 0243	0.6578 4909	0.6385 2172	0.6197 6985	72
73	0.6948 2829	0.6540 3389	0.6345 5574	0.6156 6541	73
74	0.6913 7143	0.6502 4082	0.6306 1440	0.6115 8816	74
75	0.6879 3177	0.6464 6975	0.6266 9754	0.6075 3791	75
76	0.6845 0923	0.6427 2054	0.6228 0501	0.6035 1448	76
77	0.6811 0371	0.6389 9308	0.6189 3666	0.5995 1769	77
78	0.6777 1513	0.6352 8724	0.6150 9233	0.5955 4738	78
79	0.6743 4342	0.6316 0289	0.6112 7188	0.5916 0336	79
80	0.6709 8847	0.6279 3991	0.6074 7516	0.5876 8545	80
81	0.6676 5022	0.6242 9817	0.6037 0203	0.5837 9350	81
82	0.6643 2858	0.6206 7755	0.5999 5232	0.5799 2732	82
83	0.6610 2346	0.6170 7793	0.5962 2591	0.5760 8674	83
84	0.6577 3479	0.6134 9919	0.5925 2264	0.5722 7159	84
85	0.6544 6248	0.6099 4120	0.5888 4238	0.5684 8171	85
86	0.6512 0644	0.6064 0384	0.5851 8497	0.5647 1693	86
87	0.6479 6661	0.6028 8700	0.5815 5028	0.5609 7709	87
88	0.6447 4290	0.5993 9056	0.5779 3817	0.5572 6201	88
89	0.6415 3522	0.5959 1439	0.5743 4849	0.5535 7153	89
90	0.6383 4350	0.5924 5838	0.5707 8111	0.5499 0549	90
91	0.6351 6766	0.5890 2242	0.5672 3589	0.5462 6374	91
92	0.6320 0763	0.5856 0638	0.5637 1268	0.5426 4610	92
93	0.6288 6331	0.5822 1015	0.5602 1136	0.5390 5241	93
94	0.6257 3464	0.5788 3363	0.5567 3179	0.5354 8253	94
95	0.6226 2153	0.5754 7668	0.5532 7383	0.5319 3629	95
96	0.6195 2391	0.5721 3920	0.5498 3734	0.5284 1353	96
97	0.6164 4170	0.5688 2108	0.5464 2220	0.5249 1410	97
98	0.6133 7483	0.5655 2220	0.5430 2828	0.5214 3785	98
99	0.6103 2321	0.5622 4245	0.5396 5543	0.5179 8462	99
100	0.6072 8678	0.5589 8172	0.5363 0353	0.5145 5426	100

TABLE IV.—Present Value of 1 at Compound Interest

$$v^n = (1 + i)^{-n}$$

n	½%	7/12%	⅝%	⅔%	n
101	0.6042 6545	0.5557 3991	0.5329 7246	0.5111 4660	101
102	0.6012 5915	0.5525 1689	0.5296 6207	0.5077 6152	102
103	0.5982 6781	0.5493 1257	0.5263 7225	0.5043 9886	103
104	0.5952 9136	0.5461 2683	0.5231 0285	0.5010 5847	104
105	0.5923 2971	0.5429 5957	0.5198 5377	0.4977 4020	105
106	0.5893 8279	0.5398 1067	0.5166 2486	0.4944 4391	106
107	0.5864 5054	0.5366 8004	0.5134 1601	0.4911 6945	107
108	0.5835 3288	0.5335 6756	0.5102 2709	0.4879 1667	108
109	0.5806 2973	0.5304 7313	0.5070 5798	0.4846 8543	109
110	0.5777 4102	0.5273 9665	0.5039 0855	0.4814 7559	110
111	0.5748 6669	0.5243 3801	0.5007 7868	0.4782 8701	111
112	0.5720 0666	0.5212 9711	0.4976 6823	0.4751 1955	112
113	0.5691 6085	0.5182 7385	0.4945 7715	0.4719 7306	113
114	0.5663 2921	0.5152 6812	0.4915 0524	0.4688 4741	114
115	0.5635 1165	0.5122 7982	0.4884 5242	0.4657 4246	115
116	0.5607 0811	0.5093 0885	0.4854 1855	0.4626 5808	116
117	0.5579 1852	0.5063 5512	0.4824 0353	0.4595 9411	117
118	0.5551 4280	0.5034 1851	0.4794 0723	0.4565 5044	118
119	0.5523 8090	0.5004 9893	0.4764 2955	0.4535 2693	119
120	0.5496 3273	0.4975 9629	0.4734 7036	0.4505 2344	120
121	0.5468 9824	0.4947 1047	0.4705 2955	0.4475 3984	121
122	0.5441 7736	0.4918 4140	0.4676 0700	0.4445 7600	122
123	0.5414 7001	0.4889 8896	0.4647 0261	0.4416 3179	123
124	0.5387 7612	0.4861 5307	0.4618 1626	0.4387 0708	124
125	0.5360 9565	0.4833 3363	0.4589 4784	0.4358 0173	125
126	0.5334 2850	0.4805 3053	0.4560 9723	0.4329 1563	126
127	0.5307 7463	0.4777 4369	0.4532 6433	0.4300 4864	127
128	0.5281 3396	0.4749 7302	0.4504 4902	0.4272 0063	128
129	0.5255 0643	0.4722 1841	0.4476 5120	0.4243 7149	129
130	0.5228 9197	0.4694 7978	0.4448 7076	0.4215 6108	130
131	0.5202 9052	0.4667 5703	0.4421 0759	0.4187 6929	131
132	0.5177 0201	0.4640 5007	0.4393 6158	0.4159 9598	132
133	0.5151 2637	0.4613 5881	0.4366 3262	0.4132 4104	133
134	0.5125 6356	0.4586 8316	0.4339 2062	0.4105 0434	134
135	0.5100 1349	0.4560 2303	0.4312 2546	0.4077 8577	135
136	0.5074 7611	0.4533 7832	0.4285 4704	0.4050 8520	136
137	0.5049 5135	0.4507 4895	0.4258 8526	0.4024 0252	137
138	0.5024 3916	0.4481 3483	0.4232 4001	0.3997 3760	138
139	0.4999 3946	0.4455 3587	0.4206 1119	0.3970 9033	139
140	0.4974 5220	0.4429 5198	0.4179 9870	0.3944 6059	140
141	0.4949 7731	0.4403 8308	0.4154 0243	0.3918 4827	141
142	0.4925 1474	0.4378 2908	0.4128 2229	0.3892 5325	142
143	0.4900 6442	0.4352 8989	0.4102 5818	0.3866 7541	143
144	0.4876 2628	0.4327 6542	0.4077 0999	0.3841 1465	144
145	0.4852 0028	0.4302 5560	0.4051 7763	0.3815 7084	145
146	0.4827 8635	0.4277 6033	0.4026 6100	0.3790 4389	146
147	0.4803 8443	0.4252 7953	0.4001 6000	0.3765 3366	147
148	0.4779 9446	0.4228 1312	0.3976 7453	0.3740 4006	148
149	0.4756 1637	0.4203 6102	0.3952 0451	0.3715 6297	159
150	0.4732 5012	0.4179 2313	0.3927 4982	0.3691 0229	150

TABLE IV.—Present Value of 1 at Compound Interest

$$v^n = (1 + i)^{-n}$$

n	½%	7/12%	⅝%	⅔%	n
151	0.4708 9565	0.4154 9939	0.3903 1038	0.3666 5791	151
152	0.4685 5288	0.4130 8970	0.3878 8609	0.3642 2971	152
153	0.4662 2177	0.4106 9398	0.3854 7686	0.3618 1759	153
154	0.4639 0226	0.4083 1216	0.3830 8259	0.3594 2145	154
155	0.4615 9429	0.4059 4416	0.3807 0320	0.3570 4117	155
156	0.4592 9780	0.4035 8988	0.3783 3858	0.3546 7666	156
157	0.4570 1274	0.4012 4926	0.3759 8865	0.3523 2781	157
158	0.4547 3904	0.3989 2221	0.3736 5332	0.3499 9451	158
159	0.4524 7666	0.3966 0866	0.3713 3249	0.3476 7667	159
160	0.4502 2553	0.3943 0853	0.3690 2608	0.3453 7417	160
161	0.4479 8560	0.3920 2174	0.3667 3399	0.3430 8693	161
162	0.4457 5682	0.3897 4821	0.3644 5614	0.3408 1483	162
163	0.4435 3912	0.3874 8786	0.3621 9244	0.3385 5778	163
164	0.4413 3246	0.3852 4062	0.3599 4280	0.3363 1567	164
165	0.4391 3678	0.3830 0642	0.3577 0713	0.3340 8841	165
166	0.4369 5202	0.3807 8517	0.3554 8534	0.3318 7591	166
167	0.4347 7813	0.3785 7681	0.3532 7736	0.3296 7805	167
168	0.4326 1505	0.3763 8125	0.3510 8309	0.3274 9476	168
169	0.4304 6274	0.3741 9843	0.3489 0245	0.3253 2592	169
170	0.4283 2113	0.3720 2826	0.3467 3535	0.3231 7144	170
171	0.4261 9018	0.3698 7068	0.3445 8172	0.3210 3123	171
172	0.4240 6983	0.3677 2562	0.3424 4146	0.3189 0520	172
173	0.4219 6003	0.3655 9299	0.3403 1449	0.3167 9324	173
174	0.4198 6073	0.3634 7273	0.3382 0074	0.3146 9527	174
175	0.4177 7187	0.3613 6477	0.3361 0011	0.3126 1120	175
176	0.4156 9340	0.3592 6904	0.3340 1254	0.3105 4093	176
177	0.4136 2528	0.3571 8546	0.3319 3792	0.3084 8436	177
178	0.4115 6744	0.3551 1396	0.3298 7620	0.3064 4142	178
179	0.4095 1984	0.3530 5447	0.3278 2728	0.3044 1201	179
180	0.4074 8243	0.3510 0693	0.3257 9108	0.3023 9603	180
181	0.4054 5515	0.3489 7127	0.3237 6754	0.3003 9341	181
182	0.4034 3796	0.3469 4741	0.3217 5656	0.2984 0405	182
183	0.4014 3081	0.3449 3529	0.3197 5807	0.2964 2786	183
184	0.3994 3364	0.3429 3483	0.3177 7199	0.2944 6477	184
185	0.3974 4641	0.3409 4598	0.3157 9825	0.2925 1467	185
186	0.3954 6906	0.3389 6866	0.3138 3677	0.2905 7748	186
187	0.3935 0155	0.3370 0281	0.3118 8748	0.2886 5313	187
188	0.3915 4383	0.3350 4837	0.3099 5029	0.2867 4152	188
189	0.3895 9586	0.3331 0525	0.3080 2513	0.2848 4257	189
190	0.3876 5757	0.3311 7341	0.3061 1193	0.2829 5619	190
191	0.3857 2892	0.3292 5277	0.3042 1062	0.2810 8231	191
192	0.3838 0987	0.3273 4326	0.3023 2111	0.2792 2084	192
193	0.3819 0037	0.3254 4484	0.3004 4334	0.2773 7170	193
194	0.3800 0037	0.3235 5742	0.2985 7723	0.2755 3480	194
195	0.3781 0982	0.3216 8095	0.2967 2271	0.2737 1006	195
196	0.3762 2868	0.3198 1536	0.2948 7972	0.2718 9741	196
197	0.3743 5689	0.3179 6059	0.2930 4816	0.2700 9677	197
198	0.3724 9442	0.3161 1657	0.2912 2799	0.2683 0805	198
199	0.3706 4121	0.3142 8325	0.2894 1912	0.2665 3117	199
200	0.3687 9723	0.3124 6057	0.2876 2149	0.2647 6607	200

TABLE IV.—Present Value of 1 at Compound Interest

$$v^n = (1 + i)^{-n}$$

n	¾%	⅞%	1%	1⅛%	n
1	0.9925 5583	0.9913 2590	0.9900 9901	0.9888 7515	1
2	0.9851 6708	0.9827 2704	0.9802 9605	0.9778 7407	2
3	0.9778 3333	0.9742 0276	0.9705 9015	0.9669 9537	3
4	0.9705 5417	0.9657 5243	0.9609 8034	0.9562 3770	4
5	0.9633 2920	0.9573 7539	0.9514 6569	0.9455 9970	5
6	0.9561 5802	0.9490 7102	0.9420 4524	0.9350 8005	6
7	0.9490 4022	0.9408 3868	0.9327 1805	0.9246 7743	7
8	0.9419 7540	0.9326 7775	0.9234 8322	0.9143 9054	8
9	0.9349 6318	0.9245 8761	0.9143 3982	0.9042 1808	9
10	0.9280 0315	0.9165 6765	0.9052 8695	0.8941 5881	10
11	0.9210 9494	0.9086 1724	0.8963 2372	0.8842 1142	11
12	0.9142 3815	0.9007 3581	0.8874 4923	0.8743 7470	12
13	0.9074 3241	0.8929 2273	0.8786 6260	0.8646 4742	13
14	0.9006 7733	0.8851 7743	0.8699 6297	0.8550 2835	14
15	0.8939 7254	0.8774 9931	0.8613 4947	0.8455 1629	15
16	0.8873 1766	0.8698 8779	0.8528 2126	0.8361 1005	16
17	0.8807 1231	0.8623 4230	0.8443 7749	0.8268 0846	17
18	0.8741 5614	0.8548 6225	0.8360 1731	0.8176 1034	18
19	0.8676 4878	0.8474 4709	0.8277 3992	0.8085 1455	19
20	0.8611 8985	0.8400 9624	0.8195 4447	0.7995 1995	20
21	0.8547 7901	0.8328 0917	0.8114 3017	0.7906 2542	21
22	0.8484 1589	0.8255 8530	0.8033 9621	0.7818 2983	22
23	0.8421 0014	0.8184 2409	0.7954 4179	0.7731 3210	23
24	0.8358 3140	0.8113 2499	0.7875 6613	0.7645 3112	24
25	0.8296 0933	0.8042 8748	0.7797 6844	0.7560 2583	25
26	0.8234 3358	0.7973 1101	0.7720 4796	0.7476 1516	26
27	0.8173 0380	0.7903 9505	0.7644 0392	0.7392 9806	27
28	0.8112 1966	0.7835 3908	0.7568 3557	0.7310 7348	28
29	0.8051 8080	0.7767 4258	0.7493 4215	0.7229 4040	29
30	0.7991 8690	0.7700 0504	0.7419 2292	0.7148 9780	30
31	0.7932 3762	0.7633 2594	0.7345 7715	0.7069 4467	31
32	0.7873 3262	0.7567 0477	0.7273 0411	0.6990 8002	32
33	0.7814 7158	0.7501 4104	0.7201 0307	0.6913 0287	33
34	0.7756 5418	0.7436 3424	0.7129 7334	0.6836 1223	34
35	0.7698 8008	0.7371 8388	0.7059 1420	0.6760 0715	35
36	0.7641 4896	0.7307 8947	0.6989 2495	0.6684 8667	36
37	0.7584 6051	0.7244 5053	0.6920 0490	0.6610 4986	37
38	0.7528 1440	0.7181 6657	0.6851 5337	0.6536 9578	38
39	0.7472 1032	0.7119 3712	0.6783 6967	0.6464 2352	39
40	0.7416 4796	0.7057 6171	0.6716 5314	0.6392 3216	40
41	0.7361 2701	0.6996 3986	0.6650 0311	0.6321 2080	41
42	0.7306 4716	0.6935 7111	0.6584 1892	0.6250 8855	42
43	0.7252 0809	0.6875 5500	0.6518 9992	0.6181 3454	43
44	0.7198 0952	0.6815 9108	0.6454 4546	0.6112 5789	44
45	0.7144 5114	0.6756 7889	0.6390 5492	0.6044 5774	45
46	0.7091 3264	0.6698 1798	0.6327 2764	0.5977 3324	46
47	0.7038 5374	0.6640 0792	0.6264 6301	0.5910 8355	47
48	0.6986 1414	0.6582 4824	0.6202 6041	0.5845 0784	48
49	0.6934 1353	0.6525 3853	0.6141 1921	0.5780 0528	49
50	0.6882 5165	0.6468 7835	0.6080 3882	0.5715 7506	50

TABLE IV.—Present Value of 1 at Compound Interest

$$v^n = (1 + i)^{-n}$$

n	$\frac{3}{4}\%$	$\frac{7}{8}\%$	1%	$1\frac{1}{8}\%$	n
51	0.6831 2819	0.6412 6726	0.6020 1864	0.5652 1637	51
52	0.6780 4286	0.6357 0484	0.5960 5806	0.5589 2843	52
53	0.6729 9540	0.6301 9067	0.5901 5649	0.5527 1044	53
54	0.6679 8551	0.6247 2433	0.5843 1336	0.5465 6162	54
55	0.6630 1291	0.6193 0541	0.5785 2808	0.5404 8120	55
56	0.6580 7733	0.6139 3349	0.5728 0008	0.5344 6843	56
57	0.6531 7849	0.6086 0817	0.5671 2879	0.5285 2256	57
58	0.6483 1612	0.6033 2904	0.5615 1365	0.5226 4282	58
59	0.6434 8995	0.5980 9571	0.5559 5411	0.5168 2850	59
60	0.6386 9970	0.5929 0776	0.5504 4962	0.5110 7887	60
61	0.6339 4511	0.5877 6482	0.5449 9962	0.5053 9319	61
62	0.6292 2592	0.5826 6649	0.5396 0358	0.4997 7077	62
63	0.6245 4185	0.5776 1238	0.5342 6097	0.4942 1090	63
64	0.6198 9266	0.5726 0211	0.5289 7126	0.4887 1288	64
65	0.6152 7807	0.5676 3530	0.5237 3392	0.4832 7602	65
66	0.6106 9784	0.5627 1158	0.5185 4844	0.4778 9965	66
67	0.6061 5170	0.5578 3056	0.5134 1429	0.4725 8309	67
68	0.6016 3940	0.5529 9188	0.5083 3099	0.4673 2568	68
69	0.5971 6070	0.5481 9517	0.5032 9801	0.4621 2675	69
70	0.5927 1533	0.5434 4007	0.4983 1486	0.4569 8566	70
71	0.5883 0306	0.5387 2622	0.4933 8105	0.4519 0177	71
72	0.5839 2363	0.5340 5325	0.4884 9609	0.4468 7443	72
73	0.5795 7681	0.5294 2082	0.4836 5949	0.4419 0302	73
74	0.5752 6234	0.5248 2857	0.4788 7078	0.4369 8692	74
75	0.5709 7999	0.5202 7615	0.4741 2949	0.4321 2551	75
76	0.5667 2952	0.5157 6322	0.4694 3514	0.4273 1818	76
77	0.5625 1069	0.5112 8944	0.4647 8726	0.4225 6433	77
78	0.5583 2326	0.5068 5447	0.4601 8541	0.4178 6337	78
79	0.5541 6701	0.5024 5796	0.4556 2912	0.4132 1470	79
80	0.5500 4170	0.4980 9959	0.4511 1794	0.4086 1775	80
81	0.5459 4710	0.4937 7902	0.4466 5142	0.4040 7194	81
82	0.5418 8297	0.4894 9593	0.4422 2913	0.3995 7670	82
83	0.5378 4911	0.4852 4999	0.4378 5063	0.3951 3148	83
84	0.5338 4527	0.4810 4089	0.4335 1547	0.3907 3570	84
85	0.5298 7123	0.4768 6829	0.4292 2324	0.3863 8882	85
86	0.5259 2678	0.4727 3188	0.4249 7350	0.3820 9031	86
87	0.5220 1169	0.4686 3136	0.4207 6585	0.3778 3961	87
88	0.5181 2575	0.4645 6640	0.4165 9985	0.3736 3621	88
89	0.5142 6873	0.4605 3671	0.4124 7510	0.3694 7956	89
90	0.5104 4043	0.4565 4197	0.4083 9119	0.3653 6916	90
91	0.5066 4063	0.4525 8187	0.4043 4771	0.3613 0448	91
92	0.5028 6911	0.4486 5613	0.4003 4427	0.3572 8503	92
93	0.4991 2567	0.4447 6444	0.3963 8046	0.3533 1029	93
94	0.4954 1009	0.4409 0651	0.3924 5590	0.3493 7976	94
95	0.4917 2217	0.4370 8204	0.3885 7020	0.3454 9297	95
96	0.4880 6171	0.4332 9075	0.3847 2297	0.3416 4941	96
97	0.4844 2850	0.4295 3234	0.3809 1383	0.3378 4861	97
98	0.4808 2233	0.4258 0654	0.3771 4241	0.3340 9010	98
99	0.4772 4301	0.4221 1305	0.3734 0832	0.3303 7340	99
100	0.4736 9033	0.4184 5159	0.3697 1121	0.3266 9805	100

TABLE IV.—Present Value of 1 at Compound Interest

$$v^n = (1 + i)^{-n}$$

n	$1\frac{1}{4}\%$	$1\frac{3}{8}\%$	$1\frac{1}{2}\%$	$1\frac{3}{4}\%$	n
1	0.9876 5432	0.9864 3650	0.9852 2167	0.9828 0098	1
2	0.9754 6106	0.9730 5696	0.9706 6175	0.9658 9777	2
3	0.9634 1833	0.9598 5890	0.9563 1699	0.9492 8528	3
4	0.9515 2428	0.9468 3986	0.9421 8423	0.9329 5851	4
5	0.9397 7706	0.9339 9739	0.9282 6033	0.9169 1254	5
6	0.9281 7488	0.9213 2912	0.9145 4219	0.9011 4254	6
7	0.9167 1593	0.9088 3267	0.9010 2679	0.8856 4378	7
8	0.9053 9845	0.8965 0571	0.8877 1112	0.8704 1157	8
9	0.8942 2069	0.8843 4596	0.8745 9224	0.8554 4135	9
10	0.8831 8093	0.8723 5113	0.8616 6723	0.8407 2860	10
11	0.8722 7746	0.8605 1899	0.8489 3323	0.8262 6889	11
12	0.8615 0860	0.8488 4734	0.8363 8742	0.8120 5788	12
13	0.8508 7269	0.8373 3400	0.8240 2702	0.7980 9128	13
14	0.8403 6809	0.8259 7682	0.8118 4928	0.7843 6490	14
15	0.8299 9318	0.8147 7368	0.7998 5150	0.7708 7459	15
16	0.8197 4635	0.8037 2250	0.7880 3104	0.7576 1631	16
17	0.8096 2602	0.7928 2120	0.7763 8526	0.7445 8605	17
18	0.7996 3064	0.7820 6777	0.7649 1159	0.7317 7990	18
19	0.7897 5866	0.7714 6020	0.7536 0747	0.7191 9401	19
20	0.7800 0855	0.7609 9649	0.7424 7042	0.7068 2458	20
21	0.7703 7881	0.7506 7472	0.7314 9795	0.6946 6789	21
22	0.7608 6796	0.7404 9294	0.7206 8763	0.6827 2028	22
23	0.7514 7453	0.7304 4926	0.7100 3708	0.6709 7817	23
24	0.7421 9707	0.7205 4181	0.6995 4392	0.6594 3800	24
25	0.7330 3414	0.7107 6874	0.6892 0583	0.6480 9632	25
26	0.7239 8434	0.7011 2823	0.6790 2052	0.6369 4970	26
27	0.7150 4626	0.6916 1847	0.6689 8574	0.6259 9479	27
28	0.7062 1853	0.6822 3771	0.6590 9925	0.6152 2829	28
29	0.6974 9978	0.6729 8417	0.6493 5887	0.6046 4697	29
30	0.6888 8867	0.6638 5615	0.6397 6243	0.5942 4764	30
31	0.6803 8387	0.6548 5194	0.6303 0781	0.5840 2716	31
32	0.6719 8407	0.6459 6985	0.6209 9292	0.5739 8247	32
33	0.6636 8797	0.6372 0824	0.6118 1568	0.5641 1053	33
34	0.6554 9429	0.6285 6546	0.6027 7407	0.5544 0839	34
35	0.6474 0177	0.6200 3991	0.5938 6608	0.5448 7311	35
36	0.6394 0916	0.6116 3000	0.5850 8974	0.5355 0183	36
37	0.6315 1522	0.6033 3416	0.5764 4309	0.5262 9172	37
38	0.6237 1873	0.5951 5083	0.5679 2423	0.5172 4002	38
39	0.6160 1850	0.5870 7850	0.5595 3126	0.5083 4400	39
40	0.6084 1334	0.5791 1566	0.5512 6232	0.4996 0098	40
41	0.6009 0206	0.5712 6083	0.5431 1559	0.4910 0834	41
42	0.5934 8352	0.5635 1253	0.5350 8925	0.4825 6348	42
43	0.5861 5656	0.5558 6933	0.5271 8153	0.4742 6386	43
44	0.5789 2006	0.5483 2979	0.5193 9067	0.4661 0699	44
45	0.5717 7290	0.5408 9252	0.5117 1494	0.4580 9040	45
46	0.5647 1397	0.5335 5612	0.5041 5265	0.4502 1170	46
47	0.5577 4219	0.5263 1923	0.4967 0212	0.4424 6850	47
48	0.5508 5649	0.5191 8050	0.4893 6170	0.4348 5848	48
49	0.5440 5579	0.5121 3860	0.4821 2975	0.4273 7934	49
50	0.5373 3905	0.5051 9220	0.4750 0468	0.4200 2883	50

TABLE IV.—Present Value of 1 at Compound Interest

$$v^n = (1 + i)^{-n}$$

n	1¼%	1⅜%	1½%	1¾%	n
51	0.5307 0524	0.4983 4003	0.4679 8491	0.4128 0475	51
52	0.5241 5332	0.4915 8079	0.4610 6887	0.4057 0492	52
53	0.5176 8229	0.4849 1323	0.4542 5505	0.3987 2719	53
54	0.5112 9115	0.4783 3611	0.4475 4192	0.3918 6947	54
55	0.5049 7892	0.4718 4820	0.4409 2800	0.3851 2970	55
56	0.4987 4461	0.4654 4829	0.4344 1182	0.3785 0585	56
57	0.4925 8727	0.4591 3518	0.4279 9194	0.3719 9592	57
58	0.4865 0594	0.4529 0770	0.4216 6694	0.3655 9796	58
59	0.4804 9970	0.4467 6468	0.4154 3541	0.3593 1003	59
60	0.4745 6760	0.4407 0499	0.4092 9597	0.3531 3025	60
61	0.4687 0874	0.4347 2749	0.4032 4726	0.3470 5676	61
62	0.4629 2222	0.4288 3106	0.3972 8794	0.3410 8772	62
63	0.4572 0713	0.4230 1461	0.3914 1669	0.3352 2135	63
64	0.4515 6259	0.4172 7705	0.3856 3221	0.3294 5587	64
65	0.4459 8775	0.4116 1731	0.3799 3321	0.3237 8956	65
66	0.4404 8173	0.4060 3434	0.3743 1843	0.3182 2069	66
67	0.4350 4368	0.4005 2709	0.3687 8663	0.3127 4761	67
68	0.4296 7277	0.3950 9454	0.3633 3658	0.3073 6866	68
69	0.4243 6817	0.3897 3568	0.3579 6708	0.3020 8222	69
70	0.4191 2905	0.3844 4949	0.3526 7692	0.2968 8670	70
71	0.4139 5462	0.3792 3501	0.3474 6495	0.2917 8054	71
72	0.4088 4407	0.3740 9126	0.3423 3000	0.2867 6221	72
73	0.4037 9661	0.3690 1727	0.3372 7093	0.2818 3018	73
74	0.3988 1147	0.3640 1210	0.3322 8663	0.2769 8298	74
75	0.3938 8787	0.3590 7483	0.3273 7599	0.2722 1914	75
76	0.3890 2506	0.3542 0451	0.3225 3793	0.2675 3724	76
77	0.3842 2228	0.3494 0026	0.3177 7136	0.2629 3586	77
78	0.3794 7879	0.3446 6117	0.3130 7523	0.2584 1362	78
79	0.3747 9387	0.3399 8636	0.3084 4850	0.2539 6916	79
80	0.3701 6679	0.3353 7495	0.3038 9015	0.2496 0114	80
81	0.3655 9683	0.3308 2609	0.2993 9916	0.2453 0825	81
82	0.3610 8320	0.3263 3893	0.2949 7454	0.2410 8919	82
83	0.3566 2547	0.3219 1263	0.2906 1531	0.2369 4269	83
84	0.3522 2268	0.3175 4637	0.2863 2050	0.2328 6751	84
85	0.3478 7426	0.3132 3933	0.2820 8917	0.2288 6242	85
86	0.3435 7951	0.3089 9071	0.2779 2036	0.2249 2621	86
87	0.3393 3779	0.3047 9971	0.2738 1316	0.2210 5770	87
88	0.3351 4843	0.3006 6556	0.2697 6666	0.2172 5572	88
89	0.3310 1080	0.2965 8748	0.2657 7997	0.2135 1914	89
90	0.3269 2425	0.2925 6472	0.2618 5218	0.2098 4682	90
91	0.3228 8814	0.2885 9652	0.2579 8245	0.2062 3766	91
92	0.3189 0187	0.2846 8214	0.2541 6990	0.2026 9057	92
93	0.3149 6481	0.2808 2085	0.2504 1369	0.1992 0450	93
94	0.3110 7636	0.2770 1194	0.2467 1300	0.1957 7837	94
95	0.3072 3591	0.2732 5468	0.2430 6699	0.1924 1118	95
96	0.3034 4287	0.2695 4839	0.2394 7487	0.1891 0190	96
97	0.2996 9666	0.2658 9237	0.2359 3583	0.1858 4953	97
98	0.2959 9670	0.2622 8594	0.2324 4909	0.1826 5310	98
99	0.2923 4242	0.2587 2843	0.2290 1389	0.1795 1165	99
100	0.2887 3326	0.2552 1916	0.2256 2944	0.1764 2422	100

TABLE IV.—Present Value of 1 at Compound Interest

$$v^n = (1 + i)^{-n}$$

n	2%	2¼%	2½%	2¾%	n
1	0.9803 9216	0.9779 9511	0.9756 0976	0.9732 3601	1
2	0.9611 6878	0.9564 7444	0.9518 1440	0.9471 8833	2
3	0.9423 2233	0.9354 2732	0.9285 9941	0.9218 3779	3
4	0.9238 4543	0.9148 4335	0.9059 5064	0.8971 6573	4
5	0.9057 3081	0.8947 1232	0.8838 5429	0.8731 5400	5
6	0.8879 7138	0.8750 2427	0.8622 9687	0.8497 8491	6
7	0.8705 6018	0.8557 6946	0.8412 6524	0.8270 4128	7
8	0.8534 9037	0.8369 3835	0.8207 4657	0.8049 0635	8
9	0.8367 5527	0.8185 2161	0.8007 2836	0.7833 6385	9
10	0.8203 4830	0.8005 1013	0.7811 9840	0.7623 9791	10
11	0.8042 6304	0.7828 9499	0.7621 4478	0.7419 9310	11
12	0.7884 9318	0.7656 6748	0.7435 5589	0.7221 3440	12
13	0.7730 3253	0.7488 1905	0.7254 2038	0.7028 0720	13
14	0.7578 7502	0.7323 4137	0.7077 2720	0.6839 9728	14
15	0.7430 1473	0.7162 2628	0.6904 6556	0.6656 9078	15
16	0.7284 4581	0.7004 6580	0.6736 2493	0.6478 7424	16
17	0.7141 6256	0.6850 5212	0.6571 9506	0.6305 3454	17
18	0.7001 5937	0.6699 7763	0.6411 6591	0.6136 5892	18
19	0.6864 3076	0.6552 3484	0.6255 2772	0.5972 3496	19
20	0.6729 7133	0.6408 1647	0.6102 7094	0.5812 5057	20
21	0.6597 7582	0.6267 1538	0.5953 8629	0.5656 9398	21
22	0.6468 3904	0.6129 2457	0.5808 6467	0.5505 5375	22
23	0.6341 5592	0.5994 3724	0.5666 9724	0.5358 1874	23
24	0.6217 2149	0.5862 4668	0.5528 7535	0.5214 7809	24
25	0.6095 3087	0.5733 4639	0.5393 9059	0.5075 2126	25
26	0.5975 7928	0.5607 2997	0.5262 3472	0.4939 3796	26
27	0.5858 6204	0.5483 9117	0.5133 9973	0.4807 1821	27
28	0.5743 7455	0.5363 2388	0.5008 7778	0.4678 5227	28
29	0.5631 1231	0.5245 2213	0.4886 6125	0.4553 3068	29
30	0.5520 7089	0.5129 8008	0.4767 4269	0.4431 4421	30
31	0.5412 4597	0.5016 9201	0.4651 1481	0.4312 8391	31
32	0.5306 3330	0.4906 5233	0.4537 7055	0.4197 4103	32
33	0.5202 2873	0.4798 5558	0.4427 0298	0.4085 0708	33
34	0.5100 2817	0.4692 9641	0.4319 0534	0.3975 7380	34
35	0.5000 2761	0.4589 6960	0.4213 7107	0.3869 3314	35
36	0.4902 2315	0.4488 7002	0.4110 9372	0.3765 7727	36
37	0.4806 1093	0.4389 9268	0.4010 6705	0.3664 9856	37
38	0.4711 8719	0.4293 3270	0.3912 8492	0.3566 8959	38
39	0.4619 4822	0.4198 8528	0.3817 4139	0.3471 4316	39
40	0.4528 9042	0.4106 4575	0.3724 3062	0.3378 5222	40
41	0.4440 1021	0.4016 0954	0.3633 4695	0.3288 0995	41
42	0.4353 0413	0.3927 7216	0.3544 8483	0.3200 0968	42
43	0.4267 6875	0.3841 2925	0.3458 3886	0.3114 4495	43
44	0.4184 0074	0.3756 7653	0.3374 0376	0.3031 0944	44
45	0.4101 9680	0.3674 0981	0.3291 7440	0.2949 9702	45
46	0.4021 5373	0.3593 2500	0.3211 4576	0.2871 0172	46
47	0.3942 6836	0.3514 1809	0.3133 1294	0.2794 1773	47
48	0.3865 3761	0.3436 8518	0.3056 7116	0.2719 3940	48
49	0.3789 5844	0.3361 2242	0.2982 1576	0.2646 6122	49
50	0.3715 2788	0.3287 2608	0.2909 4221	0.2575 7783	50

TABLE IV.—Present Value of 1 at Compound Interest

$$v^n = (1 + i)^{-n}$$

n	2%	2¼%	2½%	2¾%	n
51	0.3642 4302	0.3214 9250	0.2838 4606	0.2506 8402	51
52	0.3571 0100	0.3144 1810	0.2769 2298	0.2439 7471	52
53	0.3500 9902	0.3074 9936	0.2701 6876	0.2374 4497	53
54	0.3432 3433	0.3007 3287	0.2635 7928	0.2310 9000	54
55	0.3365 0425	0.2941 1528	0.2571 5052	0.2249 0511	55
56	0.3299 0613	0.2876 4330	0.2508 7855	0.2188 8575	56
57	0.3234 3738	0.2813 1374	0.2447 5956	0.2130 2749	57
58	0.3170 9547	0.2751 2347	0.2387 8982	0.2073 2603	58
59	0.3108 7791	0.2690 6940	0.2329 6568	0.2017 7716	59
60	0.3047 8227	0.2631 4856	0.2272 8359	0.1963 7679	60
61	0.2988 0614	0.2573 5801	0.2217 4009	0.1911 2097	61
62	0.2929 4720	0.2516 9487	0.2163 3179	0.1860 0581	62
63	0.2872 0314	0.2461 5635	0.2110 5541	0.1810 2755	63
64	0.2815 7170	0.2407 3971	0.2059 0771	0.1761 8253	64
65	0.2760 5069	0.2354 4226	0.2008 8557	0.1714 6718	65
66	0.2706 3793	0.2302 6138	0.1959 8593	0.1668 7804	66
67	0.2653 3130	0.2251 9450	0.1912 0578	0.1624 1172	67
68	0.2601 2873	0.2202 3912	0.1865 4223	0.1580 6493	68
69	0.2550 2817	0.2153 9278	0.1819 9241	0.1538 3448	69
70	0.2500 2761	0.2106 5309	0.1775 5358	0.1497 1726	70
71	0.2451 2511	0.2060 1769	0.1732 2300	0.1457 1023	71
72	0.2403 1874	0.2014 8429	0.1689 9805	0.1418 1044	72
73	0.2356 0661	0.1970 5065	0.1648 7615	0.1380 1503	73
74	0.2309 8687	0.1927 1458	0.1608 5478	0.1343 2119	74
75	0.2264 5771	0.1884 7391	0.1569 3149	0.1307 2622	75
76	0.2220 1737	0.1843 2657	0.1531 0389	0.1272 2747	76
77	0.2176 6408	0.1802 7048	0.1493 6965	0.1238 2235	77
78	0.2133 9616	0.1763 0365	0.1457 2649	0.1205 0837	78
79	0.2092 1192	0.1724 2411	0.1421 7218	0.1172 8309	79
80	0.2051 0973	0.1686 2993	0.1387 0457	0.1141 4412	80
81	0.2010 8797	0.1649 1925	0.1353 2153	0.1110 8917	81
82	0.1971 4507	0.1612 9022	0.1320 2101	0.1081 1598	82
83	0.1932 7948	0.1577 4105	0.1288 0098	0.1052 2237	83
84	0.1894 8968	0.1542 6997	0.1256 5949	0.1024 0620	84
85	0.1857 7420	0.1508 7528	0.1225 9463	0.0996 6540	85
86	0.1821 3157	0.1475 5528	0.1196 0452	0.0969 9795	86
87	0.1785 6036	0.1443 0835	0.1166 8733	0.0944 0190	87
88	0.1750 5918	0.1411 3286	0.1138 4130	0.0918 7533	88
89	0.1716 2665	0.1380 2724	0.1110 6468	0.0894 1638	89
90	0.1682 6142	0.1349 8997	0.1083 5579	0.0870 2324	90
91	0.1649 6217	0.1320 1953	0.1057 1296	0.0846 9415	91
92	0.1617 2762	0.1291 1445	0.1031 3460	0.0824 2740	92
93	0.1585 5649	0.1262 7331	0.1006 1912	0.0802 2131	93
94	0.1554 4754	0.1234 9468	0.0981 6500	0.0780 7427	94
95	0.1523 9955	0.1207 7719	0.0957 7073	0.0759 8469	95
96	0.1494 1132	0.1181 1950	0.0934 3486	0.0739 5104	96
97	0.1464 8169	0.1155 2029	0.0911 5596	0.0719 7181	97
98	0.1436 0950	0.1129 7828	0.0889 3264	0.0700 4556	98
99	0.1407 9363	0.1104 9221	0.0867 6355	0.0681 7086	99
100	0.1380 3297	0.1080 6084	0.0846 4737	0.0663 4634	100

TABLE IV.—Present Value of 1 at Compound Interest

$$v^n = (1 + i)^{-n}$$

n	3%	3½%	4%	4½%	n
1	0.9708 7379	0.9661 8357	0.9615 3846	0.9569 3780	1
2	0.9425 9591	0.9335 1070	0.9245 5621	0.9157 2995	2
3	0.9151 4166	0.9019 4271	0.8889 9636	0.8762 9660	3
4	0.8884 8705	0.8714 4223	0.8548 0419	0.8385 6134	4
5	0.8626 0878	0.8419 7317	0.8219 2711	0.8024 5105	5
6	0.8374 8426	0.8135 0064	0.7903 1453	0.7678 9574	6
7	0.8130 9151	0.7859 9096	0.7599 1781	0.7348 2846	7
8	0.7894 0923	0.7594 1156	0.7306 9021	0.7031 8513	8
9	0.7664 1673	0.7337 3097	0.7025 8674	0.6729 0443	9
10	0.7440 9391	0.7089 1881	0.6755 6417	0.6439 2768	10
11	0.7224 2128	0.6849 4571	0.6495 8093	0.6161 9874	11
12	0.7013 7988	0.6617 8330	0.6245 9705	0.5896 6386	12
13	0.6809 5134	0.6394 0415	0.6005 7409	0.5642 7164	13
14	0.6611 1781	0.6177 8179	0.5774 7508	0.5399 7286	14
15	0.6418 6195	0.5968 9062	0.5552 6450	0.5167 2044	15
16	0.6231 6694	0.5767 0591	0.5339 0818	0.4944 6932	16
17	0.6050 1645	0.5572 0378	0.5133 7325	0.4731 7639	17
18	0.5873 9461	0.5383 6114	0.4936 2812	0.4528 0037	18
19	0.5702 8603	0.5201 5569	0.4746 4242	0.4333 0179	19
20	0.5536 7575	0.5025 6588	0.4563 8695	0.4146 4286	20
21	0.5375 4928	0.4855 7090	0.4388 3360	0.3967 8743	21
22	0.5218 9250	0.4691 5063	0.4219 5539	0.3797 0089	22
23	0.5066 9175	0.4532 8563	0.4057 2633	0.3633 5013	23
24	0.4919 3374	0.4379 5713	0.3901 2147	0.3477 0347	24
25	0.4776 0557	0.4231 4699	0.3751 1680	0.3327 3060	25
26	0.4636 9473	0.4088 3767	0.3606 8923	0.3184 0248	26
27	0.4501 8906	0.3950 1224	0.3468 1657	0.3046 9137	27
28	0.4370 7675	0.3816 5434	0.3334 7747	0.2915 7069	28
29	0.4243 4636	0.3687 4815	0.3206 5141	0.2790 1502	29
30	0.4119 8676	0.3562 7841	0.3083 1867	0.2670 0002	30
31	0.3999 8715	0.3442 3035	0.2964 6026	0.2555 0241	31
32	0.3883 3703	0.3325 8971	0.2850 5794	0.2444 9991	32
33	0.3770 2625	0.3213 4271	0.2740 9417	0.2339 7121	33
34	0.3660 4490	0.3104 7605	0.2635 5209	0.2238 9589	34
35	0.3553 8340	0.2999 7686	0.2534 1547	0.2142 5444	35
36	0.3450 3243	0.2898 3272	0.2436 6872	0.2050 2817	36
37	0.3349 8294	0.2800 3161	0.2342 9685	0.1961 9921	37
38	0.3252 2615	0.2705 6194	0.2252 8543	0.1877 5044	38
39	0.3157 5355	0.2614 1250	0.2166 2061	0.1796 6549	39
40	0.3065 5684	0.2525 7247	0.2082 8904	0.1719 2870	40
41	0.2976 2800	0.2440 3137	0.2002 7793	0.1645 2507	41
42	0.2889 5922	0.2357 7910	0.1925 7493	0.1574 4026	42
43	0.2805 4294	0.2278 0590	0.1851 6820	0.1506 6054	43
44	0.2723 7178	0.2201 0231	0.1780 4635	0.1441 7276	44
45	0.2644 3862	0.2126 5924	0.1711 9841	0.1379 6437	45
46	0.2567 3653	0.2054 6787	0.1646 1386	0.1320 2332	46
47	0.2492 5876	0.1985 1968	0.1582 8256	0.1263 3810	47
48	0.2419 9880	0.1918 0645	0.1521 9476	0.1208 9771	48
49	0.2349 5029	0.1853 2024	0.1463 4112	0.1156 9158	49
50	0.2281 0708	0.1790 5337	0.1407 1262	0.1107 0965	50

TABLE IV.—Present Value of 1 at Compound Interest

$$v^n = (1 + i)^{-n}$$

n	3%	3½%	4%	4½%	n
51	0.2214 6318	0.1729 9843	0.1353 0059	0.1059 4225	51
52	0.2150 1280	0.1671 4824	0.1300 9672	0.1013 8014	52
53	0.2087 5029	0.1614 9589	0.1250 9300	0.0970 1449	53
54	0.2026 7019	0.1560 3467	0.1202 8173	0.0928 3683	54
55	0.1967 6717	0.1507 5814	0.1156 5551	0.0888 3907	55
56	0.1910 3609	0.1456 6004	0.1112 0722	0.0850 1347	56
57	0.1854 7193	0.1407 3433	0.1069 3002	0.0813 5260	57
58	0.1800 6984	0.1359 7520	0.1028 1733	0.0778 4938	58
59	0.1748 2508	0.1313 7701	0.0988 6282	0.0744 9701	59
60	0.1697 3309	0.1269 3431	0.0950 6040	0.0712 8901	60
61	0.1647 8941	0.1226 4184	0.0914 0423	0.0682 1915	61
62	0.1599 8972	0.1184 9453	0.0878 8868	0.0652 8148	62
63	0.1553 2982	0.1144 8747	0.0845 0835	0.0624 7032	63
64	0.1508 0565	0.1106 1591	0.0812 5803	0.0597 8021	64
65	0.1464 1325	0.1068 7528	0.0781 3272	0.0572 0594	65
66	0.1421 4879	0.1032 6114	0.0751 2762	0.0547 4253	66
67	0.1380 0853	0.0997 6922	0.0722 3809	0.0523 8519	67
68	0.1339 8887	0.0963 9538	0.0694 5970	0.0501 2937	68
69	0.1300 8628	0.0931 3563	0.0667 8818	0.0479 7069	69
70	0.1262 9736	0.0899 8612	0.0642 1940	0.0459 0497	70
71	0.1226 1880	0.0869 4311	0.0617 4942	0.0439 2820	71
72	0.1190 4737	0.0840 0300	0.0593 7445	0.0420 3655	72
73	0.1155 7998	0.0811 6232	0.0570 9081	0.0402 2637	73
74	0.1122 1357	0.0784 1770	0.0548 9501	0.0384 9413	74
75	0.1089 4521	0.0757 6590	0.0527 8367	0.0368 3649	75
76	0.1057 7205	0.0732 0376	0.0507 5353	0.0352 5023	76
77	0.1026 9131	0.0707 2827	0.0488 0147	0.0337 3228	77
78	0.0997 0030	0.0683 3650	0.0469 2449	0.0322 7969	78
79	0.0967 9641	0.0660 2560	0.0451 1970	0.0308 8965	79
80	0.0939 7710	0.0637 9285	0.0433 8433	0.0295 5948	80
81	0.0912 3990	0.0616 3561	0.0417 1570	0.0282 8658	81
82	0.0885 8243	0.0595 5131	0.0401 1125	0.0270 6850	82
83	0.0860 0236	0.0575 3750	0.0385 6851	0.0259 0287	83
84	0.0834 9743	0.0555 9178	0.0370 8510	0.0247 8744	84
85	0.0810 6547	0.0537 1187	0.0356 5875	0.0237 2003	85
86	0.0787 0434	0.0518 9553	0.0342 8726	0.0226 9860	86
87	0.0764 1198	0.0501 4060	0.0329 6852	0.0217 2115	87
88	0.0741 8639	0.0484 4503	0.0317 0050	0.0207 8579	88
89	0.0720 2562	0.0468 0679	0.0304 8125	0.0198 9070	89
90	0.0699 2779	0.0452 2395	0.0293 0890	0.0190 3417	90
91	0.0678 9105	0.0436 9464	0.0281 8163	0.0182 1451	91
92	0.0659 1364	0.0422 1704	0.0270 9772	0.0174 3016	92
93	0.0639 9383	0.0407 8941	0.0260 5550	0.0166 7958	93
94	0.0621 2993	0.0394 1006	0.0250 5337	0.0159 6132	94
95	0.0603 2032	0.0380 7735	0.0240 8978	0.0152 7399	95
96	0.0585 6342	0.0367 8971	0.0231 6325	0.0146 1626	96
97	0.0568 5769	0.0355 4562	0.0222 7235	0.0139 8685	97
98	0.0552 0164	0.0343 4359	0.0214 1572	0.0133 8454	98
99	0.0535 9383	0.0331 8221	0.0205 9204	0.0128 0817	99
100	0.0520 3284	0.0320 6011	0.0198 0004	0.0122 5663	100

TABLE IV.—Present Value of 1 at Compound Interest

$$v^n = (1 + i)^{-n}$$

n	5%	5½%	6%	6½%	n
1	0.9523 8095	0.9478 6730	0.9433 9623	0.9389 6714	1
2	0.9070 2948	0.8984 5242	0.8899 9644	0.8816 5928	2
3	0.8638 3760	0.8516 1366	0.8396 1928	0.8278 4909	3
4	0.8227 0247	0.8072 1674	0.7920 9366	0.7773 2309	4
5	0.7835 2617	0.7651 3435	0.7472 5817	0.7298 8084	5
6	0.7462 1540	0.7252 4583	0.7049 6054	0.6853 3412	6
7	0.7106 8133	0.6874 3681	0.6650 5711	0.6435 0621	7
8	0.6768 3936	0.6515 9887	0.6274 1237	0.6042 3119	8
9	0.6446 0892	0.6176 2926	0.5918 9846	0.5673 5323	9
10	0.6139 1325	0.5854 3058	0.5583 9478	0.5327 2004	10
11	0.5846 7929	0.5549 1050	0.5267 8753	0.5002 1224	11
12	0.5568 3742	0.5259 8152	0.4969 6936	0.4696 8285	12
13	0.5303 2135	0.4985 6068	0.4688 3902	0.4410 1676	13
14	0.5050 6795	0.4725 6937	0.4423 0096	0.4141 0025	14
15	0.4810 1710	0.4479 3305	0.4172 6506	0.3888 2652	15
16	0.4581 1152	0.4245 8109	0.3936 4628	0.3650 9533	16
17	0.4362 9669	0.4024 4653	0.3713 6442	0.3428 1251	17
18	0.4155 2065	0.3814 6590	0.3503 4379	0.3218 8969	18
19	0.3957 3396	0.3615 7906	0.3305 1301	0.3022 4384	19
20	0.3768 8948	0.3427 2896	0.3118 0473	0.2837 9703	20
21	0.3589 4236	0.3248 6158	0.2941 5540	0.2664 7608	21
22	0.3418 4987	0.3079 2567	0.2775 0510	0.2502 1228	22
23	0.3255 7131	0.2918 7267	0.2617 9726	0.2349 4111	23
24	0.3100 6791	0.2766 5656	0.2469 7855	0.2206 0198	24
25	0.2953 0277	0.2622 3370	0.2329 9863	0.2071 3801	25
26	0.2812 4073	0.2485 6275	0.2198 1003	0.1944 9579	26
27	0.2678 4832	0.2356 0450	0.2073 6795	0.1826 2515	27
28	0.2550 9364	0.2233 2181	0.1956 3014	0.1714 7902	28
29	0.2429 4632	0.2116 7944	0.1845 5674	0.1610 1316	29
30	0.2313 7745	0.2006 4402	0.1741 1013	0.1511 8607	30
31	0.2203 5947	0.1901 8390	0.1642 5484	0.1419 5875	31
32	0.2098 6617	0.1802 6910	0.1549 5740	0.1332 9460	32
33	0.1998 7254	0.1708 7119	0.1461 8622	0.1251 5925	33
34	0.1903 5480	0.1619 6321	0.1379 1153	0.1175 2042	34
35	0.1812 9029	0.1535 1963	0.1301 0522	0.1103 4781	35
36	0.1726 5741	0.1455 1624	0.1227 4077	0.1036 1297	36
37	0.1644 3563	0.1379 3008	0.1157 9318	0.0972 8917	37
38	0.1566 0536	0.1307 3941	0.1092 3885	0.0913 5134	38
39	0.1491 4797	0.1239 2362	0.1030 5552	0.0857 7590	39
40	0.1420 4568	0.1174 6314	0.0972 2219	0.0805 4075	40
41	0.1352 8160	0.1113 3947	0.0917 1905	0.0756 2512	41
42	0.1288 3962	0.1055 3504	0.0865 2740	0.0710 0950	42
43	0.1227 0440	0.1000 3322	0.0816 2962	0.0666 7559	43
44	0.1168 6133	0.0948 1822	0.0770 0908	0.0626 0619	44
45	0.1112 9651	0.0898 7509	0.0726 5007	0.0587 8515	45
46	0.1059 9668	0.0851 8965	0.0685 3781	0.0551 9733	46
47	0.1009 4921	0.0807 4849	0.0646 5831	0.0518 2848	47
48	0.0961 4211	0.0765 3885	0.0609 9840	0.0486 6524	48
49	0.0915 6391	0.0725 4867	0.0575 4566	0.0456 9506	49
50	0.0872 0373	0.0687 6652	0.0542 8836	0.0429 0616	50

TABLE IV.—Present Value of 1 at Compound Interest

$$v^n = (1 + i)^{-n}$$

n	5%	5½%	6%	6½%	n
51	0.0830 5117	0.0651 8153	0.0512 1544	0.0402 8747	51
52	0.0790 9635	0.0617 8344	0.0483 1645	0.0378 2861	52
53	0.0753 2986	0.0585 6250	0.0455 8156	0.0355 1982	53
54	0.0717 4272	0.0555 0948	0.0430 0147	0.0333 5195	54
55	0.0683 2640	0.0526 1562	0.0405 6742	0.0313 1638	55
56	0.0650 7276	0.0498 7263	0.0382 7115	0.0294 0505	56
57	0.0619 7406	0.0472 7263	0.0361 0486	0.0276 1038	57
58	0.0590 2291	0.0448 0818	0.0340 6119	0.0259 2524	58
59	0.0562 1230	0.0424 7221	0.0321 3320	0.0243 4295	59
60	0.0535 3552	0.0402 5802	0.0303 1434	0.0228 5723	60
61	0.0509 8621	0.0381 5926	0.0285 9843	0.0214 6218	61
62	0.0485 5830	0.0361 6992	0.0269 7965	0.0201 5229	62
63	0.0462 4600	0.0342 8428	0.0254 5250	0.0189 2233	63
64	0.0440 4381	0.0324 9695	0.0240 1179	0.0177 6745	64
65	0.0419 4648	0.0308 0279	0.0226 5264	0.0166 8305	65
66	0.0399 4903	0.0291 9696	0.0213 7041	0.0156 6484	66
67	0.0380 4670	0.0276 7485	0.0201 6077	0.0147 0877	67
68	0.0362 3495	0.0262 3208	0.0190 1959	0.0138 1105	68
69	0.0345 0948	0.0248 6453	0.0179 4301	0.0129 6812	69
70	0.0328 6617	0.0235 6828	0.0169 2737	0.0121 7664	70
71	0.0313 0111	0.0223 3960	0.0159 6921	0.0114 3346	71
72	0.0298 1058	0.0211 7498	0.0150 6530	0.0107 3565	72
73	0.0283 9103	0.0200 7107	0.0142 1254	0.0100 8042	73
74	0.0270 3908	0.0190 2471	0.0134 0806	0.0094 6518	74
75	0.0257 5150	0.0180 3290	0.0126 4911	0.0088 8750	75
76	0.0245 2524	0.0170 9279	0.0119 3313	0.0083 4507	76
77	0.0233 5737	0.0162 0170	0.0112 5767	0.0078 3574	77
78	0.0222 4512	0.0153 5706	0.0106 2044	0.0073 5751	78
79	0.0211 8582	0.0145 5646	0.0100 1928	0.0069 0846	79
80	0.0201 7698	0.0137 9759	0.0094 5215	0.0064 8681	80
81	0.0192 1617	0.0130 7828	0.0089 1713	0.0060 9090	81
82	0.0183 0111	0.0123 9648	0.0084 1238	0.0057 1916	82
83	0.0174 2963	0.0117 5022	0.0079 3621	0.0053 7010	83
84	0.0165 9965	0.0111 3765	0.0074 8699	0.0050 4235	84
85	0.0158 0919	0.0105 5701	0.0070 6320	0.0047 3460	85
86	0.0150 5637	0.0100 0664	0.0066 6340	0.0044 4563	86
87	0.0143 3940	0.0094 8497	0.0062 8622	0.0041 7430	87
88	0.0136 5657	0.0089 9049	0.0059 3040	0.0039 1953	88
89	0.0130 0626	0.0085 2180	0.0055 9472	0.0036 8031	89
90	0.0123 8691	0.0080 7753	0.0052 7803	0.0034 5569	90
91	0.0117 9706	0.0076 5643	0.0049 7928	0.0032 4478	91
92	0.0112 3530	0.0072 5728	0.0046 9743	0.0030 4674	92
93	0.0107 0028	0.0068 7894	0.0044 3154	0.0028 6079	93
94	0.0101 9074	0.0065 2032	0.0041 8070	0.0026 8619	94
95	0.0097 0547	0.0061 8040	0.0039 4405	0.0025 2224	95
96	0.0092 4331	0.0058 5820	0.0037 2081	0.0023 6831	96
97	0.0088 0315	0.0055 5279	0.0035 1019	0.0022 2376	97
98	0.0083 8395	0.0052 6331	0.0033 1150	0.0020 8804	98
99	0.0079 8471	0.0049 8892	0.0031 2406	0.0019 6060	99
100	0.0076 0449	0.0047 2883	0.0029 4723	0.0018 4094	100

TABLE IV.—Present Value of 1 at Compound Interest

$$v^n = (1 + i)^{-n}$$

n	7%	7½%	8%	8½%	n
1	0.9345 7944	0.9302 3256	0.9259 2593	0.9216 5899	1
2	0.8734 3873	0.8653 3261	0.8573 3882	0.8494 5529	2
3	0.8162 9788	0.8049 6057	0.7938 3224	0.7829 0810	3
4	0.7628 9521	0.7488 0053	0.7350 2985	0.7215 7428	4
5	0.7129 8618	0.6965 5863	0.6805 8320	0.6650 4542	5
6	0.6663 4222	0.6479 6152	0.6301 6963	0.6129 4509	6
7	0.6227 4974	0.6027 5490	0.5834 9040	0.5649 2635	7
8	0.5820 0910	0.5607 0223	0.5402 6888	0.5206 6945	8
9	0.5439 3374	0.5215 8347	0.5002 4897	0.4798 7968	9
10	0.5083 4929	0.4851 9393	0.4631 9349	0.4422 8542	10
11	0.4750 9280	0.4513 4319	0.4288 8286	0.4076 3633	11
12	0.4440 1196	0.4198 5413	0.3971 1376	0.3757 0168	12
13	0.4149 6445	0.3905 6198	0.3676 9792	0.3462 6883	13
14	0.3878 1724	0.3633 1347	0.3404 6104	0.3191 4178	14
15	0.3624 4602	0.3379 6602	0.3152 4170	0.2941 3989	15
16	0.3387 3460	0.3143 8699	0.2918 9047	0.2710 9667	16
17	0.3165 7439	0.2924 5302	0.2702 6895	0.2498 5869	17
18	0.2958 6392	0.2720 4932	0.2502 4903	0.2302 8450	18
19	0.2765 0832	0.2530 6913	0.2317 1206	0.2122 4378	19
20	0.2584 1900	0.2354 1315	0.2145 4821	0.1956 1639	20
21	0.2415 1309	0.2189 8897	0.1986 5575	0.1802 9160	21
22	0.2257 1317	0.2037 1067	0.1839 4051	0.1661 6738	22
23	0.2109 4688	0.1894 9830	0.1703 1528	0.1531 4965	23
24	0.1971 4662	0.1762 7749	0.1576 9934	0.1411 5176	24
25	0.1842 4918	0.1639 7906	0.1460 1790	0.1300 9378	25
26	0.1721 9549	0.1525 3866	0.1352 0176	0.1199 0210	26
27	0.1609 3037	0.1418 9643	0.1251 8682	0.1105 0885	27
28	0.1504 0221	0.1319 9668	0.1159 1372	0.1018 5148	28
29	0.1405 6282	0.1227 8761	0.1073 2752	0.0938 7233	29
30	0.1313 6712	0.1142 2103	0.0993 7733	0.0865 1828	30
31	0.1227 7301	0.1062 5212	0.0920 1605	0.0797 4035	31
32	0.1147 4113	0.0988 3918	0.0852 0005	0.0734 9341	32
33	0.1072 3470	0.0919 4343	0.0788 8893	0.0677 3586	33
34	0.1002 1934	0.0855 2877	0.0730 4531	0.0624 2936	34
35	0.0936 6294	0.0795 6164	0.0676 3454	0.0575 3858	35
36	0.0875 3546	0.0740 1083	0.0626 2458	0.0530 3095	36
37	0.0818 0884	0.0688 4729	0.0579 8572	0.0488 7645	37
38	0.0764 5686	0.0640 4399	0.0536 9048	0.0450 4742	38
39	0.0714 5501	0.0595 7580	0.0497 1341	0.0415 1836	39
40	0.0667 8038	0.0554 1935	0.0460 3093	0.0382 6577	40
41	0.0624 1157	0.0515 5288	0.0426 2123	0.0352 6799	41
42	0.0583 2857	0.0479 5617	0.0394 6411	0.0325 0506	42
43	0.0545 1268	0.0446 1039	0.0365 4084	0.0299 5858	43
44	0.0509 4643	0.0414 9804	0.0338 3411	0.0276 1160	44
45	0.0476 1349	0.0386 0283	0.0313 2788	0.0254 4848	45
46	0.0444 9859	0.0359 0961	0.0290 0730	0.0234 5482	46
47	0.0415 8747	0.0334 0428	0.0268 5861	0.0216 1734	47
48	0.0388 6679	0.0310 7375	0.0248 6908	0.0199 2382	48
49	0.0363 2410	0.0289 0582	0.0230 2693	0.0183 6297	49
50	0.0339 4776	0.0268 8913	0.0213 2123	0.0169 2439	50

TABLE IV.—Present Value of 1 at Compound Interest

$$v^n = (1 + i)^{-n}$$

n	7%	7½%	8%	8½%	n
51	0.0317 2688	0.0250 1315	0.0197 4188	0.0155 9852	51
52	0.0296 5129	0.0232 6804	0.0182 7952	0.0143 7651	52
53	0.0277 1148	0.0216 4469	0.0169 2548	0.0132 5024	53
54	0.0258 9858	0.0201 3460	0.0156 7174	0.0122 1221	54
55	0.0242 0428	0.0187 2986	0.0145 1087	0.0112 5549	55
56	0.0226 2083	0.0174 2312	0.0134 3599	0.0103 7372	56
57	0.0211 4096	0.0162 0756	0.0124 4073	0.0095 6104	57
58	0.0197 5791	0.0150 7680	0.0115 1920	0.0088 1201	58
59	0.0184 6533	0.0140 2493	0.0106 6592	0.0081 2167	59
60	0.0172 5732	0.0130 4644	0.0098 7585	0.0074 8541	60
61	0.0161 2834	0.0121 3623	0.0091 4431	0.0068 9900	61
62	0.0150 7321	0.0112 8951	0.0084 6695	0.0063 5852	62
63	0.0140 8711	0.0105 0187	0.0078 3977	0.0058 6039	63
64	0.0131 6553	0.0097 6918	0.0072 5905	0.0054 0128	64
65	0.0123 0423	0.0090 8761	0.0067 2134	0.0049 7814	65
66	0.0114 9928	0.0084 5359	0.0062 2346	0.0045 8815	66
67	0.0107 4699	0.0078 6381	0.0057 6247	0.0042 2871	67
68	0.0100 4392	0.0073 1517	0.0053 3562	0.0038 9743	68
69	0.0093 8684	0.0068 0481	0.0049 4039	0.0035 9210	69
70	0.0087 7275	0.0063 3006	0.0045 7443	0.0033 1069	70
71	0.0081 9883	0.0058 8842	0.0042 3558	0.0030 5133	71
72	0.0076 6246	0.0054 7760	0.0039 2184	0.0028 1228	72
73	0.0071 6117	0.0050 9544	0.0036 3133	0.0025 9196	73
74	0.0066 9269	0.0047 3995	0.0033 6234	0.0023 8891	74
75	0.0062 5485	0.0044 0925	0.0031 1328	0.0022 0176	75
76	0.0058 4565	0.0041 0163	0.0028 8267	0.0020 2927	76
77	0.0054 6323	0.0038 1547	0.0026 6914	0.0018 7030	77
78	0.0051 0582	0.0035 4928	0.0024 7142	0.0017 2377	78
79	0.0047 7179	0.0033 0165	0.0022 8835	0.0015 8873	79
80	0.0044 5962	0.0030 7130	0.0021 1885	0.0014 6427	80
81	0.0041 6787	0.0028 5703	0.0019 6190	0.0013 4956	81
82	0.0038 9520	0.0026 5770	0.0018 1657	0.0012 4383	82
83	0.0036 4038	0.0024 7228	0.0016 8201	0.0011 4639	83
84	0.0034 0222	0.0022 9979	0.0015 5742	0.0010 5658	84
85	0.0031 7965	0.0021 3934	0.0014 4205	0.0009 7381	85
86	0.0029 7163	0.0019 9009	0.0013 3523	0.0008 9752	86
87	0.0027 7723	0.0018 5124	0.0012 3633	0.0008 2720	87
88	0.0025 9554	0.0017 2209	0.0011 4475	0.0007 6240	88
89	0.0024 2574	0.0016 0194	0.0010 5995	0.0007 0267	89
90	0.0022 6704	0.0014 9018	0.0009 8144	0.0006 4762	90
91	0.0021 1873	0.0013 8621	0.0009 0874	0.0005 9689	91
92	0.0019 8012	0.0012 8950	0.0008 4142	0.0005 5013	92
93	0.0018 5058	0.0011 9953	0.0007 7910	0.0005 0703	93
94	0.0017 2952	0.0011 1585	0.0007 2138	0.0004 6731	94
95	0.0016 1637	0.0010 3800	0.0006 6795	0.0004 3070	95
96	0.0015 1063	0.0009 6558	0.0006 1847	0.0003 9696	96
97	0.0014 1180	0.0008 9821	0.0005 7266	0.0003 6586	97
98	0.0013 1944	0.0008 3555	0.0005 3024	0.0003 3720	98
99	0.0012 3312	0.0007 7725	0.0004 9096	0.0003 1078	99
100	0.0011 5245	0.0007 2303	0.0004 5459	0.0002 8644	100

TABLE V.—Amount of Annuity of 1 per Period

$$s_{\overline{n}|i} = \frac{(1+i)^n - 1}{i}$$

n	$\frac{1}{4}\%$	$\frac{7}{24}\%$	$\frac{1}{3}\%$	$\frac{5}{12}\%$	n
1	1.0000 0000	1.0000 0000	1.0000 0000	1.0000 0000	1
2	2.0025 0000	2.0029 1667	2.0033 3333	2.0041 6667	2
3	3.0075 0625	3.0087 5851	3.0100 1111	3.0125 1736	3
4	4.0150 2502	4.0175 3405	4.0200 4448	4.0250 6952	4
5	5.0250 6258	5.0292 5186	5.0334 4463	5.0418 4064	5
6	6.0376 2523	6.0439 2051	6.0502 2278	6.0628 4831	6
7	7.0527 1930	7.0615 4861	7.0703 9019	7.0881 1018	7
8	8.0703 5110	8.0821 4480	8.0939 5816	8.1176 4397	8
9	9.0905 2697	9.1057 1772	9.1209 3802	9.1514 6749	9
10	10.1132 5329	10.1322 7606	10.1513 4114	10.1895 9860	10
11	11.1383 3042	11.1618 2833	11.1851 7889	11.2320 5683	11
12	12.1663 8277	12.1943 8387	12.2224 6288	12.2788 5549	12
13	13.1967 9872	13.2299 5082	13.2632 0442	13.3300 1739	13
14	14.2297 9072	14.2685 3818	14.3074 1510	14.3855 5913	14
15	15.2653 6520	15.3101 5475	15.3551 0648	15.4454 9896	15
16	16.3035 2861	16.3548 0936	16.4062 9017	16.5098 5520	16
17	17.3442 8743	17.4025 1089	17.4609 7781	17.5786 4627	17
18	18.3876 4815	18.4532 6822	18.5191 8107	18.6518 9063	18
19	19.4336 1727	19.5070 9025	19.5809 1167	19.7296 0684	19
20	20.4822 0131	20.5639 8593	20.6461 8137	20.8118 1353	20
21	21.5334 0682	21.6239 6422	21.7150 0198	21.8985 2942	21
22	22.5872 4033	22.6870 3412	22.7873 8532	22.9897 7330	22
23	23.6437 0843	23.7532 0463	23.8633 4327	24.0855 6402	23
24	24.7028 1770	24.8224 8481	24.9428 8775	25.1859 2054	24
25	25.7645 7475	25.8948 8373	26.0260 3071	26.2908 6187	25
26	26.8289 8619	26.9704 1047	27.1127 8414	27.4004 0713	26
27	27.8960 5865	28.0490 7417	28.2031 6009	28.5145 7549	27
28	28.9657 9880	29.1308 8397	29.2971 7062	29.6333 8622	28
29	30.0382 1330	30.2158 4904	30.3948 2786	30.7568 5867	29
30	31.1133 0883	31.3039 7860	31.4961 4395	31.8850 1224	30
31	32.1910 9210	32.3952 8188	32.6011 3110	33.0178 6646	31
32	33.2715 6983	33.4897 6811	33.7098 0154	34.1554 4090	32
33	34.3547 4876	34.5874 4660	34.8221 6754	35.2977 5524	33
34	35.4406 3563	35.6883 2666	35.9382 4143	36.4448 2922	34
35	36.5292 3722	36.7924 1761	37.0580 3557	37.5966 8268	35
36	37.6205 6031	37.8997 2883	38.1815 6236	38.7533 3552	36
37	38.7146 1171	39.0102 6970	39.3088 3423	39.9148 0775	37
38	39.8113 9024	40.1240 4966	40.4390 6368	41.0811 1945	38
39	40.9109 2673	41.2410 7813	41.5746 6322	42.2522 9078	39
40	42.0132 0405	42.3613 6461	42.7132 4543	43.4283 4199	40
41	43.1182 3706	43.4849 1859	43.8556 2292	44.6092 9342	41
42	44.2260 3265	44.6117 4961	45.0018 0833	45.7951 6548	42
43	45.3365 9774	45.7418 6721	46.1518 1436	46.9859 7866	43
44	46.4499 3923	46.8752 8099	47.3056 5374	48.1817 5358	44
45	47.5660 6408	48.0120 0056	48.4633 3925	49.3825 1088	45
46	48.6849 7924	49.1520 3556	49.6248 8371	50.5882 7134	46
47	49.8066 9169	50.2953 9566	50.7902 9999	51.7990 5581	47
48	50.9312 0842	51.4420 9057	51.9596 0099	53.0148 8521	48
49	52.0585 3644	52.5921 3000	53.1327 9966	54.2357 8056	49
50	53.1886 8278	53.7455 2371	54.3099 0899	55.4617 6298	50

TABLE V.—Amount of Annuity of 1 per Period

$$s_{\overline{n}|i} = \frac{(1 + i)^n - 1}{i}$$

n	$\frac{1}{4}\%$	$\frac{7}{24}\%$	$\frac{1}{3}\%$	$\frac{5}{12}\%$	n
51	54.3216 5449	54.9022 8149	55.4909 4202	56.6928 5366	51
52	55.4574 5862	56.0624 1314	56.6759 1183	57.9290 7388	52
53	56.5961 0227	57.2259 2851	57.8648 3154	59.1704 4503	53
54	57.7375 9252	58.3928 3747	59.0577 1431	60.4169 8855	54
55	58.8819 3650	59.5631 4991	60.2545 7336	61.6687 2600	55
56	60.0291 4135	60.7368 7577	61.4554 2194	62.9256 7902	56
57	61.1792 1420	61.9140 2499	62.6602 7334	64.1878 6935	57
58	62.3321 6223	63.0946 0756	63.8691 4092	65.4553 1881	58
59	63.4879 9264	64.2786 3350	65.0820 3806	66.7280 4930	59
60	64.6467 1262	65.4661 1285	66.2989 7818	68.0060 8284	60
61	65.8083 2940	66.6570 5568	67.5199 7478	69.2894 4152	61
62	66.9728 5023	67.8514 7209	68.7450 4136	70.5781 4753	62
63	68.1402 8235	69.0493 7222	69.9741 9150	71.8722 2314	63
64	69.3106 3306	70.2507 6622	71.2074 3880	73.1716 9074	64
65	70.4839 0964	71.4556 6429	72.4447 9693	74.4765 7278	65
66	71.6601 1942	72.6640 7664	73.6862 7959	75.7868 9184	66
67	72.8392 6971	73.8760 1353	74.9319 0052	77.1026 7055	67
68	74.0213 6789	75.0914 8524	76.1816 7352	78.4239 3168	68
69	75.2064 2131	76.3105 0207	77.4356 1243	79.7506 9806	69
70	76.3944 3736	77.5330 7437	78.6937 3114	81.0829 9264	70
71	77.5854 2345	78.7592 1250	79.9560 4358	82.4208 3844	71
72	78.7793 8701	79.9889 2687	81.2225 6372	83.7642 5860	72
73	79.9763 3548	81.2222 2791	82.4933 0560	85.1132 7634	73
74	81.1762 7632	82.4591 2607	83.7682 8329	86.4679 1500	74
75	82.3792 1701	83.6996 3186	85.0475 1090	87.8281 9797	75
76	83.5851 6505	84.9437 5578	86.3310 0260	89.1941 4880	76
77	84.7941 2797	86.1915 0840	87.6187 7261	90.5657 9109	77
78	86.0061 1329	87.4429 0030	88.9108 3519	91.9431 4855	78
79	87.2211 2857	88.6979 4209	90.2072 0464	93.3262 4500	79
80	88.4391 8139	89.9566 4443	91.5078 9532	94.7151 0436	80
81	89.6602 7934	91.2190 1797	92.8129 2164	96.1097 5062	81
82	90.8844 3004	92.4850 7344	94.1222 9804	97.5102 0792	82
83	92.1116 4112	93.7548 2157	95.4360 3904	98.9165 0045	83
84	93.3419 2022	95.0282 7313	96.7541 5917	100.3286 5254	84
85	94.5752 7502	96.3054 3893	98.0766 7303	101.7466 8859	85
86	95.8117 1321	97.5863 2980	99.4035 9527	103.1706 3312	86
87	97.0512 4249	98.8709 5659	100.7349 4059	104.6005 1076	87
88	98.2938 7060	100.1593 3021	102.0707 2373	106.0363 4622	88
89	99.5396 0527	101.4514 6159	103.4109 5947	107.4781 6433	89
90	100.7884 5429	102.7473 6169	104.7556 6267	108.9259 9002	90
91	102.0404 2542	104.0470 4149	106.1048 4821	110.3798 4831	91
92	103.2955 2649	105.3505 1203	107.4585 3104	111.8397 6434	92
93	104.5537 6530	106.6577 8436	108.8167 2614	113.3057 6336	93
94	105.8151 4972	107.9688 6956	110.1794 4856	114.7778 7071	94
95	107.0796 8759	109.2837 7877	111.5467 1339	116.2561 1184	95
96	108.3473 8681	110.6025 2312	112.9185 3577	117.7405 1230	96
97	109.6182 5528	111.9251 1381	114.2949 3089	119.2310 9777	97
98	110.8923 0091	113.2515 6206	115.6759 1399	120.7278 9401	98
99	112.1695 3167	114.5818 7912	117.0615 0037	122.2309 2690	99
100	113.4499 5550	115.9160 7626	118.4517 0537	123.7402 2243	100

TABLE V.—Amount of Annuity of 1 per Period

$$s_{\overline{n}|i} = \frac{(1 + i)^n - 1}{i}$$

n	¼%	⁷⁄₂₄%	⅓%	⁵⁄₁₂%	n
101	114.7335 8038	117.2541 6482	119.8465 4439	125.2558 0669	101
102	116.0204 1434	118.5961 5613	121.2460 3287	126.7777 0589	102
103	117.3104 6537	119.9420 6159	122.6501 8632	128.3059 4633	103
104	118.6037 4153	121.2918 9260	124.0590 2027	129.8405 5444	104
105	119.9002 5089	122.6456 6062	125.4725 5034	131.3815 5675	105
106	121.2000 0152	124.0033 7713	126.8907 9217	132.9289 7990	106
107	122.5030 0152	125.3650 5365	128.3137 6148	134.4828 5065	107
108	123.8092 5902	126.7307 0172	129.7414 7402	136.0431 9586	108
109	125.1187 8217	128.1003 3294	131.1739 4560	137.6100 4251	109
110	126.4315 7913	129.4739 5891	132.6111 9208	139.1834 1769	110
111	127.7476 5807	130.8515 9129	134.0532 0000	140.7000 4000	111
112	129.0670 2722	132.2332 4176	135.5000 7349	142.3498 6255	112
113	130.3896 9479	133.6189 2205	136.9517 4040	143.9429 8698	113
114	131.7156 6902	135.0086 4391	138.4082 4620	145.5427 4942	114
115	133.0449 5820	136.4024 1912	139.8696 0702	147.1491 7754	115
116	134.3775 7059	137.8002 5951	141.3358 3905	148.7622 9912	116
117	135.7135 1452	139.2021 7693	142.8069 5851	150.3821 4203	117
118	137.0527 9830	140.6081 8328	144.2829 8170	152.0087 3429	118
119	138.3954 3030	142.0182 9048	145.7639 2498	153.6421 0401	119
120	139.7414 1888	143.4325 1049	147.2498 0477	155.2822 7945	120
121	141.0907 7242	144.8508 5532	148.7406 3745	156.9292 8895	121
122	142.4434 9935	146.2733 3698	150.2364 3958	158.5831 6098	122
123	143.7996 0810	147.6999 6754	151.7372 2771	160.2439 2415	123
124	145.1591 0712	149.1307 5912	153.2430 1847	161.9116 0717	124
125	146.5220 0489	150.5657 2383	154.7538 2853	163.5862 3887	125
126	147.8883 0990	152.0048 7386	156.2696 7463	165.2678 4819	126
127	149.2580 3068	153.4482 2141	157.7905 7354	166.9564 6423	127
128	150.6311 7575	154.8957 7872	159.3165 4212	168.6521 1616	128
129	152.0077 5369	156.3475 5807	160.8475 9726	170.3548 3331	129
130	153.3877 7308	157.8035 7178	162.3837 5592	172.0646 4512	130
131	154.7712 4251	159.2638 3220	163.9250 3510	173.7815 8114	131
132	156.1581 7062	160.7283 5171	165.4714 5189	175.5056 7106	132
133	157.5485 6604	162.1971 4274	167.0230 2339	177.2369 4469	133
134	158.9424 3746	163.6702 1774	168.5797 6680	178.9754 3196	134
135	160.3397 9355	165.1475 8920	170.1416 9936	180.7211 6293	135
136	161.7406 4304	166.6292 6967	171.7088 3836	182.4741 6777	136
137	163.1449 9464	168.1152 7171	173.2812 0115	184.2344 7681	137
138	164.5528 5713	169.6056 0792	174.0500 0516	186.0021 2046	138
139	165.9642 3927	171.1002 9094	176.4416 6784	187.7771 2929	139
140	167.3791 4987	172.5993 3346	178.0298 0673	189.5595 3400	140
141	168.7975 9775	174.1027 4818	179.6232 3942	191.3493 6539	141
142	170.2195 9174	175.6105 4786	181.2219 8355	193.1466 5441	142
143	171.6451 4072	177.1227 4529	182.8260 5683	194.9514 3214	143
144	173.0742 5357	178.6393 5330	184.4354 7702	196.7637 2977	144
145	174.5069 3921	180.1603 8475	186.0502 6194	198.5835 7865	145
146	175.9432 0655	181.6858 5254	187.6704 2948	200.4110 1023	146
147	177.3830 6457	183.2157 6961	189.2959 9758	202.2460 5610	147
148	178.8265 2223	184.7501 4893	190.9269 8424	204.0887 4800	148
149	180.2735 8854	186.2890 0353	192.5634 0752	205.9391 1779	149
150	181.7242 7251	187.8323 4646	194.2052 8554	207.7971 9744	150

TABLE V.—Amount of Annuity of 1 per Period

$$s_{\overline{n}|i} = \frac{(1 + i)^n - 1}{i}$$

n	¼%	⁷⁄₂₄%	⅓%	⁵⁄₁₂%	n
151	183.1785 8319	189.3801 9080	195.8526 3650	209.6630 1910	151
152	184.6365 2965	190.9325 4969	197.5054 7862	211.5366 1501	152
153	186.0981 2097	192.4894 3630	199.1638 3021	213.4180 1758	153
154	187.5633 6627	194.0508 6382	200.8277 0965	215.3072 5932	154
155	189.0322 7469	195.6168 4551	202.4971 3534	217.2043 7290	155
156	190.5048 5538	197.1873 9464	204.1721 2580	219.1093 9112	156
157	191.9811 1752	198.7625 2454	205.8526 9955	221.0223 4691	157
158	193.4610 7031	200.3422 4857	207.5388 7521	222.9432 7336	158
159	194.9447 2298	201.9265 8013	209.2306 7146	224.8722 0366	159
160	196.4320 8479	203.5155 3265	210.9281 0704	226.8091 7118	160
161	197.9231 6500	205.1091 1962	212.6312 0073	228.7542 0939	161
162	199.4179 7292	206.7073 5455	214.3399 7139	230.7073 5193	162
163	200.9165 1785	208.3102 5101	216.0544 3797	232.6686 3256	163
164	202.4188 0914	209.9178 2257	217.7746 1942	234.6380 8520	164
165	203.9248 5617	211.5300 8289	219.5005 3482	236.6157 4389	165
166	205.4346 6831	213.1470 4563	221.2322 0327	238.6016 4282	166
167	206.9482 5498	214.7687 2451	222.9696 4395	240.5958 1633	167
168	208.4656 2562	216.3951 3329	224.7128 7610	242.5982 9890	168
169	209.9867 8968	218.0262 8576	226.4619 1902	244.6091 2515	169
170	211.5117 5665	219.6621 9576	228.2167 9208	246.6283 2983	170
171	213.0405 3605	221.3028 7717	229.9775 1472	248.6559 4788	171
172	214.5731 3739	222.9483 4389	231.7441 0643	250.6920 1433	172
173	216.1095 7023	224.5986 0989	233.5165 8679	252.7365 6439	173
174	217.6498 4415	226.2536 8917	235.2949 7541	254.7896 3340	174
175	219.1939 6876	227.9135 9577	237.0792 9200	256.8512 5688	175
176	220.7419 5369	229.5783 4375	238.8695 5630	258.9214 7045	176
177	222.2938 0857	231.2479 4726	240.6657 8816	261.0003 0991	177
178	223.8495 4309	232.9224 2044	242.4680 0745	263.0878 1120	178
179	225.4091 6695	234.6017 7750	244.2762 3414	265.1840 1041	179
180	226.9726 8987	236.2860 3268	246.0904 8826	267.2889 4379	180
181	228.5401 2159	237.9752 0028	247.9107 8988	269.4026 4772	181
182	230.1114 7190	239.6692 9461	249.7371 5918	271.5251 5875	182
183	231.6867 5058	241.3683 3005	251.5696 1638	273.6565 1358	183
184	233.2659 6745	243.0723 2101	253.4081 8177	275.7967 4905	184
185	234.8491 3237	244.7812 8195	255.2528 7571	277.9459 0218	185
186	236.4362 5520	246.4952 2736	257.1037 1863	280.1040 1010	186
187	238.0273 4584	248.2141 7177	258.9607 3102	282.2711 1014	187
188	239.6224 1420	249.9381 2977	260.8239 3346	284.4472 3977	188
189	241.2214 7024	251.6671 1598	262.6933 4657	286.6324 3660	189
190	242.8245 2392	253.4011 4507	264.5689 9106	288.8267 3842	190
191	244.4315 8523	255.1402 3174	266.4508 8769	291.0301 8316	191
192	246.0426 6419	256.8843 9075	268.3390 5732	293.2428 0892	192
193	247.6577 7085	258.6336 3689	270.2335 2084	295.4646 5396	193
194	249.2769 1528	260.3879 8500	272.1342 9925	297.6957 5669	194
195	250.9001 0756	262.1474 4995	274.0414 1358	299.9361 5568	195
196	252.5273 5783	263.9120 4668	275.9548 8495	302.1858 8966	196
197	254.1586 7623	265.6817 9015	277.8747 3457	304.4449 9753	197
198	255.7940 7292	267.4566 9537	279.8009 8369	306.7135 1835	198
199	257.4335 5810	269.2367 7740	281.7336 5363	308.9914 9135	199
200	259.0771 4200	271.0220 5134	283.6727 6581	311.2789 5589	200

TABLE V.—Amount of Annuity of 1 per Period

$$s_{\overline{n}|i} = \frac{(1 + i)^n - 1}{i}$$

n	$\frac{1}{2}\%$	$\frac{7}{12}\%$	$\frac{5}{8}\%$	$\frac{2}{3}\%$	n
1	1.0000 0000	1.0000 0000	1.0000 0000	1.0000 0000	1
2	2.0050 0000	2.0058 3333	2.0062 5000	2.0066 6667	2
3	3.0150 2500	3.0175 3403	3.1087 8906	3.0200 4444	3
4	4.0301 0013	4.0351 3631	4.0376 5649	4.0401 7807	4
5	5.0502 5063	5.0586 7460	5.0628 9185	5.0671 1259	5
6	6.0755 0188	6.0881 8354	6.0945 3492	6.1008 9335	6
7	7.1058 7939	7.1236 9794	7.1326 2576	7.1415 6597	7
8	8.1414 0879	8.1652 5284	8.1772 0468	8.1891 7641	8
9	9.1821 1583	9.2128 8349	9.2283 1220	9.2437 7092	9
10	10.2280 2641	10.2666 2531	10.2859 8916	10.3053 9606	10
11	11.2791 6654	11.3265 1396	11.3502 7659	11.3740 9870	11
12	12.3355 6237	12.3925 8529	12.4212 1582	12.4499 2602	12
13	13.3972 4018	13.4648 7537	13.4988 4842	13.5329 2553	13
14	14.4642 2639	14.5434 2048	14.5832 1622	14.6231 4503	14
15	15.5365 4752	15.6282 5710	15.6743 6132	15.7206 3266	15
16	16.6142 3026	16.7194 2193	16.7723 2608	16.8254 3688	16
17	17.6973 0141	17.8169 5189	17.8771 5312	17.9376 0646	17
18	18.7857 8791	18.9208 8411	18.9888 8532	19.0571 9051	18
19	19.8797 1685	20.0312 5593	20.1075 6586	20.1842 3844	19
20	20.9791 1544	21.1481 0493	21.2332 3814	21.3188 0003	20
21	22.0840 1101	22.2714 6887	22.3659 4588	22.4609 2536	21
22	23.1944 3107	23.4013 8577	23.5057 3304	23.6106 6407	22
23	24.3104 0322	24.5378 9386	24.6526 4387	24.7680 6930	23
24	25.4319 5524	25.6810 3157	25.8067 2290	25.9331 8976	24
25	26.5591 1502	26.8308 3759	26.9680 1492	27.1060 7769	25
26	27.6919 1059	27.9873 5081	28.1365 6501	28.2867 8488	26
27	28.8303 7015	29.1506 1035	29.3124 1854	29.4753 6344	27
28	29.9745 2200	30.3206 5558	30.4956 2116	30.6718 6586	28
29	31.1243 9461	31.4975 2607	31.6862 1879	31.8763 4497	29
30	32.2800 1658	32.6812 6164	32.8842 5766	33.0888 5394	30
31	33.4414 1666	33.8719 0233	34.0897 8427	34.3094 4630	31
32	34.6086 2375	35.0694 8843	35.3028 4542	35.5381 7594	32
33	35.7816 6686	36.2740 6045	36.5234 8820	36.7750 9711	33
34	36.9605 7520	37.4856 5913	37.7517 6000	38.0202 6443	34
35	38.1453 7807	38.7043 2548	38.9877 0850	39.2737 3286	35
36	39.3361 0496	39.9301 0071	40.2313 8168	40.5355 5774	36
37	40.5327 8549	41.1630 2630	41.4828 2782	41.8057 9479	37
38	41.7354 4942	42.4031 4395	42.7420 9549	43.0845 0009	38
39	42.9441 2666	43.6504 9562	44.0092 3359	44.3717 3009	39
40	44.1588 4730	44.9051 2352	45.2842 9130	45.6675 4163	40
41	45.3796 4153	46.1670 7007	46.5673 1812	46.9719 9191	41
42	46.6065 3974	47.4363 7798	47.8583 6386	48.2851 3852	42
43	47.8395 7244	48.7130 9018	49.1574 7863	49.6070 3944	43
44	49.0787 7030	49.9972 4988	50.4647 1287	50.9377 5304	44
45	50.3241 6415	51.2889 0050	51.7801 1733	52.2773 3806	45
46	51.5757 8497	52.5880 8575	53.1037 4306	53.6258 5365	46
47	52.8336 6390	53.8948 4959	54.4356 4146	54.9833 5934	47
48	54.0978 3222	55.2092 3621	55.7758 6421	56.3499 1507	48
49	55.3683 2138	56.5312 9009	57.1244 6337	57.7255 8117	49
50	56.6451 6299	57.8610 5595	58.4814 9126	59.1104 1837	50

TABLE V.—Amount of Annuity of 1 per Period

$$s_{\overline{n}|i} = \frac{(1 + i)^n - 1}{i}$$

n	½%	⁷⁄₁₂%	⅝%	⅔%	n
51	57.9283 8880	59.1985 7877	59.8470 0058	60.5044 8783	51
52	59.2180 3075	60.5439 0381	61.2210 4434	61.9078 5108	52
53	60.5141 2090	61.8970 7659	62.6036 7586	63.3205 7009	53
54	61.8166 9150	63.2581 4287	63.9949 4884	64.7427 0722	54
55	63.1257 7496	64.6271 4870	65.3949 1727	66.1743 2527	55
56	64.4414 0384	66.0041 4040	66.8036 3550	67.6154 8744	56
57	65.7636 1086	67.3891 6455	68.2211 5822	69.0662 5736	57
58	67.0924 2891	68.7822 6801	69.6475 4046	70.5266 9907	58
59	68.4278 9105	70.1834 9791	71.0828 3759	71.9968 7706	59
60	69.7700 3051	71.5929 0165	72.5271 0532	73.4768 5625	60
61	71.1188 8066	73.0105 2691	73.9803 9973	74.9667 0195	61
62	72.4744 7507	74.4364 2165	75.4427 7723	76.4664 7997	62
63	73.8368 4744	75.8706 3411	76.9142 9459	77.9762 5650	63
64	75.2060 3168	77.3132 1281	78.3950 0893	79.4960 9821	64
65	76.5820 6184	78.7642 0655	79.8849 7774	81.0260 7220	65
66	77.9649 7215	80.2236 6442	81.3842 5885	82.5662 4601	66
67	79.3547 9701	81.6916 3579	82.8929 1046	84.1166 8765	67
68	80.7515 7099	83.1681 7034	84.4109 9115	85.6774 6557	68
69	82.1553 2885	84.6533 1800	85.9385 5985	87.2486 4867	69
70	83.5661 0549	86.1471 2902	87.4756 7585	88.8303 0633	70
71	84.9839 3602	87.6496 5394	89.0223 9882	90.4225 0837	71
72	86.4088 5570	89.1609 4359	90.5787 8882	92.0253 2510	72
73	87.8408 9998	90.6810 4909	92.1449 0625	93.6388 2726	73
74	89.2801 0448	92.2100 2188	93.7208 1191	95.2630 8611	74
75	90.7265 0500	93.7479 1367	95.3065 6698	96.8981 7335	75
76	92.1801 3752	95.2947 7650	96.9022 3303	98.5441 6118	76
77	93.6410 3821	96.8506 6270	98.5078 7198	100.2011 2225	77
78	95.1092 4340	98.4156 2490	100.1235 4618	101.8691 2973	78
79	96.5847 8962	99.9897 1604	101.7493 1835	103.5482 5726	79
80	98.0677 1357	101.5729 8938	103.3852 5159	105.2385 7898	80
81	99.5580 5214	103.1654 9849	105.0314 0941	106.9401 6950	81
82	101.0558 4240	104.7672 9723	106.6878 5572	108.6531 0397	82
83	102.5611 2161	106.3784 3980	108.3546 5482	110.3774 5799	83
84	104.0739 2722	107.9989 8070	110.0318 7141	112.1133 0771	84
85	105.5942 9685	109.6289 7475	111.7195 7061	113.8607 2977	85
86	107.1222 6834	111.2684 7710	113.4178 1792	115.6198 0130	86
87	108.6578 7968	112.9175 4322	115.1266 7928	117.3905 9997	87
88	110.2011 6908	114.5762 2889	116.8462 2103	119.1732 0397	88
89	111.7521 7492	116.2445 9022	118.5765 0991	120.9676 9200	89
90	113.3109 3580	117.9226 8367	120.3176 1310	122.7741 4328	90
91	114.8774 9048	119.6105 6599	122.0695 9818	124.5926 3757	91
92	116.4518 7793	121.3082 9429	123.8325 3317	126.4232 5515	92
93	118.0341 3732	123.0159 2601	125.6064 8650	128.2660 7685	93
94	119.6243 0800	124.7335 1891	127.3915 2704	130.1211 8403	94
95	121.2224 2954	126.4611 3110	129.1877 2408	131.9886 5859	95
96	122.8285 4169	128.1988 2103	130.9951 4736	133.8685 8298	96
97	124.4426 8440	129.9466 4749	132.8138 6703	135.7610 4020	97
98	126.0648 9782	131.7046 6960	134.6439 5370	137.6661 1380	98
99	127.6952 2231	133.4729 4684	136.4854 7841	139.5838 8790	99
100	129.3336 9842	135.2515 3903	138.3385 1265	141.5144 4715	100

TABLE V.—Amount of Annuity of 1 per Period

$$s_{\overline{n}|i} = \frac{(1+i)^n - 1}{i}$$

n	½%	7⁄12%	5⁄8%	2⁄3%	n
101	130.9803 6692	137.0405 0634	140.2031 2836	143.4578 7680	101
102	132.6352 6875	138.8399 0929	142.0793 9791	145.4142 6264	102
103	134.2984 4509	140.6498 0876	143.9673 9414	147.3836 9106	103
104	135.9699 3732	142.4702 6598	145.8671 9036	149.3662 4900	104
105	137.6497 8701	144.3013 4253	147.7788 6030	151.3620 2399	105
106	139.3380 3594	146.1431 0036	149.7024 7817	153.3711 0415	106
107	141.0347 2612	147.9956 0178	151.6381 1866	155.3935 7818	107
108	142.7398 9975	149.8589 0946	153.5858 5690	157.4295 3537	108
109	144.4535 9925	151.7330 8643	155.5457 6851	159.4790 6560	109
110	146.1758 6725	153.6181 9610	157.5179 2956	161.5422 5937	110
111	147.9067 4658	155.5143 0225	159.5024 1662	163.6192 0777	111
112	149.6462 8032	157.4214 6901	161.4993 0673	165.7100 0249	112
113	151.3945 1172	159.3397 6091	163.5086 7739	167.8147 3584	113
114	153.1514 8428	161.2692 4285	165.5306 0663	169.9335 0074	114
115	154.9172 4170	163.2099 8010	167.5651 7292	172.0663 9075	115
116	156.6918 2791	165.1620 3832	169.6124 5525	174.2135 0002	116
117	158.4752 8704	167.1254 8354	171.6725 3310	176.3749 2335	117
118	160.2676 6348	169.1003 8219	173.7454 8643	178.5507 5618	118
119	162.0690 0180	171.0868 0109	175.8313 9572	180.7410 9455	119
120	163.8793 4681	173.0848 0743	177.9303 4194	182.9460 3518	120
121	165.6987 4354	175.0944 6881	180.0424 0658	185.1656 7542	121
122	167.5272 3726	177.1158 5321	182.1676 7162	187.4001 1325	122
123	169.3648 7344	179.1490 2902	184.3062 1957	189.6494 4734	123
124	171.2116 9781	181.1940 6502	186.4581 3344	191.9137 7699	124
125	173.0677 5630	183.2510 3040	188.6234 9677	194.1932 0217	125
126	174.9330 9508	185.3199 9474	190.8023 9363	196.4878 2352	126
127	176.8077 6056	187.4010 2805	192.9949 0859	198.7977 4234	127
128	178.6917 9936	189.4942 0071	195.2011 2677	201.1230 6062	128
129	180.5852 5836	191.5995 8355	197.4211 3381	203.4638 8103	129
130	182.4881 8465	193.7172 4778	199.6550 1589	205.8203 0690	130
131	184.4006 2557	195.8472 6506	201.9028 5974	208.1924 4228	131
132	186.3226 2870	197.9897 0744	204.1647 5262	210.5803 9189	132
133	188.2542 4184	200.1446 4740	206.4407 8232	212.9842 6117	133
134	190.1955 1305	202.3121 5785	208.7310 3721	215.4041 5625	134
135	192.1464 9062	204.4923 1210	211.0356 0619	217.8401 8396	135
136	194.1072 2307	206.6851 8392	213.3545 7873	220.2924 5185	136
137	196.0777 5919	208.8908 4749	215.6880 4485	222.7610 6820	137
138	198.0581 4798	211.1093 7744	218.0360 9513	225.2461 4198	138
139	200.0484 3872	213.3408 4881	220.3988 2072	227.7477 8293	139
140	202.0486 8092	215.5853 3709	222.7763 1335	230.2661 0148	140
141	204.0589 2432	217.8429 1822	225.1686 6531	232.8012 0883	141
142	206.0792 1894	220.1136 6858	227.5759 6947	235.3532 1688	142
143	208.1096 1504	222.3976 6498	229.9983 1928	237.9222 3833	143
144	210.1501 6311	224.6949 8469	232.4358 0878	240.5083 8659	144
145	212.2009 1393	227.0057 0544	234.8885 3258	243.1117 7583	145
146	214.2619 1850	229.3299 0538	237.3565 8591	245.7325 2100	146
147	216.3332 2809	231.6676 6317	239.8400 6457	248.3707 3781	147
148	218.4148 9423	234.0190 5787	242.3390 6497	251.0265 4273	148
149	220.5069 6870	236.3841 6904	244.8536 8413	253.7000 5301	149
150	222.6095 0354	238.7630 7669	247.3840 1966	256.3913 8670	150

TABLE V.—Amount of Annuity of 1 per Period

$$s_{\overline{n}|i} = \frac{(1+i)^n - 1}{i}$$

n	½%	7/12%	⅝%	⅔%	n
151	224.7225 5106	241.1558 6130	249.9301 6978	259.1006 6261	151
152	226.8461 6382	243.5626 0383	252.4922 3334	261.8280 0036	152
153	228.9803 9464	245.9833 8568	255.0703 0980	264.5735 2036	153
154	231.1252 9661	248.4182 8877	257.6644 9923	267.3373 4383	154
155	233.2809 2309	250.8673 9545	260.2749 0235	270.1195 9279	155
156	235.4473 2771	253.3307 8859	262.9016 2049	272.9203 9008	156
157	237.6245 6435	255.8085 5153	265.5447 5562	275.7398 5934	157
158	239.8126 8717	258.3007 6808	268.2044 1035	278.5781 2507	158
159	242.0117 5060	260.8075 2256	270.8806 8791	281.4353 1257	159
160	244.2218 0936	263.3288 9977	273.5736 9221	284.3115 4799	160
161	246.4429 1840	265.8649 8502	276.2835 2779	287.2069 5831	161
162	248.6751 3300	268.4158 6410	279.0102 9983	290.1216 7136	162
163	250.9185 0866	270.9816 2331	281.7541 1421	293.0558 1584	163
164	253.1731 0121	273.5623 4944	284.5150 7742	296.0095 2128	164
165	255.4389 6671	276.1581 2982	287.2932 9666	298.9829 1809	165
166	257.7161 6154	278.7690 5224	290.0888 7976	301.9761 3754	166
167	260.0047 4235	281.3952 0504	292.9019 3526	304.9893 1179	167
168	262.3047 6606	284.0366 7707	295.7325 7235	308.0225 7387	168
169	264.6162 8989	286.6935 5769	298.5809 0093	311.0760 5770	169
170	266.9393 7134	289.3659 3678	301.4470 3156	314.1498 9808	170
171	269.2740 6820	292.0539 0474	304.3310 7551	317.2442 3073	171
172	271.6204 3854	294.7575 5252	307.2331 4473	320.3591 9227	172
173	273.9785 4073	297.4769 7158	310.1533 5189	323.4949 2022	173
174	276.3484 3344	300.2122 5391	313.0918 1033	326.6515 5302	174
175	278.7301 7561	302.9634 9206	316.0486 3415	329.8292 3004	175
176	281.1238 2648	305.7307 7910	319.0239 3811	333.0280 9158	176
177	283.5294 4562	308.5142 0864	322.0178 3773	336.2482 7885	177
178	285.9470 9284	311.3138 7486	325.0304 4921	339.4899 3405	178
179	288.3768 2831	314.1298 7246	328.0618 8952	342.7532 0027	179
180	290.8187 1245	316.9622 9672	331.1122 7633	346.0382 2161	180
181	293.2728 0601	319.8112 4345	334.1817 2806	349.3451 4309	181
182	295.7391 7004	322.6768 0904	337.2703 6386	352.6741 1071	182
183	298.2178 6589	325.5590 9042	340.3783 0363	356.0252 7144	183
184	300.7089 5522	328.4581 8512	343.5056 6803	359 3987 7325	184
185	303.2125 0000	331.3741 9120	346.6525 7845	362.7947 6508	185
186	305.7285 6250	334.3072 0731	349.8191 5707	366.2133 9684	186
187	308.2572 0531	337.2573 3269	353.0055 2680	369.6548 1949	187
188	310.7984 9134	340.2246 6713	356.2118 1134	373.1191 8495	188
189	313.3524 8379	343.2093 1102	359.4381 3516	376.6066 4618	189
190	315.9192 4621	346.2113 6533	362.6846 2351	380.1173 5716	190
191	318.4988 4244	349.2309 3163	365.9514 0241	383.6514 7287	191
192	321.0913 3666	352.2681 1207	369 2385 9867	387.2091 4936	192
193	323.6967 9334	355.3230 0939	372.5463 3991	390.7905 4369	193
194	326.3152 7731	358.3957 2694	375.8747 5454	394.3958 1398	194
195	328.9468 5369	361.4863 6868	379.2239 7175	398.0251 1941	195
196	331.5915 8796	364.5950 3917	382.5941 2158	401.6786 2020	196
197	334.2495 4590	367.7218 4356	385.9853 3484	405.3564 7767	197
198	336.9207 9363	370.8668 8765	389.3977 4318	409.0588 5419	198
199	339.6053 9760	374.0302 7783	392.8314 7907	412.7859 1322	199
200	342.3034 2450	377.2121 2111	396.2866 7582	416.5378 1930	200

TABLE V.—Amount of Annuity of 1 per Period

$$s_{\overline{n}|i} = \frac{(1+i)^n - 1}{i}$$

n	¾%	⅞%	1%	1⅛%	n
1	1.0000 0000	1.0000 0000	1.0000 0000	1.0000 0000	1
2	2.0075 0000	2.0087 5000	2.0100 0000	2.0112 5000	2
3	3.0225 5625	3.0263 2656	3.0301 0000	3.0338 7656	3
4	4.0452 2542	4.0528 0692	4.0604 0100	4.0680 0767	4
5	5.0755 6461	5.0882 6898	5.1010 0501	5.1137 7276	5
6	6.1136 3135	6.1327 9133	6.1520 1506	6.1713 0270	6
7	7.1594 8358	7.1864 5326	7.2135 3521	7.2407 2986	7
8	8.2131 7971	8.2493 3472	8.2856 7056	8.3221 8807	8
9	9.2747 7856	9.3215 1640	9.3685 2727	9.4158 1269	9
10	10.3443 3940	10.4030 7967	10.4622 1254	10.5217 4058	10
11	11.1010 0104	11.4041 0008	11.5668 0407	11.6401 1010	11
12	12.5075 8636	12.5946 8005	12.6825 0301	12.7710 6140	12
13	13.6013 9325	13.7048 8350	13.8093 2804	13.9147 3584	13
14	14.7034 0370	14.8248 0123	14.9474 2132	15.0712 7662	14
15	15.8136 7923	15.9545 1824	16.0968 9554	16.2408 2848	15
16	16.9322 8183	17.0941 2028	17.2578 6449	17.4235 3780	16
17	18.0592 7394	18.2436 9383	18.4304 4314	18.6195 5260	17
18	19.1947 1849	19.4033 2615	19.6147 4757	19.8290 2257	18
19	20.3386 7888	20.5731 0526	20.8108 9504	21.0520 9907	19
20	21.4912 1897	21.7531 1993	22.0190 0399	22.2889 3519	20
21	22.6524 0312	22.9434 5973	23.2391 9403	23.5396 8571	21
22	23.8222 9614	24.1442 1500	24.4715 8598	24.8045 0717	22
23	25.0009 6336	25.3554 7688	25.7163 0183	26.0835 5788	23
24	26.1884 7059	26.5773 3730	26.9734 6485	27.3769 9790	24
25	27.3848 8412	27.8098 8900	28.2431 9950	28.6849 8913	25
26	28.5902 7075	29.0532 2553	29.5256 3150	30.0076 9526	26
27	29.8046 9778	30.3074 4126	30.8208 8781	31.3452 8183	27
28	31.0282 3301	31.5726 3137	32.1290 9669	32.6979 1625	28
29	32.2609 4476	32.8488 9189	33.4503 8766	34.0657 6781	29
30	33.5029 0184	34.1363 1970	34.7848 9153	35.4490 0769	30
31	34.7541 7361	35.4350 1249	36.1327 4045	36.8478 0903	31
32	36.0148 2991	36.7450 6885	37.4940 6785	38.2623 4688	32
33	37.2849 4113	38.0665 8820	38.8690 0853	39.6927 9829	33
34	38.5645 7819	39.3996 7085	40.2576 9862	41.1393 4227	34
35	39.8538 1253	40.7444 1797	41.6602 7560	42.6021 5987	35
36	41.1527 1612	42.1009 3163	43.0768 7836	44.0814 3417	36
37	42.4613 6149	43.4693 1478	44.5076 4714	45.5773 5030	37
38	43.7798 2170	44.8496 7128	45.9527 2361	47.0900 9549	38
39	45.1081 7037	46.2421 0591	47.4122 5085	48.6198 5906	39
40	46.4464 8164	47.6467 2433	48.8863 7336	50.1668 3248	40
41	47.7948 3026	49.0636 3317	50.3752 3709	51.7312 0934	41
42	49.1532 9148	50.4929 3996	51.8789 8946	53.3131 8545	42
43	50.5219 4117	51.9347 5319	53.3977 7936	54.9129 5879	43
44	51.9008 5573	53.3891 8228	54.9317 5715	56.5307 2957	44
45	53.2901 1215	54.8563 3762	56.4810 7472	58.1667 0028	45
46	54.6897 8799	56.3363 3058	58.0458 8547	59.8210 7566	46
47	56.0999 6140	57.8292 7347	59.6263 4432	61.4940 6276	47
48	57.5207 1111	59.3352 7961	61.2226 0777	63.1858 7097	48
49	58.9521 1644	60.8544 6331	62.8348 3385	64.8967 1201	49
50	60.3942 5732	62.3869 3986	64.4631 8218	66.6268 0002	50

TABLE V.—Amount of Annuity of 1 per Period

$$s_{\overline{n}|i} = \frac{(1 + i)^n - 1}{i}$$

n	¾%	⅞%	1%	1⅛%	n
51	61.8472 1424	63.9328 2559	66.1078 1401	68.3763 5152	51
52	63.3110 6835	65.4922 3781	67.7688 9215	70.1455 8548	52
53	64.7859 0136	67.0652 9489	69.4465 8107	71.9347 2332	53
54	66.2717 9562	68.6521 1622	71.1410 4688	73.7439 8895	54
55	67.7688 3409	70.2528 2224	72.8524 5735	75.5736 0883	55
56	69.2771 0035	71.8675 3443	74.5809 8192	77.4238 1193	56
57	70.7966 7860	73.4963 7536	76.3267 9174	79.2948 2981	57
58	72.3276 5369	75.1394 6864	78.0900 5966	81.1868 9665	58
59	73.8701 1109	76.7969 3900	79.8709 6025	83.1002 4923	59
60	75.4241 3693	78.4689 1221	81.6696 6986	85.0351 2704	60
61	76.9898 1795	80.1555 1519	83.4863 6655	86.9917 7222	61
62	78.5672 4159	81.8568 7595	85.3212 3022	88.9704 2966	62
63	80.1564 9590	83.5731 2362	87.1744 4252	90.9713 4699	63
64	81.7576 6962	85.3043 8845	89.0461 8695	92.9947 7464	64
65	83.3708 5214	87.0508 0185	90.9366 4882	95.0409 6586	65
66	84.9961 3353	88.8124 9636	92.8460 1531	97.1101 7672	66
67	86.6336 0453	90.5896 0571	94.7744 7546	99.2026 6621	67
68	88.2833 5657	92.3822 6476	96.7222 2021	101.3186 9621	68
69	89.9454 8174	94.1906 0957	98.6894 4242	103.4585 3154	69
70	91.6200 7285	96.0147 7741	100.6763 3684	105.6224 4002	70
71	93.3072 2340	97.8549 0671	102.6831 0021	107.8106 9247	71
72	95.0070 2758	99.7111 3714	104.7099 3121	110.0235 6276	72
73	96.7195 8028	101.5836 0959	106.7570 3052	112.2613 2784	73
74	98.4449 7714	103.4724 6618	108.8246 0083	114.5242 6778	74
75	100.1833 1446	105.3778 5025	110.9128 4684	116.8126 6579	75
76	101.9346 8932	107.2999 0644	113.0219 7530	119.1268 0828	76
77	103.6991 9949	109.2387 8063	115.1521 9506	121.4669 8487	77
78	105.4769 4349	111.1946 1996	117.3037 1701	123.8334 8845	78
79	107.2680 2056	113.1675 7288	119.4767 5418	126.2266 1520	79
80	109.0725 3072	115.1577 8914	121.6715 2172	128.6466 6462	80
81	110.8905 7470	117.1654 1980	123.8882 3694	131.0939 3960	81
82	112.7222 5401	119.1906 1722	126.1271 1931	133.5687 4642	82
83	114.5676 7091	121.2335 3512	128.3883 9050	136.0713 9481	83
84	116.4269 2845	123.2943 2855	130.6722 7440	138.0021 9801	84
85	118.3001 3041	125.3731 5393	132.9789 9715	141.1614 7273	85
86	120.1873 8139	127.4701 6903	135.3087 8712	143.7495 3930	86
87	122.0887 8675	129.5855 3301	137.6618 7499	146.3667 2162	87
88	124.0044 5265	131.7194 0642	140.0384 9374	149.0133 4724	88
89	125.9344 8604	133.8719 5123	142.4388 7868	151.6897 4739	89
90	127.8789 9469	136.0433 3080	144.8632 6746	154.3962 5705	90
91	129.8380 8715	138.2337 0994	147.3119 0014	157.1332 1494	91
92	131.8118 7280	140.4432 5491	149.7850 1914	159.9009 6361	92
93	133.8004 6185	142.6721 3339	152.2828 6933	162.6998 4945	93
94	135.8039 6531	144.9205 1455	154.8056 9803	165.5302 2276	94
95	137.8224 9505	147.1885 6906	157.3537 5501	168.3924 3776	95
96	139.8561 6377	149.4764 6903	159.9272 9256	171.2868 5269	96
97	141.9050 8499	151.7843 8813	162.5265 6548	174.2138 2978	97
98	143.9693 7313	154.1125 0153	165.1518 3114	177.1737 3537	98
99	146.0491 4343	156.4609 8592	167.8033 4945	180.1669 3989	99
100	148.1445 1201	158.8300 1955	170.4813 8294	183.1938 1796	100

TABLE V.—Amount of Annuity of 1 per Period

$$s_{\overline{n}|i} = \frac{(1+i)^n - 1}{i}$$

n	1¼%	1⅜%	1½%	1¾%	n
1	1.0000 0000	1.0000 0000	1.0000 0000	1.0000 0000	1
2	2.0125 0000	2.0137 5000	2.0150 0000	2.0175 0000	2
3	3.0376 5625	3.0414 3906	3.0452 2500	3.0528 0625	3
4	4.0756 2695	4.0832 5885	4.0909 0338	4.1062 3036	4
5	5.1265 7229	5.1394 0366	5.1522 6693	5.1780 8938	5
6	6.1906 5444	6.2100 7046	6.2295 5093	6.2687 0596	6
7	7.2680 3762	7.2954 5893	7.3229 9419	7.3784 0831	7
8	8.3588 8809	8.3957 7149	8.4328 3911	8.5075 3045	8
9	9.4633 7420	9.5112 1335	9.5593 3169	9.6564 1224	9
10	10.5816 6637	10.6419 9253	10.7027 2167	10.8253 9945	10
11	11.7139 3720	11.7883 1993	11.8632 6249	12.0148 4394	11
12	12.8603 6142	12.9504 0933	13.0412 1143	13.2251 0371	12
13	14.0211 1594	14.1284 7745	14.2368 2960	14.4565 4303	13
14	15.1963 7988	15.3227 4402	15.4503 8205	15.7095 3253	14
15	16.3863 3463	16.5334 3175	16.6821 3778	16.9844 4935	15
16	17.5911 6382	17.7607 6644	17.9323 6984	18.2816 7721	16
17	18.8110 5336	19.0049 7697	19.2013 5539	19.6016 0656	17
18	20.0461 9153	20.2662 9541	20.4893 7572	20.9446 3468	18
19	21.2967 6893	21.5449 5697	21.7967 1636	22.3111 6578	19
20	22.5629 7854	22.8412 0013	23.1236 6710	23.7016 1119	20
21	23.8450 1577	24.1552 6663	24.4705 2211	25.1163 8938	21
22	25.1430 7847	25.4874 0155	25.8375 7994	26.5559 2620	22
23	26.4573 6695	26.8378 5332	27.2251 4364	28.0206 5490	23
24	27.7880 8403	28.2068 7380	28.6335 2080	29.5110 1637	24
25	29.1354 3508	29.5947 1832	30.0630 2361	31.0274 5915	25
26	30.4996 2802	31.0016 4569	31.5139 6896	32.5704 3969	26
27	31.8808 7337	32.4279 1832	32.9866 7850	34.1404 2238	27
28	33.2793 8429	33.8738 0220	34.4814 7867	35.7378 7977	28
29	34.6953 7659	35.3395 6698	35.9987 0085	37.3632 9267	29
30	36.1290 6880	36.8254 8602	37.5386 8137	39.0171 5029	30
31	37.5806 8216	38.3318 3646	39.1017 6159	40.6999 5042	31
32	39.0504 4069	39.8588 9921	40.6882 8801	42.4121 9955	32
33	40.5385 7120	41.4069 5907	42.2986 1233	44.1544 1305	33
34	42.0453 0334	42.9763 0476	43.9330 9152	45.9271 1527	34
35	43.5708 6963	44.5672 2895	45.5920 8789	47.7308 3979	35
36	45.1155 0550	46.1800 2835	47.2759 6921	49.5661 2949	36
37	46.6794 4932	47.8150 0374	48.9851 0874	51.4335 3675	37
38	48.2926 4243	49.4724 6004	50.7198 8538	53.3336 2365	38
39	49.8862 2921	51.1527 0636	52.4806 8366	55.2669 6206	39
40	51.4895 5708	52.8560 5608	54.2678 9391	57.2341 3390	40
41	53.1331 7654	54.5828 2685	56.0819 1232	59.2357 3124	41
42	54.7973 4125	56.3333 4072	57.9231 4100	61.2723 5654	42
43	56.4823 0801	58.1079 2415	59.7919 8812	63.3446 2278	43
44	58.1883 3687	59.9069 0811	61.6888 6794	65.4531 5367	44
45	59.9156 9108	61.7306 2810	63.6142 0096	67.5985 8386	45
46	61.6646 3721	63.5794 2423	65.5684 1398	69.7815 5908	46
47	63.4354 4518	65.4536 4131	67.5519 4018	72.0027 3637	47
48	65.2283 8824	67.3536 2888	69.5652 1929	74.2627 8425	48
49	67.0437 4310	69.2797 4128	71.6086 9758	76.5623 8298	49
50	68.8817 8989	71.2323 3772	73.6828 2804	78.9022 2468	50

TABLE V.—Amount of Annuity of 1 per Period

$$s_{\overline{n}|i} = \frac{(1+i)^n - 1}{i}$$

n	1¼%	1⅜%	1½%	1¾%	n
51	70.7428 1226	73.2117 8237	75.7880 7046	81.2830 1361	51
52	72.6270 9741	75.2184 4437	77.9248 9152	83.7054 6635	52
53	74.5349 3613	77.2526 9798	80.0937 6489	86.1703 1201	53
54	76.4666 2283	79.3149 2258	82.2951 7136	88.6782 9247	54
55	78.4224 5562	81.4055 0277	84.5295 9893	91.2301 6259	55
56	80.4027 3631	83.5248 2843	86.7975 4292	93.8266 9043	56
57	82.4077 7052	85.6732 9482	89.0995 0606	96.4686 5752	57
58	84.4378 6765	87.8513 0262	91.4359 9865	99.1568 5902	58
59	86.4933 4099	90.0592 5804	93.8075 3863	101.8921 0405	59
60	88.5745 0776	92.2975 7283	96.2146 5171	104.6752 1588	60
61	90.6816 8910	94.5666 6446	98.6578 7149	107.5070 3215	61
62	92.8152 1022	96.8669 5610	101.1377 3956	110.3884 0522	62
63	94.9754 0034	99.1988 7674	103.6548 0565	113.3202 0231	63
64	97.1625 9285	101.5628 6130	106.2096 2774	116.3033 0585	64
65	99.3771 2526	103.9593 5064	108.8027 7215	119.3386 1370	65
66	101.6193 3933	106.3887 9171	111.4348 1374	122.4270 3944	66
67	103.8895 8107	108.8516 3760	114.1063 3594	125.5695 1263	67
68	106.1882 0083	111.3483 4761	116.8179 3098	128.7669 7910	68
69	108.5155 5334	113.8793 8739	119.5701 9995	132.0204 0124	69
70	110.8719 9776	116.4452 2897	122.3637 5295	135.3307 5826	70
71	113.2578 9773	119.0463 5087	125.1992 0924	138.6990 4653	71
72	115.6736 2145	121.6832 3819	128.0771 9738	142.1262 7984	72
73	118.1195 4172	124.3563 8272	130.9983 5534	145.6134 8974	73
74	120.5960 3599	127.0662 8298	133.9633 3067	149.1617 2581	74
75	123.1034 8644	129.8134 4437	136.9727 8063	152.7720 5601	75
76	125.6422 8002	132.5983 7923	140.0273 7234	156.4455 6699	76
77	128.2128 0852	135.4216 0695	143.1277 8292	160.1833 6441	77
78	130.8154 6863	138.2836 5404	146.2746 9967	163.9865 7329	78
79	133.4506 6199	141.1850 5429	149.4688 2016	167.8563 3832	79
80	136.1187 9526	144.1263 4878	152.7108 5247	171.7938 2424	80
81	138.8202 8020	147.1080 8608	156.0015 1525	175.8002 1617	81
82	141.5555 3370	150.1308 2226	159.3415 3798	179.8767 1995	82
83	144.3249 7787	153.1951 2107	162.7316 6105	184.0245 6255	83
84	147.1290 4010	156.3015 5398	166.1726 3597	188.2449 9239	84
85	149.9681 5310	159.4507 0035	169.6652 2551	192.5392 7976	85
86	152.8427 5501	162.6431 4748	173.2102 0389	196.9087 1716	86
87	155.7532 8945	165.8794 9076	176.8083 5695	201.3546 1971	87
88	158.7002 0557	169.1603 3375	180.4604 8230	205.8783 2555	88
89	161.6839 5814	172.4862 8834	184.1673 8954	210.4811 9625	89
90	164.7050 0762	175.8579 7481	187.9299 0038	215.1646 1718	90
91	167.7638 2021	179.2760 2196	191.7488 4889	219.9299 9798	91
92	170.8608 6796	182.7410 6726	195.6250 8162	224.7787 7295	92
93	173.9966 2881	186.2537 5694	199.5594 5784	229.7124 0148	93
94	177.1715 8667	189.8147 4610	203.5528 4971	234.7323 6850	94
95	180.3862 3151	193.4246 9886	207.6061 4246	239.8401 8495	95
96	183.6410 5940	197.0842 8847	211.7202 3459	245.0373 8819	96
97	186.9365 7264	200.7941 9743	215.8960 3811	250.3255 4248	97
98	190.2732 7980	204.5551 1765	220.1344 7868	255.7062 3947	98
99	193.6516 9580	208.3677 5051	224.4364 9586	261.1810 9866	99
100	197.0723 4200	212.2328 0708	228.8030 4330	266.7517 6789	100

TABLE V.—Amount of Annuity of 1 per Period

$$s_{\overline{n}|i} = \frac{(1+i)^n - 1}{i}$$

n	2%	2¼%	2½%	2¾%	n
1	1.0000 0000	1.0000 0000	1.0000 0000	1.0000 0000	1
2	2.0200 0000	2.0225 0000	2.0250 0000	2.0275 0000	2
3	3.0604 0000	3.0680 0625	3.0756 2500	3.0832 5625	3
4	4.1216 0800	4.1370 3639	4.1525 1563	4.1680 4580	4
5	5.2040 4016	5.2301 1971	5.2563 2852	5.2826 6706	5
6	6.3081 2096	6.3477 9740	6.3877 3673	6.4279 4040	6
7	7.4342 8338	7.4906 2284	7.5474 3015	7.6047 0876	7
8	8.5829 6905	8.6591 6186	8.7361 1590	8.8138 3825	8
9	9.7546 2843	9.8539 9300	9.9545 1880	10.0562 1880	9
10	10.9497 2100	11.0757 0784	11.2033 8177	11.3327 6482	10
11	12.1687 1542	12.3249 1127	12.4834 6631	12.6444 1595	11
12	13.4120 8973	13.6022 2177	13.7955 5297	13.9921 3729	12
13	14.6803 3152	14.9082 7176	15.1404 4179	15.3769 2107	13
14	15.9739 3815	16.2437 0788	16.5189 5284	16.7997 8639	14
15	17.2934 1692	17.6091 9130	17.9319 2666	18.2617 8052	15
16	18.6392 8525	19.0053 9811	19.3802 2483	19.7639 7948	16
17	20.0120 7096	20.4330 1957	20.8647 3045	21.3074 8892	17
18	21.4123 1238	21.8927 6251	22.3863 4871	22.8934 4487	18
19	22.8405 5863	23.3853 4966	23.9460 0743	24.5230 1460	19
20	24.2973 6980	24.9115 2003	25.5446 5761	26.1973 9750	20
21	25.7833 1719	26.4720 2923	27.1832 7405	27.9178 2593	21
22	27.2989 8354	28.0676 4989	28.8628 5590	29.6855 6615	22
23	28.8449 6321	29.6991 7201	30.5844 2730	31.5019 1921	23
24	30.4218 6247	31.3674 0338	32.3490 3798	33.3682 2199	24
25	32.0302 9972	33.0731 6996	34.1577 6393	35.2858 4810	25
26	33.6709 0572	34.8173 1628	36.0117 0803	37.2562 0892	26
27	35.3443 2383	36.6007 0590	37.9120 0073	39.2807 5467	27
28	37.0512 1031	38.4242 2178	39.8598 C075	41.3609 7542	28
29	38.7922 3451	40.2887 6677	41.8562 9577	43.4984 0224	29
30	40.5680 7921	42.1952 6402	43.9027 0316	45.6946 0830	30
31	42.3794 4079	44.1446 5746	46.0002 7074	47.9512 1003	31
32	44.2270 2961	46.1379 1226	48.1502 7751	50.2698 6831	32
33	46.1115 7020	48.1760 1528	50.3540 3445	52.6522 8969	33
34	48.0338 0160	50.2599 7563	52.6128 8531	55.1002 2765	34
35	49.9944 7763	52.3908 2508	54.9282 0744	57.6154 8391	35
36	51.9943 6719	54.5696 1864	57.3014 1263	60.1999 0972	36
37	54.0342 5453	56.7974 3506	59.7339 4794	62.8554 0724	37
38	56.1149 3962	59.0753 7735	62.2272 9664	65.5839 3094	38
39	58.2372 3841	61.4045 7334	64.7829 7906	68.3874 8904	39
40	60.4019 8318	63.7867 7624	67.4025 5354	71.2681 4499	40
41	62.6100 2284	66.2213 6521	70.0876 1737	74.2280 1898	41
42	64.8622 2330	68.7113 4592	72.8398 0781	77.2692 8950	42
43	67.1594 6777	71.2573 5121	75.6608 0300	80.3941 9496	43
44	69.5026 5712	73.8606 4161	78.5523 2308	83.6050 3532	44
45	71.8927 1027	76.5225 0605	81.5161 3116	86.9041 7379	45
46	74.3305 6447	79.2442 6243	84.5540 3443	90.2940 3857	46
47	76.8171 7576	82.0272 5834	87.6678 8530	93.7771 2463	47
48	79.3535 1927	84.8728 7165	90.8595 8243	97.3559 9556	48
49	81.9405 8966	87.7825 1126	94.1310 7199	101.0332 8544	49
50	84.5794 0145	90.7576 1776	97.4843 4879	104.8117 0079	50

TABLE V.—Amount of Annuity of 1 per Period

$$s_{\overline{n}|i} = \frac{(1+i)^n - 1}{i}$$

n	2%	2¼%	2½%	2¾%	n
51	87.2709 8948	93.7996 6416	100.9214 5751	108.6940 2256	51
52	90.0164 0927	96.9101 5661	104.4444 9395	112.6831 0818	52
53	92.8167 3746	100.0906 3513	108.0556 0629	116.7818 9365	53
54	95.6730 7221	103.3426 7442	111.7569 9645	120.9933 9573	54
55	98.5865 3365	106.6678 8460	115.5509 2136	125.3207 1411	55
56	101.5582 6432	110.0679 1200	119.4396 9440	129.7670 3375	56
57	104.5894 2961	113.5444 4002	123.4256 8676	134.3356 2718	57
58	107.6812 1820	117.0991 8992	127.5113 2893	139.0298 5692	58
59	110.8348 4257	120.7339 2169	131.6991 1215	143.8531 7799	59
60	114.0515 3942	124.4504 3493	135.9915 8995	148.8091 4038	60
61	117.3325 7021	128.2505 6972	140.3913 7970	153.9013 9174	61
62	120.6792 2161	132.1362 0754	144.9011 6419	159.1336 8002	62
63	124.0928 0604	136.1092 7221	149.5236 9330	164.5098 5622	63
64	127.5746 6216	140.1717 3083	154.2617 8563	170.0338 7726	64
65	131.1261 5541	144.3255 9477	159.1183 3027	175.7098 0889	65
66	134.7486 7852	148.5729 2066	164.0962 8853	181.5418 2863	66
67	138.4436 5209	152.9158 1137	169.1986 9574	187.5342 2892	67
68	142.2125 2513	157.3564 1713	174.4286 6314	193.6914 2021	68
69	146.0567 7563	161.8969 3651	179.7893 7971	200.0179 3427	69
70	149.9779 1114	166.5396 1758	185.2841 1421	206.5184 2746	70
71	153.9774 6937	171.2867 5898	190.9162 1706	213.1976 8422	71
72	158.0570 1875	176.1407 1106	196.6891 2249	220.0606 2054	72
73	162.2181 5913	181.1038 7705	202.6063 5055	227.1122 8760	73
74	166.4625 2231	186.1787 1429	208.6715 0931	234.3578 7551	74
75	170.7917 7276	191.3677 3536	214.8882 9705	241.8027 1709	75
76	175.2076 0821	196.6735 0941	221.2605 0447	249.4522 9181	76
77	179.7117 6038	202.0986 6337	227.7920 1709	257.3122 2983	77
78	184.3059 9558	207.6458 8329	234.4868 1751	265.3883 1615	78
79	188.9921 1549	213.3179 1567	241.3489 8795	273.6864 9485	79
80	193.7719 5780	219.1175 6877	248.3827 1265	282.2128 7345	80
81	198.6473 9696	225.0477 1407	255.5922 8047	290.9737 2747	81
82	203.6203 4490	231.1112 8763	262.9820 8748	299.9755 0498	82
83	208.6927 5180	237.3112 9160	270.5566 3966	309.2248 3137	83
84	213.8666 0683	243.6507 9567	278.3205 5566	318.7285 1423	84
85	219.1439 3897	250.1329 3857	286.2785 6955	328.4935 4837	85
86	224.5268 1775	256.7609 2969	294.4355 3379	338.5271 2095	86
87	230.0173 5411	263.5380 5060	302.7964 2213	348.8366 1678	87
88	235.6177 0119	270.4676 5674	311.3663 3268	359.4296 2374	88
89	241.3300 5521	277.5531 7902	320.1504 9100	370.3139 3839	89
90	247.1566 5632	284.7981 2555	329.1542 5328	381.4975 7170	90
91	253.0997 8944	292.2060 8337	338.3831 0961	392.9887 5492	91
92	259.1617 8523	299.7807 2025	347.8426 8735	404.7959 4568	92
93	265.3450 2094	307.5257 8645	357.5387 5453	416.9278 3418	93
94	271.6519 2135	315.4451 1665	367.4772 2339	429.3933 4962	94
95	278.0849 5978	323.5426 3177	377.6641 5398	442.2016 6674	95
96	284.6466 5898	331.8223 4099	388.1057 5783	455.3622 1257	96
97	291.3395 9216	340.2883 4366	398.8084 0177	468.8846 7342	97
98	298.1663 8400	348.9448 3139	409.7786 1182	482.7790 0194	98
99	305.1297 1168	357.7960 9010	421.0230 7711	497.0554 2449	99
100	312.2323 0591	366.8465 0213	432.5486 5404	511.7244 4867	100

TABLE V.—Amount of Annuity of 1 per Period

$$s_{\overline{n}|i} = \frac{(1 + i)^n - 1}{i}$$

n	3%	3½%	4%	4½%	n
1	1.0000 0000	1.0000 0000	1.0000 0000	1.0000 0000	1
2	2.0300 0000	2.0350 0000	2.0400 0000	2.0450 0000	2
3	3.0909 0000	3.1062 2500	3.1216 0000	3.1370 2500	3
4	4.1836 2700	4.2149 4288	4.2464 6400	4.2781 9113	4
5	5.3091 3581	5.3624 6588	5.4163 2256	5.4707 0973	5
6	6.4684 0988	6.5501 5218	6.6329 7546	6.7168 9166	6
7	7.6624 6218	7.7794 0751	7.8982 9448	8.0191 5179	7
8	8.8923 3605	9.0516 8677	9.2142 2626	9.3800 1362	8
9	10.1591 0613	10.3684 9581	10.5827 9531	10.8021 1423	9
10	11.4638 7931	11.7313 9316	12.0061 0712	12.2882 0937	10
11	12.8077 0569	13.1419 9192	13.4863 5141	13.8411 7879	11
12	14.1920 2956	14.6019 6164	15.0258 0546	15.4640 3184	12
13	15.6177 9045	16.1130 3030	16.6268 3768	17.1599 1327	13
14	17.0863 2416	17.6769 8636	18.2919 1119	18.9321 0937	14
15	18.5989 1389	19.2956 8088	20.0235 8764	20.7840 5429	15
16	20.1568 8130	20.9710 2971	21.8245 3114	22.7193 3673	16
17	21.7615 8774	22.7050 1575	23.6975 1239	24.7417 0689	17
18	23.4144 3537	24.4996 9130	25.6454 1288	26.8550 8370	18
19	25.1168 6844	26.3571 8050	27.6712 2940	29.0635 6246	19
20	26.8703 7449	28.2796 8181	29.7780 7858	31.3714 2277	20
21	28.6764 8572	30.2694 7068	31.9692 0172	33.7831 3680	21
22	30.5367 8030	32.3289 0215	34.2479 6979	36.3033 7795	22
23	32.4528 8370	34.4604 1373	36.6178 8858	38.9370 2996	23
24	34.4264 7022	36.6665 2821	39.0826 0412	41.6891 9631	24
25	36.4592 6432	38.9498 5669	41.6459 0829	44.5652 1015	25
26	38.5530 4225	41.3131 0168	44.3117 4462	47.5706 4460	26
27	40.7096 3352	43.7590 6024	47.0842 1440	50.7113 2361	27
28	42.9309 2252	46.2906 2734	49.9675 8298	53.9933 3317	28
29	45.2188 5020	48.9107 9930	52.9662 8630	57.4230 3316	29
30	47.5754 1571	51.6226 7728	56.0849 3775	61.0070 6966	30
31	50.0026 7818	54.4294 7098	59.3283 3526	64.7523 8779	31
32	52.5027 5852	57.3345 0247	62.7014 6867	68.6662 4524	32
33	55.0778 4128	60.3412 1005	66.2095 2742	72.7562 2628	33
34	57.7301 7652	63.4531 5240	69.8579 0851	77.0302 5646	34
35	60.4620 8181	66.6740 1274	73.6522 2486	81.4966 1800	35
36	63.2759 4427	70.0076 0318	77.5983 1385	86.1639 6581	36
37	66.1742 2259	73.4578 6930	81.7022 4640	91.0413 4427	37
38	69.1594 4927	77.0288 9472	85.9703 3626	96.1382 0476	38
39	72.2342 3275	80.7249 0604	90.4091 4971	101.4644 2398	39
40	75.4012 5973	84.5502 7775	95.0255 1570	107.0303 2306	40
41	78.6632 9753	88.5095 3747	99.8265 3633	112.8466 8760	41
42	82.0231 9645	92.6073 7128	104.8195 9778	118.9247 8854	42
43	85.4838 9234	96.8486 2928	110.0123 8169	125.2764 0402	43
44	89.0484 0911	101.2383 3130	115.4128 7696	131.9138 4220	44
45	92.7198 6139	105.7816 7290	121.0293 9204	138.8499 6510	45
46	96.5014 5723	110.4840 3145	126.8705 6772	146.0982 1353	46
47	100.3965 0095	115.3509 7255	132.9453 9043	153.6726 3314	47
48	104.4083 9598	120.3882 5659	139.2632 0604	161.5879 0163	48
49	108.5406 4785	125.6018 4557	145.8337 3429	169.8593 5720	49
50	112.7968 6729	130.9979 1016	152.6670 8366	178.5030 2828	50

TABLE V.—Amount of Annuity of 1 per Period

$$s_{\overline{n}|i} = \frac{(1 + i)^n - 1}{i}$$

n	3%	3½%	4%	4½%	n
51	117.1807 7331	136.5828 3702	159.7737 6700	187.5356 6455	51
52	121.6961 9651	142.3632 3631	167.1647 1768	196.9747 6946	52
53	126.3470 8240	148.3459 4958	174.8513 0639	206.8386 3408	53
54	131.1374 9488	154.5380 5782	182.8453 5865	217.1463 7262	54
55	136.0716 1972	160.9468 8984	191.1591 7299	227.9179 5938	55
56	141.1537 6831	167.5800 3099	199.8055 3991	239.1742 6756	56
57	146.3883 8136	174.4453 3207	208.7977 6151	250.9371 0960	57
58	151.7800 3280	181.5509 1869	218.1496 7197	263.2292 7953	58
59	157.3334 3379	188.9052 0085	227.8756 5885	276.0745 9711	59
60	163.0534 3680	196.5168 8288	237.9906 8520	289.4979 5398	60
61	168.9450 3991	204.3949 7378	248.5103 1261	303.5253 6190	61
62	175.0133 9110	212.5487 9786	259.4507 2511	318.1840 0319	62
63	181.2637 9284	220.9880 0579	270.8287 5412	333.5022 8333	63
64	187.7017 0662	229.7225 8599	282.6619 0428	349.5098 8608	64
65	194.3327 5782	238.7628 7650	294.9683 8045	366.2378 3096	65
66	201.1627 4055	248.1195 7718	307.7671 1567	383.7185 3335	66
67	208.1976 2277	257.8037 6238	321.0778 0030	401.9858 6735	67
68	215.4435 5145	267.8268 9406	334.9209 1231	421.0752 3138	68
69	222.9068 5800	278.2008 3535	349.3177 4880	441.0236 1679	69
70	230.5940 6374	288.9378 6459	364.2904 5876	461.8696 7955	70
71	238.5118 8565	300.0506 8985	379.8620 7711	483.6538 1513	71
72	246.6672 4222	311.5524 6400	396.0565 6019	506.4182 3681	72
73	255.0672 5949	323.4568 0024	412.8988 2260	530.2070 5747	73
74	263.7192 7727	335.7777 8824	430.4147 7550	555.0663 7505	74
75	272.6308 5559	348.5300 1083	448.6313 6652	581.0443 6193	75
76	281.8097 8126	361.7285 6121	467.5766 2118	608.1913 5822	76
77	291.2640 7469	375.3890 6085	487.2796 8603	636.5599 6934	77
78	301.0019 9693	389.5276 7798	507.7708 7347	666.2051 6796	78
79	311.0320 5684	404.1611 4671	529.0817 0841	697.1844 0052	79
80	321.3630 1855	419.3067 8685	551.2449 7675	729.5576 9854	80
81	332.0039 0910	434.9825 2439	574.2947 7582	763.3877 9497	81
82	342.9640 2638	451.2069 1274	598.2665 6685	798.7402 4575	82
83	354.2529 4717	467.9991 5469	623.1972 2952	835.6835 5680	83
84	365.8805 3558	485.3791 2510	649.1251 1870	874.2893 1686	84
85	377.8569 5165	503.3673 9448	676.0901 2345	914.6323 3612	85
86	390.1926 6020	521.9852 5329	704.1337 2839	956.7907 9125	86
87	402.8984 4001	541.2547 3715	733.2990 7753	1000.8463 7685	87
88	415.9853 9321	561.1986 5295	763.6310 4063	1046.8844 6381	88
89	429.4649 5500	581.8406 0581	795.1762 8225	1094.9942 6468	89
90	443.3489 0365	603.2050 2701	827.9833 3354	1145.2690 0659	90
91	457.6493 7076	625.3172 0295	862.1026 6688	1197.8061 1189	91
92	472.3788 5189	648.2033 0506	897.5867 7356	1252.7073 8692	92
93	487.5502 1744	671.8904 2073	934.4902 4450	1310.0792 1933	93
94	503.1767 2397	696.4065 8546	972.8698 5428	1370.0327 8420	94
95	519.2720 2569	721.7808 1595	1012.7846 4845	1432.6842 5949	95
96	535.8501 8645	748.0431 4451	1054.2960 3439	1498.1550 5117	96
97	552.9256 9205	775.2246 5457	1097.4678 7577	1566.5720 2847	97
98	570.5134 6281	803.3575 1748	1142.3665 9080	1638.0677 6976	98
99	588.6288 6669	832.4750 3059	1189.0612 5443	1712.7808 1939	99
100	607.2877 3270	862.6116 5666	1237.6237 0461	1790.8559 5627	100

TABLE V.—Amount of Annuity of 1 per Period

$$s_{\overline{n}|i} = \frac{(1 + i)^n - 1}{i}$$

n	5%	5½%	6%	6½%	n
1	1.0000 0000	1.0000 0000	1.0000 0000	1.0000 0000	1
2	2.0500 0000	2.0550 0000	2.0600 0000	2.0650 0000	2
3	3.1525 0000	3.1680 2500	3.1836 0000	3.1992 2500	3
4	4.3101 2500	4.3422 6638	4.3746 1600	4.4071 7463	4
5	5.5256 3125	5.5810 9103	5.6370 9296	5.6936 4098	5
6	6.8019 1281	6.8880 5103	6.9753 1854	7.0637 2764	6
7	8.1420 0845	8.2668 9384	8.3938 3765	8.5228 6994	7
8	9.5491 0888	9.7215 7300	9.8974 6791	10.0768 5648	8
9	11.0265 6432	11.2562 5951	11.4913 1598	11.7318 5215	9
10	12.5778 9254	12.8753 5379	13.1807 9494	13.4944 2254	10
11	14.2067 8716	14.5834 9825	14.9716 4264	15.3715 6001	11
12	15.9171 2652	16.3855 9065	16.8699 4120	17.3707 1141	12
13	17.7129 8285	18.2867 9814	18.8821 3767	19.4998 0765	13
14	19.5986 3199	20.2925 7203	21.0150 6593	21.7672 9515	14
15	21.5785 6359	22.4086 6350	23.2759 6988	24.1821 6933	15
16	23.6574 9177	24.6411 3999	25.6725 2808	26.7540 1034	16
17	25.8403 6636	26.9964 0269	28.2128 7976	29.4930 2101	17
18	28.1323 8467	29.4812 0483	30.9056 5255	32.4100 6738	18
19	30.5390 0391	32.1026 7110	33.7599 9170	35.5167 2176	19
20	33.0659 5410	34.8683 1801	36.7855 9120	38.8253 0867	20
21	35.7192 5181	37.7860 7550	39.9927 2668	42.3489 5373	21
22	38.5052 1440	40.8643 0965	43.3922 9028	46.1016 3573	22
23	41.4304 7512	44.1118 4669	46.9958 2769	50.0982 4205	23
24	44.5019 9887	47.5379 9825	50.8155 7735	54.3546 2778	24
25	47.7270 9882	51.1525 8816	54.8645 1200	58.8876 7859	25
26	51.1134 5376	54.9659 8051	59.1563 8272	63.7153 7769	26
27	54.6691 2645	58.9891 0943	63.7057 6568	68.8568 7725	27
28	58.4025 8277	63.2335 1045	68.5281 1162	74.3325 7427	28
29	62.3227 1191	67.7113 5353	73.6397 9832	80.1641 9159	29
30	66.4388 4750	72.4354 7797	79.0581 8622	86.3748 6405	30
31	70.7607 8988	77.4194 2926	84.8016 7739	92.9892 3021	31
32	75.2988 2937	82.6774 9787	90.8897 7803	100.0335 3017	32
33	80.0637 7084	88.2247 6025	97.3431 6471	107.5357 0963	33
34	85.0669 5938	94.0771 2207	104.1837 5460	115.5255 3076	34
35	90.3203 0735	100.2513 6378	111.4347 7987	124.0346 9026	35
36	95.8363 2272	106.7651 8879	119.1208 6666	133.0969 4513	36
37	101.6281 3886	113.6372 7417	127.2681 1866	142.7482 4656	37
38	107.7095 4580	120.8873 2425	135.9042 0578	153.0268 8259	38
39	114.0950 2309	128.5361 2708	145.0584 5813	163.9736 2995	39
40	120.7997 7424	136.6056 1407	154.7619 6562	175.6319 1590	40
41	127.8397 6295	145.1189 2285	165.0476 8356	188.0479 9044	41
42	135.2317 5110	154.1004 6360	175.9505 4457	201.2711 0981	42
43	142.9933 3866	163.5759 8910	187.5075 7724	215.3537 3195	43
44	151.1430 0559	173.5726 6850	199.7580 3188	230.3517 2453	44
45	159.7001 5587	184.1191 6527	212.7435 1379	246.3245 8662	45
46	168.6851 6366	195.2457 1936	226.5081 2462	263.3356 8475	46
47	178.1194 2185	206.9842 3392	241.0986 1210	281.4525 0426	47
48	188.0253 9294	219.3683 6679	256.5645 2882	300.7469 1704	48
49	198.4266 6259	232.4336 2696	272.9584 0055	321.2954 6665	49
50	209.3479 9572	246.2174 7645	290.3359 0458	343.1796 7198	50

TABLE V.—Amount of Annuity of 1 per Period

$$s_{\overline{n}|i} = \frac{(1 + i)^n - 1}{i}$$

n	5%	5½%	6%	6½%	n
51	220.8153 9550	260.7594 3765	308.7560 5886	366.4863 5066	51
52	232.8561 6528	276.1012 0672	328.2814 2239	391.3079 6345	52
53	245.4989 7354	292.2867 7309	348.9783 0773	417.7429 8108	53
54	258.7739 2222	309.3625 4561	370.9170 0620	445.8962 7485	54
55	272.7126 1833	327.3774 8562	394.1720 2657	475.8795 3271	55
56	287.3482 4924	346.3832 4733	418.8223 4816	507.8117 0234	56
57	302.7156 6171	366.4343 2593	444.9516 8905	541.8194 6299	57
58	318.8514 4479	387.5882 1386	472.6487 9040	578.0377 2808	58
59	335.7940 1703	409.9055 6562	502.0077 1782	616.6101 8041	59
60	353.5837 1788	433.4503 7173	533.1281 8089	657.6898 4214	60
61	372.2629 0378	458.2901 4217	566.1158 7174	701.4396 8187	61
62	391.8760 4897	484.4960 9999	601.0828 2405	748.0332 6120	62
63	412.4698 5141	512.1433 8549	638.1477 9349	797.6554 2317	63
64	434.0933 4398	541.3112 7170	677.4366 6110	850.5030 2568	64
65	456.7980 1118	572.0833 9164	719.0828 6076	906.7857 2235	65
66	480.6379 1174	604.5479 7818	763.2278 3241	966.7267 9430	66
67	505.6698 0733	638.7981 1698	810.0215 0236	1030.5640 3593	67
68	531.9532 9770	674.9320 1341	859.6227 9250	1098.5506 9827	68
69	559.5509 6258	713.0532 7415	912.2001 6005	1170.9564 9365	69
70	588.5285 1071	753.2712 0423	967.9321 6965	1248.0686 6574	70
71	618.9549 3625	795.7011 2046	1027.0080 9983	1330.1931 2901	71
72	650.9026 8306	840.4646 8209	1089.6285 8582	1417.6556 8240	72
73	684.4478 1721	887.6902 3960	1156.0063 0097	1510.8033 0176	73
74	719.6702 0807	937.5132 0278	1226.3666 7903	1610.0055 1637	74
75	756.6537 1848	990.0764 2893	1300.9486 7977	1715.6558 7493	75
76	795.4864 0440	1045.5306 3252	1380.0056 0055	1828.1735 0681	76
77	836.2607 2462	1104.0348 1731	1463.8059 3659	1948.0047 8475	77
78	879.0737 6085	1165.7567 3226	1552.6342 9278	2075.6250 9576	78
79	924.0274 4889	1230.8733 5254	1646.7923 5035	2211.5407 2698	79
80	971.2288 2134	1299.5713 8693	1746.5998 9137	2356.2908 7423	80
81	1020.7902 6240	1372.0478 1321	1852.3958 8485	2510.4497 8106	81
82	1072.8297 7552	1448.5104 4294	1964.5396 3794	2674.6290 1683	82
83	1127.4712 6430	1529.1785 1730	2083.4120 1622	2849.4799 0292	83
84	1184.8448 2752	1614.2833 3575	2209.4167 3719	3035.6960 9661	84
85	1245.0870 6889	1704.0689 1921	2342.9817 4142	3234.0163 4289	85
86	1308.3414 2234	1798.7927 0977	2484.5606 4591	3445.2274 0518	86
87	1374.7584 9345	1898.7263 0881	2634.6342 8466	3670.1671 8652	87
88	1444.4964 1812	2004.1562 5579	2793.7123 4174	3909.7280 5364	88
89	1517.7212 3903	2115.3848 4986	2962.3350 8225	4164.8603 7713	89
90	1594.6073 0098	2232.7310 1660	3141.0751 8718	4436.5763 0164	90
91	1675.3376 6603	2356.5312 2252	3330.5396 9841	4725.9537 6125	91
92	1760.1045 4933	2487.1404 3976	3531.3720 8032	5034.1407 5573	92
93	1849.1097 7680	2624.9331 6394	3744.2544 0514	5362.3599 0485	93
94	1942.5652 6564	2770.3044 8796	3969.9096 6944	5711.9132 9867	94
95	2040.6935 2892	2923.6712 3480	4209.1042 4961	6084.1876 6308	95
96	2143.7282 0537	3085.4731 5271	4462.6505 0459	6480.6598 6118	96
97	2251.9146 1564	3256.1741 7611	4731.4095 3486	6902.9027 5216	97
98	2365.5103 4642	3436.2637 5580	5016.2941 0696	7352.5914 3105	98
99	2484.7858 6374	3626.2582 6237	5318.2717 5337	7831.5098 7406	99
100	2610.0251 5693	3826.7024 6680	5638.3680 5857	8341.5580 1588	100

TABLE V.—Amount of Annuity of 1 per Period

$$s_{\overline{n}|i} = \frac{(1 + i)^n - 1}{i}$$

n	7%	7½%	8%	8½%	n
1	1.0000 0000	1.0000 0000	1.0000 0000	1.0000 0000	1
2	2.0700 0000	2.0750 0000	2.0800 0000	2.0850 0000	2
3	3.2149 0000	3.2306 2500	3.2464 0000	3.2622 2500	3
4	4.4399 4300	4.4729 2188	4.5061 1200	4.5395 1413	4
5	5.7507 3901	5.8083 9102	5.8666 0096	5.9253 7283	5
6	7.1532 9074	7.2440 2034	7.3359 2904	7.4290 2952	6
7	8.6540 2109	8.7873 2187	8.9228 0336	9.0604 9702	7
8	10.2598 0257	10.4463 7101	10.6366 2763	10.8306 3927	8
9	11.9779 8875	12.2298 4883	12.4875 5784	12.7512 4361	9
10	13.8164 4796	14.1470 8750	14.4865 6247	14.8350 9932	10
11	15.7835 9932	16.2081 1906	16.6454 8746	17.0960 8276	11
12	17.8884 5127	18.4237 2799	18.9771 2646	19.5492 4979	12
13	20.1406 4286	20.8055 0759	21.4952 9658	22.2109 3603	13
14	22.5504 8786	23.3659 2066	24.2149 2030	25.0988 6559	14
15	25.1290 2201	26.1183 6470	27.1521 1393	28.2322 6916	15
16	27.8880 5355	29.0772 4206	30.3242 8304	31.6320 1204	16
17	30.8402 1730	32.2580 3521	33.7502 2569	35.3207 3306	17
18	33.9990 3251	35.6773 8785	37.4502 4374	39.3229 9538	18
19	37.3789 6479	39.3531 9194	41.4462 6324	43.6654 4998	19
20	40.9954 9232	43.3046 8134	45.7619 6430	48.3770 1323	20
21	44.8651 7678	47.5525 3244	50.4229 2144	53.4890 5936	21
22	49.0057 3916	52.1189 7237	55.4567 5516	59.0356 2940	22
23	53.4361 4090	57.0278 9530	60.8932 9557	65.0536 5790	23
24	58.1766 7076	62.3049 8744	66.7647 5922	71.5832 1882	24
25	63.2490 3772	67.9778 6150	73.1059 3995	78.6677 9242	25
26	68.6764 7036	74.0762 0112	79.9544 1515	86.3545 5478	26
27	74.4838 2328	80.6319 1620	87.3507 6836	94.6946 9193	27
28	80.6976 9091	87.6793 0991	95.3388 2983	103.7437 4075	28
29	87.3465 2927	95.2552 5816	103.9659 3622	113.5619 5871	29
30	94.4607 8632	103.3994 0252	113.2832 1111	124.2147 2520	30
31	102.0730 4137	112.1543 5771	123.3458 6800	135.7729 7684	31
32	110.2181 5426	121.5659 3454	134.2135 3744	148.3136 7987	32
33	118.9334 2506	131.6833 7963	145.9506 2044	161.9203 4266	33
34	128.2587 6481	142.5596 3310	158.6266 7007	176.6835 7179	34
35	138.2368 7835	154.2516 0558	172.3168 0368	192.7016 7539	35
36	148.9134 5984	166.8204 7600	187.1021 4797	210.0813 1780	36
37	160.3374 0202	180.3320 1170	203.0703 1981	228.9382 2981	37
38	172.5610 2017	194.8569 1258	220.3159 4540	249.3979 7935	38
39	185.6402 9158	210.4711 8102	238.9412 2103	271.5968 0759	39
40	199.6351 1199	227.2565 1960	259.0565 1871	295.6825 3624	40
41	214.6095 6983	245.3007 5857	280.7810 4021	321.8155 5182	41
42	230.6322 3972	264.6983 1546	304.2435 2342	350.1698 7372	42
43	247.7764 9650	285.5506 8912	329.5830 0530	380.9343 1299	43
44	266.1208 5125	307.9669 9080	356.9496 4572	414.3137 2959	44
45	285.7493 1084	332.0645 1511	386.5056 1738	450.5303 9661	45
46	306.7517 6260	357.9693 5375	418.4260 6677	489.8254 8032	46
47	329.2243 8598	385.8170 5528	452.9001 5211	532.4606 4615	47
48	353.2700 9300	415.7533 3442	490.1321 6428	578.7198 0107	48
49	378.9989 9951	447.9348 3451	530.3427 3742	628.9109 8416	49
50	406.5289 2947	482.5299 4709	573.7701 5642	683.3684 1782	50

TABLE V.—Amount of Annuity of 1 per Period

$$s_{\overline{n}|i} = \frac{(1+i)^n - 1}{i}$$

n	7%	7½%	8%	8½%	n
51	435.9859 5454	519.7196 9313	620.6717 6893	742.4547 3333	51
52	467.5049 7135	559.6986 7011	671.3255 1044	806.5633 8566	52
53	501.2303 1935	602.6760 7037	726.0315 5128	876.1212 7345	53
54	537.3164 4170	648.8767 7565	785.1140 7538	951.5915 8169	54
55	575.9285 9262	698.5425 3382	848.9232 0141	1033.4768 6613	55
56	617.2435 9410	751.9332 2386	917.8370 5752	1122.3223 9975	56
57	661.4506 4569	809.3282 1564	992.2640 2213	1218.7198 0373	57
58	708.7521 9089	871.0278 3182	1072.6451 4390	1323.3109 8705	58
59	759.3648 4425	937.3549 1920	1159.4567 5541	1436.7924 2095	59
60	813.5203 8335	1008.6565 3814	1253.2132 9584	1559.9197 7673	60
61	871.4668 1019	1085.3057 7851	1354.4703 5951	1693.5129 5775	61
62	933.4694 8690	1167.7037 1189	1463.8279 8827	1838.4615 5916	62
63	999.8123 5098	1256.2814 9029	1581.9342 2733	1995.7307 9169	63
64	1070.7992 1555	1351.5026 0206	1709.4889 6552	2166.3679 0898	64
65	1146.7551 6064	1453.8652 9721	1847.2480 8276	2351.5091 8125	65
66	1228.0280 2188	1563.9051 9450	1996.0279 2938	2552.3874 6165	66
67	1314.9899 8341	1682.1980 8409	2156.7101 6373	2770.3403 9589	67
68	1408.0392 8225	1809.3629 4040	2330.2469 7683	3006.8193 2954	68
69	1507.6020 3201	1946.0651 6093	2517.6667 3497	3263.3989 7255	69
70	1614.1341 7425	2093.0200 4800	2720.0800 7377	3541.7878 8522	70
71	1728.1235 6645	2250.9965 5160	2938.6864 7967	3843.8398 5546	71
72	1850.0922 1610	2420.8212 9296	3174.7813 9805	4171.5662 4318	72
73	1980.5986 7123	2603.3828 8994	3429.7639 0989	4527.1493 7385	73
74	2120.2405 7821	2799.6366 0668	3705.1450 2268	4912.9570 7063	74
75	2269.6574 1869	3010.6093 5218	4002.5566 2449	5331.5584 2163	75
76	2429.5334 3800	3237.4050 5360	4323.7611 5445	5785.7408 8747	76
77	2600.6007 7866	3481.2104 3262	4670.6620 4681	6278.5288 6290	77
78	2783.6428 3316	3743.3012 1506	5045.3150 1056	6813.2038 1625	78
79	2979.4978 3148	4025.0488 0619	5449.9402 1140	7393.3261 4063	79
80	3189.0626 7969	4327.9274 6666	5886.9354 2831	8022.7588 6259	80
81	3413.2970 6727	4653.5220 2666	6358.8902 6258	8705.6933 6591	81
82	3653.2278 6198	5003.5361 7866	6868.6014 8358	9446.6773 0201	82
83	3909.9538 1231	5379.8013 9206	7419.0896 0227	10250.6448 7268	83
84	4184.6505 7918	5784.2864 9646	8013.6167 7045	11122.9496 8686	84
85	4478.5761 1972	6219.1079 8369	8655.7061 1209	12069.4004 1024	85
86	4793.0764 4810	6686.5410 8247	9349.1626 0105	13096.2994 4511	86
87	5129.5917 9946	7189.0316 6366	10098.0956 0914	14210.4848 9794	87
88	5489.6632 2543	7729.2090 3843	10906.9432 5787	15419.3761 1427	88
89	5874.9396 5121	8309.8997 1631	11780.4987 1850	16731.0230 8398	89
90	6287.1854 2679	8934.1421 9504	12723.9386 1598	18154.1600 4612	90
91	6728.2884 0667	9605.2028 5966	13742.8537 0526	19698.2636 5004	91
92	7200.2685 9513	10326.5930 7414	14843.2820 0168	21373.6160 6029	92
93	7705.2873 9679	11102.0875 5470	16031.7445 6181	23191.3734 2542	93
94	8245.6575 1457	11935.7441 2130	17315.2841 2676	25163.6401 6658	94
95	8823.8535 4059	12831.9249 3040	18701.5068 5690	27303.5495 8074	95
96	9442.5232 8843	13795.3193 0018	20198.6274 0545	29625.3512 9510	96
97	10104.4999 1862	14830.9682 4769	21815.5175 9788	32144.5061 5518	97
98	10812.8149 1292	15944.2908 6627	23561.7590 0572	34877.7891 7837	98
99	11570.7119 5683	17141.1126 8124	25447.6997 2617	37843.4012 5853	99
100	12381.6617 9381	18427.6961 3233	27484.5157 0427	41061.0903 6551	100

TABLE VI.—Present Value of Annuity of 1 per Period

$$a_{\overline{n}|i} = \frac{1 - (1 + i)^{-n}}{i}$$

n	¼%	⁷⁄₂₄%	⅓%	⁵⁄₁₂%	n
1	0.9975 0623	0.9970 9182	0.9966 7774	0.9958 5062	1
2	1.9925 2492	1.9912 8390	1.9900 4426	1.9875 6908	2
3	2.9850 6227	2.9825 8470	2.9801 1056	2.9751 7253	3
4	3.9751 2446	3.9710 0260	3.9668 8760	3.9586 7804	4
5	4.9627 1766	4.9565 4601	4.9503 8631	4.9381 0261	5
6	5.9478 4804	5.9392 2327	5.9306 1759	5.9134 6318	6
7	6.9305 2174	6.9190 4273	6.9075 9228	6.8847 7661	7
8	7.9107 4487	7.8960 1269	7.8813 2121	7.8520 5969	8
9	8.8885 2357	8.8701 4144	8.8518 1516	8.8153 2915	9
10	9.8638 6391	9.8414 3725	9.8190 8487	9.7746 0164	10
11	10.8367 7108	10.8099 0934	10.7831 1107	10.7299 0271	11
12	11.8072 5384	11.7755 6295	11.7439 9442	11.6812 2198	12
13	12.7753 1555	12.7384 0915	12.7016 5557	12.6286 0280	13
14	13.7409 6314	13.6984 5542	13.6561 3512	13.5720 5257	14
15	14.7042 0264	14.6557 0959	14.6074 4364	14.5115 8762	15
16	15.6650 4004	15.6101 7990	15.5555 9167	15.4472 2418	16
17	16.6234 8133	16.5618 7442	16.5005 8970	16.3789 7843	17
18	17.5795 3250	17.5108 0125	17.4424 4821	17.3068 6648	18
19	18.5331 9950	18.4569 6842	18.3811 7762	18.2309 0438	19
20	19.4844 8828	19.4003 8396	19.3167 8832	19.1511 0809	20
21	20.4334 0477	20.3410 5587	20.2492 9069	20.0674 9352	21
22	21.3799 5488	21.2789 9213	21.1786 9504	20.9800 7653	22
23	22.3241 4452	22.2142 0071	22.1050 1167	21.8888 7289	23
24	23.2659 7957	23.1466 8952	23.0282 5083	22.7938 9831	24
25	24.2054 6591	24.0764 6648	23.9484 2275	23.6951 6843	25
26	25.1426 0939	25.0035 3949	24.8655 3763	24.5926 9884	26
27	26.0774 1585	25.9279 1639	25.7796 0561	25.4865 0506	27
28	27.0098 9112	26.8496 0503	26.6906 3682	26.3766 0254	28
29	27.9400 4102	27.7686 1324	27.5986 4135	27.2630 0668	29
30	28.8678 7134	28.6849 4879	28.5036 2925	28.1457 3278	30
31	29.7933 8787	29.5986 1947	29.4056 1055	29.0247 9612	31
32	30.7165 9638	30.5096 3303	30.3045 9523	29.9002 1189	32
33	31.6375 0262	31.4179 9720	31.2005 9325	30.7719 9524	33
34	32.5561 1234	32.3237 1967	32.0936 1454	31.6401 6122	34
35	33.4724 3126	33.2268 0814	32.9836 6898	32.5047 2486	35
36	34.3864 6510	34.1272 7025	33.8707 6642	33.3657 0109	36
37	35.2982 1955	35.0251 1366	34.7549 1670	34.2231 0481	37
38	36.2077 0030	35.9203 4597	35.6361 2960	35.0769 5084	38
39	37.1149 1302	36.8129 7478	36.5144 1488	35.9272 5394	39
40	38.0198 6336	37.7030 0767	37.3897 8228	36.7740 2881	40
41	38.9225 5697	38.5904 5217	38.2622 4147	37.6172 9009	41
42	39.8229 9947	39.4753 1582	39.1318 0213	38.4570 5236	42
43	40.7211 9648	40.3576 0612	39.9984 7388	39.2933 3013	43
44	41.6171 5359	41.2373 3056	40.8622 6633	40.1261 3788	44
45	42.5108 7640	42.1144 9659	41.7231 8903	40.9554 8999	45
46	43.4023 7047	42.9891 1167	42.5812 5153	41.7814 0081	46
47	44.2916 4137	43.8611 8320	43.4364 6332	42.6038 8461	47
48	45.1786 9463	44.7307 1859	44.2888 3387	43.4229 5562	48
49	46.0635 3580	45.5977 2521	45.1383 7263	44.2386 2799	49
50	46.9461 7037	46.4622 1042	45.9850 8900	45.0509 1582	50

TABLE VI.—Present Value of Annuity of 1 per Period

$$a_{\overline{n}|i} = \frac{1 - (1 + i)^{-n}}{i}$$

n	¼%	7⁄24%	⅓%	5⁄12%	n
51	47.8266 0386	47.3241 8154	46.8289 9236	45.8598 3317	51
52	48.7048 4176	48.1836 4589	47.6700 9205	46.6653 9401	52
53	49.5808 8953	49.0406 1076	48.5083 9739	47.4676 1228	53
54	50.4547 5265	49.8950 8341	49.3439 1767	48.2665 0184	54
55	51.3264 3656	50.7470 7110	50.1766 6213	49.0620 7651	55
56	52.1959 4669	51.5965 8106	51.0066 3999	49.8543 5003	56
57	53.0632 8847	52.4436 2048	51.8338 6046	50.6433 3612	57
58	53.9284 6730	53.2881 9656	52.6583 3268	51.4290 4840	58
59	54.7914 8858	54.1303 1645	53.4800 6580	52.2115 0046	59
60	55.6523 5769	54.9699 8730	54.2990 6890	52.9907 0584	60
61	56.5110 7999	55.8072 1623	55.1153 5106	53.7666 7800	61
62	57.3676 6083	56.6420 1035	55.9289 2133	54.5394 3035	62
63	58.2221 0557	57.4743 7673	56.7397 8870	55.3089 7627	63
64	59.0744 1952	58.3043 2244	57.5479 6216	56.0753 2905	64
65	59.9246 0800	59.1318 5451	58.3534 5065	56.8385 0194	65
66	60.7726 7631	59.9569 7996	59.1562 6311	57.5985 0814	66
67	61.6186 2974	60.7797 0580	59.9564 0842	58.3553 6078	67
68	62.4624 7355	61.6000 3900	60.7538 9543	59.1090 7296	68
69	63.3042 1302	62.4179 8652	61.5487 3299	59.8596 5770	69
70	64.1438 5339	63.2335 5529	62.3409 2989	60.6071 2798	70
71	64.9813 9989	64.0467 5224	63.1304 9490	61.3514 9672	71
72	65.8168 5774	64.8575 8427	63.9174 3678	62.0927 7680	72
73	66.6502 3216	65.6660 5824	64.7017 6423	62.8309 8103	73
74	67.4815 2834	66.4721 8103	65.4834 8595	63.5661 2216	74
75	68.3107 5146	67.2759 5945	66.2626 1058	64.2982 1292	75
76	69.1379 0670	68.0774 0035	67.0391 4676	65.0272 6596	76
77	69.9629 9920	68.8765 1050	67.8131 0308	65.7532 9388	77
78	70.7860 3411	69.6732 9670	68.5844 8812	66.4763 0924	78
79	71.6070 1657	70.4677 6569	69.3533 1042	67.1963 2453	79
80	72.4259 5169	71.2599 2422	70.1195 7849	67.9133 5221	80
81	73.2428 4458	72.0497 7901	70.8833 0082	68.6274 0467	81
82	74.0577 0033	72.8373 3675	71.6444 8587	69.3384 9426	82
83	74.8705 2407	73.6226 0413	72.4031 4206	70.0466 3326	83
84	75.6813 2072	74.4055 8781	73.1592 7780	70.7518 3393	84
85	76.4900 9548	75.1862 9442	73.9129 0146	71.4541 0846	85
86	77.2968 5335	75.9647 3060	74.6640 2139	72.1534 6898	86
87	78.1015 9935	76.7409 0294	75.4126 4591	72.8499 2759	87
88	78.9043 3850	77.5148 1803	76.1587 8329	73.5434 9633	88
89	79.7050 7581	78.2864 8243	76.9024 4182	74.2341 8720	89
90	80.5038 1627	79.0559 0268	77.6436 2972	74.9220 1212	90
91	81.3005 6486	79.8230 8532	78.3823 5520	75.6069 8300	91
92	82.0953 2654	80.5880 3685	79.1186 2645	76.2891 1168	92
93	82.8881 0628	81.3507 6377	79.8524 5161	76.9684 0995	93
94	83.6789 0900	82.1112 7253	80.5838 3882	77.6448 8955	94
95	84.4677 3966	82.8695 6959	81.3127 9616	78.3185 6218	95
96	85.2546 0315	83.6256 6138	82.0393 3172	78.9894 3950	96
97	86.0395 0439	84.3795 5432	82.7634 5354	79.6575 3308	97
98	86.8224 4827	85.1312 5480	83.4851 6964	80.3228 5450	98
99	87.6034 3967	85.8807 6919	84.2044 8802	80.9854 1524	99
100	88.3824 8346	86.6281 0386	84.9214 1663	81.6452 2677	100

TABLE VI.—Present Value of Annuity of 1 per Period

$$a_{\overline{n}|i} = \frac{1 - (1 + i)^{-n}}{i}$$

n	¼%	⁷⁄₂₄%	⅓%	⁵⁄₁₂%	n
101	89.1595 8450	87.3732 6514	85.6359 6344	82.3023 0049	101
102	89.9347 4763	88.1162 5935	86.3481 3635	82.9566 4777	102
103	90.7079 7768	88.8570 9280	87.0579 4323	83.6082 7991	103
104	91.4792 7948	89.5957 7177	87.7653 9195	84.2572 0818	104
105	92.2486 5784	90.3323 0252	88.4704 9034	84.9034 4381	105
106	93.0161 1755	91.0666 9131	89.1732 4621	85.5469 9795	106
107	93.7816 6339	91.7989 4436	89.8736 6735	86.1878 8175	107
108	94.5453 0014	92.5290 6788	90.5717 6150	86.8261 0628	108
109	95.3070 3256	93.2570 6806	91.2675 3641	87.4616 8258	109
110	96.0668 6539	93.9829 5109	91.9609 9977	88.0946 2163	110
111	96.8248 0338	94.7067 2312	92.6521 5927	88.7249 3437	111
112	97.5808 5126	95.4283 9028	93.3410 2255	89.3526 3171	112
113	98.3350 1372	96.1479 5870	94.0275 9726	89.9777 2450	113
114	99.0872 9548	96.8654 3448	94.7118 9098	90.6002 2354	114
115	99.8377 0123	97.5808 2372	95.3939 1131	91.2201 3959	115
116	100.5862 3564	98.2941 3246	96.0736 6578	91.8374 8338	116
117	101.3329 0338	99.0053 6678	96.7511 6194	92.4522 6558	117
118	102.0777 0911	99.7145 3269	97.4264 0727	93.0644 9681	118
119	102.8206 5747	100.4216 3621	98.0994 0927	93.6741 8767	119
120	103.5617 5308	101.1266 8335	98.7701 7538	94.2813 4869	120
121	104.3010 0058	101.8296 8009	99.4387 1304	94.8859 9036	121
122	105.0384 0457	102.5306 3237	100.1050 2964	95.4881 2315	122
123	105.7739 6965	103.2295 4616	100.7691 3256	96.0877 5747	123
124	106.5077 0040	103.9264 2738	101.4310 2916	96.6849 0367	124
125	107.2396 0139	104.6212 8194	102.0907 2677	97.2795 7209	125
126	107.9696 7720	105.3141 1573	102.7482 3269	97.8717 7301	126
127	108.6979 3237	106.0049 3464	103.4035 5420	98.4615 1666	127
128	109.4243 7144	106.6937 4451	104.0566 9857	99.0488 1324	128
129	110.1489 9894	107.3805 5120	104.7076 7303	99.6336 7290	129
130	110.8718 1939	108.0653 6053	105.3564 8478	100.2161 0576	130
131	111.5928 3730	108.7481 7831	106.0031 4101	100.7961 2189	131
132	112.3120 5716	109.4290 1032	106.6476 4888	101.3737 3131	132
133	113.0294 8345	110.1078 6235	107.2900 1552	101.9489 4401	133
134	113.7451 2065	110.7847 4016	107.9302 4806	102.5217 6994	134
135	114.4589 7321	111.4596 4947	108.5683 5358	103.0922 1899	135
136	115.1710 4560	112.1325 9603	109.2043 3915	103.6603 0104	136
137	115.8813 4224	112.8035 8553	109.8382 1181	104.2260 2590	137
138	116.5898 6758	113.4726 2368	110.4699 7859	104.7894 0335	138
139	117.2966 2601	114.1397 1613	111.0996 4646	105.3504 4314	139
140	118.0016 2196	114.8048 6856	111.7272 2242	105.9091 5496	140
141	118.7048 5981	115.4680 8660	112.3527 1341	106.4655 4847	141
142	119.4063 4395	116.1293 7588	112.9761 2636	107.0196 3330	142
143	120.1060 7875	116.7887 4201	113.5974 6817	107.5714 1902	143
144	120.8040 6858	117.4461 9058	114.2167 4572	108.1209 1517	144
145	121.5003 1778	118.1017 2717	114.8339 6586	108.6681 3126	145
146	122.1948 3071	118.7553 5734	115.4491 3545	109.2130 7674	146
147	122.8876 1168	119.4070 8663	116.0622 6128	109.7557 6103	147
148	123.5786 6502	120.0569 2057	116.6733 5015	110.2961 9353	148
149	124.2679 9503	120.7048 6467	117.2824 0882	110.8343 8356	149
150	124.9556 0601	121.3509 2444	117.8894 4404	111.3703 4044	150

499

TABLE VI.—Present Value of Annuity of 1 per Period

$$a_{\overline{n}|i} = \frac{1 - (1 + i)^{-n}}{i}$$

n	¼%	⁷⁄₂₄%	⅓%	⁵⁄₁₂%	n
151	125.6415 0226	121.9951 0534	118.4944 6254	111.9040 7343	151
152	126.3256 8804	122.6374 1284	119.0974 7100	112.4355 9176	152
153	127.0081 6762	123.2778 5240	119.6984 7612	112.9649 0463	153
154	127.6889 4525	123.9164 2944	120.2974 8454	113.4920 2117	154
155	128.3680 2519	124.5531 4937	120.8945 0290	114.0169 5051	155
156	129.0454 1166	125.1880 1761	121.4895 3781	114.5397 0171	156
157	129.7211 0889	125.8210 3954	122.0825 9587	115.0602 8383	157
158	130.3951 2109	126.4522 2052	122.6736 8363	115.5787 0585	158
159	131.0674 5246	127.0815 6591	123.2628 0764	116.0949 7674	159
160	131.7381 0719	127.7090 8105	123.8499 7443	116.6091 0543	160
161	132.4070 8946	128.3347 7125	124.4351 9050	117.1211 0081	161
162	133.0744 0346	128.9586 4184	125.0184 6233	117.6309 7172	162
163	133.7400 5332	129.5806 9809	125.5997 9638	118.1387 2699	163
164	134.4040 4321	130.2009 4529	126.1791 9909	118.6443 7539	164
165	135.0663 7727	130.8193 8870	126.7566 7687	119.1479 2566	165
166	135.7270 5962	131.4360 3355	127.3322 3612	119.6493 8641	166
167	136.3860 9439	132.0508 8509	127.9058 8322	120.1487 6662	167
168	137.0434 8567	132.6639 4853	128.4776 2451	120.6460 7460	168
169	137.6992 3758	133.2752 2907	129.0474 6633	121.1413 1907	169
170	138.3533 5419	133.8847 3189	129.6154 1499	121.6345 0858	170
171	139.0058 3959	134.4924 6216	130.1814 7677	122.1256 5166	171
172	139.6566 9785	135.0984 2504	130.7456 5795	122.6147 5680	172
173	140.3059 3302	135.7026 2567	131.3079 6478	123.1018 3246	173
174	140.9535 4914	136.3050 6917	131.8684 0347	123.5868 8705	174
175	141.5995 5027	136.9057 6066	132.4269 8025	124.0699 2898	175
176	142.2439 4042	137.5047 0522	132.9837 0128	124.5509 6658	176
177	142.8867 2361	138.1019 0794	133.5385 7275	125.0300 0817	177
178	143.5279 0385	138.6973 7389	134.0916 0079	125.5070 6204	178
179	144.1674 8514	139.2911 0811	134.6427 9152	125.9821 3643	179
180	144.8054 7146	139.8831 1564	135.1921 5106	126.4552 3956	180
181	145.4418 6679	140.4734 0151	135.7396 8549	126.9263 7961	181
182	146.0766 7510	141.0619 7071	136.2854 0086	127.3955 6471	182
183	146.7099 0035	141.6488 2825	136.8293 0322	127.8628 0299	183
184	147.3415 4649	142.2339 7909	137.3713 9860	128.3281 0253	184
185	147.9716 1744	142.8174 2821	137.9116 9300	128.7914 7136	185
186	148.6001 1715	143.3991 8055	138.4501 9241	129.2529 1749	186
187	149.2270 4952	143.9792 4105	138.9869 0277	129.7124 4891	187
188	149.8524 1848	144.5576 1463	139.5218 3005	130.1700 7357	188
189	150.4762 2791	145.1343 0618	140.0549 8016	130.6257 9936	189
190	151.0984 8170	145.7093 2062	140.5863 5901	131.0796 3418	190
191	151.7191 8375	146.2826 6280	141.1159 7248	131.5315 8586	191
192	152.3383 3790	146.8543 3760	141.6438 2643	131.9816 6223	192
193	152.9559 4803	147.4243 4986	142.1699 2672	132.4298 7106	193
194	153.5720 1799	147.9927 0442	142.6942 7917	132.8762 2010	194
195	154.1865 5161	148.5594 0611	143.2168 8958	133.3207 1707	195
196	154.7995 5272	149.1244 5971	143.7377 6375	133.7633 6965	196
197	155.4110 2516	149.6878 7004	144.2569 0743	134.2041 8550	197
198	156.0209 7273	150.2496 4187	144.7743 2639	134.6431 7224	198
199	156.6293 9923	150.8097 7996	145.2900 2635	135.0803 3746	199
200	157.2363 0846	151.3682 8907	145.8040 1302	135.5156 8872	200

TABLE VI.—Present Value of Annuity of 1 per Period

$$a_{\overline{n}|i} = \frac{1 - (1 + i)^{-n}}{i}$$

n	½%	⁷⁄₁₂%	⅝%	⅔%	n
1	0.9950 2488	0.9942 0050	0.9937 8882	0.9933 7748	1
2	1.9850 9938	1.9826 3513	1.9814 0504	1.9801 7631	2
3	2.9702 4814	2.9653 3733	2.9628 8699	2.9604 4004	3
4	3.9504 9566	3.9423 4034	3.9382 7279	3.9342 1196	4
5	4.9258 6633	4.9136 7723	4.9076 0029	4.9015 3506	5
6	5.8963 8441	5.8793 8084	5.8709 0712	5.8624 5205	6
7	6.8620 7404	6.8394 8385	6.8282 3068	6.8170 0535	7
8	7.8229 5924	7.7940 1875	7.7796 0813	7.7652 3710	8
9	8.7790 6392	8.7430 1781	8.7250 7640	8.7071 8917	9
10	9.7304 1186	9.6865 1315	9.6646 7220	9.6429 0315	10
11	10.6770 2673	10.6245 3669	10.5984 3200	10.5724 2035	11
12	11.6189 3207	11.5571 2016	11.5263 9205	11.4957 8180	12
13	12.5561 5131	12.4842 9511	12.4485 8837	12.4130 2828	13
14	13.4887 0777	13.4060 9291	13.3650 5676	13.3242 0028	14
15	14.4166 2465	14.3225 4473	14.2758 3281	14.2293 3802	15
16	15.3399 2502	15.2336 8160	15.1809 5186	15.1284 8148	16
17	16.2586 3186	16.1395 3432	16.0804 4905	16.0216 7035	17
18	17.1727 6802	17.0401 3354	16.9743 5931	16.9089 4405	18
19	18.0823 5624	17.9355 0974	17.8627 1733	17.7903 4177	19
20	18.9874 1915	18.8256 9320	18.7455 5759	18.6659 0242	20
21	19.8879 7925	19.7107 1404	19.6229 1438	19.5356 6466	21
22	20.7840 5896	20.5906 0220	20.4948 2174	20.3996 6688	22
23	21.6756 8055	21.4653 8745	21.3613 1353	21.2579 4723	23
24	22.5628 6622	22.3350 9938	22.2224 2338	22.1105 4361	24
25	23.4456 3803	23.1997 6741	23.0781 8473	22.9574 9365	25
26	24.3240 1794	24.0594 2079	23.9286 3079	23.7988 3475	26
27	25.1980 2780	24.9140 8862	24.7737 9457	24.6346 0406	27
28	26.0676 8936	25.7637 9979	25.6137 0889	25.4648 3847	28
29	26.9330 2423	26.6085 8307	26.4484 0635	26.2895 7464	29
30	27.7940 5397	27.4484 6702	27.2779 1935	27.1088 4898	30
31	28.6507 9997	28.2834 8006	28.1022 8010	27.9226 9766	31
32	29.5032 8355	29.1136 5044	28.9215 2060	28.7311 5662	32
33	30.3515 2592	29.9390 0625	29.7356 7265	29.5342 6154	33
34	31.1955 4818	30.7595 7540	30.5447 6785	30.3320 4789	34
35	32.0353 7132	31.5753 8566	31.3488 3761	31.1245 5088	35
36	32.8710 1624	32.3864 6463	32.1479 1315	31.9118 0551	36
37	33.7025 0372	33.1928 3974	32.9420 2550	32.6938 4653	37
38	34.5298 5445	33.9945 3828	33.7312 0546	33.4707 0848	38
39	35.3530 8900	34.7915 8736	34.5154 8369	34.2424 2564	39
40	36.1722 2786	35.5840 1396	35.2948 9062	35.0090 3209	40
41	36.9872 9141	36.3718 4487	36.0694 5652	35.7705 6168	41
42	37.7982 9991	37.1551 0676	36.8392 1145	36.5270 4803	42
43	38.6052 7354	37.9338 2612	37.6041 8529	37.2785 2453	43
44	39.4082 3238	38.7080 2929	38.3644 0774	38.0250 2437	44
45	40.2071 9640	39.4777 4248	39.1199 0831	38.7665 8050	45
46	41.0021 8547	40.2429 9170	39.8707 1634	39.5032 2566	46
47	41.7932 1937	41.0038 0287	40.6168 6096	40.2349 9238	47
48	42.5803 1778	41.7602 0170	41.3583 7114	40.9619 1296	48
49	43.3635 0028	42.5122 1380	42.0952 7566	41.6840 1949	49
50	44.1427 8635	43.2598 6460	42.8276 0314	42.4013 4387	50

TABLE VI.—Present Value of Annuity of 1 per Period

$$a_{\overline{n}|i} = \frac{1 - (1 + i)^{-n}}{i}$$

n	½%	⁷⁄₁₂%	⅝%	⅔%	n
51	44.9181 9537	44.0031 7940	43.5553 8201	43.1139 1775	51
52	45.6897 4664	44.7421 8335	44.2786 4050	43.8217 7260	52
53	46.4574 5934	45.4769 0144	44.9974 0671	44.5249 3967	53
54	47.2213 5258	46.2073 5853	45.7117 0853	45.2234 5000	54
55	47.9814 4535	46.9335 7933	46.4215 7370	45.9173 3444	55
56	48.7377 5657	47.6555 8841	47.1270 2976	46.6066 2362	56
57	49.4903 0505	48.3734 1020	47.8281 0410	47.2913 4796	57
58	50.2391 0950	49.0870 6898	48.5248 2396	47.9715 3771	58
59	50.9841 8855	49.7965 8889	49.2172 1636	48.6472 2289	59
60	51.7255 6075	50.5019 9394	49.9053 0818	49.3184 3334	60
61	52.4632 4453	51.2033 0800	50.5891 2614	49.9851 9868	61
62	53.1972 5824	51.9005 5478	51.2686 9679	50.6475 4835	62
63	53.9276 2014	52.5937 5787	51.9440 4650	51.3055 1161	63
64	54.6543 4839	53.2829 4073	52.6152 0149	51.9591 1749	64
65	55.3774 6109	53.9681 2668	53.2821 8781	52.6083 9486	65
66	56.0969 7621	54.6493 3888	53.9450 3137	53.2533 7238	66
67	56.8129 1165	55.3266 0040	54.6037 5788	53.8940 7852	67
68	57.5252 8522	55.9999 3413	55.2583 9293	54.5305 4158	68
69	58.2341 1465	56.6693 6287	55.9089 6191	55.1627 8965	69
70	58.9394 1756	57.3349 0925	56.5554 9010	55.7908 5064	70
71	59.6412 1151	57.9965 9579	57.1980 0258	56.4147 5229	71
72	60.3395 1394	58.6544 4488	57.8365 2431	57.0345 2215	72
73	61.0343 4222	59.3084 7877	58.4710 8006	57.6501 8756	73
74	61.7257 1366	59.9587 1959	59.1016 9447	58.2617 7572	74
75	62.4136 4543	60.6051 8934	59.7283 9201	58.8693 1363	75
76	63.0981 5466	61.2479 0988	60.3511 9703	59.4728 2811	76
77	63.7792 5836	61.8869 0297	60.9701 3370	60.0723 4581	77
78	64.4569 7350	62.5221 9021	61.5852 2604	60.6678 9319	78
79	65.1313 1691	63.1537 9310	62.1964 9792	61.2594 9654	79
80	65.8023 0538	63.7817 3301	62.8039 7309	61.8471 8200	80
81	66.4699 5561	64.4060 3118	63.4076 7512	62.4309 7549	81
82	67.1342 8419	65.0267 0874	64.0076 2745	63.0109 0281	82
83	67.7953 0765	65.6437 8667	64.6038 5337	63.5869 8954	83
84	68.4530 4244	66.2572 8585	65.1963 7602	64.1592 6114	84
85	69.1075 0491	66.8672 2705	65.7852 1840	64.7277 4285	85
86	69.7587 1135	67.4736 3089	66.3704 0338	65.2924 5979	86
87	70.4066 7796	68.0765 1789	66.9519 5367	65.8534 3687	87
88	71.0514 2086	68.6759 0845	67.5298 9185	66.4106 9888	88
89	71.6929 5608	69.2718 2283	68.1042 4034	66.9642 7041	89
90	72.3312 9958	69.8642 8121	68.6750 2146	67.5141 7590	90
91	72.9664 6725	70.4533 0363	69.2422 5735	68.0604 3964	91
92	73.5984 7487	71.0389 1001	69.8059 7004	68.6030 8574	92
93	74.2273 3818	71.6211 2017	70.3661 8141	69.1421 3815	93
94	74.8530 7282	72.1999 5379	70.9229 1320	69.6776 2068	94
95	75.4756 9434	72.7754 3047	71.4761 8703	70.2095 5696	95
96	76.0952 1825	73.3475 6967	72.0260 2438	70.7379 7049	96
97	76.7116 5995	73.9163 9075	72.5724 4658	71.2628 8460	97
98	77.3250 3478	74.4819 1294	73.1154 7487	71.7843 2245	98
99	77.9353 5799	75.0441 5539	73.6551 3030	72.3023 0707	99
100	78.5426 4477	75.6031 3712	74.1914 3384	72.8168 6132	100

TABLE VI.—Present Value of Annuity of 1 per Period

$$a_{\overline{n}|i} = \frac{1 - (1 + i)^{-n}}{i}$$

n	½%	⁷⁄₁₂%	⅝%	⅔%	n
101	79.1469 1021	76.1588 7702	74.7244 0630	73.3280 0792	101
102	79.7481 6937	76.7113 9392	75.2540 6838	73.8357 6944	102
103	80.3464 3718	77.2607 0648	75.7804 4062	74.3401 6830	103
104	80.9417 2854	77.8068 3331	76.3035 4348	74.8412 2677	104
105	81.5340 5825	78.3497 9288	76.8233 9724	75.3389 6697	105
106	82.1234 4104	78.8896 0355	77.3400 2210	75.8334 1088	106
107	82.7098 9158	79.4262 8359	77.8534 3812	76.3245 8032	107
108	83.2934 2446	79.9598 5115	78.3636 6521	76.8124 9699	108
109	83.8740 5419	80.4903 2428	78.8707 2319	77.2971 8242	109
110	84.4517 9522	81.0177 2093	79.3746 3174	77.7786 5801	110
111	85.0266 6191	81.5420 5005	79.8704 1043	78.2569 4303	111
112	85.5986 6856	82.0633 5606	80.3730 7868	78.7320 6458	112
113	86.1678 2942	82.5816 2991	80.8676 5583	79.2040 3764	113
114	86.7341 5862	83.0968 9803	81.3591 6108	79.6728 8505	114
115	87.2976 7027	83.6091 7785	81.8476 1349	80.1386 2751	115
116	87.8583 7838	84.1184 8671	82.3330 3204	80.6012 8559	116
117	88.4162 9690	84.6248 4182	82.8154 3557	81.0608 7970	117
118	88.9714 3970	85.1282 6033	83.2948 4280	81.5174 3015	118
119	89.5238 2059	85.6287 5926	83.7712 7235	81.9709 5708	119
120	90.0734 5333	86.1263 5554	84.2447 4271	82.4214 8052	120
121	90.6203 5157	86.6210 6602	84.7152 7226	82.8690 2036	121
122	91.1645 2892	87.1129 0742	85.1828 7926	83.3135 9636	122
123	91.7059 9893	87.6018 9638	85.6475 8188	83.7552 2815	123
124	92.2447 7505	88.0880 4946	86.1093 9814	84.1939 3523	124
125	92.7808 7070	88.5713 8308	86.5683 4597	84.6297 3696	125
126	93.3142 9920	89.0519 1361	87.0244 4320	85.0626 5259	126
127	93.8450 7384	89.5296 5731	87.4777 0753	85.4927 0122	127
128	94.3732 0780	90.0046 3032	87.9281 5655	85.9199 0185	128
129	94.8987 1422	90.4768 4873	88.3758 0776	86.3442 7334	129
130	95.4216 0619	90.9463 2851	88.8206 7852	86.7658 3442	130
131	95.9418 9671	91.4130 8554	89.2627 8610	87.1846 0371	131
132	96.4595 9872	91.8771 3561	89.7021 4768	87.6005 9969	132
133	96.9747 2509	92.3384 9442	90.1387 8030	88.0138 4072	133
134	97.4872 8865	92.7971 7758	90.5727 0092	88.4243 4507	134
135	97.9973 0214	93.2532 0060	91.0039 2638	88.8321 3084	135
136	98.5047 7825	93.7065 7892	91.4324 7342	89.2372 1604	136
137	99.0097 2960	94.1573 2787	91.8583 5868	89.6396 1856	137
138	99.5121 6875	94.6054 6270	92.2815 9869	90.0393 5616	138
139	100.0121 0821	95.0509 9857	92.7022 0988	90.4364 4649	139
140	100.5095 6041	95.4939 5056	93.1202 0857	90.8309 0709	140
141	101.0045 3772	95.9343 3364	93.5356 1100	91.2227 5536	141
142	101.4970 5246	96.3721 6272	93.9484 3330	91.6120 0861	142
143	101.9871 1688	96.8074 5261	94.3586 9148	91.9986 8402	143
144	102.4747 4316	97.2402 1804	94.7664 0147	92.3827 9867	144
145	102.9599 4344	97.6704 7364	95.1715 7910	92.7643 6952	145
146	103.4427 2979	98.0982 3397	95.5742 4010	93.1434 1340	146
147	103.9231 1422	98.5235 1350	95.9744 0010	93.5199 4706	147
148	104.4011 0868	98.9463 2663	96.3720 7163	93.8939 8712	148
149	104.8767 2505	99.3666 8765	96.7672 7913	94.2655 5010	149
150	105.3499 7518	99.7846 1078	97.1600 2895	94.6346 5239	150

TABLE VI.—Present Value of Annuity of 1 per Period

$$a_{\overline{n}|i} = \frac{1 - (1+i)^{-n}}{i}$$

n	½%	$\frac{7}{12}$%	⅝%	⅔%	n
151	105.8208 7082	100.2001 1017	97.5503 3933	95.0013 1029	151
152	106.2894 2371	100.6131 9987	97.9382 2542	95.3655 4000	152
153	106.7556 4548	101.0238 9385	98.3237 0228	95.7273 5759	153
154	107.2195 4774	101.4322 0601	98.7067 8488	96.0867 7904	154
155	107.6811 4203	101.8381 5017	99.0874 8808	96.4438 2021	155
156	108.1404 3983	102.2417 4005	99.4658 2666	96.7984 9687	156
157	108.5974 5257	102.6429 8931	99.8418 1532	97.1508 2468	157
158	109.0521 9161	103.0419 1152	100.2154 6864	97.5008 1919	158
159	109.5046 6827	103.4385 2019	100.5868 0113	97.8484 9586	159
160	109.9548 9380	103.8328 2872	100.9558 2721	98.1938 7003	160
161	110.4028 7940	104.2248 5046	101.3225 6120	98.5369 5695	161
162	110.8486 3622	104.6145 9866	101.6870 1734	98.8777 7178	162
163	111.2921 7534	105.0020 8652	102.0492 0978	99.2163 2956	163
164	111.7335 0780	105.3873 2715	102.4091 5258	99.5526 4523	164
165	112.1726 4458	105.7703 3357	102.7668 5971	99.8867 3364	165
166	112.6095 9660	106.1511 1874	103.1223 4505	100.2186 0955	166
167	113.0443 7473	106.5296 9555	103.4756 2241	100.5482 8760	167
168	113.4769 8978	106.9060 7680	103.8267 0550	100.8757 8236	168
169	113.9074 5251	107.2802 7523	104.1756 0795	101.2011 0828	169
170	114.3357 7365	107.6523 0349	104.5223 4330	101.5242 7972	170
171	114.7619 6383	108.0221 7417	104.8669 2502	101.8453 1095	171
172	115.1860 3366	108.3898 9979	105.2093 6648	102.1642 1614	172
173	115.6079 3369	108.7554 9278	105.5496 8098	102.4810 0939	173
174	116.0278 5442	109.1189 6552	105.8878 8172	102.7957 0466	174
175	116.4456 2629	109.4803 3029	106.2239 8183	103.1083 1586	175
176	116.8613 1969	109.8395 9933	106.5579 9436	103.4188 5678	176
177	117.2749 4496	110.1967 8478	106.8899 3229	103.7273 4115	177
178	117.6865 1240	110.5518 9874	107.2198 0848	104.0337 8225	178
179	118.0960 3224	110.9049 5322	107.5476 3576	104.3381 9457	179
180	118.5035 1467	111.2559 6015	107.8734 2684	104.6405 9061	180
181	118.9089 6982	111.6049 3142	108.1971 9438	104.9409 8402	181
182	119.3124 0778	111.9518 7882	108.5189 5094	105.2393 8807	182
183	119.7138 3859	112.2968 1411	108.8387 0900	105.5358 1593	183
184	120.1132 7222	112.6397 4894	109.1564 8100	105.8302 8070	184
185	120.5107 1863	112.9806 9492	109.4722 7925	106.1227 9536	185
186	120.9061 8769	113.3196 6359	109.7861 1603	106.4133 7285	186
187	121.2996 8925	113.6566 6640	110.0980 0351	106.7020 2598	187
188	121.6912 3308	113.9917 1477	110.4079 5379	106.9887 6750	188
189	122.0808 2894	114.3248 2002	110.7159 7893	107.2736 1007	189
190	122.4684 8650	114.6559 9342	111.0220 9086	107.5565 6626	190
191	122.8542 1543	114.9852 4619	111.3263 0147	107.8376 4857	191
192	123.2380 2530	115.3125 8945	111.6286 2258	108.1168 6941	192
193	123.6199 2567	115.6380 3429	111.9290 6592	108.3942 4111	193
194	123.9999 2604	115.9615 9171	112.2276 4315	108.6697 7590	194
195	124.3780 3586	116.2832 7265	112.5243 6586	108.9434 8597	195
196	124.7542 6454	116.6030 8801	112.8192 4558	109.2153 8338	196
197	125.1286 2143	116.9210 4859	113.1122 9374	109.4854 8015	197
198	125.5011 1585	117.2371 6516	113.4035 2173	109.7537 8819	198
199	125.8717 5707	117.5514 4842	113.6929 4085	110.0203 1937	199
200	126.2405 5430	117.8639 0899	113.9805 6234	110.2850 8543	200

TABLE VI.—Present Value of Annuity of 1 per Period

$$a_{\overline{n}|i} = \frac{1 - (1 + i)^{-n}}{i}$$

n	$\frac{3}{4}\%$	$\frac{7}{8}\%$	1%	$1\frac{1}{8}\%$	n
1	0.9925 5583	0.9913 2590	0.9900 9901	0.9888 7515	1
2	1.9777 2291	1.9740 5294	1.9703 9506	1.9667 4923	2
3	2.9555 5624	2.9482 5570	2.9409 8521	2.9337 4460	3
4	3.9261 1041	3.9140 0813	3.9019 6555	3.8899 8230	4
5	4.8894 3961	4.8713 8352	4.8534 3124	4.8355 8200	5
6	5.8455 9763	5.8204 5454	5.7954 7647	5.7706 6205	6
7	6.7946 3785	6.7612 9323	6.7281 9453	6.6953 3948	7
8	7.7366 1325	7.6939 7098	7.6516 7775	7.6097 3002	8
9	8.6715 7642	8.6185 5859	8.5660 1758	8.5139 4810	9
10	9.5995 7958	9.5351 2624	9.4713 0453	9.4081 0690	10
11	10.5206 7452	10.4437 4348	10.3676 2825	10.2933 1033	11
12	11.4349 1267	11.3444 7929	11.2550 7747	11.1666 9302	12
13	12.3423 4508	12.2374 0202	12.1337 4007	12.0313 4044	13
14	13.2430 2242	13.1225 7945	13.0037 0304	12.8863 6880	14
15	14.1369 9495	14.0000 7876	13.8650 5252	13.7318 8509	15
16	15.0243 1261	14.8699 6656	14.7178 7378	14.5679 9514	16
17	15.9050 2492	15.7323 0885	15.5622 5127	15.3948 0360	17
18	16.7791 8107	16.5871 7111	16.3982 6858	16.2124 1395	18
19	17.6468 2984	17.4346 1820	17.2260 0850	17.0209 2850	19
20	18.5080 1969	18.2747 1445	18.0455 5297	17.8204 4845	20
21	19.3627 9870	19.1075 2361	18.8569 8313	18.6110 7387	21
22	20.2112 1459	19.9331 0891	19.6603 7934	19.3929 0371	22
23	21.0533 1473	20.7515 3300	20.4558 2113	20.1660 3580	23
24	21.8891 4614	21.5628 5799	21.2433 8726	20.9305 6693	24
25	22.7187 5547	22.3671 4547	22.0231 5570	21.6865 9276	25
26	23.5421 8905	23.1644 5647	22.7952 0366	22.4342 0792	26
27	24.3594 9286	23.9548 5152	23.5596 0759	23.1735 0598	27
28	25.1707 1251	24.7383 9060	24.3164 4316	23.9045 7946	28
29	25.9758 9331	25.5151 3319	25.0657 8530	24.6275 1986	29
30	26.7750 8021	26.2851 3823	25.8077 0822	25.3424 1766	30
31	27.5683 1783	27.0484 6417	26.5422 8537	26.0493 6233	31
32	28.3556 5045	27.8051 6894	27.2695 8947	26.7484 4236	32
33	29.1371 2203	28.5553 0998	27.9896 9255	27.4397 4522	33
34	29.9127 7621	29.2989 4422	28.7026 6589	28.1233 5745	34
35	30.6826 5629	30.0361 2809	29.4085 8009	28.7993 6460	35
36	31.4468 0525	30.7669 1757	30.1075 0504	29.4678 5127	36
37	32.2052 6576	31.4913 6810	30.7995 0994	30.1289 0114	37
38	32.9580 8016	32.2095 3467	31.4846 6330	30.7825 9692	38
39	33.7052 9048	32.9214 7179	32.1630 3298	31.4290 2044	39
40	34.4469 3844	33.6272 3350	32.8346 8611	32.0682 5260	40
41	35.1830 6545	34.3268 7335	33.4996 8922	32.7903 7340	41
42	35.9137 1260	35.0204 4446	34.1581 0814	33.3254 6195	42
43	36.6389 2070	35.7079 9947	34.8100 0806	33.9435 9649	43
44	37.3587 3022	36.3895 9055	35.4554 5352	34.5548 5438	44
45	38.0731 8136	37.0652 6944	36.0945 0844	35.1593 1212	45
46	38.7823 1401	37.7350 8743	36.7272 3608	35.7570 4536	46
47	39.4861 6774	38.3990 9535	37.3536 9909	36.3481 2891	47
48	40.1847 8189	39.0573 4359	37.9739 5949	36.9326 3674	48
49	40.8781 9542	39.7098 8212	38.5880 7871	37.5106 4202	49
50	41.5664 4707	40.3567 6047	39.1961 1753	38.0822 1708	50

TABLE VI.—Present Value of Annuity of 1 per Period

$$a_{\overline{n}|i} = \frac{1 - (1 + i)^{-n}}{i}$$

n	¾%	⅞%	1%	1⅛%	n
51	42.2495 7525	40.9980 2772	39.7981 3617	38.6474 3345	51
52	42.9276 1812	41.6337 3256	40.3941 9423	39.2063 6188	52
53	43.6006 1351	42.2639 2324	40.9843 5072	39.7590 7232	53
54	44.2685 9902	42.8886 4757	41.5686 6408	40.3056 3394	54
55	44.9316 1193	43.5079 5298	42.1471 9216	40.8461 1514	55
56	45.5896 8926	44.1218 8647	42.7199 9224	41.3805 8358	56
57	46.2428 6776	44.7304 9465	43.2871 2102	41.9091 0613	57
58	46.8911 8388	45.3338 2369	43.8486 3468	42.4317 4896	58
59	47.5346 7382	45.9319 1939	44.4045 8879	42.9485 7746	59
60	48.1733 7352	46.5248 2716	44.9550 3841	43.4596 5633	60
61	48.8073 1863	47.1125 9198	45.5000 3803	43.9650 4952	61
62	49.4365 4455	47.6952 5847	46.0396 4161	44.4648 2029	62
63	50.0610 8640	48.2728 7085	46.5739 0258	44.9590 3119	63
64	50.6809 7906	48.8454 7296	47.1028 7385	45.4477 4407	64
65	51.2962 5713	49.4131 0826	47.6266 0777	45.9310 2009	65
66	51.9069 5497	49.9758 1984	48.1451 5621	46.4089 1975	66
67	52.5131 0667	50.5336 5040	48.6585 7050	46.8815 0284	67
68	53.1147 4607	51.0866 4228	49.1669 0149	47.3488 2852	68
69	53.7119 0677	51.6348 3745	49.6701 9949	47.8109 5527	69
70	54.3046 2210	52.1782 7752	50.1685 1435	48.2679 4094	70
71	54.8929 2516	52.7170 0374	50.6618 9539	48.7198 4270	71
72	55.4768 4880	53.2510 5699	51.1503 9148	49.1667 1714	72
73	56.0564 2561	53.7804 7781	51.6340 5097	49.6086 2016	73
74	56.6316 8795	54.3053 0638	52.1129 2175	50.0456 0708	74
75	57.2026 6794	54.8255 8253	52.5870 5124	50.4777 3259	75
76	57.7693 9746	55.3413 4575	53.0564 8637	50.9050 5077	76
77	58.3319 0815	55.8526 3520	53.5212 7364	51.3276 1510	77
78	58.8902 3141	56.3594 8966	53.9814 5905	51.7454 7847	78
79	59.4443 9842	56.8619 4762	54.4370 8817	52.1586 9317	79
80	59.9944 4012	57.3600 4721	54.8882 0611	52.5673 1092	80
81	60.5403 8722	57.8538 2623	55.3348 5753	52.9713 8286	81
82	61.0822 7019	58.3433 2216	55.7770 8666	53.3709 5957	82
83	61.6201 1930	58.8285 7215	56.2149 3729	53.7660 9104	83
84	62.1539 6456	59.3096 1304	56.6484 5276	54.1568 2674	84
85	62.6838 3579	59.7864 8133	57.0776 7600	54.5432 1557	85
86	63.2097 6257	60.2592 1321	57.5026 4951	54.9253 0588	86
87	63.7317 7427	60.7278 4457	57.9234 1535	55.3031 4549	87
88	64.2499 0002	61.1924 1097	58.3400 1520	55.6767 8169	88
89	64.7641 6875	61.6529 4768	58.7524 9030	56.0462 6126	89
90	65.2746 0918	62.1094 8965	59.1608 8148	56.4116 3041	90
91	65.7812 4981	62.5620 7152	59.5652 2919	56.7729 3490	91
92	66.2841 1892	63.0107 2765	59.9655 7346	57.1302 1992	92
93	66.7832 4458	63.4554 9210	60.3619 5392	57.4835 3021	93
94	67.2786 5467	63.8963 9861	60.7544 0982	57.8329 0997	94
95	67.7703 7685	64.3334 8065	61.1429 8002	58.1784 0294	95
96	68.2584 3856	64.7667 7140	61.5277 0299	58.5200 5235	96
97	68.7428 6705	65.1963 0375	61.9086 1682	58.8579 0096	97
98	69.2236 8938	65.6221 1028	62.2857 5923	59.1919 9106	98
99	69.7009 3239	66.0442 2333	62.6591 6755	59.5223 6446	99
100	70.1746 2272	66.4626 7492	63.0288 7877	59.8490 6251	100

TABLE VI.—Present Value of Annuity of 1 per Period

$$a_{\overline{n}|i} = \frac{1 - (1 + i)^{-n}}{i}$$

n	1¼%	1⅜%	1½%	1¾%	n
1	0.9876 5432	0.9864 3650	0.9852 2167	0.9828 0098	1
2	1.9631 1538	1.9594 9346	1.9558 8342	1.9486 9875	2
3	2.9265 3371	2.9193 5237	2.9122 0042	2.8979 8403	3
4	3.8780 5798	3.8661 9222	3.8543 8465	3.8309 4254	4
5	4.8178 3504	4.8001 8962	4.7826 4497	4.7478 5508	5
6	5.7460 0992	5.7215 1874	5.6971 8717	5.6489 9762	6
7	6.6627 2585	6.6303 5140	6.5982 1396	6.5346 4139	7
8	7.5681 2429	7.5268 5712	7.4859 2508	7.4050 5297	8
9	8.4623 4498	8.4112 0308	8.3605 1732	8.2604 9432	9
10	9.3455 2591	9.2835 5421	9.2221 8455	9.1012 2291	10
11	10.2178 0337	10.1440 7320	10.0711 1779	9.9274 9181	11
12	11.0793 1197	10.9929 2054	10.9075 0521	10.7395 4969	12
13	11.9301 8466	11.8302 5454	11.7315 3222	11.5376 4097	13
14	12.7705 5275	12.6562 3136	12.5433 8150	12.3220 0587	14
15	13.6005 4592	13.4710 0504	13.3432 3301	13.0928 8046	15
16	14.4202 9227	14.2747 2754	14.1312 6405	13.8504 9677	16
17	15.2299 1829	15.0675 4874	14.9076 4931	14.5950 8282	17
18	16.0295 4893	15.8496 1651	15.6725 6089	15.3268 6272	18
19	16.8193 0759	16.6210 7671	16.4261 6837	16.0460 5673	19
20	17.5993 1613	17.3820 7320	17.1686 3879	16.7528 8130	20
21	18.3696 9495	18.1327 4792	17.9001 3673	17.4475 4919	21
22	19.1305 6291	18.8732 4086	18.6208 2437	18.1302 6948	22
23	19.8820 3744	19.6036 9012	19.3308 6145	18.8012 4764	23
24	20.6242 3451	20.3242 3193	20.0304 0537	19.4606 8565	24
25	21.3572 6865	21.0350 0067	20.7196 1120	20.1087 8196	25
26	22.0812 5299	21.7361 2890	21.3986 3172	20.7457 3166	26
27	22.7962 9925	22.4277 4737	22.0676 1746	21.3717 2644	27
28	23.5025 1778	23.1099 8508	22.7267 1671	21.9869 5474	28
29	24.2000 1756	23.7829 6925	23.3760 7558	22.5916 0171	29
30	24.8889 0623	24.4468 2540	24.0158 3801	23.1858 4934	30
31	25.5692 9010	25.1016 7734	24.6461 4582	23.7698 7650	31
32	26.2412 7418	25.7476 4719	25.2671 3874	24.3438 5897	32
33	26.9049 6215	26.3848 5543	25.8789 5442	24.9079 6951	33
34	27.5604 5644	27.0134 2089	26.4817 2849	25.4623 7789	34
35	28.2078 5822	27.6334 6080	27.0755 9458	26.0072 5100	35
36	28.8472 6737	28.2450 9080	27.6606 8431	26.5427 5283	36
37	29.4787 8259	28.8484 2496	28.2371 2740	27.0690 4455	37
38	30.1025 0133	29.4435 7579	28.8050 5163	27.5862 8457	38
39	30.7185 1983	30.0306 5430	29.3645 8288	28.0946 2857	39
40	31.3269 3316	30.6097 6996	29.9158 4520	28.5942 2955	40
41	31.9278 3522	31.1810 3079	30.4589 6079	29.0852 3789	41
42	32.5213 1874	31.7445 4332	30.9940 5004	29.5678 0135	42
43	33.1074 7530	32.3004 1264	31.5212 3157	30.0420 6522	43
44	33.6863 9536	32.8487 4243	32.0406 2223	30.5081 7221	44
45	34.2581 6825	33.3896 3495	32.5523 3718	30.9662 6261	45
46	34.8228 8222	33.9231 9108	33.0564 8983	31.4164 7431	46
47	35.3806 2442	34.4495 1031	33.5531 9195	31.8589 4281	47
48	35.9314 8091	34.9686 9081	34.0425 5365	32.2938 0129	48
49	36.4755 3670	35.4808 2941	34.5246 8339	32.7211 8063	49
50	37.0128 7574	35.9860 2161	34.9996 8807	33.1412 0946	50

TABLE VI.—Present Value of Annuity of 1 per Period

$$a_{\overline{n}|i} = \frac{1 - (1 + i)^{-n}}{i}$$

n	1¼%	1⅜%	1½%	1¾%	n
51	37.5435 8099	36.4843 6164	35.4676 7298	33.5540 1421	51
52	38.0677 3431	36.9759 4243	35.9287 4185	33.9597 1913	52
53	38.5854 1660	37.4608 5566	36.3829 9690	34.3584 4633	53
54	39.0967 0776	37.9391 9178	36.8305 3882	34.7503 1579	54
55	39.6016 8667	38.4110 3998	37.2714 6681	35.1354 4550	55
56	40.1004 3128	38.8764 8826	37.7058 7863	35.5139 5135	56
57	40.5930 1855	39.3356 2344	38.1338 7058	35.8859 4727	57
58	41.0795 2449	39.7885 3114	38.5555 3751	36.2515 4523	58
59	41.5600 2419	40.2352 9582	38.9709 7292	36.6108 5526	59
60	42.0345 9179	40.6760 0081	39.3802 6889	36.9639 8552	60
61	42.5033 0054	41.1107 2829	39.7835 1614	37.3110 4228	61
62	42.9662 2275	41.5395 5935	40.1808 0408	37.6521 3000	62
63	43.4234 2988	41.9625 7396	40.5722 2077	37.9873 5135	63
64	43.8749 9247	42.3798 5101	40.9578 5298	38.3168 0723	64
65	44.3209 8022	42.7914 6832	41.3377 8618	38.6405 9678	65
66	44.7614 6195	43.1975 0266	41.7121 0461	38.9588 1748	66
67	45.1965 0563	43.5980 2975	42.0808 9125	39.2715 6509	67
68	45.6261 7840	43.9931 2429	42.4442 2783	39.5789 3375	68
69	46.0505 4656	44.3828 5997	42.8021 9490	39.8810 1597	69
70	46.4696 7562	44.7673 0946	43.1548 7183	40.1779 0267	70
71	46.8836 3024	45.1465 4448	43.5023 3678	40.4696 8321	71
72	47.2924 7431	45.5206 3573	43.8446 6677	40.7564 4542	72
73	47.6962 7093	45.8896 5300	44.1819 3771	41.0382 7560	73
74	48.0950 8240	46.2536 6511	44.5142 2434	41.3152 5857	74
75	48.4889 7027	46.6127 3994	44.8416 0034	41.5874 7771	75
76	48.8779 9533	46.9669 4445	45.1641 3826	41.8550 1495	76
77	49.2622 1761	47.3163 4471	45.4819 0962	42.1179 5081	77
78	49.6416 9640	47.6610 0588	45.7949 8485	42.3763 6443	78
79	50.0164 9027	48.0009 9224	46.1034 3335	42.6303 3359	79
80	50.3866 5706	48.3363 6719	46.4073 2349	42.8799 3474	80
81	50.7522 5389	48.6671 9328	46.7067 2265	43.1252 4298	81
82	51.1133 3717	48.9935 3221	47.0016 9720	43.3663 3217	82
83	51.4699 6264	49.3154 4484	47.2923 1251	43.6032 7486	83
84	51.8221 8532	49.6329 9122	47.5786 3301	43.8361 4237	84
85	52.1700 5958	49.9462 3055	47.8607 2218	44.0650 0479	85
86	52.5136 3909	50.2552 2125	48.1386 4254	44.2899 3099	86
87	52.8529 7868	50.5600 2096	48.4124 5571	44.5109 8869	87
88	53.1881 2531	50.8606 8653	48.6822 2237	44.7282 4441	88
89	53.5191 3611	51.1572 7401	48.9480 0234	44.9417 6355	89
90	53.8460 6035	51.4498 3873	49.2098 5452	45.1516 1037	90
91	54.1689 4850	51.7384 3524	49.4678 3696	45.3578 4803	91
92	54.4878 5037	52.0231 1738	49.7220 0686	45.5605 3860	92
93	54.8028 1518	52.3039 3823	49.9724 2055	45.7597 4310	93
94	55.1138 9154	52.5809 5016	50.2191 3355	45.9555 2147	94
95	55.4211 2744	52.8542 0484	50.4622 0054	46.1479 3265	95
96	55.7245 7031	53.1237 5324	50.7016 7541	46.3370 3455	96
97	56.0242 6698	53.3896 4561	50.9376 1124	46.5228 8408	97
98	56.3202 6368	53.6519 3155	51.1700 6034	46.7055 3718	98
99	56.6126 0610	53.9106 5998	51.3990 7422	46.8850 4882	99
100	56.9013 3936	54.1658 7914	51.6247 0367	47.0614 7304	100

TABLE VI.—Present Value of Annuity of 1 per Period

$$a_{\overline{n}|i} = \frac{1 - (1 + i)^{-n}}{i}$$

n	2%	2¼%	2½%	2¾%	n
1	0.9803 9216	0.9779 9511	0.9756 0976	0.9732 3601	1
2	1.9415 6094	1.9344 6955	1.9274 2415	1.9204 2434	2
3	2.8838 8327	2.8698 9687	2.8560 2356	2.8422 6213	3
4	3.8077 2870	3.7847 4021	3,7619 7421	3.7394 2787	4
5	4.7134 5951	4.6794 5253	4.6458 2850	4.6125 8186	5
6	5.6014 3089	5.5544 7680	5.5081 2536	5.4623 6678	6
7	6.4719 9107	6.4102 4626	6.3493 9060	6.2894 0806	7
8	7.3254 8144	7.2471 8461	7.1701 3717	7.0943 1441	8
9	8.1622 3671	8.0657 0622	7.9708 6553	7.8776 7826	9
10	8.9825 8501	8.8662 1635	8.7520 6393	8.6400 7616	10
11	9.7868 4805	9.6491 1134	9.5142 0871	9.3820 6926	11
12	10.5753 4122	10.4147 7882	10.2577 6460	10.1042 0366	12
13	11.3483 7375	11.1635 9787	10.9831 8497	10.8070 1086	13
14	12.1062 4877	11.8959 3924	11.6909 1217	11.4910 0814	14
15	12.8492 6350	12.6121 6551	12.3813 7773	12.1566 9892	15
16	13.5777 0931	13.3126 3131	13.0550 0266	12.8045 7315	16
17	14.2918 7188	13.9976 8343	13.7121 9772	13.4351 0769	17
18	14.9920 3125	14.6676 6106	14.3533 6363	14.0487 6661	18
19	15.6784 6201	15.3228 9590	14.9788 9134	14.6460 0157	19
20	16.3514 3334	15.9637 1237	15.5891 6229	15.2272 5213	20
21	17.0112 0916	16.5904 2775	16.1845 4857	15.7929 4612	21
22	17.6580 4820	17.2033 5232	16.7654 1324	16.3434 9987	22
23	18.2922 0412	17.8027 8955	17.3321 1048	16.8793 1861	23
24	18.9139 2560	18.3890 3624	17.8849 8583	17.4007 9670	24
25	19.5234 5647	18.9623 8263	18.4243 7642	17.9083 1795	25
26	20.1210 3576	19.5231 1260	18.9506 1114	18.4022 5592	26
27	20.7068 9780	20.0715 0376	19.4640 1087	18.8829 7413	27
28	21.2812 7236	20.6078 2764	19.9648 8866	19.3508 2640	28
29	21.8443 8466	21.1323 4977	20.4535 4991	19.8061 5708	29
30	22.3964 5555	21.6453 2985	20.9302 9259	20.2493 0130	30
31	22.9377 0152	22.1470 2186	21.3954 0741	20.6805 8520	31
32	23.4683 3482	22.6376 7419	21.8491 7796	21.1003 2623	32
33	23.9885 6355	23.1175 2977	22.2918 8094	21.5088 3332	33
34	24.4985 9172	23.5868 2618	22.7237 8628	21.9064 0712	34
35	24.9986 1933	24.0457 9577	23.1451 5734	22.2933 4026	35
36	25.4888 4248	24.4946 6579	23.5562 5107	22.6699 1753	36
37	25.9694 5341	24.9336 5848	23.9573 1812	23.0364 1609	37
38	26.4406 4060	25.3629 9118	24.3486 0304	23.3931 0568	38
39	26.9025 8883	25.7828 7646	24.7303 4443	23.7402 4884	39
40	27.3554 7924	26.1935 2221	25.1027 7505	24.0781 0106	40
41	27.7994 8945	26.5951 3174	25.4661 2200	24.4069 1101	41
42	28.2347 9358	26.9879 0390	25.8206 0683	24.7269 2069	42
43	28.6615 6233	27.3720 3316	26.1664 4569	25.0383 6563	43
44	29.0799 6307	27.7477 0969	26.5038 4945	25.3414 7507	44
45	29.4901 5987	28.1151 1950	26.8330 2386	25.6364 7209	45
46	29.8923 1360	28.4744 4450	27.1541 6962	25.9235 7381	46
47	30.2865 8196	28.8258 6259	27.4674 8255	26.2029 9154	47
48	30.6731 1957	29.1695 4777	27.7731 5371	26.4749 3094	48
49	31.0520 7801	29.5056 7019	28.0713 6947	26.7395 9215	49
50	31.4236 0589	29.8343 9627	28.3623 1168	26.9971 6998	50

TABLE VI.—Present Value of Annuity of 1 per Period

$$a_{\overline{n}|i} = \frac{1 - (1 + i)^{-n}}{i}$$

n	2%	2¼%	2½%	2¾%	n
51	31.7878 4892	30.1558 8877	28.6461 5774	27.2478 5400	51
52	32.1449 4992	30.4703 0687	28.9230 8072	27.4918 2871	52
53	32.4950 4894	30.7778 0623	29.1932 4948	27.7292 7368	53
54	32.8382 8327	31.0785 3910	29.4568 2876	27.9603 6368	54
55	33.1747 8752	31.3726 5438	29.7139 7928	28.1852 6879	55
56	33.5046 9365	31.6602 9768	29.9648 5784	28.4041 5454	56
57	33.8281 3103	31.9416 1142	30.2096 1740	28.6171 8203	57
58	34.1452 2650	32.2167 3489	30.4484 0722	28.8245 0806	58
59	34.4561 0441	32.4858 0429	30.6813 7290	29.0262 8522	59
60	34.7608 8668	32.7489 5285	30.9086 5649	29.2226 6201	60
61	35.0596 9282	33.0063 1086	31.1303 9657	29.4137 8298	61
62	35.3526 4002	33.2580 0573	31.3467 2836	29.5997 8879	62
63	35.6398 4316	33.5041 6208	31.5577 8377	29.7808 1634	63
64	35.9214 1486	33.7449 0179	31.7636 9148	29.9569 9887	64
65	36.1974 6555	33.9803 4405	31.9645 7705	30.1284 6605	65
66	36.4681 0348	34.2106 0543	32.1605 6298	30.2953 4409	66
67	36.7334 3478	34.4357 9993	32.3517 6876	30.4577 5581	67
68	36.9935 6351	34.6560 3905	32.5383 1099	30.6158 2074	68
69	37.2485 9168	34.8714 3183	32.7203 0340	30.7696 5522	69
70	37.4986 1929	35.0820 8492	32.8978 5698	30.9193 7247	70
71	37.7437 4441	35.2881 0261	33.0710 7998	31.0650 8270	71
72	37.9840 6314	35.4895 8691	33.2400 7803	31.2068 9314	72
73	38.2196 6975	35.6866 3756	33.4049 5417	31.3449 0816	73
74	38.4506 5662	35.8793 5214	33.5658 0895	31.4792 2936	74
75	38.6771 1433	36.0678 2605	33.7227 4044	31.6099 5558	75
76	38.8991 3170	36.2521 5262	33.8758 4433	31.7371 8304	76
77	39.1167 9578	36.4324 2310	34.0252 1398	31.8610 0540	77
78	39.3301 9194	36.6087 2675	34.1709 4047	31.9815 1377	78
79	39.5394 0386	36.7811 5085	34.3131 1265	32.0987 9685	79
80	39.7445 1359	36.9497 8079	34.4518 1722	32.2129 4098	80
81	39.9456 0156	37.1147 0004	34.5871 3875	32.3240 3015	81
82	40.1427 4663	37.2759 9026	34.7191 5976	32.4321 4613	82
83	40.3360 2611	37.4337 3130	34.8479 6074	32.5373 6850	83
84	40.5255 1579	37.5880 0127	34.9736 2023	32.6397 7469	84
85	40.7112 8999	37.7388 7655	35.0962 1486	32.7394 4009	85
86	40.8934 2156	37.8864 3183	35.2158 1938	32.8364 3804	86
87	41.0719 8192	38.0307 4018	35.3325 0671	32.9308 3994	87
88	41.2470 4110	38.1718 7304	35.4463 4801	33.0227 1527	88
89	41.4186 6774	38.3099 0028	35.5574 1269	33.1121 3165	89
90	41.5869 2916	38.4448 9025	35.6657 6848	33.1991 5489	90
91	41.7518 9133	38.5769 0978	35.7714 8144	33.2838 4905	91
92	41.9136 1895	38.7060 2423	35.8746 1604	33.3662 7644	92
93	42.0721 7545	38.8322 9754	35.9752 3516	33.4464 9776	93
94	42.2276 2299	38.9557 9221	36.0734 0016	33.5245 7202	94
95	42.3800 2254	39.0755 6940	36.1691 7089	33.6005 5671	95
96	42.5294 3386	39.1946 8890	36.2626 0574	33.6745 0775	96
97	42.6759 1555	39.3102 0920	36.3537 6170	33.7464 7956	97
98	42.8195 2505	39.4231 8748	36.4426 9434	33.8165 2512	98
99	42.9603 1867	39.5336 7968	36.5294 5790	33.8846 9598	99
100	43.0983 5164	39.6417 4052	36.6141 0526	33.9510 4232	100

TABLE VI.—Present Value of Annuity of 1 per Period

$$a_{\overline{n}|i} = \frac{1 - (1 + i)^{-n}}{i}$$

n	3%	3½%	4%	4½%	n
1	0.9708 7379	0.9661 8357	0.9615 3846	0.9569 3780	1
2	1.9134 6970	1.8996 9428	1.8860 9467	1.8726 6775	2
3	2.8286 1135	2.8016 3698	2.7750 9103	2.7489 6435	3
4	3.7170 9840	3.6730 7921	3.6298 9522	3.5875 2570	4
5	4.5797 0719	4.5150 5238	4.4518 2233	4.3899 7674	5
6	5.4171 9144	5.3285 5302	5.2421 3686	5.1578 7248	6
7	6.2302 8296	6.1145 4398	6.0020 5467	5.8927 0094	7
8	7.0196 9219	6.8739 5554	6.7327 4487	6.5958 8607	8
9	7.7861 0892	7.6076 8651	7.4353 3161	7.2687 9050	9
10	8.5302 0284	8.3166 0532	8.1108 9578	7.9127 1818	10
11	9.2526 2411	9.0015 5104	8.7604 7671	8.5289 1692	11
12	9.9540 0399	9.6633 3433	9.3850 7376	9.1185 8078	12
13	10.6349 5533	10.3027 3849	9.9856 4785	9.6828 5242	13
14	11.2960 7314	10.9205 2028	10.5631 2293	10.2228 2528	14
15	11.9379 3509	11.5174 1090	11.1183 8743	10.7395 4573	15
16	12.5611 0203	12.0941 1681	11.6522 9561	11.2340 1505	16
17	13.1661 1847	12.6513 2059	12.1656 6885	11.7071 9143	17
18	13.7535 1308	13.1896 8173	12.6592 9697	12.1599 9180	18
19	14.3237 9911	13.7098 3742	13.1339 3940	12.5932 9359	19
20	14.8774 7486	14.2124 0330	13.5903 2634	13.0079 3645	20
21	15.4150 2414	14.6979 7420	14.0291 5995	13.4047 2388	21
22	15.9369 1664	15.1671 2484	14.4511 1533	13.7844 2476	22
23	16.4436 0839	15.6204 1047	14.8568 4167	14.1477 7489	23
24	16.9355 4212	16.0583 6760	15.2469 6314	14.4954 7837	24
25	17.4131 4769	16.4815 1459	15.6220 7994	14.8282 0896	25
26	17.8768 4242	16.8903 5226	15.9827 6918	15.1466 1145	26
27	18.3270 3147	17.2853 6451	16.3295 8575	15.4513 0282	27
28	18.7641 0823	17.6670 1885	16.6630 6322	15.7428 7351	28
29	19.1884 5459	18.0357 6700	16.9837 1463	16.0218 8853	29
30	19.6004 4135	18.3920 4541	17.2920 3330	16.2888 8854	30
31	20.0004 2849	18.7362 7576	17.5884 9356	16.5443 9095	31
32	20.3887 6553	19.0688 6547	17.8735 5150	16.7888 9086	32
33	20.7657 9178	19.3902 0818	18.1476 4567	17.0228 6207	33
34	21.1318 3668	19.7006 8423	18.4111 9776	17.2467 5796	34
35	21.4872 2007	20.0006 6110	18.6646 1323	17.4610 1240	35
36	21.8322 5250	20.2904 9381	18.9082 8195	17.6660 4058	36
37	22.1672 3544	20.5705 2542	19.1425 7880	17.8622 3979	37
38	22.4924 6159	20.8410 8736	19.3678 6423	18.0499 9023	38
39	22.8082 1513	21.1024 9987	19.5844 8484	18.2296 5572	39
40	23.1147 7197	21.3550 7234	19.7927 7388	18.4015 8442	40
41	23.4123 9997	21.5991 0371	19.9930 5181	18.5661 0949	41
42	23.7013 5920	21.8348 8281	20.1856 2674	18.7235 4975	42
43	23.9819 0213	22.0626 8870	20.3707 9494	18.8742 1029	43
44	24.2542 7392	22.2827 9102	20.5488 4129	19.0183 8305	44
45	24.5187 1254	22.4954 5026	20.7200 3970	19.1563 4742	45
46	24.7754 4907	22.7009 1813	20.8846 5356	19.2883 7074	46
47	25.0247 0783	22.8994 3780	21.0429 3612	19.4147 0884	47
48	25.2667 0664	23.0912 4425	21.1951 3088	19.5356 0654	48
49	25.5016 5693	23.2765 6450	21.3414 7200	19.6512 9813	49
50	25.7297 6401	23.4556 1787	21.4821 8462	19.7620 0778	50

TABLE VI.—Present Value of Annuity of 1 per Period

$$a_{\overline{n}|i} = \frac{1 - (1 + i)^{-n}}{i}$$

n	3%	3½%	4%	4½%	n
51	25.9512 2719	23.6286 1630	21.6174 8521	19.8679 5003	51
52	26.1662 3999	23.7957 6454	21.7475 8193	19.9693 3017	52
53	26.3749 9028	23.9572 6043	21.8726 7493	20.0663 4466	53
54	26.5776 6047	24.1132 9510	21.9929 5667	20.1591 8149	54
55	26.7744 2764	24.2640 5323	22.1086 1218	20.2480 2057	55
56	26.9654 6373	24.4097 1327	22.2189 1940	20.3330 3404	56
57	27.1509 3566	24.5504 4760	22.3267 4943	20.4143 8664	57
58	27.3310 0549	24.6864 2281	22.4295 6676	20.4922 3602	58
59	27.5058 3058	24.8177 9981	22.5284 2957	20.5667 3303	59
60	27.6755 6367	24.9447 3412	22.6234 8997	20.6380 2204	60
61	27.8403 5307	25.0673 7596	22.7148 9421	20.7062 4118	61
62	28.0003 4279	25.1858 7049	22.8027 8289	20.7715 2266	62
63	28.1556 7261	25.3003 5796	22.8872 9124	20.8339 9298	63
64	28.3064 7826	25.4109 7388	22.9685 4927	20.8937 7319	64
65	28.4528 9152	25.5178 4916	23.0466 8199	20.9509 7913	65
66	28.5950 4031	25.6211 1030	23.1218 0961	21.0057 2165	66
67	28.7330 4884	25.7208 7951	23.1940 4770	21.0581 0684	67
68	28.8670 3771	25.8172 7489	23.2635 0740	21.1082 3621	68
69	28.9971 2399	25.9104 1052	23.3302 9558	21.1562 0690	69
70	29.1234 2135	26.0003 9664	23.3945 1498	21.2021 1187	70
71	29.2460 4015	26.0873 3975	23.4562 6440	21.2460 4007	71
72	29.3650 8752	26.1713 4275	23.5156 3885	21.2880 7662	72
73	29.4806 6750	26.2525 0508	23.5727 2966	21.3283 0298	73
74	29.5928 8106	26.3309 2278	23.6276 2468	21.3667 9711	74
75	29.7018 2628	26.4066 8868	23.6804 0834	21.4036 3360	75
76	29.8075 9833	26.4798 9244	23.7311 6187	21.4388 8383	76
77	29.9102 8964	26.5506 2072	23.7799 6333	21.4726 1611	77
78	30.0099 8994	26.6189 5721	23.8268 8782	21.5048 9579	78
79	30.1067 8635	26.6849 8281	23.8720 0752	21.5357 8545	79
80	30.2007 6345	26.7487 7567	23.9153 9185	21.5653 4493	80
81	30.2920 0335	26.8104 1127	23.9571 0754	21.5936 3151	81
82	30.3805 8577	26.8699 6258	23.9972 1879	21.6207 0001	82
83	30.4665 8813	26.9275 0008	24.0357 8730	21.6466 0288	83
84	30.5500 8556	26.9830 9186	24.0728 7240	21.6713 9032	84
85	30.6311 5103	27.0368 0373	24.1085 3116	21.6951 1035	85
86	30.7098 5537	27.0886 9926	24.1428 1842	21.7178 0895	86
87	30.7862 6735	27.1388 3986	24.1757 8694	21.7395 3009	87
88	30.8604 5374	27.1872 8489	24.2074 8745	21.7603 1588	88
89	30.9324 7936	27.2340 9168	24.2379 6870	21.7802 0658	89
90	31.0024 0714	27.2793 1564	24.2672 7759	21.7992 4075	90
91	31.0702 9820	27.3230 1028	24.2954 5923	21.8174 5526	91
92	31.1362 1184	27.3652 2732	24.3225 5695	21.8348 8542	92
93	31.2002 0567	27.4060 1673	24.3486 1245	21.8515 6499	93
94	31.2623 3560	27.4454 2680	24.3736 6582	21.8675 2631	94
95	31.3226 5592	27.4835 0415	24.3977 5559	21.8828 0030	95
96	31.3812 1934	27.5202 9387	24.4209 1884	21.8974 1655	96
97	31.4380 7703	27.5558 3948	24.4431 9119	21.9114 0340	97
98	31.4932 7867	27.5901 8308	24.4646 0692	21.9247 8794	98
99	31.5468 7250	27.6233 6529	24.4851 9896	21.9375 9612	99
100	31.5989 0534	27.6554 2540	24.5049 9900	21.9498 5274	100

TABLE VI.—Present Value of Annuity of 1 per Period

$$a_{\overline{n}|i} = \frac{1 - (1 + i)^{-n}}{i}$$

n	5%	5½%	6%	6½%	n
1	0.9523 8095	0.9478 6730	0.9433 9623	0.9389 6714	1
2	1.8594 1043	1.8463 1971	1.8333 9267	1.8206 2642	2
3	2.7232 4803	2.6979 3338	2.6730 1195	2.6484 7551	3
4	3.5459 5050	3.5051 5012	3.4651 0561	3.4257 9860	4
5	4.3294 7667	4.2702 8448	4.2123 6379	4.1556 7944	5
6	5.0756 9206	4.9955 3031	4.9173 2433	4.8410 1356	6
7	5.7863 7340	5.6829 6712	5.5823 8144	5.4845 1977	7
8	6.4632 1276	6.3345 6599	6.2097 9381	6.0887 5096	8
9	7.1078 2168	6.9521 9525	6.8016 9227	6.6561 0419	9
10	7.7217 3493	7.5376 2583	7.3600 8705	7.1888 3022	10
11	8.3064 1422	8.0925 3633	7.8868 7458	7.6890 4246	11
12	8.8632 5164	8.6185 1785	8.3838 4394	8.1587 2532	12
13	9.3935 7299	9.1170 7853	8.8526 8296	8.5997 4208	13
14	9.8986 4094	9.5896 4790	9.2949 8393	9.0138 4233	14
15	10.3796 5804	10.0375 8094	9.7122 4899	9.4026 6885	15
16	10.8377 6956	10.4621 6203	10.1058 9527	9.7677 6418	16
17	11.2740 6625	10.8646 0856	10.4772 5969	10.1105 7670	17
18	11.6895 8690	11.2460 7447	10.8276 0348	10.4324 6638	18
19	12.0853 2086	11.6076 5352	11.1581 1649	10.7347 1022	19
20	12.4622 1034	11.9503 8249	11.4699 2122	11.0185 0725	20
21	12.8211 5271	12.2752 4406	11.7640 7662	11.2849 8333	21
22	13.1630 0258	12.5831 6973	12.0415 8172	11.5351 9562	22
23	13.4885 7388	12.8750 4240	12.3033 7898	11.7701 3673	23
24	13.7986 4179	13.1516 9895	12.5503 5753	11.9907 3871	24
25	14.0939 4457	13.4139 3266	12.7833 5616	12.1978 7672	25
26	14.3751 8530	13.6624 9541	13.0031 6619	12.3923 7251	26
27	14.6430 3362	13.8980 9991	13.2105 3414	12.5749 9766	27
28	14.8981 2726	14.1214 2172	13.4061 6428	12.7464 7668	28
29	15.1410 7358	14.3331 0116	13.5907 2102	12.9074 8984	29
30	15.3724 5103	14.5337 4517	13.7648 3115	13.0586 7591	30
31	15.5928 1050	14.7239 2907	13.9290 8599	13.2006 3465	31
32	15.8026 7667	14.9041 9817	14.0840 4339	13.3339 2925	32
33	16.0025 4921	15.0750 6936	14.2302 2961	13.4590 8850	33
34	16.1929 0401	15.2370 3257	14.3681 4114	13.5766 0892	34
35	16.3741 9429	15.3905 5220	14.4982 4636	13.6869 5673	35
36	16.5468 5171	15.5360 6843	14.6209 8713	13.7905 6970	36
37	16.7112 8734	15.6739 9851	14.7367 8031	13.8878 5887	37
38	16.8678 9271	15.8047 3793	14.8460 1916	13.9792 1021	38
39	17.0170 4067	15.9286 6154	14.9490 7468	14.0649 8611	39
40	17.1590 8635	16.0461 2469	15.0462 9687	14.1455 2687	40
41	17.2943 6796	16.1574 6416	15.1380 1592	14.2211 5199	41
42	17.4232 0758	16.2629 9920	15.2245 4332	14.2921 6149	42
43	17.5459 1198	16.3630 3242	15.3061 7294	14.3588 3708	43
44	17.6627 7331	16.4578 5063	15.3831 8202	14.4214 4327	44
45	17.7740 6982	16.5477 2572	15.4558 3209	14.4802 2842	45
46	17.8800 6650	16.6329 1537	15.5243 6990	14.5354 2575	46
47	17.9810 1571	16.7136 6386	15.5890 2821	14.5872 5422	47
48	18.0771 5782	16.7902 0271	15.6500 2661	14.6359 1946	48
49	18.1687 2173	16.8627 5139	15.7075 7227	14.6816 1451	49
50	18.2559 2546	16.9315 1790	15.7618 6064	14.7245 2067	50

TABLE VI.—Present Value of Annuity of 1 per Period

$$a_{\overline{n}|i} = \frac{1 - (1 + i)^{-n}}{i}$$

n	5%	5½%	6%	6½%	n
51	18.3389 7663	16.9966 9943	15.8130 7607	14.7648 0814	51
52	18.4180 7298	17.0584 8287	15.8613 9252	14.8026 3675	52
53	18.4934 0284	17.1170 4538	15.9069 7408	14.8381 5658	53
54	18.5651 4556	17.1725 5486	15.9499 7554	14.8715 0852	54
55	18.6334 7196	17.2251 7048	15.9905 4297	14.9028 2490	55
56	18.6985 4473	17.2750 4311	16.0288 1412	14.9322 2996	56
57	18.7605 1879	17.3223 1575	16.0649 1898	14.9598 4033	57
58	18.8195 4170	17.3671 2393	16.0989 8017	14.9857 6557	58
59	18.8757 5400	17.4095 9614	16.1311 1337	15.0101 0852	59
60	18.9292 8952	17.4498 5416	16.1614 2771	15.0329 6574	60
61	18.9802 7574	17.4880 1343	16.1900 2614	15.0544 2793	61
62	19.0288 3404	17.5241 8334	16.2170 0579	15.0745 8021	62
63	19.0750 8003	17.5584 6762	16.2424 5829	15.0935 0255	63
64	19.1191 2384	17.5909 6457	16.2664 7009	15.1112 7000	64
65	19.1610 7033	17.6217 6737	16.2891 2272	15.1279 5305	65
66	19.2010 1936	17.6509 6433	16.3104 9314	15.1436 1789	66
67	19.2390 6606	17.6786 3917	16.3306 5390	15.1583 2666	67
68	19.2753 0101	17.7048 7125	16.3496 7349	15.1721 3770	68
69	19.3098 1048	17.7297 3579	16.3676 1650	15.1851 0583	69
70	19.3426 7665	17.7533 0406	16.3845 4387	15.1972 8247	70
71	19.3739 7776	17.7756 4366	16.4005 1308	15.2087 1593	71
72	19.4037 8834	17.7968 1864	16.4155 7838	15.2194 5158	72
73	19.4321 7937	17.8168 8970	16.4297 9093	15.2295 3200	73
74	19.4592 1845	17.8359 1441	16.4431 9899	15.2389 9718	74
75	19.4849 6995	17.8539 4731	16.4558 4810	15.2478 8468	75
76	19.5094 9519	17.8710 4010	16.4677 8123	15.2562 2974	76
77	19.5328 5257	17.8872 4180	16.4790 3889	15.2640 6549	77
78	19.5550 9768	17.9025 9887	16.4896 5933	15.2714 2299	78
79	19.5762 8351	17.9171 5532	16.4996 7862	15.2783 3145	79
80	19.5964 6048	17.9309 5291	16.5091 3077	15.2848 1826	80
81	19.6156 7665	17.9440 3120	16.5180 4790	15.2909 0917	81
82	19.6339 7776	17.9564 2768	16.5264 6028	15.2966 2832	82
83	19.6514 0739	17.9681 7789	16.5343 9649	15.3019 9843	83
84	19.6680 0704	17.9793 1554	16.5418 8348	15.3070 4078	84
85	19.6838 1623	17.9898 7255	16.5489 4668	15.3117 7538	85
86	19.6988 7260	17.9998 7919	16.5556 1008	15.3162 2101	86
87	19.7132 1200	18.0093 6416	16.5618 9630	15.3203 9531	87
88	19.7268 6857	18.0183 5466	16.5678 2670	15.3243 1485	88
89	19.7398 7483	18.0268 7645	16.5734 2141	15.3279 9516	89
90	19.7522 6174	18.0349 5398	16.5786 9944	15.3314 5086	90
91	19.7640 5880	18.0426 1041	16.5836 7872	15.3346 9564	91
92	19.7752 9410	18.0498 6769	16.5883 7615	15.3377 4239	92
93	19.7859 9438	18.0567 4662	16.5928 0769	15.3406 0318	93
94	19.7961 8512	18.0632 6694	16.5969 8839	15.3432 8937	94
95	19.8058 9059	18.0694 4734	16.6009 3244	15.3458 1161	95
96	19.8151 3390	18.0753 0553	16.6046 5325	15.3481 7992	96
97	19.8239 3705	18.0808 5833	16.6081 6344	15.3504 0368	97
98	19.8323 2100	18.0861 2164	16.6114 7494	15.3524 9172	98
99	19.8403 0571	18.0911 1055	16.6145 9900	15.3544 5232	99
100	19.8479 1020	18.0958 3939	16.6175 4623	15.3562 9326	100

TABLE VI.—Present Value of Annuity of 1 per Period

$$a_{\overline{n}|i} = \frac{1 - (1 + i)^{-n}}{i}$$

n	7%	7½%	8%	8½%	n
1	0.9345 7944	0.9302 3256	0.9259 2593	0.9216 5899	1
2	1.8080 1817	1.7955 6517	1.7832 6475	1.7711 1427	2
3	2.6243 1604	2.6005 2574	2.5770 9699	2.5540 2237	3
4	3.3872 1126	3.3493 2627	3.3121 2684	3.2755 9666	4
5	4.1001 9744	4.0458 8490	3.9927 1004	3.9406 4208	5
6	4.7665 3966	4.6938 4642	4.6228 7966	4.5535 8717	6
7	5.3892 8940	5.2966 0132	5.2063 7006	5.1185 1352	7
8	5.9712 9851	5.8573 0355	5.7466 3894	5.6391 8297	8
9	6.5152 3225	6.3788 8703	6.2468 8791	6.1190 6264	9
10	7.0235 8154	6.8640 8096	6.7100 8140	6.5613 4806	10
11	7.4996 7434	7.3154 2415	7.1389 6426	6.9689 8439	11
12	7.9426 8630	7.7352 7827	7.5360 7802	7.3446 8607	12
13	8.3576 5074	8.1258 4026	7.9037 7594	7.6909 5490	13
14	8.7454 6799	8.4891 5373	8.2442 3698	8.0100 9668	14
15	9.1079 1401	8.8271 1974	8.5594 7869	8.3042 3658	15
16	9.4466 4860	9.1415 0674	8.8513 6916	8.5753 3325	16
17	9.7632 2299	9.4339 5976	9.1216 3811	8.8251 9194	17
18	10.0590 8691	9.7060 0908	9.3718 8714	9.0554 7644	18
19	10.3355 9524	9.9590 7821	9.6035 9920	9.2677 2022	19
20	10.5940 1425	10.1944 9136	9.8181 4741	9.4633 3661	20
21	10.8355 2733	10.4134 8033	10.0168 0316	9.6436 2821	21
22	11.0612 4050	10.6171 9101	10.2007 4366	9.8097 9559	22
23	11.2721 8738	10.8066 8931	10.3710 5895	9.9629 4524	23
24	11.4693 3400	10.9829 6680	10.5287 5828	10.1040 9700	24
25	11.6535 8318	11.1469 4586	10.6747 7619	10.2341 9078	25
26	11.8257 7867	11.2994 8452	10.8099 7795	10.3540 9288	26
27	11.9867 0904	11.4413 8095	10.9351 6477	10.4646 0174	27
28	12.1371 1125	11.5733 7763	11.0510 7849	10.5664 5321	28
29	12.2776 7407	11.6961 6524	11.1584 0601	10.6603 2554	29
30	12.4090 4118	11.8103 8627	11.2577 8334	10.7468 4382	30
31	12.5318 1419	11.9166 3839	11.3497 9939	10.8265 8416	31
32	12.6465 5532	12.0154 7757	11.4349 9944	10.9000 7757	32
33	12.7537 9002	12.1074 2099	11.5138 8837	10.9678 1343	33
34	12.8540 0936	12.1929 4976	11.5869 3367	11.0302 4279	34
35	12.9476 7230	12.2725 1141	11.6545 6822	11.0877 8137	35
36	13.0352 0776	12.3465 2224	11.7171 9279	11.1408 1233	36
37	13.1170 1660	12.4153 6953	11.7751 7851	11.1896 8878	37
38	13.1934 7345	12.4794 1351	11.8288 6899	11.2347 3620	38
39	13.2649 2846	12.5389 8931	11.8785 8240	11.2762 5457	39
40	13.3317 0884	12.5944 0866	11.9246 1333	11.3145 2034	40
41	13.3941 2041	12.6459 6155	11.9672 3457	11.3497 8833	41
42	13.4524 4898	12.6939 1772	12.0066 9867	11.3822 9339	42
43	13.5069 6167	12.7385 2811	12.0432 3951	11.4122 5197	43
44	13.5579 0810	12.7800 2615	12.0770 7362	11.4398 6357	44
45	13.6055 2159	12.8186 2898	12.1084 0150	11.4653 1205	45
46	13.6500 2018	12.8545 3858	12.1374 0880	11.4887 6686	46
47	13.6916 0764	12.8879 4287	12.1642 6741	11.5103 8420	47
48	13.7304 7443	12.9190 1662	12.1891 3649	11.5303 0802	48
49	13.7667 9853	12.9479 2244	12.2121 6341	11.5486 7099	49
50	13.8007 4629	12.9748 1157	12.2334 8464	11.5655 9538	50

TABLE VI.—Present Value of Annuity of 1 per Period

$$a_{\overline{n}|i} = \frac{1 - (1 + i)^{-n}}{i}$$

n	7%	7½%	8%	8½%	n
51	13.8324 7317	12.9998 2472	12.2532 2652	11.5811 9390	51
52	13.8621 2446	13.0230 9276	12.2715 0604	11.5955 7041	52
53	13.8898 3594	13.0447 3745	12.2884 3152	11.6088 2066	53
54	13.9157 3453	13.0648 7205	12.3041 0326	11.6210 3287	54
55	13.9399 3881	13.0836 0191	12.3186 1413	11.6322 8835	55
56	13.9625 5964	13.1010 2503	12.3320 5012	11.6426 6208	56
57	13.9837 0059	13.1172 3258	12.3444 9085	11.6522 2311	57
58	14.0034 5850	13.1323 0938	12.3560 1005	11.6610 3513	58
59	14.0219 2383	13.1463 3431	12.3666 7597	11.6691 5680	59
60	14.0391 8115	13.1593 8075	12.3765 5182	11.6766 4221	60
61	14.0553 0949	13.1715 1698	12.3856 9613	11.6835 4121	61
62	14.0703 8290	13.1828 0649	12.3941 6309	11.6898 9973	62
63	14.0844 6981	13.1933 0836	12.4020 0286	11.6957 6012	63
64	14.0976 3534	13.2030 7755	12.4092 6190	11.7011 6140	64
65	14.1099 3957	13 2121 6516	12.4159 8324	11.7061 3954	65
66	14.1214 3885	13.2206 1875	12.4222 0671	11.7107 2769	66
67	14.1321 8584	13.2284 8256	12.4279 6917	11.7149 5639	67
68	14.1422 2976	13.2357 9773	12.4333 0479	11.7188 5382	68
69	14.1516 1660	13.2426 0254	12.4382 4518	11.7224 4592	69
70	14.1603 8934	13.2489 3260	12.4428 1961	11.7257 5661	70
71	14.1685 8817	13.2548 2102	12.4470 5519	11.7288 0793	71
72	14.1762 5063	13.2602 9862	12.4509 7703	11.7316 2021	72
73	14.1834 1180	13.2653 9407	12.4546 0836	11.7342 1218	73
74	14.1901 0449	13.2701 3402	12.4579 7071	11.7366 0109	74
75	14.1963 5933	13.2745 4327	12.4610 8399	11.7388 0284	75
76	14.2022 0498	13.2786 4490	12.4639 6665	11.7408 3211	76
77	14.2076 6821	13.2824 6038	12.4666 3579	11.7427 0241	77
78	14.2127 7403	13.2860 0965	12.4691 0721	11.7444 2618	78
79	14.2175 4582	13.2893 1130	12.4713 9557	11.7460 1492	79
80	14.2220 0544	13.2923 8261	12.4735 1441	11.7474 7919	80
81	14.2261 7331	13.2952 3964	12.4754 7631	11.7488 2874	81
82	14.2300 6851	13.2978 9734	12.4772 9288	11.7500 7257	82
83	14.2337 0889	13.3003 6962	12.4789 7489	11.7512 1896	83
84	14.2371 1111	13.3026 6941	12.4805 3230	11.7522 7554	84
85	14.2402 9076	13.3048 0875	12.4819 7436	11.7532 4935	85
86	14.2432 6239	13.3067 9884	12.4833 0959	11.7541 4686	86
87	14.2460 3962	13.3086 5008	12.4845 4592	11.7549 7407	87
88	14.2486 3516	13.3103 7217	12.4856 9066	11.7557 3647	88
89	14.2510 6089	13.3119 7411	12.4867 5061	11.7564 3914	89
90	14.2533 2794	13.3134 6429	12.4877 3205	11.7570 8677	90
91	14.2554 4667	13.3148 5050	12.4886 4079	11.7576 8365	91
92	14.2574 2680	13.3161 4000	12.4894 8221	11.7582 3378	92
93	14.2592 7738	13.3173 3954	12.4902 6131	11.7587 4081	93
94	14.2610 0690	13.3184 5538	12.4909 8269	11.7592 0812	94
95	14.2626 2327	13.3194 9338	12.4916 5064	11.7596 3882	95
96	14.2641 3390	13.3204 5896	12.4922 6911	11.7600 3578	96
97	14.2655 4570	13.3213 5717	12.4928 4177	11.7604 0164	97
98	14.2668 6514	13.3221 9272	12.4933 7201	11.7607 3884	98
99	14.2680 9826	13.3229 6997	12.4938 6297	11.7610 4962	99
100	14.2692 5071	13.3236 9290	12.4943 1757	11.7613 3606	100

TABLE VII.—Periodic Rent of Annuity Whose Present Value is 1

$$\frac{1}{a_{\overline{n}|i}} = \frac{i}{1 - (1 + i)^{-n}} \qquad \left[\frac{1}{s_{\overline{n}|i}} = \frac{1}{a_{\overline{n}|i}} - i\right]$$

n	¼%	7/24%	⅓%	5/12%	n
1	1.0025 0000	1.0029 1667	1.0033 3333	1.0041 6667	1
2	0.5018 7578	0.5021 8856	0.5025 0139	0.5031 2717	2
3	0.3350 0139	0.3352 7967	0.3355 5802	0.3361 1496	3
4	0.2515 6445	0.2518 2557	0.2520 8680	0.2526 0958	4
5	0.2015 0250	0.2017 5340	0.2020 0444	0.2025 0693	5
6	0.1681 2803	0.1683 7219	0.1686 1650	0.1691 0564	6
7	0.1442 8928	0.1445 2866	0.1447 6824	0.1452 4800	7
8	0.1264 1035	0.1266 4620	0.1268 8228	0.1273 5512	8
9	0.1125 0462	0.1127 3777	0.1129 7118	0.1134 3876	9
10	0.1013 8015	0.1016 1117	0.1018 4248	0.1023 0596	10
11	0.0922 7840	0.0925 0772	0.0927 3736	0.0931 9757	11
12	0.0846 9370	0.0849 2163	0.0851 4990	0.0856 0748	12
13	0.0782 7595	0.0785 0274	0.0787 2989	0.0791 8532	13
14	0.0727 7510	0.0730 0093	0.0732 2716	0.0736 8082	14
15	0.0680 0777	0.0682 3279	0.0684 5825	0.0689 1045	15
16	0.0638 3642	0.0640 6076	0.0642 8557	0.0647 3655	16
17	0.0601 5587	0.0603 7964	0.0606 0389	0.0610 5387	17
18	0.0568 8433	0.0571 0761	0.0573 3140	0.0577 8053	18
19	0.0539 5722	0.0541 8008	0.0544 0348	0.0548 5191	19
20	0.0513 2288	0.0515 4537	0.0517 6844	0.0522 1630	20
21	0.0489 3947	0.0491 6166	0.0493 8445	0.0498 3183	21
22	0.0467 7278	0.0469 9471	0.0472 1726	0.0476 6427	22
23	0.0447 9455	0.0450 1625	0.0452 3861	0.0456 8531	23
24	0.0429 8121	0.0432 0272	0.0434 2492	0.0438 7129	24
25	0.0413 1298	0.0415 3433	0.0417 5640	0.0422 0270	25
26	0.0397 7312	0.0399 9434	0.0402 1630	0.0406 6247	26
27	0.0383 4736	0.0385 6847	0.0387 9035	0.0392 3645	27
28	0.0370 2347	0.0372 4450	0.0374 6632	0.0379 1239	28
29	0.0357 9093	0.0360 1188	0.0362 3367	0.0366 7974	29
30	0.0346 4059	0.0348 6149	0.0350 8325	0.0355 2936	30
31	0.0335 6449	0.0337 8536	0.0340 0712	0.0344 5330	31
32	0.0325 5569	0.0327 7653	0.0329 9830	0.0334 4468	32
33	0.0316 0806	0.0318 2889	0.0320 5067	0.0324 9708	33
34	0.0307 1620	0.0309 3703	0.0311 5885	0.0316 0540	34
35	0.0298 7533	0.0300 9618	0.0303 1803	0.0307 6476	35
36	0.0290 8121	0.0293 0208	0.0295 2399	0.0299 7090	36
37	0.0283 3004	0.0285 5094	0.0287 7291	0.0292 2003	37
38	0.0276 1843	0.0278 3938	0.0280 6141	0.0285 0875	38
39	0.0269 4335	0.0271 6434	0.0273 8644	0.0278 3402	39
40	0.0263 0204	0.0265 2308	0.0267 4527	0.0271 9310	40
41	0.0256 9204	0.0259 1315	0.0261 3543	0.0263 8352	41
42	0.0251 1112	0.0253 3229	0.0255 5466	0.0260 0303	42
43	0.0245 5724	0.0247 7848	0.0250 0095	0.0254 4961	43
44	0.0240 2855	0.0242 4987	0.0244 7246	0.0249 2141	44
45	0.0235 2339	0.0237 4479	0.0239 6749	0.0244 1675	45
46	0.0230 4022	0.0232 6170	0.0234 8451	0.0239 3409	46
47	0.0225 7762	0.0227 9920	0.0230 2213	0.0234 7204	47
48	0.0221 3433	0.0223 5600	0.0225 7905	0.0230 2929	48
49	0.0217 0915	0.0219 3092	0.0221 5410	0.0226 0468	49
50	0.0213 0099	0.0215 2287	0.0217 4618	0.0221 9711	50

TABLE VII.—Periodic Rent of Annuity Whose Present Value is 1

$$\frac{1}{a_{\overline{n}|i}} = \frac{i}{1 - (1+i)^{-n}} \qquad \left[\frac{1}{s_{\overline{n}|i}} = \frac{1}{a_{\overline{n}|i}} - i \right]$$

n	¼%	⁷⁄₂₄%	⅓%	⁵⁄₁₂%	n
51	0.0209 0886	0.0211 3085	0.0213 5429	0.0218 0557	51
52	0.0205 3184	0.0207 5393	0.0209 7751	0.0214 2916	52
53	0.0201 6906	0.0203 9126	0.0206 1499	0.0210 6700	53
54	0.0198 1974	0.0200 4205	0.0202 6592	0.0207 1830	54
55	0.0194 8314	0.0197 0557	0.0199 2958	0.0203 8234	55
56	0.0191 5858	0.0193 8113	0.0196 0529	0.0200 5843	56
57	0.0188 4542	0.0190 6810	0.0192 9241	0.0197 4593	57
58	0.0185 4308	0.0187 6588	0.0189 9035	0.0194 4426	58
59	0.0182 5101	0.0184 7394	0.0186 9856	0.0191 5287	59
60	0.0179 6869	0.0181 9175	0.0184 1652	0.0188 7123	60
61	0.0176 9564	0.0179 1883	0.0181 4377	0.0185 9888	61
62	0.0174 3142	0.0176 5474	0.0178 7984	0.0183 3536	62
63	0.0171 7561	0.0173 9906	0.0176 2432	0.0180 8025	63
64	0.0169 2780	0.0171 5139	0.0173 7681	0.0178 3315	64
65	0.0166 8764	0.0169 1136	0.0171 3695	0.0175 9371	65
66	0.0164 5476	0.0166 7863	0.0169 0438	0.0173 6156	66
67	0.0162 2886	0.0164 5286	0.0166 7878	0.0171 3639	67
68	0.0160 0961	0.0162 3376	0.0164 5985	0.0169 1788	68
69	0.0157 9674	0.0160 2102	0.0162 4729	0.0167 0574	69
70	0.0155 8996	0.0158 1439	0.0160 4083	0.0164 9971	70
71	0.0153 8902	0.0156 1359	0.0158 4021	0.0162 9952	71
72	0.0151 9368	0.0154 1840	0.0156 4518	0.0161 0493	72
73	0.0150 0370	0.0152 2857	0.0154 5553	0.0159 1572	73
74	0.0148 1887	0.0150 4389	0.0152 7103	0.0157 3165	74
75	0.0146 3898	0.0148 6415	0.0150 9147	0.0155 5253	75
76	0.0144 6385	0.0146 8916	0.0149 1666	0.0153 7816	76
77	0.0142 9327	0.0145 1974	0.0147 4641	0.0152 0836	77
78	0.0141 2708	0.0143 5270	0.0145 8056	0.0150 4295	78
79	0.0139 6511	0.0141 9089	0.0144 1892	0.0148 8177	79
80	0.0138 0721	0.0140 3313	0.0142 6135	0.0147 2464	80
81	0.0136 5321	0.0138 7929	0.0141 0770	0.0145 7144	81
82	0.0135 0298	0.0137 2922	0.0139 5781	0.0144 2200	82
83	0.0133 5639	0.0135 8278	0.0138 1156	0.0142 7620	83
84	0.0132 1330	0.0134 3985	0.0136 6881	0.0141 3391	84
85	0.0130 7359	0.0133 0030	0.0135 2944	0.0139 9500	85
86	0.0129 3714	0.0131 6400	0.0133 9333	0.0138 5935	86
87	0.0128 0384	0.0130 3086	0.0132 6038	0.0137 2685	87
88	0.0126 7357	0.0129 0076	0.0131 3046	0.0135 9740	88
89	0.0125 4625	0.0127 7360	0.0130 0349	0.0134 7088	89
90	0.0124 2177	0.0126 4928	0.0128 7936	0.0133 4721	90
91	0.0123 0004	0.0125 2770	0.0127 5797	0.0132 2629	91
92	0.0121 8096	0.0124 0879	0.0126 3925	0.0131 0803	92
93	0.0120 6446	0.0122 9245	0.0125 2310	0.0129 9234	93
94	0.0119 5044	0.0121 7860	0.0124 0944	0.0128 7915	94
95	0.0118 3884	0 0120 6716	0.0122 9819	0.0127 6837	95
96	0.0117 2957	0.0119 5805	0.0121 8928	0.0126 5992	96
97	0.0116 2257	0.0118 5121	0 0120 8263	0.0125 5374	97
98	0.0115 1776	0.0117 4657	0.0119 7818	0.0124 4976	98
99	0.0114 1508	0.0116 4405	0.0118 7585	0.0123 4790	99
100	0.0113 1446	0.0115 4360	0.0117 7559	0.0122 4811	100

TABLE VII.—Periodic Rent of Annuity Whose Present Value is 1

$$\frac{1}{a_{\overline{n}|i}} = \frac{i}{1 - (1 + i)^{-n}} \qquad \left[\frac{1}{s_{\overline{n}|i}} = \frac{1}{a_{\overline{n}|i}} - i\right]$$

n	¼%	7⁄24%	⅓%	5⁄12%	n
101	0.0112 1584	0.0114 4515	0.0116 7734	0.0121 5033	101
102	0.0111 1917	0.0113 4864	0.0115 8103	0.0120 5449	102
103	0.0110 2439	0.0112 5403	0.0114 8660	0.0119 6054	103
104	0.0109 3144	0.0111 6124	0.0113 9401	0.0118 6842	104
105	0.0108 4027	0.0110 7024	0.0113 0320	0.0117 7809	105
106	0.0107 5083	0.0109 8096	0.0112 1413	0.0116 8948	106
107	0.0106 6307	0.0108 9337	0.0111 2673	0.0116 0256	107
108	0.0105 7694	0.0108 0741	0.0110 4097	0.0115 1727	108
109	0.0104 9241	0.0107 2305	0.0109 5680	0.0114 3358	109
110	0.0104 0942	0.0106 4023	0.0108 7417	0.0113 5143	110
111	0.0103 2793	0.0105 5891	0.0107 9306	0.0112 7079	111
112	0.0102 4791	0.0104 7906	0.0107 1340	0.0111 9161	112
113	0.0101 6932	0.0104 0064	0.0106 3518	0.0111 1386	113
114	0.0100 9211	0.0103 2360	0.0105 5834	0.0110 3750	114
115	0.0100 1625	0.0102 4792	0.0104 8285	0.0109 6249	115
116	0.0099 4172	0.0101 7355	0.0104 0868	0.0108 8880	116
117	0.0098 6846	0.0101 0046	0.0103 3579	0.0108 1639	117
118	0.0097 9646	0.0100 2863	0.0102 6416	0.0107 4524	118
119	0.0097 2567	0.0099 5801	0.0101 9374	0.0106 7530	119
120	0.0096 5608	0.0098 8859	0.0101 2451	0.0106 0655	120
121	0.0095 8764	0.0098 2032	0.0100 5645	0.0105 3896	121
122	0.0095 2033	0.0097 5318	0.0099 8951	0.0104 7251	122
123	0.0094 5412	0.0096 8715	0.0099 2367	0.0104 0715	123
124	0.0093 8899	0.0096 2219	0.0098 5892	0.0103 4288	124
125	0.0093 2491	0.0095 5828	0.0097 9521	0.0102 7965	125
126	0.0092 6186	0.0094 9540	0.0097 3253	0.0102 1745	126
127	0.0091 9981	0.0094 3352	0.0096 7085	0.0101 5625	127
128	0.0091 3873	0.0093 7262	0.0096 1015	0.0100 9603	128
129	0.0090 7861	0.0093 1267	0.0095 5040	0.0100 3677	129
130	0.0090 1942	0.0092 5366	0.0094 9159	0.0099 7844	130
131	0.0089 6115	0.0091 9556	0.0094 3368	0.0099 2102	131
132	0.0089 0376	0.0091 3834	0.0093 7667	0.0098 6449	132
133	0.0088 4725	0.0090 8200	0.0093 2053	0.0098 0883	133
134	0.0087 9159	0.0090 2651	0.0092 6524	0.0097 5403	134
135	0.0087 3675	0.0089 7186	0.0092 1079	0.0097 0005	135
136	0.0086 8274	0.0089 1801	0.0091 5715	0.0096 4689	136
137	0.0086 2952	0.0088 6497	0.0091 0430	0.0095 9453	137
138	0.0085 7707	0.0088 1270	0.0090 5223	0.0095 4295	138
139	0.0085 2539	0.0087 6119	0.0090 0093	0.0094 9213	139
140	0.0084 7446	0.0087 1043	0.0089 5037	0.0094 4205	140
141	0.0084 2425	0.0086 6040	0.0089 0054	0.0093 9271	141
142	0.0083 7476	0.0086 1109	0.0088 5143	0.0093 4408	142
143	0.0083 2597	0.0085 6247	0.0088 0301	0.0092 9615	143
144	0.0082 7787	0.0085 1454	0.0087 5528	0.0092 4890	144
145	0.0082 3043	0.0084 6728	0.0087 0822	0.0092 0233	145
146	0.0081 8365	0.0084 2067	0.0086 6182	0.0091 5641	146
147	0.0081 3752	0.0083 7471	0.0086 1607	0.0091 1114	147
148	0.0080 9201	0.0083 2938	0.0085 7094	0.0090 6650	148
149	0.0080 4712	0.0082 8467	0.0085 2643	0.0090 2247	149
150	0.0080 0284	0.0082 4056	0.0084 8252	0.0089 7905	150

TABLE VII.—Periodic Rent of Annuity Whose Present Value is 1

$$\frac{1}{a_{\overline{n}|i}} = \frac{i}{1 - (1 + i)^{-n}} \qquad \left[\frac{1}{s_{\overline{n}|i}} = \frac{1}{a_{\overline{n}|i}} - i\right]$$

n	¼%	⁷⁄₂₄%	⅓%	⁵⁄₁₂%	n
151	0.0079 5915	0.0081 9705	0.0084 3921	0.0089 3623	151
152	0.0079 1605	0.0081 5412	0.0083 9648	0.0088 9398	152
153	0.0078 7351	0.0081 1176	0.0083 5432	0.0088 5231	153
154	0.0078 3153	0.0080 6995	0.0083 1273	0.0088 1119	154
155	0.0077 9010	0.0080 2870	0.0082 7167	0.0087 7063	155
156	0.0077 4921	0.0079 8798	0.0082 3116	0.0087 3060	156
157	0.0077 0885	0.0079 4780	0.0081 9118	0.0086 9110	157
158	0.0076 6900	0.0079 0813	0.0081 5171	0.0086 5211	158
159	0.0076 2966	0.0078 6896	0.0081 1275	0.0086 1364	159
160	0.0075 9082	0.0078 3030	0.0080 7429	0.0085 7566	160
161	0.0075 5246	0.0077 9212	0.0080 3631	0.0085 3817	161
162	0.0075 1459	0.0077 5442	0.0079 9882	0.0085 0116	162
163	0.0074 7719	0.0077 1720	0.0079 6180	0.0084 6462	163
164	0.0074 4025	0.0076 0844	0.0079 2524	0.0084 2855	164
165	0.0074 0377	0.0076 4413	0.0078 8913	0.0083 9293	165
166	0.0073 6773	0.0076 0826	0.0078 5347	0.0083 5775	166
167	0.0073 3213	0.0075 7284	0.0078 1825	0.0083 2302	167
168	0.0072 9695	0.0075 3784	0.0077 8346	0.0082 8871	168
169	0.0072 6220	0.0075 0327	0.0077 4909	0.0082 5482	169
170	0.0072 2787	0.0074 6911	0.0077 1513	0.0082 2135	170
171	0.0071 9394	0.0074 3536	0.0076 8158	0.0081 8829	171
172	0.0071 6042	0.0074 0201	0.0076 4844	0.0081 5563	172
173	0.0071 2728	0.0073 6905	0.0076 1568	0.0081 2336	173
174	0.0070 9454	0.0073 3648	0.0075 8332	0.0080 9147	174
175	0.0070 6217	0.0073 0429	0.0075 5133	0.0080 5997	175
176	0.0070 3018	0.0072 7248	0.0075 1972	0.0080 2884	176
177	0.0069 9855	0.0072 4103	0.0074 8847	0.0079 9808	177
178	0.0069 6729	0.0072 0994	0.0074 5759	0.0079 6768	178
179	0.0069 3638	0.0071 7921	0.0074 2706	0.0079 3763	179
180	0.0069 0582	0.0071 4883	0.0073 9688	0.0079 0794	180
181	0.0068 7560	0.0071 1879	0.0073 6704	0.0078 7858	181
182	0.0068 4572	0.0070 8908	0.0073 3754	0.0078 4957	182
183	0.0068 1617	0.0070 5971	0.0073 0838	0.0078 2088	183
184	0.0067 8695	0.0070 3067	0.0072 7954	0.0077 9253	184
185	0.0067 5805	0.0070 0195	0.0072 5102	0.0077 6449	185
186	0.0067 2947	0.0069 7354	0.0072 2281	0.0077 3677	186
187	0.0067 0120	0.0069 4545	0.0071 9492	0.0077 0936	187
188	0.0066 7323	0.0069 1766	0.0071 6734	0.0076 8226	188
189	0.0066 4557	0.0068 9017	0.0071 4005	0.0076 5546	189
190	0.0066 1820	0.0068 6298	0.0071 1307	0.0076 2895	190
191	0.0065 9112	0.0068 3608	0.0070 8637	0.0076 0274	191
192	0.0065 6434	0.0068 0947	0.0070 5996	0.0075 7681	192
193	0.0065 3783	0.0067 8314	0.0070 3384	0.0075 5117	193
194	0.0065 1160	0.0067 5708	0.0070 0799	0.0075 2580	194
195	0.0064 8565	0.0067 3131	0.0069 8242	0.0075 0071	195
196	0.0064 5997	0.0067 0581	0.0069 5711	0.0074 7589	196
197	0.0064 3455	0.0066 8057	0.0069 3208	0.0074 5133	197
198	0.0064 0939	0.0066 5559	0.0069 0730	0.0074 2704	198
199	0.0063 8450	0.0066 3087	0.0068 8278	0.0074 0300	199
200	0.0063 5985	0.0066 0640	0.0068 5852	0.0073 7922	200

TABLE VII.—Periodic Rent of Annuity Whose Present Value is 1

$$\frac{1}{a_{\overline{n}|i}} = \frac{i}{1-(1+i)^{-n}} \qquad \left[\frac{1}{s_{\overline{n}|i}} = \frac{1}{a_{\overline{n}|i}} - i\right]$$

n	½%	7/12%	⅝%	⅔%	n
1	1.0050 0000	1.0058 3333	1.0062 5000	1.0066 6667	1
2	0.5037 5312	0.5043 7924	0.5046 9237	0.5050 0554	2
3	0.3366 7221	0.3372 2976	0.3375 0865	0.3377 8762	3
4	0.2531 3279	0.2536 5644	0.2539 1842	0.2541 8051	4
5	0.2030 0997	0.2035 1357	0.2037 6558	0.2040 1772	5
6	0.1695 9546	0.1700 8594	0.1703 3143	0.1705 7709	6
7	0.1457 2854	0.1462 0986	0.1464 5082	0.1466 9198	7
8	0.1278 2886	0.1283 0351	0.1285 4118	0.1287 7907	8
9	0.1139 0736	0.1143 7698	0.1146 1218	0.1148 4763	9
10	0.1027 7057	0.1032 3632	0.1034 6963	0.1037 0321	10
11	0.0936 5903	0.0941 2175	0.0943 5358	0.0945 8572	11
12	0.0860 6643	0.0865 2675	0.0867 5742	0.0869 8843	12
13	0.0796 4224	0.0801 0064	0.0803 3039	0.0805 6052	13
14	0.0741 3609	0.0745 9295	0.0748 2198	0.0750 5141	14
15	0.0693 6436	0.0698 1999	0.0700 4845	0.0702 7734	15
16	0.0651 8937	0.0656 4401	0.0658 7202	0.0661 0049	16
17	0.0615 0579	0.0619 5966	0.0621 8732	0.0624 1546	17
18	0.0582 3173	0.0586 8499	0.0589 1239	0.0591 4030	18
19	0.0553 0253	0.0557 5532	0.0559 8252	0.0562 1027	19
20	0.0526 6645	0.0531 1889	0.0533 4597	0.0535 7362	20
21	0.0502 8163	0.0507 3383	0.0509 6083	0.0511 8843	21
22	0.0481 1380	0.0485 6585	0.0487 9281	0.0490 2041	22
23	0.0461 3465	0.0465 8663	0.0468 1360	0.0470 4123	23
24	0.0443 2061	0.0447 7258	0.0449 9959	0.0452 2729	24
25	0.0426 5186	0.0431 0388	0.0433 3096	0.0435 5876	25
26	0.0411 1163	0.0415 6376	0.0417 9094	0.0420 1886	26
27	0.0396 8565	0.0401 3793	0.0403 6523	0.0405 9331	27
28	0.0383 6167	0.0388 1415	0.0390 4159	0.0392 6983	28
29	0.0371 2914	0.0375 8186	0.0378 0946	0.0380 3789	29
30	0.0359 7892	0.0364 3191	0.0366 5969	0.0368 8832	30
31	0.0349 0304	0.0353 5633	0.0355 8430	0.0358 1316	31
32	0.0338 9453	0.0343 4815	0.0345 7633	0.0348 0542	32
33	0.0329 4727	0.0334 0124	0.0336 2964	0.0338 5898	33
34	0.0320 5586	0.0325 1020	0.0327 3883	0.0329 6843	34
35	0.0312 1550	0.0316 7024	0.0318 9911	0.0321 2898	35
36	0.0304 2194	0.0308 7710	0.0311 0622	0.0313 3637	36
37	0.0296 7139	0.0301 2698	0.0303 5636	0.0305 8600	37
38	0.0289 6045	0.0294 1649	0.0296 4614	0.0298 7687	38
39	0.0282 8607	0.0287 4258	0.0289 7250	0.0292 0354	39
40	0.0276 4552	0.0281 0251	0.0283 3271	0.0285 6406	40
41	0.0270 3631	0.0274 9379	0.0277 2429	0.0279 5595	41
42	0.0264 5622	0.0269 1420	0.0271 4499	0.0273 7697	42
43	0.0259 0320	0.0263 6170	0.0265 9278	0.0268 2509	43
44	0.0253 7541	0.0258 3443	0.0260 6583	0.0262 9847	44
45	0.0248 7117	0.0253 3073	0.0255 6243	0.0257 9541	45
46	0.0243 8894	0.0248 4905	0.0250 8106	0.0253 1439	46
47	0.0239 2733	0.0243 8798	0.0246 2032	0.0248 5399	47
48	0.0234 8503	0.0239 4624	0.0241 7890	0.0244 1292	48
49	0.0230 6087	0.0235 2265	0.0237 5563	0.0239 9001	49
50	0.0226 5376	0.0231 1611	0.0233 4943	0.0235 8416	50

TABLE VII.—Periodic Rent of Annuity Whose Present Value is 1

$$\frac{1}{a_{\overline{n}|i}} = \frac{i}{1 - (1 + i)^{-n}} \qquad \left[\frac{1}{s_{\overline{n}|i}} = \frac{1}{a_{\overline{n}|i}} - i \right]$$

n	½%	⁷⁄₁₂%	⅝%	⅔%	n
51	0.0222 6269	0.0227 2563	0.0229 5928	0.0231 9437	51
52	0.0218 8675	0.0223 5027	0.0225 8425	0.0228 1971	52
53	0.0215 2507	0.0219 8919	0.0222 2350	0.0224 5932	53
54	0.0211 7686	0.0216 4157	0.0218 7623	0.0221 1242	54
55	0.0208 4139	0.0213 0671	0.0215 4171	0.0217 7827	55
56	0.0205 1797	0.0209 8390	0.0212 1925	0.0214 5618	56
57	0.0202 0598	0.0206 7251	0.0209 0821	0.0211 4552	57
58	0.0199 0481	0.0203 7196	0.0206 0801	0.0208 4569	58
59	0.0196 1392	0.0200 8170	0.0203 1809	0.0205 5616	59
60	0.0193 3280	0.0198 0120	0.0200 3795	0.0202 7639	60
61	0.0190 6096	0.0195 2999	0.0197 6709	0.0200 0592	61
62	0.0187 9796	0.0192 6762	0.0195 0508	0.0197 4429	62
63	0.0185 4337	0.0190 1366	0.0192 5148	0.0194 9108	63
64	0.0182 9681	0.0187 6773	0.0190 0591	0.0192 4590	64
65	0.0180 5789	0.0185 2946	0.0187 6800	0.0190 0837	65
66	0.0178 2627	0.0182 9848	0.0185 3739	0.0187 7815	66
67	0.0176 0163	0.0180 7449	0.0183 1376	0.0185 5491	67
68	0.0173 8366	0.0178 5716	0.0180 9680	0.0183 3835	68
69	0.0171 7206	0.0176 4622	0.0178 8622	0.0181 2816	69
70	0.0169 6657	0.0174 4138	0.0176 8175	0.0179 2409	70
71	0.0167 6693	0.0172 4239	0.0174 8313	0.0177 2586	71
72	0.0165 7289	0.0170 4901	0.0172 9011	0.0175 3324	72
73	0.0163 8422	0.0168 6100	0.0171 0247	0.0173 4600	73
74	0.0162 0070	0.0166 7814	0.0169 1999	0.0171 6391	74
75	0.0160 2214	0.0165 0024	0.0167 4246	0.0169 8678	75
76	0.0158 4832	0.0163 2709	0.0165 6968	0.0168 1440	76
77	0.0156 7908	0.0161 5851	0.0164 0147	0.0166 4659	77
78	0.0155 1423	0.0159 9432	0.0162 3766	0.0164 8318	78
79	0.0153 5360	0.0158 3436	0.0160 7808	0.0163 2400	79
80	0.0151 9704	0.0156 7847	0.0159 2256	0.0161 6889	80
81	0.0150 4439	0.0155 2650	0.0157 7096	0.0160 1769	81
82	0.0148 9552	0.0153 7830	0.0156 2314	0.0158 7027	82
83	0.0147 5028	0.0152 3373	0.0154 7895	0.0157 2649	83
84	0.0146 0855	0.0150 9268	0.0153 3828	0.0155 8621	84
85	0.0144 7021	0.0149 5501	0.0152 0098	0.0154 4933	85
86	0.0143 3513	0.0148 2060	0.0150 6696	0.0153 1570	86
87	0.0142 0320	0.0146 8935	0.0149 3608	0.0151 8524	87
88	0.0140 7431	0.0145 6115	0.0148 0826	0.0150 5781	88
89	0.0139 4837	0.0144 3588	0.0146 8337	0.0149 3334	89
90	0.0138 2527	0.0143 1347	0.0145 6134	0.0148 1170	90
91	0.0137 0493	0.0141 9380	0.0144 4205	0.0146 9282	91
92	0.0135 8724	0.0140 7679	0.0143 2542	0.0145 7660	92
93	0.0134 7213	0.0139 6236	0.0142 1137	0.0144 6296	93
94	0.0133 5950	0.0138 5042	0.0140 9982	0.0143 5181	94
95	0.0132 4930	0.0137 4090	0.0139 9067	0.0142 4308	95
96	0.0131 4143	0.0136 3372	0.0138 8387	0.0141 3668	96
97	0.0130 3583	0.0135 2880	0.0137 7933	0.0140 3255	97
98	0.0129 3242	0.0134 2608	0.0136 7700	0.0139 3062	98
99	0.0128 3115	0.0133 2549	0.0135 7679	0.0138 3082	99
100	0.0127 3194	0.0132 2696	0.0134 7865	0.0137 3308	100

TABLE VII.—Periodic Rent of Annuity Whose Present Value is 1

$$\frac{1}{a_{\overline{n}|i}} = \frac{i}{1 - (1 + i)^{-n}} \qquad \left[\frac{1}{s_{\overline{n}|i}} = \frac{1}{a_{\overline{n}|i}} - i \right]$$

n	½%	⁷⁄₁₂%	⅝%	⅔%	n
101	0.0126 3473	0.0131 3045	0.0133 8251	0.0136 3735	101
102	0.0125 3947	0.0130 3587	0.0132 8832	0.0135 4357	102
103	0.0124 4611	0.0129 4319	0.0131 9602	0.0134 5168	103
104	0.0123 5457	0.0128 5234	0.0131 0555	0.0133 6162	104
105	0.0122 6481	0.0127 6238	0.0130 1687	0.0132 7334	105
106	0.0121 7679	0.0126 7594	0.0129 2992	0.0131 8680	106
107	0.0120 9045	0.0125 9029	0.0128 4465	0.0131 0194	107
108	0.0120 0575	0.0125 0628	0.0127 6102	0.0130 1871	108
109	0.0119 2264	0.0124 2385	0.0126 7897	0.0129 3708	109
110	0.0118 4107	0.0123 4298	0.0125 9848	0.0128 5700	110
111	0.0117 0102	0.0122 6361	0.0125 1950	0.0127 7842	111
112	0.0116 8242	0.0121 8571	0.0124 4198	0.0127 0131	112
113	0.0116 0526	0.0121 0923	0.0123 6588	0.0126 2562	113
114	0.0115 2948	0.0120 3414	0.0122 9118	0.0125 5132	114
115	0.0114 5506	0.0119 6041	0.0122 1783	0.0124 7838	115
116	0.0113 8195	0.0118 8799	0.0121 4579	0.0124 0675	116
117	0.0113 1013	0.0118 1686	0.0120 7504	0.0123 3641	117
118	0.0112 3956	0.0117 4698	0.0120 0555	0.0122 6732	118
119	0.0111 7021	0.0116 7832	0.0119 3727	0.0121 9944	119
120	0.0111 0205	0.0116 1085	0.0118 7018	0.0121 3276	120
121	0.0110 3505	0.0115 4454	0.0118 0425	0.0120 6724	121
122	0.0109 6918	0.0114 7936	0.0117 3945	0.0120 0284	122
123	0.0109 0441	0.0114 1528	0.0116 7575	0.0119 3955	123
124	0.0108 4072	0.0113 5228	0.0116 1314	0.0118 7734	124
125	0.0107 7808	0.0112 9033	0.0115 5157	0.0118 1618	125
126	0.0107 1647	0.0112 2940	0.0114 9102	0.0117 5604	126
127	0.0106 5586	0.0111 6948	0.0114 3148	0.0116 9690	127
128	0.0105 9623	0.0111 1054	0.0113 7292	0.0116 3875	128
129	0.0105 3755	0.0110 5255	0.0113 1531	0.0115 8154	129
130	0.0104 7981	0.0109 9550	0.0112 5864	0.0115 2527	130
131	0.0104 2298	0.0109 3935	0.0112 0288	0.0114 6992	131
132	0.0103 6704	0.0108 8410	0.0111 4800	0.0114 1545	132
133	0.0103 1197	0.0108 2972	0.0110 9400	0.0113 6185	133
134	0.0102 5775	0.0107 7619	0.0110 4086	0.0113 0910	134
135	0.0102 0436	0.0107 2349	0.0109 8854	0.0112 5719	135
136	0.0101 5179	0.0106 7161	0.0109 3703	0.0112 0609	136
137	0.0101 0002	0.0106 2052	0.0108 8633	0.0111 5578	137
138	0.0100 4902	0.0105 7021	0.0108 3640	0.0111 0625	138
139	0.0099 9879	0.0105 2067	0.0107 8723	0.0110 5749	139
140	0.0099 4930	0.0104 7187	0.0107 3881	0.0110 0947	140
141	0.0099 0055	0.0104 2380	0.0106 9111	0.0109 6218	141
142	0.0098 5250	0.0103 7644	0.0106 4414	0.0109 1560	142
143	0.0098 0516	0.0103 2978	0.0105 9786	0.0108 6972	143
144	0.0097 5850	0.0102 8381	0.0105 5226	0.0108 2453	144
145	0.0097 1252	0.0102 3851	0.0105 0734	0.0107 8000	145
146	0.0096 6719	0.0101 9386	0.0104 6307	0.0107 3613	146
147	0.0096 2250	0.0101 4986	0.0104 1944	0.0106 9291	147
148	0.0095 7844	0.0101 0649	0.0103 7645	0.0106 5031	148
149	0.0095 3500	0.0100 6373	0.0103 3407	0.0106 0833	149
150	0.0094 9217	0.0100 2159	0.0102 9230	0.0105 6695	150

TABLE VII.—Periodic Rent of Annuity Whose Present Value is 1

$$\frac{1}{a_{\overline{n}|i}} = \frac{i}{1 - (1+i)^{-n}} \qquad \left[\frac{1}{s_{\overline{n}|i}} = \frac{1}{a_{\overline{n}|i}} - i \right]$$

n	½%	$\frac{7}{12}$%	⅝%	⅔%	n
151	0.0094 4993	0.0099 8003	0.0102 5112	0.0105 2617	151
152	0.0094 0827	0.0099 3905	0.0102 1052	0.0104 8597	152
153	0.0093 6719	0.0098 9865	0.0101 7049	0.0104 4633	153
154	0.0093 2666	0.0098 5880	0.0101 3102	0.0104 0726	154
155	0.0092 8668	0.0098 1950	0.0100 9209	0.0103 6873	155
156	0.0092 4723	0.0097 8074	0.0100 5370	0.0103 3074	156
157	0.0092 0832	0.0097 4251	0.0100 1584	0.0102 9327	157
158	0.0091 6992	0.0097 0479	0.0099 7850	0.0102 5632	158
159	0.0091 3203	0.0096 6758	0.0099 4166	0.0102 1988	159
160	0.0090 9464	0.0096 3087	0.0099 0532	0.0101 8394	160
161	0.0090 5774	0.0095 9464	0.0098 6947	0.0101 4848	161
162	0.0090 2131	0.0095 5890	0.0098 3410	0.0101 1350	162
163	0.0089 8536	0.0095 2362	0.0097 9919	0.0100 7899	163
164	0.0089 4987	0.0094 8881	0.0097 6475	0.0100 4494	164
165	0.0089 1483	0.0094 5445	0.0097 3076	0.0100 1134	165
166	0.0088 8024	0.0094 2053	0.0096 9722	0.0099 7819	166
167	0.0088 4608	0.0093 8705	0.0096 6411	0.0099 4547	167
168	0.0088 1236	0.0093 5400	0.0096 3143	0.0099 1318	168
169	0.0087 7906	0.0093 2138	0.0095 9918	0.0098 8131	169
170	0.0087 4617	0.0092 8917	0.0095 6733	0.0098 4986	170
171	0.0087 1369	0.0092 5736	0.0095 3589	0.0098 1881	171
172	0.0086 8161	0.0092 2595	0.0095 0486	0.0097 8816	172
173	0.0086 4992	0.0091 9494	0.0094 7421	0.0097 5791	173
174	0.0086 1862	0.0091 6431	0.0094 4395	0.0097 2803	174
175	0.0085 8770	0.0091 3406	0.0094 1407	0.0096 9854	175
176	0.0085 5715	0.0091 0418	0.0093 8456	0.0096 6942	176
177	0.0085 2697	0.0090 7468	0.0093 5542	0.0096 4066	177
178	0.0084 9715	0.0090 4553	0.0093 2664	0.0096 1226	178
179	0.0084 6769	0.0090 1673	0.0092 9821	0.0095 8422	179
180	0.0084 3857	0.0089 8828	0.0092 7012	0.0095 5652	180
181	0.0084 0979	0.0089 6018	0.0092 4238	0.0095 2917	181
182	0.0083 8136	0.0089 3241	0.0092 1498	0.0095 0215	182
183	0.0083 5325	0.0089 0497	0.0091 8791	0.0094 7546	183
184	0.0083 2547	0.0088 7786	0.0091 6116	0.0094 4909	184
185	0.0082 9802	0.0088 5107	0.0091 3473	0.0094 2305	185
186	0.0082 7087	0.0088 2459	0.0091 0862	0.0093 9732	186
187	0.0082 4404	0.0087 9843	0.0090 8282	0.0093 7189	187
188	0.0082 1752	0.0087 7257	0.0090 5732	0.0093 4678	188
189	0.0081 9129	0.0087 4701	0.0090 3212	0.0093 2196	189
190	0.0081 6537	0.0087 2174	0.0090 0722	0.0092 9743	190
191	0.0081 3973	0.0086 9677	0.0089 8260	0.0092 7320	191
192	0.0081 1438	0.0086 7208	0.0089 5828	0.0092 4925	192
193	0.0080 8931	0.0086 4767	0.0089 3423	0.0092 2558	193
194	0.0080 6452	0.0086 2355	0.0089 1046	0.0092 0219	194
195	0.0080 4000	0.0085 9969	0.0088 8696	0.0091 7907	195
196	0.0080 1576	0.0085 7610	0.0088 6374	0.0091 5622	196
197	0.0079 9178	0.0085 5278	0.0088 4077	0.0091 3363	197
198	0.0079 6806	0.0085 2972	0.0088 1807	0.0091 1130	198
199	0.0079 4459	0.0085 0691	0.0087 9562	0.0090 8923	199
200	0.0079 2138	0.0084 8436	0.0087 7343	0.0090 6741	200

TABLE VII.—Periodic Rent of Annuity Whose Present Value is 1

$$\frac{1}{a_{\overline{n}|i}} = \frac{i}{1 - (1 + i)^{-n}} \qquad \left[\frac{1}{s_{\overline{n}|i}} = \frac{1}{a_{\overline{n}|i}} - i\right]$$

n	¾%	⅞%	1%	1⅛%	n
1	1.0075 0000	1.0087 5000	1.0100 0000	1.0112 5000	1
2	0.5056 3200	0.5065 7203	0.5075 1244	0.5084 5323	2
3	0.3383 4579	0.3391 8361	0.3400 2211	0.3408 6130	3
4	0.2547 0501	0.2554 9257	0.2562 8109	0.2570 7058	4
5	0.2045 2242	0.2052 8049	0.2060 3980	0.2068 0034	5
6	0.1710 6891	0.1718 0789	0.1725 4837	0.1732 9034	6
7	0.1471 7488	0.1479 0070	0.1486 2828	0.1493 5762	7
8	0.1292 5552	0.1299 7190	0.1306 9029	0.1314 1071	8
9	0.1153 1929	0.1160 2868	0.1167 4037	0.1174 5432	9
10	0.1041 7123	0.1048 7538	0.1055 8208	0.1062 9131	10
11	0.0950 5094	0.0957 5111	0.0964 5408	0.0971 5984	11
12	0.0874 5148	0.0881 4860	0.0888 4879	0.0895 5203	12
13	0.0810 2188	0.0817 1669	0.0824 1482	0.0831 1626	13
14	0.0755 1146	0.0762 0453	0.0769 0117	0.0776 0138	14
15	0.0707 3639	0.0714 2817	0.0721 2378	0.0728 2321	15
16	0.0665 5879	0.0672 4965	0.0679 4460	0.0686 4363	16
17	0.0628 7321	0.0635 6346	0.0642 5806	0.0649 5698	17
18	0.0595 9766	0.0602 8756	0.0609 8205	0.0616 8113	18
19	0.0566 6740	0.0573 5715	0.0580 5175	0.0587 5120	19
20	0.0540 3063	0.0547 2042	0.0554 1532	0.0561 1531	20
21	0.0516 4543	0.0523 3541	0.0530 3075	0.0537 3145	21
22	0.0494 7748	0.0501 6779	0.0508 6371	0.0515 6525	22
23	0.0474 9846	0.0481 8921	0.0488 8584	0.0495 8833	23
24	0.0456 8474	0.0463 7604	0.0470 7347	0.0477 7701	24
25	0.0440 1650	0.0447 0843	0.0454 0675	0.0461 1144	25
26	0.0424 7693	0.0431 6959	0.0438 6888	0.0445 7479	26
27	0.0410 5176	0.0417 4520	0.0424 4553	0.0431 5273	27
28	0.0397 2871	0.0404 2300	0.0411 2444	0.0418 3299	28
29	0.0384 9723	0.0391 9243	0.0398 9502	0.0406 0498	29
30	0.0373 4816	0.0380 4431	0.0387 4811	0.0394 5953	30
31	0.0362 7352	0.0369 7068	0.0376 7573	0.0383 8866	31
32	0.0352 6634	0.0359 6454	0.0366 7089	0.0373 8535	32
33	0.0343 2048	0.0350 1976	0.0357 2744	0.0364 4349	33
34	0.0334 3053	0.0341 3092	0.0348 3997	0.0355 5763	34
35	0.0325 9170	0.0332 9324	0.0340 0368	0.0347 2299	35
36	0.0317 9973	0.0325 0244	0.0332 1431	0.0339 3529	36
37	0.0310 5082	0.0317 5473	0.0324 6805	0.0331 9072	37
38	0.0303 4157	0.0310 4671	0.0317 6150	0.0324 8589	38
39	0.0296 6893	0.0303 7531	0.0310 9160	0.0318 1773	39
40	0.0290 3016	0.0297 3780	0.0304 5560	0.0311 8349	40
41	0.0284 2276	0.0291 3169	0.0298 5102	0.0305 8069	41
42	0.0278 4452	0.0285 5475	0.0292 7563	0.0300 0709	42
43	0.0272 9338	0.0280 0493	0.0287 2737	0.0294 6064	43
44	0.0267 6751	0.0274 8039	0.0282 0441	0.0289 3949	44
45	0.0262 6521	0.0269 7943	0.0277 0505	0.0284 4197	45
46	0.0257 8495	0.0265 0053	0.0272 2775	0.0279 6652	46
47	0.0253 2532	0.0260 4228	0.0267 7111	0.0275 1173	47
48	0.0248 8504	0.0256 0338	0.0263 3384	0.0270 7632	48
49	0.0244 6292	0.0251 8265	0.0259 1474	0.0266 5910	49
50	0.0240 5787	0.0247 7900	0.0255 1273	0.0262 5898	50

TABLE VII.—Periodic Rent of Annuity Whose Present Value is 1

$$\frac{1}{a_{\overline{n}|i}} = \frac{i}{1 - (1 + i)^{-n}} \qquad \left[\frac{1}{s_{\overline{n}|i}} = \frac{1}{a_{\overline{n}|i}} - i \right]$$

n	¾%	⅞%	1%	1⅛%	n
51	0.0236 6888	0.0243 9142	0 0251 2680	0.0258 7494	51
52	0.0232 9503	0.0240 1899	0.0247 5603	0.0255 0606	52
53	0 0229 3546	0.0236 6084	0.0243 9956	0.0251 5149	53
54	0.0225 8938	0.0233 1619	0.0240 5658	0.0248 1043	54
55	0 0222 5605	0.0229 8430	0 0237 2637	0.0244 8213	55
56	0 0219 3478	0.0226 6449	0 0234 0823	0.0241 6592	56
57	0.0216 2496	0 0223 5611	0.0231 0156	0.0238 6116	57
58	0.0213 2597	0.0220 5858	0.0228 0573	0.0235 6726	58
59	0.0210 3727	0 0217 7135	0.0225 2020	0.0232 8366	59
60	0 0207 5836	0.0214 9390	0.0222 4445	0.0230 0985	60
61	0.0204 8873	0 0212 2575	0.0219 7800	0.0227 4534	61
62	0.0202 2795	0 0209 6644	0.0217 2041	0.0224 8969	62
63	0 0199 7560	0.0207 1557	0.0214 7125	0.0222 4247	63
64	0.0197 3127	0.0204 7273	0.0212 3013	0.0220 0329	64
65	0 0194 9460	0.0202 3754	0 0209 9667	0.0217 7178	65
66	0.0192 6524	0.0200 0968	0.0207 7052	0.0215 4758	66
67	0.0190 4286	0 0197 8879	0.0205 5136	0.0213 3037	67
68	0 0188 2716	0.0195 7459	0.0203 3888	0.0211 1985	68
69	0.0186 1785	0.0193 6677	0.0201 3280	0.0209 1571	69
70	0 0184 1464	0 0191 6506	0.0199 3282	0.0207 1769	70
71	0.0182 1728	0.0189 6921	0.0197 3870	0.0205 2552	71
72	0.0180 2554	0 0187 7897	0.0195 5019	0.0203 3896	72
73	0.0178 3917	0.0185 9411	0.0193 6706	0.0201 5779	73
74	0.0176 5796	0.0184 1441	0.0191 8910	0.0199 8177	74
75	0.0174 8170	0.0182 3966	0.0190 1609	0.0198 1072	75
76	0.0173 1020	0.0180 6967	0.0188 4784	0.0196 4442	76
77	0.0171 4328	0.0179 0426	0.0186 8416	0.0194 8269	77
78	0.0169 8074	0.0177 4324	0.0185 2488	0.0193 2536	78
79	0.0168 2244	0.0175 8645	0.0183 6984	0.0191 7226	79
80	0.0166 6821	0.0174 3374	0.0182 1885	0.0190 2323	80
81	0.0165 1790	0.0172 8494	0.0180 7180	0.0188 7812	81
82	0.0163 7136	0.0171 3992	0.0179 2851	0.0187 3678	82
83	0.0162 2847	0.0169 9854	0.0177 8886	0.0185 9908	83
84	0.0160 8908	0.0168 6067	0.0176 5273	0.0184 6489	84
85	0.0159 5308	0.0167 2619	0.0175 1998	0.0183 3409	85
86	0.0158 2034	0.0165 9497	0.0173 9050	0.0182 0654	86
87	0.0156 9076	0.0164 6691	0.0172 6417	0.0180 8215	87
88	0.0155 6423	0.0163 4190	0.0171 4089	0.0179 6081	88
89	0.0154 4064	0.0162 1982	0.0170 2056	0.0178 4240	89
90	0.0153 1989	0.0161 0060	0.0169 0306	0.0177 2684	90
91	0.0152 0190	0.0159 8413	0.0167 8832	0.0176 1403	91
92	0.0150 8657	0.0158 7031	0.0166 7624	0.0175 0387	92
93	0.0149 7382	0.0157 5908	0.0165 6673	0.0173 9629	93
94	0.0148 6356	0.0156 5033	0.0164 5971	0.0172 9119	94
95	0.0147 5571	0.0155 4401	0.0163 5511	0.0171 8851	95
96	0.0146 5020	0.0154 4002	0.0162 5284	0.0170 8816	96
97	0.0145 4696	0.0153 3829	0.0161 5284	0.0169 9007	97
98	0.0144 4592	0.0152 3877	0.0160 5503	0.0168 9418	98
99	0.0143 4701	0.0151 4137	0.0159 5936	0.0168 0041	99
100	0.0142 5017	0.0150 4604	0.0158 6574	0.0167 0870	100

TABLE VII.—Periodic Rent of Annuity Whose Present Value is 1

$$\frac{1}{a_{\overline{n}|i}} = \frac{i}{1 - (1 + i)^{-n}} \qquad \left[\frac{1}{s_{\overline{n}|i}} = \frac{1}{a_{\overline{n}|i}} - i\right]$$

n	1¼%	1⅜%	1½%	1¾%	n
1	1.0125 0000	1.0137 5000	1.0150 0000	1.0175 0000	1
2	0.5093 9441	0.5103 3597	0.5112 7792	0.5131 6295	2
3	0.3417 0117	0.3425 4173	0.3433 8296	0.3450 6746	3
4	0.2578 6102	0.2586 5243	0.2594 4478	0.2610 3237	4
5	0.2075 6211	0.2083 2510	0.2090 8932	0.2106 2142	5
6	0.1740 3381	0.1747 7877	0.1755 2521	0.1770 2256	6
7	0.1500 8872	0.1508 2157	0.1515 5616	0.1530 3059	7
8	0.1321 3314	0.1328 5758	0.1335 8402	0.1350 4292	8
9	0.1181 7055	0.1188 8906	0.1196 0982	0.1210 5813	9
10	0.1070 0307	0.1077 1737	0.1084 3418	0.1098 7534	10
11	0.0978 6839	0.0985 7973	0.0992 9384	0.1007 3038	11
12	0.0902 5831	0.0909 6764	0.0916 7999	0.0931 1377	12
13	0.0838 2100	0.0845 2903	0.0852 4036	0.0866 7283	13
14	0.0783 0515	0.0790 1246	0.0797 2332	0.0811 5562	14
15	0.0735 2646	0.0742 3351	0.0749 4436	0.0763 7739	15
16	0.0693 4672	0.0700 5388	0.0707 6508	0.0721 9958	16
17	0.0656 6023	0.0663 6780	0.0670 7966	0.0685 1623	17
18	0.0623 8479	0.0630 9301	0.0638 0578	0.0652 4492	18
19	0.0594 5548	0.0601 6457	0.0608 7847	0.0623 2061	19
20	0.0568 2039	0.0575 3054	0.0582 4574	0.0596 9122	20
21	0.0544 3748	0.0551 4884	0.0558 6550	0.0573 1464	21
22	0.0522 7238	0.0529 8507	0.0537 0331	0.0551 5638	22
23	0.0502 9666	0.0510 1080	0.0517 3075	0.0531 8796	23
24	0.0484 8665	0.0492 0235	0.0499 2410	0.0513 8565	24
25	0.0468 2247	0.0475 3981	0.0482 6345	0.0497 2952	25
26	0.0452 8729	0.0460 0635	0.0467 3196	0.0482 0269	26
27	0.0438 6677	0.0445 8763	0.0453 1527	0.0467 9079	27
28	0.0425 4863	0.0432 7134	0.0440 0108	0.0454 8151	28
29	0.0413 2228	0.0420 4689	0.0427 7878	0.0442 6424	29
30	0.0401 7854	0.0409 0511	0.0416 3919	0.0431 2975	30
31	0.0391 0942	0.0398 3798	0.0405 7430	0.0420 7005	31
32	0.0381 0791	0.0388 3850	0.0395 7710	0.0410 7812	32
33	0.0371 6786	0.0379 0053	0.0386 4144	0.0401 4779	33
34	0.0362 8387	0.0370 1864	0.0377 6189	0.0392 7363	34
35	0.0354 5111	0.0361 8801	0.0369 3363	0.0384 5082	35
36	0.0346 6533	0.0354 0438	0.0361 5240	0.0376 7507	36
37	0.0339 2270	0.0346 6394	0.0354 1437	0.0369 4257	37
38	0.0332 1983	0.0339 6327	0.0347 1613	0.0362 4990	38
39	0.0325 5305	0.0332 9931	0.0340 5465	0.0355 9399	39
40	0.0319 2141	0.0326 6931	0.0334 2710	0.0349 7209	40
41	0.0313 2063	0.0320 7078	0.0328 3106	0.0343 8170	41
42	0.0307 4906	0.0315 0148	0.0322 6426	0.0338 2057	42
43	0.0302 0466	0.0309 5936	0.0317 2465	0.0332 8666	43
44	0.0296 8557	9.0304 4257	0.0312 1038	0.0327 7810	44
45	0.0291 9012	0.0299 4941	0.0307 1976	0.0322 9321	45
46	0.0287 1675	0.0294 7836	0.0302 5125	0.0318 3043	46
47	0.0282 6406	0.0290 2799	0.0298 0342	0.0313 8836	47
48	0.0278 3075	0.0285 9701	0.0293 7500	0.0309 6569	48
49	0.0274 1563	0.0281 8424	0.0289 6478	0.0305 6124	49
50	0.0270 1763	0.0277 8857	0.0285 7168	0.0301 7391	50

TABLE VII.—Periodic Rent of Annuity Whose Present Value is 1

$$\frac{1}{a_{\overline{n}|i}} = \frac{i}{1 - (1 + i)^{-n}} \qquad \left[\frac{1}{s_{\overline{n}|i}} = \frac{1}{a_{\overline{n}|i}} - i\right]$$

n	1¼%	1⅜%	1½%	1¾%	n
51	0.0266 3571	0.0274 0900	0.0281 9469	0.0298 0269	51
52	0.0262 6897	0.0270 4461	0.0278 3287	0.0294 4665	52
53	0.0259 1653	0.0266 9453	0.0274 8537	0.0291 0492	53
54	0.0255 7760	0.0263 5797	0.0271 5138	0.0287 7672	54
55	0.0252 5145	0.0260 3418	0.0268 3018	0.0284 6129	55
56	0.0249 3739	0.0257 2249	0.0265 2106	0.0281 5795	56
57	0.0246 3478	0.0254 2225	0.0262 2341	0.0278 6606	57
58	0.0243 4303	0.0251 3287	0.0259 3661	0.0275 8503	58
59	0.0240 6158	0.0248 5380	0.0256 6012	0.0273 1430	59
60	0.0237 8993	0.0245 8452	0.0253 9343	0.0270 5336	60
61	0.0235 2758	0.0243 2455	0.0251 3604	0.0268 0172	61
62	0.0232 7410	0.0240 7344	0.0248 8751	0.0265 5892	62
63	0.0230 2904	0.0238 3076	0.0246 4741	0.0263 2455	63
64	0.0227 9203	0.0235 9612	0.0244 1534	0.0260 9821	64
65	0.0225 6268	0.0233 6914	0.0241 9094	0.0258 7952	65
66	0.0223 4065	0.0231 4949	0.0239 7386	0.0256 6813	66
67	0.0221 2560	0.0229 3682	0.0237 6376	0.0254 6372	67
68	0.0219 1724	0.0227 3082	0.0235 6033	0.0252 6596	68
69	0.0217 1527	0.0225 3122	0.0233 6329	0.0250 7459	69
70	0.0215 1941	0.0223 3773	0.0231 7235	0.0248 8930	70
71	0.0213 2941	0.0221 5009	0.0229 8727	0.0247 0985	71
72	0.0211 4501	0.0219 6806	0.0228 0779	0.0245 3600	72
73	0.0209 6600	0.0217 9140	0.0226 3368	0.0243 6750	73
74	0.0207 9215	0.0216 1991	0.0224 6473	0.0242 0413	74
75	0.0206 2325	0.0214 5336	0.0223 0072	0.0240 4570	75
76	0.0204 5910	0.0212 9157	0.0221 4146	0.0238 9200	76
77	0.0202 9953	0.0211 3435	0.0219 8676	0.0237 4284	77
78	0.0201 4435	0.0209 8151	0.0218 3645	0.0235 9806	78
79	0.0199 9341	0.0208 3290	0.0216 9036	0.0234 5748	79
80	0.0198 4652	0.0206 8836	0.0215 4832	0.0233 2093	80
81	0.0197 0356	0.0205 4772	0.0214 1019	0.0231 8828	81
82	0.0195 6437	0.0204 1086	0.0212 7583	0.0230 5936	82
83	0.0194 2881	0.0202 7762	0.0211 4509	0.0229 3406	83
84	0.0192 9675	0.0201 4789	0.0210 1784	0.0228 1223	84
85	0.0191 6808	0.0200 2153	0.0208 9396	0.0226 9375	85
86	0.0190 4267	0.0198 9843	0.0207 7333	0.0225 7850	86
87	0.0189 2041	0.0197 7847	0.0206 5584	0.0224 6636	87
88	0.0188 0119	0.0196 6155	0.0205 4138	0.0223 5724	88
89	0.0186 8490	0.0195 4756	0.0204 2984	0.0222 5102	89
90	0.0185 7146	0.0194 3641	0.0203 2113	0.0221 4760	90
91	0.0184 6076	0.0193 2799	0.0202 1516	0.0220 4690	91
92	0.0183 5271	0.0192 2222	0.0201 1182	0.0219 4882	92
93	0.0182 4724	0.0191 1902	0.0200 1104	0.0218 5327	93
94	0.0181 4425	0.0190 1829	0.0199 1273	0.0217 6017	94
95	0.0180 4366	0.0189 1997	0.0198 1681	0.0216 6944	95
96	0.0179 4540	0.0188 2397	0.0197 2321	0.0215 8101	96
97	0.0178 4941	0.0187 3022	0.0196 3186	0.0214 9480	97
98	0.0177 5560	0.0186 3866	0.0195 4268	0.0214 1074	98
99	0.0176 6391	0.0185 4921	0.0194 5560	0.0213 2876	99
100	0.0175 7428	0.0184 6181	0.0193 7057	0.0212 4880	100

528

TABLE VII.—Periodic Rent of Annuity Whose Present Value is 1

$$\frac{1}{a_{\overline{n}|i}} = \frac{i}{1 - (1 + i)^{-n}} \qquad \left[\frac{1}{s_{\overline{n}|i}} = \frac{1}{a_{\overline{n}|i}} - i\right]$$

n	2%	2¼%	2½%	2¾%	n
1	1.0200 0000	1.0225 0000	1.0250 0000	1.0275 0000	1
2	0.5150 4950	0.5169 3758	0.5188 2716	0.5207 1825	2
3	0.3467 5467	0.3484 4458	0.3501 3717	0.3518 3243	3
4	0.2626 2375	0.2642 1893	0.2658 1788	0.2674 2059	4
5	0.2121 5839	0.2137 0021	0.2152 4686	0.2167 9832	5
6	0.1785 2581	0.1800 3496	0.1815 4997	0.1830 7083	6
7	0.1545 1196	0.1560 0025	0.1574 9543	0.1589 9747	7
8	0.1365 0980	0.1379 8462	0.1394 6735	0.1409 5795	8
9	0.1225 1544	0.1239 8170	0.1254 5689	0.1269 4095	9
10	0.1113 2653	0.1127 8768	0.1142 5876	0.1157 3972	10
11	0.1021 7794	0.1036 3649	0.1051 0596	0.1065 8629	11
12	0.0945 5960	0.0960 1740	0.0974 8713	0.0989 6871	12
13	0.0881 1835	0.0895 7686	0.0910 4827	0.0925 3252	13
14	0.0826 0197	0.0840 6230	0.0855 3653	0.0870 2457	14
15	0.0778 2547	0.0792 8852	0.0807 6646	0.0822 5917	15
16	0.0736 5013	0.0751 1663	0.0765 9899	0.0780 9710	16
17	0.0699 6984	0.0714 4039	0.0729 2777	0.0744 3186	17
18	0.0667 0210	0.0681 7720	0.0696 7008	0.0711 8063	18
19	0.0637 8177	0.0652 6182	0.0667 6062	0.0682 7802	19
20	0.0611 5672	0.0626 4207	0.0641 4713	0.0656 7173	20
21	0.0587 8477	0.0602 7572	0.0617 8733	0.0633 1941	21
22	0.0566 3140	0.0581 2821	0.0596 4661	0.0611 8640	22
23	0.0546 6810	0.0561 7097	0.0576 9638	0.0592 4410	23
24	0.0528 7110	0.0543 8023	0.0559 1282	0.0574 6863	24
25	0.0512 2044	0.0527 3599	0.0542 7592	0.0558 3997	25
26	0.0496 9923	0.0512 2134	0.0527 6875	0.0543 4116	26
27	0.0482 9309	0.0498 2188	0.0513 7687	0.0529 5776	27
28	0.0469 8967	0.0485 2525	0.0500 8793	0.0516 7738	28
29	0.0457 7836	0.0473 2081	0.0488 9127	0.0504 8935	29
30	0.0446 4992	0.0461 9934	0.0477 7764	0.0493 8442	30
31	0.0435 9635	0.0451 5280	0.0467 3900	0.0483 5453	31
32	0.0426 1061	0.0441 7415	0.0457 6831	0.0473 9263	32
33	0.0416 8653	0.0432 5722	0.0448 5938	0.0464 9253	33
34	0.0408 1867	0.0423 9655	0.0440 0675	0.0456 4875	34
35	0.0400 0221	0.0415 8731	0.0432 0558	0.0448 5645	35
36	0.0392 3285	0.0408 2522	0.0424 5158	0.0441 1132	36
37	0.0385 0678	0.0401 0643	0.0417 4090	0.0434 0953	37
38	0.0378 2057	0.0394 2753	0.0410 7012	0.0427 4764	38
39	0.0371 7114	0.0387 8543	0.0404 3615	0.0421 2256	39
40	0.0365 5575	0.0381 7738	0.0398 3623	0.0415 3151	40
41	0.0359 7188	0.0376 0087	0.0392 6786	0.0409 7200	41
42	0.0354 1729	0.0370 5364	0.0387 2876	0.0404 4175	42
43	0.0348 8993	0.0365 3364	0.0382 1688	0.0399 3871	43
44	0.0343 8794	0.0360 3901	0.0377 3037	0.0394 6100	44
45	0.0339 0962	0.0355 6805	0.0372 6752	0.0390 0693	45
46	0.0334 5342	0.0351 1921	0.0368 2676	0.0385 7493	46
47	0.0330 1792	0.0346 9107	0.0364 0669	0.0381 6358	47
48	0.0326 0184	0.0342 8233	0.0360 0599	0.0377 7158	48
49	0.0322 0396	0.0338 9179	0.0356 2348	0.0373 9773	49
50	0.0318 2321	0.0335 1836	0.0352 5806	0.0370 4092	50

TABLE VII.—Periodic Rent of Annuity Whose Present Value is 1

$$\frac{1}{a_{\overline{n}|i}} = \frac{i}{1 - (1 + i)^{-n}} \qquad \left[\frac{1}{s_{\overline{n}|i}} = \frac{1}{a_{\overline{n}|i}} - i \right]$$

n	2%	2¼%	2½%	2¾%	n
51	0.0314 5856	0.0331 6102	0.0349 0870	0.0367 0014	51
52	0.0311 0909	0.0328 1884	0.0345 7446	0.0363 7444	52
53	0.0307 7392	0.0324 9094	0.0342 5449	0.0360 6297	53
54	0.0304 5226	0.0321 7654	0.0339 4799	0.0357 6491	54
55	0.0301 4337	0.0318 7489	0.0336 5419	0.0354 7953	55
56	0.0298 4656	0.0315 8530	0.0333 7243	0.0352 0612	56
57	0.0295 6120	0.0313 0712	0.0331 0204	0.0349 4404	57
58	0.0292 8667	0.0310 3977	0.0328 4244	0.0346 9270	58
59	0.0290 2243	0.0307 8268	0.0325 9307	0.0344 5153	59
60	0.0287 6797	0.0305 3533	0.0323 5340	0.0342 2002	60
61	0.0285 2278	0.0302 9724	0.0321 2294	0.0339 9767	61
62	0.0282 8643	0.0300 6795	0.0319 0126	0.0337 8402	62
63	0.0280 5848	0.0298 4704	0.0316 8790	0.0335 7866	63
64	0.0278 3855	0.0296 3411	0.0314 8249	0.0333 8118	64
65	0.0276 2624	0.0294 2878	0.0312 8463	0.0331 9120	65
66	0.0274 2122	0.0292 3070	0.0310 9398	0.0330 0837	66
67	0.0272 2316	0.0290 3955	0.0309 1021	0.0328 3236	67
68	0.0270 3173	0.0288 5500	0.0307 3300	0.0326 6285	68
69	0.0268 4665	0.0286 7677	0.0305 6206	0.0324 9955	69
70	0.0266 6765	0.0285 0458	0.0303 9712	0.0323 4218	70
71	0.0264 9446	0.0283 3816	0.0302 3790	0.0321 9048	71
72	0.0263 2683	0.0281 7728	0.0300 8417	0.0320 4420	72
73	0.0261 6454	0.0280 2169	0.0299 3568	0.0319 0311	73
74	0.0260 0736	0.0278 7118	0.0297 9222	0.0317 6698	74
75	0.0258 5508	0.0277 2554	0.0296 5358	0.0316 3560	75
76	0.0257 0751	0.0275 8457	0.0295 1956	0.0315 0878	76
77	0.0255 6447	0.0274 4808	0.0293 8997	0.0313 8633	77
78	0.0254 2576	0.0273 1589	0.0292 6463	0.0312 6806	78
79	0.0252 9123	0.0271 8784	0.0291 4338	0.0311 5382	79
80	0.0251 6071	0.0270 6376	0.0290 2605	0.0310 4342	80
81	0.0250 3405	0.0269 4350	0.0289 1248	0.0309 3674	81
82	0.0249 1110	0.0268 2692	0.0288 0254	0.0308 3361	82
83	0.0247 9173	0.0267 1387	0.0286 9608	0.0307 3389	83
84	0.0246 7581	0.0266 0423	0.0285 9298	0.0306 3747	84
85	0.0245 6321	0.0264 9787	0.0284 9310	0.0305 4420	85
86	0.0244 5381	0.0263 9467	0.0283 9633	0.0304 5397	86
87	0.0243 4750	0.0262 9452	0.0283 0255	0.0303 6667	87
88	0.0242 4416	0.0261 9730	0.0282 1165	0.0302 8219	88
89	0.0241 4370	0.0261 0291	0.0281 2353	0.0302 0041	89
90	0.0240 4602	0.0260 1126	0.0280 3809	0.0301 2125	90
91	0.0239 5101	0.0259 2224	0.0279 5523	0.0300 4460	91
92	0.0238 5859	0.0258 3577	0.0278 7486	0.0299 7038	92
93	0.0237 6868	0.0257 5176	0.0277 9690	0.0298 9850	93
94	0.0236 8118	0.0256 7012	0.0277 2126	0.0298 2887	94
95	0.0235 9602	0.0255 9078	0.0276 4786	0.0297 6141	95
96	0.0235 1313	0.0255 1366	0.0275 7662	0.0296 9605	96
97	0.0234 3242	0.0254 3868	0.0275 0747	0.0296 3272	97
98	0.0233 5383	0.0253 6578	0.0274 4034	0.0295 7134	98
99	0.0232 7729	0.0252 9489	0.0273 7517	0.0295 1185	99
100	0.0232 0274	0.0252 2594	0.0273 1188	0.0294 5418	100

TABLE VII.—Periodic Rent of Annuity Whose Present Value is 1

$$\frac{1}{a_{\overline{n}|i}} = \frac{i}{1 - (1+i)^{-n}} \qquad \left[\frac{1}{s_{\overline{n}|i}} = \frac{1}{a_{\overline{n}|i}} - i\right]$$

n	3%	3½%	4%	4½%	n
1	1.0300 0000	1.0350 0000	1.0400 0000	1.0450 0000	1
2	0.5226 1084	0.5264 0049	0.5301 9608	0.5339 9756	2
3	0.3535 3036	0.3569 3418	0.3603 4854	0.3637 7336	3
4	0.2690 2705	0.2722 5114	0.2754 9005	0.2787 4365	4
5	0.2183 5457	0.2214 8137	0.2246 2711	0.2277 9164	5
6	0.1845 9750	0.1876 6821	0.1907 6190	0.1938 7839	6
7	0.1605 0635	0.1635 4449	0.1666 0961	0.1697 0147	7
8	0.1424 5639	0.1454 7665	0.1485 2783	0.1516 0965	8
9	0.1284 3386	0.1314 4601	0.1344 9299	0.1375 7447	9
10	0.1172 3051	0.1202 4137	0.1232 9094	0.1263 7882	10
11	0.1080 7745	0.1110 9197	0.1141 4904	0.1172 4818	11
12	0.1004 6209	0.1034 8395	0.1065 5217	0.1096 6619	12
13	0.0940 2954	0.0970 6157	0.1001 4373	0.1032 7535	13
14	0.0885 2634	0.0915 7073	0.0946 6897	0.0978 2032	14
15	0.0837 6658	0.0868 2507	0.0899 4110	0.0931 1381	15
16	0.0796 1085	0.0826 8483	0.0858 2000	0.0890 1537	16
17	0.0759 5253	0.0790 4313	0.0821 9852	0.0854 1758	17
18	0.0727 0870	0.0758 1684	0.0789 9333	0.0822 3690	18
19	0.0698 1388	0.0729 4033	0.0761 3862	0.0794 0734	19
20	0.0672 1571	0.0703 6108	0.0735 8175	0.0768 7614	20
21	0.0648 7178	0.0680 3659	0.0712 8011	0.0746 0057	21
22	0.0627 4739	0.0659 3207	0.0691 9881	0.0725 4565	22
23	0.0608 1390	0.0640 1880	0.0673 0906	0.0706 8249	23
24	0.0590 4742	0.0622 7283	0.0655 8683	0.0689 8703	24
25	0.0574 2787	0.0606 7404	0.0640 1196	0.0674 3903	25
26	0.0559 3829	0.0592 0540	0.0625 6738	0.0660 2137	26
27	0.0545 6421	0.0578 5241	0.0612 3854	0.0647 1946	27
28	0.0532 9323	0.0566 0265	0.0600 1298	0.0635 2081	28
29	0.0521 1467	0.0554 4538	0.0588 7993	0.0624 1461	29
30	0.0510 1926	0.0543 7133	0.0578 3010	0.0613 9154	30
31	0.0499 9893	0.0533 7240	0.0568 5535	0.0604 4345	31
32	0.0490 4662	0.0524 4150	0.0559 4859	0.0595 6320	32
33	0.0481 5612	0.0515 7242	0.0551 0357	0.0587 4453	33
34	0.0473 2196	0.0507 5966	0.0543 1477	0.0579 8191	34
35	0.0465 3929	0.0499 9835	0.0535 7732	0.0572 7045	35
36	0.0458 0379	0.0492 8416	0.0528 8688	0.0566 0578	36
37	0.0451 1162	0.0486 1325	0.0522 3957	0.0559 8402	37
38	0.0444 5934	0.0479 8214	0.0516 3192	0.0554 0169	38
39	0.0438 4385	0.0473 8775	0.0510 6083	0.0548 5567	39
40	0.0432 6238	0.0468 2728	0.0505 2349	0.0543 4315	40
41	0.0427 1241	0.0462 9822	0.0500 1738	0.0538 6158	41
42	0.0421 9167	0.0457 9828	0.0495 4020	0.0534 0868	42
43	0.0416 9811	0.0453 2539	0.0490 8989	0.0529 8235	43
44	0.0412 2985	0.0448 7768	0.0486 6454	0.0525 8071	44
45	0.0407 8518	0.0444 5343	0.0482 6246	0.0522 0202	45
46	0.0403 6254	0.0440 5108	0.0478 8205	0.0518 4471	46
47	0.0399 6051	0.0436 6919	0.0475 2189	0.0515 0734	47
48	0.0395 7777	0.0433 0646	0.0471 8065	0.0511 8858	48
49	0.0392 1314	0.0429 6167	0.0468 5712	0.0508 8722	49
50	0.0388 6550	0.0426 3371	0.0465 5020	0.0506 0215	50

TABLE VII.—Periodic Rent of Annuity Whose Present Value is 1

$$\frac{1}{a_{\overline{n}|i}} = \frac{i}{1 - (1+i)^{-n}} \qquad \left[\frac{1}{s_{\overline{n}|i}} = \frac{1}{a_{\overline{n}|i}} - i\right]$$

n	3%	3½%	4%	4½%	n
51	0.0385 3382	0.0423 2156	0.0462 5885	0.0503 3232	51
52	0.0382 1718	0.0420 2429	0.0459 8212	0.0500 7679	52
53	0.0379 1471	0.0417 4100	0.0457 1915	0.0498 3469	53
54	0.0376 2558	0.0414 7090	0.0454 6910	0.0496 0519	54
55	0.0373 4907	0.0412 1323	0.0452 3124	0.0493 8754	55
56	0.0370 8447	0.0409 6730	0.0450 0487	0.0491 8105	56
57	0.0368 3114	0.0407 3245	0.0447 8932	0.0489 8506	57
58	0.0365 8848	0.0405 0810	0.0445 8401	0.0487 9897	58
59	0.0363 5593	0.0402 9366	0.0443 8836	0.0486 2221	59
60	0.0361 3296	0.0400 8862	0.0442 0185	0.0484 5426	60
61	0.0359 1908	0.0398 9249	0.0440 2398	0.0482 9462	61
62	0.0357 1385	0.0397 0480	0.0438 5430	0.0481 4284	62
63	0.0355 1682	0.0395 2513	0.0436 9237	0.0479 9848	63
64	0.0353 2760	0.0393 5308	0.0435 3780	0.0478 6115	64
65	0.0351 4581	0.0391 8826	0.0433 9019	0.0477 3047	65
66	0.0349 7110	0.0390 3031	0.0432 4921	0.0476 0608	66
67	0.0348 0313	0.0388 7892	0.0431 1451	0.0474 8765	67
68	0.0346 4159	0.0387 3375	0.0429 8578	0.0473 7487	68
69	0.0344 8618	0.0385 9453	0.0428 6272	0.0472 6745	69
70	0.0343 3663	0.0384 6095	0.0427 4506	0.0471 6511	70
71	0.0341 9266	0.0383 3277	0.0426 3253	0.0470 6759	71
72	0.0340 5404	0.0382 0973	0.0425 2489	0.0469 7465	72
73	0.0339 2053	0.0380 9160	0.0424 2190	0.0468 8606	73
74	0.0337 9191	0.0379 7816	0.0423 2334	0.0468 0159	74
75	0.0336 6796	0.0378 6919	0.0422 2900	0.0467 2104	75
76	0.0335 4849	0.0377 6450	0.0421 3869	0.0466 4422	76
77	0.0334 3331	0.0376 6390	0.0420 5221	0.0465 7094	77
78	0.0333 2224	0.0375 6721	0.0419 6939	0.0465 0104	78
79	0.0332 1510	0.0374 7426	0.0418 9007	0.0464 3434	79
80	0.0331 1175	0.0373 8489	0.0418 1408	0.0463 7069	80
81	0.0330 1201	0.0372 9894	0.0417 4127	0.0463 0995	81
82	0.0329 1576	0.0372 1628	0.0416 7150	0.0462 5197	82
83	0.0328 2284	0.0371 3676	0.0416 0463	0.0461 9663	83
84	0.0327 3313	0.0370 6025	0.0415 4054	0.0461 4379	84
85	0.0326 4650	0.0369 8662	0.0414 7909	0.0460 9334	85
86	0.0325 6284	0.0369 1576	0.0414 2018	0.0460 4516	86
87	0.0324 8202	0.0368 4756	0.0413 6370	0.0459 9915	87
88	0.0324 0393	0.0367 8190	0.0413 0953	0.0459 5522	88
89	0.0323 2848	0.0367 1868	0.0412 5758	0.0459 1325	89
90	0.0322 5556	0.0366 5781	0.0412 0775	0.0458 7316	90
91	0.0321 8508	0.0365 9919	0.0411 5995	0.0458 3486	91
92	0.0321 1694	0.0365 4273	0.0411 1410	0.0457 9827	92
93	0.0320 5107	0.0364 8834	0.0410 7010	0.0457 6331	93
94	0.0319 8737	0.0364 3594	0.0410 2789	0.0457 2991	94
95	0.0319 2577	0.0363 8546	0.0409 8738	0.0456 9799	95
96	0.0318 6619	0.0363 3682	0.0409 4850	0.0456 6749	96
97	0.0318 0856	0.0362 8995	0.0409 1119	0.0456 3834	97
98	0.0317 5281	0.0362 4478	0.0408 7538	0.0456 1048	98
99	0.0316 9886	0.0362 0124	0.0408 4100	0.0455 8385	99
100	0.0316 4667	0.0361 5927	0.0408 0800	0.0455 5839	100

TABLE VII.—Periodic Rent of Annuity Whose Present Value is 1

$$\frac{1}{a_{\overline{n}|i}} = \frac{i}{1 - (1 + i)^{-n}} \qquad \left[\frac{1}{s_{\overline{n}|i}} = \frac{1}{a_{\overline{n}|i}} - i \right]$$

n	5%	5½%	6%	6½%	n
1	1.0500 0000	1.0550 0000	1.0600 0000	1.0650 0000	1
2	0.5378 0488	0.5416 1800	0.5454 3689	0.5492 6150	2
3	0.3672 0856	0.3706 5407	0.3741 0981	0.3775 7570	3
4	0.2820 1183	0.2852 9449	0.2885 9149	0.2919 0274	4
5	0.2309 7480	0.2341 7644	0.2373 9640	0.2406 3454	5
6	0.1970 1747	0.2001 7895	0.2033 6263	0.2065 6831	6
7	0.1728 1982	0.1759 6442	0.1791 3502	0.1823 3137	7
8	0.1547 2181	0.1578 6401	0.1610 3594	0.1642 3730	8
9	0.1406 9008	0.1438 3946	0.1470 2224	0.1502 3803	9
10	0.1295 0458	0.1326 6777	0.1358 6796	0.1391 0469	10
11	0.1203 8889	0.1235 7065	0.1267 9294	0.1300 5521	11
12	0.1128 2541	0.1160 2923	0.1192 7703	0.1225 6817	12
13	0.1064 5577	0.1096 8426	0.1129 6011	0.1162 8256	13
14	0.1010 2397	0.1042 7912	0.1075 8491	0.1109 4048	14
15	0.0963 4229	0.0996 2560	0.1029 6276	0.1063 5278	15
16	0.0922 6991	0.0955 8254	0.0989 5214	0.1023 7757	16
17	0.0886 9914	0.0920 4797	0.0954 4480	0.0989 0633	17
18	0.0855 4622	0.0889 1992	0.0923 5654	0.0958 5461	18
19	0.0827 4501	0.0861 5006	0.0896 2086	0.0931 5575	19
20	0.0802 4259	0.0836 7933	0.0871 8456	0.0907 5640	20
21	0.0779 9611	0.0814 6478	0.0850 0455	0.0886 1333	21
22	0.0759 7051	0.0794 7123	0.0830 4557	0.0866 9120	22
23	0.0741 3682	0.0776 6965	0.0812 7848	0.0849 6078	23
24	0.0724 7090	0.0760 3580	0.0796 7900	0.0833 9770	24
25	0.0709 5246	0.0745 4935	0.0782 2672	0.0819 8148	25
26	0.0695 6432	0.0731 9307	0.0769 0435	0.0806 9480	26
27	0.0682 9186	0.0719 5228	0.0756 9717	0.0795 2288	27
28	0.0671 2253	0.0708 1440	0.0745 9255	0.0784 5305	28
29	0.0660 4551	0.0697 6857	0.0735 7961	0.0774 7440	29
30	0.0650 5144	0.0688 0539	0.0726 4891	0.0765 7744	30
31	0.0641 3212	0.0679 1665	0.0717 9222	0.0757 5393	31
32	0.0632 8042	0.0670 9519	0.0710 0234	0.0749 9665	32
33	0.0624 9004	0.0663 3469	0.0702 7293	0.0742 9924	33
34	0.0617 5545	0.0656 2958	0.0695 9843	0.0736 5610	34
35	0.0610 7171	0.0649 7493	0.0689 7386	0.0730 6226	35
36	0.0604 3446	0.0643 6635	0.0683 9483	0.0725 1332	36
37	0.0598 3979	0.0637 9993	0.0678 5743	0.0720 0534	37
38	0.0592 8423	0.0632 7217	0.0673 5812	0.0715 3480	38
39	0.0587 6462	0.0627 7991	0.0668 9377	0.0710 9854	39
40	0.0582 7816	0.0623 2034	0.0664 6154	0.0706 9373	40
41	0.0578 2229	0.0618 9090	0.0660 5886	0.0703 1779	41
42	0.0573 9471	0.0614 8927	0.0656 8342	0.0699 6842	42
43	0.0569 9333	0.0611 1337	0.0653 3312	0.0696 4352	43
44	0.0566 1625	0.0607 6128	0.0650 0606	0.0693 4119	44
45	0.0562 6173	0.0604 3127	0.0647 0050	0.0690 5968	45
46	0.0559 2820	0.0601 2175	0.0644 1485	0.0687 9743	46
47	0.0556 1421	0.0598 3129	0.0641 4768	0.0685 5300	47
48	0.0553 1843	0.0595 5854	0.0638 9766	0.0683 2506	48
49	0.0550 3965	0.0593 0230	0.0636 6356	0.0681 1240	49
50	0.0547 7674	0.0590 6145	0.0634 4429	0.0679 1393	50

533

TABLE VII.—Periodic Rent of Annuity Whose Present Value is 1

$$\frac{1}{a_{\overline{n}|i}} = \frac{i}{1 - (1 + i)^{-n}} \qquad \left[\frac{1}{s_{\overline{n}|i}} = \frac{1}{a_{\overline{n}|i}} - i\right]$$

n	5%	5½%	6%	6½%	n
51	0.0545 2867	0.0588 3495	0.0632 3880	0.0677 2861	51
52	0.0542 9450	0.0586 2186	0.0630 4617	0.0675 5553	52
53	0.0540 7334	0.0584 2130	0.0628 6551	0.0673 9382	53
54	0.0538 6438	0.0582 3245	0.0626 9602	0.0672 4267	54
55	0.0536 6686	0.0580 5458	0.0625 3696	0.0671 0137	55
56	0.0534 8010	0.0578 8698	0.0623 8765	0.0669 6923	56
57	0.0533 0343	0.0577 2900	0.0622 4744	0.0668 4563	57
58	0.0531 3626	0.0575 8006	0.0621 1574	0.0667 2999	58
59	0.0529 7802	0.0574 3959	0.0619 9200	0.0666 2177	59
60	0.0528 2818	0.0573 0707	0.0618 7572	0.0665 2047	60
61	0.0526 8627	0.0571 8202	0.0617 6642	0.0664 2564	61
62	0.0525 5183	0.0570 6400	0.0616 6366	0.0663 3684	62
63	0.0524 2442	0.0569 5258	0.0615 6704	0.0662 5367	63
64	0.0523 0365	0.0568 4737	0.0614 7615	0.0661 7577	64
65	0.0521 8915	0.0567 4800	0.0613 9066	0.0661 0280	65
66	0.0520 8057	0.0566 5413	0.0613 1022	0.0660 3442	66
67	0.0519 7757	0.0565 6544	0.0612 3454	0.0659 7034	67
68	0.0518 7986	0.0564 8163	0.0611 6330	0.0659 1029	68
69	0.0517 8715	0.0564 0242	0.0610 9625	0.0658 5400	69
70	0.0516 9915	0.0563 2754	0.0610 3313	0.0658 0124	70
71	0.0516 1563	0.0562 5675	0.0609 7370	0.0657 5177	71
72	0.0515 3633	0.0561 8982	0.0609 1774	0.0657 0539	72
73	0.0514 6103	0.0561 2652	0.0608 6505	0.0656 6190	73
74	0.0513 8953	0.0560 6665	0.0608 1542	0.0656 2112	74
75	0.0513 2161	0.0560 1002	0.0607 6867	0.0655 8287	75
76	0.0512 5709	0.0559 5645	0.0607 2463	0.0655 4699	76
77	0.0511 9580	0.0559 0577	0.0606 8315	0.0655 1335	77
78	0.0511 3756	0.0558 5781	0.0606 4407	0.0654 8178	78
79	0.0510 8222	0.0558 1243	0.0606 0724	0.0654 5217	79
80	0.0510 2962	0.0557 6948	0.0605 7254	0.0654 2440	80
81	0.0509 7963	0.0557 2884	0.0605 3984	0.0653 9834	81
82	0.0509 3211	0.0556 9036	0.0605 0903	0.0653 7388	82
83	0.0508 8694	0.0556 5395	0.0604 7998	0.0653 5094	83
84	0.0508 4399	0.0556 1947	0.0604 5261	0.0653 2941	84
85	0.0508 0316	0.0555 8683	0.0604 2681	0.0653 0921	85
86	0.0507 6433	0.0555 5593	0.0604 0249	0.0652 9026	86
87	0.0507 2740	0.0555 2667	0.0603 7956	0.0652 7247	87
88	0.0506 9228	0.0554 9896	0.0603 5795	0.0652 5577	88
89	0.0506 5888	0.0554 7273	0.0603 3757	0.0652 4010	89
90	0.0506 2711	0.0554 4788	0.0603 1836	0.0652 2540	90
91	0.0505 9689	0.0554 2435	0.0603 0025	0.0652 1160	91
92	0.0505 6815	0.0554 0207	0.0602 8318	0.0651 9864	92
93	0.0505 4080	0.0553 8096	0.0602 6708	0.0651 8649	93
94	0.0505 1478	0.0553 6097	0.0602 5190	0.0651 7507	94
95	0.0504 9003	0.0553 4204	0.0602 3758	0.0651 6436	95
96	0.0504 6648	0.0553 2410	0.0602 2408	0.0651 5431	96
97	0.0504 4407	0.0553 0711	0.0602 1135	0.0651 4487	97
98	0.0504 2274	0.0552 9101	0.0601 9935	0.0651 3601	98
99	0.0504 0245	0.0552 7577	0.0601 8803	0.0651 2769	99
100	0.0503 8314	0.0552 6132	0.0601 7736	0.0651 1988	100

TABLE VII.—Periodic Rent of Annuity Whose Present Value is 1

$$\frac{1}{a_{\overline{n}|i}} = \frac{i}{1 - (1 + i)^{-n}} \qquad \left[\frac{1}{s_{\overline{n}|i}} = \frac{1}{a_{\overline{n}|i}} - i\right]$$

n	7%	7½%	8%	8½%	n
1	1.0700 0000	1.0750 0000	1.0800 0000	1.0850 0000	1
2	0.5530 9179	0.5569 2771	0.5607 6923	0.5646 1631	2
3	0.3810 5166	0.3845 3763	0.3880 3351	0.3915 3925	3
4	0.2952 2812	0.2985 6751	0.3019 2080	0.3052 8789	4
5	0.2438 9069	0.2471 6472	0.2504 5645	0.2537 6575	5
6	0.2097 9580	0.2130 4489	0.2163 1539	0.2196 0708	6
7	0.1855 5322	0.1888 0032	0.1920 7240	0.1953 6922	7
8	0.1674 6776	0.1707 2702	0.1740 1476	0.1773 3065	8
9	0.1534 8647	0.1567 6716	0.1600 7971	0.1634 2372	9
10	0.1423 7750	0.1456 8593	0.1490 2949	0.1524 0771	10
11	0.1333 5690	0.1366 9747	0.1400 7634	0.1434 9293	11
12	0.1259 0199	0.1292 7783	0.1326 9502	0.1361 5286	12
13	0.1196 5085	0.1230 6420	0.1265 2181	0.1300 2287	13
14	0.1143 4494	0.1177 9737	0.1212 9685	0.1248 4244	14
15	0.1097 9462	0.1132 8724	0.1168 2954	0.1204 2046	15
16	0.1058 5765	0.1093 9116	0.1129 7687	0.1166 1354	16
17	0.1024 2519	0.1060 0003	0.1096 2943	0.1133 1198	17
18	0.0994 1260	0.1030 2896	0.1067 0210	0.1104 3041	18
19	0.0967 5301	0.1004 1090	0.1041 2763	0.1079 0140	19
20	0.0943 9293	0.0980 9219	0.1018 5221	0.1056 7097	20
21	0.0922 8900	0.0960 2937	0.0998 3225	0.1036 9541	21
22	0.0904 0577	0.0941 8687	0.0980 3207	0.1019 3892	22
23	0.0887 1393	0.0925 3528	0.0964 2217	0.1003 7193	23
24	0.0871 8902	0.0910 5008	0.0949 7796	0.0989 6975	24
25	0.0858 1052	0.0897 1067	0.0936 7878	0.0977 1168	25
26	0.0845 6103	0.0884 9961	0.0925 0713	0.0965 8016	26
27	0.0834 2573	0.0874 0204	0.0914 4809	0.0955 6025	27
28	0.0823 9193	0.0864 0520	0.0904 8891	0.0946 3914	28
29	0.0814 4865	0.0854 9811	0.0896 1854	0.0938 0577	29
30	0.0805 8640	0.0846 7124	0.0888 2743	0.0930 5058	30
31	0.0797 9691	0.0839 1628	0.0881 0728	0.0923 6524	31
32	0.0790 7292	0.0832 2599	0.0874 5081	0.0917 4247	32
33	0.0784 0807	0.0825 9397	0.0868 5163	0.0911 7588	33
34	0.0777 9674	0.0820 1461	0.0863 0411	0.0906 5984	34
35	0.0772 3396	0.0814 8291	0.0858 0326	0.0901 8937	35
36	0.0767 1531	0.0809 9447	0.0853 4467	0.0897 6006	36
37	0.0762 3685	0.0805 4533	0.0849 2440	0.0893 6799	37
38	0.0757 9505	0.0801 3197	0.0845 3894	0.0890 0966	38
39	0.0753 8676	0.0797 5124	0.0841 8513	0.0886 8193	39
40	0.0750 0914	0.0794 0031	0.0838 6016	0.0883 8201	40
41	0.0746 5962	0.0790 7663	0.0835 6149	0.0881 0737	41
42	0.0743 3591	0.0787 7789	0.0832 8684	0.0878 5576	42
43	0.0740 3590	0.0785 0201	0.0830 3414	0.0876 2512	43
44	0.0737 5769	0.0782 4710	0.0828 0152	0.0874 1363	44
45	0.0734 9957	0.0780 1146	0.0825 8728	0.0872 1961	45
46	0.0732 5996	0.0777 9353	0.0823 8991	0.0870 4154	46
47	0.0730 3744	0.0775 9190	0.0822 0799	0.0868 7807	47
48	0.0728 3070	0.0774 0527	0.0820 4027	0.0867 2795	48
49	0.0726 3853	0.0772 3247	0.0818 8557	0.0865 9005	49
50	0.0724 5985	0.0770 7241	0.0817 4286	0.0864 6334	50

TABLE VII.—Periodic Rent of Annuity Whose Present Value is 1

$$\frac{1}{a_{\overline{n}|i}} = \frac{i}{1 - (1 + i)^{-n}} \qquad \left[\frac{1}{s_{\overline{n}|i}} = \frac{1}{a_{\overline{n}|i}} - i\right]$$

n	7%	7½%	8%	8½%	n
51	0.0722 9365	0.0769 2411	0.0816 1116	0.0863 4688	51
52	0.0721 3901	0.0767 8668	0.0814 8959	0.0862 3983	52
53	0.0719 9509	0.0766 5927	0.0813 7735	0.0861 4139	53
54	0.0718 6110	0.0765 4112	0.0812 7370	0.0860 5087	54
55	0.0717 3633	0.0764 3155	0.0811 7796.	0.0859 6761	55
56	0.0716 2011	0.0763 2991	0.0810 8952	0.0858 9101	56
57	0.0715 1183	0.0762 3559	0.0810 0780	0.0858 2053	57
58	0.0714. 1093	0.0761 4807	0.0809 3227	0.0857 5568	58
59	0.0713 1689	0.0760 6683	0.0808 6247	0.0856 9599	59
60	0.0712 2923	0.0759 9142	0.0807 9795	0.0856 4106	60
61	0.0711 4749	0.0759 2140	0.0807 3830	0.0855 9049	61
62	0.0710 7127	0.0758 5638	0.0806 8314	0.0855 4393	62
63	0.0710 0019	0.0757 9600	0.0806 3214	0.0855 0107	63
64	0.0709 3388	0.0757 3992	0.0805 8497	0.0854 6160	64
65	0.0708 7203	0.0756 8782	0.0805 4135	0.0854 2526	65
66	0.0708 1431	0.0756 3942	0.0805 0100	0.0853 9179	66
67	0.0707 6046	0.0755 9446	0.0804 6367	0.0853 6097	67
68	0.0707 1021	0.0755 5268	0.0804 2914	0.0853 3258	68
69	0.0706 6331	0.0755 1386	0.0803 9719	0.0853 0643	69
70	0.0706 1953	0.0754 7778	0.0803 6764	0.0852 8234	70
71	0.0705 7866	0.0754 4425	0.0803 4029	0.0852 6016	71
72	0.0705 4051	0.0754 1308	0.0803 1498	0.0852 3972	72
73	0.0705 0490	0.0753 8412	0.0802 9157	0.0852 2089	73
74	0.0704 7164	0.0753 5719	0.0802 6989	0.0852 0354	74
75	0.0704 4060	0.0753 3216	0.0802 4984	0.0851 8756	75
76	0.0704 1160	0.0753 0889	0.0802 3128	0.0851 7284	76
77	0.0703 8453	0.0752 8726	0.0802 1410	0.0851 5927	77
78	0.0703 5924	0.0752 6714	0.0801 9820	0.0851 4677	78
79	0.0703 3563	0.0752 4844	0.0801 8349	0.0851 3526	79
80	0.0703 1357	0.0752 3106	0.0801 6987	0.0851 2465	80
81	0.0702 9297	0.0752 1489	0.0801 5726	0.0851 1487	81
82	0.0702 7373	0.0751 9986	0.0801 4559	0.0851 0586	82
83	0.0702 5576	0.0751 8588	0.0801 3479	0.0850 9756	83
84	0.0702 3897	0.0751 7288	0.0801 2479	0.0850 8990	84
85	0.0702 2329	0.0751 6079	0.0801 1553	0.0850 8285	85
86	0.0702 0863	0.0751 4955	0.0801 0696	0.0850 7636	86
87	0.0701 9495	0.0751 3910	0.0800 9903	0.0850 7037	87
88	0.0701 8216	0.0751 2938	0.0800 9168	0.0850 6485	88
89	0.0701 7021	0.0751 2034	0.0800 8489	0.0850 5977	89
90	0.0701 5905	0.0751 1193	0.0800 7859	0.0850 5508	90
91	0.0701 4863	0.0751 0411	0.0800 7277	0.0850 5077	91
92	0.0701 3888	0.0750 9684	0.0800 6737	0.0850 4679	92
93	0.0701 2978	0.0750 9007	0.0800 6238	0.0850 4312	93
94	0.0701 2128	0.0750 8378	0.0800 5775	0.0850 3974	94
95	0.0701 1333	0.0750 7793	0.0800 5347	0.0850 3663	95
96	0.0701 0590	0.0750 7249	0.0800 4951	0.0850 3375	96
97	0.0700 9897	0.0750 6743	0.0800 4584	0.0850 3111	97
98	0.0700 9248	0.0750 6272	0.0800 4244	0.0850 2867	98
99	0.0700 8643	0.0750 5834	0.0800 3930	0.0850 2642	99
100	0.0700 8076	0.0750 5427	0.0800 3638	0.0850 2435	100

TABLE VIII.—Values of $(1 + i)^{1/p}$

p	$\frac{1}{4}\%$	$\frac{7}{24}\%$	$\frac{1}{3}\%$	$\frac{5}{12}\%$	$\frac{1}{2}\%$
2	1.0012 4922	1.0014 5727	1.0016 6528	1.0020 8117	1.0024 9688
3	1.0008 3264	1.0009 7128	1.0011 0988	1.0013 8696	1.0016 6390
4	1.0006 2441	1.0007 2837	1.0008 3229	1.0010 4004	1.0012 4766
6	1.0004 1623	1.0004 8552	1.0005 5479	1.0006 9324	1.0008 3160
12	1.0002 0809	1.0002 4273	1.0002 7735	1.0003 4656	1.0004 1571

p	$\frac{7}{12}\%$	$\frac{2}{3}\%$	$\frac{3}{4}\%$	$\frac{7}{8}\%$	1%
2	1.0029 1243	1.0033 2780	1.0037 4299	1.0043 6547	1.0049 8756
3	1.0019 4068	1.0022 1730	1.0024 9378	1.0029 0820	1.0033 2228
4	1.0014 5515	1.0016 6252	1.0018 6975	1.0021 8036	1.0024 9068
6	1.0009 6987	1.0011 0804	1.0012 4611	1.0014 5304	1.0016 5977
12	1.0004 8482	1.0005 5387	1.0006 2286	1.0007 2626	1.0008 2954

p	$1\frac{1}{8}\%$	$1\frac{1}{4}\%$	$1\frac{3}{8}\%$	$1\frac{1}{2}\%$	$1\frac{3}{4}\%$
2	1.0056 0927	1.0062 3059	1.0068 5153	1.0074 7208	1.0087 1205
3	1.0037 3602	1.0041 4943	1.0045 6249	1.0049 7521	1.0057 9963
4	1.0028 0081	1.0031 1046	1.0034 1992	1.0037 2909	1.0043 4658
6	1.0018 6627	1.0020 7257	1.0022 7865	1.0024 8452	1.0028 9562
12	1.0009 3270	1.0010 3575	1.0011 3868	1.0012 4149	1.0014 4677

p	2%	$2\frac{1}{4}\%$	$2\frac{1}{2}\%$	$2\frac{3}{4}\%$	3%
2	1.0099 5049	1.0111 8742	1.0124 2284	1.0136 5675	1.0148 8916
3	1.0066 2271	1.0074 4444	1.0082 6484	1.0090 8390	1.0099 0163
4	1.0049 6293	1.0055 7815	1.0061 9225	1.0068 0522	1.0074 1707
6	1.0033 0589	1.0037 1532	1.0041 2392	1.0045 3168	1.0049 3862
12	1.0016 5158	1.0018 5594	1.0020 5984	1.0022 6328	1.0024 6627

p	$3\frac{1}{2}\%$	4%	$4\frac{1}{2}\%$	5%	$5\frac{1}{2}\%$
2	1.0173 4950	1.0198 0390	1.0222 5242	1.0246 9508	1.0271 3193
3	1.0115 3314	1.0131 5941	1.0147 8046	1.0163 9636	1.0180 0713
4	1.0086 3745	1.0098 5341	1.0110 6499	1.0122 7224	1.0134 7518
6	1.0057 5004	1.0065 5820	1.0073 6312	1.0081 6485	1.0089 6340
12	1.0028 7090	1.0032 7374	1.0036 7481	1.0040 7412	1.0044 7170

p	6%	$6\frac{1}{2}\%$	7%	$7\frac{1}{2}\%$	8%
2	1.0295 6302	1.0319 8837	1.0344 0804	1.0368 2207	1.0392 3048
3	1.0196 1282	1.0212 1347	1.0228 0912	1.0243 9981	1.0259 8557
4	1.0146 7385	1.0158 6828	1.0170 5853	1.0182 4460	1.0194 2655
6	1.0097 5880	1.0105 5107	1.0113 4026	1.0121 2638	1.0129 0946
12	1.0048 6755	1.0052 6169	1.0056 5415	1.0060 4492	1.0064 3403

TABLE IX.—Values of $s_{\frac{1}{p}|i} = \dfrac{(1+i)^{1/p} - 1}{i}$

p	$\frac{1}{4}\%$	$\frac{7}{24}\%$	$\frac{1}{3}\%$	$\frac{5}{12}\%$	$\frac{1}{2}\%$
2	0.4996 8789	0.4996 3595	0.4995 8403	0.4994 8025	0.4993 7656
3	0.3330 5594	0.3330 0978	0.3329 6365	0.3328 7144	0.3327 7932
4	0.2497 6597	0.2497 2703	0.2496 8811	0.2496 1032	0.2495 3261
6	0.1664 9332	0.1664 6448	0.1664 3566	0.1663 7805	0.1663 2050
12	0.0832 3800	0.0832 2214	0.0832 0629	0.0831 7461	0.0831 4297

p	$\frac{7}{12}\%$	$\frac{2}{3}\%$	$\frac{3}{4}\%$	$\frac{7}{8}\%$	1%
2	0.4992 7295	0.4991 6943	0.4990 6600	0.4989 1101	0.4987 5621
3	0.3326 8728	0.3325 9532	0.3325 0346	0.3323 6581	0.3322 2835
4	0.2494 5498	0.2493 7742	0.2492 9994	0.2491 8385	0.2490 6793
6	0.1662 6301	0.1662 0558	0.1661 4821	0.1660 6226	0.1659 7644
12	0.0831 1136	0.0830 7978	0.0830 4824	0.0830 0099	0.0829 5381

p	$1\frac{1}{8}\%$	$1\frac{1}{4}\%$	$1\frac{3}{8}\%$	$1\frac{1}{2}\%$	$1\frac{3}{4}\%$
2	0.4986 0160	0.4984 4719	0.4982 9297	0.4981 3893	0.4978 3143
3	0.3320 9109	0.3319 5401	0.3318 1712	0.3316 8042	0.3314 0758
4	0.2489 5218	0.2488 3660	0.2487 2117	0.2486 0593	0.2483 7592
6	0.1658 8986	0.1658 0518	0.1657 1975	0.1656 3445	0.1654 6423
12	0.0829 0627	0.0828 5968	0.0828 1273	0.0827 6585	0.0826 7231

p	2%	$2\frac{1}{4}\%$	$2\frac{1}{2}\%$	$2\frac{3}{4}\%$	3%
2	0.4975 2469	0.4972 1870	0.4969 1346	0.4966 0897	0.4963 0522
3	0.3311 3548	0.3308 6412	0.3305 9350	0.3303 2362	0.3300 5447
4	0.2481 4658	0.2479 1789	0.2476 8985	0.2474 6247	0.2472 3573
6	0.1652 9452	0.1651 2531	0.1649 5662	0.1647 8843	0.1646 2073
12	0.0825 7907	0.0824 8611	0.0823 9345	0.0823 0108	0.0822 0899

p	$3\frac{1}{2}\%$	4%	$4\frac{1}{2}\%$	5%	$5\frac{1}{2}\%$
2	0.4956 9993	0.4950 9757	0.4944 9811	0.4939 0153	0.4933 0780
3	0.3295 1834	0.3289 8510	0.3284 5470	0.3279 2714	0.3274 0237
4	0.2467 8417	0.2463 3516	0.2458 8868	0.2454 4469	0.2450 0317
6	0.1642 8684	0.1639 5492	0.1636 2496	0.1632 9692	0.1629 7080
12	0.0820 2568	0.0818 4349	0.0816 6243	0.0814 8248	0.0813 0362

p	6%	$6\frac{1}{2}\%$	7%	$7\frac{1}{2}\%$	8%
2	0.4927 1690	0.4921 2880	0.4915 4348	0.4909 6090	0.4903 8106
3	0.3268 8037	0.3263 6113	0.3258 4460	0.3253 3076	0.3248 1960
4	0.2445 6410	0.2441 2746	0.2436 9321	0.2432 6135	0.2428 3184
6	0.1626 4657	0.1623 2422	0.1620 0372	0.1616 8505	0.1613 6821
12	0.0811 2584	0.0809 4914	0.0807 7351	0.0805 9892	0.0804 2538

TABLE X.—Values of $\dfrac{1}{s_{\frac{1}{p}|i}} = \dfrac{i}{(1+i)^{1/p}-1}$ $\quad\left[\dfrac{1}{a_{\frac{1}{p}|i}} = \dfrac{1}{s_{\frac{1}{p}|i}} + i\right]$

p	$\frac{1}{4}\%$	$\frac{7}{24}\%$	$\frac{1}{3}\%$	$\frac{5}{12}\%$	$\frac{1}{2}\%$
2	2.0012 4922	2.0014 5727	2.0016 6528	2.0020 8117	2.0024 9688
3	3.0024 9861	3.0029 1478	3.0033 3087	3.0041 6282	3.0049 9446
4	4.0037 4805	4.0043 7235	4.0049 9654	4.0062 4459	4.0074 9221
6	6.0062 4696	6.0072 8756	6.0083 2795	6.0104 0824	6.0124 8788
12	12.0137 4384	12.0160 3328	12.0183 2234	12.0228 9946	12.0274 7526

p	$\frac{7}{12}\%$	$\frac{2}{3}\%$	$\frac{3}{4}\%$	$\frac{7}{8}\%$	1%
2	2.0029 1243	2.0033 2780	2.0037 4300	2.0043 6547	2.0049 8756
3	3.0058 2579	3.0066 5682	3.0074 8755	3.0087 3306	3.0099 7789
4	4.0087 3340	4.0099 8810	4.0112 3543	4.0131 0118	4.0149 0831
6	6.0145 6684	6.0166 4513	6.0187 2276	6.0218 3795	6.0249 5163
12	12.0320 4968	12.0366 2270	12.0411 9435	12.0480 4930	12.0549 0119

p	$1\frac{1}{8}\%$	$1\frac{1}{4}\%$	$1\frac{3}{8}\%$	$1\frac{1}{2}\%$	$1\frac{3}{4}\%$
2	2.0056 0927	2.0062 3059	2.0068 5153	2.0074 7208	2.0087 1205
3	3.0112 2203	3.0124 6549	3.0137 0827	3.0149 5037	3.0174 3253
4	4.0168 3567	4.0187 0147	4.0205 6648	4.0224 3021	4.0261 5513
6	6.0280 9600	6.0311 7452	6.0342 8372	6.0373 9144	6.0436 0242
12	12.0618 1437	12.0685 9580	12.0754 3856	12.0822 7820	12.0959 4852

p	2%	$2\frac{1}{4}\%$	$2\frac{1}{2}\%$	$2\frac{3}{4}\%$	3%
2	2.0099 5049	2.0111 8742	2.0124 2284	2.0136 5675	2.0148 8916
3	3.0199 1199	3.0223 8875	3.0248 6282	3.0273 3422	3.0298 0294
4	4.0298 7623	4.0335 9356	4.0373 0709	4.0410 1686	4.0447 2289
6	6.0498 0747	6.0560 0662	6.0621 9991	6.0683 8735	6.0745 6894
12	12.1096 0670	12.1232 5281	12.1368 8697	12.1505 0916	12.1641 1941

p	$3\frac{1}{2}\%$	4%	$4\frac{1}{2}\%$	5%	$5\frac{1}{2}\%$
2	2.0173 4950	2.0198 0390	2.0222 5241	2.0246 9508	2.0271 3193
3	3.0347 3244	3.0396 513d	3.0445 5985	3.0494 5791	3.0543 4565
4	4.0521 2375	4.0595 0975	4.0668 8103	4.0742 3769	4.0815 7982
6	6.0869 1473	6.0992 3739	6.1115 3716	6.1238 1418	6.1360 6860
12	12.1913 0435	12.2184 4211	12.2455 3306	12.2725 7753	12.2995 7585

p	6%	$6\frac{1}{2}\%$	7%	$7\frac{1}{2}\%$	8%
2	2.0295 6301	2.0319 8837	2.0344 0804	2.0368 2207	2.0392 3048
3	3.0592 2313	3.0640 9043	3.0689 4762	3.0737 9477	3.0786 3195
4	4.0889 0752	4.0962 2091	4.1035 2009	4.1108 0514	4.1180 7618
6	6.1483 0059	6.1605 1031	6.1726 9791	6.1848 6355	6.1970 0737
12	12.3265 2834	12.3534 3534	12.3802 9716	12.4071 1409	12.4338 8648

TABLE XI.—Values of $a_{\frac{1}{p}|i} = \dfrac{1-(1+i)^{-1/p}}{i}$

p	$\frac{1}{4}\%$	$\frac{7}{24}\%$	$\frac{1}{3}\%$	$\frac{5}{12}\%$	$\frac{1}{2}\%$
2	0.4990 6445	0.4989 0890	0.4987 5346	0.4984 4291	0.4981 3278
3	0.3327 7886	0.3326 8665	0.3325 9451	0.3324 1040	0.3322 2652
4	0.2496 1011	0.2495 4527	0.2494 8047	0.2493 5099	0.2492 2167
6	0.1664 2405	0.1663 8370	0.1663 4337	0.1662 6279	0.1661 8230
12	0.0832 2068	0.0832 0194	0.0831 8322	0.0831 4580	0.0831 0842

p	$\frac{7}{12}\%$	$\frac{2}{3}\%$	$\frac{3}{4}\%$	$\frac{7}{8}\%$	1%
2	0.4978 2308	0.4975 1381	0.4972 0496	0.4967 4249	0.4962 8098
3	0.3320 4289	0.3318 5949	0.3316 7633	0.3314 0203	0.3311 2825
4	0.2490 9251	0.2489 6351	0.2488 3468	0.2486 4172	0.2484 4912
6	0.1661 0192	0.1660 2162	0.1659 4143	0.1658 2131	0.1657 0141
12	0.0830 7108	0.0830 3379	0.0829 9654	0.0829 4075	0.0828 8506

p	$1\frac{1}{8}\%$	$1\frac{1}{4}\%$	$1\frac{3}{8}\%$	$1\frac{1}{2}\%$	$1\frac{3}{4}\%$
2	0.4958 2042	0.4953 6080	0.4949 0213	0.4944 4440	0.4935 3176
3	0.3308 5501	0.3305 8228	0.3303 1009	0.3300 3841	0.3294 9662
4	0.2482 5688	0.2480 6500	0.2478 7346	0.2476 8230	0.2473 0101
6	0.1655 8084	0.1654 6225	0.1653 4299	0.1652 2395	0.1649 8649
12	0.0828 2901	0.0827 7395	0.0827 1854	0.0826 6322	0.0825 5287

p	2%	$2\frac{1}{4}\%$	$2\frac{1}{2}\%$	$2\frac{3}{4}\%$	3%
2	0.4926 2285	0.4917 1765	0.4908 1613	0.4899 1828	0.4890 2406
3	0.3289 5689	0.3284 1922	0.3278 8360	0.3273 5001	0.3268 1843
4	0.2469 2113	0.2465 4264	0.2461 6554	0.2457 8981	0.2454 1546
6	0.1647 4987	0.1645 1409	0.1642 7915	0.1640 4503	0.1638 1173
12	0.0824 4290	0.0823 3331	0.0822 2408	0.0821 1523	0.0820 0674

p	$3\frac{1}{2}\%$	4%	$4\frac{1}{2}\%$	5%	$5\frac{1}{2}\%$
2	0.4872 4645	0.4854 8311	0.4837 3386	0.4819 9854	0.4802 7696
3	0.3257 6129	0.3247 1208	0.3236 7070	0.3226 3706	0.3216 1108
4	0.2446 7084	0.2439 3161	0.2431 9770	0.2424 6905	0.2417 4561
6	0.1633 4759	0.1628 8668	0.1624 2897	0.1619 7442	0.1615 2300
12	0.0817 9086	0.0815 7643	0.0813 6344	0.0811 5185	0.0809 4167

p	6%	$6\frac{1}{2}\%$	7%	$7\frac{1}{2}\%$	8%
2	0.4785 6896	0.4768 7437	0.4751 9301	0.4735 2474	0.4718 6939
3	0.3205 9265	0.3195 8169	0.3185 7811	0.3175 8183	0.3165 9276
4	0.2410 2731	0.2403 1409	0.2396 0589	0.2389 0266	0.2382 0435
6	0.1610 7468	0.1606 2940	0.1601 8715	0.1597 4789	0.1593 1159
12	0.0807 3287	0.0805 2544	0.0803 1937	0.0801 1463	0.0799 1123

TABLE XII.—Logarithms

N.	0	1	2	3	4	5	6	7	8	9	D
100	000000	000434	000868	ʋ01301	001734	002166	002598	003029	003461	003891	432
1	4321	4751	5181	5609	6038	6466	6894	7321	7748	8174	428
2	8600	9026	9451	9876	010300	010724	011147	011570	011993	012415	424
3	012837	013259	013680	014100	4521	4940	5360	5779	6197	6616	420
4	7033	7451	7868	8284	8700	9116	9532	9947	020361	020775	416
105	021189	021603	022016	022428	022841	023252	023664	024075	4486	4896	412
6	5306	5715	6125	6533	6942	7350	7757	8164	8571	8978	408
7	9384	9789	030195	030600	031004	031408	031812	032216	032619	033021	404
8	033424	033826	4227	4628	5029	5430	5830	6230	6629	7028	400
9	7426	7825	8223	8620	9017	9414	9811	040207	040602	040998	397
110	041393	041787	042182	042576	042969	043362	043755	044148	044540	044932	393
1	5323	5714	6105	6495	6885	7275	7664	8053	8442	8830	390
2	9218	9606	9993	050380	050766	051153	051538	051924	052309	052694	386
3	053078	053463	053846	4230	4613	4996	5378	5760	6142	6524	383
4	6905	7286	7666	8046	8426	8805	9185	9563	9942	060320	379
115	060698	061075	061452	061829	062206	062582	062958	063333	063709	4083	376
6	4436	4802	5200	5500	5900	6900	6900	7071	7443	7815	373
7	8186	8557	8928	9298	9668	070038	070407	070776	071145	071514	370
8	071882	072250	072617	072985	073352	3718	4085	4451	4816	5182	366
9	5547	5912	6276	6640	7004	7368	7731	8094	8457	8819	363
120	079181	079543	079904	080266	080626	080987	081347	081707	082067	082426	360
1	082785	083144	083503	3861	4219	4576	4934	5291	5647	6004	357
2	6360	6716	7071	7426	7781	8136	8490	8845	9198	9552	355
3	9905	090258	090611	090963	091315	091667	092018	092370	092721	093071	352
4	093422	3772	4122	4471	4820	5169	5518	5866	6215	6562	349
125	6910	7257	7604	7951	8298	8644	8990	9335	9681	100026	346
6	100371	100715	101059	101403	101747	102091	102434	102777	103119	3462	343
7	3804	4146	4487	4828	5169	5510	5851	6191	6531	6871	341
8	7210	7549	7888	8227	8565	8903	9241	9579	9916	110253	338
9	110590	110926	111263	111599	111934	112270	112605	112940	113275	3609	335
130	113943	114277	114611	114944	115278	115611	115943	116276	116608	116940	333
1	7271	7603	7934	8265	8595	8926	9256	9586	9915	120245	330
2	120574	120903	121231	121560	121888	122216	122544	122871	123198	3525	328
3	3852	4178	4504	4830	5156	5481	5806	6131	6456	6781	325
4	7105	7429	7753	8076	8399	8722	9045	9368	9690	130012	323
135	130334	130655	130977	131298	131619	131939	132260	132580	132900	3219	321
6	3539	3858	4177	4496	4814	5133	5451	5769	6086	6403	318
7	6721	7037	7354	7671	7987	8303	8618	8934	9249	9564	316
8	9879	140194	140508	140822	141136	141450	141763	142076	142389	142702	314
9	143015	3327	3639	3951	4263	4574	4885	5196	5507	5818	311
140	146128	146438	146748	147058	147367	147676	147985	148294	148603	148911	309
1	9219	9527	9835	150142	150449	150756	151063	151370	151676	151982	307
2	152288	152594	152900	3205	3510	3815	4120	4424	4728	5032	305
3	5336	5640	5943	6246	6549	6852	7154	7457	7759	8061	303
4	8362	8664	8965	9266	9567	9868	160168	160469	160769	161068	301
145	161368	161667	161967	162266	162564	162863	3161	3460	3758	4055	299
6	4353	4650	4947	5244	5541	5838	6134	6430	6726	7022	297
7	7317	7613	7908	8203	8497	8792	9086	9380	9674	9968	295
8	170262	170555	170848	171141	171434	171726	172019	172311	172603	172895	293
9	3186	3478	3769	4060	4351	4641	4932	5222	5512	5802	291
150	176091	176381	176670	176959	177248	177536	177825	178113	178401	178689	289
1	8977	9264	9552	9839	180126	180413	180699	180986	181272	181558	287
2	181844	182129	182415	182700	2985	3270	3555	3839	4123	4407	285
3	4691	4975	5259	5542	5825	6108	6391	6674	6956	7239	283
4	7521	7803	8084	8366	8647	8928	9209	9490	9771	190051	281
155	190332	190612	190892	191171	191451	191730	192010	192289	192567	2846	279
6	3125	3403	3681	3959	4237	4514	4792	5069	5346	5623	278
7	5900	6176	6453	6729	7005	7281	7556	7832	8107	8382	276
8	8657	8932	9206	9481	9755	200029	200303	200577	200850	201124	274
9	201397	201670	201943	202216	202488	2761	3033	3305	3577	3848	272
N.	0	1	2	3	4	5	6	7	8	9	D

TABLE XII.—Logarithms

N.	0	1	2	3	4	5	6	7	8	9	D.
160	204120	204391	204663	204934	205204	205475	205746	206016	206286	206556	271
1	6826	7096	7365	7634	7904	8173	8441	8710	8979	9247	269
2	9515	9783	210051	210319	210586	210853	211121	211388	211654	211921	267
3	212188	212454	2720	2986	3252	3518	3783	4049	4314	4579	266
4	4844	5109	5373	5638	5902	6166	6430	6694	6957	7221	264
165	7484	7747	8010	8273	8536	8798	9060	9323	9585	9846	262
6	220108	220370	220631	220892	221153	221414	221675	221936	222196	222456	261
7	2716	2976	3236	3496	3755	4015	4274	4533	4792	5051	259
8	5309	5568	5826	6084	6342	6600	6858	7115	7372	7630	258
9	7887	8144	8400	8657	8913	9170	9426	9682	9938	230193	256
170	230449	230704	230960	231215	231470	231724	231979	232234	232488	232742	255
1	2996	3250	3504	3757	4011	4264	4517	4770	5023	5276	253
2	5528	5781	6033	6285	6537	6789	7041	7292	7544	7795	252
3	8046	8297	8548	8799	9049	9299	9550	9800	240050	240300	250
4	240549	240799	241048	241297	241546	241795	242044	242293	2541	2790	249
175	3038	3286	3534	3782	4030	4277	4525	4772	5019	5266	248
6	5513	5759	6006	6252	6499	6745	6991	7237	7482	7728	246
7	7973	8219	8464	8709	8954	9198	9443	9687	9932	250176	245
8	250420	250664	250908	251151	251395	251638	251881	252125	252368	2610	243
9	2853	3096	3338	3580	3822	4064	4306	4548	4790	5031	242
180	255273	255514	255755	255996	256237	256477	256718	256958	257198	257439	241
1	7679	7918	8158	8398	8637	8877	9116	9355	9594	9833	239
2	260071	260310	260548	260787	261025	261263	261501	261739	261976	262214	238
3	2451	2688	2925	3162	3399	3636	3873	4109	4346	4582	237
4	4818	5054	5290	5525	5761	5996	6232	6467	6702	6937	235
185	7172	7406	7641	7875	8110	8344	8578	8812	9046	9279	234
6	9513	9746	9980	270213	270446	270679	270912	271144	271377	271609	233
7	271842	272074	272306	2538	2770	3001	3233	3464	3696	3927	232
8	4158	4389	4620	4850	5081	5311	5542	5772	6002	6232	230
9	6462	6692	6921	7151	7380	7609	7838	8067	8296	8525	229
190	278754	278982	279211	279439	279667	279895	280123	280351	280578	280806	228
1	281033	281261	281488	281715	281942	282169	2396	2622	2849	3075	227
2	3301	3527	3753	3979	4205	4431	4656	4882	5107	5332	226
3	5557	5782	6007	6232	6456	6681	6905	7130	7354	7578	225
4	7802	8026	8249	8473	8696	8920	9143	9366	9589	9812	223
195	290035	290257	290480	290702	290925	291147	291369	291591	291813	292034	222
6	2256	2478	2699	2920	3141	3363	3584	3804	4025	4246	221
7	4466	4687	4907	5127	5347	5567	5787	6007	6226	6446	220
8	6665	6884	7104	7323	7542	7761	7979	8198	8416	8635	219
9	8853	9071	9289	9507	9725	9943	300161	300378	300595	300813	218
200	301030	301247	301464	301681	301898	302114	302331	302547	302764	302980	217
1	3196	3412	3628	3844	4059	4275	4491	4706	4921	5136	216
2	5351	5566	5781	5996	6211	6425	6639	6854	7068	7282	215
3	7496	7710	7924	8137	8351	8564	8778	8991	9204	9417	213
4	9630	9843	310056	310268	310481	310693	310906	311118	311330	311542	212
205	311754	311966	2177	2389	2600	2812	3023	3234	3445	3656	211
6	3867	4078	4289	4499	4710	4920	5130	5340	5551	5760	210
7	5970	6180	6390	6599	6809	7018	7227	7436	7646	7854	209
8	8063	8272	8481	8689	8898	9106	9314	9522	9730	9938	208
9	320146	320354	320562	320769	320977	321184	321391	321598	321805	322012	207
210	322219	322426	322633	322839	323046	323252	323458	323665	323871	324077	206
1	4282	4488	4694	4899	5105	5310	5516	5721	5926	6131	205
2	6336	6541	6745	6950	7155	7359	7563	7767	7972	8176	204
3	8380	8583	8787	8991	9194	9398	9601	9805	330008	330211	203
4	330414	330617	330819	331022	331225	331427	331630	331832	2034	2236	202
215	2438	2640	2842	3044	3246	3447	3649	3850	4051	4253	202
6	4454	4655	4856	5057	5257	5458	5658	5859	6059	6260	201
7	6460	6660	6860	7060	7260	7459	7659	7858	8058	8257	200
8	8456	8656	8855	9054	9253	9451	9650	9849	340047	340246	199
9	340444	340642	340841	341039	341237	341435	341632	341830	2028	2225	198
N.	0	1	2	3	4	5	6	7	8	9	D.

TABLE XII.—Logarithms

N.	0	1	2	3	4	5	6	7	8	9	D.
220	342423	342620	342817	343014	343212	343409	343606	343802	343999	344196	197
1	4392	4589	4785	4981	5178	5374	5570	5766	5962	6157	196
2	6353	6549	6744	6939	7135	7330	7525	7720	7915	8110	195
3	8305	8500	8694	8889	9083	9278	9472	9666	9860	350054	194
4	350248	350442	350636	350829	351023	351216	351410	351603	351796	1989	193
225	2183	2375	2568	2761	2954	3147	3339	3532	3724	3916	193
6	4108	4301	4493	4685	4876	5068	5260	5452	5643	5834	192
7	6026	6217	6408	6599	6790	6981	7172	7363	7554	7744	191
8	7935	8125	8316	8506	8696	8886	9076	9266	9456	9646	190
9	9835	360025	360215	360404	360593	360783	360972	361161	361350	361539	189
230	361728	361917	362105	362294	362482	362671	362859	363048	363236	363424	188
1	3612	3800	3988	4176	4363	4551	4739	4926	5113	5301	188
2	5488	5675	5862	6049	6236	6423	6610	6796	6983	7169	187
3	7356	7542	7729	7915	8101	8287	8473	8659	8845	9030	186
4	9216	9401	9587	9772	9958	370143	370328	370513	370698	370883	185
235	371068	371253	371437	371622	371806	1991	2175	2360	2544	2728	184
6	2912	3096	3280	3464	3647	3831	4015	4198	4382	4565	184
7	4748	4932	5115	5298	5481	5664	5846	6029	6212	6394	183
8	6577	6759	6942	7124	7306	7488	7670	7852	8034	8216	182
9	8398	8580	8761	8943	9124	9306	9487	9668	9849	380030	181
240	380211	380392	380573	380754	380934	381115	381296	381476	381656	381837	181
1	2017	2197	2377	2557	2737	2917	3097	3277	3456	3636	180
2	3815	3995	4174	4353	4533	4712	4891	5070	5249	5428	179
3	5606	5785	5964	6142	6321	6499	6677	6856	7034	7212	178
4	7390	7568	7746	7923	8101	8279	8456	8634	8811	8989	178
245	9166	9343	9520	9698	9875	390051	390228	390405	390582	390759	177
6	390935	391112	391288	391464	391641	1817	1993	2169	2345	2521	176
7	2697	2873	3048	3224	3400	3575	3751	3926	4101	4277	176
8	4452	4627	4802	4977	5152	5326	5501	5676	5850	6025	175
9	6199	6374	6548	6722	6896	7071	7245	7419	7592	7766	174
250	397940	398114	398287	398461	398634	398808	398981	399154	399328	399501	173
1	9674	9847	400020	400192	400365	400538	400711	400883	401056	401228	173
2	401401	401573	1745	1917	2089	2261	2433	2605	2777	2949	172
3	3121	3292	3464	3635	3807	3978	4149	4320	4492	4663	171
4	4834	5005	5176	5346	5517	5688	5858	6029	6199	6370	171
255	6540	6710	6881	7051	7221	7391	7561	7731	7901	8070	170
6	8240	8410	8579	8749	8918	9087	9257	9426	9595	9764	169
7	9933	410102	410271	410440	410609	410777	410946	411114	411283	411451	169
8	411620	1788	1956	2124	2293	2461	2629	2796	2964	3132	168
9	3300	3467	3635	3803	3970	4137	4305	4472	4639	4806	167
260	414973	415140	415307	415474	415641	415808	415974	416141	416308	416474	167
1	6641	6807	6973	7139	7306	7472	7638	7804	7970	8135	166
2	8301	8467	8633	8798	8964	9129	9295	9460	9625	9791	165
3	9956	420121	420286	420451	420616	420781	420945	421110	421275	421439	165
4	421604	1768	1933	2097	2261	2426	2590	2754	2918	3082	164
265	3246	3410	3574	3737	3901	4065	4228	4392	4555	4718	164
6	4882	5045	5208	5371	5534	5697	5860	6023	6186	6349	163
7	6511	6674	6836	6999	7161	7324	7486	7648	7811	7973	162
8	8135	8297	8459	8621	8783	8944	9106	9268	9429	9591	162
9	9752	9914	430075	430236	430398	430559	430720	430881	431042	431203	161
270	431364	431525	431685	431846	432007	432167	432328	432488	432649	432809	161
1	2969	3130	3290	3450	3610	3770	3930	4090	4249	4409	160
2	4569	4729	4888	5048	5207	5367	5526	5685	5844	6004	159
3	6163	6322	6481	6640	6799	6957	7116	7275	7433	7592	159
4	7751	7909	8067	8226	8384	8542	8701	8859	9017	9175	158
275	9333	9491	9648	9806	9964	440122	440279	440437	440594	440752	158
6	440909	441066	441224	441381	441538	1695	1852	2009	2166	2323	157
7	2480	2637	2793	2950	3106	3263	3419	3576	3732	3889	157
8	4045	4201	4357	4513	4669	4825	4981	5137	5293	5449	156
9	5604	5760	5915	6071	6226	6382	6537	6692	6848	7003	155
N.	0	1	2	3	4	5	6	7	8	9	D.

TABLE XII.—Logarithms

N.	0	1	2	3	4	5	6	7	8	9	D.
280	447158	447313	447468	447623	447778	447933	448088	448242	448397	448552	155
1	8706	8861	9015	9170	9324	9478	9633	9787	9941	450095	154
2	450249	450403	450557	450711	450865	451018	451172	451326	451479	1633	154
3	1786	1940	2093	2247	2400	2553	2706	2859	3012	3165	153
4	3318	3471	3624	3777	3930	4082	4235	4387	4540	4692	153
285	4845	4997	5150	5302	5454	5606	5758	5910	6062	6214	152
6	6366	6518	6670	6821	6973	7125	7276	7428	7579	7731	152
7	7882	8033	8184	8336	8487	8638	8789	8940	9091	9242	151
8	9392	9543	9694	9845	9995	460146	460296	460447	460597	460748	151
9	460898	461048	461198	461348	461499	1649	1799	1948	2098	2248	150
290	462398	462548	462697	462847	462997	463146	463296	463445	463594	463744	150
1	3893	4042	4191	4340	4490	4639	4788	4936	5085	5234	149
2	5383	5532	5680	5829	5977	6126	6274	6423	6571	6719	149
3	6868	7016	7164	7312	7460	7608	7756	7904	8052	8200	148
4	8347	8495	8643	8790	8938	9085	·9233	9380	9527	9675	148
295	9822	9969	470116	470263	470410	470557	470704	470851	470998	471145	147
6	471292	471438	1585	1732	1878	2025	2171	2318	2464	2610	146
7	2756	2903	3049	3195	3341	3487	3633	3779	3925	4071	146
8	4216	4362	4508	4653	4799	4944	5090	5235	5381	5526	146
9	5671	5816	5962	6107	6252	6397	6542	6687	6832	6976	145
300	477121	477266	477411	477555	477700	477844	477989	478133	478278	478422	145
1	8566	8711	8855	8999	9143	9287	9431	9575	9719	9863	144
2	480007	480151	480294	480438	480582	480725	480869	481012	481156	481299	144
3	1443	1586	1729	1872	2016	2159	2302	2445	2588	2731	143
4	2874	3016	3159	3302	3445	3587	3730	3872	4015	4157	143
305	4300	4442	4585	4727	4869	5011	5153	5295	5437	5579	142
6	5721	5863	6005	6147	6289	6430	6572	6714	6855	6997	142
7	7138	7280	7421	7563	7704	7845	7986	8127	8269	8410	141
8	8551	8692	8833	8974	9114	9255	9396	9537	9677	9818	141
9	9958	490099	490239	490380	490520	490661	490801	490941	491081	491222	140
310	491362	491502	491642	491782	491922	492062	492201	492341	492481	492621	140
1	2760	2900	3040	3179	3319	3458	3597	3737	3876	4015	139
2	4155	4294	4433	4572	4711	4850	4989	5128	5267	5406	139
3	5544	5683	5822	5960	6099	6238	6376	6515	6653	6791	139
4	6930	7068	7206	7344	7483	7621	7759	7897	8035	8173	138
315	8311	8448	8586	8724	8862	8999	9137	9275	9412	9550	138
6	9687	9824	9962	500099	500236	500374	500511	500648	500785	500922	137
7	501059	501196	501333	1470	1607	1744	1880	2017	2154	2291	137
8	2427	2564	2700	2837	2973	3109	3246	3382	3518	3655	136
9	3791	3927	4063	4199	4335	4471	4607	4743	4878	5014	136
320	505150	505286	505421	505557	505693	505828	505964	506099	506234	506370	136
1	6505	6640	6776	6911	7046	7181	7316	7451	7586	7721	135
2	7856	7991	8126	8260	8395	8530	8664	8799	8934	9068	135
3	9203	9337	9471	9606	9740	9874	510009	510143	510277	510411	134
4	510545	510679	510813	510947	511081	511215	1349	1482	1616	1750	134
325	1883	2017	2151	2284	2418	2551	2684	2818	2951	3084	133
6	3218	3351	3484	3617	3750	3883	4016	4149	4282	4415	133
7	4548	4681	4813	4946	5079	5211	5344	5476	5609	5741	133
8	5874	6006	6139	6271	6403	6535	6668	6800	6932	7064	132
9	7196	7328	7460	7592	7724	7855	7987	8119	8251	8382	132
330	518514	518646	518777	518909	519040	519171	519303	519434	519566	519697	131
1	9828	9959	520090	520221	520353	520484	520615	520745	520876	521007	131
2	521138	521269	1400	1530	1661	1792	1922	2053	2183	2314	131
3	2444	2575	2705	2835	2966	3096	3226	3356	3486	3616	130
4	3746	3876	4006	4136	4266	4396	4526	4656	4785	4915	130
335	5045	5174	5304	5434	5563	5693	5822	5951	6081	6210	129
6	6339	6469	6598	6727	6856	6985	7114	7243	7372	7501	129
7	7630	7759	7888	8016	8145	8274	8402	8531	8660	8788	129
8	8917	9045	9174	9302	9430	9559	9687	9815	9943	530072	128
9	530200	530328	530456	530584	530712	530840	530968	531096	531223	1351	128
N.	0	1	2	3	4	5	6	7	8	9	D.

TABLE XII.—Logarithms

N.	0	1	2	3	4	5	6	7	8	9	D.
340	531479	531607	531734	531862	531990	532117	532245	532372	532500	532627	128
1	2754	2882	3009	3136	3264	3391	3518	3645	3772	3899	127
2	4026	4153	4280	4407	4534	4661	4787	4914	5041	5167	127
3	5294	5421	5547	5674	5800	5927	6053	6180	6306	6432	126
4	6558	6685	6811	6937	7063	7189	7315	7441	7567	7693	126
345	7819	7945	8071	8197	8322	8448	8574	8699	8825	8951	126
6	9076	9202	9327	9452	9578	9703	9829	9954	540079	540204	125
7	540329	540455	540580	540705	540830	540955	541080	541205	1330	1454	125
8	1579	1704	1829	1953	2078	2203	2327	2452	2576	2701	125
9	2825	2950	3074	3199	3323	3447	3571	3696	3820	3944	124
350	544068	544192	544316	544440	544564	544688	544812	544936	545060	545183	124
1	5307	5431	5555	5678	5802	5925	6049	6172	6296	6419	124
2	6543	6666	6789	6913	7036	7159	7282	7405	7529	7652	123
3	7775	7898	8021	8144	8267	8389	8512	8635	8758	8881	123
4	9003	9126	9249	9371	9494	9616	9739	9861	9984	550106	123
355	550228	550351	550473	550595	550717	550840	550962	551084	551206	1328	122
6	1450	1572	1694	1816	1938	2060	2181	2303	2425	2547	122
7	2668	2790	2911	3033	3155	3276	3398	3519	3640	3762	121
8	3883	4004	4126	4247	4368	4489	4610	4731	4852	4973	121
9	5094	5215	5336	5457	5578	5699	5820	5940	6061	6182	121
360	556303	556423	556544	556664	556785	556905	557026	557146	557267	557387	120
1	7507	7627	7748	7868	7988	8108	8228	8349	8469	8589	120
2	8709	8829	8948	9068	9188	9308	9428	9548	9667	9787	120
3	9907	560026	560146	560265	560385	560504	560624	560743	560863	560982	119
4	561101	1221	1340	1459	1578	1698	1817	1936	2055	2174	119
365	2293	2412	2531	2650	2769	2887	3006	3125	3244	3362	119
6	3481	3600	3718	3837	3955	4074	4192	4311	4429	4548	119
7	4666	4784	4903	5021	5139	5257	5376	5494	5612	5730	118
8	5848	5966	6084	6202	6320	6437	6555	6673	6791	6909	118
9	7026	7144	7262	7379	7497	7614	7732	7849	7967	8084	118
370	568202	568319	568436	568554	568671	568788	568905	569023	569140	569257	117
1	9374	9491	9608	9725	9842	9959	570076	570193	570309	570426	117
2	570543	570660	570776	570893	571010	571126	1243	1359	1476	1592	117
3	1709	1825	1942	2058	2174	2291	2407	2523	2639	2755	116
4	2872	2988	3104	3220	3336	3452	3568	3684	3800	3915	116
375	4031	4147	4263	4379	4494	4610	4726	4841	4957	5072	116
6	5188	5303	5419	5534	5650	5765	5880	5996	6111	6226	115
7	6341	6457	6572	6687	6802	6917	7032	7147	7262	7377	115
8	7492	7607	7722	7836	7951	8066	8181	8295	8410	8525	115
9	8639	8754	8868	8983	9097	9212	9326	9441	9555	9669	114
380	579784	579898	580012	580126	580241	580355	580469	580583	580697	580811	114
1	580925	581039	1153	1267	1381	1495	1608	1722	1836	1950	114
2	2063	2177	2291	2404	2518	2631	2745	2858	2972	3085	114
3	3199	3312	3426	3539	3652	3765	3879	3992	4105	4218	113
4	4331	4444	4557	4670	4783	4896	5009	5122	5235	5348	113
385	5461	5574	5686	5799	5912	6024	6137	6250	6362	6475	113
6	6587	6700	6812	6925	7037	7149	7262	7374	7486	7599	112
7	7711	7823	7935	8047	8160	8272	8384	8496	8608	8720	112
8	8832	8944	9056	9167	9279	9391	9503	9615	9726	9838	112
9	9950	590061	590173	590284	590396	590507	590619	590730	590842	590953	112
390	591065	591176	591287	591399	591510	591621	591732	591843	591955	592066	111
1	2177	2288	2399	2510	2621	2732	2843	2954	3064	3175	111
2	3286	3397	3508	3618	3729	3840	3950	4061	4171	4282	111
3	4393	4503	4614	4724	4834	4945	5055	5165	5276	5386	110
4	5496	5606	5717	5827	5937	6047	6157	6267	6377	6487	110
395	6597	6707	6817	6927	7037	7146	7256	7366	7476	7586	110
6	7695	7805	7914	8024	8134	8243	8353	8462	8572	8681	110
7	8791	8900	9009	9119	9228	9337	9446	9556	9665	9774	109
8	9883	9992	600101	600210	600319	600428	600537	600646	600755	600864	109
9	600973	601082	1191	1299	1408	1517	1625	1734	1843	1951	109
N.	0	1	2	3	4	5	6	7	8	9	D.

TABLE XII.—Logarithms

N.	0	1	2	3	4	5	6	7	8	9	D.
400	602060	602169	602277	602386	602494	602603	602711	602819	602928	603036	108
1	3144	3253	3361	3469	3577	3686	3794	3902	4010	4118	108
2	4226	4334	4442	4550	4658	4766	4874	4982	5089	5197	108
3	5305	5413	5521	5628	5736	5844	5951	6059	6166	6274	108
4	6381	6489	6596	6704	6811	6919	7026	7133	7241	7348	107
405	7455	7562	7669	7777	7884	7991	8098	8205	8312	8419	107
6	8526	8633	8740	8847	8954	9061	9167	9274	9381	9488	107
7	9594	9701	9808	9914	610021	610128	610234	610341	610447	610554	107
8	610660	610767	610873	610979	1086	1192	1298	1405	1511	1617	106
9	1723	1829	1936	2042	2148	2254	2360	2466	2572	2678	106
410	612784	612890	612996	613102	613207	613313	613419	613525	613630	613736	106
1	3842	3947	4053	4159	4264	4370	4475	4581	4686	4792	106
2	4897	5003	5108	5213	5319	5424	5529	5634	5740	5845	105
3	5950	6055	6160	6265	6370	6476	6581	6686	6790	6895	105
4	7000	7105	7210	7315	7420	7525	7629	7734	7839	7943	105
415	8048	8153	8257	8362	8466	8571	8676	8780	8884	8989	105
6	9093	9198	9302	9406	9511	9615	9719	9824	9928	620032	104
7	620136	620240	620344	620448	620552	620656	620760	620864	620968	1072	104
8	1176	1280	1384	1488	1592	1695	1799	1903	2007	2110	104
9	2214	2318	2421	2525	2628	2732	2835	2939	3042	3146	104
420	623249	623353	623456	623559	623663	623766	623869	623973	624076	624179	103
1	4282	4385	4488	4591	4695	4798	4901	5004	5107	5210	103
2	5312	5415	5518	5621	5724	5827	5929	6032	6135	6238	103
3	6340	6443	6546	6648	6751	6853	6956	7058	7161	7263	103
4	7366	7468	7571	7673	7775	7878	7980	8082	8185	8287	102
425	8389	8491	8593	8695	8797	8900	9002	9104	9206	9308	102
6	9410	9512	9613	9715	9817	9919	630021	630123	630224	630326	102
7	630428	630530	630631	630733	630835	630936	1038	1139	1241	1342	102
8	1444	1545	1647	1748	1849	1951	2052	2153	2255	2356	101
9	2457	2559	2660	2761	2862	2963		3165	3266	3367	101
430	633468	633569	633670	633771	633872	633973	634074	634175	634276	634376	101
1	4477	4578	4679	4779	4880	4981	5081	5182	5283	5383	101
2	5484	5584	5685	5785	5886	5986	6087	6187	6287	6388	100
3	6488	6588	6688	6789	6889	6989	7089	7189	7290	7390	100
4	7490	7590	7690	7790	7890	7990	8090	8190	8290	8389	100
435	8489	8589	8689	8789	8888	8988	9088	9188	9287	9387	100
6	9486	9586	9686	9785	9885	9984	640084	640183	640283	640382	99
7	640481	640581	640680	640779	640879	640978	1077	1177	1276	1375	99
8	1474	1573	1672	1771	1871	1970	2069	2168	2267	2366	99
9	2465	2563	2662	2761	2860	2959	3058	3156	3255	3354	99
440	643453	643551	643650	643749	643847	643946	644044	644143	644242	644340	98
1	4439	4537	4636	4734	4832	4931	5029	5127	5226	5324	98
2	5422	5521	5619	5717	5815	5913	6011	6110	6208	6306	98
3	6404	6502	6600	6698	6796	6894	6992	7089	7187	7285	98
4	7383	7481	7579	7676	7774	7872	7969	8067	8165	8262	98
445	8360	8458	8555	8653	8750	8848	8945	9043	9140	9237	97
6	9335	9432	9530	9627	9724	9821	9919	650016	650113	650210	97
7	650308	650405	650502	650599	650696	650793	650890	0987	1084	1181	97
8	1278	1375	1472	1569	1666	1762	1859	1956	2053	2150	97
9	2246	2343	2440	2536	2633	2730	2826	2923	3019	3116	97
450	653213	653309	653405	653502	653598	653695	653791	653888	653984	654080	96
1	4177	4273	4369	4465	4562	4658	4754	4850	4946	5042	96
2	5138	5235	5331	5427	5523	5619	5715	5810	5906	6002	96
3	6098	6194	6290	6386	6482	6577	6673	6769	6864	6960	96
4	7056	7152	7247	7343	7438	7534	7629	7725	7820	7916	96
455	8011	8107	8202	8298	8393	8488	8584	8679	8774	8870	95
6	8965	9060	9155	9250	9346	9441	9536	9631	9726	9821	95
7	9916	660011	660106	660201	660296	660391	660486	660581	660676	660771	95
8	660865	0960	1055	1150	1245	1339	1434	1529	1623	1718	95
9	1813	1907	2002	2096	2191	2286	2380	2475	2569	2663	95
N.	0	1	2	3	4	5	6	7	8	9	D.

TABLE XII.—Logarithms

N.	0	1	2	3	4	5	6	7	8	9	D.
460	662758	662852	662947	663041	663135	663230	663324	663418	663512	663607	94
1	3701	3795	3889	3983	4078	4172	4266	4360	4454	4548	94
2	4642	4736	4830	4924	5018	5112	5206	5299	5393	5487	94
3	5581	5675	5769	5862	5956	6050	6143	6237	6331	6424	94
4	6518	6612	6705	6799	6892	6986	7079	7173	7266	7360	94
465	7453	7546	7640	7733	7826	7920	8013	8106	8199	8293	93
6	8386	8479	8572	8665	8759	8852	8945	9038	9131	9224	93
7	9317	9410	9503	9596	9689	9782	9875	9967	670060	670153	93
8	670246	670339	670431	670524	670617	670710	670802	670895	0988	1080	93
9	1173	1265	1358	1451	1543	1636	1728	1821	1913	2005	93
470	672098	672190	672283	672375	672467	672560	672652	672744	672836	672929	92
1	3021	3113	3205	3297	3390	3482	3574	3666	3758	3850	92
2	3942	4034	4126	4218	4310	4402	4494	4586	4677	4769	92
3	4861	4953	5045	5137	5228	5320	5412	5503	5595	5687	92
4	5778	5870	5962	6053	6145	6236	6328	6419	6511	6602	92
475	6694	6785	6876	6968	7059	7151	7242	7333	7424	7516	91
6	7607	7698	7789	7881	7972	8063	8154	8245	8336	8427	91
7	8518	8609	8700	8791	8882	8973	9064	9155	9246	9337	91
8	9428	9519	9610	9700	9791	9882	9973	680063	680154	680245	91
9	680336	680426	680517	680607	680698	680789	680879	0970	1060	1151	91
480	681241	681332	681422	681513	681603	681693	681784	681874	681964	682055	90
1	2145	2235	2326	2416	2506	2596	2686	2777	2867	2957	90
2	3047	3137	3227	3317	3407	3497	3587	3677	3767	3857	90
3	3947	4037	4127	4217	4307	4396	4486	4576	4666	4756	90
4	4845	4935	5025	5114	5204	5294	5383	5473	5563	5652	90
485	5742	5831	5921	6010	6100	6189	6279	6368	6458	6547	89
6	6636	6726	6815	6904	6994	7083	7172	7261	7351	7440	89
7	7529	7618	7707	7796	7886	7975	8064	8153	8242	8331	89
8	8420	8509	8598	8687	8776	8865	8953	9042	9131	9220	89
9	9309	9398	9486	9575	9664	9753	9841	9930	690019	690107	89
490	690196	690285	690373	690462	690550	690639	690728	690816	690905	690993	89
1	1081	1170	1258	1347	1435	1524	1612	1700	1789	1877	88
2	1965	2053	2142	2230	2318	2406	2494	2583	2671	2759	88
3	2847	2935	3023	3111	3199	3287	3375	3463	3551	3639	88
4	3727	3815	3903	3991	4078	4166	4254	4342	4430	4517	88
495	4605	4693	4781	4868	4956	5044	5131	5219	5307	5394	88
6	5482	5569	5657	5744	5832	5919	6007	6094	6182	6269	87
7	6356	6444	6531	6618	6706	6793	6880	6968	7055	7142	87
8	7229	7317	7404	7491	7578	7665	7752	7839	7926	8014	87
9	8101	8188	8275	8362	8449	8535	8622	8709	8796	8883	87
500	698970	699057	699144	699231	699317	699404	699491	699578	699664	699751	87
1	9838	9924	700011	700098	700184	700271	700358	700444	700531	700617	87
2	700704	700790	0877	0963	1050	1136	1222	1309	1395	1482	86
3	1568	1654	1741	1827	1913	1999	2086	2172	2258	2344	86
4	2431	2517	2603	2689	2775	2861	2947	3033	3119	3205	86
505	3291	3377	3463	3549	3635	3721	3807	3893	3979	4065	86
6	4151	4236	4322	4408	4494	4579	4665	4751	4837	4922	86
7	5008	5094	5179	5265	5350	5436	5522	5607	5693	5778	86
8	5864	5949	6035	6120	6206	6291	6376	6402	6547	6632	85
9	6718	6803	6888	6974	7059	7144	7229	7315	7400	7485	85
510	707570	707655	707740	707826	707911	707996	708081	708166	708251	708336	85
1	8421	8506	8591	8676	8761	8846	8931	9015	9100	9185	85
2	9270	9355	9440	9524	9609	9694	9779	9863	9948	710033	85
3	710117	710202	710287	710371	710456	710540	710625	710710	710794	0879	85
4	0963	1048	1132	1217	1301	1385	1470	1554	1639	1723	84
515	1807	1892	1976	2060	2144	2229	2313	2397	2481	2566	84
6	2650	2734	2818	2902	2986	3070	3154	3238	3322	3407	84
7	3491	3575	3659	3742	3826	3910	3994	4078	4162	4246	84
8	4330	4414	4497	4581	4665	4749	4833	4916	5000	5084	84
9	5167	5251	5335	5418	5502	5586	5669	5753	5836	5920	84
N.	0	1	2	3	4	5	6	7	8	9	D.

TABLE XII.—Logarithms

N.	0	1	2	3	4	5	6	7	8	9	D.
520	716003	716087	716170	716254	716337	716421	716504	716588	716671	716754	83
1	6838	6921	7004	7088	7171	7254	7338	7421	7504	7587	83
2	7671	7754	7837	7920	8003	8086	8169	8253	8336	8419	83
3	8502	8585	8668	8751	8834	8917	9000	9083	9165	9248	83
4	9331	9414	9497	9580	9663	9745	9828	9911	9994	720077	83
525	720159	720242	720325	720407	720490	720573	720655	720738	720821	0903	83
6	0986	1068	1151	1233	1316	1398	1481	1563	1646	1728	82
7	1811	1893	1975	2058	2140	2222	2305	2387	2469	2552	82
8	2634	2716	2798	2881	2963	3045	3127	3209	3291	3374	82
9	3456	3538	3620	3702	3784	3866	3948	4030	4112	4194	82
530	724276	724358	724440	724522	724604	724685	724767	724849	724931	725013	82
1	5095	5176	5258	5340	5422	5503	5585	5667	5748	5830	82
2	5912	5993	6075	6156	6238	6320	6401	6483	6564	6646	82
3	6727	6809	6890	6972	7053	7134	7216	7297	7379	7460	81
4	7541	7623	7704	7785	7866	7948	8029	8110	8191	8273	81
535	8354	8435	8516	8597	8678	8759	8841	8922	9003	9084	81
6	9165	9246	9327	9408	9489	9570	9651	9732	9813	9893	81
7	9974	730055	730136	730217	730298	730378	730459	730540	730621	730702	81
8	730782	0863	0944	1024	1105	1186	1266	1347	1428	1508	81
9	1589	1669	1750	1830	1911	1991	2072	2152	2233	2313	81
540	732394	732474	732555	732635	732715	732796	732876	732956	733037	733117	80
1	3197	3278	3358	3438	3518	3598	3679	3759	3839	3919	80
2	3999	4079	4160	4240	4320	4400	4480	4560	4640	4720	80
3	4800	4880	4960	5040	5120	5200	5279	5359	5439	5519	80
4	5599	5679	5759	5838	5918	5998	6078	6157	6237	6317	80
545	6397	6476	6556	6635	6715	6795	6874	6954	7034	7113	80
6	7193	7272	7352	7431	7511	7590	7670	7749	7829	7908	79
7	7987	8067	8146	8225	8305	8384	8463	8543	8622	8701	79
8	8781	8860	8939	9018	9097	9177	9256	9335	9414	9493	79
9	9572	9651	9731	9810	9889	9968	740047	740126	740205	740284	79
550	740363	740442	740521	740600	740678	740757	740836	740915	740994	741073	79
1	1152	1230	1309	1388	1467	1546	1624	1703	1782	1860	79
2	1939	2018	2096	2175	2254	2332	2411	2489	2568	2647	79
3	2725	2804	2882	2961	3039	3118	3196	3275	3353	3431	78
4	3510	3588	3667	3745	3823	3902	3980	4058	4136	4215	78
555	4293	4371	4449	4528	4606	4684	4762	4840	4919	4997	78
6	5075	5153	5231	5309	5387	5465	5543	5621	5699	5777	78
7	5855	5933	6011	6089	6167	6245	6323	6401	6479	6556	78
8	6634	6712	6790	6868	6945	7023	7101	7179	7256	7334	78
9	7412	7489	7567	7645	7722	7800	7878	7955	8033	8110	78
560	748188	748266	748343	748421	748498	748576	748653	748731	748808	748885	77
1	8963	9040	9118	9195	9272	9350	9427	9504	9582	9659	77
2	9736	9814	9891	9968	750045	750123	750200	750277	750354	750431	77
3	750508	750586	750663	750740	0817	0894	0971	1048	1125	1202	77
4	1279	1356	1433	1510	1587	1664	1741	1818	1895	1972	77
565	2048	2125	2202	2279	2356	2433	2509	2586	2663	2740	77
6	2816	2893	2970	3047	3123	3200	3277	3353	3430	3506	77
7	3583	3660	3736	3813	3889	3966	4042	4119	4195	4272	77
8	4348	4425	4501	4578	4654	4730	4807	4883	4960	5036	76
9	5112	5189	5265	5341	5417	5494	5570	5646	5722	5799	76
570	755875	755951	756027	756103	756180	756256	756332	756408	756484	756560	76
1	6636	6712	6788	6864	6940	7016	7092	7168	7244	7320	76
2	7396	7472	7548	7624	7700	7775	7851	7927	8003	8079	76
3	8155	8230	8306	8382	8458	8533	8609	8685	8761	8836	76
4	8912	8988	9063	9139	9214	9290	9366	9441	9517	9592	76
575	9668	9743	9819	9894	9970	760045	760121	760196	760272	760347	75
6	760422	760498	760573	760649	760724	0799	0875	0950	1025	1101	75
7	1176	1251	1326	1402	1477	1552	1627	1702	1778	1853	75
8	1928	2003	2078	2153	2228	2303	2378	2453	2529	2604	75
9	2679	2754	2829	2904	2978	3053	3128	3203	3278	3353	75
N.	0	1	2	3	4	5	6	7	8	9	D.

TABLE XII.—Logarithms

N.	0	1	2	3	4	5	6	7	8	9	D.
580	763428	763503	763578	763653	763727	763802	763877	763952	764027	764101	75
1	4176	4251	4326	4400	4475	4550	4624	4699	4774	4848	75
2	4923	4998	5072	5147	5221	5296	5370	5445	5520	5594	75
3	5669	5743	5818	5892	5966	6041	6115	6190	6264	6338	74
4	6413	6487	6562	6636	6710	6785	6859	6933	7007	7082	74
585	7156	7230	7304	7379	7453	7527	7601	7675	7749	7823	74
6	7898	7972	8046	8120	8194	8268	8342	8416	8490	8564	74
7	8638	8712	8786	8860	8934	9008	9082	9156	9230	9303	74
8	9377	9451	9525	9599	9673	9746	9820	9894	9968	770042	74
9	770115	770189	770263	770336	770410	770484	770557	770631	770705	0778	74
590	770852	770926	770999	771073	771146	771220	771293	771367	771440	771514	74
1	1587	1661	1734	1808	1881	1955	2028	2102	2175	2248	73
2	2322	2395	2468	2542	2615	2688	2762	2835	2908	2981	73
3	3055	3128	3201	3274	3348	3421	3494	3567	3610	3713	73
4	3786	3860	3933	4006	4079	4152	4225	4298	4371	4444	73
595	4517	4590	4663	4736	4809	4882	4955	5028	5100	5173	73
6	5240	5313	5002	5100	5592	5610	5683	5756	5829	5902	73
7	5974	6047	6120	6193	6265	6338	6411	6483	6556	6629	73
8	6701	6774	6846	6919	6992	7064	7137	7209	7282	7354	73
9	7427	7499	7572	7644	7717	7789	7862	7934	8006	8079	72
600	778151	778224	778296	778368	778441	778513	778585	778658	778730	778802	72
1	8874	8947	9019	9091	9163	9236	9308	9380	9452	9524	72
2	9596	9669	9741	9813	9885	9957	780029	780101	780173	780245	72
3	780317	780389	780461	780533	780605	780677	0749	0821	0893	0965	72
4	1037	1109	1181	1253	1324	1396	1468	1540	1612	1684	72
605	1755	1827	1899	1971	2042	2114	2186	2258	2329	2401	72
6	2473	2544	2616	2688	2759	2831	2902	2974	3046	3117	72
7	3189	3260	3332	3403	3475	3546	3618	3689	3761	3832	71
8	3904	3975	4046	4118	4189	4261	4332	4403	4475	4546	71
9	4617	4689	4700	4831	4902	4974	5045	5116	5187	5259	71
610	785330	785401	785472	785543	785615	785686	785757	785828	785899	785970	71
1	6041	6112	6183	6254	6325	6396	6467	6538	6609	6680	71
2	6751	6822	6893	6964	7035	7106	7177	7248	7319	7390	71
3	7460	7531	7602	7673	7744	7815	7885	7956	8027	8098	71
4	8168	8239	8310	8381	8451	8522	8593	8663	8734	8804	71
615	8875	8946	9016	9087	9157	9228	9299	9369	9440	9510	71
6	9581	9651	9722	9792	9863	9933	790004	790074	790144	790215	70
7	790285	790356	790426	790496	790567	790637	0707	0778	0848	0918	70
8	0988	1059	1129	1199	1269	1340	1410	1480	1550	1020	70
9	1691	1761	1831	1901	1971	2041	2111	2181	2252	2322	70
620	792392	792462	792532	792602	792672	792742	792812	792882	792952	793022	70
1	3092	3162	3231	3301	3371	3441	3511	3581	3651	3721	70
2	3790	3860	3930	4000	4070	4139	4209	4279	4349	4418	70
3	4488	4558	4627	4697	4767	4836	4906	4976	5045	5115	70
4	5185	5254	5324	5393	5463	5532	5602	5672	5741	5811	70
625	5880	5949	6019	6088	6158	6227	6297	6366	6436	6505	69
6	6574	6644	6713	6782	6852	6921	6990	7060	7129	7198	69
7	7268	7337	7406	7475	7545	7614	7683	7752	7821	7890	69
8	7960	8029	8098	8167	8236	8305	8374	8443	8513	8582	69
9	8651	8720	8789	8858	8927	8996	9065	9134	9203	9272	69
630	799341	799409	799478	799547	799616	799685	799754	799823	799892	799961	69
1	800029	800098	800167	800236	800305	800373	800442	800511	800580	800648	69
2	0717	0786	0854	0923	0992	1061	1129	1198	1266	1335	69
3	1404	1472	1541	1609	1678	1747	1815	1884	1952	2021	69
4	2089	2158	2226	2295	2363	2432	2500	2568	2637	2705	68
635	2774	2842	2910	2979	3047	3116	3184	3252	3321	3389	68
6	3457	3525	3594	3662	3730	3798	3867	3935	4003	4071	68
7	4139	4208	4276	4344	4412	4480	4548	4616	4685	4753	68
8	4821	4889	4957	5025	5093	5161	5229	5297	5365	5433	68
9	5501	5569	5637	5705	5773	5841	5908	5976	6044	6112	68
N.	0	1	2	3	4	5	6	7	8	9	D.

TABLE XII.—Logarithms

N.	0	1	2	3	4	5	6	7	8	9	D.
640	806180	806248	806316	806384	806451	806519	806587	806655	806723	806790	68
1	6858	6926	6994	7061	7129	7197	7264	7332	7400	7467	68
2	7535	7603	7670	7738	7806	7873	7941	8008	8076	8143	68
3	8211	8279	8346	8414	8481	8549	8616	8684	8751	8818	67
4	8886	8953	9021	9088	9156	9223	9290	9358	9425	9492	67
645	9560	9627	9694	9762	9829	9896	9964	810031	810098	810165	67
6	810233	810300	810367	810434	810501	810569	810636	0703	0770	0837	67
7	0904	0971	1039	1106	1173	1240	1307	1374	1441	1508	67
8	1575	1642	1709	1776	1843	1910	1977	2044	2111	2178	67
9	2245	2312	2379	2445	2512	2579	2646	2713	2780	2847	67
650	812913	812980	813047	813114	813181	813247	813314	813381	813448	813514	67
1	3581	3648	3714	3781	3848	3914	3981	4048	4114	4181	67
2	4248	4314	4381	4447	4514	4581	4647	4714	4780	4847	67
3	4913	4980	5046	5113	5179	5246	5312	5378	5445	5511	66
4	5578	5644	5711	5777	5843	5910	5976	6042	6109	6175	66
655	6241	6308	6374	6440	6506	6573	6639	6705	6771	6838	66
6	6904	6970	7036	7102	7169	7235	7301	7367	7433	7499	66
7	7565	7631	7698	7764	7830	7896	7962	8028	8094	8160	66
8	8226	8292	8358	8424	8490	8556	8622	8688	8754	8820	66
9	8885	8951	9017	9083	9149	9215	9281	9346	9412	9478	66
660	819544	819610	819676	819741	819807	819873	819939	820004	820070	820136	66
1	820201	820267	820333	820399	820464	820530	820595	0661	0727	0792	66
2	0858	0924	0989	1055	1120	1186	1251	1317	1382	1448	66
3	1514	1579	1645	1710	1775	1841	1906	1972	2037	2103	65
4	2168	2233	2299	2364	2430	2495	2560	2626	2691	2756	65
665	2822	2887	2952	3018	3083	3148	3213	3279	3344	3409	65
6	3474	3539	3605	3670	3735	3800	3865	3930	3996	4061	65
7	4126	4191	4256	4321	4386	4451	4516	4581	4646	4711	65
8	4776	4841	4906	4971	5036	5101	5166	5231	5296	5361	65
9	5426	5491	5556	5621	5686	5751	5815	5880	5945	6010	65
670	826075	826140	826204	826269	826334	826399	826464	826528	826593	826658	65
1	6723	6787	6852	6917	6981	7046	7111	7175	7240	7305	65
2	7369	7434	7499	7563	7628	7692	7757	7821	7886	7951	65
3	8015	8080	8144	8209	8273	8338	8402	8467	8531	8595	64
4	8660	8724	8789	8853	8918	8982	9046	9111	9175	9239	64
675	9304	9368	9432	9497	9561	9625	9690	9754	9818	9882	64
6	9947	830011	830075	830139	830204	830268	830332	830396	830460	830525	64
7	830589	0653	0717	0781	0845	0909	0973	1037	1102	1166	64
8	1230	1294	1358	1422	1486	1550	1614	1678	1742	1806	64
9	1870	1934	1998	2062	2126	2189	2253	2317	2381	2445	64
680	832509	832573	832637	832700	832764	832828	832892	832956	833020	833083	64
1	3147	3211	3275	3338	3402	3466	3530	3593	3657	3721	64
2	3784	3848	3912	3975	4039	4103	4166	4230	4294	4357	64
3	4421	4484	4548	4611	4675	4739	4802	4866	4929	4993	64
4	5056	5120	5183	5247	5310	5373	5437	5500	5564	5627	63
685	5691	5754	5817	5881	5944	6007	6071	6134	6197	6261	63
6	6324	6387	6451	6514	6577	6641	6704	6767	6830	6894	63
7	6957	7020	7083	7146	7210	7273	7336	7399	7462	7525	63
8	7588	7652	7715	7778	7841	7904	7967	8030	8093	8156	63
9	8219	8282	8345	8408	8471	8534	8597	8660	8723	8786	63
690	838849	838912	838975	839038	839101	839164	839227	839289	839352	839415	63
1	9478	9541	9604	9667	9729	9792	9855	9918	9981	840043	63
2	840106	840169	840232	840294	840357	840420	840482	840545	840608	0671	63
3	0733	0796	0859	0921	0984	1046	1109	1172	1234	1297	63
4	1359	1422	1485	1547	1610	1672	1735	1797	1860	1922	63
695	1985	2047	2110	2172	2235	2297	2360	2422	2484	2547	62
6	2609	2672	2734	2796	2859	2921	2983	3046	3108	3170	62
7	3233	3295	3357	3420	3482	3544	3606	3669	3731	3793	62
8	3855	3918	3980	4042	4104	4166	4229	4291	4353	4415	62
9	4477	4539	4601	4664	4726	4788	4850	4912	4974	5036	62
N.	0	1	2	3	4	5	6	7	8	9	D.

TABLE XII.—Logarithms

N.	0	1	2	3	4	5	6	7	8	9	D.
700	845098	845160	845222	845284	845346	845408	845470	845532	845594	845656	62
1	5718	5780	5842	5904	5966	6028	6090	6151	6213	6275	62
2	6337	6399	6461	6523	6585	6646	6708	6770	6832	6894	62
3	6955	7017	7079	7141	7202	7264	7326	7388	7449	7511	62
4	7573	7634	7696	7758	7819	7881	7943	8004	8066	8128	62
705	8189	8251	8312	8374	8435	8497	8559	8620	8682	8743	62
6	8805	8866	8928	8989	9051	9112	9174	9235	9297	9358	61
7	9419	9481	9542	9604	9665	9726	9788	9849	9911	9972	61
8	850033	850095	850156	850217	850279	850340	850401	850462	850524	850585	61
9	0646	0707	0769	0830	0891	0952	1014	1075	1136	1197	61
710	851258	851320	851381	851442	851503	851564	851625	851686	851747	851809	61
1	1870	1931	1992	2053	2114	2175	2236	2297	2358	2419	61
2	2480	2541	2602	2663	2724	2785	2846	2907	2968	3029	61
3	3090	3150	3211	3272	3333	3394	3455	3516	3577	3637	61
4	3698	3759	3820	3881	3941	4002	4063	4124	4185	4245	61
715	4306	4367	4428	4488	4549	4610	4670	4731	4792	4852	61
6	4913	4974	5034	5095	5150	5210	5277	5337	5398	5459	61
7	5519	5580	5640	5701	5761	5822	5882	5943	6003	6064	61
8	6124	6185	6245	6306	6366	6427	6487	6548	6608	6668	60
9	6729	6789	6850	6910	6970	7031	7091	7152	7212	7272	60
720	857332	857393	857453	857513	857574	857634	857694	857755	857815	857875	60
1	7935	7995	8056	8116	8176	8236	8297	8357	8417	8477	60
2	8537	8597	8657	8718	8778	8838	8898	8958	9018	9078	60
3	9138	9198	9258	9318	9379	9439	9499	9559	9619	9679	60
4	9739	9799	9859	9918	9978	860038	860098	860158	860218	860278	60
725	860338	860398	860458	860518	860578	0637	0697	0757	0817	0877	60
6	0937	0996	1056	1116	1176	1236	1295	1355	1415	1475	60
7	1534	1594	1654	1714	1773	1833	1893	1952	2012	2072	60
8	2131	2191	2251	2310	2370	2430	2489	2549	2608	2668	60
9	2728	2787	2847	2906	2966	3025	3085	3144	3204	3263	60
730	863323	863382	863442	863501	863561	863620	863680	863739	863799	863859	59
1	3917	3977	4036	4096	4155	4214	4274	4333	4392	4452	59
2	4511	4570	4630	4689	4748	4808	4867	4926	4985	5045	59
3	5104	5163	5222	5282	5341	5400	5459	5519	5578	5637	59
4	5696	5755	5814	5874	5933	5992	6051	6110	6169	6228	59
735	6287	6346	6405	6465	6524	6583	6642	6701	6760	6819	59
6	6878	6937	6996	7055	7114	7173	7232	7291	7350	7409	59
7	7467	7526	7585	7644	7703	7762	7821	7880	7939	7998	59
8	8056	8115	8174	8233	8292	8350	8409	8468	8527	8586	59
9	8644	8703	8762	8821	8879	8938	8997	9056	9114	9173	59
740	869232	869290	869349	869408	869466	869525	869584	869642	869701	869760	59
1	9818	9877	9935	9994	870053	870111	870170	870228	870287	870345	59
2	870404	870462	870521	870579	0638	0696	0755	0813	0872	0930	58
3	0989	1047	1106	1164	1223	1281	1339	1398	1456	1515	58
4	1573	1631	1690	1748	1806	1865	1923	1981	2040	2098	58
745	2156	2215	2273	2331	2389	2448	2506	2564	2622	2681	58
6	2739	2797	2855	2913	2972	3030	3088	3146	3204	3262	58
7	3321	3379	3437	3495	3553	3611	3669	3727	3785	3844	58
8	3902	3960	4018	4076	4134	4192	4250	4308	4366	4424	58
9	4482	4540	4598	4656	4714	4772	4830	4888	4945	5003	58
750	875061	875119	875177	875235	875293	875351	875409	875466	875524	875582	58
1	5640	5698	5756	5813	5871	5929	5987	6045	6102	6160	58
2	6218	6276	6333	6391	6449	6507	6564	6622	6680	6737	58
3	6795	6853	6910	6968	7026	7083	7141	7199	7256	7314	58
4	7371	7429	7487	7544	7602	7659	7717	7774	7832	7889	58
755	7947	8004	8062	8119	8177	8234	8292	8349	8407	8464	57
6	8522	8579	8637	8694	8752	8809	8866	8924	8981	9039	57
7	9096	9153	9211	9268	9325	9383	9440	9497	9555	9612	57
8	9669	9726	9784	9841	9898	9956	880013	880070	880127	880185	57
9	880242	880299	880356	880413	880471	880528	0585	0642	0699	0756	57
N.	0	1	2	3	4	5	6	7	8	9	D.

TABLE XII.—Logarithms

N.	0	1	2	3	4	5	6	7	8	9	D.
760	880814	880871	880928	880985	881042	881099	881156	881213	881271	881328	57
1	1385	1442	1499	1556	1613	1670	1727	1784	1841	1898	57
2	1955	2012	2069	2126	2183	2240	2297	2354	2411	2468	57
3	2525	2581	2638	2695	2752	2809	2866	2923	2980	3037	57
4	3093	3150	3207	3264	3321	3377	3434	3491	3548	3605	57
765	3661	3718	3775	3832	3888	3945	4002	4059	4115	4172	57
6	4229	4285	4342	4399	4455	4512	4569	4625	4682	4739	57
7	4795	4852	4909	4965	5022	5078	5135	5192	5248	5305	57
8	5361	5418	5474	5531	5587	5644	5700	5757	5813	5870	57
9	5926	5983	6039	6096	6152	6209	6265	6321	6378	6434	56
770	886491	886547	886604	886660	886716	886773	886829	886885	886942	886998	56
1	7054	7111	7167	7223	7280	7336	7392	7449	7505	7561	56
2	7617	7674	7730	7786	7842	7898	7955	8011	8067	8123	56
3	8179	8236	8292	8348	8404	8460	8516	8573	8629	8685	56
4	8741	8797	8853	8909	8965	9021	9077	9134	9190	9246	56
775	9302	9358	9414	9470	9526	9582	9638	9694	9750	9806	56
6	9862	9918	9974	890030	890086	890141	890197	890253	890309	890365	56
7	890421	890477	890533	0589	0645	0700	0756	0812	0868	0924	56
8	0980	1035	1091	1147	1203	1259	1314	1370	1426	1482	56
9	1537	1593	1649	1705	1760	1816	1872	1928	1983	2039	56
780	892095	892150	892206	892262	892317	892373	892429	892484	892540	892595	56
1	2651	2707	2762	2818	2873	2929	2985	3040	3096	3151	56
2	3207	3262	3318	3373	3429	3484	3540	3595	3651	3706	56
3	3762	3817	3873	3928	3984	4039	4094	4150	4205	4261	55
4	4316	4371	4427	4482	4538	4593	4648	4704	4759	4814	55
785	4870	4925	4980	5036	5091	5146	5201	5257	5312	5367	55
6	5423	5478	5533	5588	5644	5699	5754	5809	5864	5920	55
7	5975	6030	6085	6140	6195	6251	6306	6361	6416	6471	55
8	6526	6581	6636	6692	6747	6802	6857	6912	6967	7022	55
9	7077	7132	7187	7242	7297	7352	7407	7462	7517	7572	55
790	897627	897682	897737	897792	897847	897902	897957	898012	898067	898122	55
1	8176	8231	8286	8341	8396	8451	8506	8561	8615	8670	55
2	8725	8780	8835	8890	8944	8999	9054	9109	9164	9218	55
3	9273	9328	9383	9437	9492	9547	9602	9656	9711	9766	55
4	9821	9875	9930	9985	900039	900094	900149	900203	900258	900312	55
795	900367	900422	900476	900531	0586	0640	0695	0749	0804	0859	55
6	0913	0968	1022	1077	1131	1186	1240	1295	1349	1404	55
7	1458	1513	1567	1622	1676	1731	1785	1840	1894	1948	54
8	2003	2057	2112	2166	2221	2275	2329	2384	2438	2492	54
9	2547	2601	2655	2710	2764	2818	2873	2927	2981	3036	54
800	903090	903144	903199	903253	903307	903361	903416	903470	903524	903578	54
1	3633	3687	3741	3795	3849	3904	3958	4012	4066	4120	54
2	4174	4229	4283	4337	4391	4445	4499	4553	4607	4661	54
3	4716	4770	4824	4878	4932	4986	5040	5094	5148	5202	54
4	5256	5310	5364	5418	5472	5526	5580	5634	5688	5742	54
805	5796	5850	5904	5958	6012	6066	6119	6173	6227	6281	54
6	6335	6389	6443	6497	6551	6604	6658	6712	6766	6820	54
7	6874	6927	6981	7035	7089	7143	7196	7250	7304	7358	54
8	7411	7465	7519	7573	7626	7680	7734	7787	7841	7895	54
9	7949	8002	8056	8110	8163	8217	8270	8324	8378	8431	54
810	908485	908539	908592	908646	908699	908753	908807	908860	908914	908967	54
1	9021	9074	9128	9181	9235	9289	9342	9396	9449	9503	54
2	9556	9610	9663	9716	9770	9823	9877	9930	9984	910037	53
3	910091	910144	910197	910251	910304	910358	910411	910464	910518	0571	53
4	0624	0678	0731	0784	0838	0891	0944	0998	1051	1104	53
815	1158	1211	1264	1317	1371	1424	1477	1530	1584	1637	53
6	1690	1743	1797	1850	1903	1956	2009	2063	2116	2169	53
7	2222	2275	2328	2381	2435	2488	2541	2594	2647	2700	53
8	2753	2806	2859	2913	2966	3019	3072	3125	3178	3231	53
9	3284	3337	3390	3443	3496	3549	3602	3655	3708	3761	53
N.	0	1	2	3	4	5	6	7	8	9	D.

TABLE XII.—Logarithms

N.	0	1	2	3	4	5	6	7	8	9	D.
820	913814	913867	913920	913973	914026	914079	914132	914184	914237	914290	53
1	4343	4396	4449	4502	4555	4608	4660	4713	4766	4819	53
2	4872	4925	4977	5030	5083	5136	5189	5241	5294	5347	53
3	5400	5453	5505	5558	5611	5664	5716	5769	5822	5875	53
4	5927	5980	6033	6085	6138	6191	6243	6296	6349	6401	53
825	6454	6507	6559	6612	6664	6717	6770	6822	6875	6927	53
6	6980	7033	7085	7138	7190	7243	7295	7348	7400	7453	53
7	7506	7558	7611	7663	7716	7768	7820	7873	7925	7978	52
8	8030	8083	8135	8188	8240	8293	8345	8397	8450	8502	52
9	8555	8607	8659	8712	8764	8816	8869	8921	8973	9026	52
830	919078	919130	919183	919235	919287	919340	919392	919444	919496	919549	52
1	9601	9653	9706	9758	9810	9862	9914	9967	920019	920071	52
2	920123	920176	920228	920280	920332	920384	920436	920489	0541	0593	52
3	0645	0697	0749	0801	0853	0906	0958	1010	1062	1114	52
4	1166	1218	1270	1322	1374	1426	1478	1530	1582	1634	52
835	1686	1738	1790	1842	1894	1946	1998	2050	2102	2154	52
6	2206	2258	2310	2362	2414	2466	2518	2570	2622	2674	52
7	2725	2777	2829	2881	2933	2985	3037	3089	3140	3192	52
8	3244	3296	3348	3399	3451	3503	3555	3607	3658	3710	52
9	3762	3814	3865	3917	3969	4021	4072	4124	4176	4228	52
840	924279	924331	924383	924434	924486	924538	924589	924641	924693	924744	52
1	4796	4848	4899	4951	5003	5054	5106	5157	5209	5261	52
2	5312	5364	5415	5467	5518	5570	5621	5673	5725	5776	52
3	5828	5879	5931	5982	6034	6085	6137	6188	6240	6291	51
4	6342	6394	6445	6497	6548	6600	6651	6702	6754	6805	51
845	6857	6908	6959	7011	7062	7114	7165	7216	7268	7319	51
6	7370	7422	7473	7524	7576	7627	7678	7730	7781	7832	51
7	7883	7935	7986	8037	8088	8140	8191	8242	8293	8345	51
8	8396	8447	8498	8549	8601	8652	8703	8754	8805	8857	51
9	8908	8959	9010	9061	9112	9163	9215	9266	9317	9368	51
850	929419	929470	929521	929572	929623	929674	929725	929776	929827	929879	51
1	9930	9981	930032	930083	930134	930185	930236	930287	930338	930389	51
2	930440	930491	0542	0592	0643	0694	0745	0796	0847	0898	51
3	0949	1000	1051	1102	1153	1204	1254	1305	1356	1407	51
4	1458	1509	1560	1610	1661	1712	1763	1814	1865	1915	51
855	1966	2017	2068	2118	2169	2220	2271	2322	2372	2423	51
6	2474	2524	2575	2626	2677	2727	2778	2829	2879	2930	51
7	2981	3031	3082	3133	3183	3234	3285	3335	3386	3437	51
8	3487	3538	3589	3639	3690	3740	3791	3841	3892	3943	51
9	3993	4044	4094	4145	4195	4246	4296	4347	4397	4448	51
860	934498	934549	934599	934650	934700	934751	934801	934852	934902	934953	50
1	5003	5054	5104	5154	5205	5255	5306	5356	5406	5457	50
2	5507	5558	5608	5658	5709	5759	5809	5860	5910	5960	50
3	6011	6061	6111	6162	6212	6262	6313	6363	6413	6463	50
4	6514	6564	6614	6665	6715	6765	6815	6865	6916	6966	50
865	7016	7066	7117	7167	7217	7267	7317	7367	7418	7468	50
6	7518	7568	7618	7668	7718	7769	7819	7869	7919	7969	50
7	8019	8069	8119	8169	8219	8269	8320	8370	8420	8470	50
8	8520	8570	8620	8670	8720	8770	8820	8870	8920	8970	50
9	9020	9070	9120	9170	9220	9270	9320	9369	9419	9469	50
870	939519	939569	939619	939669	939719	939769	939819	939869	939918	939968	50
1	940018	940068	940118	940168	940218	940267	940317	940367	940417	940467	50
2	0516	0566	0616	0666	0716	0765	0815	0865	0915	0964	50
3	1014	1064	1114	1163	1213	1263	1313	1362	1412	1462	50
4	1511	1561	1611	1660	1710	1760	1809	1859	1909	1958	50
875	2008	2058	2107	2157	2207	2256	2306	2355	2405	2455	50
6	2504	2554	2603	2653	2702	2752	2801	2851	2901	2950	50
7	3000	3049	3099	3148	3198	3247	3297	3346	3396	3445	49
8	3495	3544	3593	3643	3692	3742	3791	3841	3890	3939	49
9	3989	4038	4088	4137	4186	4236	4285	4335	4384	4433	49
N.	0	1	2	3	4	5	6	7	8	9	D.

TABLE XII.—Logarithms

N.	0	1	2	3	4	5	6	7	8	9	D.
880	944483	944532	944581	944631	944680	944729	944779	944828	944877	944927	49
1	4976	5025	5074	5124	5173	5222	5272	5321	5370	5419	49
2	5469	5518	5567	5616	5665	5715	5764	5813	5862	5912	49
3	5961	6010	6059	6108	6157	6207	6256	6305	6354	6403	49
4	6452	6501	6551	6600	6649	6698	6747	6796	6845	6894	49
885	6943	6992	7041	7090	7140	7189	7238	7287	7336	7385	49
6	7434	7483	7532	7581	7630	7679	7728	7777	7826	7875	49
7	7924	7973	8022	8070	8119	8168	8217	8266	8315	8364	49
8	8413	8462	8511	8560	8609	8657	8706	8755	8804	8853	49
9	8902	8951	8999	9048	9097	9146	9195	9244	9292	9341	49
890	949390	949439	949488	949536	949585	949634	949683	949731	949780	949829	49
1	9878	9926	9975	950024	950073	950121	950170	950219	950267	950316	49
2	950365	950414	950462	0511	0560	0608	0657	0706	0754	0803	49
3	0851	0900	0949	0997	1046	1095	1143	1192	1240	1289	49
4	1338	1386	1435	1483	1532	1580	1629	1677	1726	1775	49
895	1823	1872	1920	1969	2017	2066	2114	2163	2211	2260	48
6	2308	2356	2405	2453	2502	2550	2599	2647	2696	2744	48
7	2792	2841	2889	2938	2986	3034	3083	3131	3180	3228	48
8	3276	3325	3373	3421	3470	3518	3566	3615	3663	3711	48
9	3760	3808	3856	3905	3953	4001	4049	4098	4146	4194	48
900	954243	954291	954339	954387	954435	954484	954532	954580	954628	954677	48
1	4725	4773	4821	4869	4918	4966	5014	5062	5110	5158	48
2	5207	5255	5303	5351	5399	5447	5495	5543	5592	5640	48
3	5688	5736	5784	5832	5880	5928	5976	6024	6072	6120	48
4	6168	6216	6265	6313	6361	6409	6457	6505	6553	6601	48
905	6649	6697	6745	6793	6840	6888	6936	6984	7032	7080	48
6	7128	7176	7224	7272	7320	7368	7416	7464	7512	7559	48
7	7607	7655	7703	7751	7799	7847	7894	7942	7990	8038	48
8	8086	8134	8181	8229	8277	8325	8373	8421	8468	8516	48
9	8564	8612	8659	8707	8755	8803	8850	8898	8946	8994	48
910	959041	959089	959137	959185	950232	959280	959328	959375	959423	959471	48
1	9518	9566	9614	9661	9709	9757	9804	9852	9900	9947	48
2	9995	960042	960090	960138	960185	960233	960281	960328	960376	960423	48
3	960471	0518	0566	0613	0661	0709	0756	0804	0851	0899	48
4	0946	0994	1041	1089	1136	1184	1231	1279	1326	1374	48
915	1421	1469	1516	1563	1611	1658	1706	1753	1801	1848	47
6	1895	1943	1990	2038	2085	2132	2180	2227	2275	2322	47
7	2369	2417	2464	2511	2559	2606	2653	2701	2748	2795	47
8	2843	2890	2937	2985	3032	3079	3126	3174	3221	3268	47
9	3316	3363	3410	3457	3504	3552	3599	3646	3693	3741	47
920	963788	963835	963882	963929	963977	964024	964071	964118	964165	964212	47
1	4260	4307	4354	4401	4448	4495	4542	4590	4637	4684	47
2	4731	4778	4825	4872	4919	4966	5013	5061	5108	5155	47
3	5202	5249	5296	5343	5390	5437	5484	5531	5578	5625	47
4	5672	5719	5766	5813	5860	5907	5954	6001	6048	6095	47
925	6142	6189	6236	6283	6329	6376	6423	6470	6517	6564	47
6	6611	6658	6705	6752	6799	6845	6892	6939	6986	7033	47
7	7080	7127	7173	7220	7267	7314	7361	7408	7454	7501	47
8	7548	7595	7642	7688	7735	7782	7829	7875	7922	7969	47
9	8016	8062	8109	8156	8203	8249	8296	8343	8390	8436	47
930	968483	968530	968576	968623	968670	968716	968763	968810	968856	968903	47
1	8950	8996	9043	9090	9136	9183	9229	9276	9323	9369	47
2	9416	9463	9509	9556	9602	9649	9695	9742	9789	9835	47
3	9882	9928	9975	970021	970068	970114	970161	970207	970254	970300	47
4	970347	970393	970440	0486	0533	0579	0626	0672	0719	0765	46
935	0812	0858	0904	0951	0997	1044	1090	1137	1183	1229	46
6	1276	1322	1369	1415	1461	1508	1554	1601	1647	1693	46
7	1740	1786	1832	1879	1925	1971	2018	2064	2110	2157	46
8	2203	2249	2295	2342	2388	2434	2481	2527	2573	2619	46
9	2666	2712	2758	2804	2851	2897	2943	2989	3035	3082	46
N.	0	1	2	3	4	5	6	7	8	9	D.

TABLE XII.—Logarithms

N.	0	1	2	3	4	5	6	7	8	9	D.
940	973128	973174	973220	973266	973313	973359	973405	973451	973497	973543	46
1	3590	3636	3682	3728	3774	3820	3866	3913	3959	4005	46
2	4051	4097	4143	4189	4235	4281	4327	4374	4420	4466	46
3	4512	4558	4604	4650	4696	4742	4788	4834	4880	4926	46
4	4972	5018	5064	5110	5156	5202	5248	5294	5340	5386	46
945	5432	5478	5524	5570	5616	5662	5707	5753	5799	5845	46
6	5891	5937	5983	6029	6075	6121	6167	6212	6258	6304	46
7	6350	6396	6442	6488	6533	6579	6625	6671	6717	6763	46
8	6808	6854	6900	6946	6992	7037	7083	7129	7175	7220	46
9	7266	7312	7358	7403	7449	7495	7541	7586	7632	7678	46
950	977724	977769	977815	977861	977906	977952	977998	978043	978089	978135	46
1	8181	8226	8272	8317	8363	8409	8454	8500	8546	8591	46
2	8637	8683	8728	8774	8819	8865	8911	8956	9002	9047	46
3	9093	9138	9184	9230	9275	9321	9366	9412	9457	9503	46
4	9548	9594	9639	9685	9730	9776	9821	9867	9912	9958	46
955	980003	980049	980094	980140	980185	980231	980276	980322	980367	980412	45
6	0458	0503	0549	0594	0640	0685	0730	0776	0821	0867	45
7	0912	0957	1003	1048	1093	1139	1184	1229	1275	1320	45
8	1366	1411	1456	1501	1547	1592	1637	1683	1728	1773	45
9	1819	1864	1909	1954	2000	2045	2090	2135	2181	2226	45
960	982271	982316	982362	982407	982452	982497	982543	982588	982633	982678	45
1	2723	2769	2814	2859	2904	2949	2994	3040	3085	3130	45
2	3175	3220	3265	3310	3356	3401	3446	3491	3536	3581	45
3	3626	3671	3716	3762	3807	3852	3897	3942	3987	4032	45
4	4077	4122	4167	4212	4257	4302	4347	4392	4437	4482	45
965	4527	4572	4617	4662	4707	4752	4797	4842	4887	4932	45
6	4977	5022	5067	5112	5157	5202	5247	5292	5337	5382	45
7	5426	5471	5516	5561	5606	5651	5696	5741	5786	5830	45
8	5875	5920	5965	6010	6055	6100	6144	6189	6234	6279	45
9	6324	6369	6413	6458	6503	6548	6593	6637	6682	6727	45
970	986772	986817	986861	986906	986951	986996	987040	987085	987130	987175	45
1	7219	7264	7309	7353	7398	7443	7488	7532	7577	7622	45
2	7666	7711	7756	7800	7845	7890	7934	7979	8024	8068	45
3	8113	8157	8202	8247	8291	8336	8381	8425	8470	8514	45
4	8559	8604	8648	8693	8737	8782	8826	8871	8916	8960	45
975	9005	9049	9094	9138	9183	9227	9272	9316	9361	9405	45
6	9450	9494	9539	9583	9628	9672	9717	9761	9806	9850	45
7	9895	9939	9983	990028	990072	990117	990161	990206	990250	990294	44
8	990339	990383	990428	0472	0516	0561	0605	0650	0694	0738	44
9	0783	0827	0871	0916	0960	1004	1049	1093	1137	1182	44
980	991226	991270	991315	991359	991403	991448	991492	991536	991580	991625	44
1	1669	1713	1758	1802	1846	1890	1935	1979	2023	2067	44
2	2111	2156	2200	2244	2288	2333	2377	2421	2465	2509	44
3	2554	2598	2642	2686	2730	2774	2819	2863	2907	2951	44
4	2995	3039	3083	3127	3172	3216	3260	3304	3348	3392	44
985	3436	3480	3524	3568	3613	3657	3701	3745	3789	3833	44
6	3877	3921	3965	4009	4053	4097	4141	4185	4229	4273	44
7	4317	4361	4405	4449	4493	4537	4581	4625	4669	4713	44
8	4757	4801	4845	4889	4933	4977	5021	5065	5108	5152	44
9	5196	5240	5284	5328	5372	5416	5460	5504	5547	5591	44
990	995635	995679	995723	995767	995811	995854	995898	995942	995986	996030	44
1	6074	6117	6161	6205	6249	6293	6337	6380	6424	6468	44
2	6512	6555	6599	6643	6687	6731	6774	6818	6862	6906	44
3	6949	6993	7037	7080	7124	7168	7212	7255	7299	7343	44
4	7386	7430	7474	7517	7561	7605	7648	7692	7736	7779	44
995	7823	7867	7910	7954	7998	8041	8085	8129	8172	8216	44
6	8259	8303	8347	8390	8434	8477	8521	8564	8608	8652	44
7	8695	8739	8782	8826	8869	8913	8956	9000	9043	9087	44
8	9131	9174	9218	9261	9305	9348	9392	9435	9479	9522	44
9	9565	9609	9652	9696	9739	9783	9826	9870	9913	9957	43
N.	0	1	2	3	4	5	6	7	8	9	D.

Index

231568